W9-CTR-437

THE ATLAS OF ARCHAEOLOGY

St. Martins
Press

THE ATLAS OF ARCHAEOLOGY

Consultant editor, Professor K. Branigan

St. Martin's Press
New York

General Editor
Brenda Clarke
Commissioning Editor
Lynne Williams
Designer
Anne Isseyegh
Picture Research
Jenny de Gex
Production
John Moulder

Cover photograph
Paolo Koch/Vision International
Maps
Rudolph Britto

Made and printed in England by
Hazell, Watson & Viney Ltd
Aylesbury, Buckinghamshire

For information, address St. Martin's Press, 175 Fifth Avenue, New York, N.Y. 10010.

ISBN 0 312 05957 4
Library of Congress Catalog Card Number: 82-61698
First published in Great Britain by Macdonald & Co (Publishers) Ltd.

First U.S. Edition

10 9 8 7 6 5 4 3 2 1

Contributors

Introduction

Dr David Miles
Deputy Director, Oxford Archaeological Unit

Europe

Dr Sara Champion
Visiting Lecturer, Department of Archaeology, University of Southampton

Dr Tim Champion
Lecturer, Department of Archaeology, University of Southampton

The Classical World

Dr Alan W. Johnston
Lecturer, Department of Classical Archaeology, University College, University of London

Dr Malcolm A. R. Colledge
Head of Classics Department, Westfield College, University of London

Africa

Professor Thurstan Shaw
Formerly Professor of Archaeology, University of Ibadan, Nigeria

The Nile Valley

Dr Jeffrey Spencer
Assistant Keeper, Department of Egyptian Antiquities, British Museum

Dr Patricia Spencer
Archivist, Egypt Exploration Society

The Near East

Dr Charles Burney
Senior Lecturer, Near Eastern Archaeology, University of Manchester

The Indian Subcontinent

Jane McIntosh
Researcher and writer

The Far East

Graham Hutt
Researcher and writer, formerly at School of Oriental and African Studies, University of London

Gina Lee Barnes
Department of Archaeology, University of Cambridge

Anthony Christie
Senior Lecturer, School of Oriental and African Studies, University of London

The Americas

Iris Barry
Researcher and writer, formerly of the Institute of Archaeology, London

Contents

Introduction

Peoples have probably always speculated about their past, usually in such symbolic forms as myth, epic, music, dancing or painting. In contrast, the systematic, objective recording and explanation of humanity's physical and material remains – the science of archaeology – is a relatively recent phenomenon. The urge to collect the old and the curious was strong even in antiquity. Over 25 centuries ago Nabonidus, king of Babylon, dug into the ancient city of Ur and restored its ziggurat. More often the motive was greed, and resulted in tomb robbing for precious metals or to supply the antique dealers of the ancient world. The Roman historian Strabo recounts that when Julius Caesar established a colony at Corinth, the builders came upon the city's early cemeteries. These were rifled for bronze and ceramic vessels, which fetched a high price on the Roman market. Julius Caesar himself had a collection of gemstones which he gave to the temple of his clan ancestress, Venus Genetrix, for Classical temples were treasuries as well as religious centres and were stacked with antiquities in much the same way as the basements of some museums today.

In Athens, the Parthenon's collection included the throne of the Persian king Xerxes (about 519–465 BC) and a gilded sword captured in the Persian wars, while the inventories of the sanctuary of Apollo at Delos read like a museum catalogue: one golden statuette (broken); one bronze jug with a missing handle; model of a cow with only one horn. The Greeks made no attempt to do more than list their possessions; the Romans also appreciated antiquities aesthetically, as works of art, and as status symbols to decorate their town houses and villas, but not as sources of information about the past.

Occasionally there was a glimmer of deductive reasoning. Thucydides (about 460–400 BC), probably the finest and most objective of ancient historians, recorded an incident during the Peloponnesian War (431–404 BC):

> 'Delos was officially purified by the Athenians and all the graves in the island were opened up. More than half of these graves were Carian, as could be seen from the type of weapons buried with the bodies and from the method of burial, which was the same as that still used in Caria'.

Pausanias, the Greek travel writer of the 2nd century AD, also produced a rare flash of archaeological reasoning:

> 'As for the weapons in the heroic age being all made of bronze, I could argue that from Homer, from the lines about Peisander's axe and Meriones' arrow; the opinion I have given can be proved anyway from the spear of Achilles, which is dedicated in the sanctuary of Athens at Phaselis, and Memnon's sword in the temple of Asklepios at Nikomedia: the blade and the butt of the spear and the whole of the sword are made of bronze'.

In spite of this unusual insight, Pausanias was more often an uncritical traveller. He described what he saw, what he read and what he was told. Rarely were his descriptions precise and even more rarely were the travellers' tales he collected investigated for accuracy. As with most ancient writers, Pausanias took the everyday and familiar for granted. To the archaeologist, however, it is the everyday objects of people's lives which are the chief concern: the debris of flint knappers; broken potsherds swept from the kitchen; animal bones flung on to the rubbish heap; the traces of settlements and fields in the landscape. Too often archaeology is equated with the spectacular and unique: the jade burial suits of Chinese princesses; the gold death masks of Mycenaean kings; or a hoard of coins glittering on the surface of a freshly ploughed field. These may be the stuff of treasure hunters' fantasies, but they form only a minor part of archaeology.

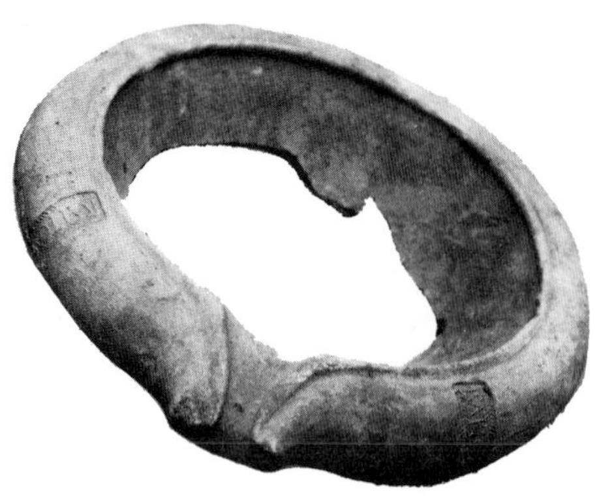

Above: A bowl, or mortarium, from a Celtic farmstead, stamped with the potter's name (detail).

Archaeology's revelations

A worn-out pot found in the ditch of a Celtic farmstead in southern England may better serve to illustrate the approach of modern archaeology. The pot was a large mixing bowl of a type called a mortarium, in which spices could have been ground with a pestle or purées mashed. Its base had been completely worn through by an energetic cook about AD 100. We can tell its age because the form of these bowls has been studied and a *typology* developed. This particular mortarium, with its heavy flange for the cook to grip, is typical of the late 1st century AD. The exact position of the mortarium in the excavation was recorded. It was well *stratified* in the bottom of a ditch, and the associated materials lying around it consisted of other types of pottery and some bronze brooches which also belonged to the same period. In the case of the mortarium there was an extra piece of evidence. The potter had stamped his name in Latin in two places on the flange: SOLLUS F(ecit), Sollus made this. Sollus's wares have been found at a number of sites in Britain, and it seems that he manufactured them at a place called Bockerley Hill, near to the important Romano-British city of Verulamium, the modern St Albans. Various techniques developed by geologists can be used to analyse the clays from which these pots were made, and their fabrics are consistent with raw materials found near Verulamium.

The worn-out mortarium therefore helps first of all to date the farmstead on which it was found. It does more than that, however. It shows that 40 or 50 years after the Roman conquest of Britain the native farmers had developed a taste for Romanized pottery, for such vessels were not made by earlier Britons. More important, it reveals that they had developed a taste for Romanized foodstuffs. The mixing bowl was a tool of the Mediterranean kitchen. Not surprisingly, on the same site there were also found fragments of amphorae, the pots which acted as the tin cans and barrels of the Classical world. In these, wine, oil and fish paste were transported from southern Italy, Spain and North Africa, and although the contents mattered most to their consumers, it is the almost indestructible container of fired clay which survives for the archaeologist to find. These pots can be interpreted into human actions, revealing cooking methods, types of foods and trading routes. The kiln which fired Sollus's mortarium was about 70 kilometres east of the farmstead, near Oxford, where the pot was dug up. Overland transport in the Roman world was slow and expensive and pots were heavy. It is likely, therefore, that the mortarium was taken first in a cart the shorter distance southwards down Watling Street, the Roman road to London. From the new bustling city of Londinium the load could have been transported by boat up the Thames and dispersed from local markets to the Celtic farmers who were increasingly demanding Romanized products.

The Sollus mortarium was just one fragment of evidence among tens of thousands excavated at a single farmstead. To its owner it was discarded rubbish; to the archaeologist it provides a link with the past as tangible as the written documents of Romans such as Cicero, the Elder and Younger Pliny, Julius Caesar, and the scores of other prodigious authors from whose pens flowed letters, memoirs, histories, and handbooks on agriculture or building. Even so, enormous areas of interest were either not written about, or, if they were, the documents have been lost. Many essential, common or garden subjects were not considered worth discussing. The activities of potters like Sollus, or of British farmers, lie outside 'the lively garrulous chronicles of history'. We have no information either about the mass of the population, about the detailed economy of Roman Britain or its rural settlements. The name of only one Romano-British villa is known from a Roman road map. Even such a tourist attraction as the tomb of Alexander in Alexandria, where the precocious conqueror's mummified body was on display, was not described by a single Classical author. Even its exact whereabouts are unknown, let alone what it looked like or what burial goods accompanied the body. No one bothered to describe the obvious.

If enormous gaps occur in our knowledge of such a well documented period as that of the Roman empire, what of the rest of human history? Current estimates put the birth of life on Earth at about 1,000,000,000 years ago. The ancestors of modern man appeared perhaps 2,000,000 years ago. The first documents were written down in the Near East about 3000 BC. If these enormous spans of time are imagined in terms of a single day during which life emerged at 12.01 am, then man only appeared on the scene at 11.57 pm and the first writing less than half a second before the stroke of midnight.

In a narrow sense, history can mean the study of the past from documents. Yet documented history accounts for no more than .25 per cent of humanity's existence. The

Above: The people of the Nazca culture of Peru etched lines and designs on to the dry surface of the land. The tracks of a vehicle to the left of the bird show the dangers of modern encroachment on the delicate tracery of ancient patterns.

vast majority of mankind's time on Earth is prehistoric, and if the most ancient records go back 5,000 years, there are peoples in Australia, Africa, parts of Asia and America who have remained in a prehistoric state into the 20th century. Others, such as the Celts of north-west Europe at the time of the Roman empire, can best be termed proto-historic, in that although some written records relating to their society do exist, they provide no more than a very limited picture.

For an understanding of our past we must therefore principally depend on archaeology.

Preservation

The body of the Egyptian boy pharaoh Tutankhamun was well preserved not because he had been mummified, but because he was buried in a dry climate and because he was not disturbed by grave robbers. Archaeologists must always bear in mind such biases in the way evidence is preserved, and if pots and flints sometimes seem to have been the most important features in the lives of peoples of the past, it is simply because they are practically indestructible.

In most of the densely occupied regions of the world, clothes, woodwork, paintings, basketry and body flesh soon rot away. Organic material can survive in exceptional conditions, however; in the aridity of Egypt, for example. The same conditions are found in desert regions of South America, and in the Nazca and Ica valleys of Peru, amazingly colourful and intricate textiles are found with burials. The famous *Nazca lines* themselves, which provide an endless source of speculation for archaeology's 'lunatic fringe', survive only because of the climate. In rainy country the textiles would have rotted, leaving little or no trace, and the delicate tracery of Nazca lines etched into the earth's surface would have been eroded away. Wet conditions can also preserve, however. Indeed, one of the chief attractions of underwater archaeology is the good state of preservation sometimes encountered in wrecked ships. And in the bogs of Denmark, bodies of Iron Age men and women have been recovered intact after lying for about two millennia in the airless conditions. In England, the peat of the Somerset Levels has preserved the oldest trackways in the world, made out of wood and dating from the Neolithic period between 4,000 and 5,000 years ago. Human bodies can be preserved so well that, for example, stubble on the chin of Denmark's Tollund Man remained clearly visible; at the opposite extreme, in acidic soil even the bones will disappear. In extreme cold nothing rots, so that the frozen tombs of Russia's Altai Mountains revealed tattooed chieftains, disembowelled and stuffed with herbs and spices. The same tombs contained Chinese carpets, lavishly bedecked horses and even delicate felt model swans, all of which had been buried about 400 BC. Russian archaeologists melted this enormous deep-freeze by pouring in thousands of litres of hot water.

Environmental archaeologists depend on the survival of plant and animal remains, and in waterlogged and dry deposits even leaves and twigs or the parts of beetles may be intact. Otherwise, plants may only be preserved if they have been carbonized by the heat from a fire. Carbonized seeds are extremely hard and resistant and, like charcoal, can survive well. Pollen is also a valuable source of evidence, allowing the botanist to reconstruct past landscapes. Plants disperse millions of pollen grains into the air, and if these fall into a suitable environment, such as a peat bog, or shallow, still lake, they will be preserved. By studying the grains under a microscope, a botanist can identify them as belonging to a genus or species of plant and in this way reconstruct the plant community of an area at a particular time.

Archaeological evidence is always affected by processes of deposition and survival. A simple example will illustrate the point. On a Roman villa or farmstead excavated in the Thames Valley of southern England, a corn-drying oven was found. Beneath it were large quantities of carbonized cereals, which by

Above: The Abbot's Way, a timber trackway laid across the marshes of the Somerset Levels in southern England about 2000 BC to link settlements on higher ground. Such trackways are preserved within the airless peat deposits and are among the earliest known roads in Europe.

themselves pointed to cereal growing as an important element in the Romano-British economy. However, several weeks later a deep well was found. In it were leather shoes, wooden objects and vast quantities of plant and insect remains. In this deposit the main economic plant was not a cereal but flax. Both these deposits reflected a different aspect of the farm economy, but taken by itself, one chance survival could have been misleading. Conditions of preservation, ancient methods of rubbish disposal and many other factors can transform the archaeological data in complex ways. Evidence cannot always be taken at face value.

Above: Tollund Man, found in a Danish peat bog in 1950, where he had lain for 2,000 years. The waterlogged and airless conditions made such preservation possible.

Underwater archaeology

Underwater archaeology often combines great technical difficulties and potential danger with spectacular results. As with the cities of Vesuvius, ancient shipwrecks can represent time capsules, captured at a particular moment. In favourable conditions, when the wreck site has not been badly disturbed, the ship and its contents may be remarkably preserved. For example, the pride of the English fleet, *Mary Rose*, which sank off Portsmouth in 1545, has revealed details of daily life in one section of 16th-century society as has no other contemporary archaeological site.

Wrecks can throw light not only on the daily life of seamen and naval technology, but also on ancient trade. A Roman merchantman from the time of the emperor Augustus (31 BC–AD 14), found at Madrague de Giens off southern France, had a cargo of about 6,000 amphorae. These pottery vessels, used as wine containers, were stamped with the name P VEVEIVS PAPVS, stamps which are often found on land sites. The mouths of the vessels were stopped with cork on which were plaster seals indicating the shipper of the wine. Such fragile seals were normally destroyed as the amphorae were opened, and therefore are rarely found on land. The seals, like the labels on modern wine bottles, remind us that it was the contents which were valued, rather than the almost indestructible container.

Underwater archaeology is not confined to shipwrecks, however, as ancient settlements in various parts of the world now lie submerged following changes in relative sea levels. The great pirate capital of Port Royal near Kingston, Jamaica, has been called the submarine equivalent of Pompeii, for on 7 June, 1692, an earthquake shook the city, which within minutes slumped into the sea.

The great campaign of excavations at Port Royal in the 1960s encountered many of the particular difficulties of underwater archaeology: an alien environment; bad visibility; the limited time in which a diver can work each day; the disposal of debris and the lifting and conserving of finds. The vital factor in the growth of underwater archaeology has been the development of the aqualung, which freed the diver for longer periods. Although much underwater archaeology has been reminiscent of the barrow-hunting which took place 150 years ago, in which glorified treasure-hunting prevailed, there has in recent years been a welcome growth of interest in both method and theory.

The origins of archaeology

Archaeology is a relatively recent science, the origins of which must be sought in that great burst of creativity, the Renaissance. The revival of interest in Classical authors by such 14th-century Italian writers as Petrarch and Boccaccio created a general fashion for things Greek and Roman. The visit to Florence in 1438 of the great Greek neo-Platonist philosopher George Gemistus Plethon inspired Cosimo de' Medici to found an academy in his honour. It was de' Medici also who started the first collection of Classical antiquities. This was a trend that spread, and soon sites were being sought out and looted for their *objets d'art*.

The conceptual leap from antique collecting to a more thoughtful study of archaeological evidence can best be seen in the work of Michele Mercati (1541–93) who was superintendent of the Vatican's botanical garden. Lucretius, the Roman author of the 1st century BC, had recorded folk memories of the technological stages through which mankind had progressed:

'Hands, tooth and nail and stones were the ancient weapons; branches ripped from forests, flames and fire, once they were known. Later the force of iron and bronze were discovered; the use of bronze was learnt before iron . . . The naked and unarmed surrendered to those equipped with weapons. Gradually the iron sword came to the fore, the bronze sickle was scorned, and they began to plough up the soil of the earth with iron'.

The discovery of new lands and new peoples, particularly in the Americas, reinforced Lucretius's words. If communities using stone tools still existed in remote regions, might they not once have existed even in Europe? Mercati compared the primitive tools brought back from overseas with the flint arrowheads and axes which he found in the soil of his homeland. For the first time documents, fieldwork and *ethnography* were combined to produce a rational explanation of the stone tools which previously had been simply the object of popular superstition – the fairy stones or thunderbolts from heaven which were hidden in the fireplace as a charm against lightning.

The reawakening interest in Classical Greece and Rome became apparent not only in literature and fine art but also in architecture, as Andrea Palladio (1508–80) drew inspiration from the ruins which he explored in Rome and elsewhere. Such early diggings can scarcely be called archaeological excavations, for they were little more than treasure hunts. This was especially true of early work at Herculaneum, the city buried along with Pompeii by the eruption of Vesuvius in AD 79. Its theatre, although embalmed in a thick layer of volcanic mud, was still not protected from the ham-fisted tunnelling parties of Prince d'Elboeuf, an Austrian general in the pay of the Bourbon kings of Naples. For seven years from 1709 this perfectly preserved theatre was hacked like a seam of coal and its riches dispersed over Europe. Excavations of a rather higher standard began at Herculaneum in 1738, revealing what Horace Walpole called '. . . one of the noblest curiosities that has ever been discovered. There is nothing of the kind known in the world'. Work started on a second buried city in 1748, the name of which became known when an inscription was found in 1763 – 'respublica Pompeianorum', the commonwealth of the Pompeians. It was about this time that Johann Winckelmann (1717–68), one of the giants of Classical art history, began to work in Rome. He completed his great book *The History of the Art of the Ancients* in 1764, and by introducing new standards to art appreciation burdened the Classical world, and its modern successors Greece and Italy, with unattainable ones. The vision of Classical perfection to which Winckelmann aspired was hardly apparent in the rugged, experienced faces of men like Marcus Celatorius whose statue, dug up at Herculaneum, shocked the idealistic art historian.

The ripples of Renaissance learning spread out across Europe. In England, Henry VIII employed the first King's Antiquary, John Leland (about 1506–52) to search out old manuscripts, many of which were lying neglected in the monasteries. As Anthony Wood said in his *Life of John Leland*, written in the late 17th century, 'he was appointed to search after England's Antiquities, and peruse the Libraries of All Cathedrals, Abbies, Priories, Colleges, etc., as also all places wherein Records, Writings and secrets of Antiquity were reposited . . . he spent more than six years in rambling to and fro in this Nation and in making researches into the bowels of Antiquity'. From the bowels emerged Leland's sensible and factual *Itinerary*, 1535–43. Equally rational was the Elizabethan antiquary William Camden (1551–1623) whose *Britannia*, 1586, contained the first English archaeological illustrations, including, not surprisingly, Stonehenge. Camden could also turn a phrase in defence of his antiquarian interests, 'In the study of Antiquity there is a sweet food of the mind well befitting such as are of honest and noble disposition'. Camden reflected the growing awareness of the past in northern Europe, an awareness based not on Classical traditions alone, but on a need to assert burgeoning nationalist identities. Druids and Stonehenge became proud symbols of the Britons' lengthy, if somewhat mixed, pedigree, even if they were, according to the 17th-century antiquary John Aubrey 'two or three degrees, I suppose, less savage than the Americans'. To some the study of antiquity seemed a quaint and scarcely useful practice. 'Magotie headed' was how one contemporary described Aubrey, and even he, the ever-curious author of *Brief Lives*, was occasionally depressed by the lack of appreciation of his work. 'This searching after Antiquities is a wearisome task . . . for nobody els hereabout hardly cares for it, but rather makes a scorn of it.' Aubrey was above all an inveterate collector of curious facts; the time was not right for synthesis. He did, however, attempt to be objective and accurate, appreciating, together with the other 'New Men' of the 17th century, the cardinal rules of Francis Bacon: observation, experimentation, recording and classification.

The 17th century also saw the appearance in Britain of all-embracing county surveys, such as Robert Plot's natural histories of Oxfordshire, 1677, and Staffordshire, 1686. These were essentially practical, designed to aid the exploitation of the land and its resources, but included details of antiquities. The discovery and surveying of ancient monuments rather than their excavation was the fashion. Even so, it is an antiquary of this time, Sir Thomas Browne (1605–82), who is usually credited as the author of the first published excavation report, with his *Hydriotaphia: Urne-Buriall, or, a Discourse of the Sepulchrall Urnes Lately found in Norfolk*, 1658. We now know that these cremation urns were Anglo-Saxon, although Browne assumed them to belong to the Roman conquerors of Britain; nevertheless he said, 'We mercifully preserve their bones, and pisse not upon their ashes'. The same earthy sensitivity was shown by John Aubrey when he discovered a burial mound, 'I never was so sacralegious as to disturbe, or rob his urne. Let his Ashes reste in peace: but I have often times wish't, that my Corps might be interred by it: but the Lawes Ecclesiastick denie it. Our bones in consecrated ground never lie quiet: and in London once in ten yeares (or thereabout) the Earth is carried to the Dung-wharf'.

The ashes were not to rest in peace for long. In England, the rational antiquarianism of the 17th century degenerated into the Gothic Romanticism of the 18th. Fieldwork of good quality continued to be carried out, particularly by the country land-agent, surveyor and self-appointed arch-Druid William Stukeley (1687–1765). However, excavation in England became fashionable at a time of cloying romanticism. Barrows were opened either in a spirit of awed mysticism or as a field sport. Dean Meriwether, for example, bagged 35 barrows in 28 days on the Marlborough Downs in 1849. The programme for the first archaeological conference ever held, at Canterbury in 1844, included the unwrapping of an Egyptian mummy and the opening of eight barrows. Lord Albert Conyngham supervised this latter operation before an audience of 200 people 'dressed in an explorer's costume'.

The rationalist tradition persisted in a few individuals, notably Thomas Jefferson (1743–1826), the third President of the United States of America. His *Notes on Virginia* was in the tradition of the English county surveys of Robert Plot, but the subsequent excavations were carried out in a spirit of scholarly enquiry alien to most of the contemporary European treasure hunters. His excavation of Indian burial mounds in Virginia was recorded in a precise, well argued report in which he noted separate layers, the age and condition of the human remains and the source of stone found in the mound. In contrast to popular opinion he argued that the mound did not house the victims of a battle but served an Indian community. But Jefferson was an exception; it was to be another century before his methods became regularly practised.

The Age of Discovery

If the 18th and earlier 19th centuries saw little in the way of scientific excavation there was no lack of spectacular discoveries. The rich, acquisitive imperialist powers of Western Europe were attracted to the ancient civilizations of the Mediterranean, while the disintegration of Turkish power made the Near East more accessible. Napoleon's invasion of Egypt in 1798 was accompanied by a scientific expedition, over 100 strong, the aim of which was to survey the country and remove anything of interest and potentially portable to the safety of France. Their most exciting discovery, a slab of black basalt found built into an Arab wall, was carved with three sets of scripts: Greek; demotic, a cursive form of ancient Egyptian; and hieroglyphic, the ancient Egyptian picture writing. This was the Rosetta Stone. It was not destined for Paris, however, but instead, with the defeat of Napoleon, became a 'proud trophy of the arms of Britain' and ended up in the British Museum. It was nevertheless a Frenchman, Jean-François Champollion, who in 1822 announced the unlocking of the ancient Egyptian code with the aid of this bilingual text.

The hunt for Egyptian antiquities was often conducted by far from sensitive hands. A former circus strong-man, Giovanni Battista Belzoni, supplied the growing demand of European museums by hacking, fighting and blasting his way into ancient tombs. He vividly and unrepentantly described his methods in his memoirs.

> 'I sought a resting place, found one and contrived to sit; but when my weight bore on the body of an Egyptian, it crushed like a band-box . . . I sunk altogether among the broken mummies, with a crash of bones, rags and wooden cases . . . every step I took I crushed a mummy in some part or other.'

It was as well for Egyptology that Belzoni's flamboyant career was prematurely terminated by a bout of dysentery in 1823 while searching for the city of Timbuktu. One commentator voiced the growing feeling of unease, at home and abroad, against those who desecrated 'time-hallowed monuments for no better purpose than the indulgence of craving acquisitiveness and the adorning of glass cases with ill-understood relics'. In Egypt in the 1830s, Auguste Mariette (1821–81) persuaded the authorities to found an archaeological service, to limit if not entirely control the tide of despoliation.

In other countries the scramble for antiquities continued. The success of the Frenchman Paul-Émile Botta (1802–70) at Assyrian sites such as Khorsabad, where he found the Palace of Sargon II (721–705 BC), roused the spirit of competition in the Englishman Sir Austen Henry Layard (1817–94). With a grant of £60 from the British ambassador in Constantinople he set off for Assyria, unhampered by any previous archaeological training. Between 1845 and 1847 Layard dug at Nimrud, in present-day Iraq, and shipped off his discoveries to the British Museum. These included two enormous bulls with human heads, weighing ten tonnes apiece. From there Layard moved on to Kuyunjik, later revealed as the site of Nineveh and previously abandoned by Botta who had found it unproductive. Layard's luck was still held, for almost immediately he discovered the Palace of Sennacherib. 'By a rough calculation about 9,880 feet or nearly two miles, of bas-reliefs, with twenty-seven portals formed by colossal winged bulls and lion-sphinxes, were uncovered in that part of the building explored by my researches.' He went on to locate the great library of Sennacherib, with its 26,000 clay tablets of *cuneiform* script, before returning to London and a career in government and the diplomatic service. The tablets appeared at an opportune moment, as Sir Henry Creswicke Rawlinson (1810–95) had recently deciphered the Babylonian script and in 1857 his work received independent verification. Much to the chagrin of their French competitors, the British successes at Nineveh were followed by further discoveries at the same site in 1854, when the palace and library of Sennacherib's grandson Assurbanipal were found. The acquisitiveness of both countries was interrupted in 1855, however, by the Crimean War.

Some of the most remarkable and unexpected discoveries were to come in the heartland of Classical civilization. Unlike many of his more scholarly contemporaries, Heinrich Schliemann (1822–90) regarded the stories of the ancient Greek poet Homer as being literally true. With the backing of two fortunes, made in Russia and California, Schliemann started his campaigns of exploration in 1868. Having little to guide him except a trusting faith in Homer, he interpreted everything he found in terms of events in the *Odyssey* or the *Iliad*. Cremations dug up in Ithaca, the home of Odysseus, must be those of the great hero and his wife, Penelope; the enormous hoard of about 9,000 gold objects, found at Hissarlik, his ancient Troy, had to be that of King Priam and Helen. In fact the Treasure of Priam was at least a thousand years earlier than the period of the Trojan Wars (around 1250 BC) and in his enthusiasm Schliemann had dug straight through the Homeric city.

From Hissarlik, Schliemann retraced the steps of Agamemnon to Mycenae, where he excavated from 1874 to 1876. Just inside the massive walls of the city Schliemann located a circle of stone slabs. With his wife, Sophia, he dug down into five shaft graves and found the bodies of 19 men, women and children laden with gold. On 28 November he sent off a telegram to King George of the Hellenes:

> 'With great joy I announce to your Majesty that I have discovered the tombs which tradition, echoed by Pausanias, specified as the graves of Agamemnon, Cassandra, Eurymedon and their companions, all killed during the feast by Clytemnestra and her lover Aegisthus . . . I have found immense treasures in the tombs, ancient

Above: Following his discoveries at Nimrud, Austen Henry Layard directed the teams of workmen required to remove massive sculptures from the palace for shipment to the British Museum.

Right: Grave circle A at Mycenae, the site of the shaft graves in which Heinrich Schliemann made his spectacular discoveries of gold masks, weapons and jewellery.

Above: 'All was mystery, dark impenetrable mystery . . . an immense forest shrouds the ruins . . . '. Copán, the classic lost city of the Maya, was discovered and mythologised by Frederick Catherwood and John L. Stephens.

objects made of pure gold. These treasures alone will be sufficient to fill a great museum which will be the most marvellous in the world and which, in the centuries to come, will attract thousands of foreigners from all countries to Greece . . .'.

Schliemann's belief in the literal truth of Homer may have been naïve, but as a businessman he knew the worth of such a discovery, and, as he predicted, tourism is now one of the cornerstones of the Greek economy. Thanks to a series of thrilling telegrams and articles strategically placed in *The Times*, Schliemann was fêted in Britain. His surprisingly dry account, *Mycenae*, was published in 1879 with a lengthy preface by Mr Gladstone, the British prime minister, and became something of a best-seller. We now know that the shaft graves pre-dated Homer's heroes by almost four centuries, but in his single-minded enthusiasm, Schliemann had discovered a Bronze Age culture of unsuspected splendour.

It was not only in Europe that there was a public demand for travellers' tales spiced with the lure of treasure. One of the most successful of the 19th-century travellers and popularizers was John Lloyd Stephens (1805–52). A lawyer and political activist involved in Andrew Jackson's 1828 presidential campaign, Stephens was dispatched by his doctor on a trip to Europe to recover from an infected throat brought on by too much public speaking. While wandering through the war-torn Balkans, Stephens, another man much influenced by Homer and the *Iliad*, sent a series of vivid letters to his friend Charles Fenno Hoffman, editor of the *American Monthly*. Hoffman took it upon himself to publish the correspondence; it was a great success and Stephens was launched on a new journalistic career. From Greece, Stephens travelled through Russia, eastern and western Europe and eventually to Cairo. Dressed as an Arab and calling himself Abdel Hasis, he crossed the Sinai desert by camel to the ruined city of Petra, the 'rose red city, half as old as time'. The traveller's wanderlust was rekindled by the romance of this once great lost city, although on his return to New York Stephens found time to write the massive *Incidents of Travel in Arabia Petraea* by 'An American'. Its exoticism appealed alike to public and reviewers (including Edgar Allan Poe) and the book was a tremendous success, earning its author more than $20,000.

Joining forces with the English artist and architect Frederick Catherwood, Stephens chose Central America as the scene for his next exploration, in 1839. After hacking their way through the jungles (both botanical and political) of Honduras (Belize) and Guatemala, Stephens and Catherwood reached the ancient Maya city of Copán.

'The city was desolate. No remnant of this race hangs around the ruins, with traditions handed down from father to son and from generation to generation. It lay before us like a shattered bark in the midst of the ocean, her masts gone, her name effaced, her crew perished, and none to tell whence she came . . . the place where we were sitting, was it a citadel from which an unknown people had sounded the trumpet of war? . . . Or did the inhabitants worship idols with their own hands and offer sacrifices on the stones before them? All was mystery, dark, impenetrable mystery and every circumstance increased it . . . an immense forest shrouds the ruins, hiding them from sight, heightening the impression and moral effect, and giving an intensity and almost wildness to the interest.'

The impact of Stephens' purple prose was reinforced, and its archaeological value certainly increased, by Catherwood's superb, intricate drawings of Copán's carved *stele* and plans of the enormous complex.

In the best tradition of heroic archaeology, Stephens decided to buy the site of Copán. In a last attempt to persuade the hesitant lease-holder to sell, the determined explorer decided to dress to impress.

'I opened my trunk and put on a diplomatic coat with a profusion of large eagle buttons. I put on a Panama hat, soaked with rain and spotted with mud, a checked shirt, white pantaloons, yellow up to the knee, and was about as *outré* as the negro king who received a company of British officers on the coast of Africa in a cocked hat and military coat, without any inexpressibles.'

The charade worked; on 17 November, 1839, Stephens bought Copán for $50.

The Gothic accounts of lost cities buried in barely penetrable jungles fired the imagination of 19th-century readers, among them Edward H. Thompson. He attracted attention to himself in 1879 with an article in *Popular Science Monthly* entitled 'Atlantis not a Myth' in which he suggested that the Maya were the remnants of the population of Atlantis. In spite of Thompson's lack of training or experience, Stephen Salisbury Jr, president of the American Antiquarian Society, arranged that he should be appointed US consul for Yucatan and given the opportunity to explore and record Mayan ruins. From 1885, in extremely arduous conditions, he cleared, planned and photographed many sites. He attracted most attention with the thousand square metres of plaster casts taken from Mayan carvings which were exhibited at the 1893 Columbian Exposition in Chicago. Thanks to newly-attracted patrons, Thompson was able to buy the hacienda at the important Mayan and Toltec site of Chichén Itzá in the Yucatan Peninsula. It was here, at the site first recorded by the Franciscan missionary Diego de Landa in the mid-16th century, that Thompson carried out his most dramatic and notorious campaign. De Landa was an enigmatic man, a religious zealot who mercilessly tortured the Indians and destroyed their writings in the name of Christianity, yet who also wrote *Relacion de las Cosas de Yucatan*, the most careful account of Mayan customs we possess. Of the great well of Cenote at Chichén Itzá, de Landa said,

'From a court in front of these stages a wide and handsome causeway runs as far as a well which is about two stones' throw off. Into this well they have had, and still have, the custom of throwing men alive as a sacrifice to the gods . . . They also threw into it a great many other things, like precious stones and things which they prized'.

The lure of treasure and human sacrifices persuaded Thompson to dredge the murky waters of the Cenote. Throughout 1904 a derrick was used to bring up tonnes of stone and mud. The foetid mixture was dumped on the shore to be sifted by Thompson and his helpers. At first only a few human bones and fragments of pottery appeared, but persistence paid. Over the next three years was found an amazing collection of weapons; tools; vessels; ceremonial objects; jewellery in gold, jade and bronze; statuettes; and small gold and bronze bells. Many of these had been ritually broken before being thrown into the well, along with the human sacrifices. Thompson at first claimed, in a flush of wishful fantasy, that the human skeletons were those of beautiful young virgins; more careful study revealed that the bones belonged to both males and females of all ages, some of them suffering from deformities. Unfortunately, Thompson's work took on more the aspect of a treasure hunt than an archaeological excavation. Many objects went missing as a result of Thompson's carelessness, and most of the others were eventually acquired by the Peabody Museum in Harvard. The whole business rankled with the Mexican government for many years, and was especially aggravated in 1926 when Theodore Willard published an account of the dredging of the Sacred Well. In the ensuing furore, Thompson left his hacienda at Chichén Itzá and returned to the United States where he died in 1936, the last of the archaeologists of the heroic age. In the 1950s the Peabody Museum at last published the Cenote finds, some of which were then returned to Mexico.

The problem of dating

Tales of buried civilizations and lost cities continue to grip the public imagination, but for antiquaries of the 19th century the real jungle to be cut away was that surrounding the problem of time. Archaeology seeks to understand the ways in which human societies have changed and adapted through time. To do this, the ordering of archaeological evidence on a chronological scale is of fundamental importance. In the early 19th century time was the great mystery, as Professor Rasmus Nyerup of Copenhagen said, 'everything which has come down to us from heathendom is wrapped in a thick fog; it belongs to a space of time which we cannot measure. We know that it is older than Christendom, but whether by a couple of years or a couple of centuries, or even by more than a millennium, we can do no more than guess'.

If the prehistoric past was fog-bound, it was at least possible to achieve some sort of relative order. Museums had been accumulating antiquities since the Renaissance, but for the most part these collections were as disorganized as the treasuries of Classical temples. Christian Thomsen (1788–1865) was appointed the first curator of the National Museum of Denmark in 1816. Confronted by a mass of artefacts he decided to arrange them on the basis of the material from which they were made – stone, bronze and iron. From there he went on to equate his three divisions of material technology with three chronological periods. The idea was not new; it had been mentioned by Classical authors such as Hesiod and Lucretius, as well as Italian and German antiquaries. Thomsen, however, formalized the concept of a Three-Age System in a book published in 1836 and translated into English in 1848 as *A Guide to Northern Antiquities*. Thomsen's scheme created order out of the previous chronological chaos, and any doubts about its relevance were overcome by a series of excavations, especially those conducted by Thomsen's assistant and successor at the National Museum, Jens Jacob Asmussen Worsaae (1821–85).

Worsaae was one of the first to appreciate that sites should not be dug like a pile of coal, simply to extract curios. Instead he carefully peeled off the layers of his burial mounds and prehistoric *shell middens*, like the successive skins of an onion. In this way he could reconstruct the relative order in which the layers and the objects in them had been deposited. He showed that the Three-Age System worked in practice as well as theory. This was the principle of stratification, appreciated intuitively by Thomas Jefferson, but becoming more widely accepted thanks to the increasing researches of geologists. It enabled archaeologists to develop a relative time scale – stone tools come before bronze, which are earlier than iron – but did not immediately solve the problem of absolute calendar dates, of the type that historians were accustomed to use.

Time was no problem, of course, for biblical fundamentalists. The absolute date of Creation was printed in the margin of the Authorized Bible for all to see: 4004 BC. It had been calculated by Archbishop Usher of Armagh (1581–1656) in 1650 on the basis of Genesis chapter 5, where we are told that Adam begat Seth in his hundred and thirtieth year and died aged nine hundred and thirty; Seth aged a hundred and five begat Enos and died aged nine hundred and twelve – and so on for seven singularly long-lived generations until we come to Noah and the Flood. Not satisfied with this lack of precision, Dr John Lightfoot refined the dating somewhat. 'Man', he said, 'was created by the Trinity on October 23, 4004 BC at nine o'clock in the morning.' If 'the poor world is almost six thousand years old', as Rosalind said in *As You Like It*, then most of humankind's span on Earth could be accounted for by the Classical civilizations and those of the Bible, such as Egypt and Assyria. The short span of prehistory was mostly filled with stock characters such as Ancient Britons, Druids or Phoenicians; only a few people, among them the so-called Scottish Primitivists, attempted to define early societies in more general and theoretical terms as 'hunting communities' or 'early farmers'.

Inconvenient discoveries of fossils, extinct animals and stone tools could be accounted for by that great catastrophe the Flood. But chinks were beginning to appear in the fundamentalist shell. In 1797 an 'Account of Flint Weapons discovered at Hoxne' was published in *Archaeologia* by John Frere (1740–1807). He wrote, 'The situation in which these weapons were found may tempt us to refer them to a very remote period indeed, even beyond that of the present world'. This was a very bold statement to make before the 18th century was out. Support of a kind came from the French geologist Georges Cuvier (1769–1832), who attempted to reconcile the fossil record with the Bible. There had been, he concluded, a whole series of floods, of which Noah's was the only documented one.

Dramatic changes were known to have taken place in the course of the Earth's history. Geologists such as William Smith (1769–1839) were documenting the existence of layers in the Earth's surface with characteristic collections of fossil animals. Cuvier and his colleagues chose to explain these changes in terms of sudden revolutions like the biblical deluge, and hence were known as the Catastrophists. The rival school of thought, initially led by the Scotsman James Hutton (1726–97) believed that slow, gradual processes observable at the present time, such as erosion and deposition, could be used to account for the changes in the Earth's surface. They were therefore called the 'Uniformitarianists'. Uniformitarianism finally won the day in scientific circles with the publication of one of the most influential books of the 19th century, Sir Charles Lyell's *Principles of Geology*, 1830–33, and with it was accepted the implication that the world was considerably older than six thousand years.

If the literal truth of the Bible was being brought into question by geologists, an even greater 'time bomb' was planted by biologists. The idea that physical changes took place in plants and animals in response to their environment had existed since the latter part of the 18th century, proposed notably by Erasmus Darwin (1731–1802) and Jean-Baptiste de Lamarck (1744–1829). It

Above: Before the beginnings of scientific classification to determine accurate dating, characters from prehistory, such as Ancient Britons and Druids, were imaginatively reconstructed.

was Charles Darwin (1809–82), grandson of Erasmus, who unleashed the full implications of evolutionary theory with his explanation of biological transformations in terms of the 'survival of the fittest'.

On the Origin of Species by Means of Natural Selection was published in 1859. Twelve years later Darwin's *Descent of Man* spelled out that evolutionary theory was as applicable to humankind as to any other animal. For several decades archaeologists had been accumulating evidence that this was so. Human remains and stone tools had been found together with the bones of extinct animals at many sites in Europe, but old preconceptions die hard and the biblical fundamentalists were not convinced. The year of reckoning proved to be 1859. Not only was *Origin of Species* published, but William Pengelly (1812–94) uncovered evidence at Windmill Hill Cave at Brixham, in Devon, south-west England, that was conclusive to all but the most fixed minds. Beneath a layer of stalagmite up to 20 centimetres thick, 'having within it relics of lion, hyaena, bear, mammoth, rhinoceros and reindeer', Pengelly found man-made flint tools together with extinct animal bones. The stratification was unquestionable. At the same time an even greater mass of evidence was presented to the Royal Society of Antiquaries in London, being the accumulated 20 years of research by Jacques Boucher de Perthes (1788–1868), a customs officer from Abbeville, in the Somme Valley. Deep in the gravel terraces of the Somme Valley, Boucher de Perthes had found flint tools and extinct animal bones. His claims were investigated by two Britons, the geologist Joseph Prestwich and the antiquarian John Evans. Both were convinced. As Evans pronounced to the Society of Antiquaries, 'This much appears to be established beyond doubt, that in a period of antiquity remote beyond any of which we have hitherto found traces, this portion of the globe was peopled by Man'.

Ordering the past

By the second half of the 19th century the combined efforts of biologists, antiquarians and geologists had shattered the rigid shell within which the European concept of time had been trapped. Evolutionary theory, the Three-Age System and the principle of stratification together provided a framework for piecing together the past. Thomsen had arranged his material into three basic technological divisions; now the concept of typological studies took on a fresh impetus. The idea of ordering material according to the sequence in which it developed is not hard to grasp; most people nowadays could arrange motor cars or women's clothes in chronological order without great difficulty. Ordering the artefacts of an alien culture is not as easy. Nevertheless, archaeologists such as the Swede Oscar Montelius (1843–1921) attempted to do this with stone tools, bronze weapons and other material, so creating finer sub-divisions within the broad span of the Three-Age System. In fact the Stone Age had been divided into the Old and New Stone Age, or Palaeolithic and Neolithic, as early as 1865 by John Lubbock (1834–1913) in his book *Prehistoric Times*. Lubbock realized that the older stone tools had been made by a chipping or flaking technique, while the later ones, including the magnificent stone axes, were often produced by polishing the surface.

Evolutionary thinking also encouraged the type of approach characteristic of the 18th-century French philosopher Montesquieu and the Scottish Primitivists, about which Dr Johnson had said 'Sir, it is all conjecture about a thing useless, even if it were known to be true'. Now ideas about different methods of subsistence – hunting, mobile pastoralism, sedentary farming and civilization – were accorded a more receptive welcome. In *Anthropology: an Introduction to the Study of Man and Civilization*, 1881, Sir Edward Tylor (1832–1917) proposed that mankind could be fitted into three cultural stages: savagery, barbarism and civilization. The same basic scheme was adopted by the American Lewis Henry Morgan (1818–81) in *Ancient Society*, 1877, but with subdivisions for the first two stages ranging from fruit and nut subsistence to the use of the bow and arrow, from pottery manufacture and the domestication of animals to iron tool production, and finally the use of the phonetic alphabet and writing in civilized society.

Such studies in technical and cultural evolution generated interest as to how these progressions had taken place. Many explanations would be seen today as blatantly racist; that hunting or wearing loin-cloths were 'in the blood', for example; others assumed that all human societies slowly climbed a sort of cultural ladder and that some were higher up it than others. One of the most pervasive ideas was that advances had permeated from certain centres of excellence, such as Egypt or the Near East. This 'diffusionist' stance was adopted by Montelius in *The Orient and Europe*, published in 1899, a book which has been called 'the first coherent view of European prehistory'. Two ideas were basic to diffusionism; that barbarian Europe had been irradiated by oriental civilization and that artefacts reflecting oriental influence could be found in barbarian, prehistoric Europe and used for cross-dating purposes.

Despite the construction of relative chronologies and the removal of the biblical buffer of 4004 BC, there remained the problem of producing absolute calendar dates, or even something approaching them, for prehistoric societies. Egypt provided the most lengthy historical chronology with its king lists stretching back as far as 3000 BC. In the late 19th century, excavation standards began to improve and a new professionalism appeared with archaeologists such as General Augustus Henry Lane-Fox Pitt-Rivers (1827–1900) in England and Frederic Ward Putnam (1839–1915) in the United States. One of the most rigorous was Sir Flinders Petrie (1853–1942) who fortunately turned his attention to Egypt, and woe betide any dilettantes who crossed his path!

> 'Let us be quit, in archaeology at least, of the brandy and soda young man who manipulates his 'expenses', of the adventurous speculator, of those who think that a title or a long purse glorifies any vanity or selfishness. Without the ideal of solid, continuous work, certain, accurate and permanent, archaeology is as futile as any other pursuit. Best of all is the combination of the scholar and the engineer, the man of languages and the man of Physics and Mathematics, when such can be found . . .'

In 1891 Petrie was digging at the palace of the pharaoh Akhenaten at Tell el-Amarna in Egypt. Among the remains that began to appear was pottery of the type that Schliemann had found at Troy, Mycenae and Tiryns. As Akhenaten is known from historical sources to have reigned in the second quarter of the 14th century BC, an absolute date could be given to Mycenaean Greece for the first time. It was not long before Egyptian objects were recognized among artefacts discovered in Greece; indeed, some had already been found by Schliemann: alabaster vases, ivory, ostrich eggs and, particularly, scarabs. These last are small seals or amulets, carved into the shape of a beetle, which often include a royal name and hence can be closely dated. On the basis of the Egyptian connection, a chronology was gradually built up for prehistoric Greece and the eastern Mediterranean, if only as far back as 3000 BC.

Dating prehistoric Europe

Archaeologists working in northern Europe and other prehistoric areas, in America, for example, were still in a chronological limbo. To introduce some form of coherence and order, elaborate relative chronologies and a kaleidoscope of 'cultures' were constructed. The archaeological 'culture' first defined by Carl Schuchhardt (1859–1943) consisted of distinctive groups of artefacts occurring together. These might include, for example, particular types of pottery, metalwork and houses. On the basis of the 5th century AD folk-movements in Europe, of Saxons, Franks, Vandals and Goths, these cultures were often equated with ethnic groups. Hence it was assumed that *Beaker folk* and *Battle Axe* cultures swept across Europe in great swathes, carrying with them the wisdom of the East. The exposition of diffusionist, culture-based prehistory was put in its most sophisticated form by the Australian archaeologist V. Gordon Childe (1892–1957) in *The Dawn of European Civilisation*, 1925, and a series of deceptively simple and readable books, such as *Man Makes Himself*, 1936, which have remained of lasting value to archaeological method and theory.

In order to fix these northern cultures in time, links needed to be found with the well-dated Mediterranean. Amber, found in the graves of Mycenae, originated on the shores of the Baltic, so the links must have existed. Beads made from faience, a simple form of glass, appeared in the north and these were thought to have been manufactured in Greece. Gradually the links, albeit tenuous and at times subjective, were forged into a chain. Megalithic (large stone) tombs were found in Spain, Brittany, the British Isles and Denmark. Childe saw these as a manifestation of Greek influence, deriving from the same tradition that produced the so-called Treasuries of Atreus, Clytemnestra and Aegisthus at Mycenae. The tradition, he argued, had been spread by traders travelling north from the east Mediterranean in search of metal ores who had left other traces of their presence: spiral decorations on the tombs of New Grange in Ireland similar to those on the grave slabs at Mycenae; copper smelting in Spain; the defensive walls of the Spanish settlement of Los Millares which 'has indeed all the aspects of an Aegean township'. 'The Iberian Peninsula', Childe wrote, 'offers the natural channel through which oriental influences . . . might penetrate to Atlantic Europe.' Another corridor along which Mediterranean influence was thought to have penetrated was through the Balkans and into the Danube basin. The civilizing influence of the Mediterranean was detected even as far north as Britain, in its Megalithic tombs, faience beads, and especially Stonehenge, about which its excavator, Professor Richard Atkinson, wrote in 1960, 'Is it then any more incredible that the architect of Stonehenge should have been a Mycenaean, than that the monument should have been designed and erected, with all its unique and sophisticated detail, by mere barbarians?'. Not surprisingly, artists' reconstructions of the building of Stonehenge usually showed the 'mere barbarians' doing the donkey-work while a Mycenaean foreman-cum-architect supervised. So even Britain, the distant land of the *Hyperboreans*, was fitted into a European network of cross-dated cultures, which ultimately led back to Egypt and its fixed, historical dates. The elaborately constructed edifice appeared relatively sound, but in 1947 an American physicist, Willard F. Libby, attacked its foundations and slowly the diffusionist tower began to buckle and collapse.

Dating techniques

Stratification and typological analysis enabled archaeologists to build up relative chronologies. Sound connections with the more ancient historical cultures back as far as 3000 BC allowed Greece, Cyprus and the Near Eastern countries to be fixed in an absolute time scale. As archaeologists moved out from the Mediterranean or further back in time, however, the relative chronologies began to float, and absolute dates relapsed into guesswork. The handicaps were especially great in parts of the world where prehistoric societies existed until recently; in America, Australia, the Pacific and much of sub-Saharan Africa.

In the late 1940s, Professor Willard F. Libby of the Institute for Nuclear Studies at the University of Chicago planted a time-bomb among the archaeological community; he discovered radiocarbon dating. Radiocarbon, or C14, dating was a time bomb in all senses of the word, because the initial impact of its discovery felt in the 1950s was followed by a possibly more effective shock wave in the later 1960s.

The basic principles of radiocarbon dating are relatively easy to understand. Cosmic radiation of the Earth's atmosphere results in the production of radioactive carbon. Normal carbon has an atomic weight of 12, while the radioactive isotope of carbon is rather heavier, with an atomic weight of 14 – hence ^{14}C. The amount of ^{14}C produced, mainly in the stratosphere, is extremely small in comparison with ^{12}C, only one part in 0.8 billion (a million, million) or two ^{14}C atoms for each square centimetre of the Earth's surface every second. The ^{14}C atoms mix evenly as carbon dioxide throughout the Earth's atmosphere, so the amount is constant across the world. Carbon dioxide, containing ^{14}C atoms, is absorbed into plants as a result of their food-making process called photosynthesis, and from them it passes up the food chain into all animals. Because ^{14}C is radioactive it decays at a constant rate. Libby originally estimated that half of a given amount of ^{14}C would decay in 5570 ± 30 years; now it is realized that the 'half-life' is more like 5730 ± 40 years. During the lifetime of a living creature its stock of ^{14}C remains in balance; it gains as much as it loses. Once the plant or animal dies, however, it ceases to absorb new ^{14}C and its existing stock is gradually depleted. Libby assumed that the amount of ^{14}C present in the atmosphere had remained constant, and therefore by measuring the level of ^{14}C remaining in material such as charcoal, seeds, wood, animal bones and other organic materials, the time of death could be calculated.

There are problems involved in collecting samples for radiocarbon dating. Obviously material must be well stratified and not re-deposited. In other words, the archaeologist must be sure that the animal bones or plant remains tested are contemporary with the deposit to be dated. Large timbers, for example, can mislead if they came from trees already old when the archaeological layer was laid down, or if the timbers were re-used from an already ancient building. A more serious handicap is that conventional radiocarbon dating requires quite large samples, and these may not always be forthcoming from sites that most need to be dated. Another limitation is that ^{14}C is present in organic material in very small quantities. With a half-life of about 5,700 years these quantities become progressively smaller, so that samples over 30,000 to 50,000 years old can only be measured with the utmost difficulty.

Some of these practical difficulties may well be overcome by a new method of radiocarbon dating. At a scientific conference in Strasbourg in 1977 it was announced that a technique of counting individual ^{14}C atoms was possible by using a *particle accelerator*. The implications for archaeology are tremendous. Samples of organic material containing as little as a milligram of carbon may be enough to provide dates, so that a fragment of bone weighing only one gram would be sufficient. This is a thousandth of the amount required by the conventional system. Material which was previously considered unsuitable for ^{14}C sampling may, in future, be utilized, including pottery tempered with chaff, building daub mixed with straw, cooking residues on pots, soot on cave walls, or even iron with a sufficiently high carbon content. The second great advantage of the atom-counting method is that the range of ^{14}C dating can be extended, perhaps as far back as 100,000 years bp (before present). Needless to say there are also snags, the initial one being cost. The massive accelerators, developed by high energy physicists, are extremely expensive. For example, the first laboratory established specifically for archaeological purposes, at the Laboratory for Art and Archaeology, Oxford, cost £500,000 to reach operational stage. Nevertheless, with such enormous possibilities for archaeology, atom-counting laboratories are being developed in Arizona, Toronto and Japan. It remains to be seen whether the method can be refined sufficiently to fulfil its promise.

The revolutionary impact of radiocarbon dating was felt in the second half of the 1960s. In its early days, radiocarbon dating seemed to support fairly well the Egyptian chronology and the prehistoric ones dependent on it. As more dates accumulated, however, discrepancies were noted in those achieved from Egyptian material for which there were firm historical contexts; the ^{14}C dates seemed to be persistently too young. At the beginning of the Egyptian historical sequence, about 3000 BC in calendar years, the ^{14}C dates averaged about 600 years later than expected. The implications for prehistoric cultures dependent on the Egyptian connection, and those even earlier, were serious. It seemed that one of Libby's basic assumptions about ^{14}C was incorrect; the level had not remained constant throughout the Earth's history, and therefore radiocarbon years could not be directly equated with calendar years.

A way of tackling the problem was found, by using a particularly gnarled and wizened inhabitant of the White Mountains of California called the bristlecone pine (*Pinus aristata*). These trees are the oldest living things on Earth, reaching ages of up to 4,600 years. At the beginning of this century, the astronomer Andrew Ellicott Douglass began to develop the science of dendrochronology, or the study of tree-rings. The idea of using tree-rings to draw up time-scales was not new; Leonardo da Vinci had tinkered with it and Charles Babbage, who invented the calculating machine, had foreseen the possibilities in 1837. Douglass put the idea into practice, however, and began to collect timber from Arizona and New Mexico. He found that the rings from suitably sensitive trees varied in thickness depending on the climatic conditions in a given year. This had two consequences. First, sequences of rings could be built up and matched, and an absolute chronology established by counting backwards; secondly, the rings encapsulated a climatic history of the region from which they came. In Colorado, for example, it was found that a period of drought had started in AD 1273 and lasted for 12 years, which exactly coincided with a drastic decline in the population of the Pueblo Indians of Mesa Verde.

The importance of the bristlecone pine was its longevity, which enabled the tree-ring sequence to be pushed far back into prehistory. By linking living specimens to the ring sequences of dead bristlecone pines, the chronology extends for over 8,000 years. This is only a localized sequence, however, applicable to the south-western United States. Elsewhere, as in Europe, independent sets of tree-rings have been studied. No European trees live for more than a few centuries; nevertheless, patterns of rings have been accumulated from the timber of oak trees, for example, found in old buildings, on archaeological sites, or preserved in marshes and rivers.

Thanks to the lengthy bristlecone pine sequence of absolute dates in which each ring represents a specific year, timber samples could be used to check radiocarbon results. In 1967 Dr Hans E. Suess, an American chemist, produced a graph for calibrating radiocarbon dates. Since then, more work has been done in laboratories at Tucson, Arizona; La Jolla, California; and Pennsylvania to develop calibration curves whereby radiocarbon dates can be translated into calendar years. The dramatic result was that sites dated before about 500 bc by radiocarbon all had to be set back by varying amounts. A sample registering about 3000 bc in radiocarbon years would more accurately belong to about 3800 BC. According to scientific convention a date is normally expressed 4952 ± 75 bp. The last two letters are written in lower case and mean 'before present' (for these purposes, present is taken as 1950) while '± 75' expresses the statistical variation that is possible in each sample. If the date is then calibrated it would be written, let us say, 3800 BC, with upper case letters.

The impact of these calibration curves in the late 1960s shattered the elaborate network of prehistoric interrelationships created for Europe, as the diffusionist structure was seen to have rested on a foundation of false assumptions. The original links between Egypt, Greece and the rest of the east Mediterranean held firm, but to the north and west there appeared what has appropriately been called an archaeological fault line. The relative chronologies of prehistoric northern Europe remained intact in relation to one another, but they all slipped down the

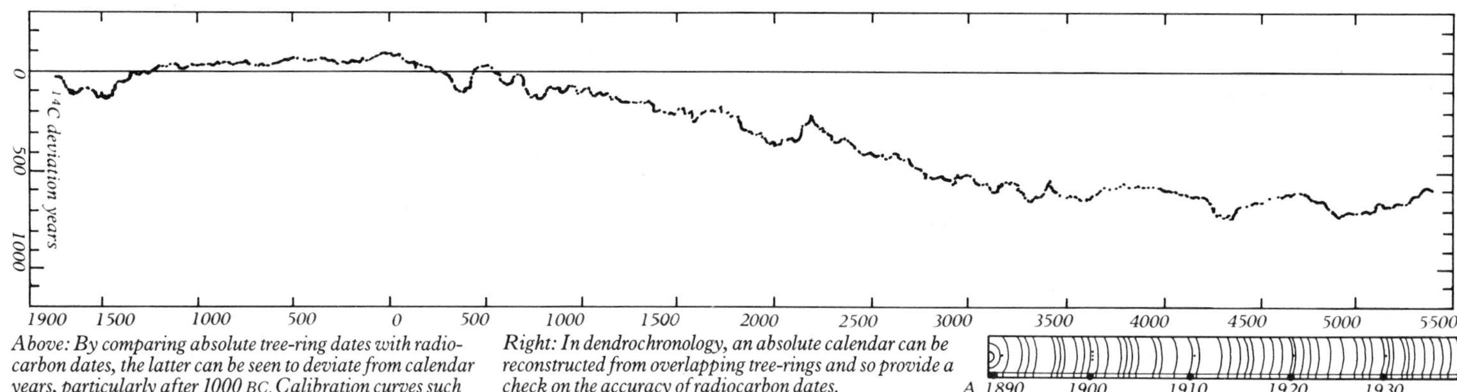

Above: By comparing absolute tree-ring dates with radiocarbon dates, the latter can be seen to deviate from calendar years, particularly after 1000 BC. Calibration curves such as this allow radiocarbon dates to be rectified.

Right: In dendrochronology, an absolute calendar can be reconstructed from overlapping tree-rings and so provide a check on the accuracy of radiocarbon dates.

A 1890 1900 1910 1920 1930

B 1870 1880 1890 1900 1910

C 1850 1860 1870 1880

Below: Bristlecone pine trees have tree-ring sequences dating back several thousand years. This factor is useful in calibrating radiocarbon dates.

time scale in relation to Greece and Egypt. Megalithic tombs in Spain, France and Britain were seen to predate those in Greece; spirals could be carved and fortifications built without any oriental influence; the 'mere barbarians' of Bronze Age Wessex could build Stonehenge without a Mycenaean overseer.

The radiocarbon revolution did more than improve dating techniques; it opened up a new perspective to archaeologists. Simple diffusionist and invasion-based explanations of change were replaced by a more open-minded analysis of the processes operating within societies. On a larger scale, themes could be studied on a world-wide basis, in the Americas, Europe, Africa, Asia and the Far East – areas that previously could not be linked by cross-cultural chronologies. The adaptive strategies of hunting and gathering communities; the spread of agriculturalists; the development of trade; and the growth of states and urbanization became subjects that could be examined universally. Radiocarbon dating thus acted as a catalyst to promote the understanding of prehistoric communities in all their complexity and ingenuity. At the same time it encouraged a world view of prehistory and a re-examination of archaeological thinking.

Other dating techniques

Radiocarbon dating is probably the most widely used of scientific dating techniques and has had the most profound impact on archaeology. Several others also exist, however. *Thermoluminescence* can be used on pottery; *archaeomagnetism* on fired material; *amino acid dating* on bone; and *fission track dating* on types of glass, notably obsidian, the naturally produced volcanic glass. One particularly important technique, especially in view of ^{14}C's short half-life, is potassium-argon dating. This works on the same principle as radiocarbon dating, but depends on the rate at which the radioactive isotope of potassium, ^{40}K, decays into the inert gas argon. It can be applied to some volcanic rocks, in which the original argon content was driven out as they were subjected to high temperatures. Once the rock has cooled, the argon content gradually increases as the ^{40}K decays. By measuring the potassium and argon content of the rock, and by no means all volcanic rocks are suitable, the approximate age of its formation can be assessed. The great advantage of this method is that as the half-life of ^{40}K is 1,300,000,000 years, it can be applied to rocks of great age. It is therefore of major importance when studying early hominid remains which are far too early for radiocarbon dating to be used.

By using potassium-argon and fission track dating in particular, it has been possible to determine the ages of many stratified beds of rock which have produced hominid remains. At Olduvai Gorge in Tanzania, for example, nine beds built up over 2,000,000 years have been found to preserve a continuous record of skeletal hominid remains and the stone tool industries with which they were associated. At Laetoli, near Olduvai, a trio of footprints fossilized in cooling lava beds has been dated and shows that hominids had become upright and bipedal 3,700,000 years ago, thereby freeing their hands for tool making, transporting materials, and promoting the complex behaviour which developed with expanding mental ability.

Development of archaeology

To the general public, archaeology often means the romance of the past – buried treasure, impressive sites, the rich and unique. For even after the heroic days of Layard and Schliemann, and the gradual development of more rigorous techniques, spectacular discoveries continued. The Minoan civilization of Knossos was revealed by Arthur Evans in 1899; the intact tomb of the boy pharaoh Tutankhamun uncovered in 1922 by Lord Carnarvon and Howard Carter; the frozen graves of the tattooed chieftains of Altai in eastern Russia discovered in 1929; the ship burial of Redwald, king of the East Angles, at Sutton Hoo in England opened in 1939. Staggering finds are still made, instanced by the buried army of 6,000 life-sized terracotta soldiers, set in battle order to guard the body of the Chinese emperor Qin Shihuangdi (reigned 221–210 BC). These were brought to light in 1979 when peasants in the Yellow River valley province of Shaanxi dug a well into the army's resting place.

Such discoveries are the stuff of archaeological legend, but represent only the tip of the iceberg. Until the radiocarbon revolution of the late 1960s, most archaeologists were concerned with the intricate and often dreary business of constructing chronologies. In particular, much effort went into typological studies, which compared masses of potsherds or the details of flint axe types. There was a tendency for such studies to become an end in themselves, a dry, academic activity of little general interest. Those who protested against this included Clyde Kluckhohn (1905–60), who said in the 1940s, 'I should like to record an overwhelming impression that many students [of Middle American prehistory] are but slightly reformed antiquaries . . . there seems a great deal of obsessive wallowing in detail of and for itself . . . proliferation of minutiae is not its own justification'.

This kind of study led into blind alleys of specialization. Many archaeologists were concerned only with a narrow field; a particular class of objects, perhaps, or a period of time or specific region. Archaeology also developed within different traditions, so that there were few common aims or even methods. In Europe, much archaeology was carried out against a background of Classical historical studies. Excavation was sometimes seen merely as providing illustrative material for theories based on sparse historical evidence. The British archaeologist Sir Ian Richmond carried out one of the most successful projects of this kind at the hill-fort of Hod Hill in Dorset. In AD 43, 40,000 Roman troops invaded Britain. One of the legions, the Second, was led by the future emperor Vespasian, and, according to the Roman historian Suetonius, Vespasian 'proceeded to Britain where he fought thirty battles, subjugated two warlike tribes, and captured more than twenty towns, besides the entire Isle of Wight'. In an attempt to flesh out this rather bald statement, Richmond excavated at Hod Hill. Within it he found the so-called Chieftain's Hut, blitzed by salvoes of Roman ballistas, which were spear-like projectiles fired from a type of mechanical cross-bow. Richmond showed convincingly that the hill-fort was one of the 20 towns captured by Vespasian and that its occupants, tribesmen of the Durotriges, were the warlike Britons who had been subjugated. The excavation provided a neat and vivid piece of historical illustration. Yet Hod Hill was a complex Celtic tribal centre with a long, unrecorded history of its own. Richmond ignored this and limited himself to spotlighting a particular historical event, simply because it had been recorded by a Roman writer.

This kind of approach kept archaeology as a handmaiden of textual history. At a more trivial level, others saw archaeology as a technique for recovering objects: Greek painted pots or bits of statuary for the art historian; curiosities to decorate the cabinets of museums; coins for the collections of numismatists. Like the modern treasure-hunter, such people failed to see that the intrinsic interest of an archaeological object is its position in the ground in relation to a whole complex of other evidence.

In contrast, archaeology developed within a very different tradition in the United States. Once they were no longer feared, indigenous Indian groups became a fit subject of study for anthropologists. Mainstream anthropologists were principally concerned with living communities, and since the days of Lewis Henry Morgan (1818–81) there had been a widespread reaction against evolutionary approaches. Consequently, the full possibilities of archaeology and the study of change through time were not regarded as important priorities, reflecting a dismissive attitude to historical studies generally. When Henry Ford said 'History is bunk!', he was probably echoing the response of many American anthropologists who believed that historical studies seldom rose above *1066*

Above: Part of the enormous army of life-size terracotta statues found at the tomb of Qin Shihuangdi (reigned 221–210 BC), first emperor of China.

Above: Aerial photographs are of significant help in revealing to archaeologists features not visible on the ground.

Right: Diagram showing the diffusion of farming in Europe. The dates given are BP (before present). The expected pattern of spread at 500-year intervals is shown by the arcs. Broken lines indicate regional variations.

Right: The levels of the ancient tell, or mound, of Jericho are marked by five men. The topmost one stands on the present surface; the next on a tower of 8000 BC. The last stands in a ditch cut into the living rock.

and all That. It is hardly surprising that in the first half of this century, archaeology in the United States was either undergoing a crisis of confidence or quietly stagnating.

A changing attitude began in the 1940s and 1950s, notably in the writings of Julian Steward and Leslie White, who saw cultural change as a major subject of anthropological interest and helped to revive interest in the possibilities of archaeology. Steward's work was also important for the interest it promoted in human ecology – the interaction of people and their environment – a theme which is still of major interest. Reaction against the study of minutiae began with increased interest in the function of objects and also in regional settlement studies. In 1946, Gordon Willey, influenced by Steward, began to survey and analyse the Viru Valley in Peru, tackling the region as a whole rather than investigating individual 'important' sites. Another American, Robert Braidwood, adopted a similar approach in Iraqi Kurdistan when he combined with biologists to look for evidence of early agriculture. In Europe, archaeological growing pains were perhaps not quite so marked. The anti-evolutionist trend had never become as firmly established, and a traditional interest in environmental factors had been maintained. Jens Worsaae had recognized the potential for studying environmental change during his excavations of Danish peat bogs in the 19th century, and in Switzerland the remains of economically important plants such as flax, wheat, and barley had been recovered from the *lake villages* revealed by the lowering of Lake Constance during the dry period of 1853–54. The British archaeologists Sir Cyril Fox, O. G. S. Crawford and Grahame Clark were influential in broadening the scope of archaeology, away from object classification to the study of man in the environment. Clark, for example, carried out the classic excavation of the Mesolithic (Middle Stone Age) settlement of Star Carr in Yorkshire, northern England, combining pollen analysis, detailed recording of artefacts and the study of animal bones to reconstruct the economy and environment of a seasonally-occupied camp site. A similar approach was adopted in the Fenlands of eastern England, where biologists and archaeologists pooled their skills to study a remarkably well preserved Romano-British landscape. Both Star Carr and the Fens were notable for the quality of their evidence, largely as a result of water-logged conditions.

Technology in the field

Such projects made use of the growth in technology which aided archaeological exploration. Aerial photography was employed after the First World War, while other significant changes included the introduction of mechanized earth-moving equipment and detectors capable of locating metal and buried features. The rapidly-expanding arsenal of scientific techniques available for dating, analysis and site location, added to the growing interest in theoretical and methodological problems, made the 1960s and early 1970s a period of remarkable stimulus in archaeology. Similar trends could be seen in other subjects, notably geography and biology, in the wake of which archaeology followed. An increasingly vociferous demand for an explicitly scientific approach came from what, to many traditionalists, seemed an alarming 'New Model Army' of young archaeologists. The New Archaeologists insisted that research aims should be explicit, that hypotheses be tested and that numeracy was essential. Archaeological data needed to be quantified and analysed statistically, using computers. At times archaeology seemed a magpie of a subject, lifting ideas from geography, biology, *cybernetics* and mathematics. The proliferation of unfamiliar jargon and the movement away from the familiar literary, historical approach was alarming to many.

A growing interest developed in systems as a whole, including the interaction and feedback between them, and a retreat from explanations based on 'discoveries', 'inventions' or 'individual genius'. This encouraged more rigorous collecting and recording of artefacts on sites, together with the search for patterning. For example, Lewis Binford,

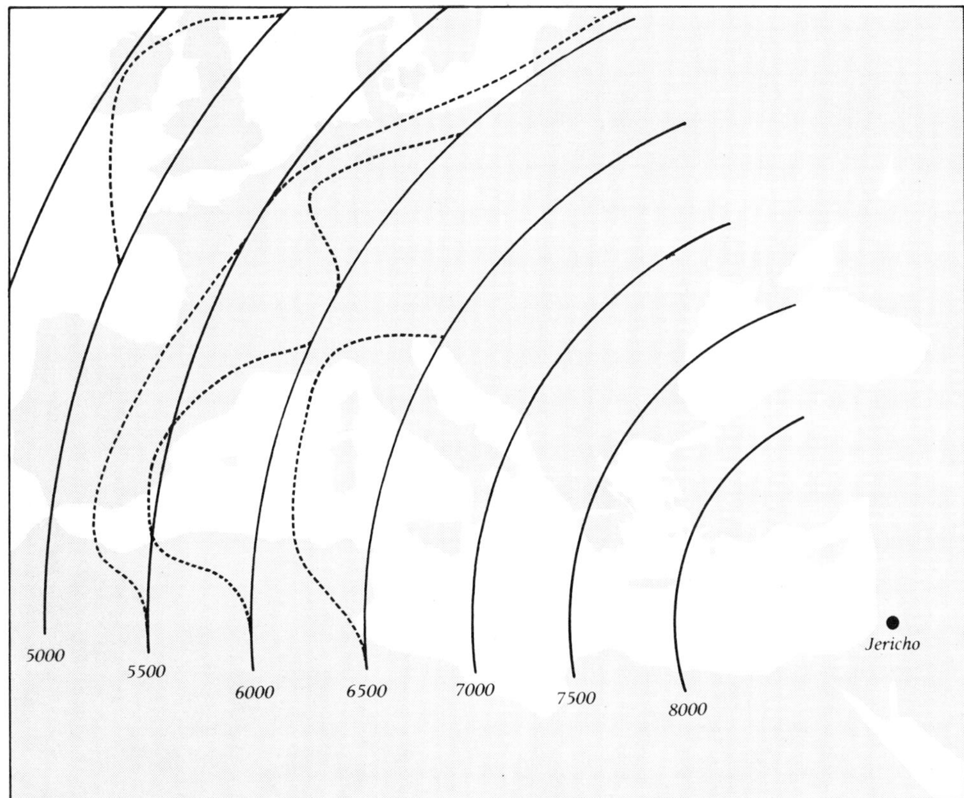

of the University of New Mexico explained the variability in some Palaeolithic flint assemblages in terms of specialized tool-kits, rather than 'culture' differences. This simply means that as different sorts of tools are found in a modern garage, kitchen and workshop belonging to the same family, so Palaeolithic groups used different flint tool-kits for different activities – plant food preparation, dismembering animals or preparing skins – and these activities could take place separately, on different sites and at different times of year in an annual cycle.

Studying the ways in which debris patterns are distributed on sites has generated an interest in *ethnology*, in particular as to how today's pre-industrial societies value and dispose of their waste products. Social anthropologists have, on the whole, ignored the material culture of the societies they studied, and there is a growing willingness on the part of archaeologists to gather anthropological data for their own purposes. Recent studies have examined bone disposal among Eskimos, stone tool manufacture in New Guinea, pottery in Guatemala and Ghana, and rubbish dispersal and food storage among African peoples. Most of these studies have focused on interpreting the economy, but there is an increasing awareness that rubbish itself reflects a society's world view. For example, among some African groups, cattle skulls are used as purifying and protective symbols. They are set around granaries, places associated with men, and are not found in parts of the settlement used by women. Such factors obviously have wider implications than economic ones alone; indeed the economy may be firmly embedded in the religious sub-system.

The need for rigorous data collection has promoted the widespread use of techniques such as sieving to recover the full range of available artefacts and biological material. Seeds, fish and bird bones, and small flints can easily remain undetected when sieving is not carried out at a site. Sampling techniques, such as those used in taking public opinion polls, have become an essential tool. By using these it is possible to make generalizations about populations as a whole, and to make comparisons between sites.

As diffusionist explanations became discredited, interest grew in taking regions as units of study. These gave statistically definable populations; appealed to the systems theorists; and coincided with a similar interest on the part of geographers, whose work began to make an important impact on archaeology. Another area of research which developed rapidly among archaeologists in the late 1960s was trade, a subject which linked local, regional and wider systems. It was stimulated by the development of techniques which made it possible to identify the source of artefacts. Pottery, for example, can be studied by using the methods of geologists. *Thin-sectioning* and *heavy mineral analysis* enable a particular set of minerals present in the clay of a pot to be identified. Providing that the minerals are sufficiently distinctive, the pottery's area of manufacture can then be located. Heavy mineral analysis made it possible to pin-point the southern English county of Dorset as the manufacturing centre of a type of Romano-British pottery known as Black-Burnished Ware. The pottery's distribution has been plotted and its trading patterns revealed. Surprisingly large quantities were bought on behalf of the Roman army and shipped by way of the west coast of Britain to Hadrian's Wall. Thin sectioning has been used on material as varied as Roman amphorae from Spain and southern Italy to Neolithic stone axes.

Another important technique is *neutron activation analysis* which identifies the trace elements in material such as obsidian and jade and again enables the sources to be located. Work on obsidian in the Mediterranean and Near East has been particularly fruitful. Obsidian is a volcanic glass found naturally in relatively few places, including some volcanic islands in the Mediterranean, such as Lipari, and in central Turkey. Identifying the source is therefore relatively straightforward. Obsidian was one of the finest materials available for Stone Age communities to manufacture into points and blades, and must have been a highly valued commodity. As early as the 8th millennium BC, fragments are known to have travelled as much as 1,000 kilometres. By measuring the proportion of obsidian at sites varying in distance from the ultimate source of supply, archaeologists can erect models to explain the kinds of interaction or trade which would best account for the pattern they had discovered. This study has enabled archaeology to contribute to a field previously entirely dominated by anthropologists. Because it is possible to analyse forms of exchange and redistribution in pre-industrial societies, the whole subject of culture studies has been opened up and looked at in social terms.

Recent work on the spread of agriculture typifies the approach of modern archaeology. Regional surveys have located early Neolithic sites across the Near East and Europe, while recovery techniques such as sieving have provided plant and animal remains. These organic materials have not only produced biological information about the earliest domesticated plants and animals, but also radiocarbon dates. When plotted, these dates create a kind of chronological contour map, showing the spread of farming across Asia, North Africa and Europe, and on the basis of the preliminary evidence a mathematical model has been constructed. The 'wave of advance' model was first developed by geneticists but has been usefully adapted by archaeologists to explain the spread of farming in terms of population growth, allowing for a limited amount of territorial expansion with each generation. The model provides a simplified reflection of reality, with variables expressed in mathematical terms which can be measured and tested. It then serves as a tool for examining change both at transcontinental and local level.

Archaeology in practice

For most people, archaeology is equated with excavation. Although important, however, digging is not the only part of archaeology. Sometimes it is not possible to excavate; often it is not even desirable. Excavation should be the last resort.

The first aim of the archaeologist is to reconstruct the settlement pattern in the parish, district, state, region or whatever unit has been selected for study. Ideally, the unit should comprise some sort of geographical or cultural entity, but the archaeologist is often circumscribed by modern political boundaries and a compromise has to be reached. Another ideal is that the land unit should be systematically and intensively surveyed; again, this is not always possible.

Archaeological sites are not rare; they exist in enormous numbers. Nevertheless, there are problems in finding them. The ease with which ancient sites can be located depends upon a number of factors, including the material used in building construction. Temporary and seasonal encampments in which shelters were made from wood, hides or cloth are notoriously difficult to find. Much easier are buildings made of stone, with roofing tiles, plaster, even mosaic pavements in the case of Roman villas. In these cases, however, the abandoned building may have acted as a local quarry, particularly in an area where stone does not naturally occur. Robbed buildings, even if once substantial, can sometimes leave little trace. The opposite occurs where buildings made of material such as sun-dried brick are regularly demolished and built over. This has happened in the mounds or tells of the Near East, at the biblical Tel Hazor and Jericho, for example, which have accumulated as man-made hills and are so prominent that even the most myopic fieldworker could scarcely miss them. Layers of occupation also build up on very different sites, such as those founded near water. In riverside cities such as London or York, modern streets may be several metres above the occupation layers of the Romans or Vikings. Each generation has built on the debris of its predecessors in order to stay as dry as possible. Accumulated layers can present a problem, and because they mask what lies beneath, excavation is necessary. Erosion of soil from hill slopes, often precipitated by farmers who have deforested the land, can bury ancient settlements in valley bottoms. In Greece, scoured limestone mountains project above silted-up valleys. Low-lying Mycenaean sites can remain buried and undetectable beneath this later fill, only appearing if discovered by accident during well-digging, laying a new road scheme, or perhaps if a stream cuts into them. The same problem arises in southern Britain, where the soils of Romano-British fields have crept down-hill and buried earlier prehistoric traces.

Land-use is the major factor in aiding or hindering the field archaeologist. Centuries of ploughing, for example, will erode the most substantial of man-made earthworks. In the traditionally arable area of the Thames Valley, even massive Neolithic henge monuments contemporary with Stonehenge, such as the Big Rings at Dorchester and the Devil's Quoits at Stanton Harcourt, have been flattened by the plough. When Devil's Quoits was excavated in 1972, the grooves of medieval furrows were found etched across the site and between them large pits into which the Neolithic standing stones had been tipped by the medieval peasants 600–700 years ago. Not surprisingly, only a very few pre-medieval earthworks survive in the Thames Valley. The plough has obliterated them as effectively as the sea washing over a child's sandcastle. As a result, early antiquaries in England believed that the higher chalk Downs, such as Salisbury Plain or the Ridgeways of Dorset and Berkshire, were the only areas of prehistoric settlement. The valleys were assumed to have been entanglements of impenetrable forest. In fact the antiquaries were misled owing to the contrast between the low-lying zone of destruction by ploughing and the higher area of preservation. Above the high tide mark of arable agriculture were the grasslands of medieval England, under which were preserved prehistoric burial mounds, settlements, trackways and fields. Unfortunately, much of this tracery of delicate earthworks has now also been destroyed, by the great ploughing campaigns at the time of the Napoleonic wars and again in recent years, stimulated by the demand for increased food production.

Woodlands and tropical forest can help to protect archaeological remains from the effects of agriculture, yet make their discovery difficult. The problems are equally great in areas of broken terrain. In the Middle East, the Dead Sea Rift valley is honeycombed with inaccessible caves and fissures so that a systematic survey is slow, hazardous and at times impossible. It is little wonder that the most spectacular discoveries, such as the Dead Sea Scrolls, have been the chance finds of local Bedouin shepherds.

Archaeologists cannot rely solely on chance finds of the spectacular, however. If the settlement pattern of a region is to be reconstructed accurately, then its survey should be systematic, with an awareness of any unavoidable bias in the evidence. In practice it is almost impossible to miss large, impressive sites with remains above ground. There may be a Machu Picchu awaiting discovery in some corner of a lost world, but that is not the problem. An archaeologist wishes to locate the full range of sites: camps belonging to the seasonal cycle of the hunter or nomadic herdsman; the hierarchy of farms, villages, religious centres or towns in a more complex society. All over the world the spectacular, the rare and the prominent have, not unnaturally, taken precedence over the everyday and the elusive. Yet it is the latter which form the foundations of any society and an understanding of it.

Preparation

The area to be surveyed can be approached in a number of different ways. In Britain and Scandinavia, existing parishes are often selected for study. These small land units are usually of early medieval origin, although accumulating evidence indicates that some may be much earlier. The advantage of the parish is that it is a coherent block of land, in terms of medieval organization at least; and it is not too large for a total survey. The main disadvantage is that parishes are not usually selected at random and so cannot be used for the statistical analysis that is necessary for generalizations to be made about a whole region.

An alternative method, where a region cannot be intensely surveyed in total, is to select a random sample. This will usually mean sub-dividing the region on the basis of geology, soil type, vegetation, altitude or other such factors. The units are then randomly selected to represent the proportions of the different sub-divisions. If 25 per cent of the region is, for example, limestone plateau, then the survey sample units will include a similar proportion of this particular land form. The size and shape of sample units have to be decided, and are influenced by such factors as the area of the sites being sought and the logistics of moving from one sample unit to the next. In practice, the use of transects, or strips of ground running at right angles to the main geological belts, often provides the simplest solution.

Before the archaeologist begins an intensive survey there is usually much background work to be done. Occasionally, in a remote, thinly occupied area this may not amount to a great deal, but in western Europe where there is an enormous variety of sources of information, this stage is very important. Chance finds may have accumulated over two or three centuries and will be recorded in journals, newspapers, museum records or national archives. Maps, especially old ones, are a rich source of information. They enable the archaeologist to study field and settlement patterns and to understand relict features in the present-day landscape. For example, a mound may be a Bronze Age barrow; it may alternatively have been built as the base for a medieval windmill. Maps and charters also incorporate place-names, which provide a rich field of study in themselves. Names such as 'black field' may indicate an ancient settlement site; the Saxon word 'chessils' means pebbles or small stones, but is often used for fields where Roman mosaic pavements lie buried. Names may also reflect the origin of a settlement. In France, Belgium and Germany, names incorporating 'acum' indicate a Roman estate; for example, Nassonacum (Nassogn) in the Ardennes, from where the emperor Valentinian issued a number of edicts. In Britain, 'wicham' names, such as Wycomb in Gloucestershire and Wickham Bushes in Berkshire, also seem to indicate Roman sites. The word probably derives from a Saxon corruption of the Roman 'vicus', meaning a small settlement or village. The impact of settlers speaking new languages sometimes results in extremes of tautology. A place called Bredon-on-the-Hill, in the English Midlands, can be literally translated from the Celtic and Old English elements as 'Hill-hill-on-the-hill'.

Maps, documentary evidence and chance discoveries all need to be examined by the fieldworker, while another rich source of information is aerial photography. Since the 1920s vast numbers of photographs have been gathered, some of which were taken for specific archaeological purposes, others as part of land-use or military surveys. The photographs are usually of two basic types: oblique shots of a specific archaeological site taken from a relatively low height, perhaps 300–500 metres; or *vertical photographs*, normally extracted from systematic higher level surveys covering a whole region, or even country. Vertical photographs will overlap by about a third and pairs of them can be used under a *stereoscope* to give a three-dimensional image of the ground. Although the vertical photographs may not be taken for archaeological purposes, they have the advantage of giving complete coverage. *Oblique photographs* will usually be taken by archaeological agencies whose aim is to achieve the best possible results. Sites can manifest themselves in a number of different ways, and the requirement may simply be to obtain a bird's eye view of a known monument, Stonehenge, for example, which was first photographed from a balloon in 1907. Upstanding earthworks show best when photographed in an oblique light, as in low winter sunlight, and if the earthwork has a dusting of snow on its crest then the contrast of highlight and shadow is even greater. Aerial survey provides a rapid means of examining upstanding archaeological sites, especially in extensive and difficult terrain. In this way, large areas of pre-Columbian ridged fields have been mapped in the tropical lowlands of eastern Bolivia, western Ecuador, Colombia and Surinam.

In some parts of the world, notably in north-west Europe, cropmarks are a major form of archaeological evidence. These are revealed as contrasts of colour and height in growing crops such as barley and wheat. The variations are brought about by disturbance of the subsoil where there are buried ditches, pits or house foundations. Once a ditch has been abandoned it gradually silts up, forming a vein of moist humic soil. If a crop such as barley has roots reaching down into this material, it may grow taller and take longer to ripen, and from the ground a vague pattern of marks may be visible. In the mid-19th century the English antiquary Stephen Stone used to ride around the Thames Valley noting cropmarks from the lofty heights of his horse. From an aircraft, however, the marks become much more coherent, just as the pattern of a carpet seems a mass of indistinguishable colour when viewed from close to, and becomes clearer when seen from further away.

Cropmarks show best on free-draining subsoils such as gravel, because in periods of low rainfall the land becomes very dry. Once the lack of soil moisture contrasts markedly with that of the buried ditch or pit then cropmarks will begin to show. On heavier clay soils, cropmarks may appear but they are more elusive. It is also necessary to have a responsive crop growing over the site. Barley is ideal because it has a long rooting system which can take advantage of the buried reservoirs of moist soil. Another advantage is its dense growth, which can therefore provide a well-defined image of the buried site, similar to the small closely-spaced dots which make up a newspaper photograph. Some crops are not responsive or are reluctantly so. For example, grassland may reveal marks, but usually only in exceptionally dry conditions. In the remarkably arid year of 1976 in Britain, vast numbers of new sites became visible under grass. In Oxford, the rings of a Bronze Age barrow cemetery appeared in the University Parks and Romano-British settlements showed under Oxford City football ground and a college cricket pitch. Archaeological features can also stimulate the opposite reaction: ancient roads, streets or stone buildings with solid walls and floors may stunt a crop. Negative cropmarks can then appear, sometimes showing the outlines of buildings with astonishing clarity. The plans of Romano-British towns such as Wroxeter (Viroconium Cornoviorum) and Silchester (Calleva Atrebatum) have been reconstructed in great detail from this kind of evidence.

A third way in which sites can be revealed in aerial photographs is as soil marks. Where the topsoil is thin and contrasts in colour with buried features, soil marks will appear when the land is ploughed. In the Somme Valley and the neighbouring region of northern France, over 1,000 Roman villas have been found from aerial photography in the past 20 years. Of course, the implications for the preservation of these sites are horrifying, because it is destructive deep ploughing which has raked through the buildings and revealed them to the aerial photographer.

More sophisticated aerial techniques which are sometimes employed by archaeologists include *false colour infra-red photography*, which can be especially useful in woodland areas. The *sumach* which colonizes abandoned Indian settlements in the woods of eastern Canada can be picked out in this way. Satellite photography of potential oil-producing regions in Alaska has also been exploited for archaeological surveys. On the whole, however, the more elaborate and expensive methods of aerial survey, developed for military surveillance purposes, are as yet not widely available to archaeology.

Field survey

Once the preliminary background survey has been carried out and the sample units defined, the archaeologist must fieldwalk the chosen area. The prosaic but essential task of asking owners for permission to have access to their land is one of the principal problems in the more heavily populated parts of the world. Diplomatic skills are a vital attribute of the successful field archaeologist. Ideally, fieldwalking should be standardized as much as possible, with people evenly spaced out but sufficiently close together to see the smallest units which are of interest, whether flint flakes, pottery sherds, buildings, or all of these. A standard walking speed should be adopted. The aim is to achieve a representative sample, not to find literally every potsherd.

The discovery rate of sites may depend on ground conditions. In remote, dry desert areas, such as the Atacama Desert of Chile, preservation may be excellent, and Stone Age tool-making sites may be found still lying on the surface. In the northern Negev Desert in Israel, pottery scatters of Bronze Age settlements are often clearly visible. In northern Europe, worm action results in the rapid formation of soil and the burial of even the most substantial sites. Agriculture can then plane away any upstanding traces. Hence fieldwalking may not give an entirely representative picture, and this is particularly the case when the artefacts from a settlement are not durable. In Britain, Iron Age and Saxon pottery is often low-fired and soft, so that it rapidly disintegrates in rain and frost. The same is true of Neolithic and Bronze Age pottery, but communities of these periods usually used durable stone tools which survive well. On farmland, sites can be most easily discovered after ploughing and light rain, for in such conditions sherds of pottery and pieces of flint are brought to the surface. Flat sites under grassland may be impossible to find simply from fieldwalking.

When fieldwalking, it is customary to collect surface material on the basis of a grid or within circular sample points. In this way, potsherds and other artefacts can be analysed to see if any pattern, either chronological or functional, is apparent in their distribution. It is sometimes advisable not to remove artefacts from a settlement as this can deplete the evidence, especially if there is neither time nor inclination to collect them systematically. Considerable discussion has taken place among archaeologists about the reliability of surface field survey. The most determined advocates of intensive systematic survey, and those who have developed the most advanced sampling strategies, are in Arizona and New Mexico, in the southwestern United States. Two factors are important here: good conditions for discovery, in that these states are dry and thinly populated; and federal funding for large-scale development projects, such as the flooding of river valleys. In Britain and the Continent, surveys are, for a variety of historical reasons, more often extensive and haphazard, and some still question the reliability of statistically-based intensive surveys. Nevertheless, there is a growing feeling that field survey should play a larger part in archaeology and that excavation must become more selective.

On the basis of regional survey it is possible to develop hypotheses about settlement patterns, population fluctuation and social organization. It is also possible to highlight areas threatened by modern development, such as urban expansion, reservoirs, road schemes and quarrying. Different attitudes to selecting sites for excavation are adopted in different parts of the world. Sometimes a spectacular site is chosen for supposed research purposes, or to boost a tourist industry; sometimes for pragmatic reasons, such as its proximity to a university, or its romantic location; or because it is threatened and some well-meaning person wants to rescue it. Ideally again, in a regional research design, a representative selection of sites should be chosen to tackle specific problems. If they can be found among sites threatened by development, then it is best to excavate these. Archaeological evidence is a finite resource and there is no point in digging an unthreatened site unnecessarily. In practical terms, funds are more often available for rescue projects.

In fact, the vast majority of archaeological sites will never be dug. During the late 1960s and 1970s an enormous increase in the number of known sites in many countries resulted from more intensive fieldwork and aerial photography. In the early 1970s the construction of an English motorway, the M5, was observed by archaeologists for the first time. As a result, the cutting of this 50-metre wide corridor, 100 kilometres long, through some of Britain's more intractable clayland produced 130 sites where only 10 had been known before. Again, in the Nene Valley of eastern England, aerial photography increased the known sites from 36 in 1931 to 434 in 1972. In 1975, an archaeological estimate as to the impact of a drainage project in the Cache River basin in Arkansas concluded that 477 sites would be directly affected – that is, bulldozed, churned up or cut about. The subsequent intensification of agriculture, it was thought, would have repercussions on about 5,748 sites.

With archaeological sites in these quantities it should be obvious that excavation of more than a handful is impossible in the foreseeable future. Any sizeable excavation is expensive and time-consuming, allowing for analysis, conservation, publication, storage and display after the dig has finished. Archaeologists have a responsibility to see that the society within which they work has sufficient information to conserve a representative sample of evidence for the future. Where that evidence is eroded by essential development, the aim should be to record as much as seems necessary. This can be achieved in a variety of ways. Some sites have to be analysed with little or no excavation, by surveying the surface evidence and by geophysical survey with *resistivity meters* and *magnetometers* to plot features below ground. A site may be sampled by excavation on a large or small scale, depending on the questions being asked of it. It always pays, however, to expect the unexpected; new information can cause an instantaneous revaluation of a site's potential.

In the last decade much of the emphasis in Europe and America has been placed on rescue excavation. This has thrived on the image of the hard-pressed archaeologist leading a frantic scramble in the mouth of a juggernaut bulldozer to salvage the delicate evidence of the past. Although this picture holds an element of truth, it generally means, should it happen, that something has gone wrong. Rescue archaeology has many different guises, but when properly planned, its excavations should be to the highest standards.

History of excavation

General Pitt-Rivers, the doyen of scientific excavators, first brought rigorous techniques of planning and recording to archaeology. Having retired from the army, and with a considerable personal fortune, Pitt-Rivers proceeded to dig barrows and settlements on his own estate on Cranborne Chase in Dorset. For their time these excavations were models of military precision and discipline. Unfortunately, few of his contemporaries had the same resources or dedication and it was 20 years before anyone attempted to imitate him. The torch was consciously taken up by Mortimer Wheeler (1890–1976) who wrote in his autobiography:

> 'Between 1880 and 1900, General Pitt-Rivers in Cranborne Chase had brought archaeological digging and recording to a remarkable degree of perfection, and had presented his methods and results meticulously in several imposing volumes. Then what? Nothing. Nobody paid the slightest attention to the old man. One of his assistants had even proceeded to dig up a lake village much as Schliemann had dug up Troy, or St John Hope, Silchester; like potatoes. Not only had the clock not gone on, but it had been set back'.

Wheeler's own campaigns between the World Wars, at the Roman town of Caerleon in Wales, the hill-fort of Maiden Castle in Dorset, and later in India at Harappa and Taxila, established the importance of rigorous excavation. His insistence on stratigraphical control led to the development of digging within a grid of boxes, with sections preserved between each. This framework, 'le système Wheeler' was useful in its day as a means of increasing excavation discipline and ensuring that layers on deep sites were understood and recorded. It had several drawbacks, however; it was over-rigid, stressed the vertical stratigraphy at the expense of across site patterning, and hindered an overall view of the site. Wheeler stressed that the baulks or sections should be removed eventually to ensure that they did not obscure features within them; it was theoretically possible that the walls of a rectangular building could lie entirely within the baulks. Needless to say, lesser excavators often left their baulks in place. 'Le système Wheeler' is still accepted uncritically in some parts of the world and must be one of the most familiar sights in archaeology. Many American excavators still clutter themselves with the trans-Atlantic equivalent, 'the five foot square'. Amazingly, a French archaeologist recently suggested, perhaps seriously, that 'le système Wheeler' might be improved by digging a network of octagonal trenches so that any stone walls would stick out somewhere.

In Germany and Scandinavia in the 1930s and 1940s, open-area excavation was pioneered, in which settlements were extensively cleared in a single large trench, thus allowing the contemporary plan to be seen all at once. This had particular advantages for the understanding of timber buildings, which could pass undetected in small boxes. It was a refugee German archaeologist, Gerhard Bersu, who introduced the open-area technique to Britain with his influential excavations at the Iron Age farmstead of Little Woodbury in Wiltshire.

Although the methods of excavation adopted will vary according to the type of site being studied, the basic aim is to unravel its layers and features in such a way as to be able to put them into chronological order and to understand their function. From the features and their associated finds, the archaeologist then attempts to understand the economic and social structure of the settlement, the changes that have taken place in it and its relationship to other sites. Some large, flat settlements, such as those seen in cropmarks, have little vertical stratigraphy. The features in them – ditches, pits, the post holes of buildings – are cut into the underlying subsoil, but there is little or no accumulation of layers. This is the type of site where open-area excavation was first developed. Once the settlement area has been defined by mapping of cropmarks, fieldwalking and geophysical surveying, an area will be selected for excavation. This may include all or part of the known site, depending on the objectives. Needless to say, the more carefully a settlement is dug, the more information will be recovered. Many area excavations are begun by removing the overlying topsoil with machinery. Some machines work without running over the cleared site and so leave a clean, undisturbed surface for the archaeologist to excavate. Others are fast but heavy, and may disturb the surface, removing the slight traces of any timber buildings. Mechanical stripping may also destroy useful evidence lying in the topsoil, such as the distribution of artefacts. Topsoil clearance by hand, in which the soil is sieved, is the most careful way of starting an excavation but is not always practicable on large sites with perhaps 20 to 50 or more centimetres of *overburden*. A sampling strategy may be the best solution, involving random units of topsoil being dug and sieved by hand, specific areas being cleared by light machinery, and larger machines being used more extensively. There are, however, many possible permutations.

Collecting finds

Once cleared, such a site will resemble an ink-blot test; a mass of dark features showing against the (it is hoped) contrasting subsoil. These features have to be disentangled by investigating their relationship to one another, on straightforward stratigraphic principles; A cuts B cuts C. Finds will be carefully recorded, soil samples sieved for animal bones, plant remains and artefacts, the features planned and every stage photographed. Some delicate finds may need the services of an on-site conservator, but more often they will be carefully packed and inspected in a museum or project laboratory. Archaeological teams vary in size, but usually include archaeological supervisors, draughtsmen, surveyors, a photographer, and the services of a zoologist, botanist and soil scientist.

Above: The grid system in operation during an excavation at St Albans, the Roman town of Verulamium, during the 1950s.

The same excavation principles apply on sites, such as towns, which have a more complex, deeper stratigraphy. Great advances have been made since the Second World War in urban archaeology, for German archaeologists took advantage of bomb damage to excavate beneath cities such as Cologne. Other spectacular successes have been at Novgorod in the Soviet Union, and the great early medieval trading centres of northern Europe: Dorestad in Holland, Hedeby in Denmark and Birka in Sweden. In Britain, a whole series of urban archaeological units sprang up in the later 1960s and 1970s at historic cities such as Winchester, Oxford, Norwich, York and London. In cities, the depth of the archaeological deposit can create difficulties. Exactly the same problems are faced on Middle Eastern tells or at sites such as Knossos on Crete or Lerna in Greece, where enormously thick deposits have built up over several thousand years. Ironically, some of the most interesting layers are often near the bottom. At English cities such as Oxford and Winchester, one of the principal subjects of research is the origins of Saxon urbanization, which took place between 1,000 and 1,500 years ago. The Saxon deposits often lie several metres beneath later medieval and post-medieval occupation. They are also elusive as the medieval habit of digging rubbish pits has destroyed much of them. In Knossos and Lerna, excavators have a similar problem, for the base of the sequence contains vital Neolithic deposits.

The technical difficulties of excavating down to these levels are immense. Even more of a dilemma at a site such as Knossos is how to reach the early deposits if important archaeological finds, such as a Minoan palace, lie on top of them. At Pompeii and Herculaneum, much of the early history of the towns still lies hidden beneath the buildings preserved by the eruption of AD 79.

In deeply stratified sites, much emphasis has been placed in the past on small trenches which cut through the whole sequence. This method gives some idea of the time-span of occupation, but provides little information about the nature of the whole settlement at any particular time. Consequently, the open-area system has been adopted with great success at sites such as Tanner Street in Winchester, although the problem still remains of how to excavate extensively on deep deposits. These operations are expensive and dangerous: several archaeologists have been killed in deep trenches which have collapsed. So far only 'key-hole' trenches have reached into the depths of Neolithic Knossos.

Organization today

The organization of archaeological projects varies enormously. During the past decade archaeology as a profession has grown significantly, particularly in Europe, North America and Australia. Third World countries, anxious to establish a national identity, also show an increasing interest in their past. But with complex problems relating to health, food and industrial development, archaeology does not always rank high in their list of priorities. Most archaeologists in Europe and North America are based within museums or universities; departments of Anthropology, History, Classics, Prehistory and Archaeology, even Physics, house them. In Britain, the expansion of archaeology in the 1960s and 1970s saw the development of professional archaeological excavation units, sometimes as independent organizations or attached to museums, universities or local government planning departments. At the same time the number of university teaching posts greatly increased.

The largest expansion of all occurred in the United States with the passing of the National Environmental Policy Act (NEPA) of 1969 and a subsequent Presidential Executive Order in 1971. These had the effect of requiring that archaeological survey and 'mitigation' should be carried out in advance of federally-funded projects. Almost overnight a new breed of 'contract' archaeologists sprang up fully armed, like Kadmos's warriors from the dragon seed. In response, the first professional Institution of Archaeologists was formed to try to maintain some sort of standards.

In Britain, a flourishing tradition of amateur archaeology stretches back to the county societies of Victorian England. Public interest has been fostered by such archaeologists as Sir Mortimer Wheeler who said, 'I was, and am convinced of the moral and academic necessity of sharing scientific work to the fullest possible extent with the man in the street and in the field. Today . . . he is in fact our employer'. The popularity of archaeology is reflected in the production of excellent BBC television programmes such as *Chronicle*. Popular interest is also strong in Scandinavian countries, particularly Denmark, where P. V. Glob has produced a series of authoritative and attractive books. Volunteers are normally welcome on professional excavations in Britain. In some parts of the world, particularly America, this is unfortunately not always the case. In most Third World countries, excavations run by Western archaeologists employ local workmen, for the host country sees foreign-financed archaeology as a means of providing employment. Excavations have been used in the same way in the United States and Britain at times of high unemployment.

Many people visualize an archaeological excavation as a romantic expedition to an exotic land. The increase of locally-based professional archaeology has made that type of project the exception rather than the rule. Short-term skirmishes are no substitute for long-term rigorous research. Rome, Athens, Ankara, Jerusalem, Amman and other cities house the Archaeological Schools of Britain, France, Germany, America and other countries. Through these, excavations and research in the host countries are organized. Increasingly, and quite properly, such countries with rich remains are organizing their own state archaeological services, retaining the finds from excavations in their own museums, and controlling strictly the work of foreign archaeologists. Unfortunately, the activities of the 'heroic' breed of archaeologists did not always lay a foundation of trust. There has also been a welcome tendency to pool international resources when tackling specific threats, in the Nile Valley, for example, and at Carthage, Mohenjo Daro, the temple of Borobadur in Indonesia, and most recently the Euphrates Valley in eastern Turkey. The only reservation about these efforts is that some donor countries attempt to achieve maximum publicity for their investment by being associated with the most spectacular rather than the archaeologically most useful.

Conservation

Conservation of its evidence is probably the greatest single problem facing archaeology today. The growth of population, increasing industrialization, the intensification of agriculture, the unscrupulousness of some art dealers and museums and irresponsibility of treasure hunters all combine to erode the evidence of the past. Agriculture is probably the single largest, if least dramatic, agent of destruction. It is also the most difficult to confront, as food production is obviously a vital necessity. As agricultural techniques become more advanced, so ancient remains are obliterated. One of the most successful archaeological surveys in recent years has been in Etruria, north of Rome, but it took place precisely because hundreds of sites were being ploughed up for the first time. Much more dramatic are the conflicts which can leave important sites wrecked. Ankgor Wat in Kampuchea has recently been used as a battlefield and so has much of Cyprus.

The phenomenal increase in the value of antiquities has encouraged a flourishing black market, as one minor example will illustrate. In 1967, a silver tetradrachm of Alexander the Great, the commonest of his silver coins, would fetch less than \$50; ten years later the price had reached \$400. Most countries with spectacular remains have laws protecting their sites and artefacts, but this does little to prevent illicit trade so long as there are customers. In some parts of the world tomb-robbing is almost a traditional occupation. Elsewhere, treasure hunting has been enormously boosted by the commercial stimulus of metal detector manufacturers. In Western Europe this is a growing plague. Roman temples and towns in particular are raked through and damaged for the coins and metalwork they contain. Irresponsible metal detecting is the archaeological equivalent of robbing eggs from a rare bird's nest, but growing opposition, including recent legislation in Britain, has so far done little to curb the practice.

In some areas, the attraction is objects other than metal. In New Mexico, *Mimbres* sites of the 1st millennium AD contain particularly attractive painted pots, and a survey in the early 1970s revealed that over 90 per cent of the sites had been looted. Sometimes artefacts of dubious origin reach the market and are of such value that they attract attention.

The UNESCO Convention on Cultural Property aims to limit the market in antiquities, but more than a few museums and dealers would agree with the attitude expressed in a letter to an American House of Representatives sub-committee that 'private acquisition and circulation of art must be allowed to exist freely and unhampered'. Fortunately, archaeology is not primarily about remarkable works of art or curios; as General Pitt-Rivers austerely said over 80 years ago: 'Common things are of more importance than particular things because they are more prevalent'. But the everyday can all too easily appear dull, especially if it consists of a dusty collection of potsherds and flint tools in a 'dingy municipal repository' of a museum. The best museums bring the past alive, whether a national museum in London, New York, Mexico City or Athens, or a small local museum providing a sense of place and identity. The evidence of the past is all around us. It is the task of archaeology to identify, appreciate and seek to protect it.

Right: Series of photographs showing several stages in the archaeological study of a specific area. The study begins with aerial photography (top) and ends with an attempt at reconstruction.

Left: An ancient landscape revealed by aerial photography. In fields of barley growing at Claydon Pike near Lechlade, Gloucestershire, in England can be seen cropmarks of Iron Age farmsteads (about 300 BC), a Roman road (the parallel lines), Roman fields and post-medieval fields. In the lower field the streets and building plots of a Romano-British village are visible. The whole area is to be quarried for gravel, and so with the backing of the mineral operators, excavations begin.

Centre left: A JCB earth-moving machine begins to strip off the ploughsoil. This stage follows detailed survey on the ground, including analysis of pottery scatters and phosphates in the soil. The enclosure ditch and circular drainage gully around an Iron Age round-house of about 300 BC is revealed.

Below: Excavation of the Iron Age farmstead with sections cut across the enclosure ditch. Twenty per cent of the ditch is randomly sampled so that pottery, animal bone and plant remains retrieved by sieving the soil can be analysed using statistical techniques.

Bottom left: Area excavation revealing an island of gravel surrounded by marsh. The island was covered with a cluster of ten Iron Age round-houses separated by linear ditches. About 30 Iron Age houses were found at Claydon Pike, once occupied by the families of Celtic herdsmen who kept cattle and sheep on the rich local pasture.

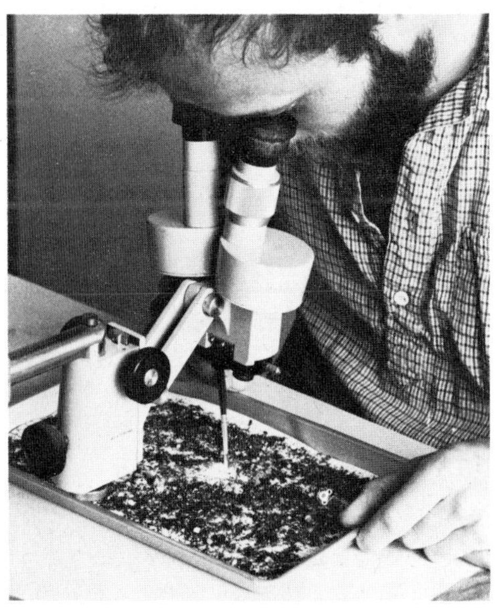

Bottom centre: Analysis. Excavation can produce vast quantities of finds. At the Claydon Pike Iron Age settlement they range from pottery, salt containers, textile equipment and quern stones to wood, beetles and animal bones. Here a botanist examines plant remains preserved by being carbonized.

Above: Reconstruction. Prehistoric farmsteads such as Claydon Pike can be much better understood by experimental or action archaeology. At Butser Hill in Hampshire, a similar farmstead has been reconstructed so that buildings, crop production and storage, domestic animals and prehistoric technology can be studied.

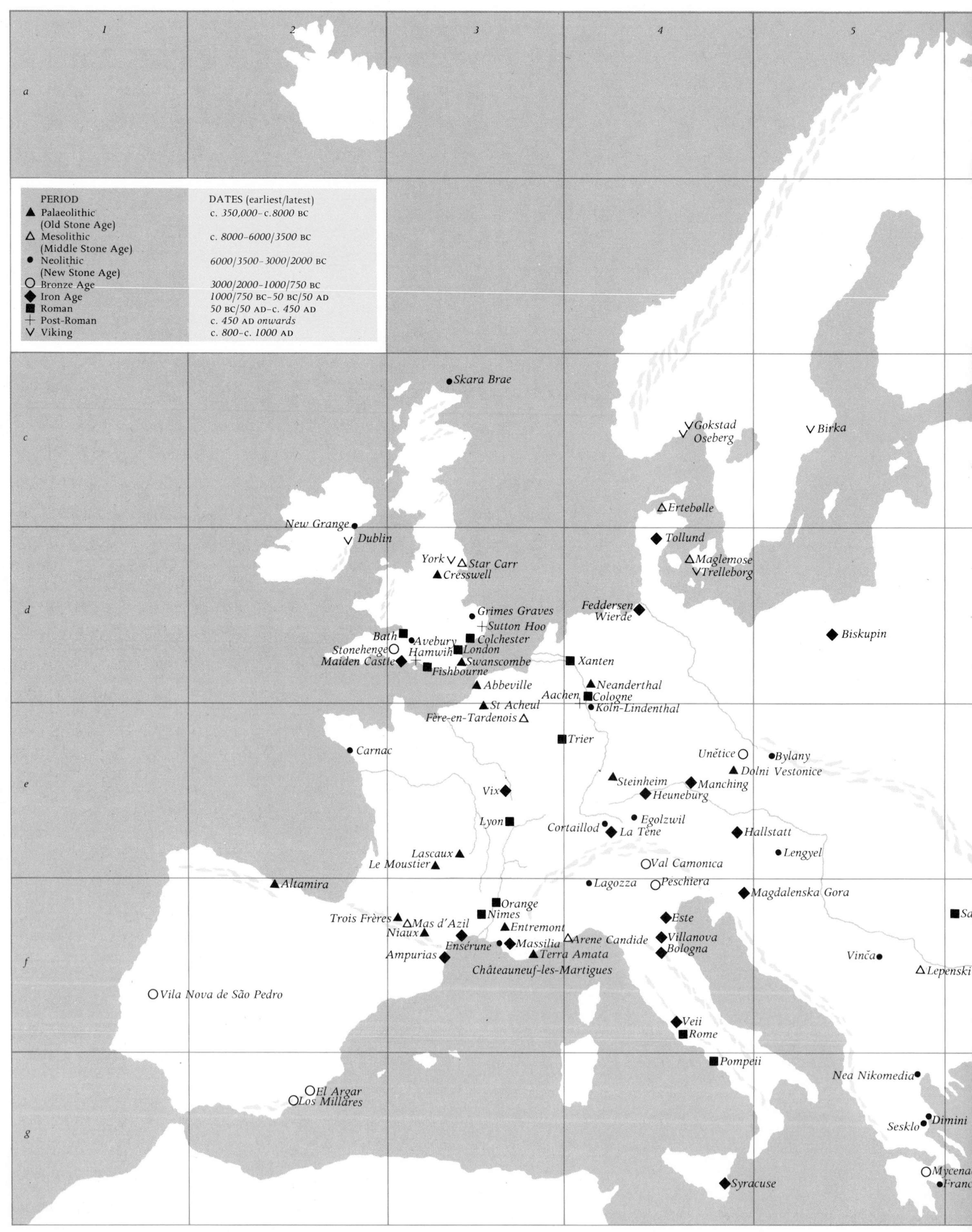

1
2
3
4
5
a
c
d
e
f
g
PERIOD
DATES (earliest/latest)
Palaeolithic (Old Stone Age) c. 350,000–c.8000 BC
Mesolithic (Middle Stone Age) c. 8000–6000/3500 BC
Neolithic (New Stone Age) 6000/3500–3000/2000 BC
Bronze Age 3000/2000–1000/750 BC
Iron Age 1000/750 BC–50 BC/50 AD
Roman 50 BC/50 AD–c. 450 AD
Post-Roman c. 450 AD onwards
Viking c. 800–c. 1000 AD
Skara Brae
Gokstad
Oseberg
Birka
Ertebølle
New Grange
Dublin
Tollund
York
Star Carr
Maglemose
Trelleborg
Cresswell
Feddersen Wierde
Grimes Graves
Sutton Hoo
Biskupin
Bath
Avebury
Colchester
Stonehenge
Hamwih
London
Maiden Castle
Swanscombe
Fishbourne
Xanten
Abbeville
Neanderthal
Aachen
Cologne
St Acheul
Köln-Lindenthal
Fère-en-Tardenois
Trier
Carnac
Unětice
Bylany
Dolni Vestonice
Steinheim
Manching
Vix
Heuneburg
Egolzwil
Lyon
Cortaillod
La Tène
Hallstatt
Lengyel
Lascaux
Le Moustier
Val Camonica
Altamira
Lagozza
Peschiera
Magdalenska Gora
Orange
Trois Frères
Nimes
Mas d'Azil
Entremont
Este
Niaux
Arene Candide
Villanova
Ensérune
Massilia
Bologna
Ampurias
Terra Amata
Vinča
Lepenski
Châteauneuf-les-Martigues
Vila Nova de São Pedro
Veii
Rome
Pompeii
Nea Nikomedia
El Argar
Los Millares
Dimini
Sesklo
Syracuse

6
7
8
Jovgorod
Kostienki
Kiev
Tripolye
Mezhirich
Chertomlyk
Olbia
Kul Oba
Seven Brothers
sa
aranovo

Europe

350,000 BC–AD 1000

The earliest evidence for man's presence in Europe comes from fragmentary remains dating to around 350,000 BC, although new finds dated by new techniques suggest a possible date of more than 1,000,000 years BC. During the Ice Ages and interglacials, man the hunter and gatherer lived in caves, rock shelters or the open air, using chipped stone implements; and from the Middle Palaeolithic practised deliberate burial, and developed artistic skills. Lascaux, which shows these skills at their best, is a classic story of accidental discovery, and still presents challenging problems for conservationists.

In warmer post-glacial times, man began to clear the forests and to domesticate particular animals. This led to the so-called Neolithic revolution – man's manipulation of his own food resources – which resulted in more permanent and larger settlements. Evidence for industrial specialization includes that for the new material, pottery. The Aldenhoven Plateau project represents this phase, in part because so many Neolithic sites have been located, partly because of the massive scale of the research and the modern salvage conditions under which it must be carried out.

The last 3,000 years BC saw great developments in social, economic and industrial organization. Intensification of farming led to the settlement of new areas; increasing industrial specialization included the development of first copper and bronze metallurgy and later iron. The appearance of élite groups living in palaces or strongholds and buried with luxurious goods in spectacular monuments demonstrates increasing social complexity. Illustrating these developments are a settlement and a burial. Biskupin is a complete village in a remarkable state of preservation, the excavation was excellent for its time, and the reconstruction imaginative. The Kul Oba excavation was one of the earliest to produce a plan and a section, and the contents are, of course, spectacular.

Within and outside the Roman empire, society and economic activities became increasingly complex, with widespread cross-cultural connections aptly demonstrated by the Vikings. The Oseberg ship burial was a quite outstanding excavation for its time, and preserved on the site were organic remains not normally available to the archaeologist.

Lascaux
FRANCE

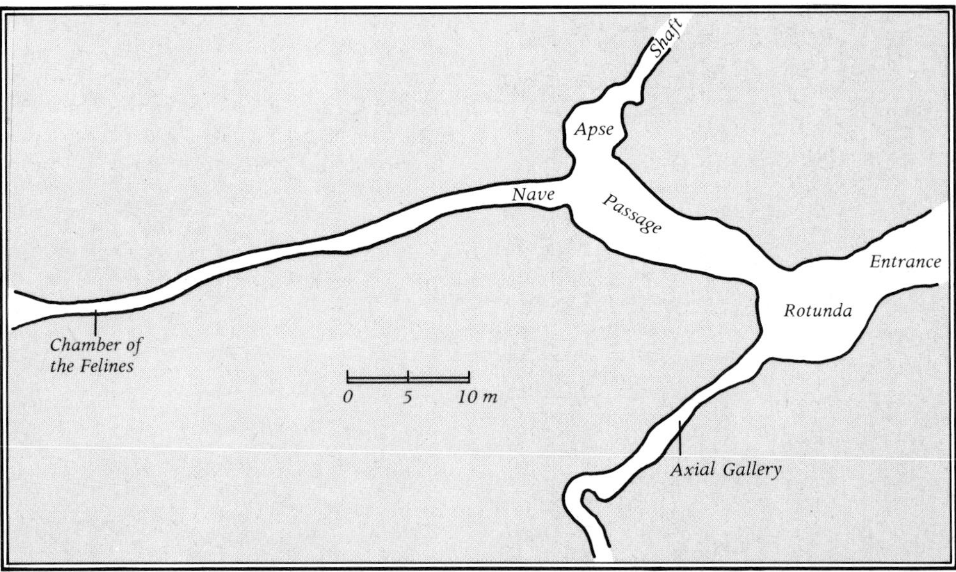

The famous cave-painting site of Lascaux is situated near Montignac in the Dordogne region of France, an area where many other painted caves have been found. The cave was decorated during the *Magdalenian* phase of the Upper Palaeolithic, that is, between about 15,000 and 14,000 BC, apparently in a temporary warm phase (Interstadial) during the last Ice Age. The story of its discovery has come to us from accounts by the boys who found it, much of it through documents collated by their schoolmaster, which happily survived a fire. Although the different accounts contain a few discrepancies, the main story emerges quite clearly.

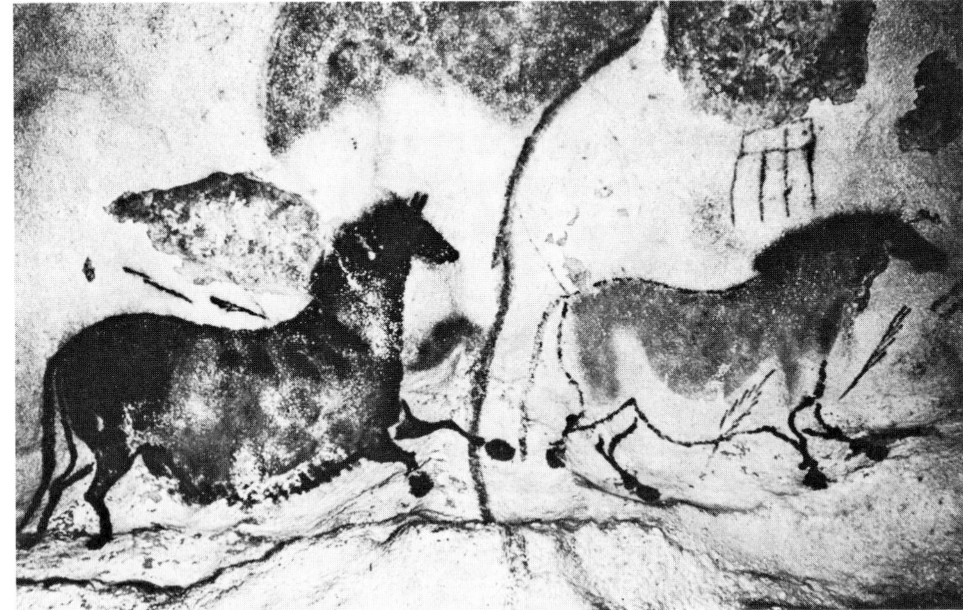

The cave's discovery

On 8 September 1940 a group of boys from Montignac found a bramble-filled hole in the Lascaux woods. They started to dig, finding the remains of an ass which had fallen into it, and threw down some stones to discover how deep the hole was. Although all four agreed to come back the next Sunday, one, a 17-year-old garage apprentice called Marcel Ravidat, returned only four days later with three different friends. This day, 12 September 1940, became the official date of discovery. Léon Laval, their old schoolmaster, tells of their first entry into the cave:

> 'On Thursday 12 September 1940 on a charming autumn afternoon four very young men, Ravidat, Marsal, Agnel and Coencas, were running through the woods well-stocked with game accompanied by their faithful dog Robot. All at once they saw the dog disappearing down a hole full of brambles and wreathed with juniper. After a long wait the dog did not reappear. Ravidat, whose faithful friend he was, decided in his turn to enter the narrow hole. It needed some courage. . . . A stone thrown down took a long time to roll down, showing how deep it was. The young speleologist, however, slid down this sort of well and eventually arrived in a large chamber whose importance he did not recognize, for he only had a box of matches for a light. Marsal and the other two friends came down in their turn with difficulty, but having no other means of exploration they climbed back as best they could to daylight, telling each other to keep the secret of their discovery'.

Ravidat's account tells of their exploration the following day:

> 'We started to explore the cave; looking right, looking left, we proceeded slowly because the lamp was not working very well. Thus it was that we crossed a large room 30 metres long, 12 metres wide and 10 metres high. Finding no obstacle in our way we arrived in a corridor, narrow but high enough. It was here that, raising the lamp to the height of the walls, we saw in the trembling glimmer of our lamp several lines in different colours. Intrigued by these coloured lines we began to examine the walls meticulously and to our great surprise discovered there several animal figures of some size. It was then that we realized we had discovered a cave with paintings. Encouraged by this success we started to run around the cave going from discovery to discovery. Our joy was indescribable. A band of savages doing a war dance could not have done better'.

They came back the following day with

Above: One of the narrow passages at Lascaux with paintings on the ceiling. Two horses and three bison can be seen, as well as a variety of obscure signs.

Left above: Two horses prance along a ceiling. The sign above the leading horse is not understood; some scholars think that the 'feathered' signs represent arrows.

Left: The head of a bison. This representation is extremely lifelike, from the horns to the nostril and dewlap. The three-pronged sign might be an arrow.

better lamps, going by different routes at 10 minute intervals 'like a handful of Indians covering their trail'. Eventually they located the famous Shaft, and Ravidat tells of his bravery thus:

> 'My friends were all too frightened that they would not be able to climb back up as they would have to climb a slippery rope. For me it was not that which made me hesitate, for I had confidence in my arms'.

Ravidat was worried whether his friends would be able to hold his 70 kilos with the strength of their arms alone, but they assured him that they could, and he climbed down several metres to the bottom of the Shaft. He located the now-famous and very unusual narrative scene drawn at the bottom, and came back up.

From that day onwards the cave was visited by people in greater and greater numbers. During the first couple of days it was bands of children: nine visited on 14 September, 20 on 15 September, and by 16 September almost all the local children knew about it, and Laval, the teacher, was told. At first he did not realize the importance of the discovery, but after seeing sketches of the paintings he, too, went down. By 21 September l'Abbé Henri Breuil, the doyen of cave art, had visited the site, accompanied by Ravidat, Marsal and Laval, and Lascaux was well and truly on the way to the fame it has enjoyed ever since. L'Abbé Glory, the archaeologist who excavated, examined and analysed the cave until his death in 1966, noted: 'The Tourist Board is active. Only eight days after the cave had been discovered, the President had put up a placard pointing out of town saying 'Lascaux cave 2 kilometres'. By 1944 the Rex Cinema in Montignac was showing *La nuit des temps*, a film on the Lascaux cave, and the increasing number of visitors was beginning to affect the paintings.

Inside the cave

What was so special about the find that Ravidat, Marsal and their friends made was that Lascaux contained one of the most spectacular collections of Palaeolithic cave paintings, all apparently executed by the same group of people over a relatively short time.

The cave itself is some 100 metres long. It consists of a long corridor with a gallery off one side and a chamber, leading to the Shaft, off the other. The different areas of the cave are known as the Rotunda, the Axial Gallery, the Passage, the Apse, the Shaft, the Nave and the Chamber of the Felines. The Rotunda contains a monumental group of figures painted in red and black, in which there are bison up to 5 metres long. The composition includes five bovines, nine horses, a so-called 'unicorn' and some smaller stags and bovines. There are also geometric signs, which have been interpreted in various ways. In the Axial Gallery appear bulls and stags, cows and horses, ibexes, and the ubiquitous signs. Painted and engraved figures in the Passage are not as clear, although there are oxen, horse and ibex, as there are in the Nave. The Chamber of the Felines contains about 30 animal figures, comprising the felines themselves, horse, bison, ibex, stag and rhinoceros, and a large number of signs. Many unfinished scrawled drawings decorate the Apse, including the only reindeer depicted at Lascaux. However, it is in the Shaft that the most unusual composition appears. Here is to be found a veritable scene, which is a rare occurrence in Palaeolithic art. A rhinoceros stands to the left of a rare human figure with outstretched arms who appears to have been thrown down by a bison. A spear has been drawn across the bison's body and it stands with its entrails pouring out.

The paintings, although of exceptional importance, were not the only finds of interest in the cave. Lying on the floor, and discovered in the limited excavations carried out by l'Abbé Glory, were some 403 pieces of flint, both tools and waste flakes of typical Magdalenian type; 28 bone tools including 16 spears of very fine manufacture; pierced and unpierced shells from beaches, including one which must have been brought 150–200 kilometres; 133 bones from local animals, mostly reindeer; and, perhaps most interesting of all, the remains of painting pigments and of 34 lamps, including two carved of pink sandstone. These were probably fuelled by grease, tallow or oil, and give clear evidence for the lighting used in the cave, doubtless during painting. Possible evidence for scaffolding came from postholes in the cave floor, and many fragments of charcoal provided raw material for radiocarbon dating. The first date, determined in 1951, was also one of the first of this kind for the Palaeolithic period: it gave a reading of 13,566 ± 900 BC. Subsequent dates of 15,240 ± 140 BC and 14,050 ± 500 BC place the activity at the cave in the 15th millennium BC.

Problems of preservation

The site at Lascaux has continued to be of interest, and not just because of the paintings. By 1955 it became clear that the constant visitation by thousands of people was affecting the cave and its paintings. Condensation from visitors' breath was actually dripping off the ceiling, bringing with it pigment from the paintings. Studies revealed an excess of carbonic gas, and a machine which maintained constant temperature and humidity was installed, linked with the turnstile which measured the number of visitors. But in the early 1960s green patches, the 'Green Sickness', began to appear on the walls, and on 20 April 1963 the cave was closed. The green algae causing the patches grew from three to 720 colonies in a few months, in spite of extra filters, and it eventually took two years' treatment to clear both bacteria and algae without damaging the paintings. The cave is no longer open to the public, although a replica is being built. It is the price that must be paid for saving some of the most spectacular art in the world.

Above: Wall painting from a side aisle at Lascaux depicting bison or wild aurochs in highly realistic style.

The Cave Artists

The question of whether the cave at Lascaux was ever inhabited on a day-to-day basis for any period of time is difficult to answer. This is partly owing to the lack of any large-scale excavations, particularly in the area immediately near the entrance. Although evidence might have been expected here, the area was built over without any significant excavation in order to provide proper access for visitors to the caves. Caves were frequently used for habitation sites in the Upper Palaeolithic period, as is shown by the hundreds of layers of occupation debris found in a number of excavated caves. However, these tended to be shallow, rather open caves or rock shelters with plenty of access to light and air, rather than the deep and often almost inaccessible caves associated with much of the cave painting. Large amounts of charcoal, and evidence for at least one hearth, were found at Lascaux, but these may reflect no more than the temporary habitation of the artists. There is little evidence for deep deposits of occupation material, so that however long the period of time taken for the painting and the presumed rituals associated with it, on balance it seems more likely that the users of Lascaux actually lived elsewhere. Both cave and open-air settlements broadly contemporary with Lascaux have been excavated in the Dordogne region. As a result, it now appears that the old idea of Palaeolithic people being essentially nomadic may not be altogether correct; they may well have been more permanently settled at this time than was once thought. Examination of reindeer bones and teeth from some sites has shown that the animals were slaughtered there all year round, so these sites at least were not seasonally occupied. Open-air sites so far excavated often consist of roughly paved areas with hearths, occupation debris and the occasional posthole, these last suggesting some sort of timber-built structure. Other sites have settings of stones in rough circles or sub-rectangles. These were not the foundations of stone walls but more probably marked the edges of skin tents. There is no evidence from France for the remarkable structures made out of mammoth bones found in Russia and dating from the Upper Palaeolithic.

Hunters, tools and weapons

The number of people living in cave or open-air sites at any one time must have varied from place to place, and estimates range from just a few, representing a nuclear family, to over a hundred. Many of the groups probably consisted of bands of about 25 to 30 people who were doubtless very effective when combining to catch food. They lived by hunting game, catching fish and gathering fruit, nuts, berries, seeds, roots and grasses. We have seen that at Lascaux the majority of animal bones were of reindeer, and in this period the reindeer is likely to have been a main source of food. Its bone and antlers were used for tools and weapons, while its skin provided clothing, bedding and tents. Other game available included bison and aurochs, horse, mammoth, bear, lion and rhinoceros. Birds and fish were also caught for food, although archaeological evidence for this is only now forthcoming as a result of advances in recovery techniques for small objects such as fish and bird bones. Bone harpoons and fish-hooks were developed during this period. Much of the game was probably brought down with bone or ivory spears, which in many cases were launched with a spear-thrower, or by projectiles tipped with a flint point. There is no clear evidence for the use of bows and arrows at this period, although the likelihood of the bow being made of organic, and therefore perishable, material means that archaeological evidence will probably not be found. Also, pictorial representation of human beings at this period is in itself so rare that the absence of a picture of a bow and arrow may not be significant. It is almost certain that several hunters combined to bring down large game, either by using missiles, or by traps, for example large pits. Meat gained from the hunt would probably be roasted in the fire, or perhaps boiled in leather containers (there was no pottery at this time) by the addition of hot stones.

Other tools in use were flint scrapers, thought to have been employed, among other things, for scraping skins. A wide variety of other flint implements existed, including *burins* and the so-called 'backed' blades. Fragments of pitch found on the backs of the latter show that they had been hafted into some kind of organic handle.

Flint was also used for engraving designs on both cave walls and pieces of bone and antler, but no types particular to this craft have been identified. Other artists' necessities were of course paints, made from natural substances such as iron oxides, ochre, haematite and manganese dioxide, and paintbrushes, which were probably tied bunches of horsehair. Artificial light was needed when painting the deeper recesses of caves, and from Lascaux come the stone lamps fuelled by grease which allowed the artist to work underground.

What is known of the tools and weapons is, of course, restricted to those objects that have survived the 15,000 years since their use. Many other likely objects in wood, bark, basketwork and leather are unknown to us because of their organic nature.

Apart from the foodstuffs and other raw materials available locally, it seems that certain objects arrived at sites some distance from their source. The Lascaux shells, for example, include one which must have travelled between 150 and 200 kilometres, while seal remains have been found in the Lartet rock shelter and at Chancelade, both of which are about 150 kilometres from the Atlantic coast. Seal is also represented at other inland cave sites. How these objects arrived at their final resting-place, by exchange, barter or visits from the inhabitants themselves, is not known, but it is unlikely that there were organized trade networks.

Burials begin

It was during the Middle Palaeolithic period that deliberate burial of the dead with grave goods started, and by the time of the Magdalenian it is clear that there was established a set of beliefs affecting the way in which the dead were treated. Many were buried in the habitation sites, in caves or rock shelters near occupation areas. Men, women and children apparently all received the same type of treatment, often being buried with necklaces and bracelets, and sprinkled with red ochre, thought by some to represent blood, thereby giving the body a chance of life in the afterworld. Work on skeletal material, where it is to hand and identifiable, suggests that infant mortality was very high and that on average women died young, under the age of 40, doubtless in many cases during childbirth. Many men were also dead by this age, and the few who lived on were likely to be dead before 60.

The Palaeolithic artists

Whatever else may be of interest, the reason for the fame of Lascaux and other well-known cave sites – such as Niaux and Les Trois Frères in France and Altamira in Spain – is their art. Apart from the sheer brilliance of the colours, composition and craftsmanship, and in the later phases the accuracy of their representation of animals, interesting observations are made on the content and meaning of the art. Many people have thought, and still think, that it was created as a kind of 'sympathetic magic': the hunters drew the animal they wished to catch, perhaps also drawing spears stuck into the body, in the hope that this very act would help them in the chase. Such an interpretation suggests that it was the act of painting wherein the importance of the art lies. In relation to this it is curious that reindeer, the animals for which there are most archaeological remains during this period, are by no means very commonly represented, while those animals which do feature frequently in the art, the aurochs, bison and horse, are not the most common food animals to judge from the bones found on the sites so far excavated. Other scholars see the sites as of general religious significance, and point to the thousands of children's footprints preserved in the clay floors of some sites as evidence for ritual dances and processions. Complete explanation of the meaning of the paintings still escapes us, however.

A further interesting feature of the paintings is the general rarity of human figures. This is a pity, since it deprives us of what would otherwise be very important information on Palaeolithic people. We are left with the enigmatic figures of the 'Sorcerers' from Les Trois Frères and Le Gabillou to taunt us with how little we know of the people who created the earliest known art.

Below: A stag, beautifully painted, with long, elaborate antlers. This flamboyant creation shows that the artist was not simply concerned to depict schematic representations. Note the 'cauliflower' texture of the surface.

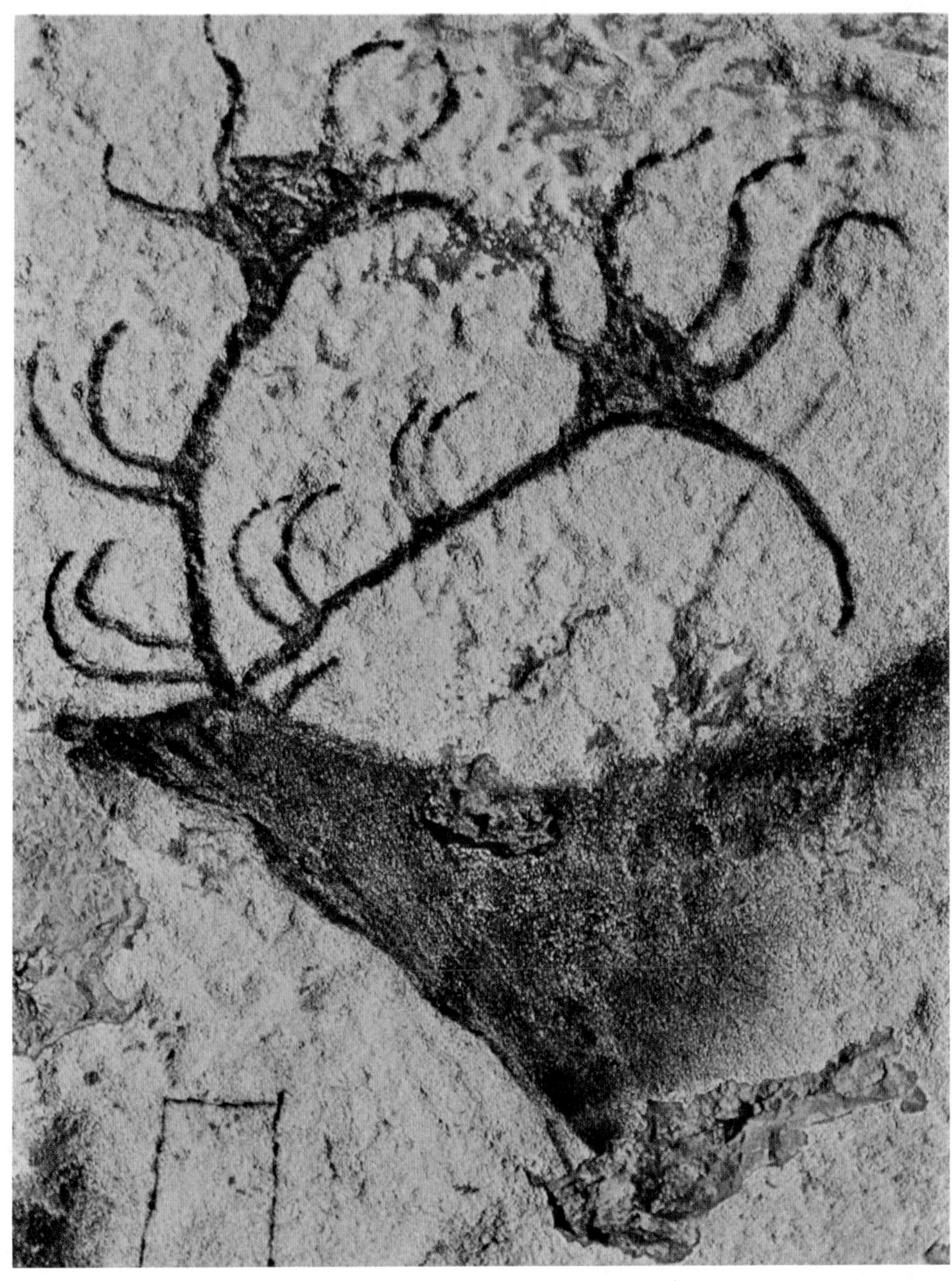

Aldenhoven Plateau

WEST GERMANY

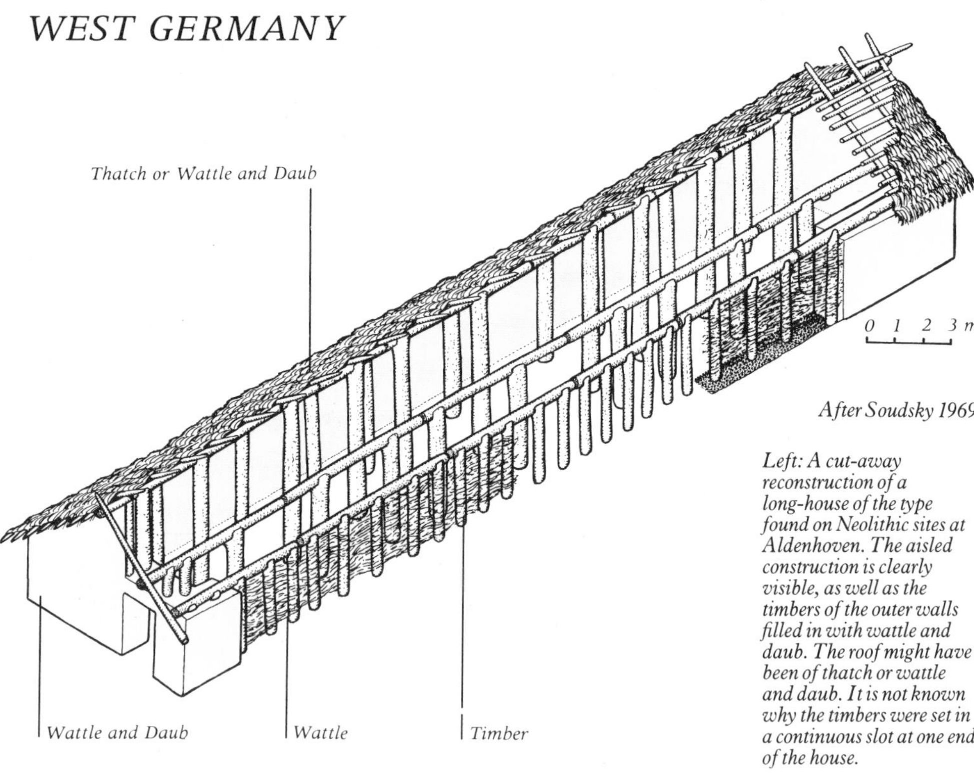

After Soudsky 1969

Left: A cut-away reconstruction of a long-house of the type found on Neolithic sites at Aldenhoven. The aisled construction is clearly visible, as well as the timbers of the outer walls filled in with wattle and daub. The roof might have been of thatch or wattle and daub. It is not known why the timbers were set in a continuous slot at one end of the house.

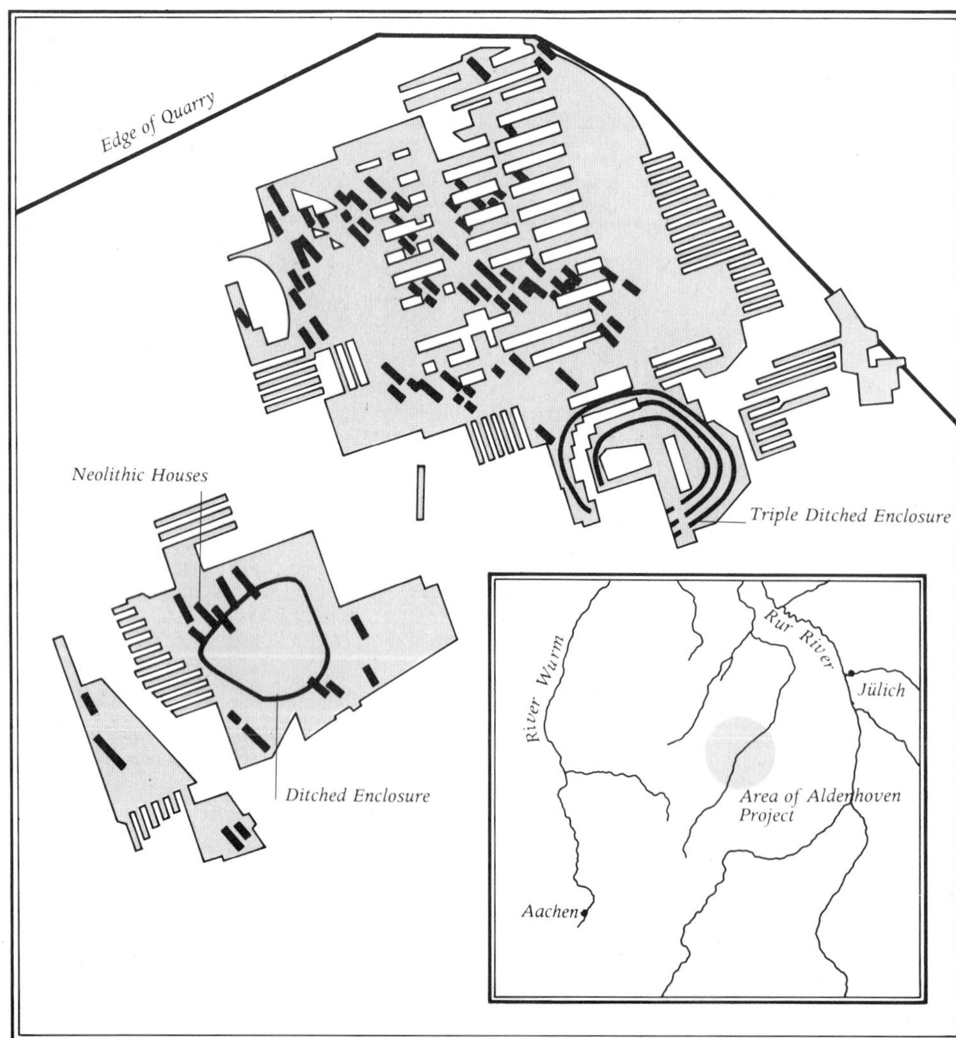

The Aldenhoven Plateau is a wide, sloping plain about 50 kilometres west of Cologne in West Germany. It forms part of the extensive lowlands which stretch north from the foothills of the middle Rhine mountains, and its archaeological importance can be traced to the fertile soils which attracted settlement at all periods, but especially during the Neolithic.

The Plateau's economic significance today derives less from agriculture than from exploitation of the underlying deposits of lignite. Lignite, or brown coal, is a substance half-way between peat and bituminous coal. It was formed much more recently than black coal and has a rather lower energy content, but lies at a considerably higher level and can be most economically exploited by large-scale open-cast mining. The deposits to the west of Cologne are near the surface and average 50–60 metres in depth, occasionally reaching 100 metres. They have been mined on an increasing scale in recent years, particularly to fuel electricity power stations.

Exploitation of the lignite deposits west of Cologne increased rapidly during the 1960s, especially in mines on the plateau to the south of Aldenhoven, where an average of a square kilometre was being mined annually in an area of great archaeological potential. Preliminary observations confirmed that ancient sites were indeed present in large numbers, and archaeological work was undertaken by the Rheinischeslandesmuseum, Bonn, and the Institute of Pre- and Proto-history of the University of Cologne.

Survey and observation

The first phase of work, up to 1971, saw the excavation of a number of sites, especially of Neolithic date. Observation of quarried areas and field surveys of areas under threat of destruction also took place. In 1971, however, it became apparent that a more organized approach would be needed. Mining activity was then concentrated in the large Zukunft West mine, where work was to take place on a wide face which included the valley of the small Merzbach stream, already recognized as a major focus of Neolithic settlement. It was therefore decided that the main object of research should be to seize this opportunity for exploring the Neolithic landscape and to excavate as completely as possible all Neolithic sites.

A second phase, of intensive excavation, was therefore initiated in October 1971, and lasted for two years. Where possible, sites were identified by field survey before mining. Because of the widespread use of flint on sites of this period, many could be recognized from surface collection of this and other artefacts; other sites, however, were found only during the course of mining. The scale of operations was vast. The mine was worked along a face 3 kilometres long by two huge mechanical excavators with rotating bucket-wheels which quarried the overburden and then the lignite for removal by conveyor-belt. The machines started at both ends of the face and every four to six weeks met in the middle. In this way the face advanced by as much as 70 metres each month. These successive faces of the mine presented a series of sections across the landscape which were carefully examined for archaeological features, and it is unlikely that many sites of any significance were missed.

Right: The remaining evidence of a Neolithic long-house on the Langweiler 9 site at Aldenhoven. The slot for containing the wall timbers can be seen in the foreground, with the lines of the internal posts behind. Each individual posthole is marked before excavation with a white label for recording purposes. In the background, the quarry workings are visible. The photograph gives a good idea of what it is like to work under such conditions, with constant constraints of time and money.

Rescue excavation

All sites were excavated, and excavation had to keep ahead of mining. During the period 1971–73, more than 2 square kilometres were mined and about 10 per cent of the area was found to be covered by traces of Neolithic settlement. In all, 244,000 square metres were dug in two years. To speed excavation, the topsoil was removed mechanically in strips 10 metres wide parallel to the working face of the mine. Spoil from the first strip was dumped over the face, and that from each successive strip was emptied on to the previous one after it had been excavated. In this way up to 100 square metres could be stripped in one hour, and 3,000 square metres of settlement excavated in one week. The pace of excavation, and the long working face of the mine, meant that on occasion four different sites were being excavated simultaneously.

As far as possible, all features were planned and sectioned by hand, but towards the end of excavation especially, some had to be dug by machine. In this case, the fill was passed through a large water sieve. Sieving tended to produce more small sherds of pottery than in those features dug by hand, but since pottery analysis was based on numbers of vessels present rather than number or weight of sherds, it is thought that this caused no distortion of the results. The scale of operations required systematic recording of features and, as on most large modern excavations, standardized forms were produced. So great was the volume of information recorded that a computerized system of data-handling was developed.

Quarrying continued at the same rate after 1973, but the face moved away from the heaviest Neolithic concentration in the Merzbach valley, and archaeological work passed into its third phase. The pace of excavation slackened, but intensive survey and observation of the mine continued, with settlements excavated as required.

To understand the significance of the sites excavated in the Merzbach valley it was necessary to see them in relation to others in a wider context, and for this purpose a research project was devised. The main area of excavations had comprised merely one part of a varied landscape, and new mining further to the east in the Hambach forest gave the opportunity to study a contemporary settlement in a different environment. A study area encompassing no less than 980 square kilometres was therefore defined, within which a smaller zone of 350 square kilometres was designated for systematic survey, the remainder being earmarked for observation. At the area's centre is a core of 85 square kilometres allocated for intensive survey and excavation. In this way, the results from the vast rescue operations instigated by the mining can be integrated into a wider research programme.

The project involves excavating all Neolithic sites in the core area, as well as intensive survey and observation. Supplementary evidence is supplied by a campaign of aerial photography, which reveals sites not visible on the ground. The environmental history of the region is also being examined, and a number of peat bogs have been found containing deposits which span the later prehistoric period and which are suitable for pollen analysis. Samples from excavated Neolithic features are being routinely examined for botanical remains, to give an insight into the crops grown at this time.

Publication of such an enormous project obviously poses problems, but the solution adopted has been to prepare reports on individual sites or topics as they are completed, rather than to wait for a single publication at the project's end. Through these, and through regular interim reports, information is thus promptly disseminated.

The Aldenhoven Plateau project has concentrated on the Neolithic period, although sites of all periods from the Bronze Age to the medieval were also found and excavated. During the 1971–73 main phase of excavation, a 1.3-kilometre-length of the valley was examined and dug. All sites happened to belong to the early Neolithic, and a total of 160 houses was excavated as well as a triple-ditched earthwork and a cemetery containing 89 graves. These results have been greatly augmented by other excavations both higher up the Merzbach valley and in other areas. Regular observation of the many sections across the landscape revealed by the mine face has also yielded important negative information, in that areas not used for settlement in the Neolithic period can be defined with equal confidence. A picture of the developing Neolithic landscape can therefore be established which is without parallel in extent or detail elsewhere in Europe.

Neolithic Farmers

The first farmers of central and western Europe belonged to the Linear Pottery culture, so called from the linear decoration on characteristic pottery which is dated about 5200–4500 BC. Houses, burials, pottery, stone tools and other artefacts of this culture are remarkably homogeneous throughout the area from Czechoslovakia and Poland to Holland, and many settlements and cemeteries are now known.

Food and subsistence

The adoption of farming was one of the most important steps in man's development, and had profound consequences both for society and for the environment. Central Europe's landscape was heavily wooded before the spread of agriculture, and it was these first farmers who were responsible for extensive clearance in order to grow crops and pasture animals. Hunting, fishing and gathering may still have played an important part in subsistence, but domesticated crops and livestock provided the bulk of food. The acidity of soil on the Aldenhoven Plateau has meant that no animal bones survive, but studies on other sites show that although sheep and pigs were kept, cattle were the most important species, providing by far the greater part of the meat. Routine sieving of excavated samples for botanical remains has also produced abundant evidence for the plants grown and exploited at Aldenhoven sites. The main crops were einkorn and emmer, two early forms of wheat, as well as millet, supplemented by legumes such as peas, beans and lentils; barley is known from other sites. Plants with seeds rich in edible oils, such as flax, were also grown, and wild fruits and nuts, among them apples and hazelnuts, were collected. The natural mixed oak forest was progressively cleared for such agriculture, and as areas were abandoned after the first farming episode, they reverted to woodland in which other species, such as hazel, flourished. These woods provided not only wild fruits, but also materials for fuel, building and many other purposes.

The growing of cereal and legume crops may have been of greater importance than the raising of animals in this economy, and settlements of these early farmers show a marked concentration on suitable soils. They clearly favoured locations in valleys which had good drainage and a plentiful water supply, and particularly exploited the fertile soils of the loess areas. Loess is a wind-blown deposit formed during the last Ice Age, and develops very fertile soils ideal for early agriculture. It is found in spreads throughout central and western Europe, and there is a high correlation between loess deposits and early farming settlements. The location of the Aldenhoven sites is thus typical, extending along the well-watered Merzbach valley on rich loess soils.

Settlements and houses

Farming was accompanied by permanent settlement, and sites of the Linear Pottery culture are now well known. Classic excavations, such as those at Köln-Lindenthal in the suburbs of Cologne in 1929 and at Bylany in Czechoslovakia in the 1950s, had already shown what houses and villages of this period were like. The sites can be extremely large – one at Olszanica in Poland extends to more than 50 hectares – and often contain numerous houses, not all of which were simultaneously in use. For example, 52 complete and 45 partial houses were found at Köln-Lindenthal, which was interpreted as a much rebuilt village consisting of up to 21 houses at a time. At Bylany the settlement was again long-lived, and in each of the phases five or six, perhaps up to ten, houses had been in use. Similar results have been obtained from excavations in Holland. The villages themselves were quite small, but constant rebuilding of the houses over a long period, not on the same foundations but close at hand, produced these very large sites.

Villages of this sort are well-known throughout central and western Europe, but have not been found at Aldenhoven, where a different pattern of settlement was revealed. The excavated area along the Merzbach valley uncovered a string of Linear Pottery sites, each of which was an individual settlement. The nearest contemporary sites were in similar valleys some distance to the north and south. This pattern of dispersed settlement along the valleys lasted for several hundred years, and only later did the first villages appear in the area.

Although the pattern of settlement varies, a remarkable similarity of house type exists throughout central and western Europe. These houses, the first substantial timber buildings of the region, must have been impressive structures although the only surviving signs are the post-holes for their massive oak uprights. They were generally between 5 and 7 metres wide, and between 10 and 30 metres long, although some known examples exceed 40 metres. The walls are marked by the lines of post-holes, or in some cases by continuous *bedding trenches*. In addition there are three internal lines of posts to support the roof and provide partitions. The design was derived from a rather simpler style of architecture current among the early farmers of south-eastern Europe, but adapted to the very different climate of more northerly areas. To counteract rain and snow, the rather shallow-pitched roof of southern Europe had to be made much steeper. As this greatly increased the weight and the problem of pressure from strong winds, so three lines of internal posts were introduced to support and strengthen the roof. The buildings were frequently orientated into the prevailing winds, with doors at the sheltered south-eastern end. As experience in these new building techniques increased, it was found that such structural problems could be better and more easily solved by strengthening the walls, with the result that some of the rather later buildings are much simpler, showing fewer internal posts or none at all.

Right: Typical pottery from a Neolithic site on the Aldenhoven Plateau. It belongs to a class called Linear Pottery or Linearbandkeramik, which is widespread on Neolithic sites in central and western Europe. The forms shown here are the globular pot with lug handles (left), the small, knobbed narrow-necked jar (centre) and the open bowl (right). The name for the pottery derives from the long incised bands which decorate all three pots, forming spirals on the knobbed jar and waves on the other two. These decorated bands are frequently filled in with lines of dots or slashes, and between them, as on the bowl, may be lines of impressed marks made with the end of an animal or bird bone.

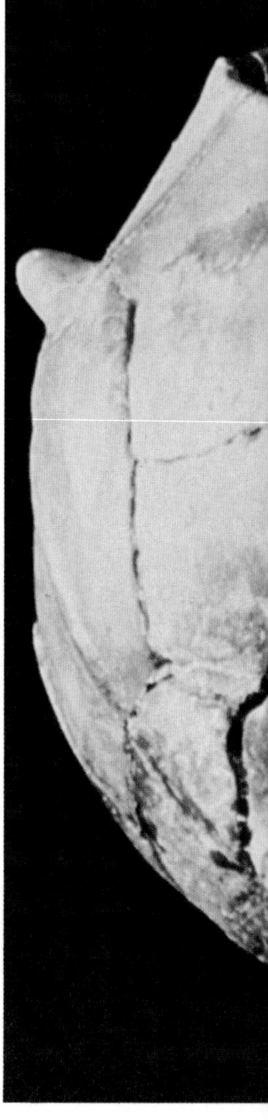

Little is known of internal features, although hearths are occasionally found. Some houses may have been fitted with upper floors at one or both ends.

The houses themselves were built in oak, with the walls in wattle and daub, or, in some cases, planks. The roof was thatched with reeds, possibly resting on more wattling. Oak, hazel and reed would all have been plentiful, but would have been needed in very large quantities. About 80 oaks may

have been needed for an average-sized house, involving the clearance of half a hectare; 1.5 hectares of reed swamp and many hectares of hazel coppice would also have been required. Construction was a considerable undertaking, perhaps involving more than 2,000 man-hours, for some of the largest timbers may have needed 12 men to lift them.

This high degree of woodworking skill was achieved with comparatively primitive tools; stone axes, adzes, chisels and wedges were used, but saws, augers and drills were unknown. Joints would have been made by notching, or by cutting mortices and tenons, and secured by tying. Other technologies that had been fully mastered included the making and polishing of stone tools, and the production of pottery, which involved considerable skill in the control of heat during the firing process. It is doubtful, however, whether any high degree of craft specialization existed at this stage.

Community life

Just as individual families were largely self-sufficient within the community, so individual communities were largely self-reliant for subsistence needs. Trade was not, however, totally absent. Stone suitable for making tools of particularly high quality occurs rarely, and was highly prized. Certain types of flint, and also obsidian, a glassy rock of volcanic origin, were traded over long distances. *Spondylus* shells from the Mediterranean are also found, particularly in cemeteries. Like the valuable stone tools, they were exchanged between communities by people of some status.

Little is known about the religion or ritual of these northern farmers, whereas in south-eastern Europe, clay figurines of a religious nature are found in some numbers. Cemeteries have, however, been discovered. They frequently occur within a short distance of the settlement site, and contain inhumation burials, some of which are provided with grave goods.

An insight into social organization can be gained from the cemeteries. There are no extreme differences in the style or wealth of burials, but some indications of difference in status are revealed. Polished stone tools, especially those made from imported stone, and *spondylus* shells are regularly found only in the burials of older men. This may indicate no more than specialization of labour by sex, but the likely value and prestige of such items probably suggests that older men occupied a higher status within the community than younger men or women. There are, however, no signs of any more complex organization or a more developed hierarchy.

Such a picture of a comparatively egalitarian society, in which special status was ascribed by virtue of age and sex rather than by ancestry, fits well with what is known of these early farmers. There are few signs of such massive undertakings as appeared in later communities, who were able to mobilize and direct huge efforts to building large ceremonial or funerary monuments. Building a house would undoubtedly have been a considerable project, requiring communal help, but with less labour involved than in other communal efforts, such as harvesting.

Biskupin

POLAND

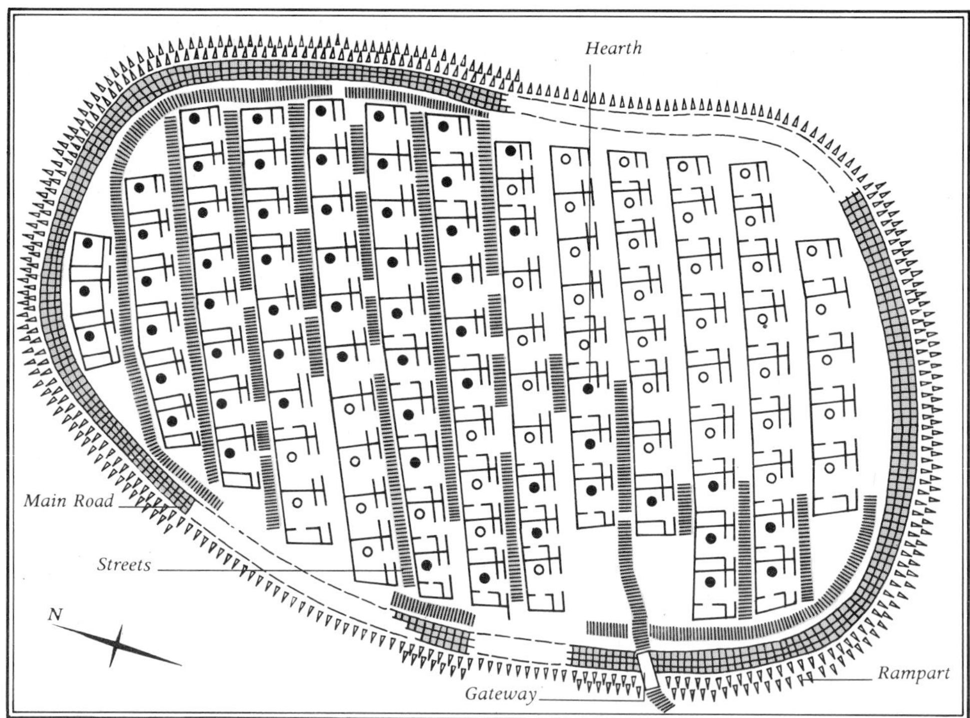

The site of Biskupin is now on a peninsula in a lake of the same name near Gniezno, some 230 kilometres west of Warsaw in Poland. The site was originally on an island, and may have been located there because the chain of lakes in this region formed a passage through what is thought to have been heavy forest. Traces of Upper Palaeolithic and Mesolithic activity exist in the area, and the site itself was occupied from the Neolithic period to the medieval. However, its principal period of habitation was during the Lusatian phase, the early Iron Age of Poland, from the 8th to the 5th centuries BC.

The site of Biskupin is of exceptional importance because of its nature and state of preservation. It consists of a settlement comprising about 2 hectares of closely-packed wooden houses and streets, enclosed by a timber box-frame rampart and a series of timber breakwaters. The timber has been preserved in much of its detail because of the presence of water, so that the plan and partial elevation of the structures can be seen on the ground. On most sites there would only remain holes for upright posts and perhaps the shadows of horizontal timbers.

The early excavations

The history of the excavations is an interesting one, although tragic in parts. Investigations began in 1933 under the direction of Józef Kostrzewski, and during that decade most of the island and an area of surrounding land were bought by the University of Poznań. These early excavations were extensive and methodical. Finds and structures were collected and annotated, a film record was made, a certain amount of *in situ* reconstruction was carried out, and many of the finds were displayed for visitors.

The invasion of Poland by the Nazis at the start of the Second World War was a disaster for Polish archaeology, not least for the site at Biskupin. The Nazis took away or destroyed plans, sections, notes, photographs, the inventory book, the contents of the darkroom and a large quantity of finds. The reconstructions were dismantled, and after a two-month investigation by the *SS-Ausgrabungen Urstätt*, of which no records remain, 80 per cent of the area of pre-war excavation was filled in with sand. Eight members of the original excavation team died in concentration camps or other theatres of the war.

Post-war excavations therefore started among innumerable difficulties. For the 1946 season it was necessary to borrow tools and equipment and to seek funds outside the University. The small team concentrated on installing technical workshops, clearing the filled-in areas, rebuilding the reconstructions and displaying those finds which remained. In 1947 the new excavations started in earnest, with the opening of 670 square metres of fresh ground and the clearing of 3,000 square metres of filled-in trenches. Specialist scientists were brought in to deal with matters of geology and morphology, palaeobotany and archaeozoology. More houses were reconstructed, and some experiments were made with techniques of potting, boneworking and food preparation.

The methodical nature of the excavations both before and after the war was remarkable and unusual for its time. It is clear from the excavation reports and notes that extensive written, drawn and photographic records were kept. A plan of the site was drawn before excavation began, and the area was divided into squares so that the recording of finds would be more accurate. After the turf had been removed, the layers were lifted in sequence and all the material was sieved in order to recover even very small remains. A pump was necessary in the lower levels to keep the water down to a workable depth while excavation and recording continued. All structures were planned at the scale of 1:10, important finds were measured three-dimensionally, and ordinary finds were coded according to area, feature and layer. In the upper levels, finds appeared to be mixed and there was no apparent stratigraphy. Here the site was dug in 24 levels, each 10 centimetres deep, and every find was assigned to its particular level.

In 1947 a test area was dug in exceptional detail in an attempt to refine the evidence for length of phases and interior changes of level. Every find, down to the smallest sherd, was measured in three dimensions. Special emphasis was laid on the recovery of the abundant environmental evidence, such as seeds, fish and animal bones. Such material, and the conclusions that could be drawn from it, remained of very great importance for many years. A study of the Biskupin excavations could teach much to excavators all over the world about techniques of recovery and recording.

Results of the investigations

The site's main structures belonged to the early Iron Age, although within this period there were two major phases of occupation, differing little in their nature and extent. During the earlier phase, which has a radiocarbon date of 720 ± 150 BC, the site was enclosed by a timber box-framed rampart filled with earth some 3 metres wide and up to 6 metres high. The defences included a breakwater, 6.8 metres wide, made of timbers set at an angle of 45° which, with the rampart, made up 34 per cent of the total area of the site. The gateway was 8 metres long and 3 metres wide at the inside, although less at its outer end. Evidence from the timber remains suggests that there was some sort of superstructure, although its exact form cannot be certainly reconstructed. Originally, a causeway led from this gate to the lakeside, 120 metres away. Within the rampart, and running round the entire site to a length of 417 metres, was a road made of logs measuring nearly 3 metres in width. Twelve of these log-built 'corduroy' roads ran across the site, each between 72 and 97 metres long and 2.7 metres wide, giving access to the houses. An open space or 'square' near the entrance gate had no structures in the early phase.

The rest of the site consisted of rows of houses, 104 to 106 in all, each comprising a main room and a porch, the latter taking up 25 per cent of the total house area. This porch may have been used for keeping a few animals, for working, or perhaps for both activities. The main room in some of the houses was divided into two; a smaller room (2 metres by 7) for sleeping, and the larger one, which contained the stone or clay hearth, for living and working. Grain may have been stored in the houses at an upper level, reached by a ladder, since there is no evidence for separate granaries during this phase. Each row of houses was apparently under one continuous roof.

In the later phase, which has a radiocarbon date of 560 ± 150 BC, the settlement contracted a little, losing one transverse street and some of the houses. The houses were smaller, and there is evidence that the 'square' near the entrance gate had structures on it, although their nature is uncertain. There were also three buildings of an apparently agricultural character.

Among the finds were pottery sherds from all phases, bones of both wild and domesticated mammals and birds, fishbones, and the remains of 140 varieties of plant. Also recovered were bronze and iron ornaments and tools; stone tools; clay loomweights and spindlewhorls; beads of glass and amber; objects of bone and horn; hundreds of fragments of moulds from metalworking; toys and possible cult objects of clay; and many wooden objects, including the remains of a plough, and floats for fishing nets. From all these finds it is possible to reconstruct a fairly detailed picture of life in Biskupin during the Iron Age.

Subsequent occupation on the site included a proto-historic open settlement, a 7th-century AD military establishment with an oak palisade, and an early medieval village which had an earth and timber wall and protective ditches.

Parts of the site have been reconstructed, and there is an on-site museum. Such attractions have made Biskupin one of Europe's most interesting archaeological sites.

Left: Part of the waterlogged rampart at Biskupin. On the right can be seen the lines of posts forming a breakwater; in the centre is the box-framed rampart of intricate construction. On the left is part of one of the 'corduroy' timber roads which ran around the entire settlement, linked to the houses by side streets. The remarkable state of preservation of the timbers can be clearly seen.

Right: A reconstruction, on the Biskupin site itself, of one of the houses found during excavation. The walls and floors were of timber, as were most of the 'fixtures and fittings'. The door is made of wattle. The compartment on the right may have been used as a sleeping area or for a few animals. The central hearth is made of stone, which allowed an internal fire in an all-timber construction. The roof has been reconstructed with a thatch, although there is no direct evidence of the material used. Large logs served as fireside stools.

Iron-Age Settlement

The site at Biskupin is unique in its plan and detail, so that although other well-excavated sites of the same period exist in the area, we must look at life in Biskupin, as far as it can be reconstructed, before attempting a general view of the Polish Iron Age.

We have already seen that the people of Biskupin lived in houses very much alike, and that apparently no family or group was set apart by having a larger or different style of dwelling. The population is thought to have totalled between 700 and 1,000 people, and although there is some evidence of the periodic rebuilding of houses, there is nothing to suggest that most of the structures were not all inhabited simultaneously.

The excavation has made it clear that the site must have been set out according to a preconceived plan, with the roads and houses laid out at the same time. This suggests a highly developed central organization. It has been calculated that 7,155 cubic metres of timber were used in the construction of the defences, roads and houses, with another 10,000 cubic metres of earth and clay. These are not trifling amounts, and the organization required to hew and quarry, transport and construct these materials must have been considerable. It is difficult to deduce from the evidence of Biskupin alone whether this organization implies a central authority in the form of a chief or chiefly clan living elsewhere in a different type of structure; whether such a chief lived in Biskupin in a house no different from those of more humble rank (a situation not without anthropological parallel); or whether society was egalitarian and democratic, taking such decisions communally. It is evident that the enclosure of the tightly-packed houses with massive and formidable defences implies a need felt by society to protect itself. Moreover, since there is no evidence for purely sporadic occupation, the need for protection must have been more than short-term.

Left: Stone-lined burial of the Lausitz culture, showing a typical group of pottery jars, bowls and handled cups.

Right: An on-site reconstruction of the gateway with a tower; the rampart with a parapet; and two rows of houses.

Below: External view of one of the settlement buildings reconstructed on the Biskupin site.

Food and technology

Economic and industrial activity at Biskupin can be well demonstrated, although the improvement since the main period of excavation in recovery techniques for certain sorts of evidence, such as fishbones and seeds, might alter to a certain extent the ratios of some foods to others. Among mammals, the bones of domesticated animals predominated. Those of cattle were the most common, followed by pig and then sheep or goat, with horse and dog also present. A very small percentage (1.2) of wild animal bones was recovered from the early excavations, although among later finds the percentage increased to 23.26. These included red and roe deer, boar, bear, beaver, hare, aurochs, wolf and fox, as well as partridge and goose. The variation in ratios between different years of the excavation demonstrates that evidence gathered from other sites after one season of work may be suspect unless corroborated by further results. There was evidence for fishing, both from net sinkers, floats and hooks, and from the finds of bones and scales. Species discovered were sheatfish, pike, perch, bream, roach and carp.

The economy was clearly broad-based, since there was much evidence for the use and cultivation of plants such as wheat, barley, millet, peas, beans and lentils, the oleaginous rape and poppy, as well as other edible and useful plants such as flax. There is no evidence for any of these plants being imported: indeed, the find of a plough strongly suggests an active concern with agriculture.

Evidence of industry and technology from the site demonstrates that many manufacturing procedures took place at Biskupin itself. For example, the important finds of hundreds of fragments of moulds from the *'lost wax' process* of bronze-casting are clear evidence for on-site metalworking. The plans of these

finds show that 84 per cent of the mould fragments came from only five of the houses. Such concentration implies a few specialists rather than a general ability to work metal. Similar craft specialization can be suggested from finds of other types. For example, the loomweights and spindlewhorls, which are almost exclusively associated with the later Iron Age phase of the site, are concentrated in a few houses, suggesting specialist weaving families. However, a close similarity in the distribution of grinding stones might rather imply either a sexual discrimination in the houses (the activities of weaving and food preparation being considered as women's tasks), or even a basic difference in function of some of the structures, despite their similarity of type. Leatherworking may also have been a fairly specialized craft, if the presence of bone or horn awls demonstrates the piercing and sewing of hides, since large numbers of these were found in some structures although single examples occurred in a number of houses. Half-finished bone objects were also clustered in certain structures or areas. For example, several groups of unfinished arrowheads were recovered from one road.

Apart from the metal ores, few imported materials appeared on the site. Amber, probably from the Baltic, was made into beads, although only a few examples were found. Glass in the form of beads may also have come in from outside, since there is no evidence of glassworking on the site. A suggestion in the original site report that the blue glass beads came from Egypt reflects opinion prevalent 30 years ago; it is now considered more likely that they would have been made in the Balkans, or even in the Polish region itself.

Burials and beliefs

Evidence of the spiritual life of Biskupin is little and ambiguous. No burials are definitely associated with the site, but since only a few fragments of human bones appeared among the finds, presumably a cemetery awaits identification somewhere nearby. Finds of miniature vessels, figurines of birds, clay wheels and the like may reflect religious practices, but many of these objects could be toys, as the excavators suggest. An interesting feature is that some 75 per cent of the miniature pots were found outside the houses, on the roads or on and beyond the defences. Whether this represents children playing outside the house, or offerings to spirits being placed beyond the doors, must remain unanswered.

If we look at Biskupin in the context of the Polish early Iron Age, we find that the occupation of defended settlement sites is common in the area at this time. Many of the sites were on hilltops or slopes, but a number, like Biskupin, were placed on islands or lakesides. None of the others, however, shows the same sort of regular plan as Biskupin's tightly-packed structures and single building type. It is clear from sporadic finds of post-holes and pits from the period that other groups of people lived on undefended sites, but these are less easy to locate than sites with defences still visible, and therefore are not well-known.

Burial was in the form of cremation as a rule, the ashes being placed in an urn and buried in a flat cemetery along with many, often hundreds, of others. The nature of the settlements and burials, extensive and rarely with vastly differing components, suggests only minor social distinctions. And yet there are occasional finds of rich burials with horse-gear, or gold-inlaid weapons and imports from outside the immediate area, which imply the existence of chieftains. We have also seen that the planning and construction of the defended sites suggest some kind of central authority. Further south, in southwest Germany, there is for the same period certain evidence of ranked societies with rich chiefs. While the evidence from Poland does not suggest an exact parallel for that sort of society, there may well have been social distinctions that are not clearly revealed in the archaeological record. Certainly the people of the Lusatian culture were not cut off from the rest of Europe at this time. Imports from Hungary, Italy and the east Alpine region suggest an external exchange of some sort, although the details remain, for the moment, tantalizingly obscure.

Kul Oba

USSR

The Scythian tumulus at Kul Oba lies some 6.5 kilometres east of Kerch in the Crimea, USSR, and was excavated in 1830 with a precision and accuracy remarkable for its time. Indeed, the survival of a measured plan and elevation of the burial vault reveals the sort of valuable information that is normally lost to us from such early investigations. In this case the excavator was Paul Dubrux, a French emigrant who entered Russian service in 1797. Working his way through the civil service, health commission and customs, he found himself in Kerch, and conceived a plan to work on the antiquities of the region. The discovery of Kul Oba was, however, accidental, and we have Dubrux's own account of it.

According to Dubrux, orders had been issued during the early days of September to carry to Kerch 300 or 400 sazhens (600 to 800 metres) of stones. These were to be used in the construction of barracks for retired sailors being sent to Kerch from Sevastopol. Around 10 or 12 September, M. Stempkovsky, the governor of Kerch, asked Dubrux to accompany him to a mountain summit lying to the east, where 200 infantrymen were hewing the stones from the top of two hillocks. In examining the shape of the topmost hillock (that further to the east), Dubrux recognized that it contained a tomb. Having been employed in excavating mounds around Kerch for over 14 years, Dubrux was convinced that he was right, and he informed Stempkovsky of his suspicions. The governor then ordered the captain in command to put more workmen on the north side, where Dubrux, from the form of the tumulus, presumed that the entrance should be.

> 'On the 19th the governor was informed that a cut stone construction had been found; and returning there immediately we easily recognized the entrance or the passage of a vault, the door to which could be seen at the end; but as the three courses of enormous stones which covered this sort of vestibule were only held up by timber posts which were reduced to dust, and because these stones, almost hanging, had no support other than that which they mutually gave each other, the order was given to uncover this passage and, on Monday 22nd at 4 o'clock, the vault could be penetrated through an opening made at the height of the door by removing some of the stones which held it closed.'

Problems in excavating

From the beginning of the excavation Dubrux was plagued by two major problems: the dangerous state of the burial vault and the treasure-seeking local inhabitants. He regretted that the vault could not be preserved, and was light-hearted about his own escape from becoming 'a victim of my passion for antiquity and my punctuality in executing the orders given me by M. Stempkovsky . . .'. This referred to an incident which happened at 4 pm on 24 September, when an enormous stone detached itself from the vault and fell to the spot where Dubrux had been standing with two workmen a few minutes previously. He had left 'because of a fairly brisk argument with an officer who had taken our light from us in order to look around, thus saving our lives'.

Although the work was observed by several hundred curious spectators, Dubrux felt that the excavation was safe from burglary since they had also witnessed the frightened workmen rushing to escape a major collapse, and the incident in which he himself was nearly killed. However, as a precaution, on the 24th he left the entrance closed with large stones, and spoke to the officer of police who, with two soldiers, was keeping watch to stop people entering the tomb. The officer 'said that the nights were very cold, that the guards hadn't eaten, etc. I replied that I had not the right either to place or to relieve a guard, that orders must be taken from the governor'. Dubrux reported to the governor, and, when the question of the guard arose, said that he thought nobody would try to enter after that day's collapses. He learnt later that the guard had been lifted immediately he had left the site, and that tomb robbers were already at work while he was making his report.

When the excavators arrived the following morning, they found that the remaining rubble had been cleared and that the paving had been torn up. Dubrux informed the governor, who gave strict orders for the tomb to be guarded by day and patrolled by night. Nevertheless, more robbers arrived that night, posted a sentinel, and hid behind the hill when patrols approached. The same thing happened every night until the 28th, when the collapsing walls seriously wounded two of the robbers and frightened the rest off.

Dubrux later heard rumours that small gold objects were being sold in the town, and eventually managed to see much of what had been robbed, in return for a promise not to give the thieves away. He discovered the identity of one of those robbers who had been present the first night, and managed to persuade him to send back to the governor a whole piece of gold weighing more than 340 grams.

The burial chamber

Dubrux's investigations revealed that the tumulus was 53 metres in diameter. It contained an almost square burial vault, 4.60 by 4.26 metres, made up of eight courses of stone blocks to a height of 5.30 metres. A short passage or lobby led into it from the north. The chamber contained three burials at one level, and a fourth dug into the floor in the north-west corner. Since this last was found and looted by the robbers, its contents and its true stratigraphical relationship with the other graves cannot be reconstructed. However, it is said that the skeleton was decayed, and that some 55 kilograms of gold and electrum were robbed from this grave alone. Only 7 kilograms were recovered, including the well-known deer plaque.

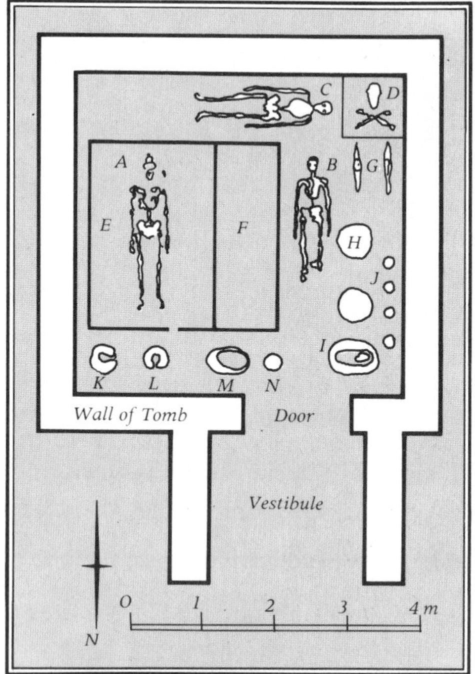

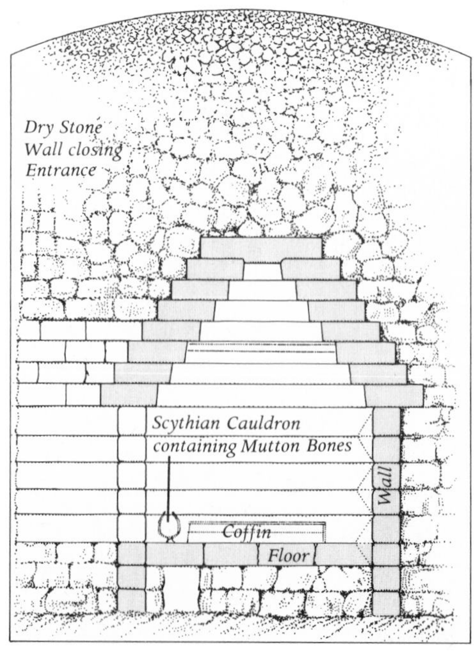

Left: Gold mount of a Scythian riding a horse. Its detail is remarkably clear and instructive, from the bridling of the horse to the rider's clothing. We can see his decorated trousers and top, as well as his spear, long hair and beard.

Left above: Key

A King's (?) skeleton
B Queen's (?) skeleton
C Man's (groom, guard) skeleton
D Sunken space with bones of horse, helmet, greaves
E Coffin of cypress or juniper
F Compartment for king's arms
G Two iron spearheads
H Two silver-gilt basins with 6 other vessels inside
I Scythian cauldron containing mutton bones
J Four amphorae
K Bronze hydria
L Bronze amphora
M Cauldron
N Bronze dish

Above: Fragments of the ivory veneer from an inner coffin at Kul Oba. The scene shows part of the Judgement of Paris, and is considered one of the most beautiful Greek drawings in existence. Its presence in this grave shows how important was the Greek world to wealthy Scythians.

Left: Cross section through the Kul Oba tumulus, showing its vaulted roof.

In the south-west corner of the chamber, a hollow in the floor contained horse-bones, a helmet, and the remains of greaves. In a partly open timber box of cypress or juniper, 2.84 metres square and 0.27 metres deep, lay the body of a male, orientated south-north with his head at the south. Beside this sarcophagus lay a female buried in a wooden coffin. Along the south wall, the body lying east-west, lay another male who is variously described as a slave or a groom. These burials probably belonged to the 5th or 4th century BC.

The male in the timber box, a king or high-ranking noble, was wearing a pointed felt cap decorated with two embossed gold strips, and a twisted neckring with terminals in the form of mounted Scythians. He wore rings on his arms and wrists. In the open part of his box lay his sword, the blade of which was 78 centimetres long, with a gold-mounted hilt and sheath; a whip with gold handle and gold thread twisted in with the leather; gilded greaves; and a gold-mounted whetstone. Five gold statuettes lay beneath his head, and a gold bowl was beside him. The female skeleton, probably his consort, wore a diadem of electrum, a heavy gold neckring and necklace, and heavily decorated bracelets. She was hung about with pendants and medallions of gold, and had between her knees the famous electrum vase with depictions of Scythians, as well as a gold-handled bronze mirror. Between her and the 'groom' lay seven knives, six with ivory handles and one with a gold.

The floor was strewn with stamped gold plaques, presumably attachments from wall-hangings, and clothes. There were arrowheads, two bronze cauldrons, four wine amphorae, three silver flasks, two drinking horns, a handled cup, and fragmentary remains of painted wood and engraved ivory from outer and inner coffins.

Dubrux made plans and sections of the burial vault, and recorded most of the finds. Those from his excavations are in the Hermitage Museum, Leningrad, along with some others originally robbed from the grave on the night of 24 September 1830 and subsequently sold or donated to the museum.

In 1875 further investigations were carried out by Lutzenko, the director of Kerch museum. His workmen sieved some of the rubble which blocked the tomb and found a few objects, but the general state of the monument after the collapses and the robbing left little to be newly gleaned. Although a few trenches were located, there was nothing in them to suggest any further burials. The site is now hardly recognizable, and we therefore rely entirely on Dubrux's original and, for its time, very advanced account for our information on this fabulously wealthy tomb.

The Scythians

In spite of the rich finds at Kul Oba and in other Scythian royal graves, the Scythians themselves remain something of an enigma. Accounts of them have been written by both ancient historians and modern archaeologists, yet many details of their lives, and indeed their very identity, remain unknown. The Greeks considered the Scythians to be any barbarians from eastern Europe, although Herodotus, the Greek historian of the 5th century BC, tried to distinguish between Scyths and non-Scyths. His distinction remained inconsistent, however, since he clearly used the name to describe the restricted group of 'real' Scyths (including the Royal Scyths) as well as the general group of tribes sharing Scythian culture. A related problem is that some of the so-called Scyths were nomadic and others were settled. Were they all Scyths? Further difficulties concern their origins: had they migrated from further east, or did they emerge from indigenous populations? These questions remain unanswered and are evidently associated with the differing usages of the name 'Scythian'.

As the groups which generally shared Scythian culture varied, so the social and economic basis for their way of life must have varied too. The nomads spent their time looking after their horses, which were used both for riding and as a source of food, and their cattle herds, which they moved around from pasture to pasture. They hunted and collected wild vegetables and fruit. The settled Scyths may have had a not dissimilar diet, since it is said that they produced food not for their own consumption but for export.

Scythian women were kept very much confined to the wagons and tents. The males carried swords, shields and the characteristic 'gorytus', a bow-case which held both bow and arrows. Armed with these they raided their enemies, captured their women, and drank out of cups made from their victims' skulls. Scythian kings were polygamous, and their sons could inherit their father's wives. There was clearly an exceedingly wealthy aristocracy, and we know very much less about the lower ranks of Scythian society.

Burial customs

Much of what archaeologists know of the Scythians has been discovered from the graves of their kings or aristocracy. These enormously rich tombs, most of which were at least partially plundered in antiquity, are the sole evidence of Scythian presence in some areas. Fortunately, we know something of their burial rites from the writings of Herodotus:

'The tombs of the kings are in the land of the Gerrhi. There, when their king dies, they dig a great square pit. When they have prepared this they take up the corpse, its body smeared over with wax and its belly slit open, cleaned out, and filled with chopped frankincense, parsley and anise, and then sewn up again, and bring it on a wagon to another tribe. Those who receive the corpse when it is brought do as the Royal Scythians. They cut a piece out of their ears, cut their hair short, slash their arms, slit their foreheads and noses, and thrust arrows through their left hands. Then they convey the corpse to another tribe among their subjects, and the tribe first reached goes with them. When they have gone round all the tribes with the corpse, they are among the Gerrhi, who live farthest off of all their subjects, and among the tombs.

When they have laid the corpse upon a mattress in its chamber, they stick spears into the ground on all sides. Then they lay beams across and cover them with wicker, and in the remaining space of the tomb they strangle and bury one concubine, the cupbearer, a cook, a groom, an attendant and a messenger; they also bury the pick of everything else and golden vessels. They use no silver or bronze. When they have done this they heap up a great mound, vying with one another and full of eagerness to make it as great as they can. Then when a year has passed they do as follows. They take the most suitable of the other attendants – these are true-born Scythians and are called to attend him by the king himself, for they have no bought slaves – and strangle 50 of them and 50 of the finest horses. They take out their entrails, clean them, fill them with chaff and sew them up. Then they put half the rim of a wheel with the hollow side upwards on two stakes, and the other half-rim on two others, fixing many such frames, drive stout stakes lengthwise through the horses to their necks and hoist them onto the rims. The front rims support the horses' shoulders and the rear ones their thighs and bellies, while both pairs of legs hang free. They put reins and bridles on the horses, draw these forward and tie them to pegs. Then they hoist every one of the strangled youths on to his horse, after driving a vertical stake through him by the spine to the neck, and part of this stake that projects downward they fasten into a socket in the other stake that runs through the horse. When they have set up riders in this style round the tomb they ride off'.

Not all graves correspond exactly to this description but there are certainly some, such

Right: A silver rhyton found among the treasures at Kul Oba, and made by Greeks for the Scythians. The terminal is in the form of the head, forelegs and front body of a ram. The vessel would have been used as a drinking horn for wine, although the Scythians usually drank from the wide end rather than in the Greek style of piercing the terminal and pouring the stream of wine into the mouth.

Below: The terminals of a gold torc, or neck-ring, inlaid with blue enamel and found round the neck of the 'king'. The Classical decoration on the body of the torc, for example on the palmettes, contrasts with the riders and horses on the terminals which must have been made to appeal particularly to the Scythians.

as Kostromskaya in the Kuban region of the USSR, where there are skeletons of sacrificed horses. Apparently, after the burial had been completed, the mourners repaired to a tent where hemp seeds were scattered on a fire, releasing fumes which were inhaled with extreme pleasure! The lavish attention given to the burials contrasts with the lack of temples or permanent shrines, of which no traces survive until a later period. However, since the gods worshipped by the Scythians were those of the elements – fire, water, earth, air – with the Sun and Moon, rites may have taken place in the countryside without the need for permanent sanctified places.

Settlements

Since many of the Scythians appear to have been nomadic, the lack of evidence for permanent settlements in some areas is hardly surprising. It seems that covered wagons were used for journeys, although it is uncertain whether these were, like caravans, lived in all the time, or whether temporary tented settlements were set up. However, there are a number of hill-forts or fortified settlements which date from the 7th century BC onwards, and these must represent either a permanent settlement for some Scythian group, or a base from which periodic, nomadic activities were initiated. One such site is at Kamenskoe on the River Dnieper, where a defensive bank enclosed 12 square kilometres of settlement. Of this, three per cent was taken up by a citadel containing house types different from those on the rest of the site. Everywhere on the site were remains of metal-working – iron and copper slag, crucibles, furnaces and the remains of workshops. Other, undefended, sites in the area have also produced evidence for metal-working, and it is possible that here we see a production area permanently occupied by specialist craftsmen who manufactured the tools, weapons and jewellery used and worn by the nomadic tribesmen. Sites of the period which have been excavated show different types of house plan. Circular, sunken-floored structures were found at Nemirov, while log-built, rectangular houses with sub-divisions were seen at Kamenskoe.

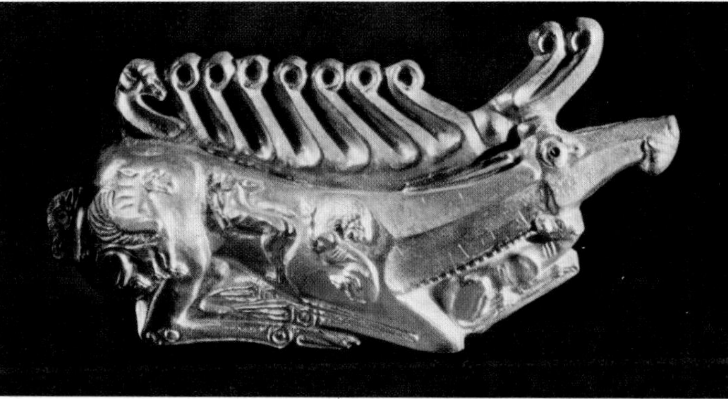

Right: A gold stag, possibly the centrepiece of a shield. The piece is typical of the Scythian art style, with the antlers repeated as a decorative pattern along the animal's back. The antler at the rear has a ram's-head terminal. The stag's legs are tucked beneath its belly, and the joints emphasized with decoration. A winged beast is superimposed on its rump, a lion and a hare on its belly, and a dog lies below its neck. Their presence is not understood.

Right: The famous Kul Oba electrum vase, found between the 'queen's' knees. The whole vase shows intimate scenes of Scythian warriors. Here, for example, a warrior helps to bandage the wounded leg of his comrade. Other scenes include one man aiding another with a sore tooth or mouth; a warrior fixing his bowstring; and two warriors in conversation, leaning on their spears.

Although the objects found in the burials may not be entirely representative of all the material in use during a Scythian's lifetime, there are many clues, and the settlement material, although still sparse, also yields useful information. There is evidence of spades, hammers, picks and axes, some in wood and some in iron. Ladders, and the wagons themselves, are evidence of wood-working, which was probably a highly-skilled specialist craft. The emphasis on horses is evident in the wealth of saddles, saddle blankets and bridles that have been preserved in the frozen tombs of Pazyryk in Siberia. There the bodies were so well preserved, after more than 2,000 years of freezing, that it was possible to see their all-over tattooing. The designs for tattoos, rugs, felt hangings and saddles mirror those found on wood carvings and on local gold and electrum ornaments. These complex designs, in which fantastic animals twist about and attack each other, seem to have a mixed origin from both the Far East and Asia, forming an art style which is probably the most well-known aspect of Scythian culture.

The Scythians' relationship with the Greeks in the Black Sea area was clearly advantageous to both sides. The Greeks, in search of agricultural products such as wheat and cattle, were able to provide the Scythians with wine (one of the amphorae at Kul Oba had a Thasos stamp) and other trappings of a civilized society. Rich ornaments and vessels were made by Greek craftsmen for the Scythian market, of which the Kul Oba vase is one example. Its pictures of Scythians talking, stringing a bow, dressing a wounded leg and attending to a sore mouth or tooth are Greek in style and workmanship, but the subject matter was evidently aimed at Scythian taste. The architecture of the Kul Oba tomb itself may perhaps be seen as of Greek inspiration, and many of the other grave-goods, such as the gold torc and the painted and engraved coffins, are clearly Greek. For those Scythians in contact with Greeks, therefore, the trappings of civilization were mixed with the instincts of the nomadic horseman.

Oseberg

NORWAY

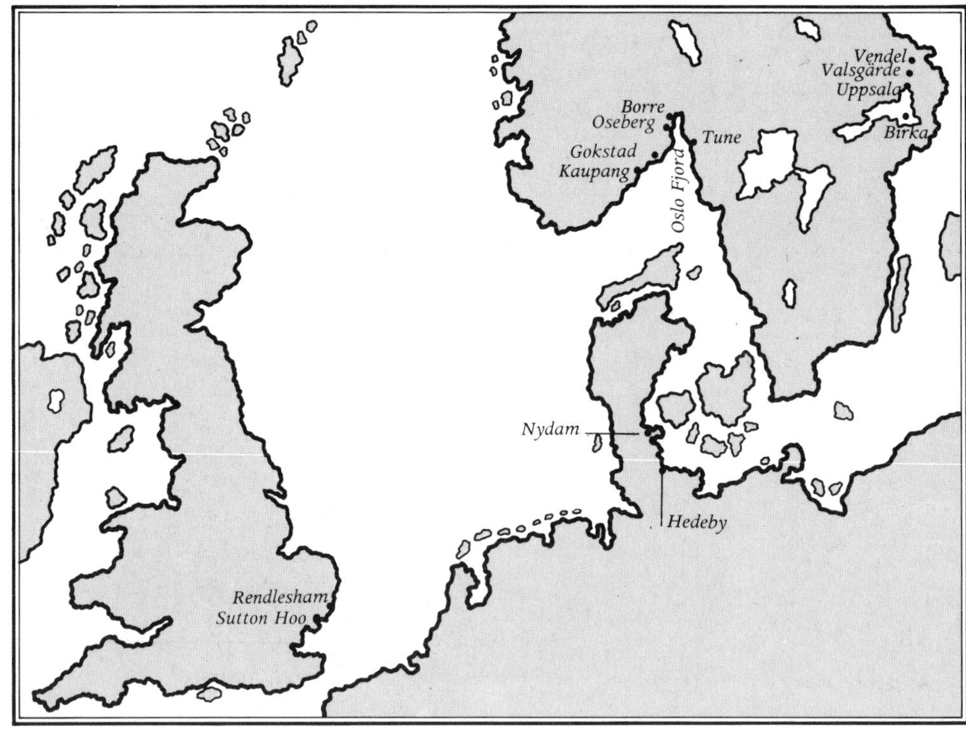

Saturday 8 August 1903 was the birthday of Gabriel Gustafson, director of the Archaeological Museum at the University of Oslo. It was also the day on which reports first reached the museum of what was to be Norway's most spectacular archaeological discovery. The accounts described how agricultural workers had dug into a mound at Oseberg, about 70 kilometres south of Oslo on the west side of the Oslo Fjord, and suspected that they had found the remains of a ship. Gustafson began a scientific excavation on the following Monday, and within a few days had confirmed the existence of a Viking ship-burial in a remarkable state of preservation. Despite great interest in the site and considerable pressure to excavate it immediately, he wisely decided to defer further work until the following year.

Gustafson spent the winter in organizing and financing the excavation. Two other recent discoveries of ship-burials in the Oslo Fjord, at Tune in 1867 and at Gokstad in 1880, had shown what could be expected. The blue clay subsoil in which the ships had been buried, and the peat which comprised the mounds on top, ensured almost perfect preservation of the ships and their rich contents. Realizing the potential of the site, Gustafson brought together one of the first excavation teams to consist of specialists drawn from different disciplines, including engineers, draughtsmen, a geologist and a botanist. He also made careful arrangements to conserve the many objects of organic materials he expected would be found.

Excavation began again on 13 June 1904 with a team of 15 men, later reduced to nine. Shortly afterwards, Haakon Shetelig, director of the Archaeological Museum at Bergen, was recruited as Gustafson's assistant. The mound was meticulously excavated, and, by the standards of the time, the quality of the records kept was high. Oseberg was also one of the first excavations in which extensive use was made of photography as a regular means of documenting the work's progress. Over 200 photographs were taken, giving a vivid picture of the working conditions.

The ship burial

The clay and peat of the mound, which had originally been 6 metres high and 40 metres in diameter, had indeed ensured remarkable preservation of the contents. The ship had been moored by rope to a large stone and had survived well, although damaged by pressure from the mound. Greater damage had been done by grave-robbers, who had tunnelled into the mound to reach the ship's prow. Their main target had been the wooden grave-chamber at the stern, which had originally contained the remains of two women. The older female, aged about 60–70, had been left alone, but the relics of the younger one, perhaps aged 25–30, had been greatly disturbed and the personal jewellery expected in the burial of a woman of such status was missing.

Preservation was so good that many types of organic material were recovered. These included not only wooden objects and textiles, but also plant and fruit remains. Apples, walnuts, hazelnuts, wheat, cress and woad had all been placed in the grave. The peat of the mound was also examined, and from the *diatoms*, mosses and plant remains recovered, it was possible to deduce that the burial had taken place in late August or early September.

Conservation and publication

Actual excavation was finished by 22 September 1904, but much remained to be done. Gustafson was faced with an unprecedented volume of organic material in need of conservation, as well as the problem of the ship itself. This was dismantled and the timbers impregnated to prevent them from shrinking and cracking. Eventually, by the evening of 16 December 1904, everything had been removed to Oslo.

The preparation of the finds for public viewing was a long process, but Gustafson continued to press the government for funds to carry out conservation and to provide adequate accommodation for their display. The ship itself took three years to restore, and the first selection of finds went on show in a new Oseberg Gallery at the University Museum, Oslo, in 1912. Unfortunately, Gustafson did not live to see the completion of the project he had initiated with such foresight and enthusiasm. After his death in 1915 he was succeeded as director of the museum by A. W. Brøgger, the son of the geologist who had been involved in the ship's initial excavation.

Brøgger was instrumental in establishing the Viking Ship Museum near Oslo, in which the ships from Oseberg and Gokstad took pride of place. He also assumed the enormous task of publishing the finds, which he did in collaboration with Shetelig, Hjalmar Falk and S. Grieg. With the aid of government finance, the four magnificent and lavishly illustrated volumes of *Osebergfundet* appeared between 1917 and 1928, some of the copies including summaries in English or German. The standard of this report is remarkably high, with a full description of the actual excavation, as well as detailed treatment of the ship and finds, accompanied by numerous drawings and photographs. Of particular importance are Shetelig's sections on the ship and on the styles of artistic decoration associated with it. The latter section proved a major contribution to art historical studies. In it, Shetelig presented a masterly analysis of the decoration and attempted to define the work of different craftsmen. He then tried to apply to the styles the newly developed *typological method* of the famous Swedish archaeologist Oscar Montelius

Top right: The excavation team at Oseberg on 21 September 1904. The director of the project, Gabriel Gustafson, stands third from the left.

Centre right: The Oseberg ship on 20 September 1904, towards the end of the excavation. The wooden grave chamber had by then been removed from the ship's centre.

Bottom right: The Oseberg ship fully restored. The vessel was adaptable for sailing or rowing, while its open design and shallow draught are typical of early Viking ships.

(1843–1921) who had himself visited the excavation. The various styles and craftsmen were thus arranged into a chronological order of artistic development.

The quality of the volumes themselves was also very high, betokening a sumptuousness that could not have been achieved without the generous support of the newly independent state of Norway, and which is beyond the reach of most modern archaeological reports. They form a suitable monument to Gustafson, who appreciated the potential of the site.

Finds from the ship

Although ship-burials had been discovered before, they had seldom been found with the quantity of artefacts that survived in the 9th-century AD interment at Oseberg. The ship contained a burial chamber at the stern end, in which two women had been buried amid beds, pillows, blankets and eiderdowns. There were also several chests and barrels. One barrel still contained apples, whereas one of the chests had been opened and its contents, probably personal jewellery and ornaments, had been stolen by grave-robbers. In the ship's bows was a collection of objects of the greatest archaeological importance, including a four-wheeled wagon with carved wooden panels and four sledges, three of them highly decorated. Two of these became known as Gustafson's and Shetelig's sledges. There were also tents, beds, a chair, a loom, reels and tablet-weaving plaques. Some of the equipment, including oars, an anchor-stock, gangplanks and a large baler, was clearly related to the ship itself. Further aft were domestic items, such as a knife and axes, wooden plates and jugs, iron cauldrons and a rotary quern. The carcass of an ox was laid out on two wooden planks.

The grave was also notable for its wealth of decoration. In addition to the panels on the wagon and sledges, there were four posts, magnificently carved with animal heads, the true function of which is unknown. The ship itself also had highly decorated panels on stem and stern. One of the most unusual finds was a pictorial textile panel, somewhat similar to the Bayeux Tapestry. Although such panels were common in the Viking period, few survive. This one depicts a variety of scenes, especially battles with horses, carts, wagons and warriors armed with spear and shield.

Viking Life and Death

The Oseberg ship-burial is one of the most spectacular finds of the Viking period, but its archaeological importance extends beyond the mere richness and artistry of the goods deposited. It also tells us a great deal about the society, economy and, particularly, the technical achievements of the period.

Burial in a ship was a rite given only to those among the highest levels in Viking society. (It has indeed been suggested that the young woman buried at Oseberg was queen Åsa, grandmother of king Harald Finehair.) But with certain variations, especially as to the practice of inhumation or cremation, it had a long usage in Scandinavia, and occasionally further afield. Some of the best known examples are the aristocratic cemeteries, in use from the 5th century BC onwards, at Vendel and Valsgärde near Uppsala in eastern Sweden, where the men were buried with elaborate armour and weapons. The most richly-furnished of all ship-burials was found outside Scandinavia, however, at Sutton Hoo in Suffolk, England. Here Redwald, king of the East Angles, was buried in AD 625 amid a treasure of enormous value and exquisite workmanship. This included arms and armour, drinking vessels, imported silver bowls and dishes, as well as royal emblems.

Burial rites

The rites accompanying such burials cannot be fully reconstructed from archaeological evidence alone, but there exists a remarkable account of a cremated ship-burial among Swedish settlers on the River Volga in south Russia in AD 922. This was witnessed and recorded by the Arab ambassador Ibn Fadlan. He describes how the dead man was temporarily buried with food and drink while special clothes were prepared and a slave selected to accompany him. When the preparations were complete, the body was dressed, adorned and placed on a bed in the ship with other offerings of weapons and food. The slave was killed and placed beside the body. After the ship and all its contents had been consumed by fire, a mound was raised over the ashes. Despite the use of cremation, there are many points of similarity to the Oseberg burial, such as the food and other offerings and the slave killed to accompany the dead person.

It is impossible, without specific testimony, to reconstruct with certainty the beliefs that underlay these rites. The use of a ship for burial was probably chosen as a sign of Viking mastery of the sea, but may also have symbolized the belief in death as a journey. The dead woman was well prepared for such a voyage, since the Oseberg ship had been newly repaired and fitted out with oars and a rudder. It was also supplied with meat, fruit and other provisions, as well as cooking and eating utensils. In a contemporary variant on this theme, women of high class in Denmark were sometimes buried on a wagon similar to the one in the Oseberg burial. The secure mooring of the ship might, however, indicate a safe refuge for the dead to await some future resurrection, or the ship may simply have been thought of as being the largest of the goods deposited with the dead.

Social structure

Whatever the beliefs involved, the use of ship-burial from the 6th century onwards was one custom which marked the status of higher ranks in early Viking society. Those lower in the social scale were furnished with simpler graves. During this period, social structure was becoming more hierarchical, and larger political units were beginning to appear. The centres of these emerging powers were frequently marked by concentrations of rich cemeteries, such as those at Old Uppsala, Vendel and Valsgärde at the seat of Svear power in east Sweden, or the Sutton Hoo cemetery near the East Anglian royal centre of Rendlesham in England. The ship-burials around Oslo Fjord, at Gokstad, Oseberg, Tune and Borre, mark another such centre, although nothing is known of the area in which those interred once lived.

Closely associated with this new social

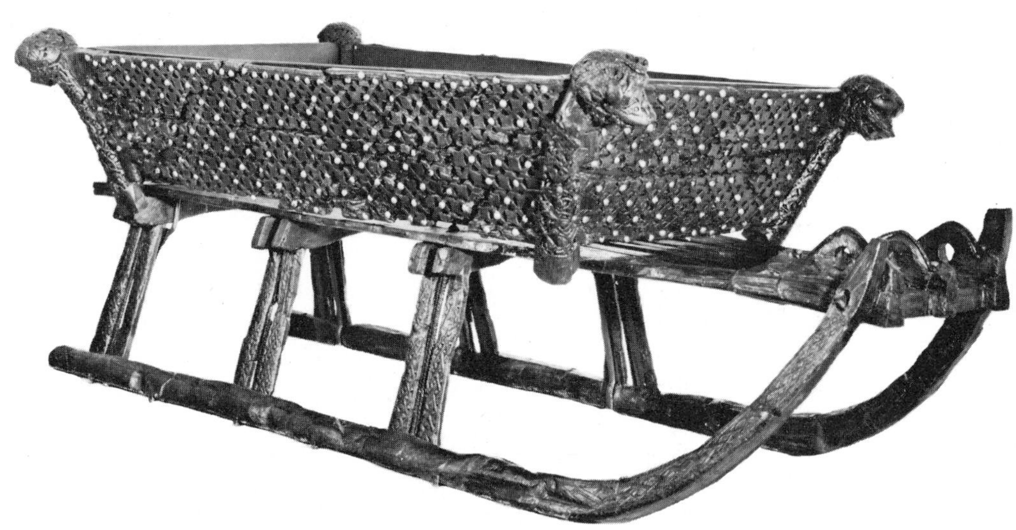

Above: Gustafson's sledge, one of four from the Oseberg burial. The fine carving on three of the sledges, and on the ship and the waggon, were the work of a royal 'school' of carvers. Sledges were an important means of transport in the north, especially in winter, when travel would often be easiest across frozen lakes and rivers. Skis and skates from the period are also known.

Left: A carved wooden animal post from the Oseberg ship-burial. The carving is meticulously executed, and its use of established animal motifs has led to its artist being nicknamed the 'Academician'. Another animal-head post in the burial was carved with new motifs, especially the writhing animals which were to become one of the main themes of Viking art. These motifs are found on wood and metal alike, although little woodwork has been preserved. This is one of the finest Viking objects to survive, and is a reminder of how much has been lost.

Right: Fragment of a textile with pictorial designs, from the Oseberg burial. The almost perfect conditions in the burial preserved this unique survival of what may have been a widespread Viking craft. The long, narrow bands of tapestry probably adorned the walls of the grave chamber, and Viking houses may well have had similar hangings. The tapestry is bordered by bands of geometric designs, between which a procession of riders, soldiers and horse-drawn carts moves from right to left. The meaning of the scenes is not known. The material was brightly coloured in yellow, black and red.

order was the first appearance of towns in Scandinavia, as centres of craft production and especially of maritime trade. These new sites, which flourished in the 9th century, commanded the trade routes and took advantage of good harbours. Hedeby, near Schleswig, and Birka served southern Jutland and east Sweden respectively, while on the Oslo Fjord itself, south of Oseberg, was the site of Kaupang. The cemetery excavated here contained numerous ship-burials and many imported ornaments, especially from England and Ireland. These coastal towns were the market centres for Viking traders, and so were in contact with the whole of Europe, from Ireland in the west to Russia in the east.

The wealth of the Vikings, best seen in their imported goods and lavish burials, was firmly rooted in a stable agricultural economy and the growing exploitation of local resources. Little is yet known about farming settlements of the time, but the main elements of the subsistence economy are seen in the meat, grain, wild fruit and nuts offered in the Oseberg burial. However, the main commodities for export were not agricultural, but materials such as iron, tar, wax and especially furs and slaves.

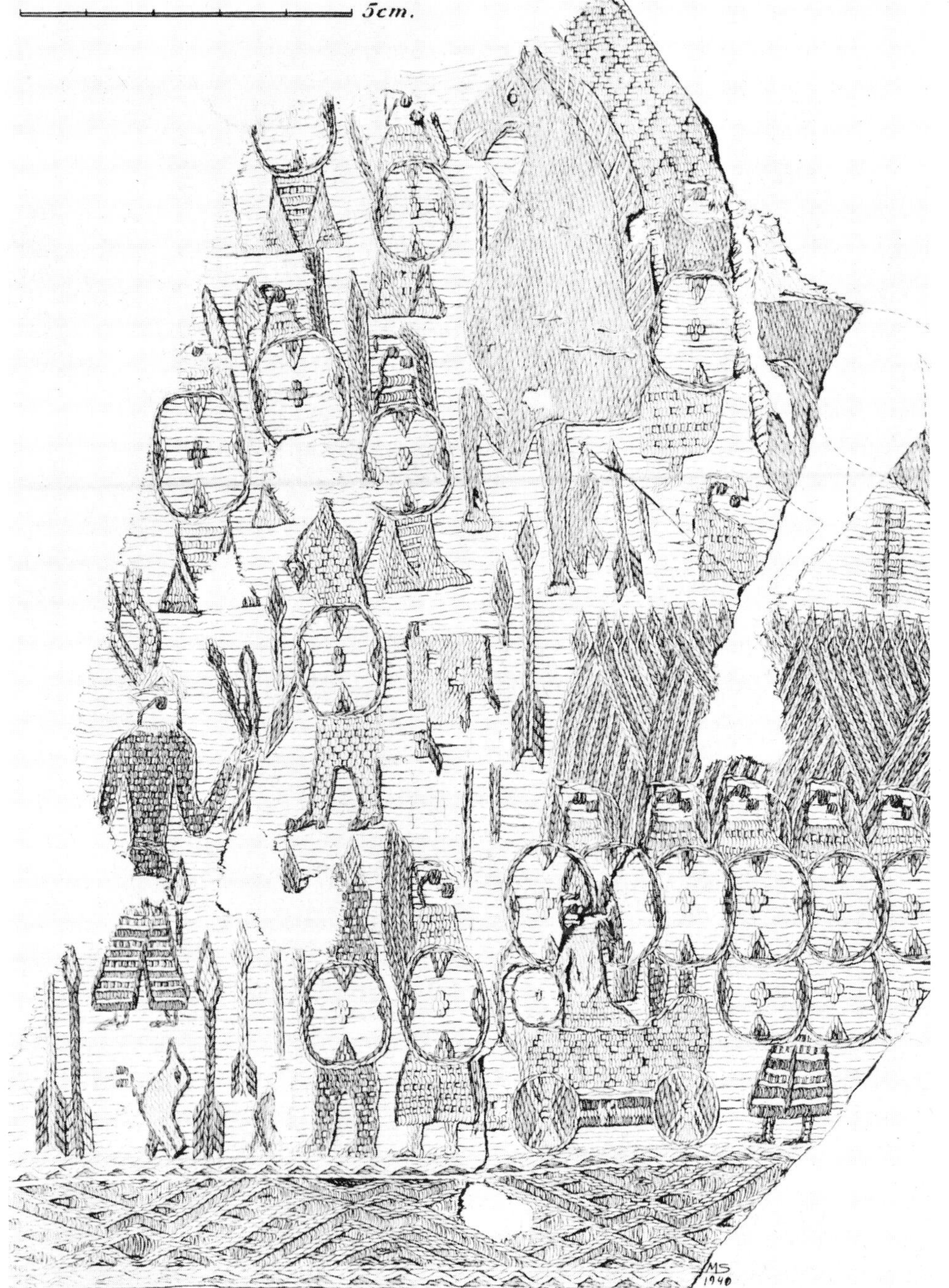

The art of Oseberg

The emergence of the new hierarchies stimulated artistic growth in Scandinavia, and the finest expression of an art based on interlaced animals and birds appears on decorated metal ornaments found in the 7th-century boat graves at Vendel and Valsgärde in Sweden. This style is developed in wood into something even finer at Oseberg. Here, carvings which show tightly-packed animals gripping each other are of local inspiration, but some motifs seem derived from *Carolingian* art. Shetelig's analysis of this 'Vestfold school' at Oseberg showed no fewer than ten individual craftsmen, some traditional, some innovative. Since this style is seldom found outside the rich graves of south Norway, the artists may have been specialist craftsmen working only for royal or aristocratic patrons. In much the same way, although weaving was certainly a domestic craft, the complex pictorial pieces such as the Oseberg panel may also have been produced by highly-skilled specialists.

The special conditions of the Oseberg burial have preserved evidence of the technical mastery of the period, especially in wood. At a more humble level than the supremely skilled decorative wood-carving was the production of wooden domestic items such as plates. For transport needs, wooden wagons and sledges were produced, but the greatest achievement was in boatbuilding, and the surviving ships demonstrate how these skills developed.

Viking ships

The Oseberg vessel, with its near contemporary at Gokstad, marks a significant step in the history of Viking ships. To judge by the example from Nydam near Schleswig, ships of the 5th century were little more than very long rowing boats with no provision for a mast or a keel. By the 9th century, however, the technical skill of construction had advanced greatly. The Oseberg ship was built of oak, the planks being lashed to the strakes to give greater elasticity in rough water. It was provided with a full keel and a mast, and its fine, low lines gave it great speed. A replica of the Gokstad ship, which was essentially similar to that from Oseberg, was tested in a voyage from Bergen to Newfoundland, which took place in 1893. It was completed in under a month, speeds of 11 knots were achieved, and the captain praised the design and handling of the vessel.

The development of such fast ocean-going ships was obviously vital to later Viking seafaring, but it should not be supposed that these were the only type of vessel known at the time. Special ships may well have been chosen for the burial of prestigious people, and we know little of the history of sailing vessels designed for cargo purposes, few of which have survived. The techniques for building these vessels may well also have improved over this period, and in any case there is clear evidence of the seafarers' growing ability to undertake long journeys away from land.

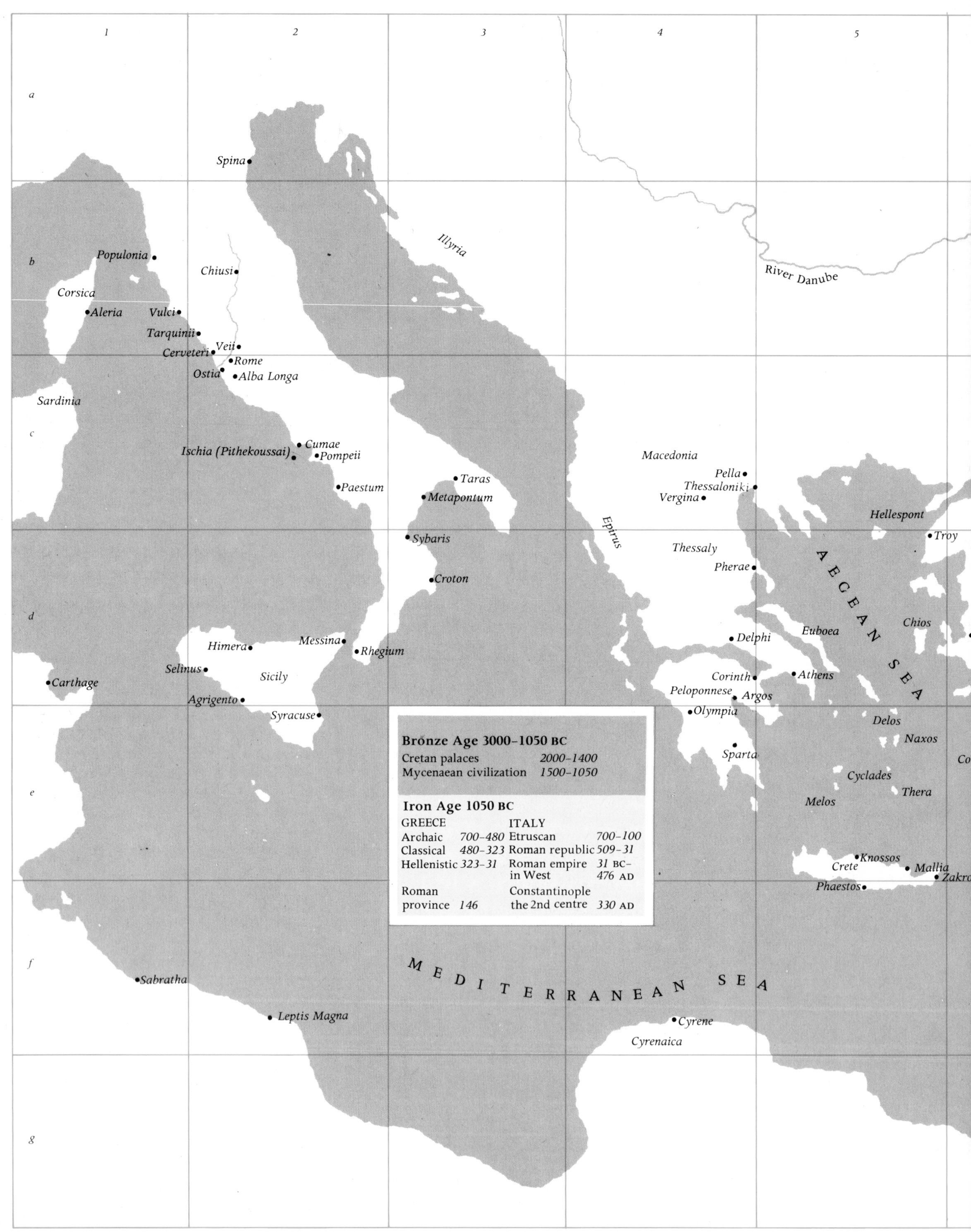
1
2
3
4
5
a
b
c
d
e
f
g
Spina
Illyria
River Danube
Populonia
Chiusi
Corsica
Aleria
Vulci
Tarquinii
Cerveteri
Veii
Rome
Ostia
Alba Longa
Sardinia
Cumae
Ischia (Pithekoussai)
Pompeii
Paestum
Taras
Metapontum
Macedonia
Pella
Thessaloniki
Vergina
Hellespont
Troy
Epirus
Sybaris
Thessaly
Pherae
AEGEAN SEA
Croton
Chios
Euboea
Delphi
Himera
Messina
Rhegium
Selinus
Sicily
Carthage
Corinth
Athens
Peloponnese
Argos
Agrigento
Syracuse
Olympia
Delos
Naxos
Sparta
Cyclades
Thera
Melos
Knossos
Crete
Mallia
Zakro
Phaestos
Sabratha
MEDITERRANEAN SEA
Leptis Magna
Cyrene
Cyrenaica
Bronze Age 3000–1050 BC
Cretan palaces 2000–1400
Mycenaean civilization 1500–1050
Iron Age 1050 BC
GREECE
Archaic 700–480
Classical 480–323
Hellenistic 323–31
Roman province 146
ITALY
Etruscan 700–100
Roman republic 509–31
Roman empire in West 31 BC–476 AD
Constantinople the 2nd centre 330 AD

The Classical World

2000 BC-AD 500

Greece and Italy figure impressively in the history of archaeology, for sites of great importance abound there. Those described here cover much of the range, but cannot hope to be wholly representative.

Pompeii, captured in an instant by the eruption of Vesuvius, is a rare kind of site. Rare too are the unplundered burials of Cerveteri, a major Etruscan city, and of Vergina, home of the early kings of Macedon. More typical are the complex levels of the Roman Forum or the Agora of Athens, both riddled with the pits of later generations. So few Greek or Roman sites are of a single period that it is rare to discover the complete plan, let alone elevation, of any structure. The sand-blown glories of Leptis Magna approach that ideal, and reveal an important North African city of the Roman empire. Knossos, which flourished under first Cretan and then Greek-speaking lords, is the largest of the centres of the Minoan civilization.

At all ten sites, archaeological problems remain. One example concerns some of the earliest known coins found in the sanctuary of Artemis at Ephesus in 1904. Their dating is disputed because of the absence of pottery in the deposit and the quagmire conditions in which the material was extracted. At Metapontum, a Greek agricultural colony in the instep of Italy, the ancient drainage system has been of use in drying out such deep levels. Metapontum is an excellent example of a planned site offering a range of structures, from temples to field drains. Much the same could be said of the Agora of Athens. Delphi could be said to be the spiritual counterpart of the Agora, a powerful force in early Greek thought and politics, as well as the source of some of the finest marble sculpture of the 6th century BC. Ephesus and Vergina for the most part exemplify the later Greek period, the former owing its rebuilding to a military successor of Alexander the Great, the latter being the burial place of some of the famous conqueror's family.

Knossos

CRETE

Crete is best known for its Minoan palaces, which date between 2000 and 1400 BC. The most impressive palace is that of Knossos, which lies 6 kilometres south of the island's present capital Iraklion. Knossos is associated in legend with king Minos and the monstrous Minotaur which lived in the labyrinth until it was slain by the Greek hero Theseus. The minotaur was part man and part bull, a fact which has made the archaeological discovery of bull cults at the palace of Knossos all the more intriguing.

The Minoan palaces capture the imagination, but Knossos also offers excavators material from the whole of prehistory, going back to the early Neolithic period and including the entire historical period, apart from a gap between 550 and 400 BC.

Knossos stands on a knoll on the west bank of a stream known as the Kairatos. Vines and olives grow well in the soils of the area. To the south is the striking peak of Mount Juktas, where the largest of the Minoan hilltop shrines once stood. At Arkhanes, at its foot, archaeologists have excavated a large settlement, including a variety of burials and buildings of a royal nature. The port serving Knossos was Amnisos. It, too, has been partly excavated during recent years.

The work of Arthur Evans

Knossos is irrevocably linked with the name of the great British archaeologist Sir Arthur Evans (1851–1941), who excavated the palace in association with the British School at Athens. Evans was not the first nor the last investigator of the site, although earlier soundings were never more than casual. Evans had a broad background in European archaeology and, in 1884, he became Keeper of Antiquities at the Ashmolean Museum at Oxford in England. He was also a noted numismatist and his interest in Crete stemmed partly from his studies of engraved seal stones from the island.

Evans purchased some land at Knossos in 1894 from a local Muslim land-owner, but progress was tough. He wrote that the 'native Mahometans' had 'almost inexhaustible powers of obstruction'. However, the establishment of a Greek administration in 1898 gave him and other archaeologists their chance. He began digging in 1900.

He planned on a large scale. A gross of bottles of fruit salts was merely part of his

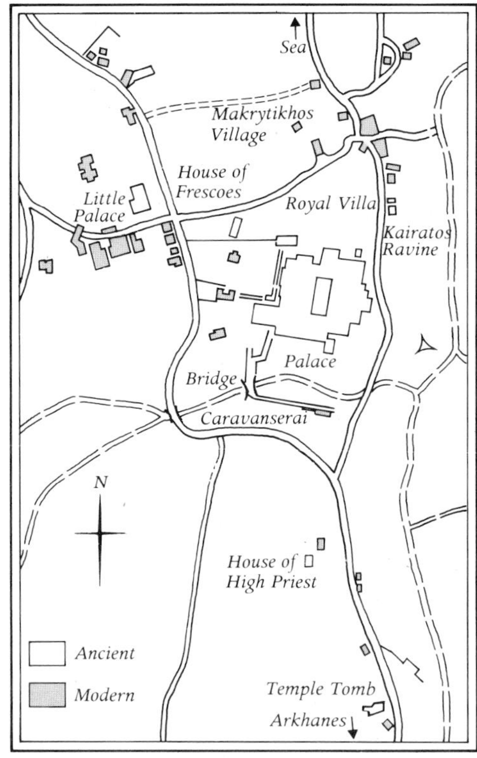

equipment! Excavation proceeded quickly. It is estimated that 130 cubic metres of earth were removed each day. Evans's assistant, a Scot named Duncan MacKenzie, wrote up the day books. He had previously worked at the site of Phylakopi on the Aegean island of Melos. Evans himself produced the annual reports, from which we learn of his care in excavating, notably in sifting earth. (In this context, his interest in seal stones and, eventually, in fragments of inscribed clay tablets should not be forgotten.)

By present standards, however, the reports are lacking in detail and Evans's final publication, *The Palace of Minos*, is more an account of the civilization of Bronze Age Crete than a record of the work undertaken at the site. In some disputed areas we could also wish for better records and treatment of the finds. Little was kept and less published, although we need not doubt that Evans's judgements are representative.

Later excavations

In 1928 the British School at Athens became responsible for excavating at Knossos and much has been done since then. One notable excavation involved 6-metre-deep soundings in the central court of the palace to investigate the 4,000 years preceding the palace period. There was also the work of a succession of investigators in the cemeteries, especially those of the late 2nd and early 1st millennium BC.

In 1978 the initial building work for the medical faculty of the University of Crete predictably hit on a cemetery. This yielded graves a few metres ahead of the bulldozer, ranging from the Minoan to the Roman period, including rich and unusual material from the period 800–600 BC. A 'rescue' dig was conducted before the erection of an extension to the on-site archaeological storeroom, in which startling evidence of human sacrifice has been unearthed.

The Neolithic sequence stretches from about 6000 to 3000 BC. Even in the earliest pre-ceramic phase, there is evidence of a sizeable settlement at Knossos and contacts with the Cyclades, islands to the north in the Aegean Sea. The changes in the 3rd millennium, quickening towards its end, were more striking. Metal and stone-working techniques were acquired and housing became more sophisticated. One variety of tomb, a roofed roundhouse for communal burials called 'tholos', is particularly characteristic. As these tholoi became full, charnel-houses were attached to them to accommodate the accumulated bones. Most of these early tholoi are found in southern Crete, but a late example of around 1800 BC has been excavated at Knossos.

The Minoan palaces

The earliest palaces were built between 2000 and 1800 BC at Mallia, east of Knossos on the north coast, at Phaistos in south-central

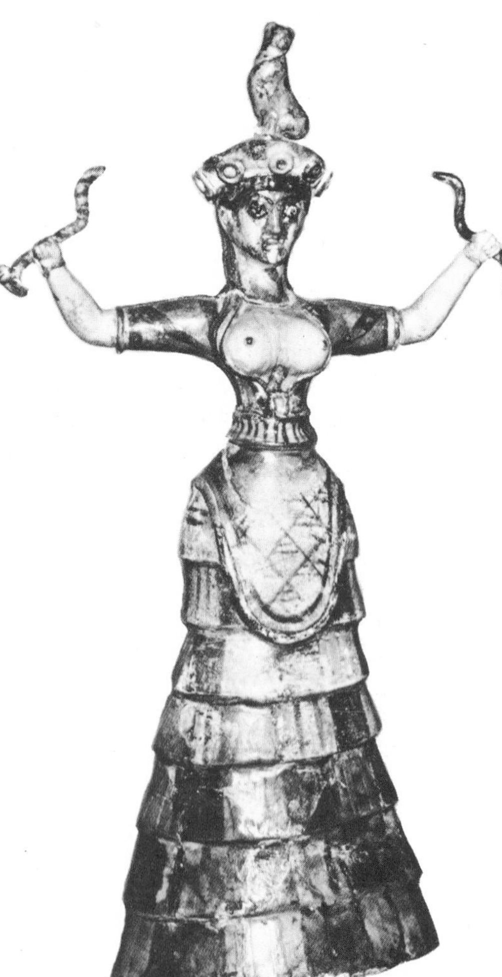

Crete and at Knossos itself. Their architectural sophistication is noteworthy, with rooms ranged around a central court in a number of storeys. In each case the west range had its own monumental façade, behind which were cult rooms and stores. Earthquakes destroyed these palaces in about 1700 BC, but they were rapidly replaced in much the same form.

Minoan palace society reached its peak of sophistication in the subsequent period. At Knossos a series of roomy villas was built around the palace, and a model recently found at Arkhanes affords a good idea of their original appearance. Destruction came to most Cretan sites around 1450 BC. It occurred a generation or so after the titanic explosion of the volcano on the nearby island of Thera (now Santorini).

The palace at Knossos survived until about 1375 BC. The decipherment of *Linear B* texts has proved that, in this last period, Knossos was run by Greek-speaking people, presumably from the mainland, who also controlled much of the island. A fire finally destroyed the palace at Knossos, but its cause has not yet been clearly determined.

Impressive works of art have come from Knossos. At its best Minoan pottery combines simple functionality with wonderful, disciplined floral and faunal decoration – a spirited reflection of the magnificent wall paintings in the palaces. A wide range of styles and moods is revealed, including sacred processions, bull sports, and birds and animals in rural settings. Setting a similar tone are carved black vases, made of a form of talc called steatite. These were perhaps used in rituals. The best examples of these pieces come from the royal quarters at Aghia Triada, near Phaistos, and Zakro, on the east coast of Crete.

From the 'Little Palace' at Knossos came a Steatite bull's head (a ritual vessel?) with fiery, bloodshot pupils painted on its rock-crystal eyes. The famous snake goddess, found in a sacred deposit in the palace, is made of faience (coloured, glazed earthenware). She is the most elegant of a number of deities from the palace, some of which were found still standing on a bench in a small shrine.

The work of Sir Arthur Evans at Knossos was particularly significant because it uncovered a major civilization about which practically nothing was known before the excavation. However, Evans's decision to restore parts of the palace has been both praised and condemned. Although conjectural in part, the rebuilding has given us a glimpse of the cool grandeur of the palace. It also arrested the decay of the *gypsum* used for paving and other purposes, which is highly susceptible to weathering. The timber beams and columns long since perished were also replaced.

Above: Linear 'B' tablet. Michael Ventris detected that the language of archival clay tablets found by Evans was Greek, although written in a syllabic script already in use in Crete. Here, lists of animals follow the heading 'livestock at Wato', a place probably in west Crete, far from the administrative centre.

Below: Many large storage jars were found in the palace, some decorated. This piece is from the magazines in the west wing. Its distinctive formalized style of the later 15th century BC is largely confined to the Knossos area and western Crete. This 'Palace style' is far more restrained than earlier work. The doubled edges of the axes, a regular companion of the bull's horns, are an artistic convention.

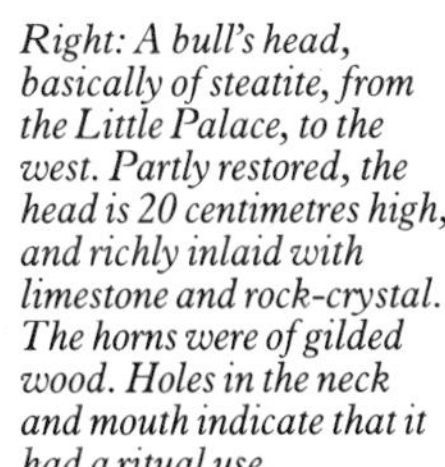

Right: A bull's head, basically of steatite, from the Little Palace, to the west. Partly restored, the head is 20 centimetres high, and richly inlaid with limestone and rock-crystal. The horns were of gilded wood. Holes in the neck and mouth indicate that it had a ritual use.

Far left: Although only 34 centimetres high, the snake goddess stands far above lesser rivals in terracotta. Found in the treasury of the shrine in the palace's west wing, the figure is made of faience, in typical Minoan garb: c. 1650 BC.

The Minoans

The social structure of Minoan Crete can be judged at present only from the archaeological record. This is because the early scripts of the island's hieroglyphic and *Linear A* have yet to be deciphered.

Life in the palace

Greek legend tells of king Minos, and the poet Homer referred to a fine dancing floor made for the king's daughter Ariadne by Daedalus, the legendary artist, craftsman and engineer. A royal family probably did rule at Knossos and the Linear B tablets prove that there was a single overlord.

The houses around the palace suggest that numbers of aristocratic dependants lived there. There was also probably a substantial agricultural population, concerned largely with sheep farming and the production of cereals, wine and oil. Such commodities are listed in Linear B tablets and were stored in the pithoi (clay jars) and cists (stone chests) which were prominent features of the palace from an early date. Strict attention to correct conduct is also indicated by the use of seals to denote personal property, a custom which was established well before the first palace was built. Evidence of regular armed forces is rare, but one palace fresco shows black warriors, who possibly formed a mercenary force. Total estimates of the population are difficult to arrive at, but Crete was certainly heavily populated in the middle of the 2nd millennium, as archaeological surveys on various parts of the island have shown.

Palace life was influenced by Near Eastern cultures. Egyptian tomb paintings show people from the land of Keftiu (Cretans) bearing gifts to the pharaohs. The most substantial remains of a return trade are copper ingots from Cyprus and elephant tusks from Syria found in a storeroom at Zakro. Eastern influence is also apparent in wall painting and script.

Certain aspects of Cretan architecture, however, are totally home-grown, especially the basic construction technique of wooden beam and rubble walls, which were designed to withstand earthquakes. At Knossos many walls have a face of squared stones, for which gypsum from the surrounding hills was regularly used. The face of the west front of the palace was particularly well fitted, although the blocks, as at Mallia, touch only along their front edges. Mud-brick was also widely used and most walls were plastered and normally painted; roofs were flat. Columns, tapering downwards, were used in various ways, notably on staircases, which also acted as light wells for inner rooms. Rooms were often spacious and fitted with light partitions for arrangement at will.

Thought was given to drainage, with particular regard to the violence of rains in Crete. And the toilet facilities of the royal apartments set a standard rarely upheld before the present century. Baths were more rudimentary. Evans found several 'lustral basins' in the palace. These were large, square baths with steps leading down into them, but they lacked plug-holes. Terracotta bathtubs were also found, in one of which was a cache of Linear B tablets. The tubs were also used for burials, although a version modelled on wooden coffins and often painted was more common.

Military matters seemed to have been of little concern to the Minoans. Arms are rare in tombs before the Mycenaean period, from which there is a series of rich warrior graves from the Knossos area. Some earlier frescoes show warriors, and Minoan paintings from the island of Thera depict Cretan-inspired naval scenes which could reflect Minoan sea power. The Greek historian Thucydides, writing about 1,000 years later, mentioned a 'thalassocracy' (sea power) in Minoan times. However, the picture is much clearer during the period of Mycenaean domination, when the tablets list vast arsenals, including war chariots. Throughout the palace period, the lack of defences suggests that there was a large measure of security in Crete.

Most weapons and armour were made of bronze – about nine parts of copper to one of tin. The source of the tin is a mystery, because there is none in the Aegean area. Blades made of obsidian were still in favour for general use. The obsidian, a glassy, black volcanic stone, came from the island of Melos. The abrasive emery, obtained from Naxos, assisted the cutting edge of metal tools, not least the drills of gem-engravers and makers of stone vases.

Worship, sacrifice and burial

The religious side of Minoan life appears to have been elaborate. Of course this is only conjecture, because we cannot be sure, without historical texts, what were the chief activities in the worship of the deities.

Cult activity is evident in the multi-room shrines on hilltops, with their fire altars and many bronze and terracotta figurines, especially of animals. A steatite vase from Zakro, once gilded, shows wild goats sporting around such a shrine which is adorned with symbols seen in so many Minoan contexts – double-axes and stylized bulls' horns. In one house at Knossos real bulls' skulls were found by an altar. Other small but important shrines were found in the palaces. Both Knossos and Zakro had depositories for cult equipment.

Macabre and disturbing discoveries in 1979 have shaken the picture of a peaceful and civilized Crete. At Arkhanes, at the foot of Juktas, Greek archaeologists have excavated a large, free-standing temple of unique, aisled plan, complete with the remains of a life-size cult statue. Bull sacrifice was probably a regular rite here. However, just before the temple was burned down, at the same time as the destruction of the first palace at Knossos, human offerings were made, apparently to appease the deity. The evidence cannot be given here, because it has yet to be fully published, but a sacrificial victim, with a knife still lodged in its skeleton, was found draped across an altar-like construction.

Meanwhile, at Knossos, a deposit of human bones has been unearthed. These were of two adolescents and show every sign of having been butchered and split open for the extraction of the marrow. They are grim reminders that scholars can still be surprised, even if the interpretations of these finds have not gone unchallenged.

However, this evidence makes the king seem a more sinister character, and we recall the legend of how Athens was forced to send seven of its youths and seven of its maidens as tribute to king Minos every year. The king may have been regarded as divine. This is suggested by the all-pervading presence of the double-axe and horns in the palace, as well as the strongly religious aspect of the west wing.

Both Knossos and Phaestos have theatre-like areas with ranges of steps designed to accommodate spectators. Many explanations have been offered as to their purpose. The most plausible is that the king welcomed visitors and dispensed justice there. The formal layout of the paths into the palace strongly suggests order and protocol.

The Minoans inhumed their dead, and various types of tomb construction are now known. In the Knossos area, chamber tombs are regular, although few belonging to the palace period have been found. Katsamba, on the coast west of Amnisos, has yielded wealthy burials. In recent years, hundreds of burials have also been cleared at Arkhanes. There is a wide range of types, with some extremely rich, intact inhumations from tholoi of an elaborate kind, more typical of Mycenaean Greece. Noteworthy finds include stone bowls, gold jewellery and imported Egyptian objects.

Paradoxically, perhaps the most spectacular of Minoan artefacts come from a Mycenaean tholos tomb at Vapheio, south of Sparta on the Greek mainland. Here a pair of gold cups embossed with scenes of hunted and captured bulls recalls the workmanship and rituals of Minoan Crete. They are almost certainly trade objects or royal gifts which originated at Knossos.

Right: Minoan fresco artists delighted in flora and fauna. The fragmentary nature of their work, including the famous 'Bluebird' fresco here, is all the more to be regretted.

Below: The palace and its outlying satellite buildings stand on a rise by the gully of the Kairatos stream, which was massively bridged to bring the main track from the south into the precincts. The 'horns of consecration' are an ever-present decorative feature underlining the importance of the bull cult.

Below: Sir Arthur Evans superintended the reconstruction work carried out in the palace and results reliably reflect the original, especially the coolness of the rooms, lit by broad light-wells through columned staircases.

Delphi

GREECE

Delphi flourished from 700 to 200 BC and became one of Greece's most important sanctuaries, largely because of Apollo's oracle. Called 'the navel of the world', the site stands on the steep slopes of Parnassos, home of the Muses. It lies just below the highest point of the pass on the road which skirts the south side of Parnassos on its way from Boeotia to the Bay of Krisa on the northern shore of the Gulf of Corinth.

Legend tells of a crack in the ground at Delphi from which vapours emerged. Anyone purified by these vapours could predict the future. The crack was the home of a dragon, Python, the guardian of the oracle. But Python was killed by the sun god Apollo, whose temple was eventually built over the crack. The predictions were made by an elected priestess, the Pythia, who inhaled the vapours as she sat on a tripod placed over the opening in the ground.

The ruins

In modern times many people, including the poet Lord Byron, visited the site during their Grand Tour. However, exploration was hampered because the village of Kastri had been built over ancient Delphi. As the 19th century progressed, interest in the site, not to say international rivalry, developed over the excavation rights. American, French and German groups were all prepared to dig there in the 1880s. Eventually it was decided to allot the site to France. France had to contribute half a million francs and assist in the rehousing of the villagers, who left reluctantly. Then Théophile Homolle, head of the French School of Archaeology at Athens, opened the first trenches in 1893.

Like all excavations of its time, Delphi suffered from lack of care in detail, an overwhelming interest in unearthing statues and inscriptions, and far from prompt or full publication of the finds. It is only in the last 50 years that attention to scientific principles has been more apparent. For example, when the well-known bronze statue of a charioteer was unearthed in 1896 admirers crowded into the photograph, but little heed was paid to the precise context in which the statue lay, causing a continuing debate as to the date when it was overthrown and buried.

Sorting out strata on a steeply sloping site is difficult, but evidence does exist. Today mere scraps of such evidence remain to be gleaned in the main sanctuary, and much of this is of an architectural nature, such as the

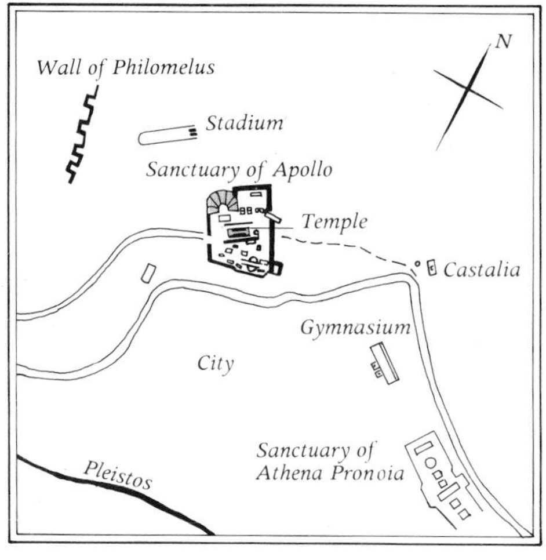

run of a drain which was blocked by later phases, or the reuse of blocks from a building that must, therefore, be of an earlier date. Substantial structures also still stand over what may be important lower levels.

Delphi is very much an architectural site. Building blocks lie scattered throughout the area and not all of them have moved downhill. The fitting together of these blocks has perhaps contributed most to our knowledge of the sanctuary. The account of the site written by Pausanias in the 2nd century AD is also of basic importance – indeed it overinfluenced the first excavators. The main problem is that he described just one moment in the shifting history of Delphi.

In piecing together the jigsaw the inscriptions are also helpful. Many walls were covered with texts proclaiming the setting free of slaves, actually their 'sale' to Apollo, or honouring various citizens. When inscriptions run over to a second block, the architectural join is evident. And when several texts on one monument refer to a single city, we can be sure that the monument was some form of dedication by that city. Archaeologists can, therefore, identify the blocks of the many repositories for offerings which are called treasuries. These are like small temples. In a number of cases their locations can be established via the text of Pausanias and the foundations *in situ*. One such was the first all-marble structure on the Greek mainland, which was contemporary with the first large temple of Artemis at Ephesus, constructed in about 550 BC. Other treasuries were set up by Corinth, Thebes, Sikyon, Athens, Klazomenai, Massalia (Marseilles), Spina on the Po delta and Caere (Cerveteri) in Etruria.

The importance of Delphi

How did Delphi become such a focus of religious attention? Archaeologically the answer

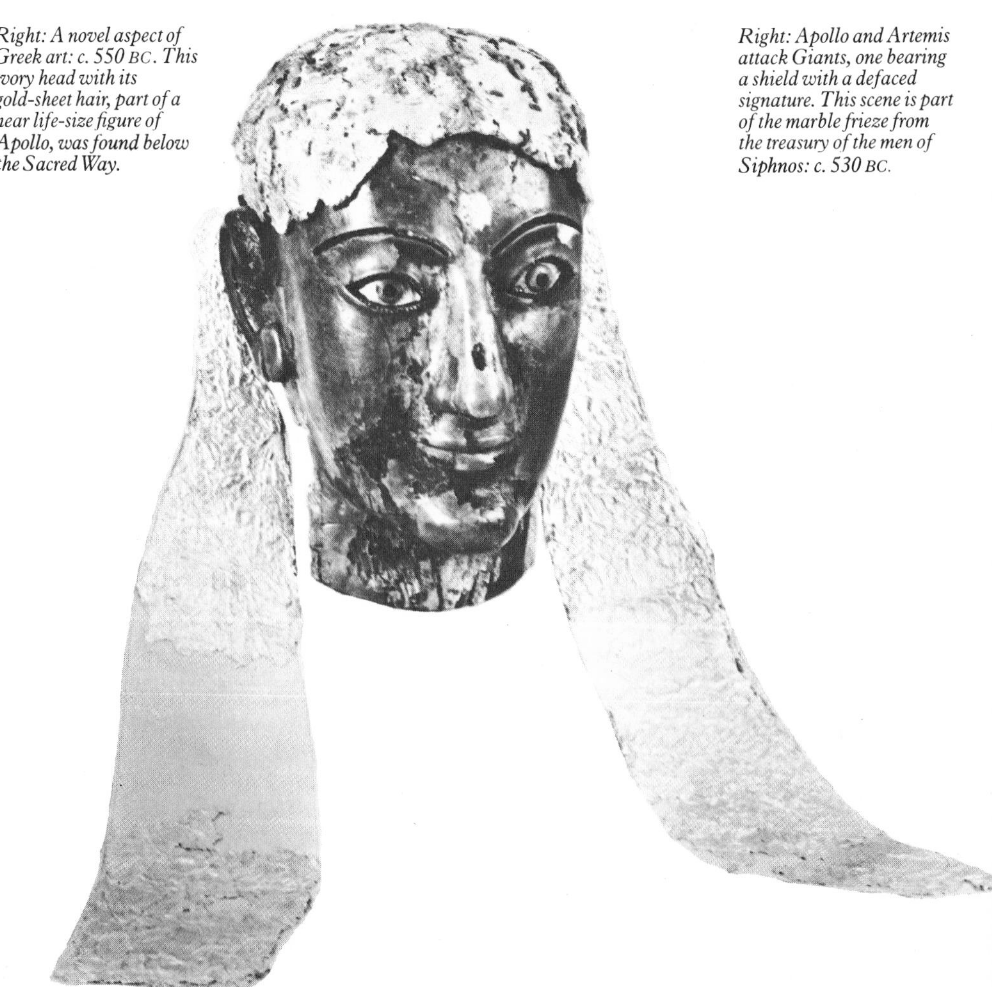

Right: A novel aspect of Greek art: c. 550 BC. This ivory head with its gold-sheet hair, part of a near life-size figure of Apollo, was found below the Sacred Way.

Right: Apollo and Artemis attack Giants, one bearing a shield with a defaced signature. This scene is part of the marble frieze from the treasury of the men of Siphnos: c. 530 BC.

is not clear. The spring of Kastalia, below the twin cliffs of the Phaedriades, is a natural focus for human activity. There was probably a cult in the Bronze Age on the site later occupied by the sanctuary of Athena Pronoia (of Forethought) east of the Apollo shrine, where perhaps there was merely domestic habitation in the late Bronze and early Iron Age. The Apollo cult arrived here only in the latter period, replacing, according to legend, Ge, Mother Earth. It was in the 8th century that structures and finds reappear – a period when Greece as a whole recovered some material prosperity. The Greek historian Herodotus wrote that Midas was the first foreigner to make a dedication at Delphi in about 700. Just at this time artefacts from beyond the Greek world, especially ivories and bronzes made in the Near East, began to be taken to Delphi, Olympia and other sites. Much of the Greek pottery of this period was of Corinthian origin, which may well indicate a measure of Corinthian influence at Delphi at a period when the oracle was being regularly consulted by would-be emigrants, who came largely from states bordering the Gulf of Corinth.

The sanctuary blossomed in the 6th century after an ill-documented Sacred War, fought between rival local peoples, with allies from much of mainland Greece. A new temple of Apollo arose, after a fire in 546, on an enlarged terrace fronted with a magnificent wall of polygonal masonry.

Fighting flared twice more between Delphiots and neighbouring Phokians, during the hostilities between Athens and Sparta in the 440s and for a longer period in the 350s when the Phokians used treasures stored in the sanctuary to pay mercenaries. Once more the temple had to be rebuilt, by subscriptions raised among all the Greek city-states, after it had been destroyed in 373. But it was perhaps the Pythian games rather than the oracle that became the attraction for visitors in the following centuries. Many statues dedicated in the sanctuary were dispatched to Rome, notably by Nero, who visited the games in AD 66–67. What survived to be excavated had mostly been hidden beneath the earth long before. Small finds too are rarer than at Olympia or the Athenian Acropolis.

Archaeologists have found a few pits containing dedications deliberately buried after some catastrophe or to make way for new offerings. The most significant find of dedications is a hoard recently put on display in the Delphi museum after extensive restoration work. It was found in 1939 in a pit under the Sacred Way, the path which winds uphill to the sanctuary of Apollo. It seems to consist of a variety of dedications salvaged from a fire in a treasury in about 460 BC, although the richest objects in the hoard are of the earlier 6th century. They include a life-size bull in sheet silver with gold detail and fragments of carved ivory which once decorated some large piece of furniture with floral patterns and mythological scenes. There are also several half life-size statues of Apollo, in which ivory heads and limbs are combined with gold drapery and hair. These are the sole surviving examples of a technique that the sculptor Pheidias later used for the Zeus at Olympia and the Athena Parthenos.

Visitors and Citizens

The sanctuary of Apollo was administered by a council of Amphiktyons, meaning 'dwellers around', with representatives from central Greece chosen by race, not by city. The council was originally concerned only with the temple of Demeter near Thermopylae and Delphi was added later. The citizens of Delphi were entrusted with some of the day-to-day running of affairs. Evidence of this comes from inscribed accounts of the 4th century, which show complex financial arrangements, replete with double-checks.

Laws concerning behaviour and procedures in the sanctuary were also set up. One law of about 400 BC has been shown to be a re-publication of a 6th-century original. In the 330s the Amphiktyons also issued coins in an attempt to tidy up book-keeping, and incidentally getting a good rate of exchange against the Attic drachma – few coinages were accepted in other states. They also give us a clue about the survival rate of Greek coins. Earlier, rare issues of about 480 show golden drinking vessels captured from the Persians, while the reverse has the panelled ceiling of Apollo's temple.

The inscriptions concerning the rebuilding of the temple after 373, though fragmentary, show the protracted nature of the undertaking. They also reveal the great financial effort made by the Peloponnesian states, whose finances were in better shape than those of Athens at the time, and the enormous expense of hauling blocks up from the port below. Each piece of work was let out to contract, as normal in Greece. There are also hints that a prime concern was to provide adequate shelter for the oracle.

Unfortunately, however, neither these inscriptions nor any other texts give an accurate idea of the layout of the central chamber of the temple, and little can be gleaned from the remains on the ground. The temple was plundered for the lead and bronze of its dowels and clamps and the squared blocks were also sought and re-used for new buildings, so much so that the lower sanctuary of Athena gained the name Marmara, meaning 'quarries'. Most details of the temple's elevation can be reconstructed, but the oracular shrine remains elusive.

The oracle

One of the features associated with the workings of the oracle is the ecstatic state of the priestess or the Pythia, who was Apollo's mouthpiece. Her ecstasy was induced by vapours which rose from a water source under the temple. No such source exists today, but a channel routed under the foundations could perhaps have been tapped. The Pythia's utterings were meaningless to laymen and so they were 'translated' by the priests and given to the petitioners, who had performed a series of preliminary rites, including payment of a fee, at individual or corporate rates. Oedipus, Agamemnon, Philip of Macedon and his son Alexander all allegedly consulted the oracle. The Pythia told Alexander: 'My son, none can resist thee'. The ambiguity of some predictions was well illustrated when Croesus asked whether he should wage war against Persia. He was told that war would destroy a great empire, but his empire, and not Persia's, was destroyed.

Above: The plunging view from the rear of the theatre, over the foundations of the temple of Apollo, into the Pleistos ravine. The theatre, now bereft of its stage buildings, dates from the 4th century.

A privilege of 'prior consultation' was granted to a large number of people and states. At first the oracle could be consulted only on one day in early March, but eventually monthly access was possible. We are not sure whether this applied during the winter months when Apollo was thought to be absent from Delphi.

Sculptures and trophies

The dramatist Euripides hinted at the oracular arrangements in his *Ion*. He also described some of the sculptures of the temple. Sculpture from Delphi bulks large in the corpus of Greek art of the period 550–470. From the temple and treasuries there are relief sculptures and others in the round, most notably a Caryatid (one of a pair) and a long frieze from the treasury of the Siphnians. This frieze was set up in about 530. The islanders financed it from the windfall profits of their silver mines. The Athenian treasury of about 500, which was restored in 1903–06, has small, finely composed carvings depicting the deeds of Heracles and the

Athenian hero Theseus. This was 'programmed' sculpture, designed more to boost the pride of the city than to honour Apollo.

Much the same can be said for a good proportion of other offerings of this and later periods. Little remains, but the narrative of Pausanias rounds out the gaps. There are also many inscribed bases, now shorn of their statues, which have attachments for the feet of bronze heroes and deities. Visitors can see the huge socket for the 15 metre-high gold statue of Apollo set up by the Amphiktyons on the temple terrace and paid for by a fine imposed on the Phokians. There are also the blocks of the round base on which stood the huge serpent column, which is now in the square of Sultan Ahmet in Istanbul. The column commemorated the victory over the Persians in 480–79.

The bronze charioteer still exists. It was just part of one of several groups offered by the rulers of Syracuse and Gela to advertize their wins at games at Olympia and Delphi. At the very entrance of the sanctuary, Athenian and Spartan tableaux rivalled one another as expressions of thanks to Apollo for victory over the old enemy.

Not till the 4th century are statues of contemporary figures found. Pausanias of Sparta, victor at Plataia in 479, was convicted of sacrilege for inscribing his name in an epigram on the base of the serpent column. His compatriot Lysander, architect of the defeat of Athens in 405, was criticized for placing his own likeness in the same row as that of Apollo in a commemorative offering.

Trophies captured from the enemy were also displayed. The remains of several trophies have been found at Olympia. At Delphi the Athenians placed 'equipment' won from the Persians in the graceful small stoa which they erected in front of the polygonal wall. Inscriptions cut on the wall in later years show where the spoils hung, because when they were removed, the uninscribed areas stood out. We are still not sure of the nature of the objects, nor whether they were won after Marathon or Plataia.

Recently a similar dedication has been discerned from scraps of an inscription on

Above: The temple of Apollo, housing the oracle, dominates the reconstructed sanctuary. Offerings fill the rest, standing free or guarded in small treasuries.

the impressive stoa to the west of the sanctuary. The occasion was the victory of the Aetolian confederation over the invading Gauls in 280 after their sack of nearby Kallion, which was partly excavated ahead of the rising waters of the Mornos dam. The Gauls were trounced in the face of foul weather and a rock fall in the sanctuary.

The brooding physical power of the site must be considered in any account of its history. Thunderstorms, earthquakes and avalanches are common. The Persians were deterred by rock falls when they sent a detachment to investigate the wavering loyalties of the Delphiots in 480. In 1905 the newly restored temple of Athena was shattered by a similar collapse. Both sets of boulders were left as they lay.

The feet of thousands of visitors have also caused extensive erosion and stricter controls may have to be introduced, only 15 years after the site was fenced in.

The Agora

ATHENS, GREECE

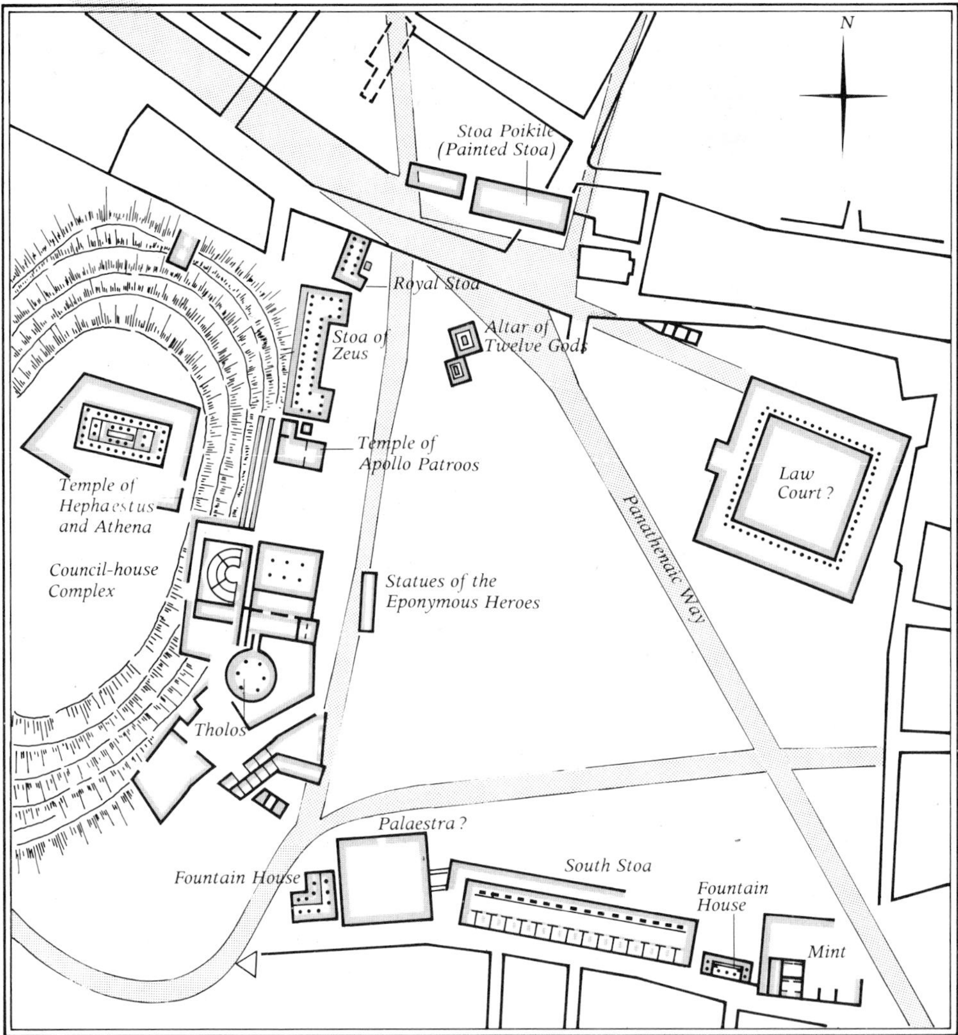

The Agora lay at the foot of the Acropolis in ancient Athens. It was a market place and the centre of Athenian public and cultural life. Here Socrates and Plato taught, Zeno explained the philosophy of the Stoics and, centuries later, St Paul preached Christianity.

The site has been inhabited almost without break since the Mycenaean period and there is evidence of even earlier settlements, a fact which makes the Agora an extremely complicated site archaeologically. Successive generations of Athenians have dug pits, built houses and demolished and destroyed those of earlier periods. By the late 19th century, the lower slopes of the north side of the Acropolis were a mixed area of houses and workshops. When the Athens to Piraeus railway was cut in 1891, part of the line passed between the rise on which stands the temple of Hephaestus, which had more recently been the Church of St George and the first National Museum, and the massive remains of a large Hellenistic stoa (covered colonnade) to the east.

Archaeologists were not given the opportunity to work on the line at first, but some, including the German Wilhelm Dörpfeld, did observe the proceedings and records were made of the structures which had been cut through. These comprised the first substantial excavations of the Agora.

American excavations

In the 1920s the American School of Classical Studies in Athens negotiated at length with successive Greek governments for permission to excavate the Agora. This was granted in 1929 and work began in 1930, with the Rockefeller Foundation contributing most of the large sums needed to expropriate the broad area that was thought to cover the ancient centre. Excavation has continued annually, apart from the war years, and further extensions of the area are envisaged. No other Greek city centre, inhabited for such a long period, has been so methodically unearthed.

Initial finds from above ground included architectural fragments and inscribed stones built into the houses that were pulled down. Below, not surprisingly, the remains of the Athenian Agora were in a sorry state. Little above foundation level was found *in situ*. The depth of archaeological deposit increases down the slope, but generally, the history of a thousand years was often found compressed into a small space. Structures had often been robbed even of their foundations, and modern pits are frequent. To compensate, the accumulated rubbish from many ancient wells added substantially to our knowledge of Athenian and imported artefacts.

The Agora is mentioned by numerous ancient authors, but the fullest account is given by the Greek traveller Pausanias, who wrote his *Guide to Greece* in the 2nd century AD. It was this work that largely determined the extent of the expropriated area. One nagging problem remained; the failure to find the historically important Royal Stoa where expected. In 1970 it was found, and proved to be a modest structure just fitting between the railway cutting and the road to the north, beyond the original area.

Conservation and restoration

In a full programme of conservation, three particularly constructive items may be singled out. The least obvious is the planting of the Agora with trees and plants such as would have been found in antiquity. More visible is the greensward outlining the square of the Roman 'palaestra', which formed part of the gymnasium on the south side, and breaking the long lines of the stoa, which belongs to an earlier date. Most obvious is the rebuilt Stoa of Attalus on the east side. This is a most carefully built replica (incorporating earlier buildings under the floor), now used as museum, sales desk, storerooms and offices. It is, in short, the headquarters of the excavations, and also used by the Greek archaeological inspectorate of the area. The records are a pleasure to consult, with detailed record cards for the objects filed alongside the day-books in which their discovery is logged.

One helpful factor is the precise dating that Athenian pottery can normally provide. This is because changes of shape and style, and the work of individual artists, have been studied in great detail. Many sherds can be dated within the limits of a single generation. One hazard is a deceptive 'natural rock surface' that can turn out to be merely compacted hard-pan.

The rise of Athens

Athens boasted of not having been destroyed at the end of the Bronze Age (about 1100 BC) and archaeology has found little to confound that claim. However, it remained, as did the rest of Greece, much in the doldrums during the ensuing centuries, although there are

Above: A large amphora, painted in strict Geometric style, from a rich female tomb of c. 850 BC on the south side of the Agora. Other goods are of eastern origin.

Right: A drinking cup from the Agora, signed by the potter Gorgos in c. 510 BC. A tondo figure in the bowl is a fine red-figure study of an aristocratic youth.

Below: Evidence of democracy. A vote of ostracism (top) against Pericles, scratched on a sherd in the 440s, and a more humble citizen's bronze 'identification card'.

signs that it was a leading power around 800 BC. Another recession followed. Athens generally took little part in the Greek expansion that occurred around 700 BC, and did not send out colonies, although it is clear that the population of the Attic countryside increased markedly.

It was in the 6th century BC, and notably under the autocrat Peisistratus and his sons, that wealth increased. In particular, the pottery trade captured Mediterranean markets. However, one of the sons, Hippias, was responsible for first bringing a Persian army to mainland Greece, in 490 BC, attempting to regain power which had been wrested from him in 510, in part by a genuine democratic movement. He was thwarted when the Persians were defeated at the battle of Marathon.

Athens played a leading part in repulsing the subsequent Persian invasion of 480 BC at Salamis and Plataia, and then led the freedom struggle of the Asiatic Greeks, an alliance that gradually turned into an Athenian empire of the Aegean. It was the finances of this alliance which contributed largely to Pericles' building programme on the Acropolis and elsewhere. The later war against Sparta ended in Athenian humiliation, at Syracuse in 413 and behind the city's own walls in 405. The 4th century developed as a constant power struggle, often fuelled by Persian gold, between the mainland states, until the final intervention of Philip II of Macedon in 338. The influence of Athens was then reduced. Nonetheless, as a former super-power, it continued to bask in that reflected glory during the ensuing centuries when new leaders, the kings of Macedon, Syria and Pergamum, held the stage.

One of the more significant historical finds from the Agora is a scrap from an inscribed statue base found in 1936. It belongs to the lost bronze figures of Harmodius and Aristogeiton, known from Roman copies and reflections in the minor arts. This pair killed the brother of Hippias in 514, an event which was later promoted as the dawn of Athenian democracy (although this dawn is more realistically associated with the social and political reforms of Cleisthenes in 507 BC). The Persian king Xerxes removed the original bronzes during the invasion of 480, but they were speedily replaced and Alexander the Great arranged the eventual return of the originals.

The Persian destruction of 480 BC left sporadic traces for the excavators of the Agora. For example, the stock of one potter's shop was smashed and thrown into a well. Many similar events, as well as various institutions of Athenian public life can be illustrated from the finds. These range from a child's commode, through inscribed lead assessment dockets for the cavalry force, to voters' tickets and ballots, as well as tangible remains of the institution of ostracism. 'Ostracism' was a practice used at Athens between 487 and 416 BC in which, by popular, written vote, the most unacceptable politician could be removed for a ten-year period. It was so called because the votes were recorded on 'ostraka', or broken sherds of pottery. Examples inscribed with the names of some of the most illustrious Athenian leaders have been found in the Agora excavations. They reveal how political abuse and gerrymandering are to be found in the most infant of democracies.

The City

Key

1 To Acropolis
2 Mint
3 South and Middle Stoas
4 Statues of Athenian Heroes
5 Stoa of Zeus
6 Record Office
7 Council Chamber
8 Tholos
9 Temple of Hephaestus and Athena
10 Temple of Aphrodite
11 Royal Stoa
12 To Dipylon Gate
13 Panathenaic Way
14 Altar of the 12 gods
15 Tyrannicides
16 Speakers' Rostrum
17 Stoa of Attalus

The Agora in the Hellenistic period, about 150 BC

The Agora had no special status until after 600 BC. Burials, some of them rich, and traces of housing and shrines indicate that the site formed part of the settlement pattern which lay at the foot of the Acropolis and comprised Athens at the time. Its various nuclei grew up on the main routes from the Acropolis to the farmland and neighbouring towns which lay beyond. In the 6th century, the Agora acquired a new function as an administrative and commercial centre. The site lies in front of the marshy ground of the Eridanos stream, at the spot where the Sacred and Dipylon gates were later built, and where began the annual procession in honour of the city's patron goddess, Athena Polias. The procession then made its way up to the old Mycenaean walls of the Acropolis, where a new temple was built for the goddess around 570 BC.

Civic buildings

The first 'civic' structures of the Agora are scarcely impressive, or as closely datable as archaeologists would like. The changes were connected with a process of political change, which transformed Athens from a set of autocratically controlled villages into a city governed by the votes of an assembly and a democratically elected council. The most important of these reforms were introduced by Cleisthenes in 507 BC and to this period can be assigned the first phase of the Bouleuterion, or Council House. This was the seat of the newly constituted governing body of the state, elected annually from all male citizens. The civic buildings remained concentrated on this west side of the Agora in the 5th century. Here the round Tholos was built, to house several cults and serve as a civic dining-hall. There was also the temple of Hephaestus on the hill behind, the temple of the Mother of the Gods, later the record office, and the Stoa of Zeus, an ambitious building, unusually decorated with sculpted *acroteria*.

The south stoa, of much the same date, was a multi-purpose structure of partly preserved mud-brick. The whole appearance of the Agora changed drastically when the massive Middle Stoa and the Stoa of Attalus were erected in the 3rd and 2nd centuries BC. Gifts of the *nouveau riche* kings of Pergamum, these buildings were erected in the Hellenistic spirit of carefully planned and rectangular civic centres.

In the Classical Agora, two appendages of the little Royal Stoa should be noted. In front of the north end is a large cracked block. This is the stone on which the annually elected Athenian officers took their oath (although they remained fully accountable to the Assembly for their conduct). In front of the south end of the Royal Stoa is a slotted base on which were once set up some of the city's statutes. This public display of legal codes was one of the first steps by which the common people were able to assert their rights. At Athens in particular the posting of laws and acts proliferated, and most were committed to stone. Indeed, the inscriptions also incorporated information about the terms under which they were carved and positioned. Many of these notices were set up on the Acropolis, on the steps of the Parthenon, for example. Some were later re-used, for such purposes as cover stones for major drains in the Agora area.

An important measure of the 440s BC enjoined the allies of Athens to use only Attic weights, measures and coins. We know this from tantalizing scraps found in some allied cities which tell how the statute was to be set up in front of the mint at Athens. Recent supplementary excavations have made it clear that there was a mint operating in the south-eastern corner of the Agora from at

Right: Viewed from the slopes of the Acropolis, the battered remains of the Agora date from many periods. The 5th-century temple of Hephaestus and an early Byzantine church catch the eye, while the Panathenaic Way ascends the slope in the foreground.

least the 4th century, so that this commercial statute of the 440s may well have been set up there.

Temples

Such finds have given us a tangible picture of Athenian life over a number of centuries. In the 5th century Athens achieved prosperity as head of an alliance of Greek states called the Delian league. The contributions to the fighting fund against Persia were originally lodged with Apollo on Delos, but they were transferred to Athena in 454, for security reasons. Athens continued to ask for contributions long after peace with the Persians had eventually been concluded in 449 BC.

At that time, work began on the temple of Hephaestus, the god of blacksmiths and potters, although the temple was jointly dedicated to Athena, another patron of artisans, especially metalworkers. The most striking metallurgical find from Athens was from a pit near the temple, in which the mould for a cult statue of Apollo was placed prior to its casting around 550 BC. This find represents very early evidence for the use of the *lost wax* technique in the production of large metal pieces.

The temple had cult statues made by Alcamenes, pupil of the great sculptor Pheidias. An inscription tells us that they were made around 420 BC and cost more than five and a half talents. Regrettably, the only echo of their appearance now surviving is to be found in the figure of Hephaestus on a small Roman lamp. However, there are many other interesting shrines in the Agora. Several have no temple, but are merely areas marked off by a fence or boundary marker. Some contain altars, such as the important altar of the Twelve Gods, lying by the Panathenaic Way at the centre of the town. There are also ancient tombs, the occupants of which were later heroised, above which offerings would be left. More odd are the 'wandering temples of Attica', to use the words of Homer Thompson, doyen of the American excavation team. The phrase refers to at least three temples of the 5th century BC, which were moved block by block from various locations in Attica into the Agora during the Augustan period. The most prominent example is the temple of Ares, which once stood in the large town of Acharnai. It was moved to a central position in the Agora and is now marked off by a pebble area. Scraps of its exquisite marble sculpture also remain.

Artisans and slaves

More mundane activities at the Agora were largely commercial. Potters' and cobblers' shops and sculptors' studios have been traced, but the main market would have been a simple open-air gathering in the broad areas beside the Panathenaic Way. It has left little archaeological trace, although post-holes for booths have been discovered outside the Dipylon, the most used of the Athenian gates.

As overseas trade, notably in grain, grew during the 5th century, special marts were constructed in Piraeus, the seaport which served Athens. An inscription of 375 tells us that public slaves were appointed to adjudicate in those cases when suspect coin was being offered, both in the Agora and in Piraeus.

The Agora was also equipped, from an early date, with fountain houses. Water was led in substantial terracotta pipes to the solidly constructed fountains which are depicted on many Attic water-jugs of the late 6th century. The women carry the jugs on their heads. However, it should not be imagined that women were frequently seen in the streets of ancient Athens, except for slaves and good-time girls.

Metapontum

ITALY

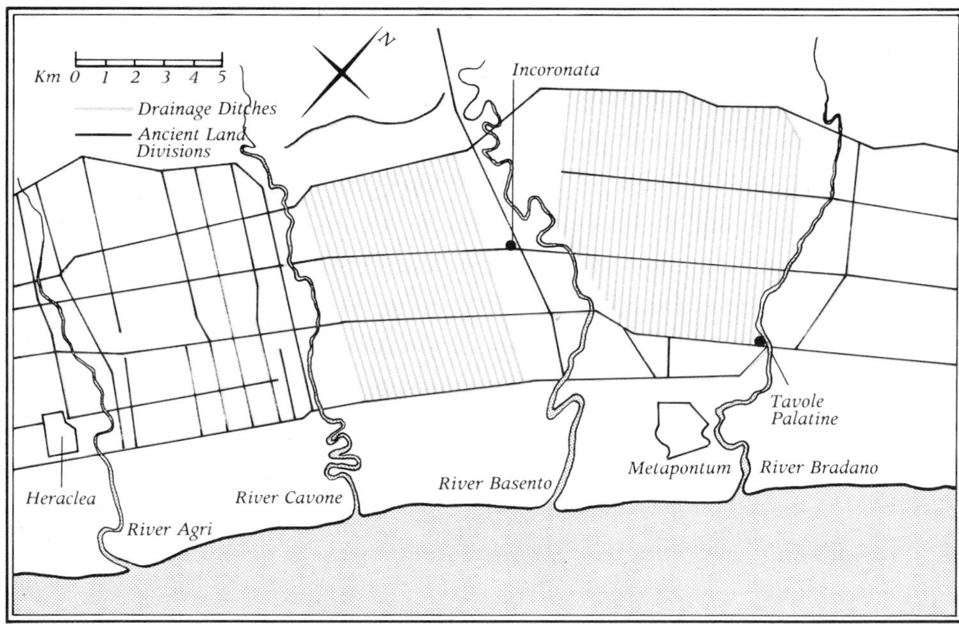

'Magna Graecia', or Great Greece, was the term applied to the colonies which were sent out from Greece to Sicily and southern Italy during the period 750–600 BC. The most successful of these colonies were Syracuse, in west Sicily, Taras (Tarentum) in the heel of Italy, and Sybaris, situated in the instep. Metapontion, or Metapontum to use its romanized name, lies between Taras and Sybaris, flanked by two substantial rivers, the Bradano and Basento, the valleys of which afford easy routes into the mountainous hinterland.

Excavation

In the 18th and 19th centuries, the malarial nature of the coast deterred visitors. In that respect the Duc de Luynes, who excavated in the years following 1826, was a bold pioneer. Ample remains were still visible to guide his work in and around the central temple of Apollo. In the late 19th century and up to 1939, further work was done. But it is only since 1965 that substantial campaigns have been conducted – with increasing tempo. This work, under the guiding hand of Professor Dinu Adamesteanu, has drawn on a number of international teams, notably from Belgium and Texas.

The site has the great advantage that overbuilding is light and most modern tourist development lies on land which was under the sea in antiquity. The work has not proceeded, however, without problems. A plan to build what would have been the largest petro-chemical complex in Europe partly over the site was shelved mainly because of the oil crisis in 1974. One major problem was that the upper levels in the centre of the ancient city were lost when soil was removed in bulk to prepare land for, among other things, strawberry planting. In 1908 large quantities of stones from the temples were sold off to provide building material, despite the protests of archaeologists. The first ballast for the nearby railway had a similar origin. More recently deep ploughing has removed many features seen clearly in earlier air photographs.

As in much of Italy, illicit excavation is endemic, although the Superintendency of Antiquities pursues an enlightened policy of

employing as much local labour as possible. This means that the excavation season has been extended to limits unknown in other parts of the world.

Another real problem is that of drainage. As at Sybaris, excavation at any depth in much of the city area demands constant pumping. In Italy the problem has been eased by the relatively inexpensive well-point system, which involves a given area being isolated within a set of tubes driven into the ground, through which the water is drawn off. At Metapontum an added bonus has been the discovery of the main drain of the Agora, or city centre, which has now been put back into service.

Air photography has also contributed largely to the discovery of one group of ancient remains rarely encountered in Greek archaeology, namely the field systems of the city's population. Only at Chersonesos in the Crimea has similar research been carried out, with surprisingly similar results. Air photographs of an area stretching 14 kilometres inland, and beyond the Basento River as far south as the territory of the colony Siris (which was destroyed by fellow Greeks in the 6th century) have revealed a sequence of strips 200 metres apart. Some are still visible on the ground. Selective excavation has confirmed this regular land planning, which dates back to about the mid-6th century.

One of the scientifically more intriguing discoveries in the central part of the city is an industrial area. In particular there is a series of kilns, which are reasonably well preserved and replete with kiln furniture and misfired pots. Ceramics of all kinds were produced, most noticeably red-figured vases in a style imitating that of Athens of the later 5th century. Works by previously identified painters have been found here and so their place of manufacture has been located. It has been surmised that the red-figure technique had been introduced to Italy (with impressive results) through the colony of Thurii, which was founded with considerable Athenian support on the old site of Sybaris in 443. The results of clay analyses of some of the figured vases, to define whether they are of Athenian or local manufacture, will be of particular interest. Such studies are still in their infancy. But enough data has been collected to show that the clays from some areas are readily distinguishable, while those from others are less distinctive. The analysis shows the content of individual trace elements in the clays, while their geological origin can be ascertained by inspecting *thin sections* of the rock under a microscope.

Magna Graecia

Various more or less reliable literary sources refer to the foundation of Greek colonies in Magna Graecia. Occasionally a plausible reason is given to explain why the settlers left home, which was often the central strip of Greece, between the Gulf of Corinth and the Cyclades. Archaeology has now shown that the initial ventures west were made in the first half of the 8th century in search of the mineral wealth of central Italy. The aims of the Greeks who established colonies in the heel of Italy and in Sicily are less clear.

These migrations occurred long after the Mycenaeans had departed from their trading posts at Taranto, Lipari and Thapsos, north of Syracuse. After 735 BC a series of foundations of a more agricultural nature followed. Many of the Greek settlements flourished in the 6th century and the stronger ones prospered until, in the years after 410, the Carthaginians made devastating inroads into Sicily and, between 425 and 375, the colonies in Italy suffered at the hands of indigenous tribes. For example, one of the many temples at Selinus, a city in western Sicily, was fitted with a mosaic bearing a Punic (Carthaginian) motif. And the name of Posidonia was changed to Paestum when local Lucanian people took control.

Selinus is a typical Greek site, on a low hill by the sea. Paestum, however, is on virtually flat ground, like two other Italian colonies – Sybaris, whose wealth became a by-word and attracted the destructive attentions of her neighbours in 510, and Metapontum.

The Greeks first occupied the Metapontum area around 740 BC. But the colony by the shore was not founded before 650, when men from Achaia and Troizen in central Greece established their farming settlement. The traditional date of the city's foundation is 773 BC, but there is little to support this.

The colony had a solid, unspectacular history, thriving between 550 and 450 BC, although references in contemporary written sources are rare. Like other colonies, Metapontum suffered heavily from the inroads of local Lucanian tribes in the 4th century. A would-be protector, Kleonymos of Sparta, was called in by the Tarentines in 303. But he abused his powers, taking vast sums from the inhabitants. The city also changed hands several times in the Punic Wars of the late 3rd century, when it was in full decline. It may have been Hannibal himself who first built the Castrum, a small fortified area within the old walls, to house his garrison.

Right: Painted, mould-made terracotta friezes decorated a number of shrines in the Metapontum area. These two fragments of the earlier 6th century are contrasting in type. On the right is a heroic scene, with warrior, charioteer and winged horses, 20 centimetres high from the San Biagio sanctuary. An early phase of temple C in the Agora was decorated with the wedding procession above. It is led by a lantern-bearer, and the pair in the mule-cart behind may well have some more divine significance than a simple Metapontine couple.

Left: Crop-marks from aerial photos such as this can be interpreted to suggest the grid plan of both the city and land-division of Metapontum. The heart of the town lies north of the railway just right of centre, where the one temple then excavated and the theatre can be seen.

A Prosperous Colony

Left: Once repaired from its many fragments, the secret of this misshapen pot was revealed. Smashed by a disconsolate potter, its remains were found beside one of the kilns excavated near the Agora in 1973. The painting on this rejected water-jar (hydria) was finely executed in the red-figure technique. Greeks fight Amazons in the main upper register. The painter is known from more successful pieces, and the find is significant for the history of this school in the late 5th century.

Right: The substantial remains of a temple of Hera stand on a low bluff on the south bank of the River Bradano. Lying outside the city walls, the temple is the most grandiose of several such extra-mural shrines, located at significant points of early Greek penetration – water sources, cult sites and native habitation areas. Parts of the two long sides of the colonnade survive and gave rise to the evocative sobriquet 'the Knights' Tables'. About 500 BC.

Back from the ancient shoreline the land rises, and on the first bluffs beside the river valleys lie some of the most interesting sites in the area. By the Bradano River is a sanctuary of Hera with the best preserved of the colony's monuments, the temple which is generally termed the Knights' Tables. It was once known as the school of Pythagoras, after the famous Samian philosopher and politician, who in fact ended his days at Croton in the heel of Italy.

Beside the Basento River more recent work has uncovered two important sites. On the left bank, where one of the rare all-year springs flows, was a sanctuary dedicated to the nymph of the source, centred on a fountain-house. Here was found votive pottery of a rare type, imitating mainland Greek black-figured ceramics. On the right bank there was also material from a shrine, including a unique, large, terracotta, pedestalled basin, decorated in relief with scenes from myth and dating to the later 7th century. The whole hilltop here is littered with local and Greek sherds of an earlier period, about 750–650. Excavation has shown that a local settlement on the hill was supplemented by Greek traders. This is evidenced by the large numbers of big oil and wine jars, mainly from Athens and Corinth, found on site. Such material corroborates evidence from many parts of Sicily and southern Italy suggesting that there were sustained Greek trading interests in the west from about 750 onward. The present evidence suggests that the trading post at Metapontum was abandoned at much the same time that the colony was planted in the plain below where, so far, nothing before 650 has been found.

Metapontum is, therefore, one of the later of a series of subsistence colonies planted on the south coast of Italy, mainly by Achaeans from the northern Peloponnese. On the first coins of Metapontum there are legends written in a script which is typical of that area. The badge on these silver coins, minted in an unusual *repoussé* technique used from about 550 onward, is an ear of corn – a simple statement of the source of wealth in the colony, the agricultural planning of which has been revealed by air photography. The frontiers also were protected against local peoples with a series of forts erected in the early 6th century. The presence of Greeks had a profound effect on the local population. During the course of the 6th century, they began to take up Hellenic habits of art, architecture and probably social structure as well.

Right: Few coins of the mint of Metapontum do not carry an ear of corn on one of their faces. This is a striking indication of the importance of agriculture to the city's inhabitants. At Sybaris, to the south, the bull has a similar significance. Coinage arrived in the area c. 550 BC and a piece such as this, weighing 8 grams, was the most common denomination. Early coins are broad and very thin, with the same design in intaglio on the reverse, a striking contrast with the dumpy beans from the deposit at Ephesus. Silver, about 500 BC.

Organization

Written sources reveal little of Metapontum's political life and information has to come from the excavations. The city itself was walled, probably as early as the 6th century, and good traces of the circuit remained until recently. So too did parts of the theatre, along with the foundations of a temple of Apollo of the late 6th century. Aerial photography made clear the rectilinear plan of the town – a system of colonial planning now known from a number of western sites. Intensive excavation in the Agora area is beginning to provide a clearer picture of its appearance and history.

The theatre in fact replaced an earlier structure: this had a circular shape with tiers of seats facing across a central gangway. It must have been an assembly room for the citizens, and as such is truly a unique find. It certainly seems too large to have housed merely a select Council. It is not surprising that it was replaced by a conventional theatre in the 4th century, because theatres elsewhere were used regularly for meetings of the popular assembly. More imposing is the surrounding wall of the zone, which presents a Doric façade, at least in its final form. It was thrown down in a violent earthquake and found lying in more or less correct order, so inviting reconstruction. The Agora proper lay between the theatre and the temples to the north-west. The whole occupies an area set apart for public buildings

when the colony was founded. On the sea side the remains of a substantial stoa (covered colonnade) of the 4th century have recently been cleared.

Religion

The area of the Apollo temple has become particularly significant. We now know that a row of four temples stood here. Obviously it was once a most impressive sight, fronting the wide Agora, while the solid main drainage channel, which was itself faced with reused architectural blocks, ran behind it. Some of the deities worshipped here can be tentatively identified from inscriptions on votive pottery and on terracotta destined for particular roofs. Two temples are aligned with the known street grid. The other pair, and the earlier phase of a third, have a slightly different orientation. A similar shift of axis has been observed in other Greek colonies. We can only speculate why the priests of Apollo allowed a change, while those of Athena and temple D remained conservative in orientation.

Temple D is the most recently found. It is also the most significant, because it is in the Ionic order, not the Doric style which is normal in Italy. A mere three blocks remain *in situ*, but fortunately several column drums, capitals and the like have been recovered. The stone robbers also left enough undisturbed earth in the original packing trenches for the building to be dated to the early 5th century. This was the most flourishing period of the colony. It is becoming increasingly clear that the temples were not kept in a good state of repair long into the 4th century and, by the 1st century BC, burials were encroaching on nearby land.

The inhabitants expressed their piety mainly in the form of terracotta figurines, found in thousands in the refuse pits of the various sanctuaries. The figurines are now bereft of their original paint, as indeed are most of the architectural terracottas and what little limestone and marble sculpture has survived. The rarity of marble in the area should be noted; a number of cult statues were made with marble heads and limbs, but the torsos were probably made of wood or plaster. One such head in the Getty Museum, Malibu (near Los Angeles), which has been dated to about 440 BC, is 'allegedly from Metapontum'.

Water was obviously an important resource for the community and shrines were often sited at major springs. Around 450 a short series of coins was struck figuring a river god, portrayed unusually as a Minotaur, with the legend 'from the games of Achelous'. Achelous was the Greek river-god *par excellence*, and Metapontum held games in his honour, as did other towns. But Metapontum also issued commemorative coins on this one occasion, perhaps giving us a hint of the purpose of one branch of Greek minting.

Defence

There is little evidence of military power. The city is curiously absent in written accounts of the hostilities between Taras and newly-founded Thurii. One echo that remains is part of a warrior's equipment, which comprised fragments of a shield with a willow core, and a fine helmet with a bold ram's head crest-holder – all fashioned from a single sheet of bronze. The crest itself was of sheet silver, not the most readily available material in southern Italy. The whole was a splendid parade helmet, of a type found elsewhere in the area, not least in the hinterland of Metapontum, where the colony's influence was so strong between 550 and 450 BC.

Vergina

GREECE

In the historical period, the successive capitals of the kingdom of Macedonia were Pella and Thessaloniki. However, ancient texts name Aigai as the capital before Pella and indicate that Aigai was not fully eclipsed until the reign of Alexander the Great (336–323 BC). But where was Aigai?

There were two possible locations: Edessa, which lies east of Pella; and Vergina, which is 50 kilometres west-south-west of Thessaloniki, in the foothills of the extensive Mount Olympus massif. By the later 1970s, historical considerations led to the view that the town of Vergina was the likeliest contender.

Confirmation of Vergina's significance came in the late 1970s with the discovery of two unlooted royal burial chambers dating to the later 4th century BC. Its significance was further increased by the strong likelihood that one of these tombs houses the remains of Philip II of Macedon, the father of Alexander the Great.

Excavating the burial chambers

The extensive tumulus cemeteries of Vergina had been known for a long time, and Professor Manolis Andronikos of the University of Thessaloniki excavated many of them between 1957 and 1962. His work contributed much to the study of Macedonia in the early Iron Age. During this period, Macedonia was almost wholly independent of Greece to the south, which supplied only the occasional pot in the years down to 600 BC. In 1952 Professor Andronikos also sank shafts into one much larger mound at Vergina, five times the size of the rest, without making any significant finds.

He then turned his attention to the slight remains of a large dwelling, which had already been partly cleared by a Frenchman, Léon Heuzey, in 1861 and by Konstantinos Rhomaios in 1937. The dwelling had been of palatial size, with spacious rooms surrounding a large central court. Some mosaics were found and the pottery showed that it had been built in the 3rd century BC. In 1963 Andronikos gave it as his conclusion that: 'although the palace was not in the capital of the Macedonian state, it still constitutes an excellent example of the royal grandeur of the Macedonian kings who succeeded Alexander'.

Andronikos returned to the great mound, particularly to its southern edge, late in the 1977 season. Prospects seemed as bleak as before, until, in early October, he found stone blocks. Soon a handsomely-built chamber of a type already known in the area was revealed. The door, as was to be expected, had been broken in and the contents were looted. But Andronikos was more than adequately compensated by finding painted friezes on the upper walls of the chamber. These were not only rare, but were also of high quality.

The dig continued and another tomb was located farther into the mound. The excited archaeologists found that its door was still in position and there was no visible sign of forced entry. The only way in was to remove slabs from the roof and be lowered down. Andronikos entered the tomb on 8 November and found himself amid the decayed remnants of what was obviously an important and intact burial. The antechamber to the tomb was next entered and a second cremation burial inside a gold casket was dis-

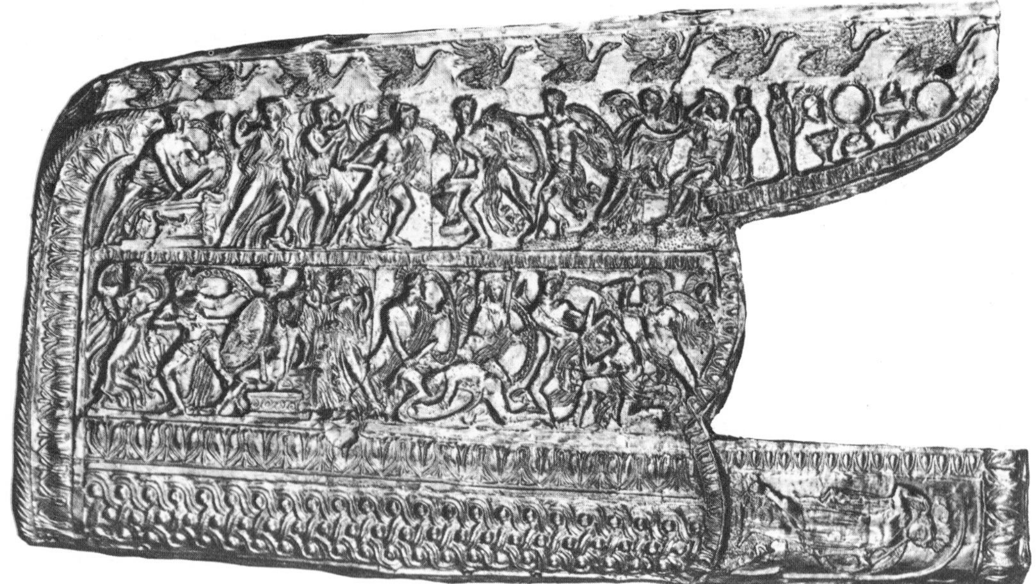

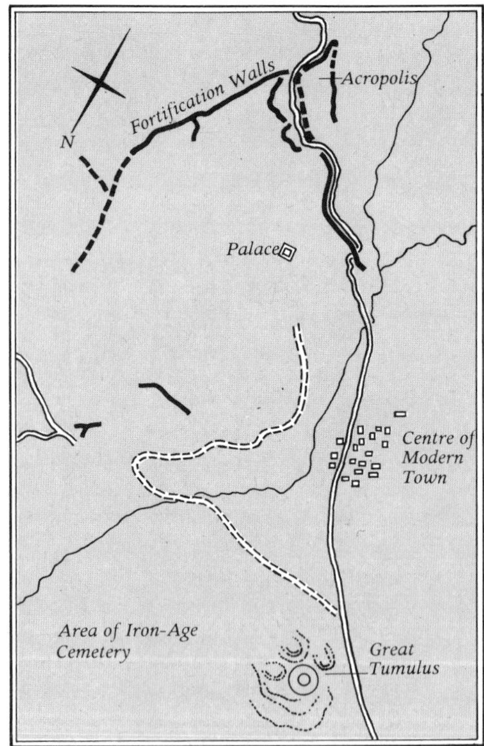

Above: A leather case for bow and quiver. Basically a utilitarian object, this example has been covered in a gilded silver casing with embossed and chased detail. Such pieces were previously best known from rich tomb finds in south Russia, where Scythian bowmen and Greek art combined. Northern conquests may well have brought this example into the hands of the Macedonian kings, although it was found with the female burial in the antechamber. The scene shows fierce fighting amid altars, in a city with women and children present – perhaps the sack of Troy?

Top right: One of a set of finely carved ivory heads, part of a larger ensemble, from the main chamber. Each head is only 3 centimetres high. Restoration of the whole is awaited. However, it is clear that the features of the heads reflect those of members of the Macedonian royal house, as known from coins, medallions and larger scale representations. Straining necks and upturned eyes are characteristic of major sculpture of the later 4th century. Seemingly deliberate damage to the right eye (a wound?) reinforces the impression that this likeness is of Philip II.

Right: The splendours of a royal burial are illustrated in the casing of the cremated bones which were placed in the main tomb's antechamber. A marble box holds a golden casket (a unique imitation of a marquetry chest) complete with the royal Macedonian sunburst symbol on its lid. Within, the bones were found wrapped in a shroud of purple and gold, finely decorated with floral designs. The condition of preservation within the airtight containers was remarkable, and this unique find has been admirably restored by skilled laboratory staff.

covered, as well as more frescoes. A third tomb was also found, but it was too late in the season to do more than take a brief glimpse of the unplundered burial. Only a few objects were removed. The rest were sealed as they lay until the chamber could be cleared in 1978.

In 1980 the façade of a further tomb was located, and the construction of the great mound encourages the belief that yet more tombs may be there. The large tumulus, in fact, covers three smaller ones. The tumulus being excavated is on the edge of the mound and it is not easy to reach the lowest levels because of the thick layers of compacted stone in the make-up.

The richness of the finds had one happy result: there is now no lack of funds for conservation work to be carried out at Thessaloniki Museum. The work requires a wide range of expertise which was previously in little demand in Greek archaeology, notably the treatment of the cloth wrapping the ashes found in the casket from the antechamber, and the reconstruction of the amazingly complex ceremonial shield of gold, glass and ivory. The frescoes also demand careful treatment. No tomb paintings quite as early as these, or of such quality, have been found in Macedonia before. In view of the importance of the site, it remained under armed guard during the excavations.

Ancient Macedon

The kingdom of Macedon, centred on the lower valleys of the Haliakmon and Axios rivers, emerged as a force in Greek affairs after 500 BC under Alexander I. The Makednes (or Macedonians) were one of a large number of tribes in northern Greece. Their rise during the 5th century was probably connected with the exploitation of precious metals in the neighbouring mountains. However, internal quarrels and warfare with nearby tribes, not least the Thracians, meant that a united kingdom was not established in this area until well into the 4th century. In that century the Greek cities of Thebes, north-west of Athens, and Pherai, in Thessaly, had brief periods of dominion. No doubt it was from their experience that Philip II obtained his military and political training.

Militarily, Philip created a strong army based on the use of cavalry, a deep phalanx and the long Macedonian pike. Politically, by adroit interference in affairs to the south, he gradually expanded his kingdom. In 346 he concluded a peace treaty with the rest of Greece more or less on his own terms. When opposition welled up again, he defeated its forces at Chaeronea in Boeotia in 338 after a bitter battle. He then turned to a long-cherished Greek dream, an invasion of Persia. However, he was assassinated in 336, possibly by agents of Alexander's mother. The success of Alexander in carrying out his father's project is well known.

By this time the capital had been transferred from Aigai to Pella, which was closer to the sea. Excavation has shown that it had grown and prospered in the 4th century and the figured mosaics in some of its houses are noteworthy.

Macedon became a magnet for Greek artists and scholars. Euripides spent his last days with king Archelaos (reigned 413–399 BC), Aristotle was the tutor of the young Alexander, and leading Greek sculptors worked at his court. The finds at Vergina amply confirm the spending power and taste of the royal Macedonian family.

From the fill of the mound came finds, such as pieces of smashed gravestones, which are worth special attention. One painted example of the 5th century is in full Greek style. The fact that it was 'Greek' should be stressed, because the origins of the Macedonians has been the subject of debate. The stone could be the work of a hired Greek artist, but the names cut on other stones are all fully Greek in pedigree. These monuments may have been shattered in 274–73 by the Gallic troops of king Pyrrhos of Epiros, because the historian Plutarch wrote that they sacked the royal tombs. Hence we can infer that the great mound was heaped up by the subsequent Macedonian king, Antigonus Gonatas (reigned 276–239 BC). Certainly it would be most unusual to find a cemetery so despoiled by Greek hands.

Grave Evidence

The king who ruled the Macedonians was only one member of a broad aristocratic élite. We might expect, therefore, to find many rich tombs deriving from the period of Macedonian ascendancy. Hence the theory that the main burial found at Vergina is that of king Philip II needs to be substantiated.

First we should consider the building found beside the edge of the smaller tumulus. In view of the quality of its marble architecture, it is possible that it housed a cult associated with the burials under the tumulus. Also, significant remains, including weaponry, horse harness and traces of a mud-brick altar, were found on top of 'Philip's tomb'. These items are echoes of the heroic status accorded to Greek warriors at Troy and to Achilles in particular. The rites observable in the burial itself suggest a similar intention.

Evidence from the tomb

The first reports of the tomb mentioned a 'casket' of gold, a find so unusual in Macedonia that it was thought to have been a mistake for 'urn'. However, the receptacle for the cremated remains in both burials in the main chamber was indeed a miniature gold chest of a type unparalleled in other Greek cemeteries. Both have the Macedonian sunburst emblem on the lid.

The bones in the larger casket are those of a man of about 40 years. (Philip II was 46 when he died.) Andronikos believes that they were washed in wine after having been collected from the pyre – another echo of the funeral of Achilles. Study of the skull, using established police methods, may make it possible to reconstruct the features, which can then be compared with known portraits of Philip. The second casket contained the bones of a woman wrapped in a purple and gold embroidered cloth. The bronze receptacle in the third chamber held the bones of a 12-year-old boy.

The offerings in an average Greek grave of the 5th and 4th centuries were rarely lavish. Most Athenians considered that a few vases, possibly decorated, a mirror or strigil (an instrument which men used for scraping sweat and dust from their skin) were sufficient. At Vergina, however, the tombs contained an extraordinarily rich variety of objects, and ceramics played a minor role. The vases were largely metallic and the amount of precious metals indicates the high status of the dead. The pottery does, however, help to date the tombs more accurately than the other finds. One Attic red-figured vase, together with some glazed pieces, point to a dating for the main burial in the third quarter of the 4th century. On similar criteria, the youth's burial should be earlier.

The tomb buildings have façades resembling pretentious civic or religious buildings. The arched roof of the main tomb is an early example of an architectural form that was later to influence Rome and all subsequent cultures.

Above the columns of the façade in tomb 3 there are traces of wooden boards. These were no doubt originally painted. Fortunately, however, the frescoes on the plaster of the façade of tomb 2, and inside tombs 1 and 2, have survived. The paintings throw a completely new light on a subject known previously from some descriptions in texts, echoes in mosaic work and contemporary Etruscan tombs, and Roman copies, notably at Pompeii and Herculaneum. Most impressive is a hunt over open ground, passing a grave-marker. This theme recalls some Athenian white-ground painted vases of the previous century. The heads are closer to those of a Pompeian masterpiece, a mosaic showing Alexander in battle against the Persian Darius. This mosaic was based on an original of about 325 BC. Its equal is a scene in tomb 1 which shows the rape of Persephone by Hades and is a bold composition of almost impressionistic lines.

Other evidence

Only a selection of further finds has yet been published. Among the metal vessels there are unusual shapes, such as a lantern and a plate of the kind used in most Greek households for serving fish but here uniquely made of silver. Some of the vessels are truly exquisite, with incised or repoussé (raised) decoration. A number have their weight noted on the underside. Andronikos has suggested that one piece, a kind of torque made of gilded silver, may be the royal diadem. Wreaths found in each casket display consummate workmanship. They are composed of interlacing gold foliage, on which a tiny gold bird or minute gold bees have settled.

For different reasons the discovery of a

The unplundered tomb and antechamber, later 4th century BC

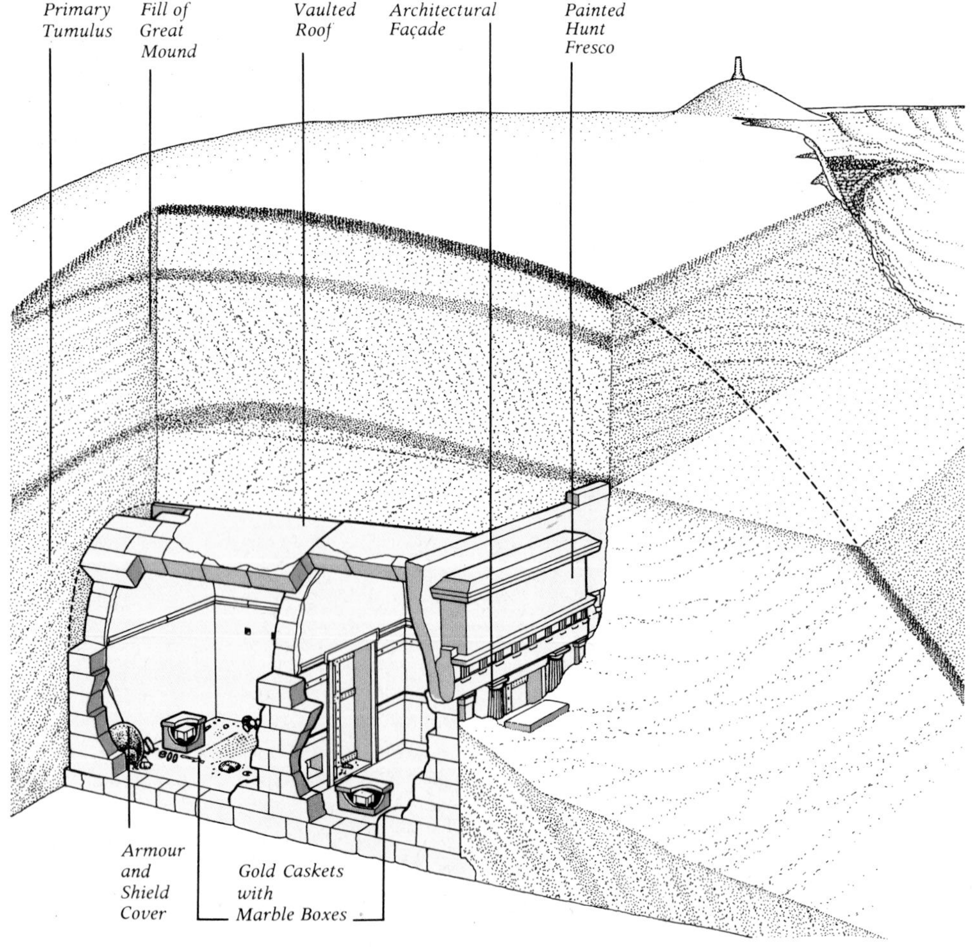

Left: The intact burials were found in an area well away from the centre of the Great Mound. This was piled in the 3rd century BC over a series of three smaller mounds, such as had covered burials in the Vergina cemeteries for many hundreds of years. Not shown are the scant remains of a brick altar found above the vault together with objects from the cremation pyre, including acorns from the gold wreath shown opposite. Such burial chambers, with architectural façade, are typical of Hellenistic Macedonia. However, this is one of the earliest examples of the true vault yet known from the Greek world.

bronze tripod, with the lion's claw feet so beloved of the Greeks, was unexpected. On artistic grounds it can be dated to the 5th century. This is confirmed by an inscription that was found on the rim, on which a cauldron would have stood, after it was cleaned. It read, 'from the games of Hera at Argos'. Such phrasing is found on a number of bronze vessels given as prizes in various athletic contests held under divine auspices in Greece. This piece must have been a treasured heirloom won by a member of the Greek royal house of Macedon in about 440 BC. A similar prize, from games in Boeotia, was discovered in a hoard of bronzework found at Epirus, the birthplace of Alexander's mother, which is west of Macedonia. It is striking that another tomb, found in the Epirus area and also in 1978, contained armour of the same date. In certain respects it is as impressive as that in the main tomb at Vergina. In both tombs the excavators found helmets and corselets of iron, which were virtually unknown elsewhere in the Greek world. The corselet from the Illyrian tomb is modelled, with the musculature of the body beneath. The Vergina corselet is simpler, but it has gold studs fashioned as lions' heads on the front. The spears are also finely decorated and the sword has an ivory pommel, bound in gold.

The most remarkable of the military objects at Vergina is a shield, found disintegrated behind a large bronze cover. It was composed of bands of ivory, glass and gold, with a carved ivory centrepiece, all set on a leather frame, and is the most luxurious piece of 'parade armour' known from the Greco-Roman world. It makes us think beyond the Eros-emblazoned shield of the Athenian statesman Alcibiades to Homer's description of the wondrously inlaid shield which was made for Achilles by the divine smith Hephaestus.

A series of small ivory heads was found in the main tomb. They resemble known work in marble – work attributable to artists associated with the sculptors Praxiteles and Lysippus. Portraits of Philip and Alexander have been identified with some certainty.

In view of all this evidence for a burial of the later 4th century BC, accompanied by the most lavish grave goods made in immaculate style, it seems likely that here, indeed, is the final resting place of Philip II. Two final points can be added. No coins of Philip have been reported. This is all to the good, because it has recently been demonstrated that much of his coinage was issued posthumously by Alexander. Another point is that in one of the pairs of greaves (leg guards), the left leg is markedly shorter than the right. Philip is known to have been lame. Nonetheless, a case for a later burial, that of his son Philip, can still be argued.

Above: Among the offerings in precious metals from the two intact burials were intricately constructed wreaths of gold. This one was found within the gold casket for the cremated bones in the inner chamber. It is a confection of oak leaves and acorns, probably made in a workshop local to the old royal capital.

Left: The rifled tomb 1 has given us our most precious remains of Greek free painting, best known previously from mere descriptions in ancient authors. This excerpt shows Hades abducting Persephone on his chariot. It displays a fine sense of depth and shade in its almost impressionist fresco technique.

Ephesus

TURKEY

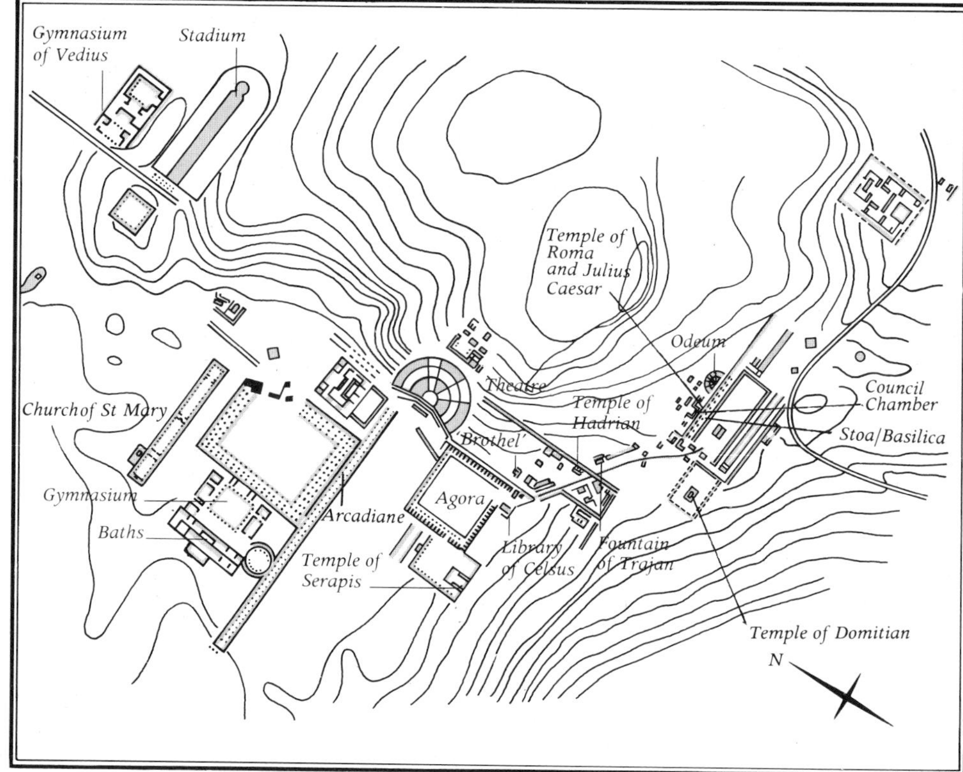

The Temple of Artemis at Ephesus was one of the Seven Wonders of the World. The site is near the Turkish village of Selçuk, about 50 kilometres south of the modern port of Izmir. It lies on the south side of the River Caystrus, largely to the west of the isolated Panayir hill and in the narrow valley between it and the long crest of the Bulbul hill to the south. Ephesus was once a port, but constant silting necessitated drainage works and even a change of position when Lysimachus, one of Alexander the Great's more successful heirs, moved the population downstream in 294 BC. Such removals were not rare in Classical Greece. In the 4th century BC, the towns of Rhodes and Kos were re-sited at strategically and commercially important points, and in order to remain near the sea, Ephesus and Priene, to its south, were relocated in the same general period. Halicarnassus, site of another Wonder of the World, achieved prominence also because of its coastal situation. Today, the ruins of Ephesus, Priene and Miletus lie stranded several kilometres from the sea, and it was this problem of silting which led to their being abandoned in late antiquity.

Excavation and discoveries

Little of the earlier settlement at Ephesus has been revealed. This is partly because the later city has attracted most attention, and partly because some of it must underlie later buildings. The Artemisium, as the Temple of Artemis is called, was itself not readily found, for literary sources give conflicting hints as to its location. When in 1863–69 an Englishman, John Wood, inched his way towards it, the temple lay 6 metres below the surface at a spot that must have been close to the ancient shoreline. Wood's excavations were not uneventful. He had to contend with unsatisfactory lodgings, cholera, a broken collar-bone, trench collapse, an assassination attempt and murder. Both Wood and D. G. Hogarth, who succeeded him at the site in 1904–05, sent back to the British Museum substantial chunks of decorated marble. Hogarth also located the remains of earlier phases of the temple, erected, according to the Greek historian Herodotus, with the aid of funds provided by king Croesus of Lydia around 550 BC. For its time the temple was the largest marble structure ever attempted.

As Hogarth dug deeper into the waterlogged mire of the lowest 'levels', constant pumping was needed to effect even the pretence of proper excavation. He was rewarded by discovering several early phases of the sanctuary, the date and interpretation of which are still a matter of debate. Rich votive deposits were also found. The Austrian Archaeological Institute, which had begun work at Ephesus in 1895, started supplementary work in the area of the altar beyond the temple's west end in 1965. The Austrian excavations have concentrated on the new town, where finds of an earlier period have not been lacking. It seems that the sacred way, which runs around the 150-metre high Panayir hill, was flanked by the graveyards of Ephesus before it became a main artery in the Hellenistic town.

Above: Marble figure of Artemis, the finest of echoes of her cult statue. Although it bears traces of Greek archaic art, the 'breasts' seem to be a garbled version of the original.

Among the excavated finds, sculpture takes a leading place. Dating back to the years around 600 BC are some finely cut ivory figurines of priests and priestesses from the Artemisium. Sculpted fragments which come from reliefs cut on the lower column drums of the temple itself are enough to show that they represented petrified processions to the shrine. When the temple was burnt down in 356 BC, by one Herostratus who desired immortality for his name, rebuilding took place along previous lines. The brash young Alexander the Great offered financial assistance towards this, but was refused by an offended citizenry. Larger remnants of the sculpted drums of this later temple have been recovered. One, a subtly composed and finely achieved work, seems to show Hermes leading Alcestis from the underworld. A bronze youth found in the gymnasium by the har-

Above: The view west from the theatre on the Panayir hill shows the extent of silting of the Caystrus river valley. Prominent are the Arcadiane and harbour bath complex.

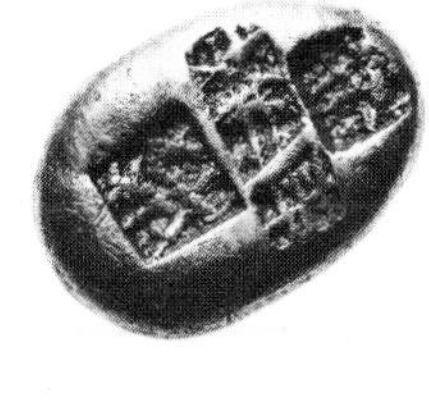

Left: Two very early Greek coins of electrum. Technical aspects and Artemis's creatures, the stag and bee, betray Ephesus as their source: c. 590 BC.

bour may be of the same date. It was found in 1896, and had been placed in one of the niches around the walls, where the Romans often displayed copies of famous Greek originals. The battered bronze shows a sturdy youth cleaning his strigil, or body-scraper, after exercise. The style is close to that of Alexander's official sculptor, the Athenian Lysippus, but debate continues as to whether it is a Greek original or Roman copy.

Fragments of a frieze from the altar of the Artemisium depict warrior Amazons, and these lead us to a fascinating episode which occurred about 440 BC – or at least to an anecdote related by the Roman author Pliny which was set at that time. Four leading sculptors, including the Greek masters Pheidias and Polycleitus, competed in a contest to cast a statue of an Amazon, probably wounded, in battle against Theseus. This was to be dedicated in the Artemisium. While the story is difficult to accept in all details, Roman copies of three Amazon types datable to the period in question do exist, and the matter has been one of the more lively topics of art-historical debate for over a century.

The history of Ephesus

Late literary sources say that the first Greek inhabitants came from Athens around 1000 BC. Similar information about Miletus has received some confirmation by finds of the early Iron Age, but at Ephesus the only material dated earlier than about 800 BC consists of some Mycenaean vases. Some are from a tomb on the hill of St John, farther up the silted estuary, where there was perhaps a native Carian town which the Greeks found on their arrival.

When Lysimachus moved the town in 294 BC, he threw a strong defensive wall around the Panayir and Bulbul hills, using the crest of the latter as the main defensive line on the south. This wall dates largely from the 3rd century BC and illustrates several aspects of Hellenistic fortification techniques. However, very little standing within its compass is as early as the wall, since the city changed overlords several times in the 3rd century, played second fiddle to Pergamum in the 2nd century and suffered terribly at the hands of both Romans and Asiatics in the 1st century BC. It recovered only after the visits of Antony and Cleopatra, and its elevation to capital of the Roman province of Asia in 30 BC. Later destructions were as violent but not always man-made. A series of earthquakes in the 3rd century necessitated large-scale rebuilding, so that much of the building material which has remained above ground to the present day had already seen service in earlier structures. For example, part of a basilica of the 2nd century AD was transformed into the church of St Mary, where a general council of the Christian Church was held in 431. In the realm of legend, catacombs cut on the Panayir hill may relate to the story of the Seven Sleepers of Ephesus. These were reputedly persecuted Christians who took refuge in a cave outside the walls and slept there for two centuries before awakening to the amazement of all.

Left: Mural painting of Socrates. On the steep lower slopes of the Bulbul hill have been found remains of houses of the Roman period. The wall of one large room was originally painted with this and other panels in the 1st century BC, before later replastering. The figure of Socrates is 34 centimetres high; he sits carefully posed on a bench with lion's paw feet. Details are picked out by highlights. While the features are typical of marble portraits of Socrates – beard, snub nose, balding (he was likened to the satyr Silenus) – the inspiration for this figure may be from a lost original of the 3rd century BC.

Right: The temple of Artemis was the crowning glory of the city of Ephesus. In view of the slight remains, any reconstruction has to be imaginative. The cult statue of the deity may have been displayed in the window of the pediment, to observe the rites carried out at the monumental altar below. The harbour may have reached close to the temple in the Classical period. In port are a couple of square-rigged merchantmen and two triremes. Behind is the Panayir hill; to the right is the Hellenistic city.

City of Diana

The population of Ephesus certainly included non-Greeks, as was the case with other Greek cities in the area. Even its name may be derived from a word related to the Hittite 'apusa', meaning bee, the significance of which is discussed below. The first Greek settlement may have been called Koressos. Lysimachus certainly gave to the city which he established the short-lived title of Arsinoeia, after his wife, the daughter of Ptolemy I.

An Athenian origin may be reflected in common aspects of cult and dialect. The constitution of independent Ephesus was also modelled largely on Athenian lines, providing for a sovereign assembly of the people and having the year named after the chief annual magistrate, whose title at Ephesus was the Prytanis. The influence of successive conquerors was obviously felt, and it is unfortunate that almost all clear evidence for the workings of the Ephesian constitution derive from the Roman period.

Town planning and building

As in many other cities built or rebuilt during the Hellenistic period, Ephesus had a 'Hippodamian' plan. This was based on a rectangular street grid, named after the architect Hippodamus who so planned the city of Miletus after its destruction by the Persians in 494 BC. At Ephesus the street grid was laid down almost in spite of the contours. Only the old sacred way around the Panayir hill was allowed to interrupt the pattern. It has been shown that some of the visible structures had early phases, notably the theatre and the civic square in the east of the town, but otherwise we know very little of the appearance and life of Ephesus during the Hellenistic period. Much is swamped under Roman remodelling, and the overwhelming majority of surviving inscriptions are of the same period. One inscription belongs to the period of conflict between Rome and king Mithridates of Pontus, in the 80s BC, and shows the Ephesians grovelling to the eventual Western victors, protesting loyalty.

Excavation has, however, thrown light on two basic types of Hellenistic building at Ephesus, the stoa and the brothel. Visitors are confidently shown, as an example of the latter, a building which lies a little way back from the main street down by the harbour. Its identification as a brothel was based on the presence of small rooms leading off a court, and in particular from an inscription on a block re-used in the superstructure which refers to a latrine and neighbouring bordello. Closer scrutiny of the building's history reveals that the block was blamelessly, if a little foolishly, brought from an original position elsewhere. In fact the development of the house shows the typical stages undergone by many of the Ephesian buildings so far excavated.

The stoa in question lies in the civic centre or agora, and is one of an original pair. It fitted neatly into the Hellenistic grid plan, but was substantially altered in the 1st century AD to form a more Romanized basilica structure, and was given wings which cut across the earlier streets. Other buildings in this area include a council chamber, erected after Ephesian independence had been drastically curtailed by the Roman take-over of Asia. There are also symbols of that Roman suzerainty – small temples of the goddess Roma and the god Julius Caesar, raised on podia in the Italian manner. A not too rare twist of archaeological fate has also preserved parts of a huge cult statue of the Roman emperor Domitian, whose temple was proudly erected south of the square. His subsequent fall from favour brought about obliteration of everything associated with him. The statue was smashed and consigned to the cellar, where, ironically, it was far better

preserved than if it had been anywhere else.

Many of the structures on the main streets of Ephesus were given by individual benefactors, and some were still being erected well into the 5th century AD. One of the buildings is the Arcadiane, a marble-paved avenue leading from the Panayir hill to the harbour. Named after the emperor Arcadius, it was noted for having street lighting. Our sources do not name the many structures from which the emperor took stone blocks to act as capitals for its flanking colonnades. From an earlier age comes the library of C. Julius Polemeaenus, a Sardian who became Roman consul in AD 92. Enough of the façade of this building survived to justify restoration. Although small by the standards of the libraries at Alexandria or Pergamum, holding some 12,000 scrolls, it was still richly decorated, especially the two-storey front which was adorned with free-standing sculpture in the manner of a Roman theatre. In 1904, excavators found in the basement the austerely furnished lead sarcophagus of the donor. This proved a rare exception to the rule of burial outside the city walls in the Greco-Roman world.

Other forms of less academic recreation were also amply provided. Ephesus boasts a series of bath buildings, often with gymnasia attached, while individual houses could also have their own bathroom suites. Down by the harbour was a massive complex with a spacious arena. This comprised a square with covered running tracks on each side, a smaller gymnasium and a set of large bathrooms fronting the old quay. The main town latrines have seats reserved by special inscriptions, and an elegant epigram praises successful achievement.

Another sidelight on life in Ephesus is to be found in the *Acts of the Apostles*, chapter 19. At a stormy debate held in the theatre, the populace raised the cry 'Great is Diana of the Ephesians' in response to the effect that Christian missionary work was having on sales of souvenirs of the Artemis cult. The 'town clerk', as the Authorized Version has it, appealed to the complainants to take recourse to law, thereby ending the probably typical meeting.

The temple of Artemis was in one sense the most massive of sacred buildings in Ephesus, although the tumbled blocks of a temple to the Egyptian deity Serapis, beyond the library, are of immense size. The Serapis temple honoured a god extremely popular in the Greco-Roman world, and is built on a high podium in the Corinthian architectural style. Serapis did not, however, eclipse the glory of Artemis. Her cult was founded in an open grove, and, because there is much in its worship that is non-Greek, possibly on the site of a native shrine. The bee is found as a votive offering and also appears regularly on Ephesian coins. It may owe its place to Hittite elements. The name 'Megabyzos', given to some priests, is of Persian origin. They were eunuchs and one of that name ran a banking service from the temple. Some temple servants had the name Essenes, a term also used for royal bees.

The original enclosure with its altar and cult-statue – 'the image that fell down from Jupiter' – was followed by a sequence of temples. The first enormous building, of about 550 BC, had a ground plan measuring 55 by 115 metres and a column height of some 19 metres. It was clearly built to rival a huge temple dedicated to Hera on the neighbouring island of Samos. However, at Ephesus, marble was used for much of the temple, and it is no surprise that it took about a century to complete. The setting of foundations on such marshy sites as Samos and Ephesus, and the emplacement of blocks of as much as 40 tonnes, were substantial architectural feats. Dwarfed by the stone forest of some 130 columns, the citizens of Ephesus could be rightly proud of 'their' goddess.

Cerveteri
ITALY

Cerveteri is a town some 70 kilometres northwest of Rome and 6 kilometres from the sea. Its 270-hectare cemetery, 'ancient Caere', is also one of the major Etruscan cemetery sites, and is an archaeological site where excavators work a night shift. These excavators are tomb robbers, or 'clandestini', who carry out organized and informed work under the cover of darkness in order to feed the world's art markets with illegally recovered and exported material.

The Etruscans were a people who built up a major civilization in north-central Italy, which flourished between 700 and 200 BC. It had a great influence on the early development of Roman art, architecture and government. The Etruscans, like the ancient Egyptians, provided valuable gifts for their dead, placing them for the most part in solidly-built or rock-cut chambers, which would have stood the test of time well had they not been the target of tomb robbers, not only of the present day but also in antiquity. The ancient looter can be distinguished archaeologically by the lack of deposited humus under disturbed offerings. The ancient robbers also rejected most ceramic material, but this is now well worth finding because of the prices it can fetch.

In part, Caere lies under modern Cerveteri. Most of the cemeteries are on spurs flanking the town, pushing out from the Tuscan hills into the plain that Caere controlled. To either side, Monte Abatone and the hill called Banditaccia are equally rich in burials, although the latter has the more impressive funerary monuments. Farther up the coast are the other rich Etruscan cemeteries of Tarquinia and Vulci.

In broad terms, all these towns flourished between 800 and 300 BC and they were all systematically exploited – one can hardly say excavated – between 1825 and 1875. To those diggings we owe the great advances made in the study of Greek and Etruscan art in the 19th and early 20th centuries. They also provided the basis of the collections of Greek vases and Etruscan bronzes in the British Museum, the Louvre in Paris, the Hermitage in Leningrad, the Vatican and the Antikenmuseum in Munich.

One of the richest and earliest burials, indeed one of the few ever found intact, was discovered in 1836 on the seaward slope below the town, where the first burials were consigned. Called the Regolini-Galassi Tomb after its discoverers, Father Regolini and General Galassi, it belongs to the horizon of princely tombs of the 7th century BC that graced many cemeteries of central Italy, including those at Cumae, on the Bay of Naples, and probably Rome. Like most Etruscan tombs it was used more than once. This point raises a major difficulty in the study of Etruscan cemeteries – the isolation and dating of single depositions, a problem by no means confined to Etruria. Under the terms of their contract, Regolini and Galassi were obliged to devote one tenth of the finds to the local church. Nor were they their own best allies in causing the roof of the chamber to collapse, contrary to the regulations in force and to the detriment of the objects below. The records made at the time by excavators and visitors alike were little better than minimal.

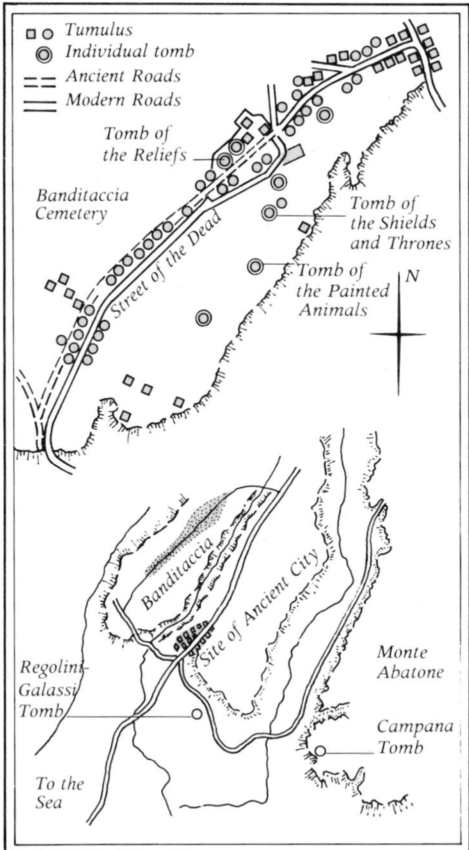

Modern techniques

The inroads of illegal excavation have been appalling, yet there are insufficient public funds either to dig or to protect the sites fully. At Vulci, experiments have been made in licensing private societies to dig, while detection techniques developed by the Lerici Foundation have been used at both Tarquinia and Cerveteri. The Lerici Foundation was set up in 1947 by Carlo Lerici. It later pioneered the use of the *proton magnetometer* in Italy and, somewhat incidentally, it developed a device to aid prospecting in cemeteries. This was a probe which was pushed into the chamber of any tomb located by *resistivity techniques*. A miniature camera built into the probe scanned the interior to determine the contents and wall decoration. The resulting photographs were of rather better quality than those taken by clandestini to show to prospective buyers.

Recently the Foundation has located and excavated Iron Age huts amid later burials in the cemetery of Tarquinia, contributing to the question of the location of the early town. Previously its staff were busy salvaging many of the tombs which they had pinpointed at Tarquinia and Cerveteri. In a small cemetery at Cerveteri half the located tombs, in total around 50, were looted in 1960. Only one, which was rather poorly furnished, was found intact. Yet even the records of their excavation seem to have been unsatisfactory and little has yet been published.

Cerveteri's finds

It is difficult to assess the amount of metalwork originally put in Caeretan chambers because of the depredations of tomb robbers. Scraps of iron and bronze merely hint at what might have been. People of the earlier Villanovan civilization, which developed into that of the Etruscans in Etruria, often put bronzework in their tombs. And we know from other centres that styles and objects imported from the East were soon copied with some skill in gold, silver and bronze. The few *fibulae*, mirrors and weapons from Caeretan tombs tell us little, although an interesting selection of pieces left in one tomb of about 600 BC included many small gold fibulae, four bronze vessels, a set of dice, a pair of sandals and a wooden water bottle and stool.

What has survived in quantity is pottery. The finds amply illustrate the ceramic history not only of Etruria but also of Greece. Scores of vessels of Etruscan 'bucchero', with its dark grey soapy surface, were put in tombs of the 7th and 6th centuries, along with imitations of Corinthian ware, and some originals. Then Attic vases, often of high quality, become frequent. From some tombs which had already been robbed, as many as 300 vases or other fragments have been recovered.

In general terms, the cemeteries show a sharp increase in wealth in the 7th century and this was sustained as far as the early 4th century. Greek and Latin authors fill out the evidence a little. We hear of Carthaginians and Caeretans combining to defeat at sea Greeks operating as pirates out of Aleria on Corsica in about 540. In turn, Hieron of Syracuse followed up the victory over Carthage at Himera in 480 with a naval success against the Etruscans off Cumae in 474. This seriously weakened Etruscan control over Campania.

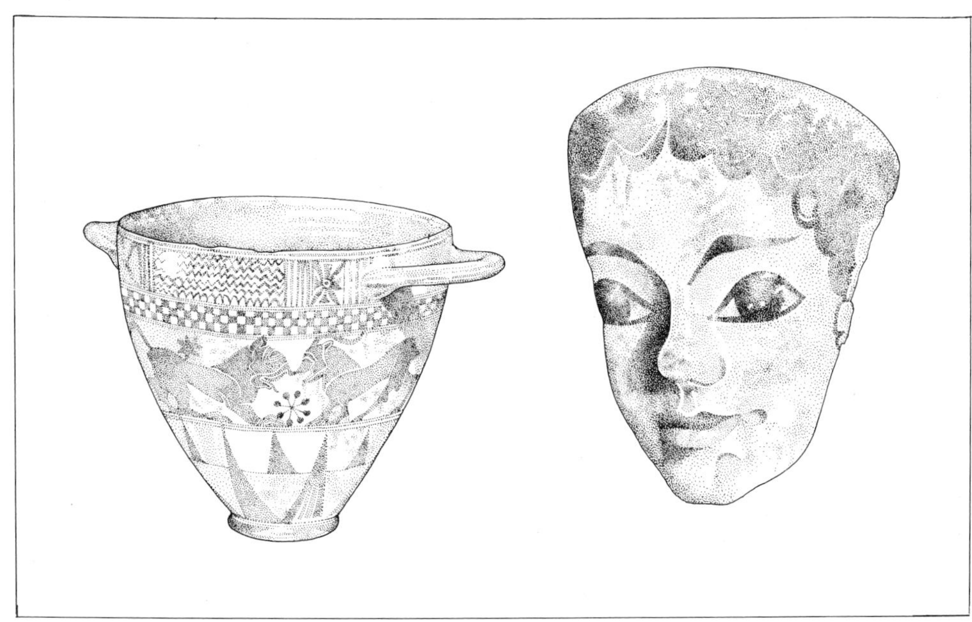

It must have been in the later 6th century that the Caeretans dedicated their treasury at Delphi, in Greece, where we also find individual Etruscan offerings. Another Syracusan, Dionysios, attacked and pillaged Caere in 384, shortly after a Gallic invasion of Italy, when the Romans sent the sacred objects of Vesta to Caere for safe keeping. The town became a satellite dependency of Rome in 353 and subsequently sank into historical oblivion.

Left: Much Etruscan art is highly dependent on Greek models. The cup (skyphos) is a fine example of Corinthian work, found in a rich tomb of c. 650 BC. Such pieces were soon imitated by Etruscan potters. The large clay head, with freshly preserved colouring, formed part of the decoration of a temple on the town plateau of Cerveteri. It reflects Greek work of the mid-6th century BC.

Right: A superb terracotta funerary couch found in the necropolis of Cerveteri during the mid-19th century, although unfortunately, no precise record exists of the exact spot. It was made in the later 6th century BC, when couches were already being cut in the stone of burial chambers to receive corpses. This piece acted as an ash urn and represents a noteworthy mingling of life and death, husband and wife 'at table' together in the Etruscan manner, unlike the male preserve of Greek symposia. Near life-size, it was probably originally painted in a variety of colours.

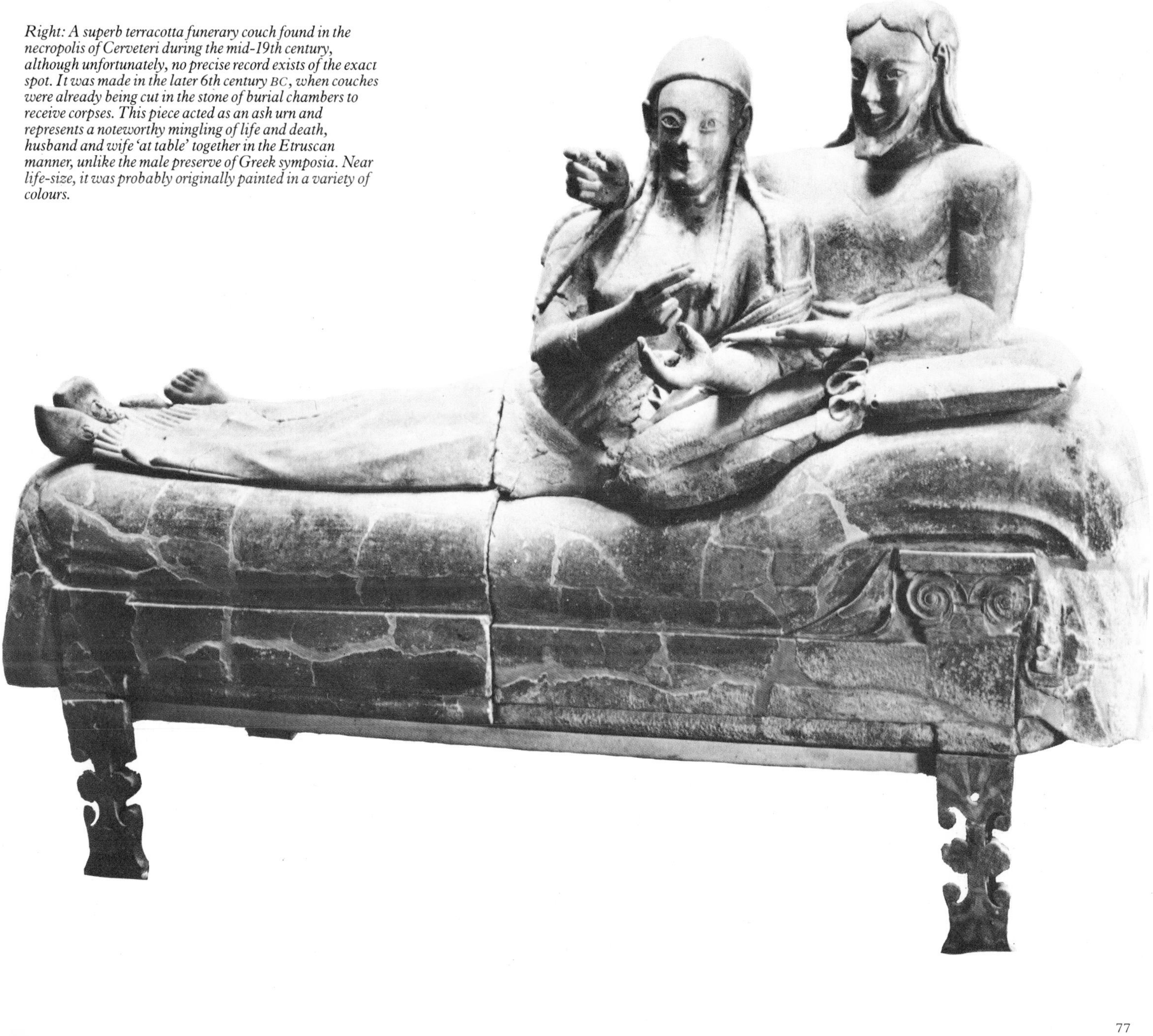

The Etruscans

Twelve states, from the River Tiber in the south to the River Arno in the north, constituted the Etruscan heartland. They were politically independent and each was governed by one or more leading families. Information about the Etruscans is mostly gleaned from later Greek and Latin texts, augmented by contemporary Etruscan inscriptions.

The origins of the Etruscans

The Etruscans spoke a language that was not of Indo-European origin, unlike most dialects spoken in the Italian peninsula. It is known almost wholly from material dug up in Etruria, and finds from Caere and its territory have contributed much to the stock of interpretations that have been made. The Etruscan alphabet is close to a Greek version brought to Italy in the 8th century, but it has some affinity with that found in Lydia in Asia Minor. A stone from the Aegean island of Lemnos bears a text with verbal forms very close to Etruscan. Add to that the statement of the Greek historian Herodotus that Etruscans, who were called Tyrrhenians in Greek, emigrated from Lydia to Italy and a good case for an Anatolian origin of these powerful people seems to have been made.

However, a major snag is that the archaeological record nowhere reveals evidence of an Etruscan invasion, let alone in the years from which the above parallels are drawn. Instead, Etruscan culture appears to have grown steadily from late Bronze Age roots via the Villanovan culture, as did other less distinctive Italian societies. We should note though that some places settled by the Etruscans have Indo-European names.

The rise of Etruria

The early tombs at Caere are of the 9th century BC. They are simple cremation pits or shafts with few offerings, vases and bronzes. The increasing richness of tombs of the 7th century is very striking at Cerveteri, though it is paralleled at Populonia to the north and Praeneste and Ostia to the south. The cause of the change may have been political, with the rise of a restricted wealth-earning class. But it was surely prompted initially by the exploitation of local resources, notably metals in central Italy. In the Tolfa hills north of Caere, rich deposits of iron and copper were found and Populonia and Vetulonia were even richer in iron. Local demand for tools, weapons, and luxury goods no doubt existed, but it seems most likely that Greek traders developed this lucrative market. Greek expansion west began in the early 8th century, and by 760 there was a colony on north Ischia, where slag from Elba has been identified in iron foundries.

At Caere the new wealth is displayed in the Regolini-Galassi Tomb. The tomb grew in stages, with a long chamber and open antechamber being converted into two chambers with side rooms, while the whole was covered with a tumulus of increased size. It set the standard for future chamber tombs. Steps led down via a passage to a room with side chambers and a further room at the end. There were three burials in the tomb. A male cremation was deposited in the right-hand room, with the charred remnants of his chariot. The remains of a female inhumation lay in the main chamber, the body lying on a mattress on a stone couch, draped in a gold-encrusted pall. The antechamber was occupied by an inhumed male resting on a bronze couch, with a light hearse nearby. Numbers of bronze and silver vessels, some from the Near East, accompanied the inhumations and the 390 or so recorded finds included a few Greek vases. From such evidence archaeologists have shown the development of the family vault in Etruria and the emphasis laid on proper burial. Less attention went on housing, even for the gods.

Beliefs and rites

We know little about the temples of Caere. Small by Greek standards, they were largely made of mud-brick and wood. The walls were decorated with painted terracotta. Dedications often took the form of terracotta or bronze figurines. A kiln found close to one of the temples was probably used for firing the figurines. We know so little about towns that we cannot yet say whether they had central market areas, as in Greece, or whether they had an overall plan. A hint of what might have been lies in the rows of chamber tombs along well-defined streets at Orvieto, an order that was also imposed on the Banditaccia cemetery from about 550 onward.

The most important religious finds come from Pyrgi, one of Caere's ports. Though this name is Greek, it is Carthage that has left the more tangible mark, and indeed another of its sea-ports to the north is called Punicum in a later route map of the Roman empire. The remains of two temples were found at Pyrgi in 1959–66, both poorly preserved. The finds included fragments of a terracotta pediment depicting a scene from the Greek legend of the Seven against Thebes, one of the most striking examples of Etruscan indebtedness to the Greek repertoire. Between the temples was an altar, a well and a shallow pit, in the centre of which were three gold sheets and the gilded nails by which they were once posted. The sheets were inscribed and had been buried out of piety, because they contain details of the dedication in about 500 BC of a temple to the goddess Uni (Hera) by one Thefarie Velianas. Two dedications are in Etruscan. The third, with the Carthaginian goddess Astarte substituted for Uni, is in Punic. This not only eases the translation of the Etruscan texts, but also dramatically proves Carthage's interests in the Etruscan ports. At the same time there is

Left: A thin gold plaque, once nailed up in a shrine in the port of Pyrgi. Its Etruscan inscription records the setting up of a cult to Uni by Thefarie Velianas. Another plaque bears a similar text in the Punic of Carthage, Cerveteri's trading partner.

Far left: Tomb structures increasingly echo domestic architecture. In the Tomb of the Reliefs, couches for the bodies have stone pillows, while the walls are decorated with carved offerings and utensils, together with household pets.

Above: Banditaccia, one of Cerveteri's main cemeteries, became a veritable city of the dead, with countless tombs, mainly rock-cut vaults topped with earth mounds, lining distinct streets. The large mound on the left covers a number of such vaults.

Below: The earliest known monumental tomb at Cerveteri, the Regolini-Galassi tomb, was part cut, and part built. A long passage leading to the burial chamber was soon converted into a second chamber, and crude side rooms added. It belongs to the period 700-650 BC. A 19th-century view of the tomb's entrance is shown (left).

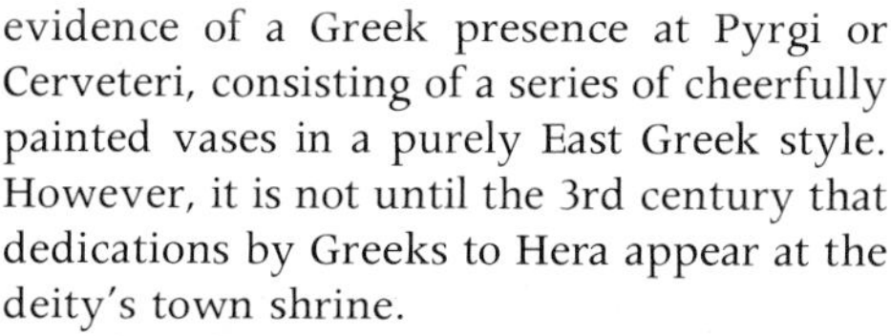

evidence of a Greek presence at Pyrgi or Cerveteri, consisting of a series of cheerfully painted vases in a purely East Greek style. However, it is not until the 3rd century that dedications by Greeks to Hera appear at the deity's town shrine.

Although incineration and single burials survive, inhumation in chambers is the main burial rite. Stone couches, separate types for males and females, were placed inside the chambers, which could be in use for up to 150 years, although there is no evidence that previous interments were moved over. Most tombs were covered by an earth mound which could increase in size as new tombs were put under its cover. They could be cut into to provide new chambers, or they could be shaved away for the paths that were laid down in the regularization of the cemetery. Individual mounds were often given a neat surround of worked stone.

Few painted tombs have been found at Caere. More striking is the architecture of the chamber itself. This imitates the interior of an Etruscan house, with wood and brick translated into stone. Stone beds are sometimes accompanied by thrones, and nails on the wall demonstrate that offerings were hung from them. The Tomb of the Reliefs has a selection of objects carved on the pillars. Stone figures have also been found, and it has been suggested that ancestor cults were observed in some chambers or, perhaps, above them, as access to the top of the mound was regularly provided.

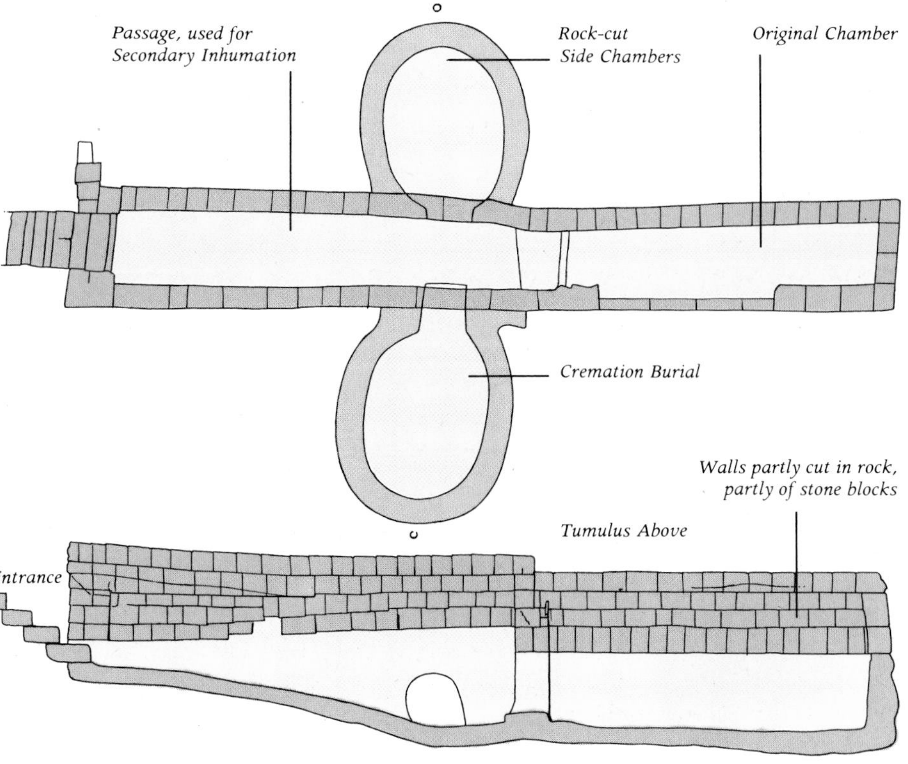

Palatine Hill and Forum

ROME, ITALY

Rome stands on the River Tiber about 27 kilometres from the sea. It is one of the world's most beautiful cities and contains two of the most fascinating and complex of all archaeological sites.

The ancient city occupied an area encompassing seven hills with lower ground between them on the south bank of the river. The sites present special problems to archaeologists because they are large, because they possess some enormous monuments in stone, brick and concrete, and because they have been continuously occupied since at least the 8th century BC.

Some ancient buildings, particularly those of the Roman imperial period, have remained standing. But attitudes towards existing buildings have varied over the centuries. Romans of the regal and republican periods (until 31 BC) generally had little respect for earlier structures, except for the most venerable. In the imperial period (until AD 476), this attitude continued and whole areas were swept away in order to build on a grand scale, although it was recognized that the finest monuments should be preserved.

Throughout the medieval period, however, ancient structures were used as sources of building materials and the Forum, once the heart of ancient Rome, became a meadow. In the Renaissance and its aftermath, many took a keen interest in Roman antiquities, but such people were hardly less destructive, because the maltreatment or demolition of ancient buildings continued, while treasure hunters dug haphazardly. Sculptures were also often damagingly 'restored'.

More scientific excavation began on the Palatine hill, by legend the first of Rome's seven hills to be occupied, only in the 18th century. At the same time, tentative work began in the Forum below, where cattle still grazed. But it is really only since 1870 that this work has been carried out methodically. From 1924 the Forum area was cleared, revealing some of its original splendour, and between 1931 and 1937, the monumental centre of ancient Rome, the Senate House, which had become a church, was restored to the state it had been around AD 300.

The Palatine and Forum areas of Rome are in the centre of a city which, from 200 BC to AD 476, when Rome was taken over by the German chief Odoacer, had been the centre of an enormous empire. These sites are thus of great significance in Western history.

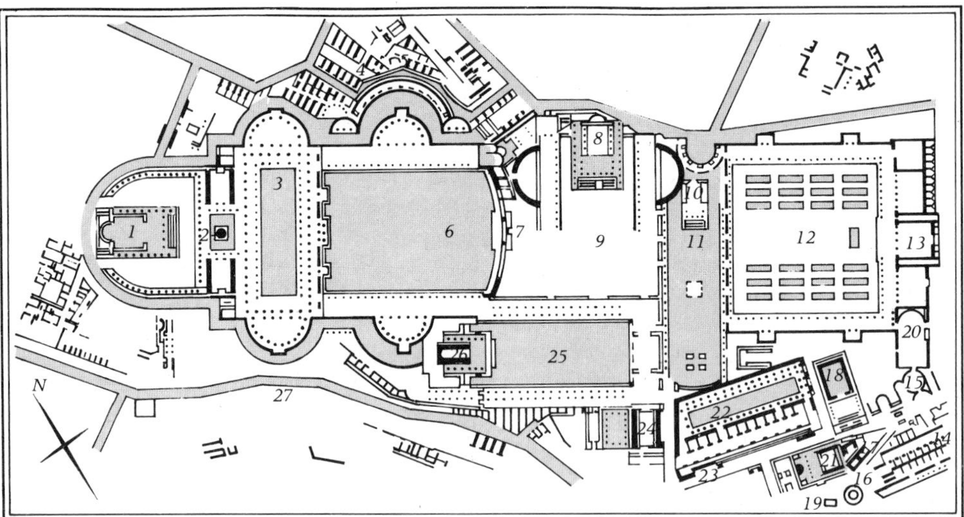

Archaeologists have revealed that Rome's beginnings were small and its growth slow. The earliest settlements seem to have grown up from about the 9th century BC, both on the Palatine and on four other hills. Doubtless the site of Rome was chosen because it was defensible. It lay at an ancient crossroads, overlooking rich farmland. It also guarded the lowest practicable Tiber crossing and was accessible by boat from the mouth of the Tiber.

Later legends told how Rome was founded by Latins under Romulus from nearby Alba Longa (near Castelgandolfo) in 753 BC. They relate how the Palatine was occupied and how the Sabines soon joined the Latins to form one nation. Excavators have found evidence on the Palatine of newcomers' huts built in the 8th century BC from wood posts, wattle and thatch and the associated pottery is similar to that of Alba Longa. As for Romulus, monuments supposedly associated with him were later preserved. These are the Lupercal cave below the Palatine, where he and his brother Remus were suckled by a she-wolf, his thatched hut on the Palatine, and his 'tomb' in the Forum. The black marble which perhaps covered the tomb lay over early material, including a stone with the earliest known Latin inscription dating to the 6th or 5th century BC. The 'palace', or Regia, of Numa, the successor of Romulus, was also preserved and ruins survive.

The Forum

By 700 BC the hill communities were using the marshy Forum area as a cemetery. Later, Roman law forbade burial within city or town limits. But, from about 670 BC, hut dwellers, perhaps bringing the cult of Vesta with them, began to occupy the Forum and to improve its drainage.

Within 100 years, the Forum was transformed from a dwelling area into a pebbled main market place with adjoining roads, including the Sacra Via (Sacred Way). It contained shrines, such as those of Jupiter, Saturn and possibly Castor and Pollux, with terracotta ornament, and the Great Drain (Cloaca Maxima) which now crossed the Forum. The better houses, built on the surrounding hills, were of plastered mud-brick roofed with clay tiles. This advance was surely connected with the legendary seizure and control of 6th-century Rome by kings from Etruria to the north. The Etruscans stimulated trade, political development and craftsmanship. But, according to tradition, they were expelled in 510 BC.

The Romans created a republican government dominated by a Senate of ex-magistrates who met in the Curia, or Senate House. They established state cults and fought hostile neighbours. A stone wall, the Servian, ringed Rome around 378 BC. In 338 BC the first speakers' platform, the Rostra, which was made from ships' prows, was built in the Forum. Soon afterwards, the earliest part of the Tullianum, the prison below the Capitol, was constructed.

As the Romans built up their empire, architects in the capital experimented with Etruscan and Greek traditions and Italian concrete construction. Similarly, artists used Italian and Greek elements. The Forum acquired basilicas including the Basilica Aemilia, the Porcia and the Sempronia, for public and legal business, a variety of statuary and, in 78 BC, a Record Office, or Tabularium, where state archives were stored. The Palatine, where remnants of shrines and late republican period houses with wall paintings have been found, became a fashionable residential area for such figures as the orator Cicero.

Major change began during civil wars in the 1st century BC and the assumption of dictatorial powers by Julius Caesar who, in 46 BC, dedicated the Basilica Julia and a new Forum on purchased land. With its rectangular, porticoed plan, its statuary and temple to a cult connected with its founder, it proved to be the first of a series of essentially similar, although increasingly grandiose, 'imperial' Fora, which were extensions made to the old Forum. The extensions were made by various emperors following the collapse of republican government and the establishment of one-man rule by Caesar's great-nephew Augustus, who ruled from 31 BC to AD 14.

The main building material became brick-faced concrete, disguised by veneers of stucco and marble so that it appeared to be stone throughout. This was a sop to the Greek traditions admired by Romans, who also adapted the Greek decorative *Doric*, *Ionic* and *Corinthian* architectural forms and added their own, *Tuscan* and *Composite*.

Augustus, as well as completing an enclosure called the Saepta in the Roman Forum, dedicated the second 'imperial' Forum with its temple of Mars Ultor (Mars the Avenger) in 2 BC. Vespasian (reigned AD 69–79) added the third, with a temple of Peace. Here Septimius Severus (reigned 193–211) attached to a wall a huge marble plan of Rome, of which precious fragments survive.

Vespasian's hated younger son Domitian (reigned 81–96) erected a triumphal arch with reliefs, which still survives in the Roman Forum, to honour his elder brother Titus. He also provided the fourth 'imperial' Forum, including a temple to Minerva, goddess of wisdom and war. But his successor Nerva dedicated it in AD 97 and it is usually called the 'transit' Forum or Transitorium, because it led into the Forum of Vespasian.

The greatest of all the Fora was that of Trajan (reigned 98–117). It included a great basilica, Greek and Latin libraries, a mass of buildings rising up the Quirinal hill, a covered market accessible at three levels and Trajan's surviving column. This column, intended at first as a viewing platform, was converted into a war memorial when a figured relief spiral was carved on the exterior. The reliefs show campaigns in Dacia and are a major source of information on the Roman army.

Later emperors maintained and restored Fora structures, such as the house of the Vestal Virgins, built by Nero between AD 64 and 68, and the temple of Saturn, or the Senate House, rebuilt by Diocletian (reigned 284–305). The well-preserved temple of the deified Antoninus and Faustina was erected in the Roman Forum between AD 138 and 161, as were also the triumphal Arch of Septimius Severus with relief panels dated AD 203; Maxentius's circular brick temple, thought to have been dedicated to his son Romulus Maxentius who died about 309; the towering 'New' basilica begun by Maxentius and completed by Constantine (reigned 306–337); and the final monument, a usurped column dedicated to the Byzantine emperor Phocas in 608. It is clear that successive emperors tried to impress the Senate and the people of Rome by undertaking these great public works in the Forum.

Left: Key

1 Temple of Trajan
2 Trajan's Column
3 Basilica Ulpia
4 Trajan's Market
5 Via Biberatica
6 Forum of Trajan
7 Arch of Trajan
8 Temple of Mars Ultor
9 Forum of Augustus
10 Temple of Minerva
11 Forum of Nerva
12 Forum of Peace
13 Temple of Peace
14 House of the Vestal Virgins
15 Temple of Romulus
16 Temple of Vesta
17 Regia
18 Temple of Antoninus and Faustina
19 Spring of Juturna
20 Library
21 Temple of Caesar
22 Basilica Aemilia
23 Sacred Way (Sacra Via)
24 Senate House (Curia)
25 Forum of Caesar
26 Temple of Venus Genetrix
27 Clivus Argentarius

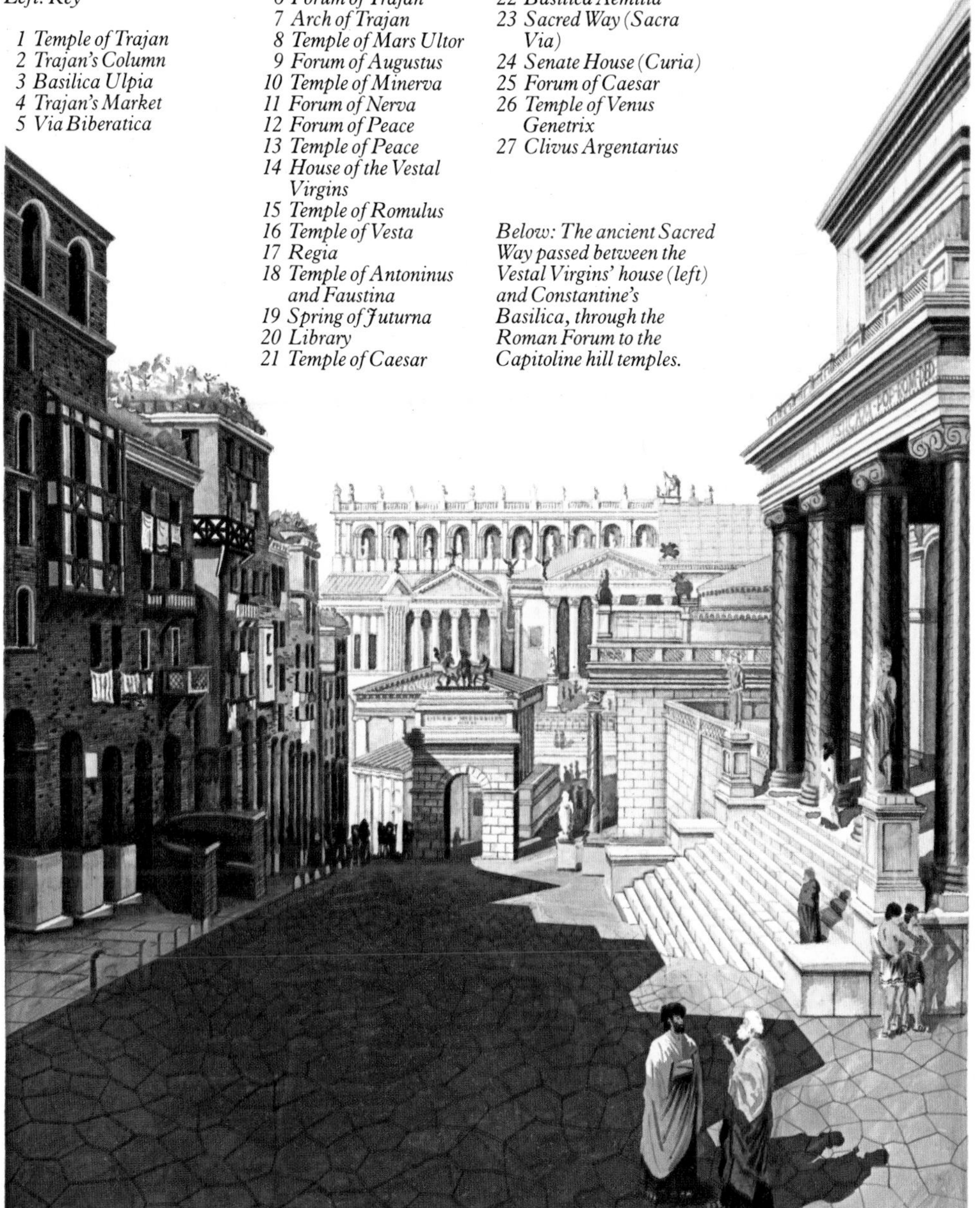

Below: The ancient Sacred Way passed between the Vestal Virgins' house (left) and Constantine's Basilica, through the Roman Forum to the Capitoline hill temples.

The Palatine

The Roman emperors established themselves on the Palatine. Augustus's residence, if correctly identified, was modest. It was a late republican dwelling of about 50 BC, with slightly later wall paintings of architecture and mythological scenes in the second of four styles used between about 200 BC and AD 100. The building was later reverently preserved.

Augustus's gloomy successor, Tiberius (reigned AD 14–37), raised the first truly palatial complex, in concrete disguised by rich ornament, on the north-western flank of the hill. He was followed by Nero (reigned 54–68), who set nearby a part of his first palace, the Domus Transitoria, which included a fountain or nymphaeum, but both structures were destroyed by fire.

It eventually fell to Domitian to cover the Palatine with a palace worthy of the hub of empire. A vast construction on several levels, it contained courts, innumerable halls and chambers often of most imaginative design, a racecourse, or stadium, and rich decoration in marble, stucco, paint and mosaic. The palace, called the Domus Augustana, remained the residence of rulers until the end of antiquity.

The City Centre

Roman society had as its nucleus Latin and Sabine tribes of Indo-European origin. These tribes had settled in Italy probably during the second millennium BC. But Rome's population steadily became more mixed through the acquisition of foreign slaves, often subsequently freed and allowed to remain, and through the many Indo-European and Semitic subjects who flowed into the capital from the empire. Over the centuries, Italian influence declined. From the AD 100s, many emperors were not even of Italian origin.

The stages of Rome's development are reflected in the monuments of the Palatine and Forum. Documentation from elsewhere in the city and empire and a wealth of surviving Greek and Latin literature, especially that dating from about 200 BC to AD 565, have further enriched our knowledge.

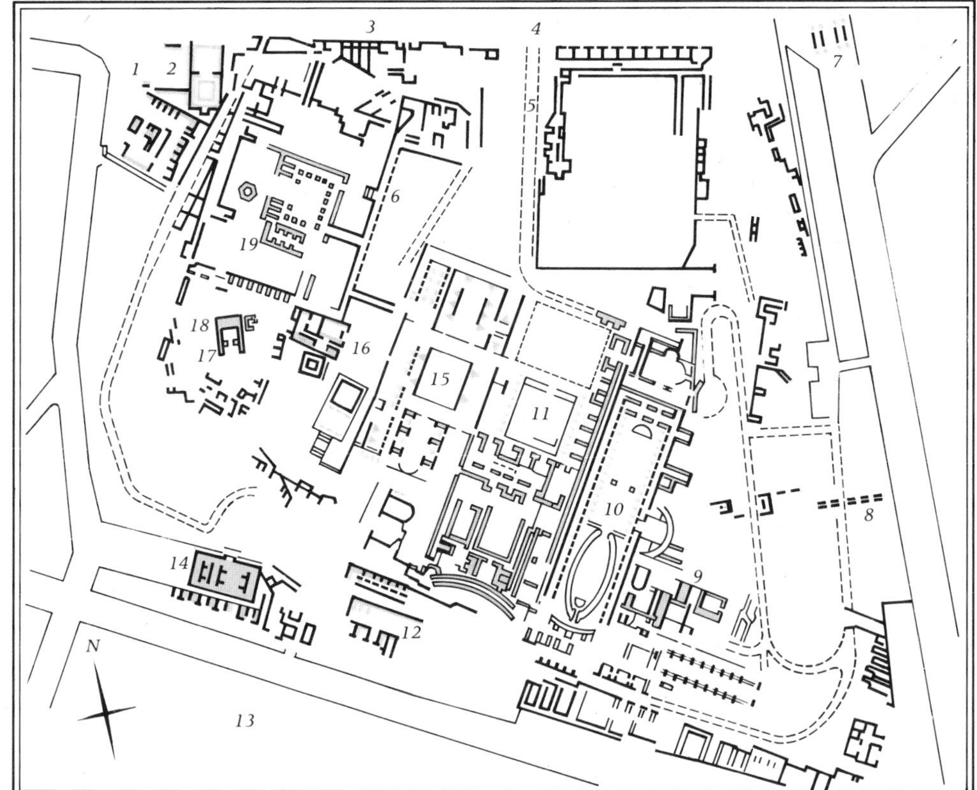

Government and economy

The government passed through three major phases. A regal period, traditionally until 510 BC, corresponded with those of the early settlements and Etruscan occupation. During this period, a Senate of elders or heads of families was created, together perhaps with some magistracies and divisions into voting groups by kinship and wealth.

The succeeding republican phase, which lasted until 31 BC, was the period when Rome acquired most of her empire. It saw the establishment of the consuls, who were two senior executive magistrates with equal power, and lesser magistrates in the praetors, aediles, tribunes and quaestors. These were elected annually by the body of free adult males holding citizenship. These men were organized into group voting divisions to run Rome, the state and its irregular, *ad hoc* army. Ex-magistrates became life members of the Senate. This was an advisory but influential body which was traditionally conservative in outlook. In crises a dictator could be appointed for a limited term.

The strains of empire and senatorial divisions led to civil war, from which Octavian emerged to become absolute ruler in 31 BC and soon became emperor, taking the name Augustus. Constitutionally the emperor was merely a republican magistrate with powers superior to any other. The remaining republican magistrates continued to function under his control together with the prefecture of the city of Rome, although the people lost their votes and influence. But the emperor, as controller of finances and head of a reorganized police force in Rome and of the standing army in two sections (the legions being made up of Roman citizens and the auxiliaries containing non-citizens) tended to act beyond his powers. Nevertheless, the Republican-period Romans had had a great respect for the rule of law. This persisted under the emperors and constrained them. At the end of antiquity, two emperors, Theodosius and Justinian, made important collections of laws, which still survive. Republican magistrates and, later, emperors were normally drawn from the uppermost, senatorial section of society. Beneath this were the other grades: businessmen who belonged to the Roman order of equites, or knights; poorer citizens; free persons without citizenship; freed slaves or 'freedmen', whose sons could attain full citizenship; and

Above: Two marble spiral relief bands in the middle section of Trajan's Column, erected in Trajan's Forum AD 106–113. They show Roman auxiliaries among Dacian tombs and (above) attacking a fort.

Far left (top): Key

1 Vicus Tuscus
2 Temple of Augustus
3 Via Nova
4 Roman Forum
5 Clivus Palatinus
6 Cryptoporticus
7 Arch of Constantine
8 Aqueduct
9 Baths of Septimius Severus
10 Stadium (Hippodrome)
11 Domus Augustana
12 Paedogogium
13 Circus Maximus
14 Antiquarium
15 Palace of Domitian
16 House of Augustus ('Livia')
17 House of Romulus (?)
18 Temple of Cybele
19 Palace of Tiberius

Far left: Part of the shopping centre on the Quirinal hill adjoining Trajan's Forum, dedicated in AD 113, with brick-faced hemicycle and roofed market.

Left: Colossal marble head with an unworldly gaze, 2.60 metres high, from a statue of Constantine I. Erected c. AD 324–337, it was found in his Basilica.

slaves, whose tasks ranged from comfortable teaching and doctoring posts to appalling work in the mines.

Rome's economy changed enormously over the years. Agriculture and foreign trade became important during the regal period and remained so. Coinage in bronze, silver and sometimes gold was introduced in the 3rd century BC. Although late for the ancient world, it facilitated trade and army payments. War booty brought wealth until at least the AD 100s and some internal taxation was introduced. The acquisition of provinces enabled Romans to exploit their resources, tax them and bring products and any profits to Rome. But senators, through snobbishness, were not permitted to engage directly in trade.

As the city grew, light industries of numerous kinds sprang up, contributing further wealth. At her zenith in the first 200 years after the birth of Christ, Rome had a population of perhaps a million and it had a complex money economy. Serious upheavals in the 3rd century, however, led to disadvantageous policies, including an increased dependence on barter and payment in kind, attempts to freeze prices and the fixing of people in jobs.

Technology and religion

The Romans reached a comparatively high point of technological achievement over a wide range of activities. In many cases they took over and improved techniques already in use among Greek and other societies. Their greatest technological achievement, lavishly exemplified in Rome's monumental centre, lay in the exploitation of volcanic dust from central Italy to make concrete architecture on a grand scale, with vaults and domes roofing enormous spans and brick facings that were clad in rich decoration.

Rome was also the centre of religious cults. Roman religion was less a matter of belief than of ritual observance, carried out by colleges of priests and priestesses. These were chosen or elected, under the general supervision of the chief priest, or pontifex maximus, who lived in the old Forum throughout the republican period until the emperors usurped his functions.

In and around the Roman Forum were shrines of ancient cults, such as those of Vesta, with an everlasting fire kept going by virgin priestesses, of Jupiter, Saturn, Castor and Pollux, the spring Juturna and the 12 leadings gods headed by Jupiter.

In the imperial Fora, Julius Caesar contributed a temple of Venus Genetrix ('the Mother'), Augustus the temple of Mars Ultor, Vespasian the temple of Peace, and Domitian the temples of Minerva and Janus Quadrifons ('the four-faced'). The imperial cult, which involved the worship of selected deceased emperors and their associates, led to the building of a temple of Vespasian and Titus below the Capitol, one of Trajan at the end of his Forum, and one in the old Forum of Antoninus and Faustina, which is still largely complete. Maxentius added a temple dedicated to his son Romulus Maxentius.

The final transformation came in the 6th century, following Constantine's conversion to Christianity. As the empire adopted Christianity and was threatened by barbarian ravages, the Romans began to transmute Forum buildings into churches, a sign of the new age.

Pompeii

ITALY

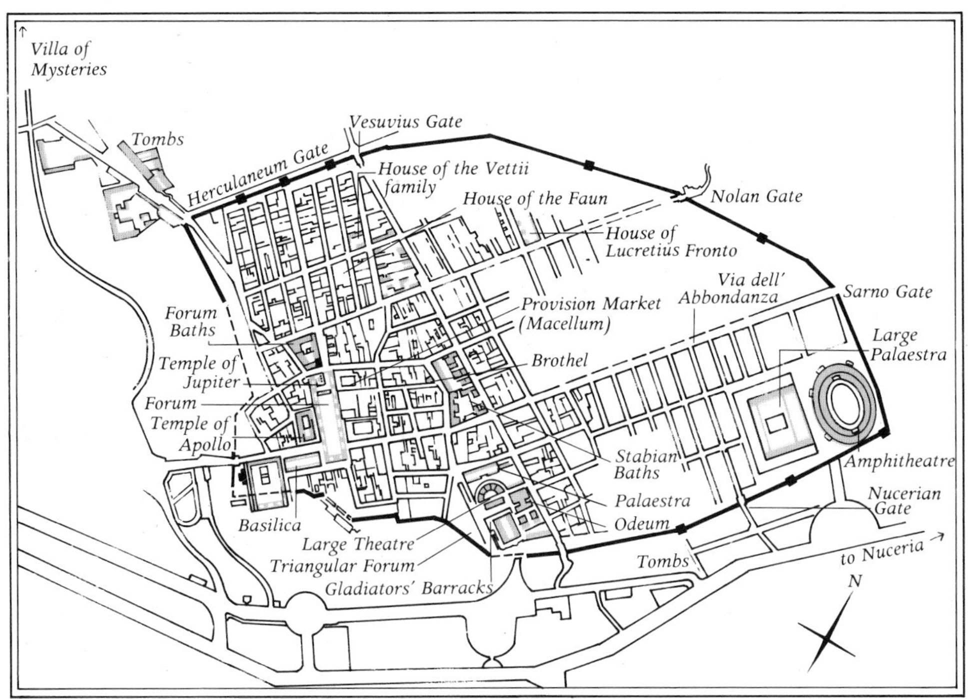

In the days of the Roman republic and early empire, a number of towns flourished around the central Italian Bay of Naples, between the Campanian coast and the volcano Vesuvius. One of these was Pompeii.

In AD 79, Vesuvius exploded. From the sky, lava pebbles, pumice, ash and sulphurous gases rained down on Pompeii, burying it quickly. This sudden catastrophe preserved for hundreds of years an astonishingly vivid picture of Roman daily life. When disaster struck, some people were cooking bread, and the carbonized loaves were found in the ovens. Others were eating meals of eggs and fish, the remains of which were found on dining-room tables. Some 2,000 people were killed, about one-tenth of the population.

Excavation

After Pompeii's rapid burial, there was at first a considerable amount of pillage, but soon the town sank into oblivion. It even remained unrecognized in 1594 when a water channel was dug across the ruins and antiquities were brought up. Nevertheless, scholarly speculation began. In 1709, well diggers discovered the nearby Roman town of Herculaneum, which had been buried at the same time by a mud flow caused when heavy rains turned loose volcanic ash into hot liquid mud. With the stimulus of this discovery, Pompeii, too, was soon found and at first suffered the depredations of hunters after antiquities.

The brilliant Italian excavator Giuseppe Fiorelli, who was director of the work from 1860 to 1875, laid a scientific basis for modern exploration. He divided the city area (about 64 hectares in all) into regions, city blocks and numbered houses, so that the position of any discovery could be pinpointed easily. This system is still in use.

Second, he noticed odd cavities in the hardened ash and pumice. He hit upon the idea of forcibly blowing a liquid plaster into these cavities. After the plaster had hardened, he removed the casts and found that the holes were spaces left by perished corpses of humans and animals. The casts reproduced the outward appearance of the corpses with horrifying perfection. They preserved not only the contorted expressions and postures of the agonies of death, but also such details as Pompeian hair-styles.

Third, Fiorelli and his successor introduced the modern approach of trying to leave and preserve discoveries where they were found, instead of removing the interesting items and leaving the rest to decay.

Recent additions to these successful Italian techniques have included an investigation of the plants that grew in Pompeii. There has also been a British project to store information about Pompeii on computer, the recent policy having been to involve international co-operation in the excavations.

Historical evidence

Pompeii had already existed for hundreds of years when it was so suddenly buried. We do not know when the site was first settled, because the earliest strata have not yet been excavated, but its name appears to be of ancient Italian origin. Nevertheless, in the 6th century BC, it had already acquired an international character. Local Italian pottery indicated contact with neighbouring agricultural communities in the Sarno River valley. Etruscan wares suggested commerce with the Etruscan town of Capua. Temples to Apollo and Hercules of Archaic Greek form demonstrate a powerful Greek influence. They also perhaps indicate the presence of Greek settlers from the nearby Greek colony of Cumae, who would have been anxious to exploit Pompeii's commercial potential, situated as it was in a most fertile region.

In 474 BC the Greek colonists of southern Italy and Sicily expelled the north Italian Etruscans, leading to Greek control over Pompeii and heralding a period of prosperity. The town, which was laid out essentially on Greek grid-plan lines, expanded rapidly to fill the area within the surviving defensive walls. These were built in an attempt to keep out encroaching Italian tribesmen, the Samnites, who spoke Oscan, a language akin to Latin.

By about 400 BC, the Samnites had engulfed Pompeii. Their peasant culture was to be an important component in that of Pompeii for the next 300 years. At the same time, the Samnites recognized the quality of Greek culture and borrowed from it freely. At first they warred with Rome until, in 290 BC, the Romans established control of central Italy. Subsequent Roman success in conquering Hannibal and the Carthaginians, and then Greece and Asia Minor, opened up new opportunities for the Campanian merchants.

By about 150–100 BC Pompeii had become extremely prosperous. Constructions belonging to this 'Samnite' period can often be recognized by brown *tufa* blocks, from a nearby town, Nocera, which were used for building. The Forum (public square and market place) was enlarged and surrounded by a portico, or colonnade, of equally spaced columns. At the north end of the Forum there was the temple of Jupiter and in the southwestern corner stood a *basilica* for public and legal business, the name having been found scrawled on the wall. It is the earliest known example of the type. Elsewhere other temples were built. The Triangular Forum received its Doric columns, and the Large Theatre and Stabian Baths, as originally

Above: View south-east along the important street now called the Via di Mercurio. This formed part of the grid-plan of streets in the sixth quarter (Regio), off which large rectangular private houses open at right angles. Among them are those of Meleager and Castor and Pollux, with colonnaded gardens (peristyles). The street has pavements for pedestrians; in the distance is the Arch of Caligula.

Left: Part of a great painted frieze in the so-called dining room (triclinium) of the Villa of the Mysteries outside the Herculaneum Gate, c. 50–0 BC. It consists of almost life-size figures against a background of 'Pompeian' red. Forest deities, Silenus (to the left) and Pans, look on as a bride-to-be shows her fear before a marital initiation ceremony which involves a ritual whipping to beat out evil.

planned, constitute some of the earliest examples of their forms. Enormous houses, like the House of the Faun (named after a bronze statue of a dancing faun found there), sprawled over a whole city block. The room walls of these houses were plastered and often painted to imitate marble masonry.

Grievances over the denial of Roman citizenship, however, led Pompeii to join other towns in fighting the 'Social' War against Rome in 90–89 BC. Pompeii itself was besieged by Lucius Cornelius Sulla (138–78 BC). The outcome was the unification of all Italy south of the River Po. But Pompeii suffered when Sulla became dictator of Rome, through the confiscation of territory for Sulla's veteran soldiers, although their presence led to the raising of Pompeii's civic status to that of a Roman 'colony' in 80 BC.

Further building followed. The Forum was refurbished and its principal temple was rebuilt and dedicated to the 'Capitoline triad' of the Romans; Jupiter, Juno and Minerva. The Stabian Baths were improved and new structures included more houses, a small covered theatre, the Forum baths and an amphitheatre for blood sports. Inaugurated in 70 BC, this amphitheatre is the earliest known in the Roman world. Pompeii was comparatively unscathed by the Roman civil wars that brought the first emperor Augustus to power in 31 BC.

With Augustus's establishment of the Pax Romana (Roman Peace), the town prospered as never before. The Forum porticoes were reconstructed in limestone. A market-hall (macellum) for meat and fish was built, and a central building erected by the patroness Eumachia for the use of wool merchants arose beside it. The Large Theatre was remodelled, the imperial cult was introduced, a huge exercise area (palaestra) was provided near the amphitheatre, and an aqueduct and water system was created. At the same time, private houses were built and refashioned.

But troubles were approaching. In AD 59, as the Roman historian Tacitus tells us, the emperor Nero closed the amphitheatre for 10 years after a bloody riot. This event is actually commemorated in a surviving wall-painting from a house in the city.

On 5 February 62, an earthquake shook the city inflicting widespread damage. Recovery was slow and reconstruction was still in progress in AD 79. By then only the amphitheatre, the temple of Isis and some private houses had been fully restored. Furthermore, many fine old houses were subdivided and some turned to industrial uses. From 20 August 79, for four days, the unhappy Pompeians felt renewed tremors. The springs dried up, and many fled. Finally, Vesuvius erupted on the morning of 24 August. What followed is documented archaeologically and by an eye-witness, Pliny the Younger, who wrote to Tacitus describing the explosion and how his uncle, Pliny the Elder, the scientist, approached too close and was killed.

The eruption froze Pompeii in time and captured an enormous amount of information about Roman daily life in August 79. The sudden burial made Pompeii quite different from most other sites which declined and decayed slowly before final burial.

Pompeii contained other treasures. For historians of architecture, Pompeii stresses the role of Campania in the development of Roman architecture. For art historians, the assorted rich murals proved a revelation.

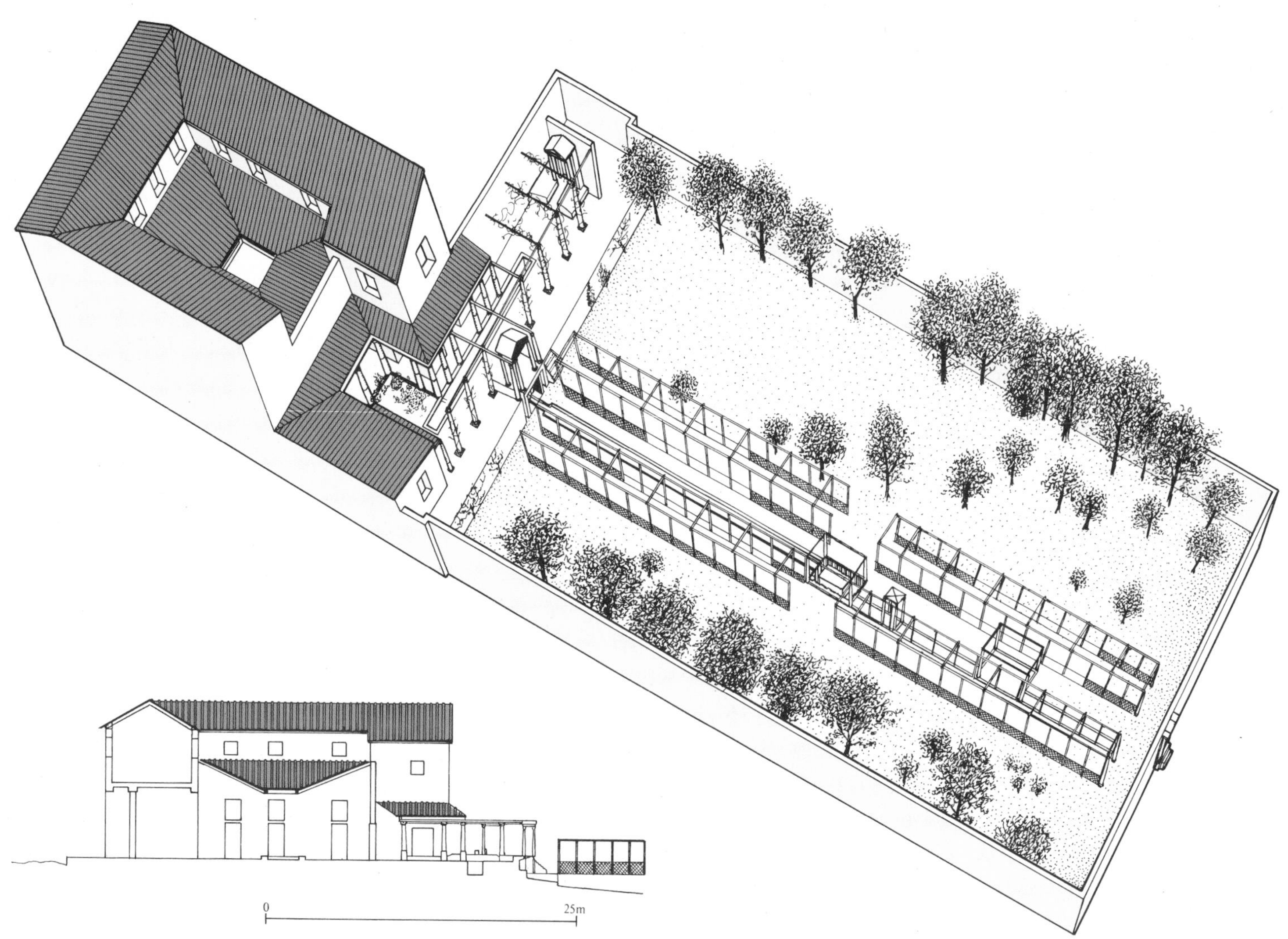

Roman Life

Visitors can now walk around Pompeii, down its narrow, paved streets, into the impressive Forum and through open doorways, one of which has a mosaic warning to 'beware of the dog'. The houses vary in style but some are spacious and elegant, with central gardens in which the flowers planted are the same as those that grew in ancient Pompeii. There are also the baths, theatres, a brothel, shops, restaurants, factories, and so on.

It takes only a little imagination to conjure up the sounds and smells of the bustling and prosperous town of Pompeii in AD 79. And, like the Pompeians, visitors are aware of the menace of the still-active Vesuvius which dominates the horizon.

Life in ancient Pompeii

For the historian the discoveries at Pompeii have illuminated a wide variety of aspects of ancient life, particularly when set beside literary references and comparable material from elsewhere.

Pompeii is exceptionally rich in inscriptions. These comprise official texts, inscriptions denoting ownership and assorted graffiti. From these it is clear that, after 80 BC, the town had a standard type of administration, based on that of Rome. There were two chief magistrates (duoviri), lesser officials elected annually by all free Pompeian citizens, and a senate. Elections must have been lively, and slogans still cover the walls of many buildings. One reads 'The petty thieves support Vatia for aedile' – aedile being a magistrate in charge of public buildings.

Portrait sculpture of leading citizens abounded in public and private places. The composition of the élite changed over the years. After 80 BC there was a preponderance of Romans, but later the old Samnite families re-emerged, followed by a rise of previously insignificant persons and freed slaves, whose sons could attain Roman citizenship. Also present were the usual urban proletariat, of mixed origin, the local Italian peasantry and a sizable slave population, often of Greek background. Pompeii's population probably totalled about 20,000.

The town's economy depended largely on local farming, and the richness of the Campanian soil contributed greatly to its prosperity. A wide variety of products, including fruit, vegetables and grain as attested by wall-paintings and plant remains, were doubtless for local consumption. Real local wealth, however, was surely derived from the export of olive oil and wines, transport jars (amphorae) for which have been found in southern France. This trade was controlled by local landed families.

Wool was processed and sold in Pompeii. After the earthquake of AD 62 fulleries (cloth-fulling mills) multiplied. They were often installed in large, old houses whose owners had moved out, suggesting that economic changes were taking place. Local industry seems to have been small-scale, but bronze working and pottery making flourished. Pompeii also drew wealth from its position as a distribution centre for its region.

The extremely varied religious life of Pompeii is best documented for the last 200 years of its existence. An important Italian element was present from early times. It was manifested in the worship of the chief god Jupiter and his associates Juno, Minerva, Mars, Mercury, Venus and the like. Through centuries of interaction between Italian and Greek cultures, these deities had been strongly

Above: Interior of a tavern for serving hot and cold drinks (thermopolium), with vats sunk into the counter (right) and painting of protective deities.

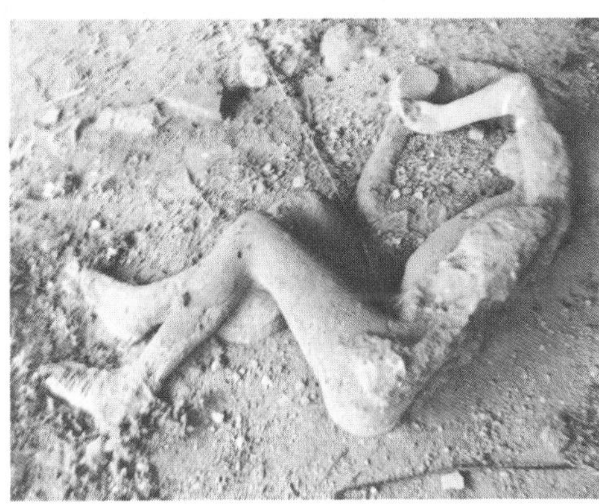

Right: Body of a beggar who died outside the Nucerian Gate, reconstituted in plaster from the cavity left in the hardened ash by his decomposed remains.

Left: Reconstruction of the house of Loreius Tiburtinus, with a square open court, or atrium (left), colonnade (peristyle) in the centre, and garden.

Hellenized and such Greek gods as Zeus, Hera, Athena, Ares, Hermes and Aphrodite were accepted as their counterparts or, like Apollo, shared.

The cults of all these divinities were latterly largely a matter of observance, intended to propitiate or flatter, rather than belief. Colleges of priests, elected or selected, controlled worship. Italian popular religion was also present in almost every Pompeian home in the form of a household shrine, or lararium. This contained figures of the household gods, the Lares and the Penates, before whom daily offerings were made.

But very different cults were also present. There was a group of 'mystery' religions, such as those of the Anatolian Cybele and Sabazios, the Egyptian Isis and her consort Serapis, or the (originally) Iranian Mithras. The last, brought in through the Roman conquest of the eastern Mediterranean, was characterized by the belief that, through initiation into some hidden knowledge or 'mystery', the initiate could improve life in this world and/or the next. In this respect it was not unlike Christianity, and there may have been Christians in Pompeii before AD 79. A later import was the Imperial cult. This involved worship of the emperor or his associates who were pronounced divine after death, or of his Fortune or spirit during life.

The funerary practices of Pompeii were similar to those of other Roman towns and cities. Believing in an after-life, however shadowy, the Pompeians were concerned to make some provision for the dead, who could be either burned or buried. Roman law prohibited the placing of tombs within the city limits and so cemeteries lined the roads leading out of it. The tombs often had considerable architectural distinction.

Various kinds of entertainment were available. Some, including concerts, literary readings, lectures and the public orations beloved of antiquity, were doubtless presented at the small, covered theatre. More popular shows, such as farces, mimes and ballets, were staged at the Large Theatre.

Pompeians could cultivate their bodies as well as their minds. For cleansing, there were public baths. For eating and drinking, there were bars. And, for exercise, there was an enormous open gymnastics yard (palaestra) surrounded by colonnades, and another smaller one.

Pompeii also had a brothel with paintings on the walls depicting the inmates plying their trade. Most popular of all, however, was the amphitheatre, in which an endless procession of people and wild animals was killed for public amusement. Near the amphitheatre archaeologists found a house converted into a barracks for gladiators. In the house 60 gladiators, together with a well dressed woman visitor, were overcome by ashes and fumes and perished.

Architecture and art

Architectural historians have learned much from the buildings at Pompeii, from the Greek temple remains of the Archaic period, through centuries of Samnite cultural domination, to the opening-out of the town's horizon in its last 200 years. The town builders were not innovators and they tended to preserve Greek methods and forms. Yet in its basilica and amphitheatre, Pompeii has the earliest known examples of these forms, while other structures are early examples of their type.

Rich documentation survives concerning the development of housing. The simple local house was built around a hall, or atrium. This hall was open to the sky with a cistern beneath it and the rooms faced inwards. Other buildings, enlarged from the 2nd century BC onwards, are distinguished by the addition or incorporation of features of Greek houses, such as rectangular courtyards and gardens, surrounded by a columned, covered walk.

Pompeii possessed an extraordinarily wide range of items of art or craftsmanship, including silverware, jewellery, and portraiture and other sculpture in marble and other stones and in bronze. But the most exciting discovery was Pompeii's wall-painting. During the final 200 years, varied and richly coloured murals were painted on the walls of buildings, including private houses.

Critical analysis and research by archaeologists and art historians have made it possible to see how styles and themes changed over the years. Between about 200 and 80 BC, most wall painting tended to imitate stone masonry. However, between about 80 and 30 BC, a dramatic change occurred. Wall surfaces were often framed by paintings of solid-looking features, such as pillars, window frames and doorways. In the panels were painted vistas of buildings or landscapes, often portraying Greek mythological scenes.

Following this period, the architecture becomes fantastic, while in the fourth and final stage from the time of Nero, elements from the previous two are mixed and contemporary scenes are included. The panels, containing architectural scenes and figures, often convey an illusion of reality and depth. These painted Pompeian ensembles give us yet another insight into ancient life.

Leptis Magna

LIBYA

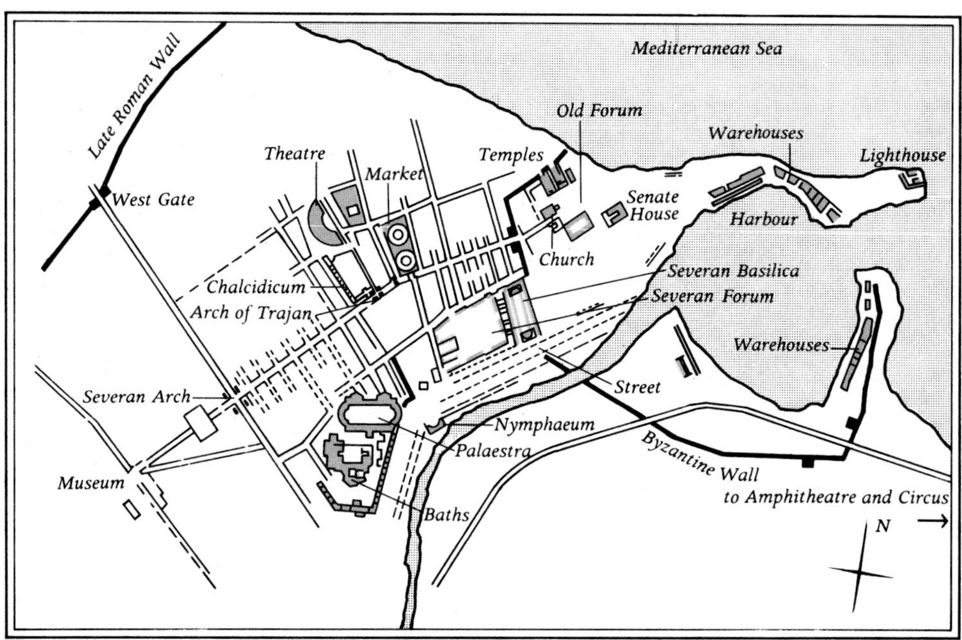

The ancient city of Leptis Magna lay on the North African coast in a desolate part of what is now Libya. It is about 140 kilometres east of the Libyan capital Tripoli.

With the arid Sahara forming its hinterland, the site was at first made habitable only by the presence of water, from wells, from rainfall and sometimes from the Wadi Lebda. Although the Phoenicians originally founded the city, it became prominent under the Romans and the present ruins are primarily those of a flourishing Roman imperial city of the 1st to early 3rd centuries AD.

Leptis Magna was abandoned in late antiquity. Its very whereabouts were forgotten in Europe until a curious event brought it back to Western notice. Pirates captured a learned Frenchman and held him as a slave at Tripoli from 1668 until 1676. On his release he wrote a history of the area that included a description of Leptis Magna, which he had clearly visited. A trickle of other hardy scholars followed, while the ruins were plundered for material for buildings in Tripoli, Paris and London. Serious archaeological exploration, inspired by the obvious importance of the site and the quality of its surviving monuments, began with the Italian occupation of Libya from 1913.

Uncovering the site

The site presents comparatively few problems to the excavator for several reasons. The city stood on dry sandy soil, its major buildings were made of stone and it was not re-occupied after its abandonment in late antiquity. Further, it was covered only by wind-blown sand, a dry and fairly gentle blanket which helped to preserve the carved stone, cement and plaster beneath. Indications of where to dig are provided by the outlines of structures and streets visible in the sand and by ruins which still rise above the surface. Hence the main problems are the removal of vast quantities of sand, the preservation of stone structures and the conservation of artefacts, particularly marble sculptures, mosaics and wall painting.

The first man to explore the site scientifically was Salvatore Aurigemma, who worked there between 1913 and 1919. Systematic excavation began in 1920 under a leading figure of Romano-African archaeology, the Italian Pietro Romanelli. He was followed in turn by other Italian directors.

In 1951 Libya became independent and the Libyan Department of Antiquities was created. It set about the conservation of the monuments, with continuing Italian cooperation. Many monuments have been restored, including, recently, the Four-Way arch. Meanwhile, from 1946, British archaeological missions and the British Society for Libyan Studies have also been at work, under John Ward-Perkins and his successors. The British have taken a particular interest in the buildings of the Severan period (the early 3rd century AD) and in the numerous inscriptions found. A museum was erected on the site, but the most notable finds, particularly the finest Roman marble sculptures, are now in Tripoli museum.

The city's history

Information provided by monuments and inscriptions from the site, combined with references in Greek and Roman texts, helps us to piece together the city's history. Leptis Magna began life, perhaps by the 7th century BC, as a trading post established by Semitic colonists from Phoenicia. It came under the general control of the great Phoenician city of Carthage. A Greek attempt to gain a foothold nearby in about 520 BC was soon repulsed, and the population and character of Leptis remained Punic (Carthaginian) into Roman times.

Eventually Leptis became the administrative centre of a group of three colonies named the 'Tripolis', which the Greeks called 'the Trading Posts' (Emporia). The other two colonies were Oea (Tripoli) and Sabratha. They acquired a constitution with chief magistrates called 'shophetim' in the Punic language, and Latinized to 'sufetes', and collectors, called 'muhazim' along Carthaginian lines. Relics of this period are few. There are traces of a warehouse, some later Punic inscriptions, a little sculpture and some Punic graves. Doubtless the Punic town extended from the Old (Roman) Forum and west harbour area over to the left bank of the Wadi Lebda, which is as yet unexcavated.

After Rome destroyed Carthage in 146 BC, the 'Emporia' were controlled by Numidia, a kingdom in what is now north-eastern Algeria, and trade with Rome began. Forty years later Leptis made a treaty of 'friendship and alliance' with Rome. Siding with the losers in the Roman civil wars, the three towns were incorporated by Julius Caesar into the newly created Roman province of New Africa in 46 BC. The towns were fined and punished by a reduction to 'stipendiary' or subject status. After further fighting, Octavian emerged in 31 BC as the outright victor. He took the name Augustus and became first emperor of the Romans, reigning until AD 14. The three towns were incorporated into an enlarged province of Africa and settled down into a long period of peace and prosperity, retaining their Punic constitutions. Leptis also received a limited 'freedom'.

The first architectural blossoming at Leptis came under Augustus, as dated monuments demonstrate. Limestone and sandstone were the favoured materials. The core of the expanding Roman town was the Old Forum, a rectangular space paved by about 5 BC. This old forum may have been erected over an earlier market area. At its north-west end, in normal Roman fashion, architects built temples, the ruins of which still stand. The designs were similar to those found in Rome, with a frontal approach, high podium, pillared porch and hall for statuary. On its east side stood the basilica, a building for business and the administration of justice. From here to the south-west ran the typically Roman axial main street, or cardo, the basis for the division of space into rectangular areas (insulae).

In 9–8 BC a market was erected at the expense of a wealthy local citizen, Annobal Rufus. Its delightful design comprised two octagonal pavilions with counters, one of which is marked with standard measures, in a porticoed rectangular court. Rufus also sponsored a fine sandstone theatre in AD 1–2. Another citizen built the limestone, porticoed Chalcidicum in AD 11–12, which was probably another market.

This burst of building continued into the reign of Tiberius (AD 14–37), with a temple of Rome and Augustus in the Old Forum, two arches and paving for all the streets. Before long an amphitheatre was added, the largest in North Africa. A charming limestone arch erected to the emperor Trajan in AD 109–110 perhaps commemorated the raising of the city's status to that of a 'colony'. A Trajanic forum and basilica are also mentioned in an inscription.

A fine complex, the Hadrianic Baths, was dedicated during the reign of Hadrian in AD 126–127, and restored with increased use of marble under Commodus (AD 180–193). The symmetrical plan, with an open-air swimming bath, a cold room (frigidarium), a warm bathroom (tepidarium), a barrel-vaulted hot room (caldarium), changing rooms and well preserved latrines, all echo the great baths of imperial Rome.

But the most splendid buildings were those donated by her greatest sons, the emperor Septimius Severus (AD 193–211) and his dynasty (until AD 235), to honour his birthplace, to which he granted 'Italian' status – that is, it received exemption from land-tax. The harbour was refurbished and, on reclaimed land between the Wadi and cardo, there arose a magnificent new urban complex, a colonnaded street, an exotic fountain (nymphaeum), and a splendid forum with adjoining basilica for public and legal business. The Forum was a rectangular space, about 100 by 60 metres. It incorporated an imposing temple of the Italian type. The decoration was particularly lavish, with statuary, mythological reliefs on the column bases in the front of the temple and, between limestone arches of the arcaded colonnade around the court, marble reliefs of Medusa heads. The Basilica was enriched with carved marble *pilasters* inside, again depicting religious figures and scenes. At a major street crossing in the city, a four-way arch was erected. It was covered with figured reliefs celebrating the achievements of the Severan house and its deities. Across the Wadi an earlier structure, the Hunting Baths, was refurbished with wall-painting and mosaics.

The early 3rd century was the high point of the city's fortunes, because the favour it had received at Severan hands was more than its local economy could sustain. During the following 50 years of anarchy the inhabited area shrank and sands began to encroach. Economic decline was made worse by tribal unrest, particularly in the 4th century as the empire became Christianized. The 'late Roman wall' was built in response to this unrest. Worse followed in 455 when Germans of the Vandal tribe occupied North Africa and demolished the city walls. The Vandal kingdom lasted until the East Roman (or 'Byzantine') emperor Justinian took Africa and established a feeble Byzantine administration (AD 533–643). Justinian's work at Leptis included the enclosure of the shrunken town within a wall and the raising of several churches. The Arab invasion of AD 643 brought the end of Leptis Magna.

The most significant archaeological discoveries concerned the marble relief decoration of the Severan buildings. Here both materials and craftsmen turned out to have been imported from Asia Minor, as the types of marble, style of execution and choice of motifs all indicate. This use of craftsmen from one province of the empire in another, and their unusual work, has shed much light on Roman art and imperial patronage.

Below: Fine sandstone theatre dedicated by Annobal Rufus in AD 1–2, with semi-circular seating and a stage decorated with statuary and columns.

Roman Africa

The excavations at Leptis, together with passages in ancient literature, provide vivid glimpses of life in the city, particularly between the time of Augustus and that of Septimius Severus. The city lay in the province of Africa which was administered by a governor of 'proconsular' rank. The province was divided into three sections or 'dioceses', of which the Tripolitana regio, including Leptis, Oea and Sabratha, probably formed one.

The city paid a normal range of Roman taxes through two departments. One was for taxes on seaborne goods and death duties. The other was for land goods and taxes on the freeing and sale of slaves. Roman governors relied heavily on individual cities and towns and their officials for the smooth running of imperial administration and the collection of taxes. As a result they allowed the previous Phoenician constitution, with magistrates and council, to continue unchanged. However, after Trajan had granted 'colonial' status, titles were Romanized and the still widely-spoken Punic language ceased to be used for official inscriptions. And, later, special officials, called curatores, were sent by Commodus to restore the Hadrianic Baths.

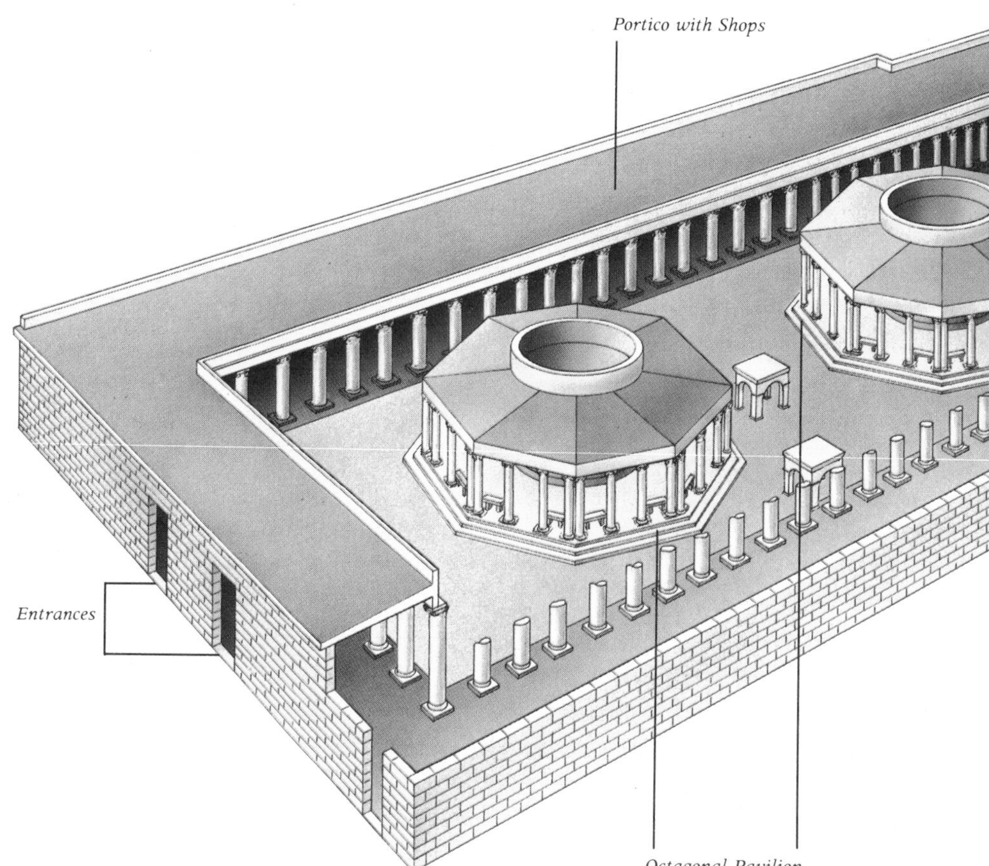

The people

The population was primarily Punic in character, and divided into the strata usual in a Roman city. These were a small, rich, educated and politically dominant landowning élite; an urban bourgeoisie; a proletariat, and a mass of domestic and agricultural slaves. Free adult males normally had local citizenship. They were divided into 11 voting-groups for electing annually the local magistrates. Law and order needed little enforcement within the city. Major troubles were usually the result of inroads by Berber tribesmen, who were held at bay by detachments of the imperial army elsewhere in the province.

City life in general imitated that of Rome. The Forum provided a focus. Here speeches, elections and general gossiping took place, while various public and legal business was transacted in the adjoining Basilica. The lavish Hadrianic Baths provided another popular place for meeting as well as bathing. Its fine communal latrine, upholstered in marble, is a reminder of the Roman disregard for privacy in this respect.

Other forms of Roman entertainment were also provided. There was Annobal Rufus's theatre for mimes and ballets, and a circus for races between four-horse chariots driven by charioteers each sporting one of four standard colours (red, white, green and blue). There was also an amphitheatre for combats between wild beasts and human beings.

Above: Marble relief of Septimius Severus and his sons entering Leptis. From his Arch: c. AD 203–207.

Farming, trade and technology

The city's economy was based on agriculture and trade. The Carthaginians had introduced a money economy and olive farming. From that time, olives remained the basis of an increasingly successful local agriculture, supplemented by figs, almonds, peaches, pomegranates and vines. In fact Julius Caesar imposed on the city an annual fine of three

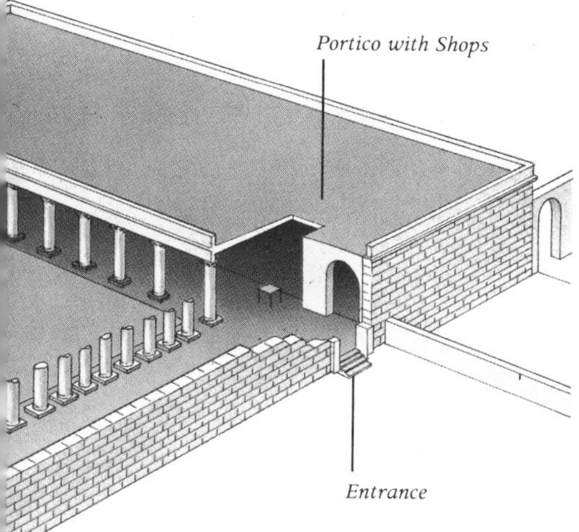

Left: Reconstructed view of the remarkable Market of Leptis, built by a leading citizen, Annobal Rufus, in 9-8 BC. The design of two pavilions within a rectangle is also found at Pompeii. Annobal Rufus first built the two octagonal pavilions. The surrounding porticoes were added in AD 31–37. Around AD 200 the south pavilion was rebuilt in marble, further entrances were added, and the porticoes were given granite Corinthian columns. Market stalls occupied the pavilions and porticoes.

Left: The ruined remains of Annobal Rufus's splendid market place. Rufus's two pavilions in fine grey limestone had central circular drums, with platforms for displaying wares. Surrounding these were octagonal colonnades with capitals of local Ionic, or 'Romano-Punic', type. Between the columns were further stone benches, visible here, on which could be displayed the various commodities for sale.

Above: Leopard-hunting fresco in the cold room (frigidarium) of the Hunting Baths: 3rd century AD.

million pounds of olive oil for backing the wrong side during the civil wars. The great single crop olive farms which spread across the hinterland in Roman times were doubtless often owned by residents of Leptis and elsewhere, who ran them through bailiffs and cheap hired labour or slaves, or through renting them to tenants who paid in kind. On the coast there seems to have been some mixed farming.

Further wealth was brought by the great trans-Saharan caravan trade, some of which passed through Leptis. Items travelling northwards included gold, precious stones, ebony, ivory (commemorated by a sculptured elephant in a Leptis street), negro slaves, wild beasts and Tripolitanian ostriches. Items which were taken southwards into the interior included Roman pottery, lamps and glassware. A well-known product of Leptis itself was garum, a strong sauce made from the entrails of salted fish.

A wide range of simple technological skills was present at Leptis, particularly agricultural. Further, Phoenician skills in water management were developed in the Roman period. Concrete dams or barrages were built across wadis to control the unpredictable flow. An important group of works was concentrated on the Wadi Caam, 20 kilometres east of Leptis, and from the reservoir here, an underground cement-lined aqueduct carried water to Leptis.

In the city, from the time of Augustus onwards, the cutting and carving of the local limestone and sandstone for building became an important craft. However, for grand projects involving the use of imported marble, highly skilled craftsmen were brought in from elsewhere.

Beliefs and customs

Religious beliefs and customs reflected the largely Punic character of the population. The people continued to worship Phoenician deities, although often under the guise of Roman names. The patron deities of Leptis were Liber Pater, who was really the Phoenician Satrapis, and the equivalent to the Greek and Roman Bacchus, or Dionysus, and Hercules, the Phoenician Melqart. Liber Pater had an Augustan temple facing the Old Forum, and both deities were pictured in the Severan temple and basilica reliefs.

The Roman imperial cult – the worship of deceased, deified emperors and of the emperor's family or spirit – arrived with the Old Forum temple dedicated to Rome and to the dead Augustus in AD 14–19. Another small shrine was dedicated to the 'Di Augusti' (deified emperors) in AD 43. The huge temple in the Severan Forum may well have been dedicated to the Septimian family, or 'gens', from which the emperor sprang, although no inscription survives. The north Syrian god Jupiter Dolichenus was given a fine temple above the harbour of Leptis, while the Phrygian 'Magna Mater' (Great Mother, or Cybele) had a shrine by the Old Forum.

Christianity also arrived. Leptis had a bishop by the end of the 2nd century, and, from the 4th century onwards, Christianity became the dominant religion of the city, outlasting paganism. This was reflected in the appearance of sizable basilical churches, such as the Old Forum church (a converted Trajanic temple).

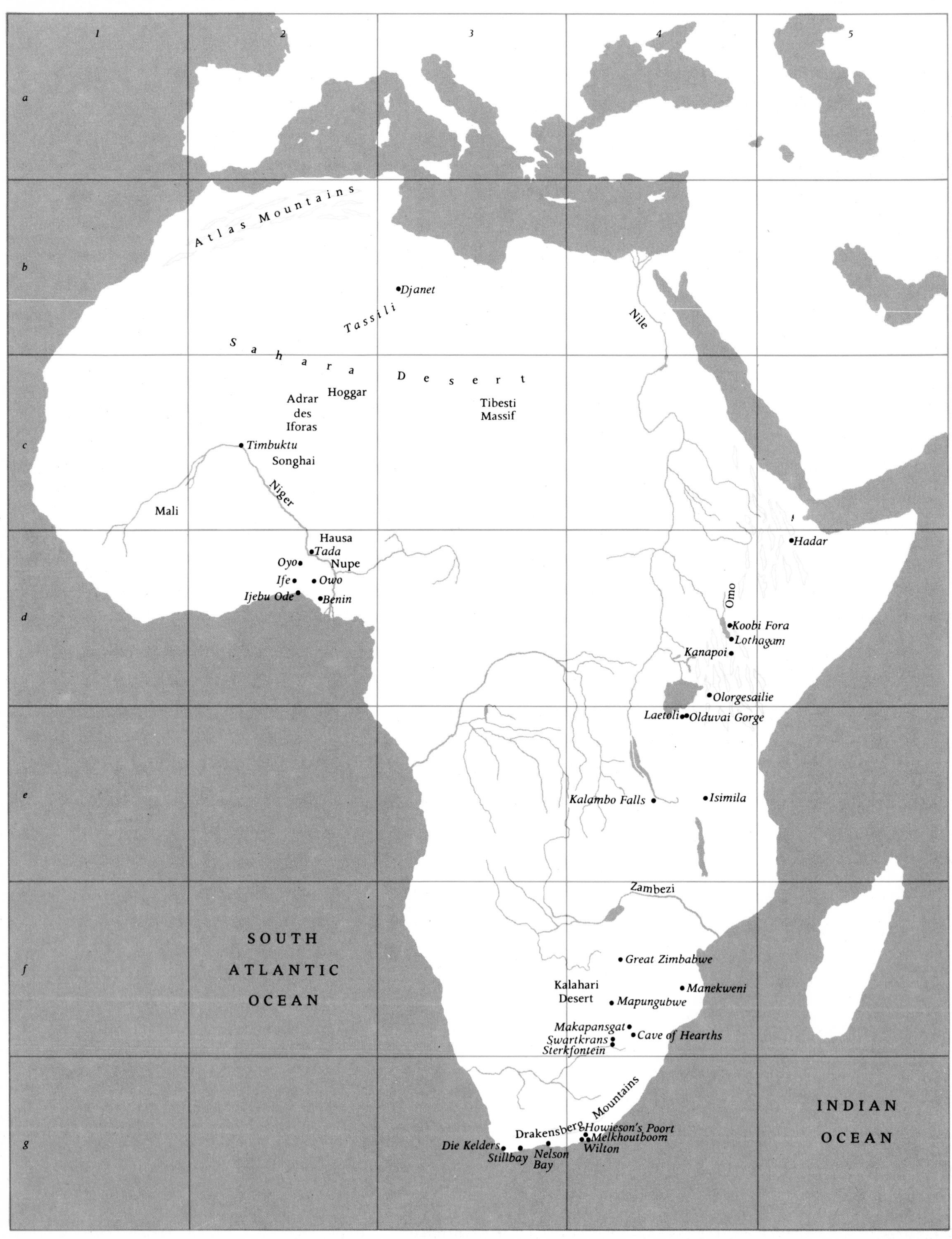
1
2
3
4
5
a
b
c
d
e
f
g
Atlas Mountains
Djanet
Tassili
Sahara Desert
Hoggar
Adrar des Iforas
Tibesti Massif
Nile
Timbuktu
Songhai
Niger
Mali
Hausa
Tada
Nupe
Oyo
Ife
Owo
Ijebu Ode
Benin
Hadar
Omo
Koobi Fora
Lothagam
Kanapoi
Olorgesailie
Laetoli
Olduvai Gorge
Kalambo Falls
Isimila
Zambezi
SOUTH ATLANTIC OCEAN
Great Zimbabwe
Kalahari Desert
Manekweni
Mapungubwe
Makapansgat
Swartkrans
Sterkfontein
Cave of Hearths
Drakensberg Mountains
Howieson's Poort
Melkhoutboom
Wilton
Die Kelders
Stillbay
Nelson Bay
INDIAN OCEAN

Africa

2,000,000 BC-AD1600

To illustrate the archaeology of Africa, sites have been chosen from the Sahara Desert, Nigeria, Tanzania, Zimbabwe and South Africa. Olduvai Gorge, in Tanzania, is among the most important in the world for the part it has played in unravelling the story of early man. At the southern end of the continent, Nelson Bay Cave serves to illuminate the history of the indigenous peoples long before any European settlers arrived. The Saharan sites show examples of artistic achievement thousands of years ago. Those in Nigeria and Zimbabwe provide instances of pre-European urbanization, metallurgy and long-distance trade.

Olduvai Gorge is justly renowned for the discoveries made there which throw light upon the emergence of man. As a result, it is now part of the East African tourist route, and thousands of visitors annually make a pilgrimage there. It also has a special place in the history of archaeological research in Africa, as one of the first sites outside North and South Africa to be investigated by a professional archaeologist – thanks to the fact that Louis Leakey's home was close by in Kenya. Olduvai has now received attention for over 50 years, and illustrates how archaeological results of the greatest value may only be achieved after a planned programme of many years' research, rather than from one or two seasons' work, however lucky or brilliantly executed. Olduvai also illustrates superbly the difference made to archaeology by the post-war revolution in chronology brought about by *radiometric dating*. To understand human evolution we need to know accurately when different developments took place. Thanks to *potassium-argon dating* and the hominid footprints discovered at Laetoli, not far from Olduvai, we now know that at least 1,000,000 years separated the achievement by man's ancestors of an upright, bipedal walking gait and the making of the earliest stone tools. Formerly it had been supposed that upright walking had concurrently or immediately freed the hands for the development of manual dexterity and increased cerebral control, resulting in tool-making and brain-enlargement. Africa is now the continent most favoured as 'the cradle of mankind', with the hypothesis that hominids arose east of a line from Khartoum to Cape Town, evolved and diversified there, and spread thence to Asia, Europe and other parts of Africa in the early part of the Pleistocene period.

Environmental change, particularly that resulting from climatic causes, is regarded as the agent most likely to have exerted those selective pressures which favoured the emergence and development of man's adaptive powers. Such environmental change can still be seen working at Nelson Bay Cave and at the Saharan sites. Nelson Bay Cave itself was formed by sea-wave action when sea-level was higher than at present, more than 100,000 years before it was first occupied by man. From about 100,000 years ago, man had the use of fire and took advantage of caves and rock-shelters as ready-made living sites – unlike his Olduvai predecessors. The work at Nelson Bay Cave is a good example of modern archaeological practice; the concern not simply with artefacts, but also with the use of many different scientific techniques to collect and analyse all kinds of data which help to reconstruct the contemporary environment. Efforts are then made to interpret in behavioural terms the relationship between this environment and the archaeological remains, throwing light upon the way of life of the people concerned. The Saharan sites, which also give so much evidence of environmental change, not only show the artistic abilities of the people who lived there, but also contribute evidence of a major economic change in Africa – the change from dependence on food hunted or collected to a subsistence in which pastoralism and domestic cattle also played a part. This change had important social as well as economic consequences, as for the first time it made possible the accumulation of wealth – in the hands of whoever could gain and control it.

The centralization of wealth was one of the conditions for the creation of Great Zimbabwe and of ancient Ife. In the former, cattle still represented an important reservoir of wealth, but in both societies the domestication of indigenous crops had developed to the point of making possible a large permanent settlement which was also a centre of religious ritual and of long-distance trade. In both cases there developed a considerable measure of social stratification, and works of art were produced by skilled craftsmen to add to the prestige of rulers and the impressiveness of ritual.

Olduvai Gorge
TANZANIA

South-east of Lake Victoria in East Africa lies the high grassland plain of Serengeti, in northern Tanzania. For hundreds of thousands of years, rivers of part of this plain drained into an inland lake of fluctuating size and position. From some two million years ago, early men and near-men lived around the lake shores. They did so because, like other animals which lived in this rather arid area, they could not survive far from water, having no means to carry it.

As the lake rose and fell and changed its position, sometimes as the result of earthquakes and volcanic activity, deposits of sand, gravel and silt brought in by the rivers and streams were laid down on the lake bed. Sometimes deposits of volcanic ash and cinder were formed when nearby volcanoes erupted. These various deposits grew hundreds of metres thick, and bones of animals and near-men which lived there, as well as some stone tools of early men, were incorporated in the deposits. The lake finally dried up, but the flat surface of the grassy plain concealed the thick stream- and lake-deposits below, together with all the keys to man's early history which they contained. However, as a result of further earth movements, a new depression formed farther east. As a result, a new stream cut a gorge about 75 metres deep through the old deposits. On the sides of the gorge were stratified layers of lake- and stream-deposits, containing fossil bones and artefacts. It was a giant natural excavation, revealing a section through the water-laid and volcanic deposits. The gorge was named Olduvai by the local Masai herdsmen after a type of wild cactus which flowered there in profusion. When the gorge first became known to Europeans the name was anglicized to Oldoway, but has now reverted to the more correct form.

When Tanganyika (the mainland part of Tanzania) was a German colony before World War I, a German entomologist named Kattwinkel became the first man to make the gorge known to science. He is said to have nearly fallen over its precipitous side when chasing butterflies on the Serengeti plain. Kattwinkel found some fossils, which had been eroded out of the old lake beds exposed in the side of the gorge, and took them back to Berlin. As a result, in 1913 the German geologist Hans Reck visited the gorge and revealed it as an important source of fossil fauna of the *Pleistocene* epoch. World War I intervened, and Reck was unable to return to Olduvai until 1931. By this time Louis Leakey was 28 and had begun his career as an archaeologist and palaeontologist.

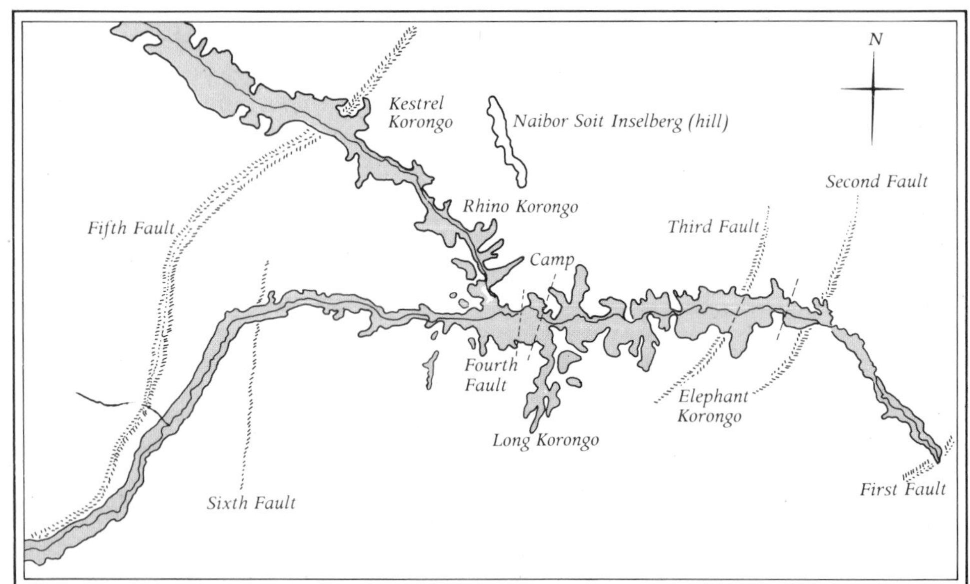

The work of the Leakeys

Leakey was born of missionary parents in neighbouring Kenya. He went to school in England at the age of 16 and on to Cambridge University. As part of his postgraduate work he carried out archaeological researches in Kenya, and became interested in Olduvai Gorge across the Tanganyika border. Reck revisited Olduvai with Leakey in 1931 and, in a scientific sense, 'bequeathed' the gorge to him. Reck had said that there was no evidence of human culture, namely artefacts, in the gorge deposits; there were only fossil bones. Leakey soon demonstrated that this was not true. In fact early Stone Age tools were abundant and there was much evidence of artificial stone flaking.

In 1945 Leakey was appointed Curator of the Coryndon Museum in Nairobi. With the museum as a base, Louis Leakey and his wife Mary conducted widespread archaeological excavations and researches in the field, although there was little money available. Some of their work was conducted at Olduvai Gorge. There they collected fossils and artefacts, studied the geology, and carried out small-scale excavations. Studies of Stone Age tools were dominated at that time by an evolutionary concept of development proceeding through a succession of stages, each of which was characterized by a 'type fossil'. As a result of his studies of stone tools from the various layers at Olduvai, Leakey published a scheme of 11 stages in 1951. The stages ranged from the crudest choppers – cobbles with a few flakes struck off to make a sharp cutting edge – to a series of 'hand-axes' (well-made, oval-shaped and pointed general-purpose cutting tools) and 'cleavers' (straight-edged cutting tools). Except for two bits of cranium and a couple of teeth, no bones of fossil men or near-men were found before 1959, in spite of the large number of fossil animal bones recovered.

Views on human evolution at this time were divided. The famous Piltdown forgery had not yet been exposed, although experts regarded it as increasingly anomalous, because it fitted less and less well into the human 'family tree' as more and more Australopithecine remains were discovered. Piltdown 'man' had been 'discovered' in 1912 and it was not until 1953 that it was shown to consist of a comparatively modern human skull and an ape's jaw. Before World War I, people had supposed that the 'missing link' in human evolution was a creature with a well-developed brain but with many ape-like characteristics. The theory was that man's brain had become more developed than those of his ape-like ancestors, and that it was the brain which had 'led the way' in human evolution. It was only after a brain of human type and size had developed that other human characteristics began to appear and the ape-like ones to disappear.

However, fossils found in South Africa from 1924 onwards began to show that this was not how things actually happened. As a group these fossils came to be called the Australopithecines, or 'Southern Apes', although they were given a bewildering variety of scientific names at first. These creatures had small brains, about a third the size of modern human brains. Nevertheless, they habitually walked on two feet in the human style, rather than using the forelimbs as well, as apes usually do when on the ground. Most of the remains consisted of skulls, jaws and teeth, because these are the toughest bony parts of the body and have a better chance of survival as fossils than other bones. However, it was possible to infer the habitual upright gait of Australopithecines from the shape of the base of the skull and the angle at which it must have sat on the spine. Scientists also found that the Australopithecines' front teeth were modified, from the ape-like form, in the human direction.

There seemed to be two types of Australopithecines. One was slender, light-boned and supposedly omnivorous. It is sometimes referred to as the 'gracile' Australopithecine. The other, called the 'robust' type, was thick-boned, heavily built and supposedly vegetarian. Hence the genus *Australopithecus* came to be divided into two species, *A. africanus* (the gracile type) and *A. robustus* (the robust type). Some people suggested that these were not two contemporaneous species but merely the female and male of one. A few still hold this interpretation.

One day at Olduvai in 1959, Louis Leakey stayed in camp because he had fever. On an exposed surface of Bed I, the lowest of the rock beds in the gorge, Mary Leakey saw embedded the palate of an undoubted hominid (a man or man-like creature). She rushed back to camp and told Louis. Fever forgotten, he went to the site and confirmed its importance. After a wait of three days for the arrival of a film team from Nairobi, the palate and the surrounding area were excavated, and the greater part of a hominid skull was found. This skull, when restored, proved to be comparable to the robust Australopithecines of South Africa. Leakey named it *'Zinjanthropus boisei'*. 'Zinj' or 'Zanj' is an old name for East Africa, so Zinjanthropus means 'Man of East Africa', while the term 'boisei' was in honour of Charles Boise who had put up the money for the Leakeys' research at the time that the skull was found. It was the most complete Australopithecine skull found up to that time, and, because of its enormous jaws and huge molar teeth, it was popularly nicknamed 'Nutcracker Man'. Scientifically it has now been placed in the Australopithecine group and is properly called *Australopithecus (Zinjanthropus) boisei.*

The ascent of man

This find marked a turning point in the course of researches into man's origins in Africa. Not only did it mean that much more money became available for more extensive work at Olduvai, largely from the American National Geographical Association, but it also stimulated work in suitable fossil-bearing localities in northern and southern Ethiopia and in northern Kenya, together with further detailed investigations at the South African Australopithecine sites. All these places have yielded a veritable harvest of fossil hominids. The interpretation of the finds is still proceeding and experts are far from being in agreement about them.

Various scientific aids have come to the assistance of the archaeologist, the most important of which are *potassium-argon dating* and *palaeomagnetism*. By potassium-argon dating, scientists can measure how long ago a volcanic deposit was laid down, whether in the form of a laval flow, like basalt, or in the form of an ash or cinder layer, which geologists call a 'tuff'. By a happy chance, volcanoes in the neighbourhood of Olduvai, and of the Ethiopian and Kenyan sites, erupted at intervals of tens and hundreds of thousands of years. The volcanic deposits were 'sandwiched' between the water-laid, fossil-bearing deposits. Hence, although the sands, gravels and silts cannot be dated, their age can be bracketed between two datable volcanic deposits. The South African cave sites do not have this advantage. But in recent years, advances have been made in dating them by palaeomagnetism and by the faunal evidence. At Olduvai *Australopithecus boisei* has been firmly dated between the basalt at the base of Bed I, dated at 1.9 million years old, and the tuffs above which average 1.7 million years in age.

Not far from where the skull of 'Nutcracker Man' was found, at a slightly lower level in Bed I, other fossil remains were found. They included a juvenile mandible contrasting strongly with what we should expect from *A. robustus* because it is much more like that of *A. africanus;* parts of a skull suggesting a size slightly bigger than *A. africanus;* and hand bones and an almost complete foot. The hand bones are quite close to those of modern man, and the foot indicates habitual upright walking, with shin bones that support this theory. The remains came from several individuals. Leakey claimed that they were sufficiently 'human' to be classified in the genus *Homo* and he called the species *habilis*, or 'Handy man'. Other palaeontologists have maintained that *H. habilis* is just an East African version of the gracile Australopithecine, *A. africanus*. One of their reasons was that they did not accept the possibility of two co-existent man-like creatures in the Lower Pleistocene epoch at Olduvai. Leakey thought that it was possible, particularly if the two creatures had different life-styles and occupied separate ecological niches.

From about 1.5 million years ago, a new type of early man, which scientists call *H. erectus*, appears in a number of places in Africa. *H. erectus* had a fully-upright pelvis and a brain that was twice as large as that of the Australopithecines, but only about two-thirds the size of modern human brains. Bones of early men of this type were found in the upper part of Bed II at Olduvai. These remains have an estimated age range of 1,000,000–700,000 years, although more recent finds of two *H. erectus* skulls from northern Kenya have been dated to 1.5 million years ago. As yet, the only *H. erectus* remains found outside Africa are about 750,000 years younger.

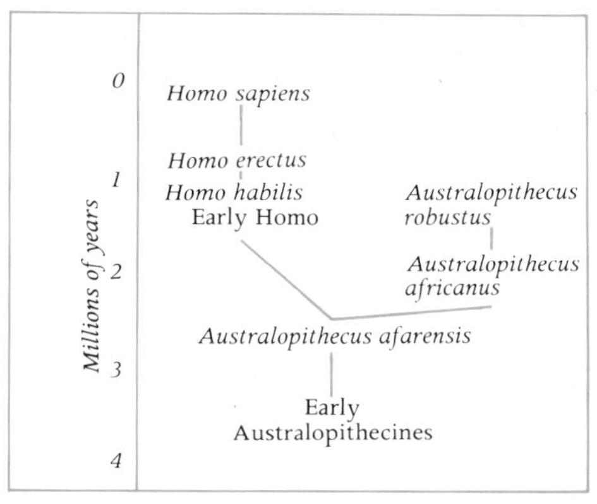

Scientists had usually traced the ancestry of modern man (*H. sapiens*) through *H. erectus* to *Australopithecus africanus*. It had been supposed that in the Lower Pleistocene epoch, it was *A. africanus* who made the stone tools and not *A. robustus*. With the discovery of *H. habilis* Leakey claimed that neither of these Australopithecines was ancestral to *H. erectus* and neither was a tool-maker.

Shortly before Louis Leakey died in 1972, his son Richard was excavating east of Lake Turkana in northern Kenya, in deposits extending further back in time than those at Olduvai. There he discovered a skull, known as ER 1470, which was more than 2 million years old but showed remarkable human characteristics. Since then, other finds appear to confirm this sort of antiquity for a human ancestor, which would, therefore, seem to be ancestral to *H. habilis* and *H. erectus*, leading on to modern man. With the new dating of the South African fossils, it is now possible to see that *A. africanus* dates to 3 to 2.5 million years ago and *A. robustus* to 1 to 1.5 million years ago. Hence *taxonomists* are now inclined to believe that *A. africanus* is ancestral to *A. robustus*. Discoveries at Hadar in Ethiopia have revealed an upright walking hominid, which is believed to be ancestral to the two known Australopithecines. This hominid was dated to 3 million years ago and named *Australopithecus afarensis*. The earliest ancestral Australopithecine remains come from west of Lake Turkana and are dated to 5.5 and 4 million years ago. It looks now, therefore, as if *A. africanus* and *A. robustus* were not in the line of human ancestry. Thus a human descent 'tree' can be illustrated as above.

The precise taxonomic position of many of the large number of recently discovered hominid fossils is often a matter of debate among the experts. Hence the way in which the genealogical 'tree' of human ancestry should be drawn remains controversial. There is no doubt that a clearer pattern will emerge following further research.

The First Steps

The significance of Olduvai lies both in the discoveries that were made there by the Leakeys and in the way these discoveries, combined with those in South Africa, turned attention from Asia to Africa as 'the cradle of mankind'. These discoveries also shed light on man's origins and gave tremendous stimulus to such studies in other parts of Africa, to the financing of research in this field and to popular interest in the subject.

How did the early men and near-men live at Olduvai? Around two million years ago, the climate was probably a little wetter than today. The Australopithecines probably lived in a terrain covered with rather lusher vegetation, in the midst of a strange collection of animals. Many belonged to the same species that now live in East Africa. But there were also unfamiliar and now extinct animals, including giant baboons, tree-cropping chalicotheres (hoofed mammals), the elephant-like *Deinotherium* and an oddly-antlered relative of the giraffe. Lions and hyaenas, as well as the now extinct sabre-toothed tiger, preyed upon all this game, and their prey would have included the hominids. The Australopithecines and early men had long adapted their way of life to the African savanna and were predominantly vegetarians. The lake shores and banks of streams supported gallery forests which helped to supply this vegetarian diet.

The use of rudimentary tools had probably long been established as an habitual behaviour pattern among the earliest Australopithecines, just as it is among chimpanzees, who, for example, use grass stems and twigs to 'fish' for termites in a termites' nest. But who made the stone tools of two million years ago? We do not know whether the Australopithecines were tool-makers as well as tool-users, but the tools were most likely made by early representatives of the genus *Homo*. These are probably best described as

Above: Mary Leakey examining hominid footprints, 3,700,000 years old, made by three individuals including a child. They are preserved in volcanic ash, now 15 centimetres deep, at Laetoli, Tanzania.

Above: Quartz biface showing (left) one flat face and (right) a side view of the sharp cutting edge. This type of stone tool had a long history, and was formerly called a 'hand-axe' because it is believed that it was not hafted, but held in the hand, in the manner shown for skinning (right).

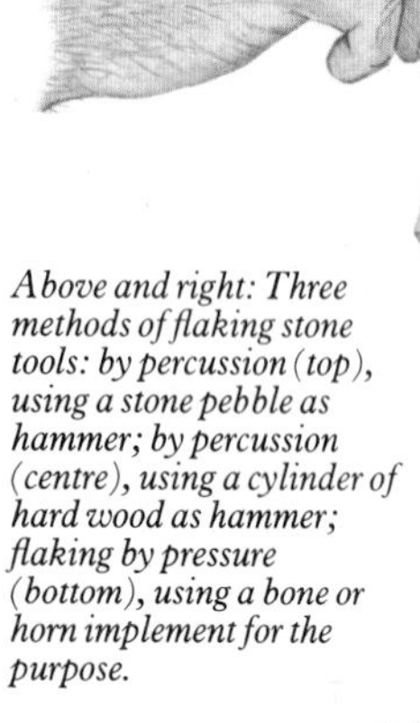

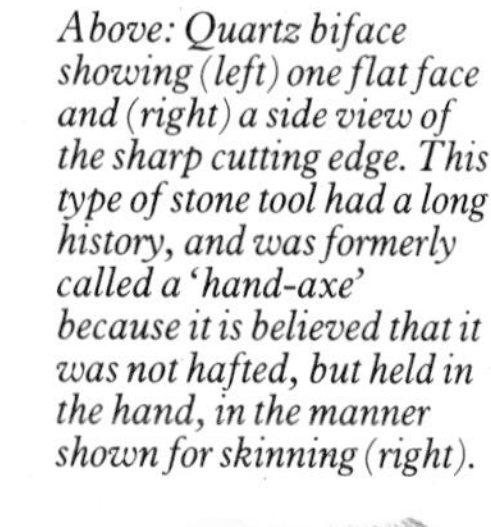

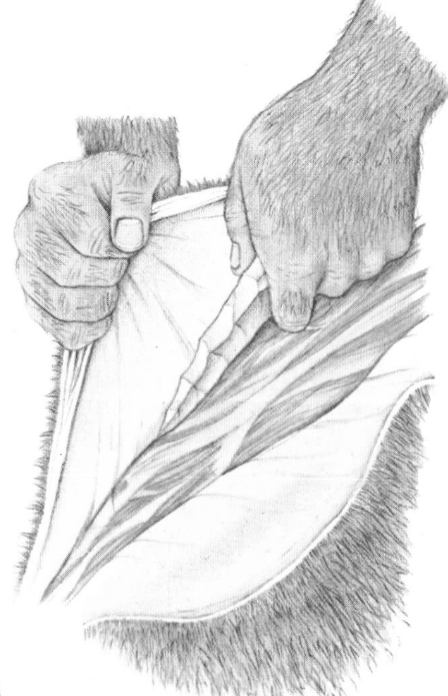

Above and right: Three methods of flaking stone tools: by percussion (top), using a stone pebble as hammer; by percussion (centre), using a cylinder of hard wood as hammer; flaking by pressure (bottom), using a bone or horn implement for the purpose.

scavenger hunter-gatherers, and the stone tools helped them to procure food. It is interesting to speculate whether there was any competition for food or territory between Australopithecines and early men and whether confrontations ever took place.

Social innovations

To begin with, early men would have hunted small and slow animals, but even this activity involved important modifications of behaviour and social organization. This would have been the task of the males, who were stronger and fleeter, unencumbered with children. Therefore, instead of every adult foraging for himself or herself, the first sexual division of labour would have arisen, with men doing the hunting and women and children doing most of the foraging, which almost certainly still provided the larger proportion of the diet. Such a division of labour led to the practice of sharing food, which was a profound social modification. Because hunters had to travel over considerable distances, certainly farther than pregnant or nursing mothers and small children could move, a home base, however temporary, became necessary. This was another important social innovation. In Bed I at Olduvai an artificially piled-up circle of lava blocks was uncovered. This may represent the foundation of some kind of shelter, perhaps the world's oldest 'home' of which we have evidence.

Development of tools

In deposits formed around a million years ago, by which time *Homo erectus* had become well-established in Africa, we can recognize tools of a more sophisticated design than the cruder 'Oldowan' choppers and flake tools found in the lower levels of Bed I at Olduvai. These, known to archaeologists as 'Acheulean', include bifaces (or 'handaxes') – oval or pointed tools skilfully flaked over both surfaces to give a sharp cutting edge – and 'cleavers', which are similarly fashioned but which have a straight, transverse cutting edge. Although Acheulean-type tools appear later than the Oldowan and are generally associated with *Homo erectus*, the succession is by no means clear-cut. This is because rudimentary bifaces begin to appear in the Developed Oldowan stone industries.

Partly as a result of excavations and studies carried out at Olduvai, the old concept of rigid stages of tool development characterized by 'type-fossils' gave way to a consideration of the characteristics of complete *assemblages* of artefacts, taking them all into account and the relative proportions in which various tools occurred. This approach has been further modified by the idea of the 'activity variant' – that is, that the characteristics of a particular assemblage are determined by the activity that they represent, such as butchering a carcass or preparing vegetable foods, and that the same people may have used one set of tools for one job and another for another. Microscopic examination of the damage along the edges of the tools has helped to determine what those jobs may have been. At Olduvai the sites where artefacts have been found have been divided into four groups. First, there are living floors, in which the occupation debris is found on an old land surface with a vertical distribution of only a few centimetres. Second, there are butchering or kill sites, where artefacts are associated with the skeleton of a large mammal or with a group of smaller mammals. Third are sites with diffused material, where artefacts and bones are found throughout a considerable thickness of deposit. Finally, there are stream channel sites, where occupation debris has become incorporated in the filling of a former channel. Many of the finds of Oldowan and Acheulean artefacts elsewhere have been made in situations like the third and fourth type above. Obviously the study of such occurrences as living floors or butchering sites, such as occurred at Olduvai, can tell us much more about the life and behaviour of the toolmakers.

We do not know whether the earliest representatives of *Homo* at Olduvai possessed anything which can be called human speech, but the latest ones almost certainly did. Nor do we know just when the change took place from the female 'coming on heat' like the apes and only being amenable to sexual intercourse at such times, to accepting the advances of the males at all times. It probably happened early on and it must have had profound social consequences for 'family life', as also did the habitual adoption of frontal copulation in place of the rear-entry position that is normal among apes. We have no idea of how the earliest men viewed the world or life and death; it is only much later that we find evidence of intentional burial of the dead.

Below: A view of Olduvai Gorge and the surrounding Serengeti Plain. The river which gouged out the gorge in prehistoric times performed a giant natural excavation of the site.

Nelson Bay Cave
SOUTH AFRICA

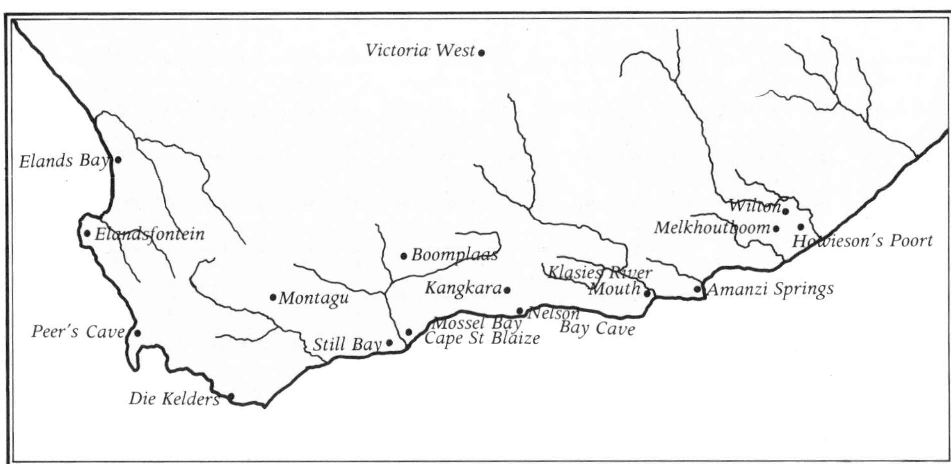

Nelson Bay Cave is situated on the coast of South Africa, some 450 kilometres east of Cape Town, on the western side of the Robberg Peninsula at Plettenberg Bay, near to the junction of the peninsula with the mainland. The cave was formed by sea-wave action more than 200,000 years ago. At that time the sea-level was some 15 metres higher than at present, during an interglacial period when less of the oceans' water was locked up in the polar ice-caps. During subsequent glacial periods, with more of the Earth's water held in the ice-sheets, the sea retreated, leaving the cave high and dry inland. It is now on the coast, with its floor some 20 metres above present sea-level, and is roughly rectangular in shape, about 18 metres wide and 35 metres from front to back.

There are many caves and rock shelters in this most southerly part of Africa, both along the coast and inland. For more than 50,000 years man found that they provided useful shelter and took advantage of what they offered; his lost or discarded artefacts accumulated in deposits which slowly built up on the cave floors. Archaeologists have excavated in them and thereby discovered something about the people who lived or camped there. Some caves gave one sort of picture, some another, partly because they were used at different periods in the past, at different times of year, or for different purposes. Nelson Bay Cave, however, gave an exceptionally continuous and complete picture over the last 20,000 years, with an earlier occupation more than 50,000 years ago.

The excavations

The first excavations at the site were undertaken from 1964 onwards by Ray Inskeep, then of the Department of Archaeology in the University of Cape Town, later of the Pitt-Rivers Museum, University of Oxford. Inskeep's work on interpreting the results of the finds in the cave are still continuing, as his most recent excavation took place only in 1979. In 1970 and 1971, R. G. Klein of the University of Washington, Seattle, excavated an area that went deeper into the cave. The results of these two complementary sets of excavations have very considerably increased our knowledge of the early South Africans who occupied the cave.

The rock floor of the cave slopes downwards from the back towards the front. Human activity and natural agencies have combined over the years to build up the series of layers deposited on top of it.

At the base lies the former beach, 12 metres above the present sea-level. The lowest cultural layer, of black and pale brown loams, dates to 50,000 BC and more. Here there was an abundance of Middle Stone Age artefacts, but no bone or other organic materials had been preserved. There were no artefacts found in the sterile grey loam, but there was plenty of bone material, all of land animals, found in the middle cultural layer. Here were also occupation deposits with Late Stone Age artefacts, dating from 16,000–10,000 BC. The upper cultural layer, 10,000 BC–AD 100, revealed Late Stone Age material with shellfish remains and bones of both fish and marine animals and land animals.

The Middle Stone Age

What prehistorians of Africa call the 'Middle Stone Age' is not the same as the 'Middle Palaeolithic' of Europe. It comes later in time than the *Acheulean* tradition of handaxes and cleavers. The African Middle Stone Age spans from around 75,000 BC, or perhaps even earlier, to around 20,000 BC. Its stone industries are characterized by the further development of a specialized flaking technique (known technically as *levallois*) which had begun in an earlier period, and by the production of knife-like blades (long, parallel-sided flakes), triangular flakes and carefully made points. It is difficult to believe that these were not used to tip projectiles such as throwing-spears and javelins, or perhaps even arrows in the case of the smallest stone points.

It certainly looks as if something of a technical revolution took place in the Middle Stone Age, in the making of composite implements of more than one material, of wood and stone, for example. Perhaps this brought more efficient hunting methods, a more effective social organization and an increase in population. At Nelson Bay Cave the Middle Stone Age occupation is not dated, as it is too old for effective *radiocarbon* determination, but people apparently began making use of the cave, perhaps between 100,000 BC and 75,000 BC, soon after the sea had retreated from another high stand that occurred much later than the one which had formed it.

The Middle Stone Age artefacts came from the lowest layer containing cultural material, but unfortunately at this level bone was not preserved. This not only deprives us of knowledge of any bone industry the Middle Stone Age people may have had, but also of the opportunity to reconstruct the meat part of their diet and the animals living near the cave. The upper part of the Middle Stone Age layer contained an industry of the kind known from elsewhere as of 'Howieson's Poort type', containing a number of kinds of stone tools not present in the earlier Middle Stone Age industry below.

The study of sediments in caves tells us about the climatic conditions prevailing at the time they were laid down. Such study of the Nelson Bay Cave sediments suggests that at the beginning of the Middle Stone Age occupation there the climate was temperate; later it became cold or very cold and wet, but at the end of the period conditions were dry and warm.

The Middle Stone Age layer is succeeded by a layer above it with no artefacts at all. This sterile layer between the Middle and Late Stone Ages, covering the time-span 35,000–30,000 to 15,000–10,000 BC, has been found in no less than a dozen of the sites which have been investigated along the Cape coast and inland from it. Nobody is sure of the explanation. It was not a period when the climate in this area was so severe as to drive out human occupants. However, it was a period when the last glacial maximum had caused the sea to retreat some 70 to 80 kilometres south of the present coastline. If the Middle Stone Age people were exploiting coastal resources of food, they may have left the area of Nelson Bay Cave and followed the retreating coastline southwards. It is impossible to prove whether or not this is true, because the supposed occupation sites now lie under the sea.

The Late Stone Age

Above the sterile layer comes one containing artefacts differing from those of the Middle Stone Age, and there are abundant bone remains. We are now within the range of radiocarbon dating, and by this means the layer is dated as lasting from 16,000 to 10,000 BC. The stone industry was previously unknown, and has been called the 'Robberg', after the peninsula in which it occurs: it is characterized by small keeled scrapers and the appearance of 'backed' tools. The latter are tools in which one side of a stone blade is left sharp and the other is intentionally blunted (or backed) by steep flaking, often in such a manner as to meet the unblunted side in a point. Such artefacts are believed to have been used among other purposes for the points and barbs of arrows. The bones all come from land animals, two of which are now extinct. Bones from the large, gregarious migratory species are present as well as the smaller, less gregarious, non-migratory ones. At this time, the sea was coming nearer and the climate fostered a grassy vegetation on the coastal plain where all these animals grazed. Some of the bones have been ground and polished to make implements. During the occupation of the cave by the makers of the Robberg industry, the climate was rather cold and damp.

During the succeeding 2,000 years or so the climate was becoming warmer and drier and the grassy environment was giving way to a more closed type of habitat. The occupants of the cave were now makers of the 'Albany' stone industry, named after the Albany district of the eastern Cape, of which the remains overlie the Robberg. The Albany industry is characterized by large flakes and scrapers, usually in quartz, and an absence of backed pieces. There is a greater use of bone than before, with pointed and spatulate tools, double-ended points (probably 'fish-gorges', a kind of fish-hook), beads and pendants. Bush-meat obtained by hunting remained an important ingredient of the diet, but the coast was near enough now for the exploitation of marine resources also, particularly shell-fish and the Cape fur seal.

The upper part of the topmost cultural layer of the cave, the lower part of which contained the Albany industry, yielded abundant remains of the Late Stone Age industry, long recognized in South Africa and designated the 'Wilton'. At Nelson Bay Cave it lasted from about 8000 BC until about 2000 BC and was succeeded in the front part of the cave by the 'Post-Wilton' during the next 2,000 years. Wilton assemblages are characterized by small stone scrapers and 'segments' (backed pieces in the shape of a segment of a circle). These occurred in the Wilton levels of Nelson Bay Cave, and use was made of quartz and chalcedony, but the industry was dominated by larger quartzite flakes and tools. There were also shell pendants and a bone industry.

In the succeeding Post-Wilton period, the use of quartz and chalcedony ceases, and scrapers and segments disappear, leaving the large quartzite industry to flourish. Grooved stone net-sinkers appear, a new type of shell pendant and bored stones; the bone industry is much more varied and prolific. Both in the Wilton and Post-Wilton levels, abundant shell-fish remains and bones of fish and marine animals attest to the exploitation of the resources of shore and sea, which had now returned close at hand. Finally, right at the end of the cave's occupation, in the 1st century AD, the bones of domesticated sheep, and perhaps of dog, are found for the first time. Pottery also makes its appearance at this period.

Above: African Middle Stone Age points made from stone. The delicacy and symmetry with which they had been flaked suggest that they were hafted as knives or spearheads with some kind of vegetable gum mastic. The smallest may be an arrowhead, indicating the use of the bow.

Right: A selection of pendants, made of sea shell, from Nelson Bay Cave. Similar pendants were also found at the inland site of Melkhoutboom.

Stone-Age Life

Nelson Bay Cave is unique among the excavated sites along the southern Cape coast in that it provides a long sequence of Late Stone Age levels over a period of more than 16,000 years. By providing such a long sequence it helps to tie together the less complete sequences excavated at other sites in the southern Cape. It is a site of particular significance and satisfaction to prehistorians because it was the first place where the Robberg stone industry was identified.

The wealth of faunal material preserved has made it possible for prehistorians to detect patterns in the animal population of the time. These can be related to the changing food-getting habits of the human occupants and to changes in the environment. The latter can in turn be related to what is known of changes in climate and sea-level, and the results of studying the cave sediments. This makes it possible to construct a much fuller picture of the life of the users of the cave and their relationship to the natural world around them, instead of merely cataloguing changes in their stone implements.

Stone-Age life

If we try to reconstruct the life of the Middle Stone Age people we have less evidence than for the Late Stone Age. For one thing we know very little about what these people looked like. They were certainly fully human, very little different, essentially, from modern human beings, and quite unlike even the most advanced forms of 1,000,000 to 500,000 years before, who were mentioned in connection with Olduvai Gorge.

Middle Stone Age people were probably of medium to small stature, and it is likely that they had brown skins and tightly-curled hair. They had the use of fire, but probably only used skins for clothing during the coldest times of the southern winter. We can imagine the women and children going out to forage for wild nuts and vegetable products, while the men went off to hunt with their spears and javelins tipped with beautifully-made stone points. At other times they would have been seeking out the stone suitable for such implements, and at others sitting down and fashioning them. It is difficult to say much more.

For the people who made the Robberg, Albany, Wilton and Post-Wilton industries we have much more information. We still do not know much about their physical characteristics, but the earlier folk represented the generalized continuum of the population which later diverged into the negroid, pygmy and bushmanoid peoples. It seems most likely that by the time the occupants of Nelson Bay Cave were making the Wilton-type stone implements, they had acquired physical characteristics not unlike those of today's speakers of San languages (formerly called 'Bushmen'), with yellowish-brown skins, tightly-twisted 'peppercorn' hair and small stature. They probably spoke an ancestral Khoisan language. There were no burials found in the cave excavations, and so we have no information on this point, or on the occupants' funerary practices.

During all this time the basic division of labour, between the women and children on the one hand and the men on the other, probably remained the same, with the former doing the bulk of the collecting and the latter doing the hunting. However, within this broad pattern, there were marked changes in the details.

The makers of the Robberg industry principally hunted the big gregarious migratory antelopes grazing on the grassy plains, and tended to ignore the smaller non-gregarious non-migratory ones. The Albany people reversed this pattern and came to depend almost entirely on the smaller animals which browsed all the year round in what was now a more closed habitat. It is difficult to be sure whether this change is reflected in the change in the artefacts, with the disappearance in the Albany of the backed pieces of the Robberg, and the Albany emphasis on the larger, heavier quartzite pieces. Perhaps the latter have something to do with the increasing use of shell-fish, and the bone industry supplied the points for the hunting projectiles. However, the relationship in the changes is not exact and we cannot be sure.

Changes in environmental conditions would certainly have affected the kind of adaptations that man made, and the artefact changes may represent these in a broad and general sense, but the particular adaptation chosen may have been one of a number of options. Although it is useful to use names like Robberg, Albany and Wilton to designate the different industries, they should not be thought of as totally discrete entities with a clean break between them implying sudden change.

Evidence of hunting and fishing

The abundance in the Wilton levels of 'segments', probably used for arrow points and barbs, strongly suggests hunting with the bow. The bone remains indicate systematic hunting of grysbok (a small, grey South African antelope). The exploitation of marine resources was put on a completely different footing in Wilton times, with the first appearance in these levels of a number of species of fish and sea-birds not found lower down; there is a great variety and abundance of fish. The importance of fishing is also shown by the bone fish-gorges and grooved sinkers. The former implies hook-and-line fishing; the latter may have been used for the same purpose or for fishing with nets.

The most striking evidence of the importance of fish in the Wilton people's diet comes from the tidal fish traps which occur along a 1,800-kilometre stretch of this coast. These consist of a wall of stones built near the low tide mark parallel to the shore, with each end curving back in the direction of the land. The wall is built to a height about a metre below the level of the sea at high tide. Fish swim over the wall at high tide and some fail to retreat over it again as the tide falls. At low tide they are either stranded or easily caught in very shallow water. The construction of such fish traps implies a measure of social co-operation and an investment of energy in capturing food from the tides.

From ethnographic evidence we can see that people who hunt large migratory animals tend to be organized in fairly large groups, hunting over a wide territory. Those who hunt smaller non-migratory animals tend to be grouped in smaller units using a smaller territory. Thus the former type of social organization is more likely to have been that of the Robberg people, and the latter that of the Wilton people, who would therefore have been 'thicker on the ground' than the Robberg people, but living in smaller communities.

Many hunting and gathering peoples follow a seasonal pattern of movement, following the game animals they hunt and knowing the times of year when the botanical resources of different places can best be exploited. Did the occupants of Nelson Bay Cave follow such a pattern? We cannot be sure, but it is quite likely that the Robberg people did, and only occupied the cave when the large migratory animals were near at hand. However, in Wilton and late Albany times, there is some evidence that the techniques of exploiting the area's food resources had been perfected to the point when all-the-year-round occupation was possible. The presence of bones of the yellowtail fish implies occupation in October–March, since it is only during these months that it frequents Plettenberg Bay. *Oxygen isotope examination* of some of the shell-fish implies an occupation from May to October. Analysis of the size range of seal mandibles also suggests all-the-year-round occupation.

The hunters and fishers of Nelson Bay would have developed skills in using a variety of raw materials in addition to stone. Plant fibres must have been spun or twisted into strings and ropes for fish- and trap-lines, and for making nets which would have been used for carrying objects as well as for fishing and hunting. String would also have been used for bows and for various kinds of bindings used in hafting some of the stone tools; preparations of resin were made into

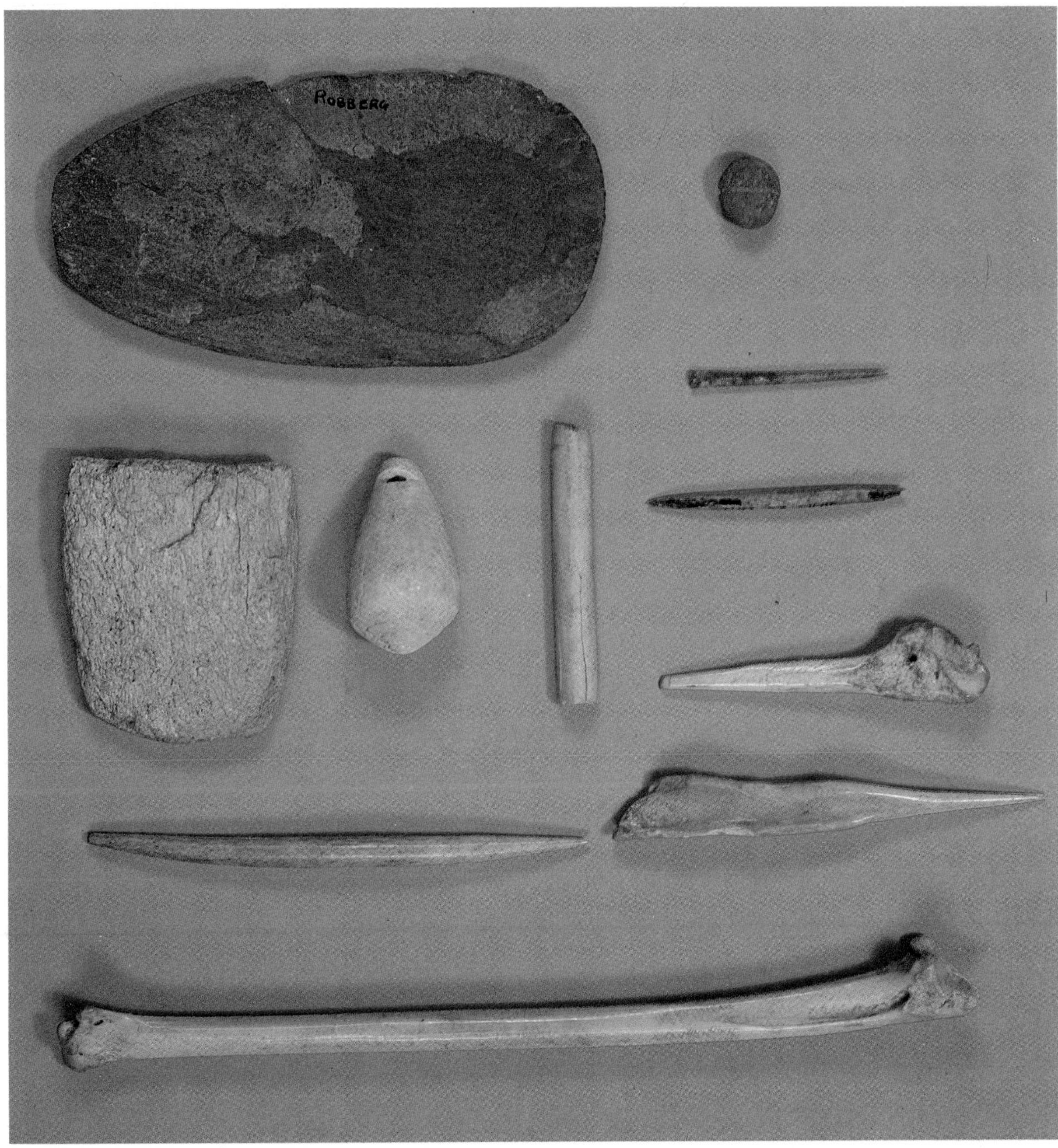

Right: A selection of artefacts from the southern coast of Africa, all dated within the last 8,000 years. They include a decorated bird bone (bottom), a variety of points and awls, a bone ring, tubular bone (a bead?), a shell pendant, a spatulate bone tool for working skins, a shale palette and a tiny shale sinker for a fishing line.

a mastic for the same purpose. Wood was worked with the stone tools in making bows, arrows and other objects; stone scrapers were used in preparing leather from skins. Care and skill was lavished on the making of beads and pendants and in making and decorating a variety of objects in bone and ivory.

Right at the end of the sequence, domesticated sheep and pottery appear, indicating the beginning of a new way of life. The sheep must have been introduced from somewhere, because there are no potential wild ancestors in Africa from which domesticated sheep could have been bred. Sheep were first domesticated nearly 10,000 years ago in south-west Asia and their use had spread to the Khartoum area by about 3500 BC. They were later brought into East Africa by negroid peoples moving southwards, but the earliest they are known in the Transvaal is in the 4th century AD. No early occurrences of sheep are known in the thousands of square kilometres between Nelson Bay Cave and the Transvaal, so how the sheep reached the southern Cape coast – for this is not an isolated find of sheep at this kind of date – remains a problem for archaeologists.

The pottery is quite unlike that of the earliest farmers in the Transvaal and East Africa. Theoretically, pottery-making could have been an indigenous development in the southern Cape, but it seems more likely that it arrived from elsewhere by the same route, whatever that was, as the sheep.

Future work

The profitable results from Nelson Bay Cave obtained in the ways described confirm the need to sort out some of the long-standing problems in the later Stone-Age prehistory of South Africa by a similar strategy. That is, archaeologists should be building up sequences that are valid for limited regions and not trying to extrapolate them over vast areas. They should be placing less reliance on surface collections and stone tool typology and more on excavated sequences and numerical *taxonomy*. Thirdly, they must extract the maximum amount of information that can be gained concerning environmental conditions. There is an element of luck here, of course, in the conditions of preservation. The non-survival of bone in the Middle Stone Age levels at Nelson Bay Cave prevents our being able to make the same kind of reconstruction that is possible with the later material.

Tassili
ALGERIA

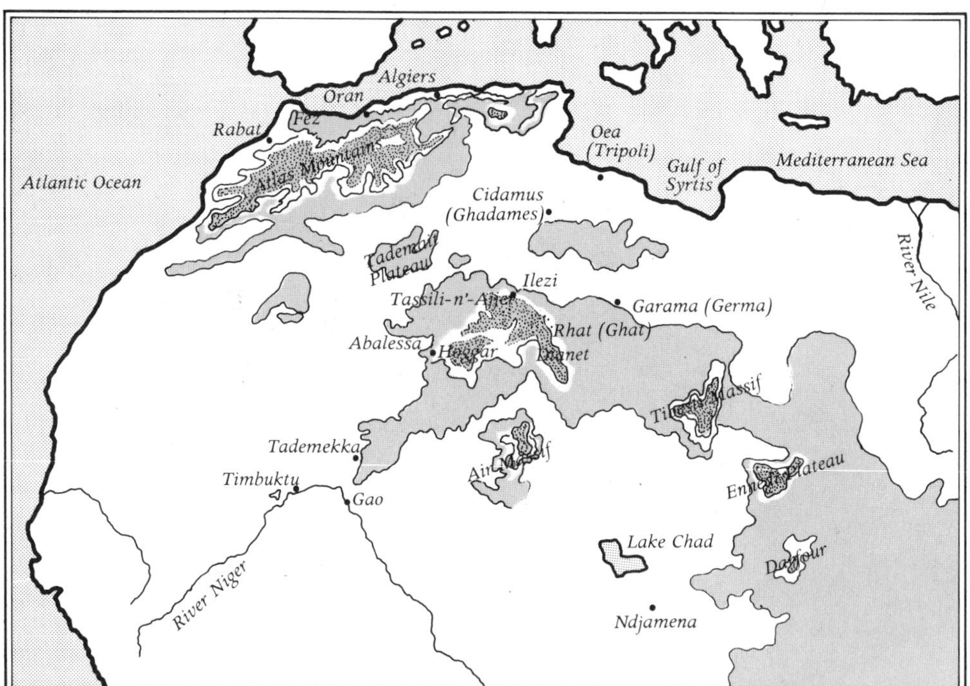

Many people think of the Sahara Desert as an endless waste of sand, the only features being dune after sandy dune. It is not like that at all. There is tremendous variety in the Sahara, which is not surprising in view of its vast size – some 5,000 kilometres from the Atlantic to the Nile and 1,500 kilometres from north to south. Vast areas of nothing but sand there indeed are, sometimes known as 'sand seas', or 'ergs', but even in these there are differences. In some places the sand is flat and fairly firm; in others it is soft and a snare even for four-wheel-drive vehicles. In some places there are isolated dunes on a flat expanse; in others ridge after ridge of dunes rise in monotonous regularity, but even the dunes vary in size and orientation.

Above: The great shelter at Jabbaren, with the expedition's tents pitched under its overhang.

Landscape and climate

Outside the sand areas there are four other kinds of terrain in the Sahara. There are flat expanses of clay and silt ('sebka') left behind by former lakes now dried up. The everlasting north-east trade winds, which blow over much of the Sahara for most of the year, scour out the fine particles of clay which are so light that they can be carried hundreds of kilometres down onto the West African coast and out into the Atlantic. Another type of terrain consists of expanses of pebbles and boulders, known as 'regs'. A third consists of nothing but rock, bare and equally uninviting: sometimes these are gently-sloping surfaces without much feature ('hamadas'); sometimes they rise in dramatic cliffs, gullies and peaks ('jebels'). The latter are found among the various highland or mountain massifs which occur in the Sahara. Lastly, there are the oases, sometimes in unexpected places, with springs or pools fed by underground reservoirs.

The highland areas of the Sahara have been immensely important in the human history of what is now the desert. This is because, rising above the surrounding plains, they have a higher rainfall and catch much more of the little moisture that is available. The effect was more marked in the past, when the climate was wetter than at present and more rainfall was available. This made possible the growth of types of vegetation which have since disappeared. The vegetation in turn, together with the greater availability of water, supported an abundance and variety of wild animals which could not survive in those areas today; and one of those animals, making use of vegetation and preying upon the others, was man. It became evident a long time ago that this must have been the case, as there exist in the Sahara engravings on rocks of animals such as elephant, rhinoceros, giraffe and even hippopotamus in areas at present far too dry for them.

The reasons for a formerly wetter climate are complex, and details often controversial, but it is generally agreed that they are linked with the same global changes which in northern latitudes manifested themselves as Ice Ages. When the northern ice-cap was at its fullest extent southwards, all the different climatic belts, with their corresponding vegetation belts, tended to be compressed towards the equator. A consequence was that the Atlantic storm track came in south of the Atlas Mountains, instead of to the north as now, making the northern Sahara wetter; whereas the present savanna zone south of the desert, which today receives a fair quantity of seasonal monsoon rain from the south-west, became desert, as the dry north-east trade winds blew in more southerly latitudes than at present. On the other hand, during a northern 'interglacial' period, when the ice-sheets retreated further north, the southern Sahara received more of the seasonal monsoon rain. The relationship between the two sources of rain and the two weather systems is a complex one, but it can be seen how, with such fluctuations, the Sahara Desert could have been a wetter region in the past than it is now.

There are two principal highland massifs in the Sahara; the Hoggar, pretty well right in the middle of the Sahara, and Tibesti, further to the east. Tibesti is the more rugged and mountainous and rises higher (to nearly 3,500 metres) than the Hoggar (just under 3,000 metres); it is also larger in size (100,000 square kilometres) than the Hoggar (12,500 square kilometres). Tibesti is more or less surrounded by sand deserts, although to the south-east lies the Ennedi plateau (rising to 1,450 metres). The Hoggar on the other hand is surrounded by a large area of rocky uplands, with that known as the Adrar des Iforas extending to the south-west, and the Air and Djado plateaus extending to the south and south-east respectively. To the immediate south of the Hoggar lies the Tassili du Hoggar, and to the north-west lies the Tassili n' Ajjer. It is this Tassili with which we are concerned. In the Tuareg language, 'Tassili' means 'plateau of the rivers'.

Today, the plains surrounding the highland massifs receive virtually no rain. The average is 25 millimetres or less on the lower slopes of the Hoggar, up to a height of 1,000 metres. Above 2,000 metres the average is 100 millimetres to 200 millimetres but this can vary greatly from one year to another. Tamanrasset, at 1,376 metres, had an average of 48.5 millimetres over a 50-year period, but in that time there were 12 years with less than 25 millimetres and 12 years with more than 75 millimetres. Tibesti has the same kind of pattern, although, lying further east, it receives rather less rain than the Hoggar. However, these figures show the importance of altitude in attracting rain in the Sahara, and it can be readily imagined how in a wetter period these highlands would have benefited most.

We can paint a broad general picture of the area remembering that there were local and latitudinal differences, especially between the northern and southern Sahara because of the interacting northern and southern weather systems and sources of rain. There had been great aridity for thousands of years up to about 10,500 BC, but then it became progressively wetter over most of Africa between the tropics. One result was that the ensuing permanency of water supplies and vegetation in the Sahara enabled large animals such as elephant, rhinoceros, giraffe and hippopotamus to live there, together with a great variety of antelope and other smaller animals, as well as the predators who preyed upon them. There was a somewhat drier interval around 5000 BC but moist conditions returned until 3000–2500 BC when a process of desertization set in, from which the Sahara never fully recovered. During these moister periods comparatively large numbers of people were able to live in the Sahara. They have bequeathed to us enormous numbers of engravings and paintings on the readily available rock surfaces, not only in the Hoggar and Tibesti highlands, but also in other rocky areas such as the Mauretanian Adrar in the west and Jebel Uweinat in the east, at the point where Libya, Egypt and Sudan meet.

Lhote's investigations

The engravings and paintings of the Tassili n'Ajjer first became known to Europeans in the early 1930s as a result of the discoveries of a French camel-corps officer. His findings fired the imagination of Henri Lhote, a student of the famous Abbé Breuil, the acknowledged expert on the world-renowned cave paintings of France.

World War II interrupted Lhote's investigations, and it was not until 1956 that he was able to organize an expedition of sufficient size to tackle the exploration of the rock surfaces in this vast area and to record the prehistoric paintings and engravings found upon them.

Lhote took with him four artist-draughtsmen and a photographer, but before the end of the 16 months that the expedition lasted, some of the original personnel had been replaced; the health of some did not stand up to the rigours involved and they had to be evacuated. The difficulties and obstacles and hardships were formidable: directing loaded camels over the pass of Tafalelet alone was a bruising and exhausting experience – and that steep, rock-strewn defile had to be traversed many tens of times. Such was the casualty-rate among the camels that at one point the local Tuareg refused to hire any more to Lhote, and he could only use donkeys to assist the men who had to travel on foot each month to obtain food and other supplies from Djanet. Later in the expedition, supplies were brought in by parachute drop, with the co-operation of the French army. The winters were bitterly cold, with snowfalls and ice at 1,500 metres. The summer was unbearably hot, with shade temperatures, even at that altitude, of 49°C. Lhote decided to continue the expedition over one summer when he found that there was so much to do, so much to explore, so much to record and he did not want to go through the whole arduous business of moving all the necessary equipment out and back again a second time.

The paintings were recorded by taking tracings directly from the rock face and filling in the background tints of the rock, transferring these tracings to drawing paper, and then returning to the rock face to fill in the colouring. A painting's 'match' could then be directly tested, sometimes in the different light falling on the rock face at different times of day. In this way copies were made as accurate as possible. Most paintings lay under overhanging projections of rock, and these, together with the extreme aridity, had helped to preserve them. Nevertheless, the paintings had often accumulated a layer of dust and dirt in the course of thousands of years, so that the rock surfaces had to be swabbed down first in order to make the paintings appear clearly, or to appear at all.

Phases and styles

The prime significance of Lhote's expedition was to reveal just how great is the wealth of rock art in the Tassili and to bring back recordings of it. It is difficult to appreciate this art fully without seeing a large number of reproductions of it. Secondly, from this mass of material, Lhote identified at least 16 art phases and 30 different styles. Unfortunately, such phases cannot yet be precisely equated with phases of prehistoric occupation derived from the excavation of the artists' settlements.

Before Lhote's expedition it had been recognized that Saharan rock art could be divided into four stages. First there is the Hunting Period, with representations, usually engravings, of wild animals such as elephant, rhinoceros, giraffe, hippopotamus and the extinct North African buffalo. The period probably antedates 5000 BC. Following this is the Pastoral Period from about 5000 BC to 1000 BC. The third is the Horse Period (from about 1000 BC) when horses, carts and chariots appear. Finally there is the Camel Period, when camels are shown, probably not before the 3rd century AD.

The Lhote expedition recognized many additional different points of style among the Tassili paintings after the first of the periods listed. Before the Pastoral Period there are six stages in the 'Round-Headed Man' style. The first shows small human figures with schematic bodies and round heads, with horns and plumes, all painted in violaceous ochre; animals are uncommon, and are mostly elephants and mouflon sheep. Next comes the more evolved 'Style of the Little Devils', in yellow ochre with a red ochre outline. The figures from the Middle Period of 'Round-Headed Men' look like Martian 'space-men' of science fiction with yellow ochre and a red outline. The fourth stage, known as the Evolved Phase of 'Round-Headed Men' includes polychrome figures with rather thick limbs. The body markings may represent body painting or *cicatrization* (which provided evidence for Lhote that these artists were negroes). The 'Decadent Phase' with 'debased' Martian style figures and more lavish use of white ochre within yellow-ochre outlines is followed by the Final Phase, in which Lhote saw an Egyptian influence.

At the beginning of the Pastoral Period comes the Style of the Hunters with Painted Bodies, and thereafter the main 'classical' Pastoral style. Most of the paintings are on a fairly small scale, but there are some almost life-size ones. Cattle are the favourite subject of these artists, and it is clear from their numbers and the quality of their representations that they were important in the lives of the artists' community. They are in a naturalistic style. Wild animals are treated no less skilfully and include elephant, rhinoceros, hippopotamus, giraffe, gazelle, ardvaark, lion, ostrich and fish.

After the Pastoral Period come what Lhote called the 'Style of the Judges', in which he also saw Egyptian influence, and the 'Style of the Elongated Men' carried out in white ochre. In the earlier part of the Horse Period, there are representations of chariots; the horses have their legs extended in what is known as the 'Flying Gallop'. In the later Horse Period is a style which shows mounted men and human figures of 'bi-triangular' shape.

The Painters

The rock art of Tassili provides the basis, if rightly interpreted, of reconstructing much of the way of life of the artists. However, as we have seen, the art stretches over a very long period of time and was executed by different groups of people.

The rock shelters where the majority of paintings occur were indeed used intermittently as sheltered camping places over the last 8,000 years or so, but whereas charcoal from such occupations can be dated by *radiocarbon determinations,* the paintings themselves remain undated in absolute terms – and the rock walls often contain paintings and engravings of different ages.

The richness of detail in many of the figures – of dress, of ornament, of arms and accoutrements, of stance or action and of feature, together with the portrayal of artefacts such as grass huts, canoes and masks – is all potential material for reconstructing the ways of life of the ancient inhabitants of the Sahara. Many of the scenic compositions readily suggest an interpretation of what they portray, but there is still room for a great deal of analysis and interpretation, using the kind of numerical and statistical techniques which have been applied in recent years to French cave art and to the rock art of the San hunters of the Drakensberg in South Africa.

This kind of analysis may throw further light on the motivation of the original artists, who may sometimes have been working 'just for pleasure' or producing 'art for art's sake', although prehistoric art usually occurs in the context of magic and religion. It is easy to see many examples of Saharan rock art as connected with desires for success in hunting or fertility in cattle, with 'rites of passage' such as marriage and initiation ceremonies. Others represent male and female deities and their mythologies, portraying ceremonial rituals. But at present these interpretations all remain somewhat conjectural. There were no areas in the Tassili that could be identified as 'sanctuaries', or paintings which had an obviously magical character.

Whether all the paintings and engravings were done by people of the same biological stock remains controversial, as does the question of whether some of them were negroids, or fair-skinned caucasoids such as the Tuareg who inhabit the Tassili today. Lhote saw the representations of masks and other features as indicating the handiwork of negroids; he may be right, but it is dangerous to argue about the identity of a prehistoric people from the kinds of artefacts made by certain peoples thousands of years later. Similarly, in certain kinds of adornments and in bird-headed figures Lhote saw 'Egyptian influence'; again, he may be right, but the 'influence', if there was any, could have been the other way round.

Lhote certainly believed that the Round-Headed figures were executed by negroes, whose territory would have extended much further north than today. In the wetter conditions of the time they would have lived by hunting the plentiful wild game, principally with bows and arrows tipped with flint or bone points, and by collecting wild vegetable food – a job principally of the women and children. They utilized the grain of wild grasses and ground it between stones. The abundance or scarcity of game and wild food varied with the seasons, necessitating an annual move to places and altitudes where food was most easily obtained. This involved camping for shorter or longer periods of time at the various conveniently situated rock shelters along the way. Sometimes groups joined together for dancing, for masked performances of a ritual or religious nature, for marriage exchange between bands and other communal purposes. The rock art may well have been carried out in celebration of these events or as part and parcel of them.

The Pastoral Period

In the Pastoral Period many elements of this way of life persisted but the new feature

Above left: 'The Great Martian God', nickname given to an example from the so-called 'Decadent Period' of the 'Round Heads'.

Above: Procession of bi-triangular men from the period of the 'Flying Gallop' chariots and of mounted horses.

Below left: 'The White Lady' of Aouanret, attributed to the period of 'Evolved Round Heads'. The figure is interpreted as a goddess in ceremonial dress.

above all was the cattle. Where the cattle came from is not yet certain. Lhote believed they came from the east, from the Nile valley, but there is a possibility that wild cattle were domesticated locally. As for the cattle-herders, Lhote saw them as light-skinned caucasoids similar to the Tuareg, but there may well have been a mixture of both biological stocks; one cannot be certain from the art.

Hunting of wild game and the collecting of wild food remained part of the subsistence economy, while the cattle provided an additional source of food. This probably did not happen regularly, but rather when a festival or a gathering justified a slaughtering. Cattle-herding would have involved protecting the animals from predators, watering them daily and moving them from pasture to pasture wherever grazing was to be found, especially around the lower slopes of the Tassili.

During the Pastoral Period, a fluctuating frontier between the southern and northern weather systems was gradually moving from its most southerly to its most northerly position. At the same time there was some overlap of the two systems in the Hoggar and Tassili. This would have had the advantage of reducing the extreme conditions of either winter rains or summer rains alone. And it helps to account for what was still a modest annual rainfall being able to support the vegetation on which the cattle were able to find sustenance all the year round. Nevertheless, there would still have been some pattern to the seasons and also a measure of unpredictability, resulting both in the development of regular transhumant patterns of movement and of occasional emergencies in which new pastures had to be sought.

When the northern rains were plentiful during the winter, the pastoralists would have taken advantage of the grazing it afforded on the lower slopes of the Tassili and in the surrounding plains, avoiding the bitter cold of the mountains. When summer rains came, longer-lasting pasturage would have been found in the hills, and the hot plains would have been avoided. Rights to water-holes and to areas of grazing would have been important, and sometimes there were conflicts between different groups of cattle herders.

The art from Tassili portrays these conflicts, and many other aspects of daily life: hunters with their bows and arrows, women standing before their cooking pots, men with axes ready to chop wood, people sitting in a circle conversing, couples making love. We can picture many other activities not recognizably portrayed, including men working on their weapons, making bows and arrows, chipping flint to make stone implements or grinding stones to make into axes. People also worked hides and leather; women made dresses and ornaments, including beads from pieces of ostrich egg shell. Some people made pots and baked them, while others did body-painting or tattooing.

It was altogether a richer and more varied life than one might expect in the middle of the Sahara thousands of years ago. And in the background, either near at hand or away in a distant grazing ground, were the cattle, always the cattle; cattle must have been in everyone's consciousness. We do not know how the ownership of cattle was organized, whether communally by the group, by families or by individuals. But since cattle represented wealth, which it had not been possible to accumulate in the same way before, ownership was a very important social as well as economic matter; it could have been the basis of status or social distinctions, either for families or individuals.

Great Zimbabwe

ZIMBABWE

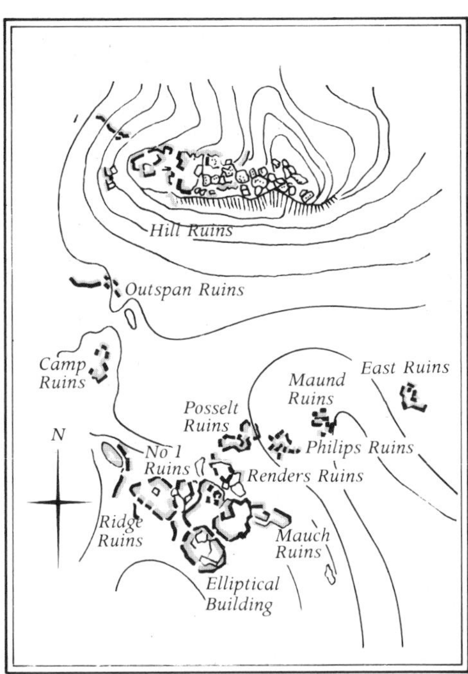

Great Zimbabwe lies in the country which was formerly called Rhodesia, and which took its present name from this ancient site. The archaeological site is therefore now referred to as 'Great Zimbabwe', and not 'Zimbabwe', in order to distinguish it from the name of the country.

Great Zimbabwe is situated on a high, tsetse-free granite plateau, 900–1,200 metres high, which lies between two great eastward-flowing rivers, the Zambezi to the north and the Limpopo on the south. It is woodland savanna country, stretching eastwards to the Eastern Highlands, which overlook the hotter, wetter, more densely vegetated Mozambique plain. To the west the savanna grades off into hotter, drier scrub, and ultimately into the Kalahari desert. The plateau lies within the country of the Shona-speaking people, from whose language the name is derived – either *'dzimba dza babwe'* (houses of stone) or *'dzima woye'* (chiefs' houses, or graves). Thus the name originated as a group term, rather than one for a particular spot. In fact there are some 200 stone ruins or 'zimbabwes' on the plateau, of which Great Zimbabwe is only the best known and most impressive.

Some of the ruins ('Khami type ruins') differ from those of Great Zimbabwe and comparable sites in not having free-standing walls. Instead they have terrace-walling to support platforms for huts of pole-and-dagga (puddled earth). They are later in date (16th and 17th century AD) than the Great Zimbabwe type ruins. The Dhlo-Dhlo ruins are later still, dating from the late 17th and early 18th centuries.

Early Zimbabwe

The gleam of gold runs through the history of Great Zimbabwe. There are gold deposits on and around the plateau, many of them displaying signs of ancient exploitation. Even richer are the Matabeleland goldfields to the west. It has long been appreciated that something of Great Zimbabwe's importance was derived from the export of gold down the Sabi River valley to the port of Sofala on the East African coast.

The Arab writer Masudi, who visited the East African coast in the 10th century, mentions the port of Sofala and the trade in gold which was important there. In the 16th century the Portuguese, who had supplanted the Arabs at Sofala, heard tales of large stone buildings inland, inhabited by members of the ruling Mwene Mutapa's family and court. The Portuguese later made contact with these to the north of Great Zimbabwe near the Zambezi River. They connected the ruins with stories of the biblical Queen of Sheba, King Solomon, and the Phoenician sailors who exploited the mines of Ophir for gold and silver, and who also brought back ivory, apes and peacocks. The Portuguese themselves may have adopted such ideas from Arab sources on the East African coast. In the 1530s the captain of Sofala mentioned that his Muslim informants referred to the Great Enclosure as being 'ancient'.

Zimbabwe 'discovered'

The first outsider to reach Great Zimbabwe was Carl Mauch, a German geologist, in 1871. He enthusiastically adopted the 'King Solomon's Mines' idea, as also did Cecil Rhodes. Theodore Bent, a traveller and amateur antiquarian, dug in the ruins in 1891 and was disgusted to find that 'everything was native'. In spite of this he compared finds with odd 'parallels' from the eastern Mediterranean and Arabia and declared: 'a northern race coming from Arabia built the ruins'.

In 1896 a company called Rhodesia Ancient Ruins Ltd was formed to dig for gold. It was granted digging rights in Matabeleland and other ruins, Great Zimbabwe excepted. The company made four or five finds of gold in the order of 5–20 kilograms but most finds were of less than 300 grams. In 1902 the company's activities were terminated. A local journalist called Hall was appointed curator of Great Zimbabwe and dug around indiscriminately looking for exotic objects.

The first professional archaeologist to excavate at Great Zimbabwe was David Randall-MacIver, who came to the conclusion that the ruins were 'essentially of African construction and of no great antiquity'. This led to a violent controversy with Hall, who was backed by the whole white establishment of southern Africa. In 1929 the British Association met in South Africa, and in connection with this meeting, commissioned a careful and experienced archaeologist, Gertrude Caton-Thompson, to investigate Great Zimbabwe. She carried out extensive excavations there and at four other sites, coming to the conclusion that Great Zimbabwe was 'of African construction and of medieval date' – a conclusion that was equally rejected by South African whites.

In the late 1950s, the architect Anthony Whitty carried out the first complete large-scale survey of the Great Zimbabwe buildings, and demonstrated a sequence of building styles. Poorly-coursed walling preceded regularly-coursed walling of dressed stones, followed by uncoursed piled-and-wedged walling. In the same period two archaeologists, Keith Robinson and R. F. Summers, carried out excavations, and were assisted by the new radiocarbon dating technique which had been unavailable to previous excavators. As a result of their excavations, of study of the finds, of Whitty's work on the walls, and of radiocarbon dates, they saw four distinct 'periods' at Great Zimbabwe.

The first of these was a rather slight occupation of the Hill from about ad 100 to about ad 300 (radiocarbon dates) by the earliest iron-using people in the area. The second, said to have lasted from about ad 350 to ad 1050 was characterized by clay figurines of long-horned cattle. The third occupation of the Hill, put at ad 1050–1450, showed a number of fresh characteristics and was tentatively attributed to the arrival of ancestors of the present Shona people. It was at this period that stone walling began. The fourth period, set at ad 1450 to ad 1800, saw most of the wall-building, and it was attributed to the arrival of a different group of people, identified as the Rozwi. To this period also were assigned the soapstone carvings of birds, bowls and phalli, ornaments of gold, copper and iron, Nanking ware from China, glass beads from India, Indonesia and Europe, iron gongs and copper ingots.

In 1964 the archaeologist Peter Garlake was appointed senior inspector of monuments and carried out a survey of stone ruins throughout the country. He also analysed all

Right: The Conical Tower, inside the Elliptical Building, erected in the finest architectural style. Investigations have proved that it is completely solid. Originally, the top was decorated with a dentelle-patterned frieze.

Below: Two styles of wall building at Great Zimbabwe. On the left is irregularly coursed walling of undressed blocks; on the right, regular coursed walling of carefully-dressed stones. The exterior of the great Outer Wall of the Elliptical Building (right) at its north-eastern end reaches its greatest height and width. Here the workmanship is of the highest quality. The wall is surmounted by a chevron-patterned frieze.

the imported objects discovered at Great Zimbabwe, especially the glazed ceramics, and found none which could be unequivocally dated to later than the 14th century. He was able to feel more confident in such a conclusion since by this time a number of up-country 'fair' sites, or temporary trading stations of the Portuguese, had been excavated to the north of Great Zimbabwe. These spanned the period from the late 16th to the 18th centuries, and produced not a single sherd of Chinese *celadon ware* such as had been found at Great Zimbabwe. Neither had a single item characteristic of these later Portuguese trading sites been found at Great Zimbabwe. There was therefore a strong presumption that by the late 16th century, Great Zimbabwe was of no economic importance, if indeed it had not been abandoned entirely.

Archaeology and politics

More nonsense has been written about Great Zimbabwe, and it has generated more heat and controversy, than any other archaeological site in Africa. This has largely been because the results of archaeology have impinged upon local and national economics and politics, and in turn, economics and politics have impinged on archaeology by trying to smear, distort or suppress unwelcome findings.

The reasons for this situation stem from the fact that Great Zimbabwe is built, impressively, of stone. Stone has not been a traditional building material for most of Africa in areas south of the Sahara and Ethiopia, and north of the Zambezi. Monumental stone buildings are associated in European minds with their concept of 'civilization'; in fact monumental stone building has been one of the elements sometimes included when attempts have been made to define 'civilization'.

Great Zimbabwe came to the knowledge of Europeans at a time when *diffusionist* ideas were current, with the result that a white concept of black 'backwardness' did not allow any elements of culture or civilization to indigenous Africans. European economic and political ascendancy was thus justified and rationalized by a continued belief in black inferiority, and by the continued popularity of diffusionist ideas for the first 40 years of the 20th century. Such ideas came to be opposed both by the results of modern archaeological research and by attitudes generated in the climate of political independence newly achieved in black African countries. Thus Great Zimbabwe became a symbol for both sides of the struggle. Whites saw it as an earlier instance of a superior culture being imposed on an indigenous population by immigrant foreigners. Blacks, claiming Great Zimbabwe for themselves and with archaeology on their side, saw it as giving the lie to the whites' assertions about the lack of black civilization. Thus, when black aspirations were fulfilled in independence, Zimbabwe provided a prestigious indigenous name for the country.

The investigations at Great Zimbabwe produced three important results. To begin with they solved what had been called for a century 'The Mystery of Zimbabwe'. This was achieved by the inter-disciplinary pooling of data and methods of interpretation from a number of research disciplines, freed from racially-inspired prejudices and preconceptions. Of these disciplines, archaeology has been the major contributor, using analysis of cross-cultural imports, the new radiocarbon dating techniques, faunal analysis and ideas drawn from ecology and the 'new geography'. Assistance has also come from historians in collecting, examining and interpreting oral traditions, and relating these to early historical records.

Secondly, as has been found elsewhere in the world, the understanding of a unique or striking archaeological site can only be achieved by setting it in the context of the ecological, economic and social conditions that produced it. Inter-relationships of resources, their manner of exploitation, the trade network and settlement patterns must be examined, and, as far as they are 'visible' in the surviving records of a pre-literate society, so must social institutions and religious beliefs. Finally, the solution to the 'mystery' of the monuments of Great Zimbabwe lies unequivocally in their construction by Africans from the 13th to the 15th centuries AD, and in indigenous developments at earlier stages of the same society.

Above: The only surviving doorway at Great Zimbabwe, in the Western Enclosure on the Hill, showing the overriding wall carried on stone lintels.

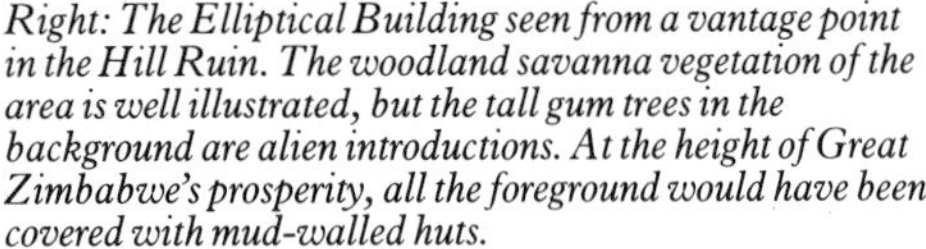

Right: The Elliptical Building seen from a vantage point in the Hill Ruin. The woodland savanna vegetation of the area is well illustrated, but the tall gum trees in the background are alien introductions. At the height of Great Zimbabwe's prosperity, all the foreground would have been covered with mud-walled huts.

The Wall Builders

The ruins at Great Zimbabwe are divided into those on the Hill (formerly called the 'Acropolis') and those in the Valley. The Acropolis has been renamed because the word implies a defended citadel, and the walls of Great Zimbabwe were not designed or sited for a military or defensive purpose, however much they may so appear at first sight. Wall-building on the plateau probably began simply with the joining up of natural rocky outcrops by lengths of wall to make stock pens. Most of Great Zimbabwe's walls, however, were probably built primarily for prestige, to impress the beholder with the power of whoever held authority there. The most impressive of the Valley Ruins is the 'Elliptical Building' or 'Great Enclosure', containing the conical Tower.

Any attempt to picture life at Great Zimbabwe must take into account which period is under review. It seems that the earliest farmers to arrive on the plateau comprised a small group of Bantu-speaking peasants who settled on the Hill in the 4th and 5th centuries AD. They cleared patches of neighbouring land with their iron hoes and on them grew sorghum (kaffir-corn) and millet. In south-west Mashonaland, the Leopard's Kopje culture appeared in the 9th to 10th centuries AD. People of this culture practised a type of mixed farming in which cattle were important, as shown by the cattle bones found in the middens, by clay figurines of cattle, and by the ceremonial burial of cattle carcases. An untypical group of these people appeared on the Hill at Great Zimbabwe and built there during the 10th to the 12th centuries a small village of pole-and-dagga houses.

In the 13th century, Great Zimbabwe ceased to be an ordinary peasant village and became the central settlement of an élite which had grown out of the peasant stock and gained control of the community. This process was probably connected with religious beliefs and the need to ensure fertility of the land and herds. It would also result from the local trade network which had grown up because of Great Zimbabwe's position at the centre of an ecologically diverse area. The religious specialist (a long-standing Bantu functionary) responsible for fertility thus becomes the centre of the redistributive system. He gains wealth from it, uses it to recruit an élite supporting his state, and employs religious sanctions to enforce obedience. His power would therefore be only quasi-political, and not backed by military sanction. Such a process would be very similar to that which, it is supposed, produced the power of the Oni at Ife. The concept also fits in with the tradition of a Mbire ruler moving north from the Great Zimbabwe area to become the 'sacred king' of Mwene Mutapa.

Prosperity through trade

It is likely that at the beginning of the 13th century, Great Zimbabwe was no more important than other 'territorial headquarters' on the plateau. However, once trade developed between the Matabeleland goldfields to the west and the coast to the east, Great Zimbabwe, lying near the head of the Sabi river valley, was strategically placed to exploit it. The injection of wealth from long-distance trade would greatly increase the power of any ruler. He would be able to enhance his status and that of his court and reinforce their position by employing craftsmen such as goldsmiths, stone carvers and stone masons. The masons constructed important public works designed to impress the more lowly and bolster the prestige of the exalted. These buildings also marked off sacred places where rituals of public and secret ceremonies served to establish communication with the supernatural powers.

The 14th and 15th centuries witnessed the greatest flowering of Great Zimbabwe, as its trade expanded and new building took place. This period coincides with that of great prosperity at Kilwa and other East African sites. Gold flowed through Great Zimbabwe down to the coast at Sofala, whence it was taken by coastal ships to Kilwa, there to enter the wider world of Islamic and Indian Ocean trade. In return, luxury imports made their way back to Great Zimbabwe, and among the items recovered there is a Kilwa coin of the Sultan al-Hassan bin-Suleiman, dated AD 1320–33. It was gold which paid for the foreign imports of glass beads and Chinese porcelain, for, as well as deriving wealth from the gold deposits exploited locally, Great Zimbabwe may have benefited from a 'middleman' position between the richer Matabeleland goldfields and the coast.

The importance of cattle

In 1971–72, Mrs. L. Hodges, former curator of the Zimbabwe Ruins Museum, excavated on the slope below the Hill. Among her finds was a large quantity of animal bones belonging to the main period of occupation. When analysed, the following interesting results were produced. There were nine species of wild animals represented by a total of 26 animals; five dogs; 25 sheep or goat; and 585 cattle. Thus the food remains were completely dominated by cattle; they were all butchered on the site and 75 per cent were immature animals.

The importance of cattle to the Great Zimbabwe economy was later confirmed by Garlake's excavation of a large stone ruin site at Manekweni, much closer to the coast, in Mozambique. Although 200 kilometres from the plateau, Manekweni's affinity to the Great Zimbabwe-type ruins was revealed by its similar pottery. At this site it was possible to see how the people pursued a *transhumant* pattern of movement with their cattle, according to the availability of water at different times of the year. Similarly, Garlake was able to see that in the plateau ruins of Great Zimbabwe type, settlement distribution was clearly influenced by agricultural fertility and access to the coast. The greatest concentrations of settlement were along the north-east and south-east edges of the plateau. Few were found along the eastern edge where access to the sea was blocked by the Eastern Highlands, and comparatively few along the 'spine', or watershed, of the plateau.

Although Great Zimbabwe is the most impressive, and may have had some sort of suzerainty over the others, there were probably a number of semi-autonomous 'headquarters' of territories recognized as belonging to the occupying group. These headquarters are marked either by a very large enclosure surrounded by many smaller ones, or by a major enclosure with no others for a considerable distance, or a tight cluster of several small ruins far from any major one. On this basis, some ten headquarters or 'centres' can be identified. Each has a territory stretching from the watershed to the low veldt, and each contains a high, middle and low belt, with boundaries roughly 60 kilometres from each centre. This would allow cattle owners to take advantage of the better-watered low veldt and coastal plain in the dry season, when there was less danger from tsetse; and to retreat to the high veldt in the rains.

Viewing the Great Zimbabwe-type ruins on the plateau in this light may provide a better explanation for their distribution than that of gold exploitation. Some of the richest goldfields with many ancient workings have few or only small ruins nearby, and one large group of ruins coincides only with a very low quality goldfield.

Revealing the history

Garlake's examination of stone ruins all over Zimbabwe enabled him to recognize seven different building styles. This, when set alongside the dating of the imports, led him to another conclusion. He suggested that the third and fourth 'periods' of Robinson and Summers represented a single, stable continuum, without change of population, which had lasted from the early 13th to the mid-15th centuries, and had arisen naturally from the earlier indigenous culture of mixed farmers. Finally, he suggested a different reason from 'the Portuguese stranglehold at the coast' for the eclipse of Great Zimbabwe. After all, even if the Portuguese had replaced the Arabs at Sofala, they still wanted gold and ivory from the interior and were prepared to pay for it. It seems more likely that the decline of Great Zimbabwe resulted from some failure in the subsistence base. This may have been caused by a series of droughts or crop failures; or the exhaustion of land more and more intensively cultivated over hundreds of years without manuring and with shorter and shorter fallows as population increased; or a disastrous epidemic among the cattle herds of some disease such as rinderpest or trypanosomiasis.

Study of the oral traditions of Zimbabwe, particularly by D. P. Abraham and E. A. Alpers, has helped to fill out this picture. The first Shona were traditionally known as Mbire, who established themselves in the Great Zimbabwe area. They introduced the worship of a supreme god (Mwari) and cults of spirits ('mhodoro'); the later Torwa dynasty ruled around Great Zimbabwe and supported these cults. However, the Mbire may not have been an immigrant group but may simply have arisen from the indigenous people responsible for what archaeologists know as the Leopard's Kopje culture. According to tradition, the Mbire kingdom became afflicted with a shortage of salt, and the ruler of the time found it in the middle Zambezi valley. This may be symbolic of the kind of subsistence breakdown suggested above. The Mbire king conquered this middle Zambezi area, settled there and became known as the Mwene Mutapa ('master pillager'). Subsequently, the Mbire in the Great Zimbabwe area and the Guruhuswa in Matabeleland defected from the Mwene Mutapa empire. It was this scene that the Portuguese found early in the 16th century when they recorded information about the sacred king of 'Monomotapa'.

The decline of Great Zimbabwe

The population at Great Zimbabwe may never have exceeded 3,000 adults, but by the mid-15th century it was nevertheless too large to be supported by the immediately surrounding land. Decades of over-exploitation to feed the numbers of people concentrated around the royal and sacred buildings had resulted in the land becoming exhausted. The scarcity of wild game found in the food refuse excavated below the Hill suggests that nearly all the easily available game had been hunted out. Timber for buildings and for firewood had been used up; shorter and shorter fallows for agricultural land led to falling crop yields; overgrazing and over-dependence on cattle produced a dangerous situation when grazing became scarce. So the Mbire decided to move north to a territory which had not been exploited so intensively for so long. An additional reason for Great Zimbabwe's decline may have been the prosperity in the middle Zambezi area of the Ingombe Ilede people, for they had direct access to the Urungwe copper ores and to the Zambezi valley trade route to the coast.

However, although the 'power and the glory' passed away from Great Zimbabwe, an aura of sanctity remained, and is preserved in local traditions. In 1871, Carl Mauch was told about a ceremony held on the Hill some 30 or 40 years previously, involving a large concourse of people, a priest and the sacrifice of cattle. Although the Mbire had departed, their gods remained.

Ife

NIGERIA

Many people have heard of the ancient kingdom of Benin, in southern Nigeria (not to be confused with the modern Republic of Benin, which takes its name from the Bight of Benin, itself named after the ancient kingdom). They know of it largely because of the 'Benin bronzes' which are well known throughout the world and can be seen in many museums, following their removal from Benin after the British Punitive Expedition of 1897. Fewer people have heard of Ife, also in southern Nigeria, because its works of art are fewer in number and have mostly remained in their country of origin. Yet they are older than the Benin works, and the gradually unfolding story of the development and decline of Ife is in many ways more interesting than that of Benin.

Ife is situated at the centre of a northward bulge in the equatorial forest of south-western Nigeria, a geographical position which may have had something to do with its rise to pre-eminence. Unlike Benin, which the Portuguese visited in 1485, Ife was unknown to Europeans until the 19th century. The Arab traveller Ibn Battuta may be referring to Ife when in the 14th century he wrote of 'Yufi'. Describing the Niger River, he says that it 'descends from Timbuktu to Gao, then to the town of Muli in the land of the Limis, which is the frontier province of Mali; thence to Yufi, one of the largest towns of the negroes, whose ruler is one of the most considerable of negro rulers'.

To all immediate outward appearances, Ife is no different from a number of similar small Yoruba towns. There is a 'wall' system of earth ramparts, but some of these at least date from the time of the Yoruba wars of the 19th century. There is no surviving craft tradition such as there is at Benin. Yet Ife is widely recognized among Yorubas as their 'holy city', where, according to tradition, the world was created. There are many sacred shrines and groves in and around the town, and it is said to have a thousand gods. Rulers of the other kingdoms and principalities of Yorubaland validate their authority by claiming to have received it from the Oni (king) of Ife.

Frobenius's finds

There is certainly something exceptional about the works of art which have come to light at Ife. Three very remarkable stools carved out of quartz were given to a British official by the Oni in 1896, and in 1910 the German explorer and anthropologist Leo Frobenius obtained a number of terracotta heads and a copper-alloy head dug up from the grove of Olokun, the deity of the sea. He claimed that the latter represented Poseidon, the Greek god of the sea, and that Ife was the lost Atlantis, an early Greek colony which lost touch with its homeland after the Carthaginians gained control of the western Mediterranean. Frobenius based his claim on the style of extreme naturalism exhibited by the sculptures, which is unusual in the African tradition.

Most people remained sceptical of Frobenius's claims until interest was aroused once again in 1938 and 1939 by the accidental discovery in building operations, not far from the present palace of the Oni, of 17 life-size copper-alloy heads in the same naturalistic style, one of which was closely similar to the already-known Olokun head. On a smaller scale, there was also the head and torso of a complete figure apparelled in royal regalia. All these metal objects, fashioned with delicate artistry and great technical skill, had been made by the lost wax casting process. In this, a model of the desired object is first made in wax on a clay core. The wax is then covered with clay and the whole thing heated so that the wax runs out. The clay is baked into a hard mould and molten copper or brass is poured into the space left by the wax, thereby taking its form. After cooling, the clay mould is broken off.

These new finds renewed speculations about their origin and age; few people subscribed to Frobenius's Atlantis theory, but estimates ranged from the 5th to the 18th centuries AD. The Nigerian Antiquities Department undertook a certain amount of excavation, but although they recovered a large number of terracottas, did not succeed in advancing towards the solution of the main problem. Then in 1957, further accidental finds of copper-alloy castings were made, among them a complete standing figure, 47 centimetres high, similar to the one found earlier of which only the head and torso remained. Also found were a joined male-and-female figure ('the royal pair'), a complicated casting only 12 centimetres high portraying a female figure coiled round a pot on top of a stool carved in quartz, a pair of human-headed staffs and three double-headed ovoid mace-heads; most of these heads were shown gagged.

Whereas there are no more than 30 of these remarkable metal castings from Ife, there is a larger number of stone carvings, amounting in all to some 200. One of the most remarkable is the 'Opa Oranmiyan', or staff of Oranmiyan (a legendary prince of the royal house), which is a tapering standing pillar studded with a pattern of iron nails. Nearly 2,000 complete or partial terracottas are known.

Potsherd pavements

Since 1957 a number of important excavations have been carried out by members of the Antiquities Department and the University, many on the sites of accidental finds. These excavations have yielded more than two dozen radiocarbon dates and have helped to date the heyday of ancient Ife. One of the site's characteristic features is the presence of pavements made up of broken pieces of pottery set on edge. Such potsherd pavements are not confined to Ife but are far more numerous there than anywhere else. As a result of discovering numerous potsherd pavements and obtaining radiocarbon dates associated with them, or from levels above and below them, we can now see that the 'pavement-building period' lasted from the early 12th into the 15th century AD. It therefore seems most likely that these centuries represent the period when Ife flourished, and it was perhaps during the later part that the greatest works of art were produced, above all the copper and brass castings. If we can rely on *thermoluminescent dates* from the remains of the clay cores surviving in some of the castings, these also indicate a date of manufacture in the 14th and 15th centuries.

The plans of potsherd pavements recovered suggest that they were employed principally for the courtyards of houses. Semi-circular 'cut-outs' at the edge of some pavements almost certainly indicate earth platforms which were used as shrines or altars, in the form still used at Benin today. Most potsherd pavements are patterned, some with simple herring-bone arrangements, some with more elaborate chequer-board or other patterns picked out with white quartz stones. Sometimes the pattern conforms to the central positioning of a ceremonial pottery vessel. One of these portrays a shrine with a naturalistic-style head of metal or terracotta in the centre, flanked on either side by highly-conventionalized anthropomorphic figures. This helps to give us an idea of what the purpose of such sculptures may have been, as does information from another excavation, at the site of the burial of a former Oni. Although the actual grave could not be opened, a kind of rectangular mortuary chapel was revealed. This was floored with a potsherd pavement and a central post supported its roof. Around the edges of the pavement was set a series of pottery jars which had lids surmounted by various terracotta sculptures, predominantly animal heads carrying some of the same royal emblems as on the metal royal figures. The animals were facing inwards. Most of the terracottas have been found accidentally, or after re-burial, so that any clue as to their

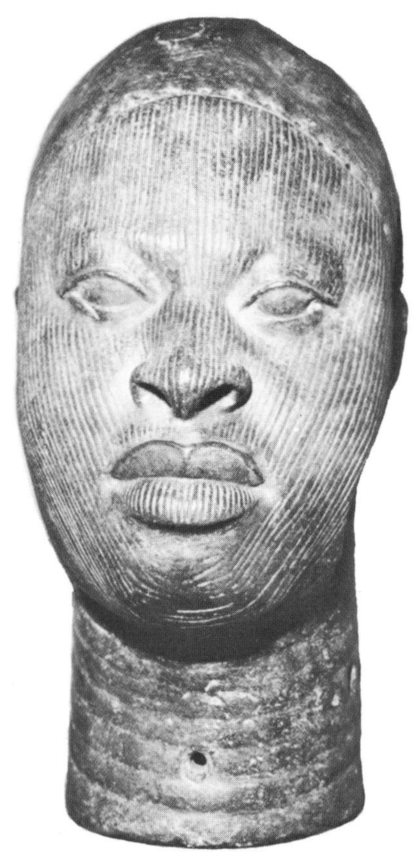

Left: Brass head from Wunmonije Compound, with the finely striated face found on much Ife sculpture. Traces of white and red paint can be seen on some of these metal heads. In the neck can be seen two of the four nail-holes by which it was originally attached, probably to a clothed wooden body. The grooves around the neck are considered to be marks of beauty among the modern Yoruba. Height: 30 centimetres.

Right: Seated copper figure from the Nupe village of Tada on the River Niger. It is one of a collection of seven metal figures kept there, but this is the only one closely resembling the Ife copper and brass heads in style. The figures, together with two at Jebba, are said to have been brought from Idah by the Nupe founder-hero Tsoede in the 16th century. But a number of experts believe that they originated from Ife and Owo in Yorubaland, and that their position at Jebba and Tada, where the trade route to the north crossed the River Niger, indicates the importance of this route. Height: 52 centimetres.

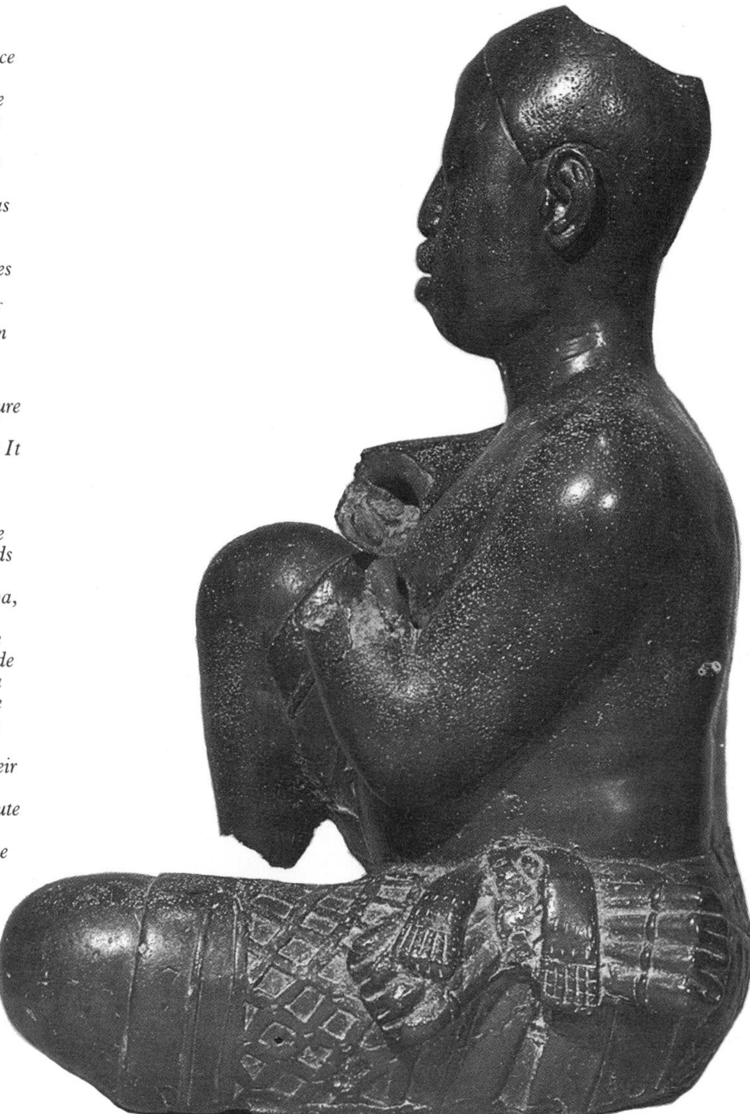

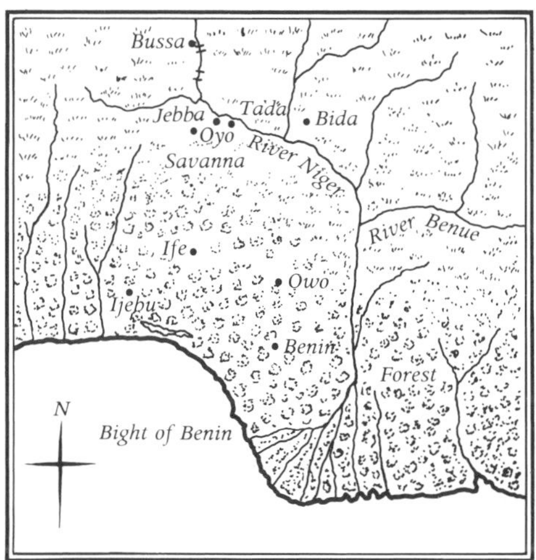

original purpose was lost; in this archaeological excavation the terracottas were found in their original positions, so that more informed speculation about their function was possible.

Ceremonial centre

The significance of Ife lies not merely in the achievements of its artists and craftsmen. It is also an example of indigenous African urbanization and centralization of authority, which may have come about in the following way.

By the middle of the 1st millennium AD there was a long-established agricultural population in Yorubaland, using an iron technology. Such a population is likely to have had three characteristics. The first follows from the premise that all settled agricultural populations in pre-scientific times feel that, as part of their agricultural practice, they must do something to ensure fertility of the land and of their crops. Such fertility is usually believed to depend on the goodwill of supernatural powers. Ordinary folk may not feel confident in their ability to handle such supernatural powers, or may be afraid to do so, and therefore are happy to delegate the job, for a consideration, to specialists who do have the confidence and know-how. The second point is that in different ecological zones – savanna, forest, river valley, coast – the inclination will be to specialize in products most favoured in those zones. This will tend to happen most in areas of ecological diversity, such as that at the centre of which Ife was situated. It will also tend to foster an internal system of exchange for the products of the different ecological zones. Finally, there is likely to be a population increase, which in turn will encourage the use of more intensive agricultural practices and more efficient exploitation of the various ecozones.

Thus the production of complementary resources from neighbouring societies favours the growth of mutual interdependence, occupational specialization, and arrangements to redistribute resources to ensure that supplies are available to all.

Now when these two needs come together – that for ensuring the fertility of the land and that for arranging redistribution – we are well on the way to the creation of a ceremonial centre, at which a specialist in 'supernatural' farm management becomes associated with the exchange system. In some such way as this, Ife established itself as a ceremonial centre. Tributes to the Oni, given in return for his supernatural services to all the different sectors of the community, and his largesse to his court, retainers and the subordinate chiefs who owed him loyalty, served to redistribute the resources of the region, but also to concentrate a lion's share in Ife and in the hands of the Oni.

The Kingdom of Ife

In the absence of written records, it is difficult to portray everyday life in ancient Ife. Reconstructions of life in ancient Egypt or Mesopotamia, for example, are to a considerable degree based on written evidence. Our knowledge of the religious ideas and daily life of the ancient Egyptians is based, not just on temple and tomb construction and on grave goods, but also on the inscriptions and illustrations in the tombs and in *Books of the Dead*. For Ife we have no corresponding information: we must base our reconstructions entirely on artefacts and excavations. What is more, there has been only a minute quantity of excavation in Ife compared to that in Egypt. There are a few pot-burials, probably of commoners, and hints of shaft graves, but preservation is poor. The excavation of what was probably a royal burial was stopped by the reigning Oni of Ife. The sensible choice of a mud architecture tradition rather than one of stone makes it more difficult to identify shrines and temples.

However, an attempt to recreate everyday life in the ancient kingdom is not impossible. The first fairly clear picture is of a stratified society. At the bottom of the social structure were royal and domestic slaves; next came a large number of commoners whose main occupation was agriculture or handling agricultural produce and who would be called upon to serve as soldiers in time of war. At the top was the Oni, surrounded by a court of elders and aristocrats, war-leaders and administrators.

Agriculture and food

Agriculture would have been the most important economic activity. Many peasant farmers probably lived in Ife and went out to their farms in the surrounding countryside, 'camping' on them at the busiest times of the year. Villagers from further afield also probably grew more food than was necessary for their own needs and would head-load it along the bush-paths to the Ife market. The most important activities were the growing of yams, beans, okra and other vegetables, together with the harvesting of palm-nuts from which palm-oil would be made. Guinea corn (sorghum) may have been grown in more northerly areas. The diet in general was good, adequate in quantity and variety. Most households kept a few chickens and goats, and guinea-fowl were available, but beef was rare and pork unknown. However, hunters supplemented the meat supply with wild game, large and small, and the large African snails collected from the forest were an important source of protein. Thus with staple foods of yams and palm-oil, made tasty by a great variety of peppers and relishes, the diet of the Ife people was sounder and more balanced than that of many who live on the products of a farming system dominated by a single food resource. Kola nuts were grown partly for local consumption but primarily for export. Palm wine provided a happy alcoholic drink, itself not without nutritional value.

Hunters and traders

Hunters were important in another aspect of the economic life of the community: they acquired the elephant tusks which provided ivory for export northwards into the Islamic world. In exchange came imported copper and brass, salt, textiles, hides and luxury goods. The social position of the hunters is not known, but economically they were an important class. They may have been 'independent' but with ownership of the ivory being the sole prerogative of the Oni, as at Benin. We do not know, either, the precise status of the traders. Much of the local exchange network would have been handled in the markets and by 'petty traders', often women. It would be interesting to know, however, if there were any who could be called professional long-distance traders, or merchants, and whether any non-Yoruba merchants lived in the town to handle such trade, to collect local exportable goods and to supervise the selling of their imports. This, after all, was the pattern in the trading towns of the Sahel to the north, which would have formed Ife's trading contacts. On the other hand, and certainly on the analogy of Benin which is likely to have derived many of its ideas and practices from Ife, the Oni would have exercised strict control over all the most important items of long-distance trade. For whether or not he or his agents were themselves actively engaged in such trade, he would have derived from it the wealth and power to sustain his state, as well as prestige items to advertise it.

The Oni

The well-being of the people of the Ife kingdom was vested in the person of the Oni. He was responsible for ensuring the goodwill of the tutelary deities, of the powers responsible for the fertility of the land and crops, of the ancestors watching over the current generation, and above all of his predecessors in office, the former Onis. His daily prayers and sacrifices, as well as those offered at important festivals, were to this end. His dignity was evidenced not in a marble palace but in the reverence in which he was held, in the numbers of those who waited upon him, in the tributes brought to him, and in the special regalia with which he was adorned on ceremonial occasions. His palace consisted of many ranges of rooms around typical Yoruba *impluvia* courtyards, with cool shady verandahs looking out on to potsherd pavements. It was maintained and annually re-thatched, the labour and grass being supplied by villagers from a wide area, as part of an annual ceremony. As in the smaller but comparable houses of the more wealthy and important, there were shrines and altars in a number of the courtyards. The most important of all, however, was that containing the altars of the previous Onis, on which stood their images in wood, terracotta or brass. On the occasion of some of the more important festivals, slaves were bound and gagged and sacrificed as part of the religious procedure. The slave population was drawn from criminals and those captured in war. It seems likely, with the persistent demand of the Islamic world for negro slaves, that they were also exported to the north.

Technology and crafts

We do not know exactly how the practice of various arts and crafts was organized, or what was the social status of specialized craftsmen. Pottery was a women's craft, sometimes as a part-time activity, sometimes concentrated in particular pottery-making villages. Modelling in terracotta, however, may have been a men's craft, as also woodcarving and leather-making. Iron-smelting was important where good raw material was available, but is likely to have been undertaken during the dry season among men of an agricultural community. Blacksmithing may have been associated with smelting, or there may have been independent blacksmiths more widely distributed. Basketry may have been a spare-time activity of both men and women, but weaving is likely to have been concentrated in certain villages or districts. The highly specialized, highly skilled crafts of making glass beads and bangles, and of brass-casting by the lost-wax method, were probably under the control of the Oni. It is likely that part of his prerogative would be to have possession or distribution of the products of these workshops. The artisans may have been slaves, but were probably independent craftsmen organized in guilds.

Left: Artist's reconstruction of a house in Ife, based on the archaeological evidence from excavations. Terracottas stand on the altars; cult objects hang above them; the recess is decorated with a mosaic of potsherd discs and in it stands a diviner's iron staff.

Right: Terracotta head found by Frobenius in 1910 in the Olokun Grove, Ife. It appears to come from a figure, and has not only an unusual hairstyle, but also raised dots resembling keloid scarifications along the eyebrows. This latter feature is not found on other Ife heads. Height: 17 centimetres.

The evidence of trade

When the Islamic world sent its commercial probings south of the Sahara, and these, at however many removes, reached the West African forests, Ife was in a good position to gain advantage from, and exploit, them. The Arabs sought and obtained gold from the western part of West Africa, but there is no gold in any useful quantity in Nigeria. However, they also had an insatiable desire for ivory, and almost as great a demand for negro slaves. Other tropical products, such as kola nuts, were also welcome. In return, commodities such as salt and hides were offered, and luxury goods such as fine textiles, beads and brass vessels. Eventually there developed a demand for brass and copper metal as such, for there is virtually no copper in the forest region of West Africa and people there wanted to be able to cast objects in this metal themselves. A hint of the northward pattern of trade appears along the River Niger around Tada, just outside the present Yoruba area. Here stands a group of very remarkable copper and copper-alloy statues, one of which is in exactly the style of the Ife heads. This stretch of the Niger probably represents the crossing point on the river for overland routes leading north-east through the Hausa states, or the embarkation point for the river route upstream into the territories of Mali and Songhai. Once external trade injects wealth into a local trading system, the power of the chiefs who control its distribution increases out of all proportion. The power, wealth and importance of the Oni of Ife grew, and this encouraged the growth of a court, with court functionaries, and court artisans producing objects of prestigious as well as religious significance.

There were probably many causes for a decline in Ife's prosperity after the 16th century and for the break in continuity which left no craft traditions surviving. Chief among these were the rise to power of the Nupe along the River Niger to the north of Yorubaland, and the rise of Oyo, a Yoruba offshoot of Ife situated in the savanna country to the north-west. These two powers succeeded in coming between Ife and the source of its wealth in the north. To the south, the new forest powers of Benin and Ijebu Ode grew rich from trade with the Europeans who had recently arrived on the coast, and blocked Ife's access to this alternative source of wealth. Ife was commercially surrounded; prosperity declined, together with political influence, although its position as the ceremonial centre remained. The Yoruba wars of the 19th century further disrupted Ife's traditions, since we know that for a time the town was uninhabited.

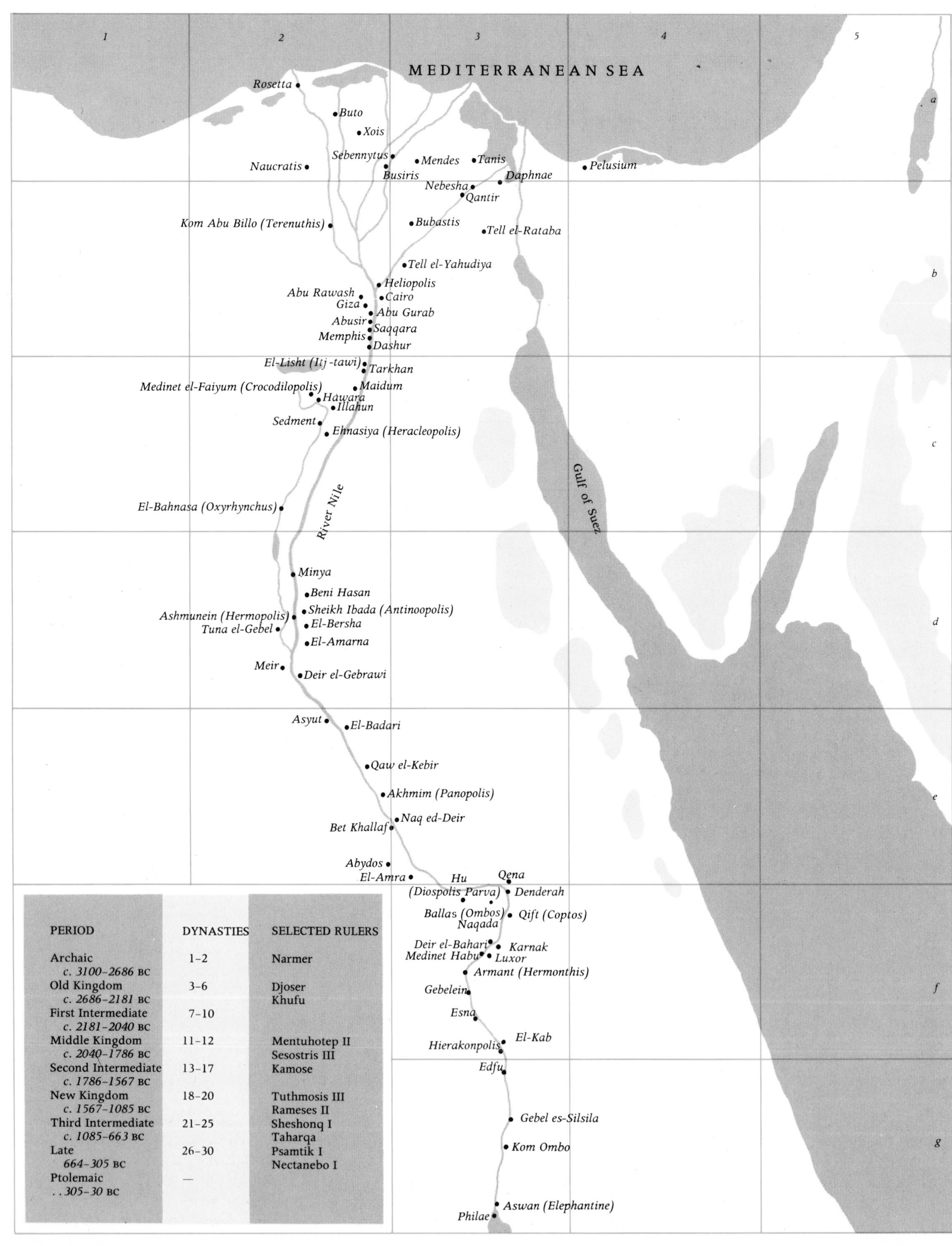

PERIOD	DYNASTIES	SELECTED RULERS
Archaic *c. 3100–2686* BC	1–2	Narmer
Old Kingdom *c. 2686–2181* BC	3–6	Djoser Khufu
First Intermediate *c. 2181–2040* BC	7–10	
Middle Kingdom *c. 2040–1786* BC	11–12	Mentuhotep II Sesostris III
Second Intermediate *c. 1786–1567* BC	13–17	Kamose
New Kingdom *c. 1567–1085* BC	18–20	Tuthmosis III Rameses II
Third Intermediate *c. 1085–663* BC	21–25	Sheshonq I Taharqa
Late *664–305* BC	26–30	Psamtik I Nectanebo I
Ptolemaic *. . 305–30* BC	—	

The Nile Valley

3100 BC - 30 BC

The valley of the River Nile is a remarkable phenomenon, consisting of a narrow strip of fertile land enclosed on either side by inhospitable deserts. The soil of the valley is river silt, deposited by the annual flooding of the Nile on which life in ancient Egypt depended. The population of Egypt has always been concentrated near to the river, and the deserts were regarded as frontier areas, to be controlled and exploited. However, the desert fringes were much used as cemeteries by the inhabitants of the nearby cultivated land.

Archaeological sites in Egypt are generally easy to locate because most are extremely large. Towns in the Nile valley have usually left stratified mounds of ruins, hiding domestic, religious and administrative buildings. Desert cemeteries are marked by the hollows of tomb shafts, and by the scatter of potsherds on the surface. Many sites, however, possess monuments so conspicuous that their existence has always been evident. Among these are the pyramids of Giza and Saqqara, as well as the temples of Karnak and Abydos.

The sites described in this section are justly famous, and each has its own importance. Abydos and Saqqara possess remarkable tombs of the Archaic Period, in addition to later monuments. At the latter site, the beginning of stone architecture is seen in the Step Pyramid, and its refinement is found in the magnificent group of pyramids at Giza. A different kind of site is exemplified by Karnak, the main religious complex of ancient Thebes, with its various additions from the Middle Kingdom to the Graeco-Roman Period. The Valley of the Kings, across the Nile from Karnak, houses the royal tombs of the New Kingdom. These are cut into the valley cliffs and take the form of narrow corridors, the walls of which are covered with funerary inscriptions. The site was originally chosen in an attempt to gain security from tomb-robbers, but only a single tomb remained relatively intact to modern times.

The chronology of ancient Egypt has been established with a fair degree of accuracy, thanks to a number of pieces of evidence supplied by the Egyptians themselves. First, there are the lists of kings compiled at certain stages of Egyptian history, and carved on the walls of temples and tombs. A more detailed king-list is given in the sadly damaged Turin Papyrus, helping us to reconstruct the correct sequence of rulers. Astronomical records made by the Egyptians provide fixed points to link the sequence of kings to a scale of years. Other valuable sources include the writings of ancient historians, particularly those of Manetho, an Egyptian of the 3rd century BC, and the Greek Herodotus. Scientific dating methods have been used in Egypt, but they rarely provide a date as accurate as can be determined from other evidence.

The dating of uninscribed material depends on standard archaeological techniques, particularly the establishment of typologies to cover not only portable finds such as tools, pots and beads, but also to trace the evolution of burial customs and architecture. Inscribed monuments can often be dated from the royal names upon their walls, but care must be taken to check that the names are original, and not cut by a later king above the erased inscription of one of his predecessors.

Archaeology in the Nile valley has developed from the rough approach of early explorers to a precise science, employing archaeological techniques similar to those used elsewhere. The method of excavation depends on the kind of site. For example, the stratified town-sites of the valley require a far more detailed approach than the desert cemeteries. Excavation techniques cannot be standardized, but must always be varied to suit local circumstances. In addition, there is little point in excavating a site well if the results are never published for the benefit of other scholars. Sadly, some reports fail to appear, or do so only after years of delay. Another serious problem is the high cost of publishing results of fieldwork, which has placed many volumes well beyond the means of the individual Egyptologist, making access to specialist libraries even more necessary.

Archaeology involves not simply the excavation of fresh sites; it also includes the surveying and copying of monuments which are already known. Every one of the five sites described in this section has inscribed monuments which have been copied only inadequately, or have never been copied at all. What Egyptian archaeology now requires is a concentrated effort to record all exposed monuments and to excavate those sites which are threatened by environmental problems.

Giza

EGYPT

The ancient monuments of Giza lie only 8 kilometres from the city of Cairo, beyond the modern suburb to which the site owes its name. At the western limit of the cultivated land the ground rises steeply to the desert, upon which stand the three large 4th-dynasty pyramids which are the best-known structures of the site.

The pyramids

The large and conspicuous pyramids of Giza have attracted visitors since the Graeco-Roman period. However, the investigations carried out by numerous archaeological expeditions over a long period of time have served to tell us a great deal about how and why the pyramids and their attendant temples and private cemeteries were built.

The Giza pyramids were all completely plundered in antiquity, and the Arabs reopened them during the Middle Ages in search of treasure. Indeed, the present entrance to the Great Pyramid of Khufu (about 2600 BC) consists in its outer part of a forced tunnel made under the direction of the Caliph El-Ma'mun in the latter part of the 9th century. The first European explorers were travellers rather than archaeologists, but some of them entered the Great Pyramid and made brief descriptions of the internal passages. The entrance is situated on the north side, from which a sloping passage descends to an unfinished chamber in the bedrock. But following a change in plan, it was decided to place the burial chamber in the masonry of the pyramid itself. Hence a new passage, known as the Ascending Corridor, was constructed on an upward slope from the initial entrance tunnel into the heart of the monument. For almost 40 metres this corridor is only 1.2 metres high, but it then opens into a lofty passage, called the Grand Gallery, which is 8.54 metres in height and has an impressive *corbelled* roof. A horizontal passage at the beginning of this gallery leads off to a granite chamber with a gabled roof. This chamber was planned for the burial, but again it was abandoned. The true burial chamber lies at the upper end of the Grand Gallery, and still contains an empty and lidless sarcophagus.

Not all of these passages were accessible until they were cleared by early explorers. A Genoese sea captain, Giovanni Caviglia, cleared the lower end of the original descending passage in 1817 and found that the rough pit from the top of the Ascending Corridor communicated with the lower tunnel. This formed an escape-route for the workmen who sealed the former corridor. The lowest of the five *relieving compartments* above the burial chamber was found by a British traveller called Nathaniel Davison in 1793, but the remaining four compartments were only discovered by a British colonel, Howard Vyse, in 1837.

Right: The Valley Temple of Khafre, showing the monolithic columns of red granite. The temple lies at the foot of the Causeway running from the pyramid: 4th dynasty, c. 2600 BC.

The Second Pyramid of Giza, belonging to Khafre (late 2500s BC), had already been opened by Giovanni Belzoni in 1818, but Vyse settled at the site to make a thorough investigation of all the pyramids. His methods were rough, involving the extensive use of gunpowder to blast tunnels into the masonry, but at least he kept careful notes and made drawings of the monuments which he later published. He succeeded in entering the pyramid of Menkaure, the Third Pyramid, in which he found a fine basalt sarcophagus. After Vyse had completed his work, there were no more chambers to be discovered in the pyramids. More careful scholars had now to explain the details of the structures.

Methodical surveying of the Giza pyramids was carried out in 1880–81 by the British archaeologist Sir Flinders Petrie, who was later to be regarded as the founder of scientific Egyptian archaeology. Petrie's survey revealed the astonishing accuracy of the pyramids, both in the jointing of the masonry and in their correct alignment to the compass points. The industry of Petrie was amazing. He worked at all hours, gathered a vast amount of material, and had his own ways of keeping visitors at a distance:

'It was often most convenient to strip entirely for work, owing to the heat and absence of any current of air, in the interior. For outside work in the hot weather, vest and pants were suitable, and if pink

Left: The Great Sphinx of Giza, carved from the rock in an ancient quarry near the Causeway of the pyramid of Khafre: 4th dynasty, c. 2600 BC.

Below: Key

1 *Pyramid of Menkaure*
2 *Funerary Temple*
3 *Workmen's Quarter*
4 *Pyramid of Khafre*
5 *Funerary Temple*
6 *Mastabas of dynasties IV and V*
7 *Pyramid of Khufu*
8 *Funerary Temple*
9 *Boat Graves*
10 *Mastabas of dynasties IV and V*
11 *Shaft of Hetepheres*
12 *Causeway*
13 *Rock Tombs*
14 *Temple of the Sphinx*
15 *Valley Temple*
16 *Sphinx*
17 *Building of Amenophis II*
18 *Causeway*
19 *Valley Temple*
20 *Causeway*

Above: Diorite statue of king Khafre, found in his Valley Temple: 4th dynasty, c. 2600 BC.

they kept the tourist at bay, as the creature seemed to him too queer for inspection'. In addition to the survey and measurement of the pyramids, Petrie also explained the changes in design which were a feature of all three monuments, and the methods by which the entrances had been sealed. Pyramids were generally closed by portcullises – that is, stones let down from the roof of a corridor to block access – and by granite plug-blocks inserted into the entrance passage in order to fill it completely with stone. Because the Great Pyramid possessed a corridor sloping upwards to the chamber, the plugs had to be stored inside the pyramid until required, as Petrie understood. A later scholar, the German Ludwig Borchardt, suggested that the great height of the Grand Gallery was intended to allow space for a false floor of wood upon which the plug-blocks could be stored without obstructing the funeral procession. The same scholar investigated the pyramid of Khafre.

Other finds at Giza

As the complexities of the pyramids were explained, through the combined efforts of many archaeologists, attention was transferred to the remaining monuments of Giza. Each pyramid had originally possessed two temples linked by a causeway, although not all these elements survive. The plan of Khufu's Mortuary Temple has been traced but the Valley Temple still lies buried. The temples of Khafre are in a better state, especially the Valley Building, which retains its fine colonnades of square granite pillars. It was in this temple that the magnificent statue of the king was discovered, one of 23 statues which had originally been set at intervals along the pillared hall. The temples of the pyramid of Menkaure, excavated by the American George Reisner for the Boston Museum, were found to have been economically completed in mud-brick after the death of the king. From the Valley Temple came many statues, including some fine groups showing Menkaure with queen Khamerernebty II, or with various divinities.

Several expeditions have worked upon the cemeteries which surround the Great Pyramid, particularly the Austrian team led by Hermann Junker, and the Americans under Reisner. These excavations revealed regular streets of tombs to the east and west of the pyramid, containing the burial-places of the king's relatives and of high officials. Thanks to the careful procedure adopted, the excavators made some particularly interesting discoveries, chief among which was the finding of a *shaft-tomb* for the burial of queen Hetepheres, mother of Khufu. In the burial chamber was a rich assortment of objects, including sheets of inscribed gilding from decayed wooden furniture. By the painstaking removal of these fragments layer by layer, it was possible to collect all the pieces. From them, the shape of the original furnishings were reconstructed in new wood, upon which the gilding could be replaced.

In more modern excavations, Egyptian archaeologists opened a pit to the south of the Khufu pyramid in 1954. There they found parts of a dismantled wooden boat, 43.5 metres in length as now reconstructed. Such boats were provided with the royal burial for religious reasons, and it is likely that another still remains within a similar pit farther to the west. Other excavations at the site have revealed chapels of the New Kingdom, dedicated to the Great Sphinx, a rock-cut image of a lion with a human head which is a portrait of Khafre. In later times the Great Sphinx was considered to be the guardian of the Giza cemetery.

The development of Giza really began when Khufu selected the site for his pyramid tomb, and had the surrounding private cemeteries laid out in a regular plan on either side. The neat appearance of this layout was upset by the building of later tombs in between pre-existing ones, because, in the Late Period especially, great numbers of private burial-places were constructed all over the Giza plateau. Khafre and Menkaure followed Khufu in building their pyramids at Giza, but they could not equal the Great Pyramid in size, nor in accuracy of construction. The explanation of the pyramids, their temples, and the surrounding tombs of private individuals have been the major achievements of archaeologists at Giza. Much remains to be discovered and excavation is continuing at the site. By the gradual recovery of new material, combined with careful study of the monuments which have long been known, our understanding of this famous cemetery is steadily improving.

Pyramid Builders

The intriguing question that most people pose about the pyramids of Giza is how they were built. The great size of the monuments – the Great Pyramid of Khufu was originally 146 metres high and had a base length of 230 metres – seems to represent an achievement beyond the powers of the simple tools available in the 4th dynasty. Even more remarkable is the accuracy of construction, the sides of the Great Pyramid being aligned north-south and east-west with a maximum error of only one-twelfth of a degree. Similar accuracy is seen in the jointing of the casing blocks and the granite stones of the internal chambers.

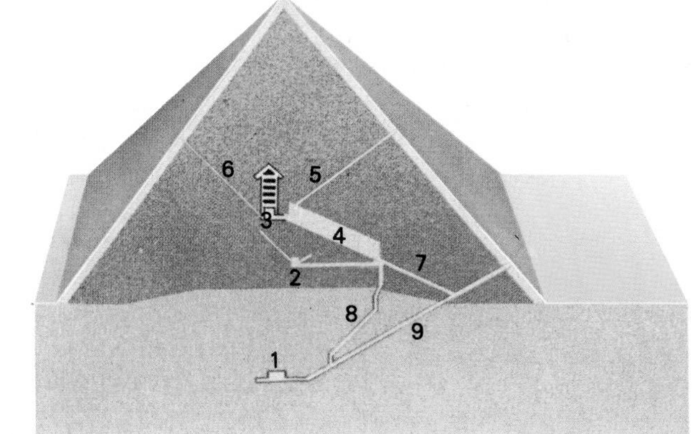

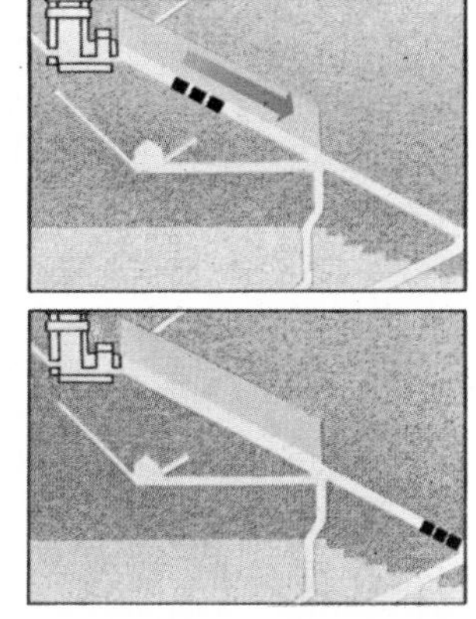

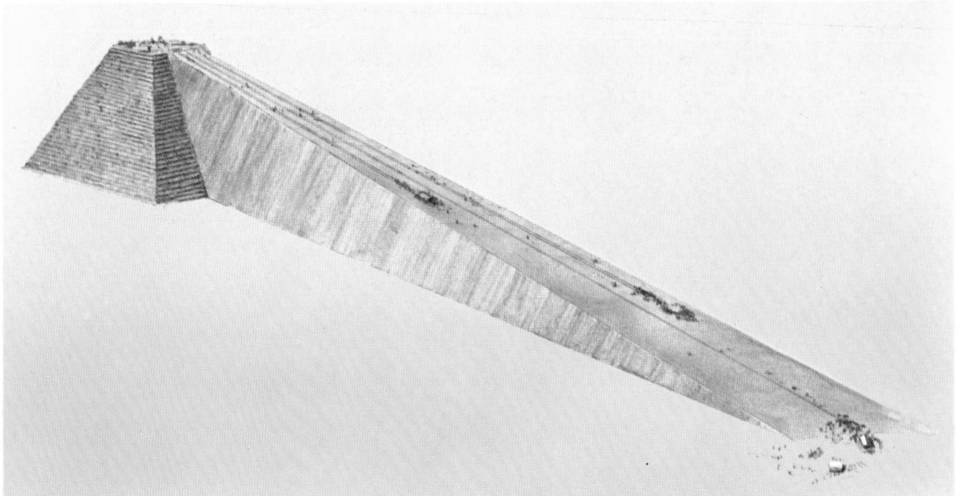

Above: Section of the Great Pyramid, showing the unfinished burial chambers (1, 2), actual burial chamber (3) with two ritual shafts (5, 6), and the Grand Gallery (4). The pyramid was sealed from inside by lowering stone 'plugs' into the Ascending Corridor (7). The workmen left through the shaft (8) and the Descending Corridor (9). The pyramids were built by using ramps of earth to raise the stone to the required level. The ramp was lengthened as the structure rose, to retain the same angle of slope.

Construction techniques

The construction was achieved by fairly simple, straightforward methods. The orientation of the pyramid was determined from star observations, at which we know the Egyptians were quite adept. To raise the stones to the required height as construction proceeded, ramps of earth were laid and the blocks were dragged up them. As the level of the monument rose, the ramp was lengthened so as to maintain the same angle of slope. The blocks for the core of the pyramid, averaging 2.5 tonnes each in weight, were quarried locally by pounding them out from the bedrock of the plateau. Near the pyramid of Khafre is part of an ancient quarry with some blocks still in place. Fine white limestone for the outer casing was brought from Tura on the opposite side of the Nile valley. The granite blocks for internal apartments were quarried at Aswan, about 800 kilometres to the south. Some granite blocks weighed up to 50 tonnes, which shows clearly that the Egyptians had mastered the skill of placing great weights with precision. Their tools were extremely simple, including levers, rollers, ropes, and wooden cradles on which to rest the blocks. The stones were not produced to a fixed size, but, as everywhere in Egyptian architecture, they were individually cut to fit the space reserved for them. Once the pyramid had been built to its full height, the enveloping ramp could be removed and, as this was done, the casing stones were trimmed to a flat surface. The pyramids of Khafre and Menkaure both possessed some casing stones of granite, some of which, on the Menkaure pyramid, have never been smoothed.

The workmen employed on the pyramids were organized in gangs, each of which had a distinctive name. Examples include: 'The craftsmen-gang. How powerful is the White Crown of Khnum-Khufu!' and, rather surprisingly, 'The gang, Menkaure is drunk'. Flinders Petrie located a barracks to the west of the Khafre pyramid, in which he suggested about 4,000 men could have been accommodated. These would have been the skilled workers. The larger mass of seasonal labour, possibly up to 100,000 men, would have been employed only during the months of the Nile floods, when they were unable to work in the fields. Because there was no coinage at this period in Egypt, the workmen were paid with supplies of food. Brief inscriptions were painted upon some of the blocks from the quarries, sometimes mentioning the gang responsible for cutting the stone, or its intended destination. In one of the relieving compartments above Khufu's burial chamber these marks had not been removed from the stones, and among them was the only instance of the king's name to have been found upon his pyramid.

Religious cults

During the Old Kingdom, each of the pyramids of Giza had its own staff of priests for the upkeep of the offering-cult on behalf of its owner, to ensure his continued well-being. The priests lived in special pyramid-cities established close to the temples in which they served. The city of the priests of Menkaure was, at first, situated close to his Valley Temple. It consisted of a cluster of mud-brick houses, but the later growth of the city led to its encroachment into parts of the temple itself. The inhabitants of these settlements were granted certain privileges, such as relief from taxation, as a favour in view of their services in the temples. From the Menkaure city came an inscription of Pepi II, who reigned some 400 years after the pyramid was built, re-establishing the privileges of the local priests, and it is possible that the temple was rebuilt at this stage. In the Mortuary Temple the priests would have presented offerings of food and drink to the statue of the dead king. As payment, they would have received a share of these foodstuffs after their ritual use had been completed. Each of the pyramids of Giza originally had such a cult, including the small pyramids of the queens which lie close to the monuments of Khufu and Menkaure.

Another town for mortuary priests was built not far from the Menkaure complex, to serve the tomb of queen Khentkawes, a rock-cut sepulchre with a superstructure in the form of a huge sarcophagus. Like the city of Menkaure, this settlement consisted of mud-

Above: Painted limestone stela from the tomb of Wepemnefert, who is shown seated before a table of food-offerings: 4th dynasty, c. 2600 BC.

brick dwellings, which originally must have possessed wooden roofing. The royal mortuary cults lasted a long time. But, inevitably, they were eventually abandoned and the temples themselves subsequently fell into ruin.

The large cemeteries to the east and west of the Great Pyramid exhibit clearly the Egyptian concept of the tomb as a dwelling-house, since the whole necropolis was laid out like a planned town. Each tomb had its own offering chapel, sometimes built against the outside of the superstructure, or occasionally incorporated within it. As in the case of the pyramid temples, mortuary priests were employed to officiate at these chapels. In the later part of the Old Kingdom, the original control over the layout of the necropolis was relaxed, with the result that minor tombs were added on the peripheries. Burial at Giza became popular again in the Late Period (after 600 BC), when there was an archaistic revival of interest in the earlier monuments, and even the rooms of the old pyramid temples were used to contain Roman mummies.

The Sphinx

Considerable interest was taken in the Sphinx from the New Kingdom onwards, when it was identified with the Sun god Re-Horakhty. In front of the chest of the figure is a famous stela (stone slab) of Tuthmosis IV, who reigned in the 18th dynasty (about 1420 BC). It states that Tuthmosis, when still a young prince, was resting one day in the shadow of the Sphinx. He had a dream in which he was promised the kingship if he would undertake to clear the figure of sand. After his accession to the throne, Tuthmosis kept his promise, and set up the memorial inscription between the paws of the colossal image.

In the same dynasty, Amenophis II built a small chapel in honour of the Sphinx, to which Seti I of the 19th dynasty made additions. Amenophis had also visited Giza, when he was heir to the throne. He had been so impressed by the monuments there that, when he became king, he ordered the shrine to be built. A long inscription in this building states that Amenophis 'stopped at the sanctuary of Horakhty, so that he might pass some time going over it looking at the skill of this sanctuary of Khnum-Khufu and Khafre'.

Late Period developments

Admiration for the earlier works of Giza was not restricted to royalty. Numerous votive inscriptions set up by private individuals to the Sphinx have been recovered. In the Late Period the archaic revival of the time prompted the restoration of the burial-place in the pyramid of Menkaure. The same may well have been carried out for Khufu and Khafre. In the burial chamber of the Third Pyramid, Colonel Howard Vyse found part of the lid of a wooden coffin, inscribed for Menkaure. However, the style of this object, which is today in the British Museum, shows it to belong to the Late Period restoration of the tomb and not to the original 4th-dynasty interment. Also in the Late Period, the chapel of one of the queens' pyramids beside that of Khufu was enlarged to serve as a small temple of Isis.

Giza has a long history of tourism and the texts of the 18th dynasty show that it was a place to be visited and admired even then. Much later, the Greek historian Herodotus came to the site and left interesting observations concerning the pyramids. In his time (400s BC), Giza was still in regular use as a burial-place and the site must have been busy with tomb-construction gangs and the visits of mortuary priests. Owing to the perpetuation of the funerary cult, an Egyptian cemetery was not an undisturbed, silent place. Only after the last burials had been made, and the most recent offering-cult had been abandoned, did the necropolis lapse into an obscurity of some 2,000 years.

Saqqara

EGYPT

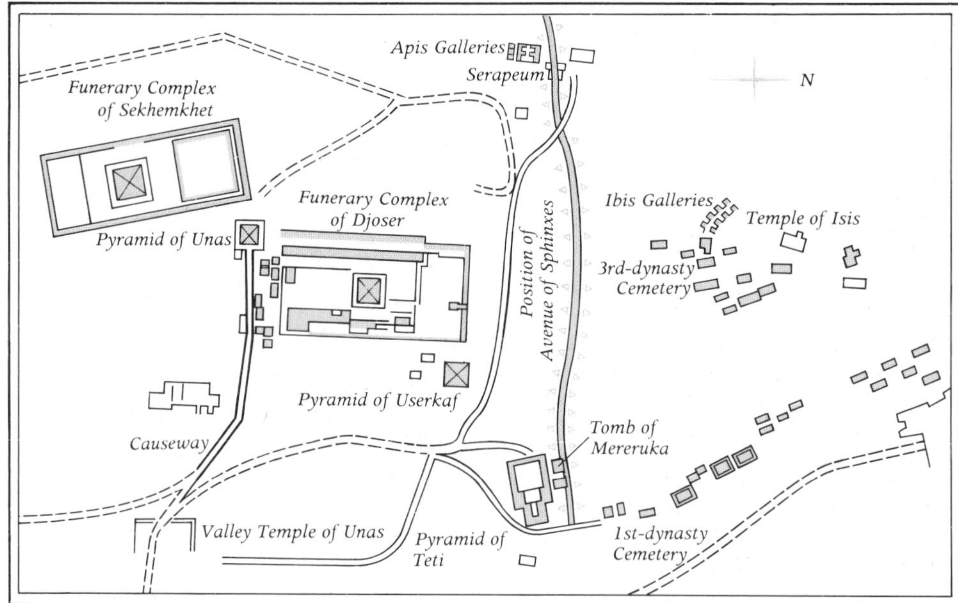

The archaeological site known as Saqqara occupies a desert plateau on the fringe of the Nile valley, some 30 kilometres south of modern Cairo. Saqqara was the necropolis of Memphis, the ancient capital city of Egypt, which lay a short distance to the south-east surrounded by cultivated land. The site is extremely large, including a strip of desert some 6 kilometres long. It is really only a section of an almost continuous burial-ground which extends from Giza in the north to Dashur in the south. The modern name Saqqara may derive from the name of the god Sokar, a divinity of the Memphite necropolis. Saqqara was a cemetery in constant use throughout the course of Egyptian civilization, although it is particularly noted for its important monuments of the Early Dynastic Period (3100–2686 BC), the Old Kingdom (2686–2181 BC) and the Late Period (after 600 BC).

The large area of the site has been a considerable problem in its exploration. Despite the many expeditions which have set out to work there over the last 150 years, some of the regions have never been investigated.

Mariette's excavations

Large-scale excavation at Saqqara really began in 1850, with the work of the French scholar Auguste Mariette, who had originally been sent by the Louvre in Paris to purchase Coptic manuscripts in Egypt. The chance observation of the head of a limestone sphinx protruding from the sand convinced Mariette that he was on the track of the temple of Serapis. This temple had been mentioned by the early Greek geographer Strabo as having an approach lined with sphinxes.

Immediately, Mariette made arrangements to excavate. He gradually unearthed a long avenue of similar figures leading to the ruins of a temple built by king Nectanebo II and dedicated to Osiris-Apis, the sacred bull of Memphis. Eventually the excavations led to the discovery of the underground burials of the bulls themselves, mummified and enclosed in huge granite sarcophagi. First to be found were the tombs of the Late and Ptolemaic Periods (about 664–30 BC), situated in vaults on either side of a lofty subterranean corridor. Subsequent clearance led Mariette to the older galleries of the 19th to 22nd dynasties (1320–730 BC), and to a number of isolated burials of slightly earlier date. Two of these burials remained intact and yielded an extremely impressive array of jewellery.

Mariette's later excavations at Saqqara unearthed monuments of much greater age than the Serapeum, as the burial-place of the sacred bulls is now known. Over large areas of the site he cleared the tombs of high officials belonging to the Old Kingdom, particularly the 5th and 6th dynasties (about 2560–2260 BC). These tombs, generally built of limestone, had rock-cut burial chambers beneath a rectangular superstructure, within which there was usually a decorated offering-chapel. From the chapels, Mariette gathered a rich harvest of inscribed stelae and statues, including some of the most famous examples of Egyptian art. His methods were not those of modern archaeology and he sometimes excavated only part of a tomb. But the rules of careful excavation had not been established in his time. Unfortunately, he did not live to complete the publication of his work, neither on the Serapeum nor on the tombs of the Old Kingdom.

Later excavations

The discoveries of Mariette had demonstrated the great potential of Saqqara, and more scholars were attracted to continue the work of excavation. The pyramids of the 5th and 6th dynasties were opened, resulting in the discovery of the religious spells now known as the Pyramid Texts. Further large tombs were cleared to reveal fine coloured reliefs depicting life in the Old Kingdom. But it was not until 1924 that the systematic excavation of the most conspicuous monument at Saqqara was initiated, namely the Step Pyramid of king Djoser. The work of clearance lasted many years. It was carried out by two Britons, Cecil Mallaby Firth and James Edward Quibell, and the French Egyptologist Jean-Philippe Lauer. It brought to light the great complexity and extent of this 3rd-dynasty (27th century BC) royal mortuary structure. The pyramid stands within a vast enclosure, surrounded by a panelled wall of limestone. Beneath the monument was a labyrinth of passages, some belonging to the original structure, while others were the work of later plunderers. The burial chamber itself lay at the foot of a deep pit under the pyramid, and could be reached by a descending passage from the north side, where the mortuary temple stood. In view of the importance of the early stone buildings within the enclosure, a great deal of work has been carried out on their reconstruction. Those architectural elements which had fallen down were replaced in their original positions.

In more recent excavations carried out by the Egyptian-born Zakaria Goneim, who was chief inspector of Antiquities at Saqqara, another Step Pyramid complex of the 3rd dynasty was discovered. It belonged to king Sekhemkhet, but this monument had never been completed. Only small areas of the complex were cleared by Goneim, although the work has since been resumed.

The temples of the Old Kingdom pyramids at Saqqara were investigated by Firth and Quibell. Firth worked in 1928–29 on the temples of kings Userkaf and Unas, while Quibell had cleared the temple of the pyramid of king Teti some 20 years before. It would be impossible to mention here all the scholars who have worked in some part of the Saqqara necropolis. But we should at least mention the explorations of the Swiss archaeologist Gustave Jéquier on the pyramids of the 5th and 6th dynasties in the southern part of the site, begun in 1924, and

Top: Sarcophagus of an Apis bull in the Serapeum, situated in a burial-vault to one side of the main passage. Late Period, c. 350 BC.

Above: Relief from the wall of a tomb-chapel, showing food being brought for the benefit of the deceased: 5th dynasty, c. 2400 BC.

the more recent excavation by the Egyptian Antiquities Service of the great Causeway of the Unas pyramid. Each pyramid was equipped with two temples, linked by such a causeway, but only in the complex of Unas is this feature well preserved.

An extremely important excavation for the early history of Saqqara was that carried out by the British Egyptologist Walter Bryan Emery at intervals between 1936 and 1956 in the north-eastern sector. There a series of large brick-built tombs was discovered. They belonged to the 1st dynasty, around 3000 BC, when Egypt had just been united into a single kingdom for the first time. These tombs were the burial-places of important officials of the realm, and they contained numerous fine items of funerary equipment. In later years Emery discovered the burials of the sacred Isis-cows, mothers of the Apis bulls whose tombs had been found by Mariette more than a century earlier.

The excavations at Saqqara have provided a vast quantity of information about the development of the necropolis and about such varied aspects of Egyptian civilization as daily life, architecture, funerary beliefs, art and technology. We can now assemble a picture of the steady growth of the cemetery, and begin to trace the development of the Egyptian tomb and of the artefacts found within the monuments. The cemetery began with the 1st-dynasty tombs of nobles, along the edge of the plateau. Their isolation was soon ended by the construction of more brick tombs during the next two dynasties, until the whole northern area of the site was so crowded that the later tombs were built on top of the 1st-dynasty monuments.

With the advent of the 3rd dynasty (about 2600 BC), the Step Pyramid of Djoser was erected. It dominated the site, as indeed it still does. There followed a series of royal tombs during the Old Kingdom, as successive rulers chose this place to build their pyramids. Among these monuments is the pyramid of Unas, the earliest to contain inscriptions. The tombs of private individuals clustered around the pyramids. Many of these tombs contained exquisite reliefs upon the walls of their offering-chapels. Because both royal and private tombs were equipped with statues, many fine examples of Egyptian sculpture have been found at Saqqara. They include the limestone statue of Djoser himself and the wooden figure of Ka-aper (a priest and important state official of about 2500 BC) in the Cairo Museum, and the unnamed squatting scribe, now in the Louvre. The last two of these statues still retain inlaid eyes of coloured stones. Private tombs continued to be built at the site down to Graeco-Roman times, and many have yielded examples of Egyptian material culture, particularly coffins, amulets, jewellery and vessels of stone, pottery and metal.

The use of Saqqara as a necropolis for sacred animals led to the construction of temples for their cult. These were revealed by the excavations of Mariette, and, more recently, of Emery and the Egypt Exploration Society. In the New Kingdom, the Apis bull was probably the only animal buried at the site. During the Late and Ptolemaic periods, however, a vast extension of animal-cults took place, with the result that ibises, baboons, cows, hawks, dogs and cats were all interred there. Many of these underground cemeteries have only recently been exposed by excavation. From some of them came large numbers of bronze objects, particularly figures of gods and items of temple equipment. The fact that important discoveries can still be made after such a long period of exploration shows the size and potential of this great site, where it is certain that much remains to be discovered.

Royal Tombs

The large necropolis of Saqqara has yielded much information about ancient Egyptian life. This is because the Egyptians considered tombs to be the eternal dwellings of the dead, and built them to reflect this concept.

Features of the tombs

The royal pyramids of Saqqara rise above the surrounding tombs of the nobility, paralleling the comparative social positions of the king and his subjects during life. Officials of highest rank generally had a tomb close to the royal pyramid, while lesser individuals had smaller tombs farther away. This relationship can be seen in the earliest monuments, the brick tombs of the 1st-dynasty nobles.

In some cases these large structures are surrounded by small graves for servant-burials, because the personal household staff of the noble were deliberately slain so that the servants could accompany their master to the next world. This practice did not last beyond the 1st dynasty at Saqqara, but the Egyptians never lost the belief that the after-life would be basically the same as daily life in Egypt. Hence the needs of the dead were identical to those of the living. For this reason the Egyptians provided all the kinds of objects which the deceased might require. Most essential was a supply of food and drink, without which the spirit of the tomb-owner could not survive.

Supplies of food were placed in the tombs, especially those of the 1st and 2nd dynasties found by Emery. But the Egyptians also wished to provide fresh offerings at the tomb, if not on a daily basis, then at least on special feast-days. For this reason, every tomb had to combine both an offering-place and the burial-chamber, the latter normally being underground. The brick tombs of the 1st and 2nd dynasties at Saqqara had special recesses in their eastern sides at which offerings could be presented. Later, in the Old Kingdom, this offering-place was incorporated within the tomb superstructure to form an enclosed chapel. The first chapels had few rooms, but by the 6th dynasty they had become so extensive that the whole superstructure might be filled with separate chambers. Within these chapels was a room in which the offering ritual was to take place, in front of a large inscribed stela in the form of a doorway, carved in stone. The deceased could emerge through this to receive the benefit of the food and drink provided.

Similar magic surrounded the placing of statues in tombs. The fine sculptures recovered by Mariette were not intended for admiration. They were originally sealed into hidden chambers in the tombs, close to the offering-chapel. There they functioned as a substitute for the body of the deceased should it be destroyed. The Egyptians believed that the preservation of the body was essential for survival in the next world, but a tomb-statue provided insurance against the damage which thieves in search of jewellery could cause to the mummy. The statue-chamber was linked to the chapel only by small holes in the wall, to enable the benefit of the offerings to pass through to the image. Exactly the same arrangement existed in the pyramid-temple of Djoser, where the limestone figure of the king was enclosed in a sealed chamber.

Above: Statue of Mereruka in his decorated tomb-chapel. Such statues were to act as substitutes for the body, should it be destroyed: 6th dynasty, c. 2250 BC.

The royal pyramids of the Old Kingdom were each provided with two temples. The upper one, close to the pyramid and normally on its east side, was for the celebration of the funerary cult. In this respect, it was a much more elaborate equivalent of the private tomb-chapel. This temple was reached by ascending a long stone-walled causeway from the Valley Temple which lay on the edge of the cultivated land. The Valley Temple served as a reception point for the king's body, where it was probably embalmed before being taken up the causeway for interment inside the pyramid.

Large staffs of priests were recruited for service in the temples, and many private tombs at Saqqara belonged to priests who served the royal pyramids on the same site. Offerings at private tombs could be supplied by relatives, or by a hired group of mortuary priests. The concept of supplying offerings is central to the understanding of Egyptian

Above: Wooden figure of Ka-aper, from his tomb at Saqqara. The arms were carved separately and joined to the figure; the eyes are inlaid with quartz and obsidian: 5th dynasty, c. 2400 BC.

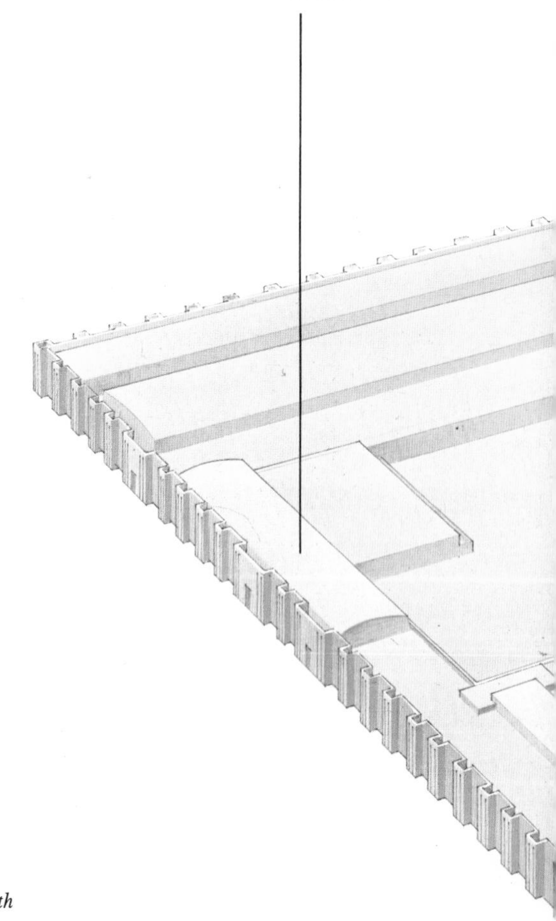

funerary practices, and was a major influence on tomb-design at Saqqara and elsewhere. The tombs of later ages at the site were similarly equipped with offering-places of some type, but it is for the decorated chapels of the Old Kingdom that the necropolis is best known.

The tombs of Saqqara provide us with examples of the technological progress of the Egyptians, especially in the field of architecture. The brick tombs of the early 1st dynasty had an open-pit substructure, roofed with wood, and their superstructure could only be built after the burial. A stairway entrance to the pit was soon introduced, allowing the tomb to be constructed in advance of burial. By the end of the dynasty, rock-cut burial chambers were in use. From this time onwards, burial apartments were always cut into the bedrock, following the increased skill of the local stonemasons at underground tunnelling.

The building of the Step Pyramid for king Djoser represents the earliest attempt of the Egyptians to create a large monument entirely in stone. Their caution in the use of the new material is shown by the fact that they laid the blocks in alternate *header and stretcher* courses, as with the mud-bricks they had formerly used. Many architectural forms in the buildings around the complex were inspired by earlier Egyptian architecture in wood and reeds, here translated – even 'fossilized' – into stone. The Egyptian stonemason used copper chisels for the finer work, but the rough dressing of blocks or the sinking of tomb-shafts in the rock was achieved with stone implements. Large gangs of workmen must have been almost continuously employed on tomb-construction in the necropolis. Some of them, no doubt, also indulged in robbing tombs. This pursuit was extremely common, and the tomb-builders and mortuary-priests must fall under the greatest suspicion, for they would know the location of wealthy burials. They also had the opportunity to gain access to the cemetery for legitimate reasons.

Animal cults

By late times the northern part of Saqqara had become so intensely overcrowded that the Ptolemaic galleries for animal burials frequently broke into older shafts. The development of animal cemeteries at the site provided a whole new industry, involving not only masons for the cutting of tombs, but also embalmers, priests, and people to look after the live animals which were kept near to the site.

The oldest cult, that of the Apis bull of Memphis, was extremely important and royalty provided for the burials. On death, the sacred bull was mummified in Memphis and then transported on a sledge in a great funeral procession to Saqqara, for burial in the Serapeum. Outside the burial vaults stood the temple with its priestly staff, to perpetuate the cult of the Apis, while farther to the north lay the separate temple to Isis-mother-of-the-Apis, close to the more modest burial-place of the sacred cows. Inscriptions were set up in both catacombs recording details of the burials and the names of some of the people involved. At this period, the cemetery must have been a centre of intense activity, with domestic quarters for the staff of the temples and others involved in the animal cults situated around the edge of the plateau. It gives some idea of the span of Egyptian civilization to realize that, to these individuals, the Step Pyramid of Djoser was already an ancient monument over 2,000 years old.

Saqqara is an archaeological site of such complexity that separate portions of it can be treated as individual units. Excavation has therefore tended to follow this pattern. Complete excavation of the site would hardly be practicable, even if it were desirable, although the excavation of particular areas could help to clarify our picture of the history of this great necropolis.

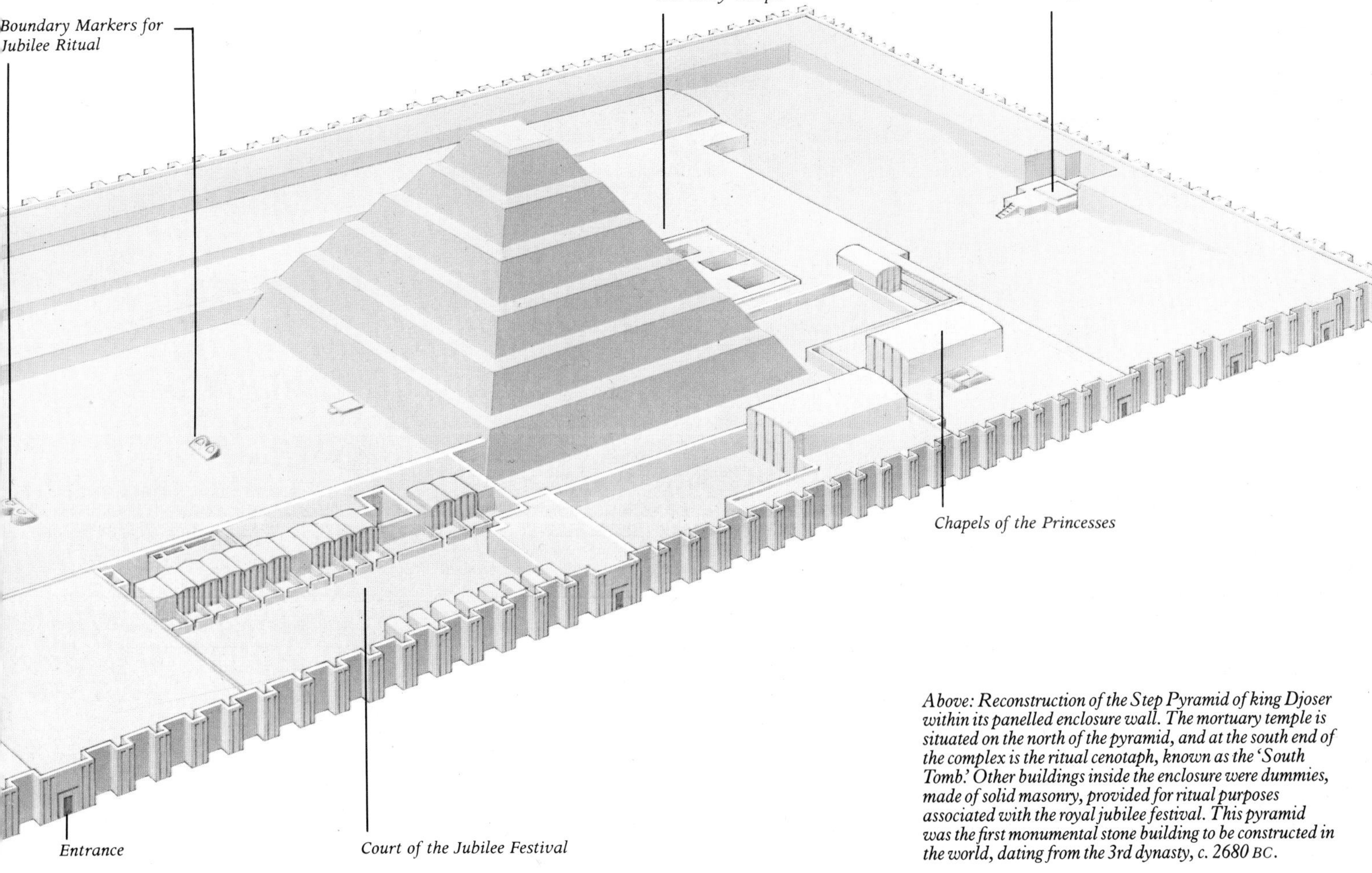

Above: Reconstruction of the Step Pyramid of king Djoser within its panelled enclosure wall. The mortuary temple is situated on the north of the pyramid, and at the south end of the complex is the ritual cenotaph, known as the 'South Tomb.' Other buildings inside the enclosure were dummies, made of solid masonry, provided for ritual purposes associated with the royal jubilee festival. This pyramid was the first monumental stone building to be constructed in the world, dating from the 3rd dynasty, c. 2680 BC.

Karnak
EGYPT

Karnak is the name of a modern Egyptian village situated on the east bank of the Nile, some 600 kilometres south of Cairo. The name of the village has been transferred to the nearby complex of temples which was once the centre for the cults of the gods of the ancient city of Thebes. Little survives today of the town itself other than the temples at Karnak and Luxor. Karnak consists mainly of three large temple enclosures, each encircled by a brick boundary wall. The largest, measuring some 480 × 550 metres, was dedicated to the god Amun, the principal Theban deity and, from the Middle Kingdom onwards, the state god of Egypt.

Thebes was the name given to the town by the Greeks. To the Egyptians, it was known as 'Southern Heliopolis' or, simply, 'The City'. The town seems to have been of little importance in ancient Egypt prior to the Middle Kingdom. Tombs of the Old Kingdom have been found on the west bank of the river, and some statues of Old Kingdom kings have been recovered at Karnak, but it was not until the throne of Egypt passed, in the Middle Kingdom, to a Theban family that the town began to grow in importance and the local god Amun became the state god. Naturally, his home temple benefited from his new status and the kings of the Middle Kingdom enlarged and embellished his temple at Karnak, although few traces now remain of this early brick temple. The kings of the 18th dynasty also originated in Thebes and they soon began to rebuild the Karnak temple, in stone, on a grand scale. The temple which can be seen today is largely the work of the New Kingdom kings, with later additions.

The temple of Amun remained the principal Egyptian cult-centre even in later dynasties when the administrative capital was situated elsewhere. It continued in use until the pagan gods were ousted by the rise of Christianity in the early centuries AD.

The site of Karnak was never lost and its monuments, because of the scale on which they were built, were never completely buried in sand. However, the identity of the ancient city was forgotten until early European travellers began to explore the monuments of the Nile valley. The earliest expeditions to work at Karnak were employed in copying the texts and scenes on the temple walls. The military expedition of Napoleon, in 1798, was accompanied by another army, of scholars and artists, who

Above: Amun-Re crowning queen Hatshepsut. This scene is carved on one of Hatshepsut's obelisks at Karnak: 18th dynasty, c. 1490 BC.

Right: Avenue of sphinxes leading to the first pylon of the temple of Amun. The heads are of Amun's sacred animal, the ram. Figures of a king stand between their paws: 19th dynasty, c. 1270 BC.

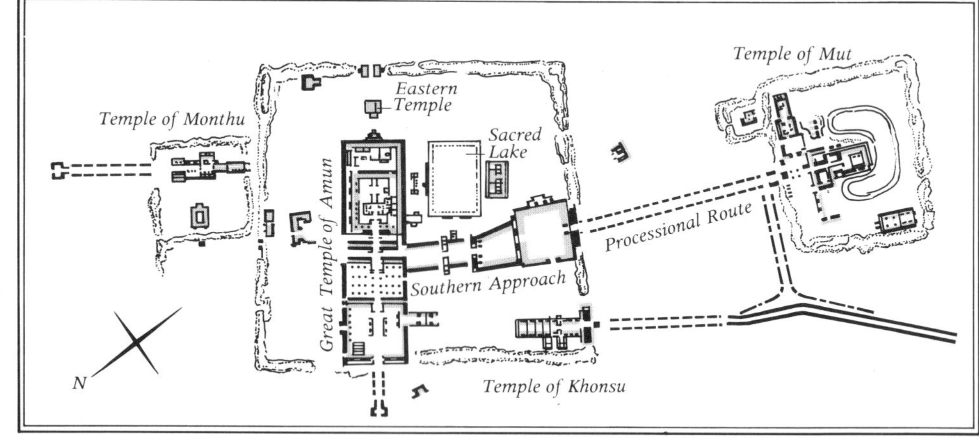

made copies of the temple reliefs at Karnak. In 1842, the Prussian scholar, Richard Lepsius, included parts of Karnak in his monumental record of the standing remains of ancient Egypt.

Excavation at Karnak

Scientific excavation and reconstruction at Karnak, as opposed to previous hunts for treasure, started in 1895 when the French Egyptologist, Georges Legrain, began work on the huge task of clearing and restoring the Amun temple. In 1899 an earthquake caused 11 of the columns of the great Hypostyle Hall to collapse, and these had to be re-erected. Following the same methods of construction as those of the ancient Egyptians, Legrain had earth ramps constructed. The huge column-drums were dragged up the ramps and replaced, one on top of another. Legrain also rebuilt the second *pylon* of the temple which had completely collapsed, and he removed from the fill of the third pylon thousands of blocks which came from earlier temples and shrines. It was a common practice on the sites of Egyptian temples to re-use blocks in this way. When Amenophis III built the third pylon he cleared the area in which it was to stand and used the blocks from the demolished buildings for the fill of his own construction. From this pylon have been recovered the fine limestone *way-*

station of Sesostris I, the quartzite and granite sanctuary of Hatshepsut and a building erected by the father of Amenophis III, Tuthmosis IV, which can have stood only for a few years.

Legrain's most spectacular discovery occurred in 1903 when he found a cache of statues, stelae and temple equipment buried in the court between the south wall of the temple and the seventh pylon. This cache was the result of a general clear-out in the temple in the Ptolemaic period. It included royal statues from the Old Kingdom onwards, as well as private statues, stelae, discarded temple equipment and more than 17,000 bronze figures. It is not difficult to see why it was necessary from time to time, even in such a large temple as that of Amun at Karnak, to remove from the temple itself some of the many statues which had been dedicated to the god. These sacred objects, however, had to be disposed of within the temple precincts.

Legrain's work was cut short by his death in 1917 but it has been continued by other French Egyptologists, particularly Henri Chevrier and Pierre Lacau, who have been responsible for the publication of the findings in parts of the temple. Work is still in progress at Karnak, and much remains to be done.

The Amun temple is not, however, the only one on the Karnak site. There are also two other enclosures. One is dedicated to the worship of Amun's wife, the goddess Mut, and the other to the Theban god, Monthu. The temple of Mut is largely destroyed, but was excavated between 1895 and 1898 by Margaret Benson, daughter of a British Archbishop of Canterbury, and her friend Janet Gourlay. A team from the American Brooklyn Museum is currently re-excavating the temple. The temple of Mut is the main source of the lioness-headed statues of the goddess Sekhmet, with whom Mut was identified. These statues adorn the Egyptian collections of the world's museums. The temple was built in the reign of Amenophis III, as was the temple of Monthu which was excavated by the French Institute in Cairo. This temple is also largely destroyed.

The temple of Amun

The temple of Amun is the principal monument at Karnak and, to most visitors, Karnak is synonymous with the Amun temple. Any building which may have existed on the site in the Old Kingdom would have been made of brick and none has survived. A few traces of the Middle Kingdom temple have been found, mainly stone door-jambs and lintels, many of which bear the name of Sesostris I. In the 18th dynasty a major reconstruction took place, in the reigns of Tuthmosis I, Hatshepsut and Tuthmosis III. The rear portion of the temple, from the fourth pylon backwards, is the work of these rulers. They also began the construction of the southern approach, a feature unique to Karnak, which led to the temple of Mut. Amenophis III built the third pylon, but his major contribution to the cult of Amun was the erection of the fine temple at Luxor, a short distance to the south of Karnak. His son, Akhenaten, later spurned the cult of Amun, and built a separate temple for his solar god, the Aten, to the east of the enclosure of Amun. Blocks from this temple were found to have been re-used in the fill of later pylons of the Amun temple. The temple of Amun, as it appeared at the end of the 18th dynasty, is depicted in the tomb of the Theban official Neferhotep.

In the 19th dynasty the great Hypostyle Hall was completed and decorated by Seti I and Rameses II. Later kings made additions to the temple, including the erection of the first pylon and the massive brick enclosure wall in the 30th dynasty and the provision by Philip Arrhidaeus, regent for the short-lived boy-king Alexander II, of a new granite sanctuary.

Excavation at Karnak will go on for many years to come. The Amun temple itself is not accurately and completely copied and there are areas of the enclosure which have never been excavated. There is still much that can be learned about the history and development of Egypt's principal temple complex.

Left: A detail from the illustration opposite, showing the official Neferhotep at the entrance to the temple of Amun. Behind him are the flagstaffs in front of the third pylon of Amenhotep III. This was the entrance to the temple in the late 18th dynasty. Behind the pylon is one of the many obelisks at Karnak: 18th dynasty, c. 1350 BC.

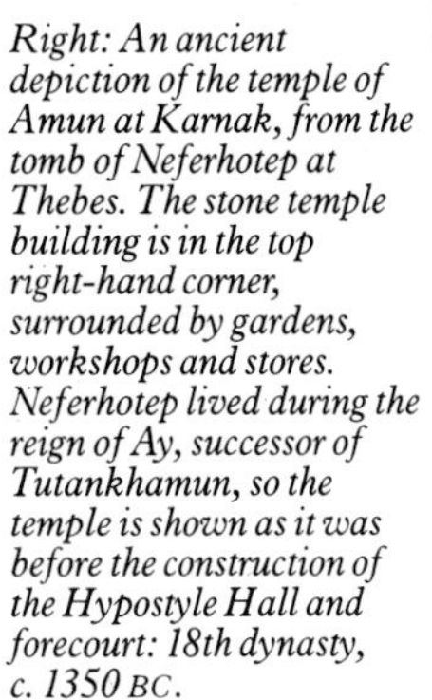

Right: An ancient depiction of the temple of Amun at Karnak, from the tomb of Neferhotep at Thebes. The stone temple building is in the top right-hand corner, surrounded by gardens, workshops and stores. Neferhotep lived during the reign of Ay, successor of Tutankhamun, so the temple is shown as it was before the construction of the Hypostyle Hall and forecourt: 18th dynasty, c. 1350 BC.

Temples and Priests

Egyptian state religion was, to a large extent, ritualistic in nature, and was practised mainly by the official priesthood. There was no onus on the people either to believe in, or to worship, the gods. In fact, the general public were not allowed into the temple enclosures. All that was visible to them of the temple was the brick encircling wall over which they could glimpse the tops of pylons, obelisks and flagstaffs. The only people allowed into the temple were the priests and, of course, the king who was, in theory at least, the High Priest of every Egyptian god. As such he was supposed to officiate at the daily ritual of each temple. This was clearly impracticable and so the role of chief officiant was delegated to one of the priests. However, it was always the figure of the king who was depicted on the temple walls, offering to the god and performing the temple rituals.

Religious rituals

Ancient Egyptians regarded it as essential to propitiate the god by daily offerings. Provided the ritual was performed satisfactorily each day, the god would bestow benefits on the king and Egypt. Every day, in all the temples in the land, a similar ritual was performed. The priest entered the temple, having first been ritually purified with sacred water. He walked the length of the temple to the shrine at the rear, and opened the doors to reveal the image of the god. The divine effigy was purified, anointed and attired in its regalia, and then given a meal. After completing the ritual, the priest withdrew backwards, sweeping the floor with a brush to remove any trace of his footprints. The offerings made to the god, which were not, of course, consumed, were then offered to the other images in the temple, the reliefs and statues of other gods, kings and highly-favoured officials. Finally the offerings reverted to the priests themselves as part of their payment.

In addition to this daily ritual, major festivals were held during which the image of the god was taken out of its shrine and placed in another in the form of a barque. This was carried on the shoulders of the priests and borne in procession out of the temple and into the streets of the town. There it was paraded, usually on the way to visit the temples of other deities. For example, the priests carried the image of Amun to the temple of Mut so that he could visit his wife, or to the temple at Luxor. The image even crossed the Nile to call at the temples on the west bank.

Gods often travelled even farther afield. Once a year the falcon-god Horus used to travel the 130 or so kilometres from his temple at Edfu to visit his wife, the goddess Hathor at Denderah. However, even when the god appeared in these processions, ordinary people were not allowed to see his image, which remained concealed within the shrine.

Most temples, however, had at least one point at which the public could communicate, through the priesthood, with the god. At Karnak the Eastern Temple, at the rear of the Amun temple, was dedicated to 'Amun-Hearer-of-Prayers'. As this name suggests, people could go with their supplications to this aspect of the god.

Egyptian gods resolved problems either by choosing one of two alternatives placed before them, or by moving towards or away from a suppliant. For example, the young prince who was later to become Tuthmosis III was standing in the hall between the fourth and fifth pylons of the Amun temple, in his capacity as a priest, when the image of the god which was being carried past in procession suddenly lurched towards him. This was taken as a sign by those who witnessed it that the god wished Tuthmosis, the son of a concubine of Tuthmosis II, to be the next king.

The ritual life of the temple figures prominently in scenes depicted on the walls of the temples. The king is often shown making offerings to the gods, or participating in

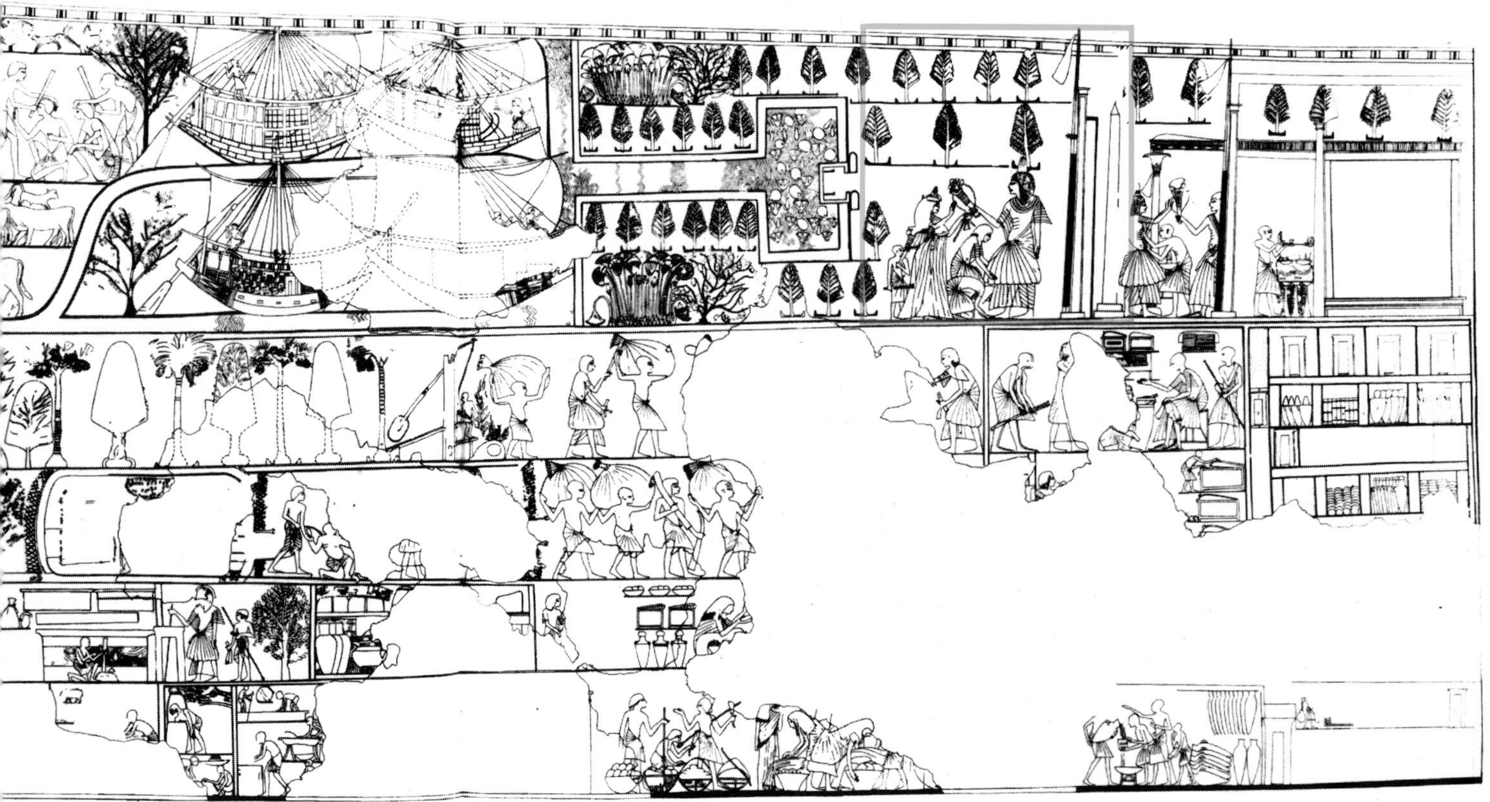

religious festivals. The king could also be depicted being crowned by Amun or taking part in the 'Sed'-festival (or jubilee festival) in which the power of the king was renewed and re-confirmed. Other important rites which are represented include those which took place at the foundation of the temple and its dedication to the god. The information which can be gained from temple reliefs is not, however, confined to religious life. At Karnak, in particular, there are building texts describing in detail the work of various kings. From studying these, it is possible to establish exactly when each part of the temple was built.

There are also historical records, relating especially to foreign campaigns. The Annals of Tuthmosis III are inscribed on the walls of the Amun temple and describe 19 years of military action by the king in the Near East. The military exploits of Seti I and Rameses II are shown in reliefs on the exterior walls of the Hypostyle Hall. In addition, kings often set up, in the temple precinct, stone stelae recording important events. They were usually military in nature although more peaceful occurrences, such as royal marriages or decrees affecting the temple itself, could also be recorded.

The power of the temple

As well as being involved in daily rituals and festivals, the temple of Amun also controlled a vast administrative estate. All the temples at Thebes were administratively subordinate to the Karnak temple of Amun, which also owned and controlled land as far away as the delta in the north and Nubia in the south. This extensive land-ownership involved the temple of Amun in agricultural and mercantile transactions for which it had to employ a secular staff. There were administrators and scribes based in the various estates and in temple-owned barges which plied up and down the Nile with produce from the estates. Even the area within the temple enclosure wall was not devoted entirely to religious buildings. For example, it also contained workshops where temple equipment was made, as well as storehouses for offerings and tribute and houses for the priests. Here also were the pens in which were kept the sacred geese of Amun.

Most of the gods of ancient Egypt had one or more sacred animals and the gods were themselves often depicted in animal form. Amun had two sacred animals, the ram and the goose. The god himself was normally depicted in human form but he could also be shown with a ram's head. Indeed, the sphinxes of Amun which line the path from the quay to the first pylon of the temple are ram-headed. The sacred geese of Amun were kept in a pen within the temple precincts and a staff was appointed to care for them. At Edfu, where the sacred animal of Horus was a falcon, one of the falcons belonging to the temple was displayed to the people of the town from the top of the temple pylon. It is not known, however, whether the same custom was followed with Amun's geese at Karnak.

In the New Kingdom it was Amun, the state-god, who was held to be responsible for all the king's decisions in war, and it was at the instigation of Amun that foreign conquests were made. This meant that all the tribute and plunder from military campaigns was taken first to the temple of Amun where it was displayed before the god and offered to him. This naturally resulted in a great deal of wealth flowing into the treasuries of the Amun temple so that, year by year, the temple became wealthier and more powerful, and the family who controlled the priesthood of Amun at the end of the 20th dynasty eventually challenged the power of the king. The High Priest of Amun, Herihor, began to write his name and titles in a *cartouche* and to claim kingly status. However, the emergence of a strong king, Smendes, at the start of the next dynasty soon put a stop to the pretensions of the priests of Amun. Herihor's successors did not follow his example. This episode is an indication of the potential power wielded by the temple of Amun and illustrates the unique position which Karnak held during the dynastic period in Egypt.

Valley of the Kings

EGYPT

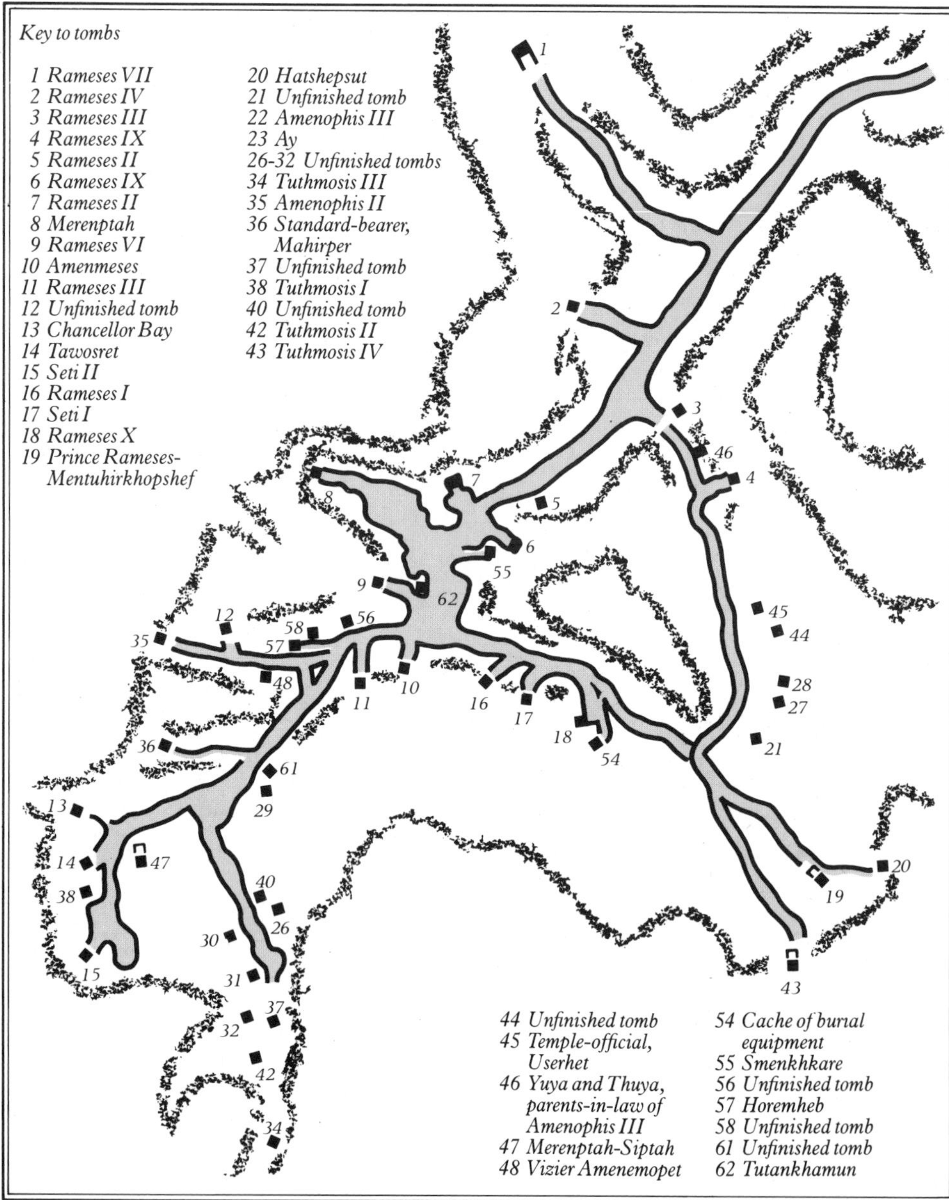

The Valley of the Kings is the name given today to the burial site of the pharaohs of the New Kingdom (about 1567–1085 BC), on the west bank of the Nile at Thebes. The Valley itself is a dried-up watercourse, or 'wadi', of the Nile and is reached by a long winding path from the cultivated area to the back of the Theban cliffs. The Valley has two branches. Almost all the tombs are in the main branch, but two, those of Amenophis III and Ay, are in the secondary branch, the West Valley. Most of the queens of the New Kingdom were not buried in the Valley. The exceptions are the queens Hatshepsut and Tiwosret, both of whom ruled as pharaohs. In the 18th dynasty there seems to have been no special burial ground for the queens, while in the 19th and 20th dynasties they were buried, along with other members of the royal family, in the separate Valley of the Queens.

The Valley of the Kings is dominated by a pyramid-shaped peak in the cliffs which was deified by the Egyptians and regarded as the protectress of the Valley.

Robbers, tourists and archaeologists

Prior to the New Kingdom the kings were buried under pyramids, which were made of stone in the Old Kingdom and of brick in the Middle Kingdom. The main reason for the change to rock-cut tombs was a wish to conceal and protect them from tomb robbers who flourished in ancient Egypt in every period. Needless to say, this device was not successful and robbers had entered all the royal tombs in the Valley, including that of Tutankhamun, long before modern times.

The existence of the Valley was never forgotten and it was known to have contained the tombs of the ancient kings. Hence, from an early period, the Valley was visited not only by robbers but also by tourists. By the time of the 26th dynasty (about 550 BC) some of the tombs were already open and by the Graeco-Roman Period they were being visited regularly by travellers who inscribed graffiti on the walls. A Jesuit scholar who visited the Valley in the 18th century found 10 tombs open and five others in a ruined state, and an English traveller, Richard Pococke, made plans of nine of the Valley tombs in 1738. The expedition which accompanied Napoleon's army listed 11 tombs in the main Valley and discovered another, that of Amenophis III, in the West Valley (tomb No. 22). The other tomb in the West Valley, of king Ay (No. 23), was found by the Italian Giovanni Battista Belzoni in the 1810s. This colourful character started his career as a strong-man in a circus, and became the main source of antiquities for the British consul general in Egypt, Henry Salt, whose collection is now in the British Museum. Belzoni was the first 'excavator' in the Valley, although his methods were hardly scientific, because his main object was to acquire antiquities for his patron. He did, however, discover the sites of many of the royal tombs including that of Seti I (No. 17), one of the Valley's most impressive tombs. Belzoni sent the fine sarcophagus from this tomb to England, and it is now in the Sir John Soane's Museum, London.

Scenes from the tombs were reproduced in large volumes produced by the Prussian archaeologist Richard Lepsius and the French scholar Jean François Champollion in the early 19th century. Hand-copies of the scenes in most of the tombs were published by the French Egyptologist Eugene Lefébure in the late 19th century. However, with the exception of the tomb of Rameses VI, none have been adequately copied even today, and accurate plans exist only for a few tombs.

Most tombs were, of course, plundered within a few centuries, and often within only a few years, of the burial. This led, in the 21st dynasty, to a major effort to collect, rewrap and rebury the royal mummies. They were all removed from their desecrated tombs and reburied in two separate hiding-places. One group, including the mummies of Tuthmosis IV, Amenophis III, Merenptah, Siptah, Seti II, Rameses IV, Rameses V and

Rameses VI, was placed in a side-room of the tomb of Amenophis II, whose body was left in his sarcophagus. This group remained miraculously undisturbed until the tomb was opened and excavated in 1898 by Victor Loret, a Frenchman who was at that time director general of the Egyptian Antiquities Service. The other royal mummies were removed to the Cairo Museum but it was decided to leave Amenophis II in the sarcophagus of his Valley tomb. Unfortunately this proved to be too great a temptation to local tomb robbers and, in 1901, the burial place was again desecrated and the body searched for treasure. For a while Amenophis remained in his tomb but was removed to Cairo in 1939, in a sleeping-car on the Luxor-Cairo train. The only king who still rests in the Valley is Tutankhamun.

The second group of rewrapped mummies, including those of Ahmose, Amenophis I, Tuthmosis I, Tuthmosis II, Tuthmosis III, Seti I, Rameses II and Rameses III, was buried in a Middle Kingdom tomb shaft at Deir El-Bahari. This cache was discovered in 1871 but not, unfortunately, by the Egyptian Antiquities Service. Instead it was found by a family of local tomb robbers who had the intelligence not to attempt to sell the royal mummies themselves nor to flood the antiquities market all at once. For several years they sold off small items found with the mummies until the Antiquities Service perceived, in 1881, that the family had a secret source for the objects they were selling. Eventually one of the men was persuaded to reveal the location of the cache and the mummies were removed to Cairo. As the ship bearing the bodies sailed downstream from Luxor, grieving people lined the banks of the Nile, just as their ancestors had mourned the deaths of the kings 3,000 years earlier.

In 1902 a wealthy American businessman, Theodore Davis, was granted the concession to excavate in the Valley of the Kings. His teams, which included the brilliant British archaeologist Howard Carter, found and excavated the tombs of Hatshepsut (No. 20), Tuthmosis IV (No. 43), Siptah (No. 47), Horemheb (No. 57), Yuya and Thuya, the parents-in-law of Amenophis III (No. 46) and the problematical tomb No. 55. No. 55 is a small tomb which contained an assorted collection of funerary equipment dated to the *Amarna Period.* It is probably the burial-place of the brother and short-lived predecessor of Tutankhamun, Smenkhkare.

Above: View of the limestone cliffs of the Valley of the Kings at Thebes. The rulers of the New Kingdom were buried here in rock-cut tombs: 18th – 20th dynasties, c. 1567 – 1085 BC.

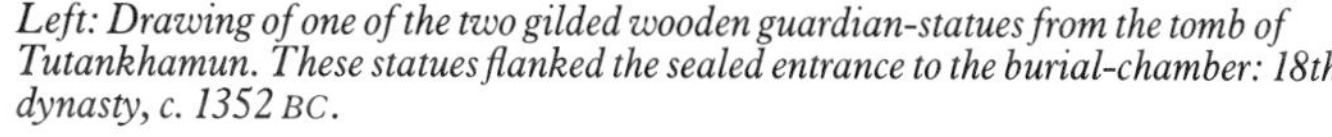

Left: Drawing of one of the two gilded wooden guardian-statues from the tomb of Tutankhamun. These statues flanked the sealed entrance to the burial-chamber: 18th dynasty, c. 1352 BC.

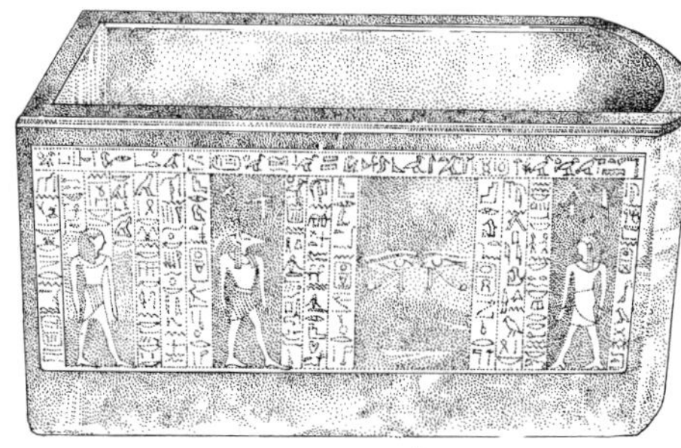

Right: Drawing of the quartzite sarcophagus of Amenhotep II. On the side are depicted some of the four sons of Horus, and two magical eyes to enable the dead king to see out: 18th dynasty, c. 1425 BC.

Tutankhamun's tomb

The most famous tomb in the Valley is, of course, that of Tutankhamun (No. 62), excavated by Howard Carter on behalf of Lord Carnarvon. This was not a fortuitous discovery as Carter had already spent five years systematically clearing the Valley floor in an endeavour to find further tombs. He was rewarded in 1922, when, on clearing away some workmen's huts, he found the stairway entrance to the tomb of Tutankhamun.

The tomb itself is small by the standards of the Valley and was almost certainly not intended as a royal burial-place. It consists of four chambers, only one of which, the sarcophagus chamber itself, was decorated, and each room was packed full of, in Carter's own words, 'wonderful things'. Although the tomb had been entered shortly after the funeral, it had been resealed and remained undiscovered until modern times. It was fortunate that this excavation was under the control of so painstaking a worker as Carter.

The mass of objects packed tightly together in the small space would, undoubtedly, have been picked through for 'treasures' by earlier excavators and many of the interesting, but fragile, artefacts would have been lost. Carter spent 10 years in removing the objects from the tomb and conserving them in the nearby tomb of Seti II (No. 15), which was turned into a store and laboratory during the excavation. Each object was numbered and recorded in detail on an index card. Carter's meticulous records are now in the Griffith Institute in Oxford and work has recently begun on the mammoth task of publishing properly the contents of the tomb. With the exceptions of the stone sarcophagus and the outer coffin, within which the king's mummy still lies, all the objects were taken to the Cairo Museum. Recently a few have been transferred to the new Luxor Museum.

The discovery of the tomb of Tutankhamun, although it dominated the world's headlines and is still the most famous of Egyptian finds, provided little additional information on the history of the period. It was also a great disappointment to scholars that no *papyri* were found in the tomb.

In 1914, when the concession to excavate in the Valley passed from Davis to Lord Carnarvon, the former stated that, in his opinion, there were no more tombs to be found in the Valley. In view of the fact that the tomb of Tutankhamun was discovered eight years later, it may seem rash to repeat such a statement today. However, Carter's systematic search of the Valley makes it highly unlikely that any more royal tombs await discovery.

Royal Burials

When the Egyptians decided, in the reign of Amenophis I, to try and hide the burial-places of kings in rock-cut tombs, they set themselves a problem. To ensure continued existence after death, the dead king had to receive offerings, and so there had to be a temple in which his cult could be celebrated.

In the Old and Middle Kingdoms the royal mortuary temple was situated within the pyramid complex, adjacent to the actual burial beneath the pyramid. However, if the site of the tomb was to be kept secret the cult-centre of the dead pharaoh had to be separated from the burial-place. Accordingly the royal mortuary temples of the New Kingdom were built on the low desert at the edge of the cultivated land, on the other side of the Theban cliffs. It was in these temples that the royal cult, as well as that of Amun, to whom the temples were also dedicated, was celebrated. Each temple had its own priesthood and several of the royal cults flourished for many years after the deaths of the pharaohs. Only four of these temples are at all well preserved today. They are those of Hatshepsut, Seti I, Rameses II (the Ramesseum) and Rameses III. Other temples were used as quarries for the building projects of later kings. For example, the mortuary temple of Amenophis III, which once stood behind the famous Memnon *colossi*, was dismantled in the reign of Merenptah and the blocks used to build the temple of this king.

Top: A painted wall-scene in the tomb of Horemheb, last king of the 18th dynasty. Osiris, god of the dead, is followed by Anubis and Horus: 18th dynasty, c. 1320 BC.

The layout of tombs

The first pharaoh actually to be buried in the Valley of the Kings was Tuthmosis I. An interesting text in the tomb of one of his officials, Ineni, describes the great secrecy that surrounded the excavation of the tomb. The earliest tombs in the Valley are all similar in plan, being of a 'hook'-shape culminating in a burial-chamber containing the sarcophagus. During the reign of Tuthmosis III, when several of the tombs were constructed, the burial-chamber was of an oval shape to imitate the cartouche, an oval figure in which the names of the king were written. However, the sarcophagus-chamber of his son, Amenophis II, is rectangular, as are those in subsequent tombs.

Various methods were tried from time to time to attempt to outwit the tomb robbers. In some royal tombs there is a well in the main passage. This probably served both as a security device and to fulfil religious requirements. In the 18th and 19th dynasties, the tombs had small entrances which could be blocked and concealed after the burial. However, by the 20th dynasty, it had become obvious that concealment was impossible, and so the tombs had large, decorated entrances and corridors. Another device can be seen in the tombs of Horemheb, Seti I and Setnakhte (No. 14). These tombs each have a false burial-chamber, intended to make robbers think they had reached the end of the tomb, whereas, in fact, a concealed stairway in the floor of this chamber led on to the true burial-place. Needless to say, these devices did not fool the robbers, who were usually local men and had often worked on the construction of the tombs.

From the reign of Ay the regular tomb-plan had a straight axis, the exception being

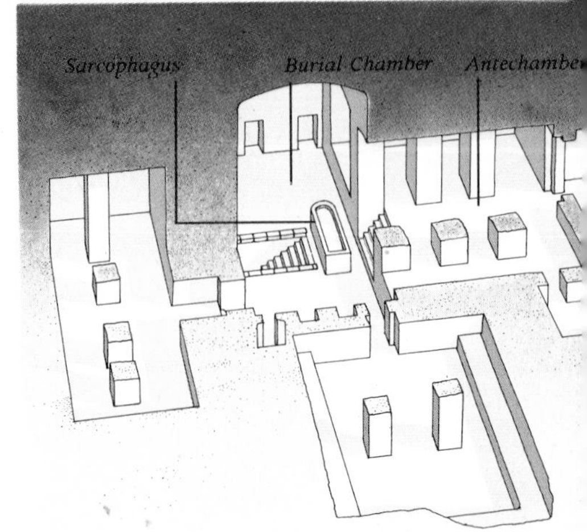

that of Rameses II (No. 7) which turns at a right-angle.

Workmen and plunderers

The work of the royal tombs in the Valley of the Kings was a continuous operation. The workmen were provided with a special walled village in another wadi, a short walk from the Valley. Known today as Deir El-Medineh, this village, and the tombs of its inhabitants, provides a fascinating insight into the lives of the craftsmen who worked on the royal tombs.

Their village, unlike most ancient Egyptian villages, was enclosed by a wall and guarded at night. The men were paid for their work in food and other necessities, and there was at least one occasion on which these workmen went on strike because they had not been paid. Because their pay took the form of provisions, their reluctance to carry on working under the hot Egyptian sun can be readily understood. Each day the men were led to work along a path on the top of the cliffs, the sides of which are covered in ancient graffiti, and at night they were led home again. The royal tomb under construction at any one time was known simply as 'The Tomb', and the men engaged on its construction were divided into two gangs.

The life of these men was undoubtedly hard, and they had to live in an isolated desert valley. But they had one compensation which is not to be underestimated for an ancient Egyptian. This was their right to excavate and decorate their own tombs, with the help of their fellow workmen. The rock-cut tombs, surmounted by small pyramids, which the workmen erected on the cliff overlooking their village, are exquisitely painted and many are well-preserved.

If the main activity in the Valley during the day was the preparation of 'The Tomb', then the main occupation at night was, undoubtedly, the robbing of earlier tombs. Even during the 20th dynasty, when the Valley was still being used as the royal cemetery, tomb robbing had become such a problem that an official enquiry was set up at Thebes. All the royal tombs were inspected, both those in the Valley and those of earlier kings on the cliffs at Dira abu'l Naga, and a record was made of the state in which the tombs were found. Investigations then began into the robberies which had taken place. The account of these proceedings is preserved in a series of papyri, most of which are now in the British Museum. Each of the accused was brought before the court and had to swear an oath that he was about to tell the truth. These oaths make interesting reading, because they indicate the kinds of punishments in store for those who would be found guilty. For example, two such oaths are: 'If I speak falsehood, may I be mutilated and may I be sent to Kush' (to work in the quarries), and 'If I speak falsely, may I be mutilated and placed upon the stake' (impaled).

Each of the accused, and they included both men and women, was asked to give information voluntarily and, if they refused, they were 'persuaded' to speak by various means of applied pressure. Usually a confession followed, but if the accused still pleaded ignorance of the crime, he was released and allowed to go free. Once a guilty robber had been persuaded to confess, he gave details of the men involved and the division of the plunder. An extract from one of the papyri is as follows.

'The incense-roaster of the estate of Amun, Shedsukhonsu was brought. The Vizier said to him, "Tell me the men who were with you in the tombs". He said, "As for me, I was sleeping in my house when Amenkhau . . . Userhetnakht . . . Perpatjau . . . and Nesamun . . . came to where I was at night. They said to me 'Come out. . . .' They took me with them. We opened the tomb and we carried off a shroud of gold and silver, (worth) one deben. We broke it and we placed it in a basket and we brought it down. We divided it and made it into six parts".'

It was not only the royal tombs which suffered at this time. There were also confessions to the robbing of the royal mortuary temples, particularly the Ramesseum, usually with the connivance of one or more of the temple officials. The robbers naturally concentrated on valuable items made of gold or other precious metals and, when robbing tombs, they rifled the bodies of the dead for the jewellery which they knew they would find between the mummy wrappings. In view of this persistent and continuous plundering, it is surprising that anything at all has been found in the royal tombs.

The objects originally buried with a king formed a combination of his personal effects and ritual items necessary for his continued survival after death, as can be seen in the contents of the tomb of Tutankhamun. Several of the ritual objects from this tomb can be compared with less well-preserved finds from other royal tombs. For example, the guardian statues of Tutankhamun are paralleled by similar statues of Rameses I and Rameses II, now in the British Museum. Triple shrines can also be seen on an ancient plan of the tomb of Rameses IV, now in Turin, Italy. Despite centuries of plundering, many objects which were not regarded as valuable by the robbers have been recovered from the tombs in the Valley, and so it is possible to form an idea of the wealth buried beside each pharaoh in his lonely tomb in the Valley of the Kings.

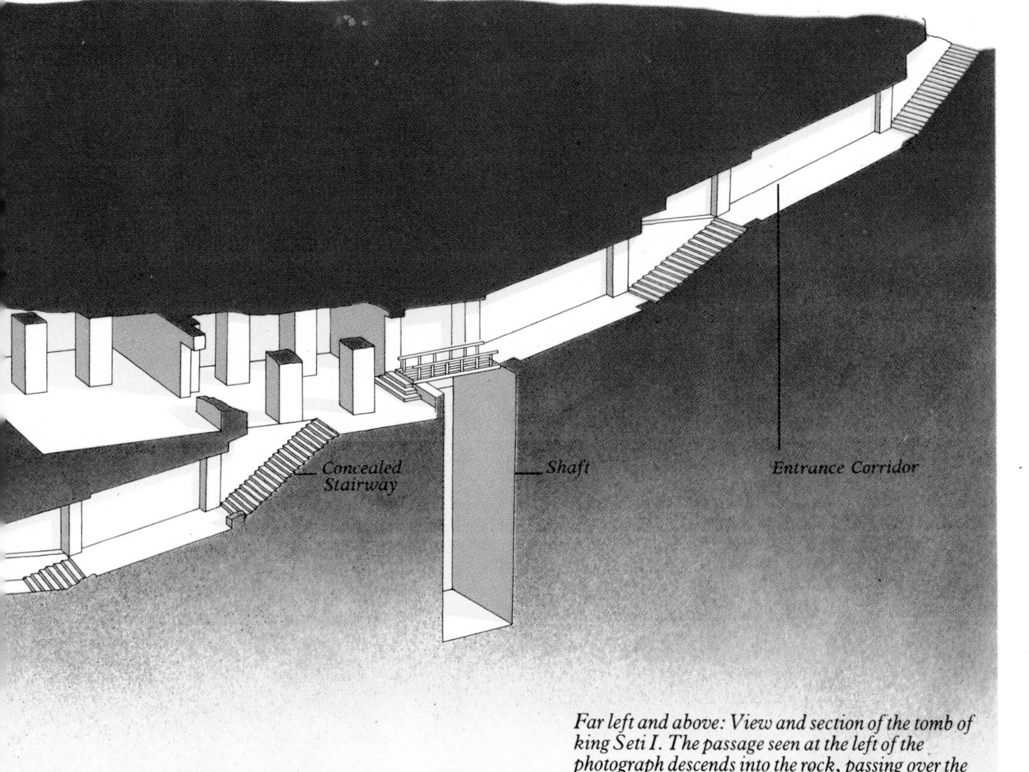

Far left and above: View and section of the tomb of king Seti I. The passage seen at the left of the photograph descends into the rock, passing over the ritual-shaft, and leading to a false-end to the tomb, designed to outwit tomb-robbers. The true burial-chamber is reached by descending the concealed stairway, which gives access to a deeper level. The walls of the passages and chambers are covered with finely-decorated scenes and texts: 19th dynasty, c. 1290 BC.

Abydos

EGYPT

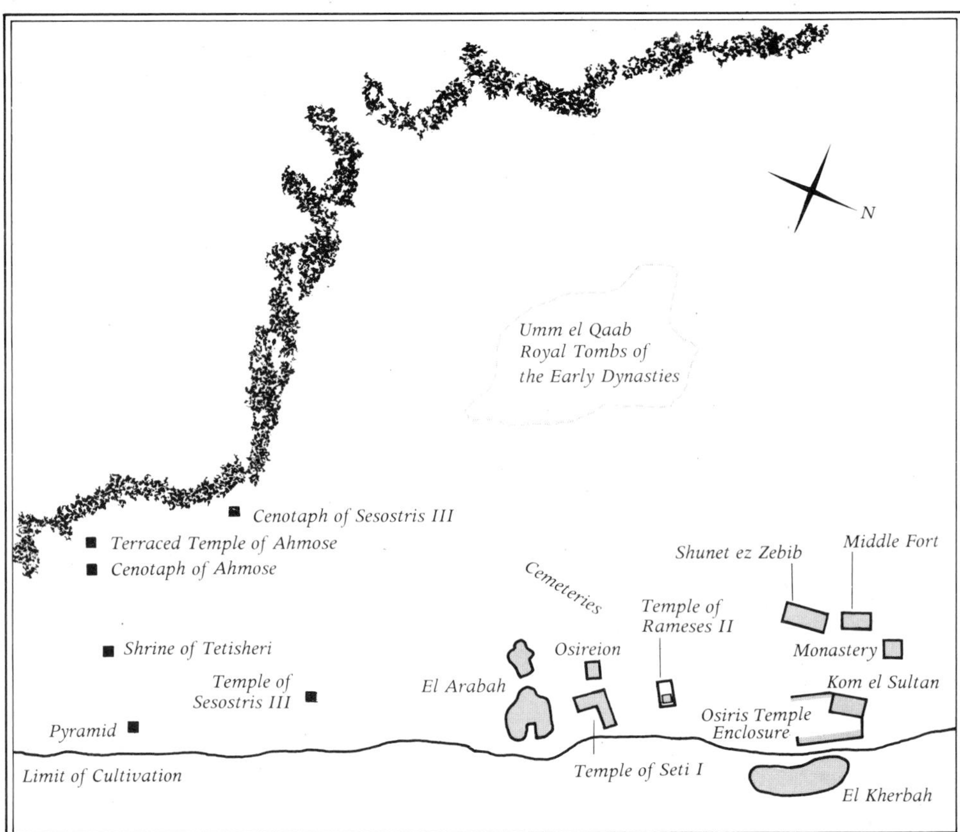

The ancient town of Abydos (the Greek version of Abdju, the Egyptian name) stands on the west bank of the Nile in Upper Egypt. It was one of the most important religious centres in the *Pharaonic Period*. Abydos was in the Thinite *nome*, the capital of which was Thinis, although the site of this town is not known. Because Abydos was not the nome-capital, it would not have been a major administrative centre on either a local or a national level. Its importance was based entirely on the fact that it was regarded as being one of the burial-places of the god Osiris.

A sizable town-mound must once have existed at Abydos, because the site has been occupied continuously. However, only a small part of the mound remains today, near the temple of Osiris. The disappearance of the town-mound is not solely the result of the passing of time and the effects of the weather. It is also due to the activities of Egyptian farmers who regard town-mounds as a convenient source of highly fertile soil, the product of decayed mud-brick buildings. Because of the relatively small area of the town which survives, archaeologists have tended to concentrate instead on the extensive cemeteries of the site, and on the temple remains.

Excavations at Abydos

As at Saqqara, the first work carred out at Abydos was by the French Egyptologist and founder of the Egyptian Antiquities Service, Auguste Mariette. He excavated in the private cemeteries and recorded parts of the temples of Seti I and Rameses II. Mariette's methods were later to be faulted by Flinders Petrie and other excavators. But they were not unreasonable for one of his time, and were infinitely preferable to those of another French 'archaeologist', Emile Amélineau, who rummaged his way through the cemeteries between 1895 and 1898. Unfortunately, Amélineau discovered at Abydos the most important burial-ground of the Early Dynastic Period, that of the first kings of the united land of Egypt. All the kings of the 1st dynasty (about 3000 BC), and two of those of the 2nd dynasty, were buried at Abydos. Amélineau looted these tombs of their fine pottery, stone vessels and other objects which were sold in Paris in 1904. Although many of the items ended up in the Louvre in Paris, others were dispersed among private collections and Amélineau's publication of his work at Abydos is totally inadequate.

Fortunately he was followed at Abydos by Sir Flinders Petrie who, by careful and systematic excavations, was able to salvage many objects from the destroyed tombs, which were brick-built and probably had low tumulus superstructures. Petrie was the first excavator in Egypt to use scientific methods, and to insist that all objects, even those of no apparent value or interest, should be carefully preserved and properly recorded. Petrie himself established typologies of objects which he illustrated from his own collection, now housed in the museum which bears his name at University College, London. He insisted on rapid publication of his findings so that the material he had discovered could be quickly made available to other scholars, and he trained other Egyptologists on his excavations to follow his methods.

Petrie not only rescued the Early-Dynastic royal tombs, but also excavated the Osiris temple, the main cult-centre at Abydos. This temple was in continuous use and was repeatedly rebuilt from the Old Kingdom to the 26th dynasty. Petrie was able to reconstruct the plans of the various stages of the temple's history. He also excavated in the private cemeteries. His work at Abydos was carried out for the Egypt Exploration Fund of London (now the Egypt Exploration Society) and was continued in 1904 under the direction of Edward Ayrton, Charles Currelly and Arthur Weigall, who made other important discoveries. They excavated two monuments which they regarded as Early-Dynastic 'forts', but we now know that these monuments were connected with the early royal tombs. They were probably the structures in which the royal cult was celebrated. In the same season the excavators revealed two cenotaphs, of the 12th-dynasty king, Sesostris III, and the founder of the 18th dynasty, Ahmose. These were underground tombs in which neither king was buried. They also found a dummy pyramid and an offering chapel built by Ahmose in memory of his grandmother Tetisheri, regarded as the ancestress of the 18th dynasty.

The Egypt Exploration Society is still involved with Abydos today, copying the reliefs of the temple of Seti I. This work was begun in 1927 by a British-born Canadian artist, Amice Calverley, who produced four folio volumes of the finely painted relief-work, but left the publication unfinished. Recently the task of completing the record of this temple has been taken up again by the Society.

The private cemeteries at Abydos were excavated, with varying degrees of proficiency, by the British Egyptologist John Garstang in 1900 (for the Egyptian Research Account), the Britons David Randall-MacIver and Arthur Mace between 1899 and 1901, and the Swiss Henri Naville and the Briton

Right: The Osireion, cenotaph of Seti I, situated behind his mortuary temple. It imitates the form of the tomb of Osiris, god of the dead: 19th dynasty, c. 1290 BC.

Above: A small ivory figurine of king Khufu, found in the temple of Osiris. It is the only known representation of the builder of the Great Pyramid: 4th dynasty, c. 2600 BC.

Thomas Peet from 1909 to 1912 (all for the Egypt Exploration Fund).

The importance of the excavations

The excavations at Abydos have provided many insights into the religious and funerary customs of the ancient Egyptians, as well as many artefacts with both historic and artistic value. The royal cemetery of the earliest kings has yielded the oldest examples of Egyptian stelae. At the entrance to each tomb was a pair of stone stelae, inscribed with the name of the dead monarch. The finest example is the one surviving stela of king Uadji, which is now in the Louvre.

Another impressive artefact which was recovered from the archaic cemetery in fact dates from the 13th dynasty (about 1700 BC), by which time the identities of the royal tomb-owners had been forgotten. Because Abydos had become renowned as the burial-place of Osiris, it was decided that one of the royal tombs, that of king Djer, was the actual tomb of the god. The 13th-dynasty king Khendjer, therefore, had made a basalt bier depicting the mummiform figure of Osiris and this was placed in the tomb of Djer. The bier was discovered by Emile Amélineau and is now in the Cairo Museum.

Thousands of private stelae, which can be seen in most Egyptological collections, also came from Abydos. If an Egyptian could not be buried there, near to Osiris, he built a brick chapel and placed within it a stela which depicted himself, and often members of his family, and bore the standard Egyptian offering-formula.

One of the smallest, but also one of the most important finds which Flinders Petrie made in the Osiris temple was an ivory statuette, only just over 7 centimetres high, bearing the name of Khufu. This is the only known representation of the builder of the Great Pyramid of Giza. Another small ivory figure from the temple depicts an Early-Dynastic king wearing the crown of Upper Egypt and the cloak of the 'Sed'-festival, or royal jubilee. The latter figure came from a brick chamber in which a whole range of objects was found, particularly ivories and items of green glazed faience. These objects had probably been given to the temple during the Early Dynastic Period and were discarded towards the end of the 2nd dynasty.

One interesting custom in ancient Egypt, which is well illustrated at Abydos, was the placing of foundation deposits under the corners, or doorways, of religious buildings at the time of their foundation. The Osiris temple has provided examples of these dated from the 6th to the 20th dynasties. The deposits of Sesostris I are remarkably uniform, consisting of a shallow pit lined with bricks in which were placed an ox-head and other ox-bones, pottery, and bricks containing plaques of various materials, inscribed with the name of the king, and describing him as 'Beloved of Khentamentiu'. By the time of the New Kingdom, the ox-bones were usually omitted from the deposits and model tools were included. The discovery of these deposits was of great value to Petrie as they enabled him to reconstruct the plans of the earlier temples.

The fact that the Osiris temple underwent such continuous rebuilding should not imply that it was constantly falling into disuse and, therefore, had to be rebuilt. It is rather an indication of the high esteem in which the god was held that successive kings preferred to rebuild his temple completely rather than, as at other sites, make additions to the buildings of their predecessors.

The Necropolis

Abydos was associated with the chief god of the dead, Osiris, especially from the Middle Kingdom onwards. Osiris was not the native god of the town, but originated at Busiris in the Nile delta. However, by the Old Kingdom he was already being identified in the Pyramid Texts with the local Abydene deity named Khentamentiu. From the 12th dynasty (1991–1786 BC) the temple of Abydos was dedicated to the composite god, Osiris-Khentamentiu. Once this link between Osiris and Abydos was established, the area became a favoured burial-place, because all who could afford it wished to be interred in the domain of the god.

Abydos also came to figure prominently in funerary rituals, which included a symbolic journey to the site for burials made in other parts of Egypt. Khentamentiu was also regarded as a patron of the dead. This made his assimilation with Osiris a fairly straightforward matter. His name means, 'The Chief of the Westerners,' because the Egyptians regarded the west as the abode of the dead.

The main temple of Abydos was situated in the northern part of the site, surrounded by the ancient town. In the cemeteries close to the temple, vast numbers of private stelae were set up on behalf of individuals who could not achieve their ambition of burial at Abydos, but nevertheless wished to place some memorial in the precincts of Osiris. From the Middle Kingdom, it was thought that burial at Abydos conferred special benefits on the deceased, but even a cenotaph was considered to be advantageous. The sacred route from the temple to the area of Umm el-Qaab, which tradition had identified as the burial-place of Osiris himself, was lined with such private monuments. The building of tombs and cenotaphs seems to have encroached upon the temple area itself, because a brick wall was built across part of the 'temenos', or precinct, as if to restrict the funerary monuments to that quarter.

People who lived during the Middle Kingdom had, in fact, identified one of the 1st-dynasty royal tombs with the tomb of Osiris, because the true ownership of these monuments had been long forgotten. Already in the 12th dynasty the cult of the god included ritual processions to the tomb, at which the burial ceremonies of Osiris were re-enacted. A certain Ikhernofret, priest of Osiris at Abydos, says in his memorial inscription:

'Also, I organized the great procession and I followed the god at his goings-forth. I caused the boat of the god to sail and Thoth directed the journey. I prepared the bark, "Rising in Truth", of the lord of Abydos with a cabin, his beautiful regalia being set in place when he proceeds to the

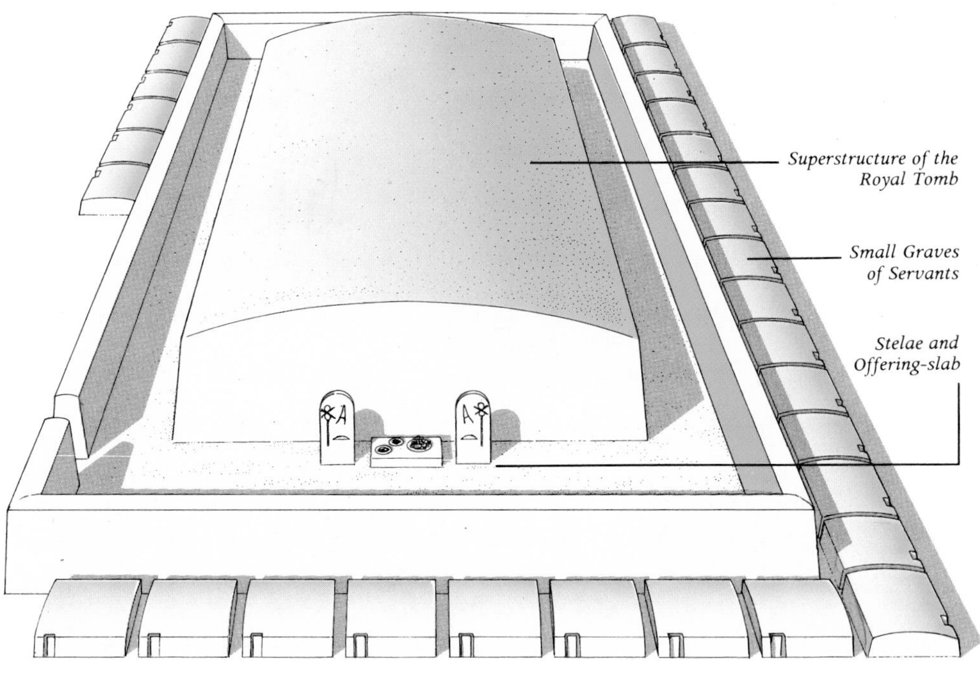

Above: Reconstruction of the tomb of Meretneith, showing the funerary stelae and subsidiary burials of servants: 1st dynasty, c. 3050 BC.

Below: The goddess Isis shown in fine-relief in the mortuary temple of Seti I. She holds a musical instrument called a sistrum: 19th dynasty, c. 1290 BC.

Right: Rameses II consecrating an offering. He stands before an altar piled high with food gifts for the god: 19th dynasty, c. 1270 BC.

district of Peker. And I cleared the path of the god to his tomb in Peker'.

This refers to the preparation of the boat-shrine in which the image of the god was transported, and to the procession to the tomb. In the following dynasty, king Khendjer provided the stone image of Osiris lying upon the funeral couch, to be placed within the cenotaph of the god. With the continuance of these rituals and the extensive supply of offerings at the tomb during the New Kingdom, the area around the sacred burial-place became covered by heaps of pottery offering-vessels, from which derives the Arabic name Umm el-Qaab, 'Mother of Pots'.

Not only private individuals wished to benefit from the construction of funerary monuments at Abydos. In the 12th dynasty, king Sesostris III built an extensive underground tomb there, together with an associated temple. A similar cenotaph was constructed in the 18th dynasty by Ahmose. Both of these dummy tombs were supposed to confer benefits upon their owners, even though they were actually buried elsewhere. The inscription upon the stela of Ahmose, set up in the nearby cenotaph of queen Tetisheri, states that her burial was at Thebes.

Mortuary temples

In the 19th dynasty (1320–1200 BC), considerable attention was paid to the site by Seti I and Rameses II, both of whom constructed temples here. These buildings did not form part of the main cult-temple of Osiris-Khentamentiu, but were separate buildings with a special purpose. They were really mortuary temples, like those of Thebes, in which the cult of the dead king could be combined with that of the gods. Building these temples at Abydos was another attempt to secure additional benefits by having the cult of the king perpetuated in the domain of Osiris himself. This was particularly appropriate, because the Egyptians believed that the dead king became identical with Osiris. Hence the cult of the god was really a form of royal ancestor-worship. Not only Seti and Rameses, but also their predecessors shared this identification with Osiris. Consequently, in the temples of the 19th dynasty at Abydos the rituals were carried out for the royal ancestors in addition to the major deities who possessed shrines within the buildings.

The temple of Seti I is unusual in having seven sanctuaries. The central one is dedicated to the state-god Amun-Re; to his right are the shrines of Horakhty, Ptah, and the deified king Seti himself; to the left are those of Osiris, Isis and Horus. Although not in the central position, the sanctuary of Osiris was the most important.

Both temples incorporated an unusual feature which confirms their link with the ancestor cult. This was a list of the names of many foregoing rulers of Egypt, back to the 1st dynasty. In the temple of Seti, where the list is well preserved, king Seti and prince Rameses are shown invoking their ancestors. This aspect of the Osiris cult, the identity of the god with the dead king, was one of the reasons for the stability of the kingship in Egypt and the emphasis placed on continuity and permanence. At the back of the temple, Seti I constructed his underground cenotaph as a replica of the tomb of Osiris. It consisted of a subterranean burial chamber upon an island surrounded by water. This tomb was originally covered by a mound, with probably a sacred grove of trees, but it is now open to the sky. It possesses an impressive series of square pillars upon the central platform, and the walls of the burial chamber were inscribed with religious texts in the reign of king Merenptah. The temple of Seti itself is well preserved, and contains some of the finest reliefs in Egypt, depicting the rituals which ensured the well-being of the gods and of the king.

The popularity of the Osiris cult continued until the latest times, and became even more influential. In the religious life of Abydos, it is highly appropriate that the worship of the god should have led to the cult of the royal ancestors, because the tomb identified as the burial-place of Osiris had really belonged to king Djer of the 1st dynasty, and the area of Umm el-Qaab was the cemetery of the earliest of Egypt's royal dead.

1
2
3
4
5
a
b
c
d
e
f
g
TURKEY
Samsun
Alaca Hüyük
Boğazköy
Sungurlu
River Halys
Sardis
Konya Plain
Hacilar
Beyşehir
Carşamba River
Çatal Hüyük
Taurus Mountains
Amanus Mountains
Tarsus
Mersin
Cilicia
Gaziantep
Carchemish
Khorsabad
Nineveh
Nimrud
Mosul
MEDITERRANEAN SEA
Minet-el-Beida
Ugarit
Cyprus
Ebla
River Euphrates
Assur
River Tigris
Byblos
Kadesh
Mari
Sidon
Tyre
Hazor
Sippar
Ashdod
Jericho
Jerusalem
Lachish
Babylon
Red Sea

The Near East

7000 BC - 330 BC

These sites of the Near East have been selected as illustrating the emergence of the first permanent settlements, the growing complexity of economic patterns, and the rise of the first empires. Among them, only Çatal Hüyük is prehistoric and therefore has no written records. Interpretation of the other five sites has been greatly amplified by the discovery of tablets and other inscriptions.

Çatal Hüyük may well represent a more sophisticated community than known elsewhere to date in the Neolithic Near East. Its wall paintings, the recovery of which stimulated improved techniques for conservation in the field and after recovery, and reliefs were the work of talented artists. This fact sets Çatal Hüyük apart from all other known contemporary sites.

Ur was one of the leading Sumerian cities, sustained by intensive farming and by trade along the Euphrates River and down to the Gulf – trade which was recorded in countless clay tablets, especially those from the houses of merchants. Leonard Woolley excavated the sacred precinct with its massive temple-tower, or ziggurat, exemplifying the theocratic character of the Mesopotamian city-states and the empire of Ur.

Ugarit was a cosmopolitan centre of industry and trade in the 2nd millennium BC, where peoples of differing language and religion co-existed peacefully. More completely excavated than most major Near Eastern sites, Ugarit emerges from its abundant archives as more commercially orientated and less state-controlled than the centres of great empires. Here the alphabet developed, and Canaanite texts relevant to the Old Testament have been recovered.

The excavation of Boğazköy, its defences, temples and reliefs, as well as archives from the citadel and chief temple, has revealed the previously unknown Hittite state, which was the leading Anatolian power of its day. On the other hand, the site of Nineveh suffered the consequences of being excavated, by Layard, at a very early date (1845–51). Nineveh was supported by the tribute and labour of the subject peoples of the Assyrian empire, of which it was the chief city (705–612 BC). Persepolis was not a city, but the ceremonial shrine of the Achaemenid dynasty, rulers of the Persian empire that stretched from the Danube to the Indus.

Çatal Hüyük

TURKEY

Çatal Hüyük is a settlement mound (the Turkish term 'hüyük' means mound) which stands in the flat, largely fertile Konya plain of central Turkey. The mound extends over 13 hectares at an altitude of 900 metres, 57 kilometres south-east of Konya. Standing 15 metres above the plain, Çatal Hüyük is a landmark comparable with many others of the 300 or more prehistoric settlement mounds which occur in this level stretch of the Anatolian plateau.

The uniqueness of this site, evident even before the first day of excavation, is its solely Neolithic occupation, extending from the later 7th to the middle 6th millennium BC. This made it the clear choice for James Mellaart, assistant director of the British Institute of Archaeology in Ankara, to excavate. Mellaart was determined to lay bare the secrets of the prehistoric cultures of Anatolia, hitherto known only through a few sites, notably Mersin in the Cilician plain.

Mellaart's work

Mellaart arrived in Turkey in 1951 and soon embarked on a lengthy series of surveys (1951–53) from the Konya plain westwards to the Aegean Sea. The surveys were conducted on foot, of necessity leaving some very remote areas for later exploration, among these the banks of the Çarşamba River, where stands Çatal Hüyük. Indeed, Mellaart's outstanding contribution to approaches in Near Eastern archaeology has perhaps been in applying the field survey as a means of discovery. This has led to the plotting of distribution maps and thence to a far clearer understanding of successive cultural phases, as well as contemporary cultural provinces. Such previous investigations, except for the Chicago Oriental Institute survey in the plain of Antioch, had normally been of limited extent and related to excavations in progress. Mellaart showed that single-mindedness and will-power, together with time, were more efficacious than funds when it came to filling in large blanks on the archaeological map. A few hundred pounds proved sufficient for him to make a vast zone of the southern plateau of Anatolia accessible to the archaeological profession and a wider public alike. Others will undoubtedly refine his results, and amplify them with environmental and other data; but their work will surely be less impressive in the ratio of manpower and money to results.

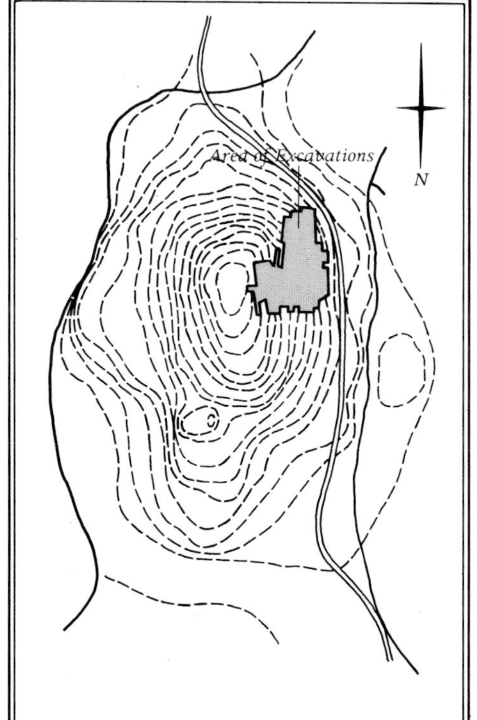

Above right: On the north and east walls of a shrine in Level VII of Çatal Hüyük was painted this unique landscape of a terraced town, depicting either individual houses or blocks of houses and shrines. In the background stands a volcano in eruption.

Right: Female clay figure, found in a grain-bin in the latest of the Çatal Hüyük shrines. This surely represents the moment of giving birth as one of the focal themes of Neolithic religion.

Far right: Hands frequently appear on the richly coloured wall paintings of Çatal Hüyük shrines, rendered by various methods.

Çatal Hüyük itself was completely unknown before 1958, although it is just conceivable that some lingering folk memory survived locally, for the painting of red hands on some doorways in the nearby modern village echoes the Neolithic wall paintings. It is worth relating Mellaart's account of the discovery of the site, on a cold November day in 1958, just before nightfall, when he reached the double mound.

'Much of the eastern (Neolithic) mound was covered by turf and ruin-weed (*peganum harmala*), but where the prevailing south-westerly winds had scoured its surface bare there were unmistakable traces of mud-brick buildings, burned red in a conflagration contrasting with patches of grey ash, broken bones, potsherds and obsidian tools and weapons. To our surprise these were found not only at the bottom of the mound, but they continued right up to the top, some 15 metres above the level of the plain.'

Surface indications alone guided Mellaart as to where he should first dig, although the exposure of the first wall painting on almost the first day of excavations came as a complete surprise. Once adjacent areas for excavation had been selected, their limits were determined not by any rigid grid, but by the orientation of the buildings exposed, the walls of which had been hardened by repeated burning. Throughout the four seasons' work at Çatal Hüyük, emphasis was laid on the uncovering of whole structures rather than on the excavation of predetermined grid squares. The most serious difficulties arose from the demands of conserving

the wall paintings, many of which comprised numerous layers. Considerable success was achieved in lifting off successive layers, although inevitably the techniques required were developed largely on site.

The levels at Çatal Hüyük

The origins of Çatal Hüyük remain uncertain, for the deepest levels are still unexcavated. However, 14 building levels have been explored, spanning at least several hundred years. The evidence of radiocarbon dating can be supplemented by that of the number of layers of plaster, over 100 in one level, in the mural decoration of the shrines, for it seems a reasonable presumption that replastering took place annually. Çatal Hüyük VII, perhaps dating from around 6500 BC, is the earliest level to have yielded a coherent plan. Here, 120 layers of plaster have been traced and a similar number tends to be found in separate buildings within the same level. All the buildings uncovered to date can be classified as houses, shrines or associated store-rooms. Workshops surely existed, but elsewhere in the settlement.

Mellaart has often stressed that only about a thirtieth of the total area of Çatal Hüyük has been excavated. Consequently there has been speculation as to whether or not he happened to come upon a sacred area, unrepresentative of the settlement as a whole. Until work is permitted again, this must remain one of many unsolved conundrums.

The town, as it must be called, had a compact and perhaps reasonably regular plan, although it is impossible to be sure whether one remarkable wall painting represents a panorama of the town or simply the layout of a few of the blocks of buildings. Mellaart's description of this as a landscape painting is reinforced by the volcano in the background, identifiable with Hasan Dağ in central Anatolia. Regularity of plan is made the more plausible by the uniform dimensions of the mud bricks. In Çatal Hüyük VI, bricks are 8 x 16 x 32 centimetres, suggesting the human hand and foot as the likeliest units of measure: four hands (8 centimetres) made up one foot (about 32 centimetres). Timber-framed structures inspired the development of mud-brick architecture until Level V, when mud-brick walls became load-bearing. Vestiges of the timber frame were abandoned in Çatal Hüyük II. The only access to each house or shrine was by ladder through a small opening in the roof, and the way to the store-rooms, entry-passages and light-shafts was from the main room through a small open doorway. A measure of security was thus provided by the very pattern of the town's growth. The small rectangular houses were built up against each other, their blocks providing an irregular perimeter, so that there was no need for a defensive wall.

Paintings and artefacts

The wall paintings of Level III, among the first to be uncovered, depicted the ritual or magic of hunting. Agriculture, equally if not more significant as a means of subsistence, is not depicted on any of the known paintings or reliefs. Some shrines, especially in Level VII, are relief-decorated rather than painted.

If one artefact deserves mention, it is the clay statuette of the 'mother goddess' from Level II, whose massive proportions within a small scale resemble certain modern sculpture. She represents a tradition originating in the Old Stone Age, or Palaeolithic times, and widespread in and beyond the Near East in Neolithic times. The artists of Çatal Hüyük could equally portray an ebullient *joie de vivre*, as in scenes with leaping or dancing figures clad only in a leopard-skin loincloth.

The discoveries at Çatal Hüyük demonstrate that, given the favourable environment of the Konya plain, urban life could and did flourish on the Anatolian plateau almost as early (from about 8000 BC) as at Jericho, the earliest known town. The people of Çatal Hüyük also developed an art derived in many respects from their Palaeolithic ancestors.

Mellaart worked out a cultural sequence based principally on the evidence from his surveys and from his excavations at Çatal Hüyük and earlier at Hacilar, to the west. According to this, the great site of Çatal Hüyük is termed Early Neolithic. In spite of the older occupation found at Hacilar, an example of the transitional phase from food-gathering to food-producing remains yet to be disclosed on the Anatolian plateau.

The Town

By any reasonable definition, Çatal Hüyük has to be called a town, the size and layout of which strongly imply social cohesion through organized government. It may be that the site was chosen as the focal point for gathering together herds of wild aurochs (*bos primigenius*), so becoming pre-eminent among the communities in the Konya plain.

Peoples and classes

The study of skeletal remains has shed light on the ethnic affinities, life-span and pathology of the people of Çatal Hüyük. Highly significant is the presence of three races, found nowhere else together in this period, namely Eurafricans (59 per cent), proto-Mediterraneans (17 per cent) and Alpines (24 per cent). The first two were of Upper Palaeolithic origin; the Alpines represented an intrusive element. A maximum population of 6,000 has been suggested for Çatal Hüyük in its heyday. It is hard to avoid the conclusion that life expectancy was much lower on average than the available skeletal remains may suggest, for infant mortality would inevitably be high, and it is impossible to know the scale of emigration. Malaria was the likeliest cause of the endemic anaemia which appears to have afflicted the people. Neither kingship nor class structure can be proved at Çatal Hüyük, although a priestly caste is implied by the shrines. A class of craftsmen almost certainly flourished.

Agriculture and economy

The people of Çatal Hüyük adapted to life in the Konya plain after earlier inhabiting the neighbouring foothills of the Taurus Mountains. They were primarily dependent on cattle-breeding and on irrigation-based agriculture, which was technically easy in the grasslands along the river.

Wall paintings depicting men in leopard skins dancing and brandishing bows or baiting stags or bulls made a marked impact at the time of the excavations (1961–65). Yet it seems that hunting was much less significant than was once supposed. Its decline may

Below: Houses and shrines in Çatal Hüyük. The arrangement in cellular plan (right), in blocks which could be extended, may indicate extended families. Access was by roof and wooden ladder, which allowed for security and privacy, but made impracticable the introduction to the shrines of animals for sacrifice. The buildings were of timber frame design (below left), with mud brick filling. Not until Level II was the timber frame abandoned, surviving only as mud brick piers. The decoration of the shrines varies greatly, from scenes of hunting and dancing to representations of ornate woven hangings. These last are comparable with surviving carbonized fragments of woollen fabrics, some of fine shawl weave.

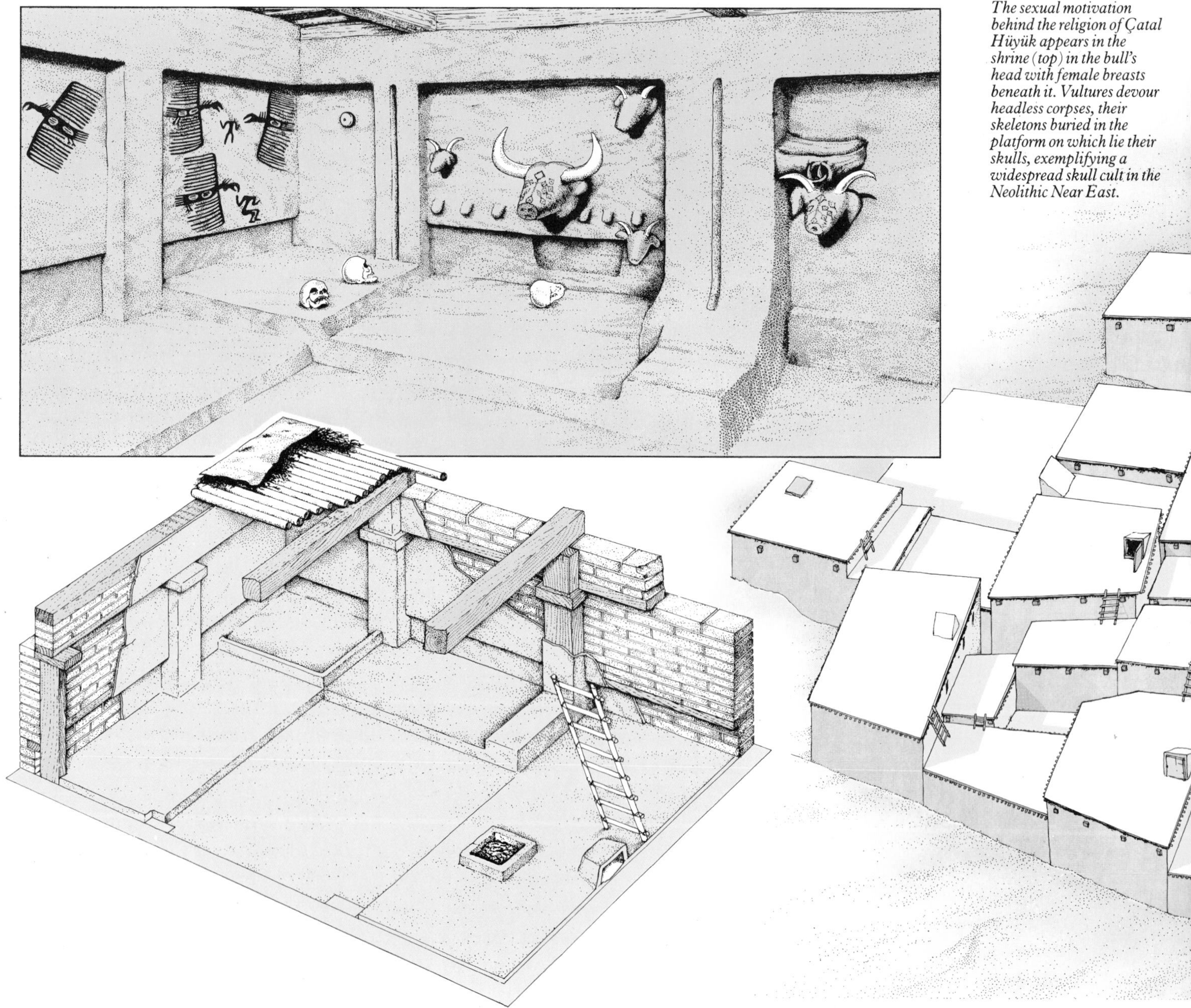

The sexual motivation behind the religion of Çatal Hüyük appears in the shrine (top) in the bull's head with female breasts beneath it. Vultures devour headless corpses, their skeletons buried in the platform on which lie their skulls, exemplifying a widespread skull cult in the Neolithic Near East.

have been quite rapid, even though the supply of meat survived. Study of the animal bones has revealed physical changes, especially in the cattle, which indicate progressive domestication, although the sheep remained wild. The economy depended on cattle for more than 90 per cent of its meat supply and the cattle also provided transport. This was surely a local trend, contrasting with the predominant use of sheep and goats elsewhere in the Neolithic Near East.

The staple crops of Çatal Hüyük were varieties of wheat and six-row naked barley. Protein came from a variety of vegetables, including field peas. Vegetable oils and fruits, with hackberry to make wine, supplemented the diet. The cultivation of flax for linen has not been proved, although sheep may have been exploited chiefly for their wool and leopard skins for loincloths, headdresses or wall-hangings.

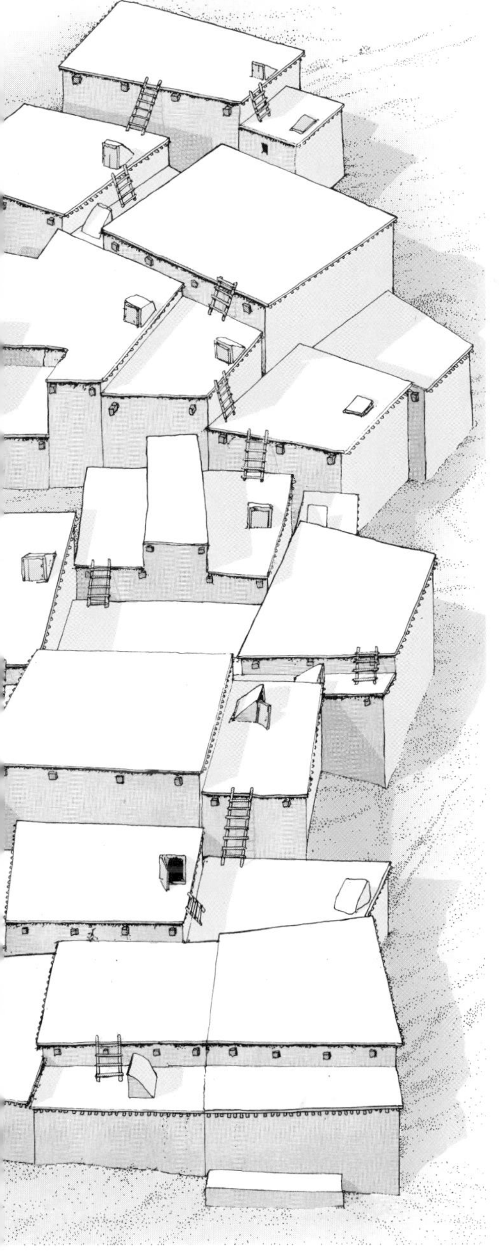

The precise sources of many of the stones and minerals used at Çatal Hüyük are as yet unknown. Copper and obsidian, for example, occur widely in the Taurus Mountains and the volcanic areas of central Anatolia respectively. Shells of Mediterranean origin demonstrate far-flung commercial contacts, even if the volume of imports was necessarily small. Tabular flint, used for ceremonial daggers, came from nowhere closer than the Gaziantep area, far to the east.

Arts and crafts

The versatility of Çatal Hüyük craftsmen was remarkable. They fashioned artefacts of wood, bone, metals, clay or stone, and they wove textiles, the oldest surviving anywhere. The textiles, preserved by charring, include three fabrics, one being a fine shawl material made from two-ply woollen yarn. The wall paintings depict clothing worn by goddesses and men, as well as richly decorated woven hangings. These may well have been contemporary, although they probably eventually supplanted the comparably patterned wall paintings, one of which shows a stitched border. Minerals were used for dyes, and stamp-seals may have been partly used for printing patterns. Animal hides remained a significant material for clothing.

Tools, weapons, vessels, statuettes and ornaments of many types of stone were produced by chipping, grinding, polishing and drilling. But it remains an enigma how the fine perforation of many obsidian beads, or the polishing of the obsidian mirrors set in lime plaster was achieved. The most labour-saving material, clay, was not widely used for making vessels. Wood and basketry were especially popular alternatives at Çatal Hüyük, while limestone was also used. Pottery can readily be put into proper perspective at Çatal Hüyük, as its simple forms largely copy leather bags, a traditional Neolithic type in the Near East. Reeds, available on the site, were easily woven into mats and coiled baskets.

Among the major surprise discoveries at Çatal Hüyük have been the traces of use of lead with pendants in Level IX, and copper with beads in Level VIII. Tubes for string skirts were also made of copper. The process mostly involved hammering lumps of native copper, but slag found in Çatal Hüyük VIA provides exciting evidence of extraction of copper from ore by smelting, which is the birth of true metallurgy.

Wood-workers produced a remarkably modern-looking range of eating vessels and platters. Fir and perhaps other soft woods were gouged out with obsidian tools and emery and sand were used for the final smoothing. Hard woods, such as oak and juniper, were used in building, with greenstone axes, adzes and chisels the tools for squaring the timbers. Thus began the millennia-long Anatolian tradition of woodworking. The curious inward overhang of the walls in many Çatal Hüyük buildings was a survival from wholly timber construction. The ultimate abandoning of this archaic form in favour of entirely mud-brick buildings may perhaps reflect incipient deforestation through felling.

Religion

In the shrines the reliefs of females giving birth are partially self-explanatory, although it would be rash to assume that modern man can grasp more than a few of the thoughts of his Neolithic forebears. There seems little doubt that this was a matriarchal religion, but to jump from that conclusion to assertions of a matriarchal society is possibly over-bold. However, the supremacy of the female may be hinted at by the placing of these birth panels above bulls' heads on the shrine wall, for the association of the bull's head with masculinity seems incontrovertible. The bull was later to become the emblem of the storm- or weather-god of the Hittites and other Anatolian peoples.

Figurines are also found in the shrines. Those of boars, often covered with stab wounds, surely indicate the seeking of sympathetic magic in hunting rites, while crude female figurines were inserted in the brickwork of the shrines, doubtless to bring fertility. Superior in workmanship are the carved stone and modelled clay statuettes which were part of the cult equipment. Broken-off stalactites or stalagmites, usually associated with the statuettes, must have come from caves in the Taurus Mountains, and imply a cult of the Earth.

Life was inevitably short for most of the people, with death and disease ever present in their lives. Children and others came to place their hands on the reliefs, and it is tempting to see these as the sick seeking a cure.

Exposure of the dead to the mercies of vultures is depicted on wall paintings, one of which shows a reed-and-timber structure, a charnel-house in which lay skulls and headless corpses. Elsewhere, detached skulls occur in the shrines. Red ochre was used to paint either the skull or the entire skeleton, revealing a clear link with Palaeolithic burials, while the cult of the human skull in the Neolithic Near East was widespread, being first recognized at Jericho. The dead of successive generations of the same family, though perhaps only its leading members, were buried within the platforms of the shrines with appropriate grave-goods – the men with a dagger in their belt, the women with jewellery. In death, at least, the people of Çatal Hüyük shared a common heritage with other, less sophisticated, communities.

Ur

IRAQ

The extensive ruins of Ur (modern Tell el-Mugayyar) are situated in southern Iraq, halfway between Baghdad and the Persian Gulf. Today the site lies south of the River Euphrates, but in the days of its greatness, Ur stood on the very bank of the river, on which it depended for drinking water, irrigation and communication.

As with many other Mesopotamian sites, this important city of ancient southern Mesopotamia (Sumer) had a very long history. There is evidence of occupation over at least 5,000 years, from prehistoric times to the restorations and extensions carried out by the neo-Babylonian kings (626–539 BC). Impressive as the sacred precinct, or 'temenos', must have been even in that last period, the greatest days of the city of Ur occurred in the 3rd and early 2nd millennia BC, approximately 3100–1750 BC.

Leonard Woolley

When Leonard Woolley, the British excavator of Ur, began work in 1923, the site was already familiar to the Christian world as 'Ur of the Chaldees'. It was from Ur that Abraham's family had migrated by stages to the Promised Land of Canaan. Woolley had originally trained in theology, and was therefore naturally attracted to the idea of revealing the secrets of Ur. It was a task to which he was well fitted, not only by his experience in the field, initially in Egypt, but also by his gifts as a publicist which enabled him to raise repeatedly the finances required for continuing the excavations over 12 successive seasons. As his leading assistant during six seasons at Ur, Sir Max Mallowan was in a position to judge Woolley's ability to make his finds accessible to a wider public. He wrote:

> 'Woolley was an incomparable showman, a man of knowledge endowed with a vivid imagination which sometimes got the better of him, but as a rule he did not deviate too far from probability. He was at his best when guiding the visitors to Ur through the houses. . . (his) observations missed nothing and his imagination grasped everything'.

The excavations at Ur rested firmly on joint support from the British Museum and the University of Pennsylvania Museum, Philadelphia. This is reflected in the handsome collections of material from Ur, especially from the so-called Royal Cemetery, to be seen in the British Museum and in Philadelphia, with an equal third share in the Baghdad Museum. No such division of finds from a dig in the Near East is permitted today, since the countries of origin are understandably anxious to preserve their heritage for themselves.

It was perhaps also easier for Woolley to raise funds, year by year, than for most of his successors. Unencumbered by ties of family or professional duties in England, he was free to devote his energies entirely to the excavations, to writing up the results and to lecturing between seasons, with a view to raising money for continuing the work. Additionally, the years since the Ur expedition, and particularly since the 1973 boom in oil prices, have seen a very large rise in wages paid to the local work force. This has affected all excavations in the Near East to varying degrees.

The financial aspect touches on the scale of the excavations at Ur, which would be enviable indeed for the present-day director, who can ill afford a labour force of 60 men. As Woolley himself said:

> 'We could not in that time excavate the whole of Ur, for the site is immense and to reach the earlier levels we often had to dig very deeply so that, although work was always done at high pressure and the number of men employed was the maximum consistent with proper supervision – at one moment it topped 400 – only a minute fraction of the city's area was thoroughly explored . . .'.

Woolley gave as his reason for ending the excavations in 1934 the fear that results would become repetitive.

Woolley's achievements

Apart from the exploitation of his discoveries through popularization, Woolley's major achievement lay in the use of special techniques for the recovery and preservation of organic materials and metals. The use of paraffin wax was brilliantly developed in recovering delicate harps and lyres, and in preserving jewellery in its original arrangements on the skulls of those who had been buried in the Royal Cemetery. Referring to this operation, Woolley described it as slow work . . .

> 'A few heads on which the original order of the beads and gold work was best preserved were laboriously cleaned with small knives and brushes, the dirt being removed without disturbing any of the ornaments . . . and then boiling paraffin wax was poured over them, solidifying them in one mass. The lump of wax, earth, bone and gold was then strengthened by waxed cloth pressed carefully over it, so that it could be lifted from the ground by undercutting'.

Such patient recovery and conservation in the field was a new advance in practical archaeology.

Woolley was one of the greatest of all Near Eastern excavators, even if, absorbed in the work at Ur, he underrated the significance of other excavations. Like all the best directors he drove his men hard, though not beyond what he demanded of himself. He saw the city of Ur as a living community, and imparted something of his vision to all who cared to read or, if fortunate enough to visit the excavations, to listen to what he himself had to say about it.

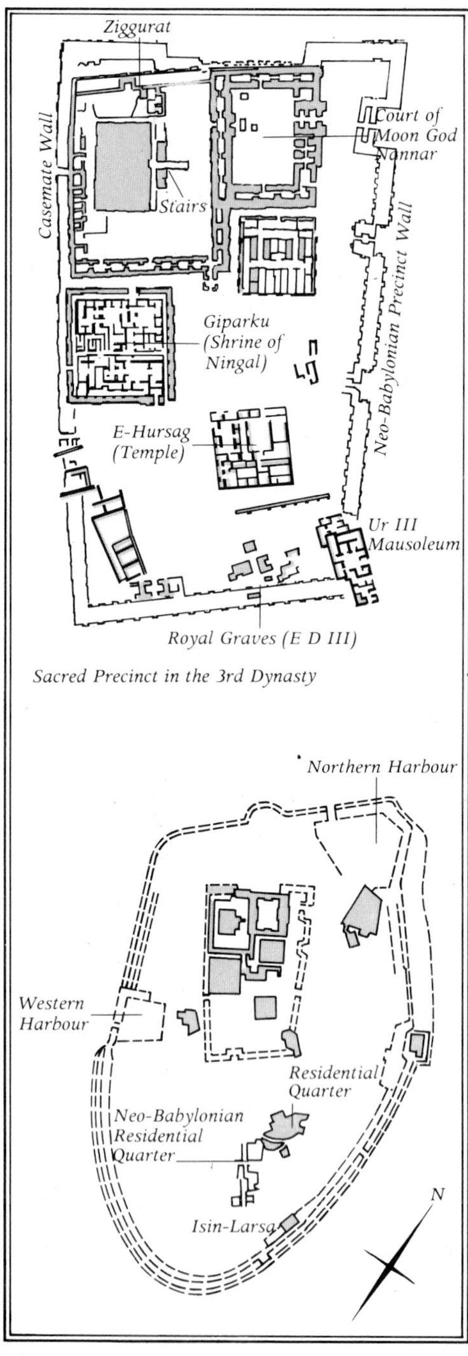

Above: Detailed plan of the sacred precinct (top) during the 3rd dynasty of Ur (Ur III). A plan of the city is shown beneath it.

Historical setting

Further studies have brought improved knowledge of chronology and of the cultural sequence throughout Mesopotamia from the 6th millennium BC onwards. In this light, Woolley's interpretation of the prehistoric strata of Ur has been revised, although Ur has added to the evidence more fully provided by nearby Eridu, where a continuous sequence of temples has been distinguished from about 5500 to about 3000 BC. Reed huts found close to virgin soil illustrate a way of life little different from that of the marsh Arabs of the Tigris-Euphrates delta today, although this habitat is now threatened by drainage. In the early 3rd millennium BC, Ur was the focus of a tract of farming land and salt marshes extending over 9,000 hectares, of which no more than 6,000 seem to have been suitable for cultivation. The town itself probably had an area of about 20 hectares. A considerable expansion of the city took place towards 2500 BC, along with many other cities in Mesopotamia, and it is to this time that the famous Royal Cemetery can be attributed. The greatest days of Ur were during the 108 years of the 3rd dynasty (Ur III), ending about 2000 BC as a result of economic decline and attacks from Amorites from the north-west and Elamites from the east. The town's fortifications were themselves evidence of manpower organization on a vast scale, and were the work of Ur-Nammu, founder of Ur III.

The city remained a prosperous commercial community for 250 years after the fall of Ur III, commanding as it did the sea trade through the Gulf up the River Euphrates. Evidence of this is supplied by the clay tablets which comprise the office records of merchant households, although these tablets were not unique in Mesopotamia. Other cities, notably Larsa, Sippar and Mari, have yielded textual evidence of internal and external trade in various periods, especially in the so-called Old Babylonian period (about 2000–1600 BC). Yet at Ur alone has been uncovered an extensive area of residential quarters, not planned to any overriding design but with a fairly standard house-plan for the homes of richer families. The rooms ranged round an interior courtyard and had two storeys, forming the typical layout of a traditional dwelling in Iraqi towns today.

Later periods reveal largely restorations and additions to the great buildings of the sacred precinct of Ur III. Interpreting these remains involved not so much the uncovering of successive strata as of dissecting an architectural complex which had endured many centuries, with alterations not entirely unlike those found in medieval cathedrals. It seems that neo-Babylonian Ur witnessed a final period of grand architecture which deliberately echoed past splendours.

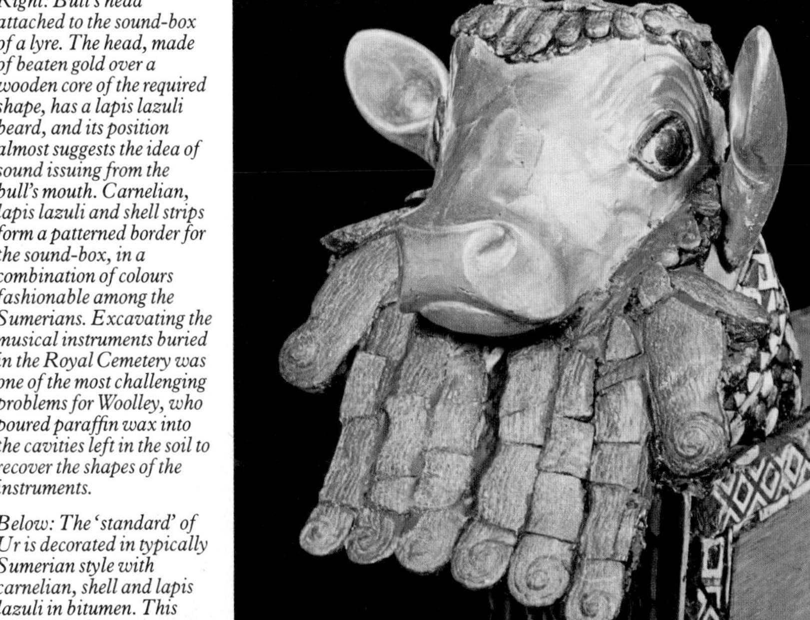

Right: Bull's head attached to the sound-box of a lyre. The head, made of beaten gold over a wooden core of the required shape, has a lapis lazuli beard, and its position almost suggests the idea of sound issuing from the bull's mouth. Carnelian, lapis lazuli and shell strips form a patterned border for the sound-box, in a combination of colours fashionable among the Sumerians. Excavating the musical instruments buried in the Royal Cemetery was one of the most challenging problems for Woolley, who poured paraffin wax into the cavities left in the soil to recover the shapes of the instruments.

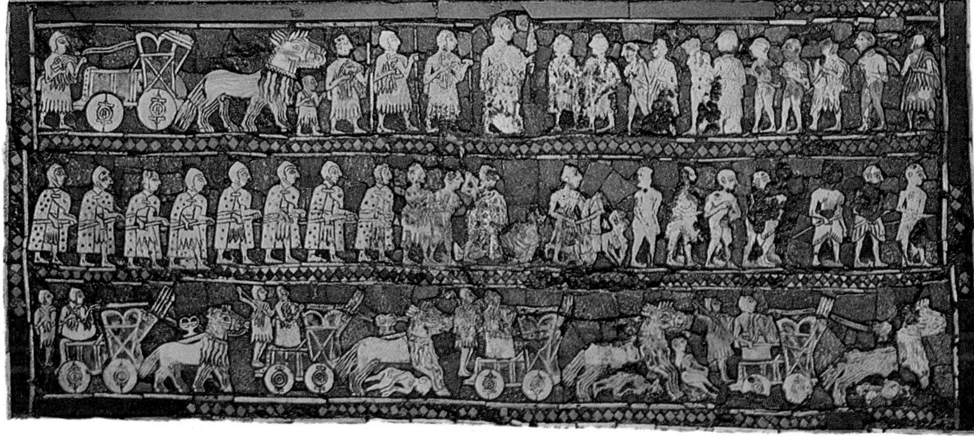

Below: The 'standard' of Ur is decorated in typically Sumerian style with carnelian, shell and lapis lazuli in bitumen. This 'war' side shows wagons drawn by onagers, horses not yet being in use in Mesopotamia.

Right: Inlaid gaming board with counters. Games and musical instruments were found at Ur, revealing how the Sumerians spent their leisure.

Above: Reconstruction of the jewellery worn by queen Puabi (Shubad). It comprises beaten gold, carnelian, pearls and lapis lazuli.

The City of Ur

Right: This ceremonial wig-helmet from the tomb of Meskalamshar was beaten from a single sheet of 15-carat gold. Use of the repoussé technique was rare at this period and suggests that the Sumerian goldsmiths may have learned the modern technique of dissolving silver from the surface of a silver-gold alloy. The details are chased, not engraved, and the perforations are for attachment of a leather lining.

Left: Reconstruction of a house typical of those belonging to the merchants of Ur in the early 2nd millennium BC. They lived in substantial two-storey houses of typically Near Eastern plan, with a central court where pack animals and merchandise could be received.

It has long been agreed that the government of the Sumerian (southern Mesopotamian) city-states was largely theocratic. However, it is no longer generally accepted that the temple of each city owned all the land. The temple was perhaps rather more the leader among the great landowners, although during the later 4th millennium BC its corporate strength probably dominated late prehistoric Mesopotamia.

The relationship of the deities to the land and the livelihood of those working on it was originally extremely close, and indeed remained so. Nanna, the moon-god of Ur, was close to the herdsmen whose stockbreeding dominated the territory north of the marshes and around the city. Only later, after about 3000 BC in the Early Dynastic period, was this primitive view of the gods overlaid by another stratum, when they became rulers governing cities. The emergence of classes in society, the lords and their retainers, is reflected in the concept of 'lord' and 'ruler' coming to be applied to the gods.

Population estimates are always difficult, and sometimes impossible, to make. Most of Ur's inhabitants were crowded in residential quarters, where disease must have acted to curb the natural increase. Population growth might otherwise have caused even greater friction between neighbouring cities than is known to have occurred, often over rights to water for irrigation. Tablets from Lagash suggest that about 2400 BC, at the close of the Early Dynastic period, there were 100,000 free citizens, of whom 25,000 only worked on the temple estates. Of the 33,500 slaves, a third worked for the temples.

The city of Ur was at the centre of the empire founded by Ur-Nammu and extended by his successors until economic collapse within and pressure from enemies without brought about the city's decline, siege and fall about 2000 BC, under Ibbi-Sin, who was taken prisoner by the Elamites. Political allegiance to Ur was enforced by governors appointed over 40 districts, although military garrisons were soon made directly answerable to the king. Yet, elaborate as the civil service was, there seems to have been no over-riding nationalist or patriotic loyalty to give permanence to Ur III. Sumerian was re-established as the official language, following the dominance of Akkadian under Sargon I, king of Agade (Akkad) who reigned in the 24th century BC.

The tablets of Ur

Ur provides the oldest group of tablets, termed 'Archaic' by the excavators from the style of their seal impressions, which are sufficient in number and content to give a coherent outline of Sumerian agriculture and economic administration around 3000 BC. The tablets number over 220 and come from the south-east slope of the site, from rubbish tips. Although the teaching and profession of scribes are not specifically mentioned, yet practice writing exercises were found side by side with economic texts. A storehouse, temples and a palace are all recorded for this period at Ur, as are officials of the king, although he remains a shadowy figure.

These Archaic tablets from Ur deal with the grain, livestock, fish, reeds, trees or land allotted to individuals. Where two persons share the same name, they are distinguished by using their occupation – chief bricklayer, carpenter, smith, gardener, cook, kitchen supervisor, maltster, physician – as an additional name. Sheep and goats in the territory of the city appear to have been kept in large flocks, and were probably distributed by a central body. A wide divergence between large estates and smaller holdings is shown by the variation in yields, from 1.2 to 0.9 *gur* per unit of land for barley, and from 1.1 to 0.7 *gur* for wheat. Thus barley, which is more resistant to salt, was perhaps already supplanting wheat as the main cereal crop. Unfortunately, there is no certainty on the size of the *gur*, which ranged from 370 litres around Ur in the time of the Archaic texts, about 3000 BC, to only 150 litres at Lagash about 2400 BC. Twelve thousand man-days may have been required for planting all the available land with barley. Irrigation, too, demanded regularly organized labour, although less work was required than further upstream, where more silt was deposited annually. Of the 20 kilometres of canals around Ur, half needed cleaning every year.

Trade and commerce

Trade is documented at Ur, especially around 2600–1750 BC. The Royal Cemetery provides ample evidence of the industrial sector of the Sumerian economy in the mid-3rd millennium BC. Beads of carnelian, lapis lazuli and shell were made of materials from eastern Iran, Afghanistan and the Gulf respectively. Gold, used with extravagance in the jewellery, headgear, drinking vessels, ritual weapons and musical instruments of Ur, seems to have come at least in part from south-eastern Anatolia. Silver came from Elam and the Taurus Mountains; copper partly from Oman, by way of the entrepôt of Dilmun (Bahrein); while tin, used for bronze, seems on recent evidence to have originated in Afghanistan, and may well therefore have been imported with the lapis lazuli. Cedar wood, which was used for roofing large buildings, had to come overland from the Amanus mountain range in north-west Syria, now within Turkey. From there it had to be floated down the Euphrates, as, too, did building stone.

Fine examples of this foreign trade are the etched carnelian beads found among the jewellery of Queen Pu-abi and others buried in the shaft graves of the Royal Cemetery. These prove connections with the Indus civilization of Pakistan, mainly by sea, but there is also textual evidence to support the archaeological data. Both Sargon and, later on, Ur-Nammu, record the mooring of ships from Magan (Oman or the Makran coast of south-east Iran) and Meluhha (perhaps the west coast of India) at the quaysides of Agade and Ur respectively.

Under the Akkadian kings and their successors of Ur III, the temples and the secular

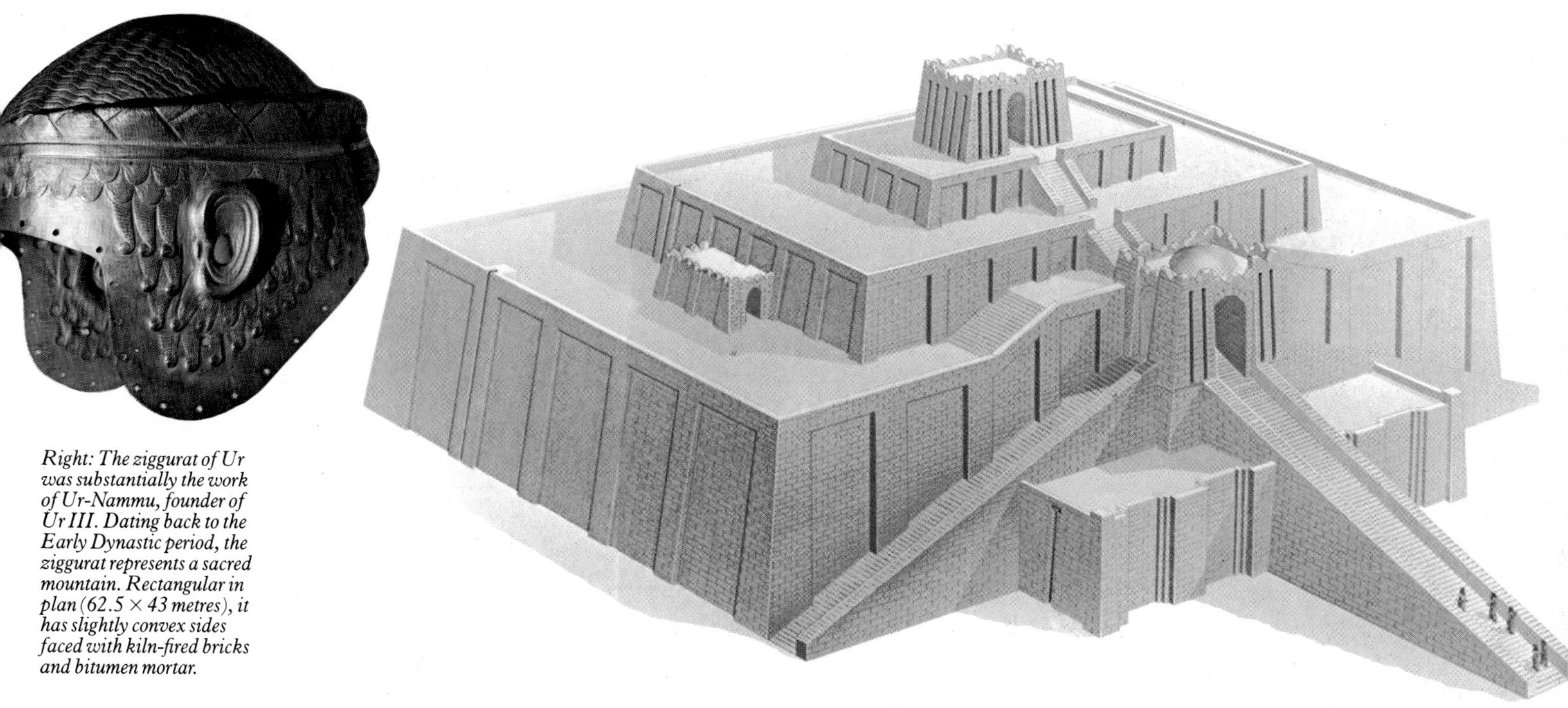

Right: The ziggurat of Ur was substantially the work of Ur-Nammu, founder of Ur III. Dating back to the Early Dynastic period, the ziggurat represents a sacred mountain. Rectangular in plan (62.5 × 43 metres), it has slightly convex sides faced with kiln-fired bricks and bitumen mortar.

authority were deeply involved in commercial ventures, although private merchants were growing more prominent by the time of Ur III. The economic records of this period number thousands, and carry precise details not only of labour to a fraction of a man-day but also of many commodities and materials, as well as the nature of the transaction.

Although it is so well documented, the Old Babylonian period was one of contracting geographical horizons. Political and economic factors alike accounted for this change, culminating in the loss of access to the Gulf for the cities of Mesopotamia, with the rise of the Sea Lands dynasty. A long era of economic eclipse followed for Ur and the other cities of the south. At its zenith, however, Mesopotamia overcame its scarcity of raw materials and a market economy evolved. This shared the benefits of a semi-industrialized society throughout and beyond the Tigris-Euphrates basin. Ur joined in the general prosperity, its merchants no more inclined than those of other cities to accept official regulation of prices. In the Old Babylonian residential quarter, family businesses flourished.

Manufacturing

Metallurgy, the wheel and the sail have been associated with much of the material achievements of the Sumerians. Ships indeed plied up and down the Euphrates and its side channels, which were straightened or deepened where necessary. Around Ur, as elsewhere, many of the canals were essentially natural watercourses.

The Royal Cemetery of Ur illustrates the wide range of techniques commanded by the Sumerian metal-workers. Fundamental was the wide use of tin-bronze, especially for tools and weapons, which made possible a degree of mass production, with prototypes copied in due course in surrounding lands. The goldsmiths of Ur have left examples of their mastery of engraving, *chasing, repoussé, filigree, granulation*, sweating, soldering and *cloisonné*. The famous helmet of Meskalamshar was fashioned by repoussé, with the main shape hammered out from within, and the details of the hair chased. A dagger sheath imitating raffia is the outstanding example of filigree. Granulation was used on daggers and finger-rings. Electrum, an alloy of silver with gold, was very popular.

Soft conch shells from the Gulf were used with bitumen or bituminous paste in three different techniques for decorating the surfaces of gaming boards and the sound-boxes of lyres. Small squares (tesserae) of lapis lazuli were set in bitumen as a background to the 'standard' of Ur. The 'standard' is actually a wooden box, possibly the sound-box of a stringed musical instrument. Its inlaid mosaic shows the Sumerian army at war on one side and a scene of peace on the reverse. On the side depicting war, the king and his leather-helmeted spearmen are shown in heavy wooden wagons with solid wheels. These appear too cumbersome to have served as chariots, as their turning circle has been proved to have been very wide. They are drawn by animals normally identified as onagers, the wild asses still found in Iraq. It was some centuries before the horse came into use in Mesopotamia.

The builders of Ur were advanced in their techniques. Arches, vaults and domes, as well as the more rudimentary corbelling, are all to be seen in the chambers of the Royal Cemetery's shaft graves.

The royal burials and ziggurat

Woolley deliberately postponed excavation of the Royal Cemetery until his workmen had become well enough trained to tackle it. But the 16 royal burials are distinguished from the private graves by their more elaborate plan and by the presence of human sacrifices. The suggestion that these were substitute kings and queens is attractive, if inadequately documented. Of this gory custom the Great Death Pit, with a cup beside each victim, is the most vivid example, although unique. The theory that some drug was imbibed by the victims seems reasonable from the positions of the skeletons.

The prestige of the Ur III monarchy, celebrated in coronation hymns, is demonstrated by the royal mausoleum. This was built of fired bricks, with stairs leading down into the subterranean chamber where were housed rich offerings later looted at the sack of Ur by the Elamites.

The royal tombs of the greatest kings of Ur were located close to the massive temple-tower (ziggurat) conceived by the Sumerians as a sacred mountain. Enlarged by Ur-Nammu, its core was of a much earlier date, built with the plano-convex bricks distinctive of the Early Dynastic period (about 3000–2340 BC). Many tiny crescent moons of copper found in its excavation demonstrate its association with the cult of the city god Nanna, the moon-god. Rising perhaps 30 metres above the rest of the city, the ziggurat of Ur provided an impressive focus for the tens of thousands who lived around it.

Ugarit

SYRIA

The ancient Canaanite city of Ugarit, usually called Ras Shamra in connection with its oldest levels, is important not so much for any significance in the excavation techniques or recording used at the site, as for the wide ranging impact created by the discoveries made there. Excavations were opened in 1929 by the French archaeologist Claude Schaeffer and have since continued for over 30 seasons, with interruptions caused by war. From the start, the results have made Ugarit one of the most important of all Near Eastern sites, at least for the period of its heyday in the Late Bronze Age, around 1600–1170 BC.

Situated on the Mediterranean coast of northern Syria, 12 kilometres north of the modern port of Latakia and with its own ancient harbour town of Minet-el-Beida, Ugarit was very well placed for maritime trade westwards across the Mediterranean. Its position also encouraged trade by land with the middle Euphrates valley to the east, the coastal towns of the Levant to the south, and with Anatolia.

Schaeffer's work

The contribution of Schaeffer's expedition to Near Eastern archaeology has been strengthened by the very large proportion of the city ruins which have been exposed, amounting to well over two thirds. French archaeologists in the Near East, like their German counterparts, have greatly benefited from the willingness of their government to grant enough financial support for the expedition on site and between seasons also; this has been so for decades, and indeed as far back as the days, in the mid-19th century, when Paul-Emile Botta was working in Assyria. It is improbable that funds on an appropriate scale could have been raised over so many seasons in the United Kingdom.

Claude Schaeffer, director of the excavations at Ras Shamra/Ugarit, spent the years of World War II working in Oxford, England. In 1948 he published *Stratigraphie comparée et chronologie de l'Asie occidentale*, which collated all the available information on Ugarit and its surrounding regions. Although his theory of the relevance of earthquakes to *absolute chronology* is not widely supported, this book helped to underline the wide significance of Ugarit, which was also emphasized by a journal devoted exclusively to discoveries from this one site.

It was already recognized that the clay tablets discovered in the pre-World War II seasons were significant for a different field of research. In a series of lectures to the British Academy, published in 1939 as *The Cuneiform Texts of Ras Shamra-Ugarit*, Schaeffer discussed the light cast by some of these tablets on Canaanite religion and thus on the Old Testament. It is therefore scarcely surprising that a vast literature has since appeared from many biblical scholars. Other sites, especially Mari and more recently Ebla, have aroused great interest among biblical researchers; but the information they reveal about the Old Testament is less direct than that derived from the texts of Ugarit, situated as the city was at the northern extremity of Canaan.

Texts written in the local language, Ugaritic, and in a *cuneiform* alphabetic script with 30 signs, also give a clearer understanding of the development of the alphabet and some support for the Greek tradition of a Phoenician origin. Syllabic writing began in southern Mesopotamia in the 4th millennium BC.

The history of Ugarit

The main period of occupation at Ugarit was in the later 2nd millennium BC, conventionally termed the Late Bronze Age and subdivided into three phases (Late Ugarit I–III). Its history, however, extended back into the 7th millennium BC, as is shown by burnished plaster floors typical of Jericho and many other prehistoric settlements throughout the Levant. After successive cultural influences from Mesopotamia, the sequence of occupation at Ugarit can be related to that in the Amuq plain of north-west Syria, now within Turkey. In the late 4th and 3rd millennia BC, Ugarit, although a prosperous community, was less important than Byblos further south on the coast near Beirut, which had direct maritime trade with Egypt.

Around 1900 BC when the Canaanites settled in Palestine, Ugarit shared cultural connections with the area, most clearly in its pottery. The Canaanites introduced the Middle Bronze culture from the region of the Levant coast and brought hitherto unsurpassed prosperity and urban growth. Moreover, the metal industry was developing. In

Right: Stele depicting the storm-god Ba'al, leading member of the Canaanite pantheon, who brandishes a weapon representing lightning. The god's posture owes much to Egyptian iconography. Numerous statuettes of divinities, commonly termed Reshef, Adad or Ba'al, were cast in the bronzesmith's workshops of Ugarit, which continued a long tradition of metallurgical skills earlier in evidence at Byblos to the south. Although Ugarit lay at the extreme north of Canaan, Ba'al and other divinities figure in literary texts which survive in the cuneiform archives of the 14th and 13th centuries BC. These provide direct background to the Old Testament.

Left: Cuneiform tablet exemplifying the 200-year overlordship of the Hittite kings in the rich trading city of Ugarit. When still soft, the clay tablet was impressed with the convex face of a typical royal Hittite seal. This example carries the monogram of the viceroy of north Syria, whose headquarters were at Carchemish on the Euphrates. The central design, with 'Hittite' hieroglyphs of Luvian (Indo-European) origin, is surrounded by two concentric lines of cuneiform. Such seals have helped towards decipherment of the hieroglyphic writing so typical of the Hittite state and its successors in Syria during the 1st millennium BC.

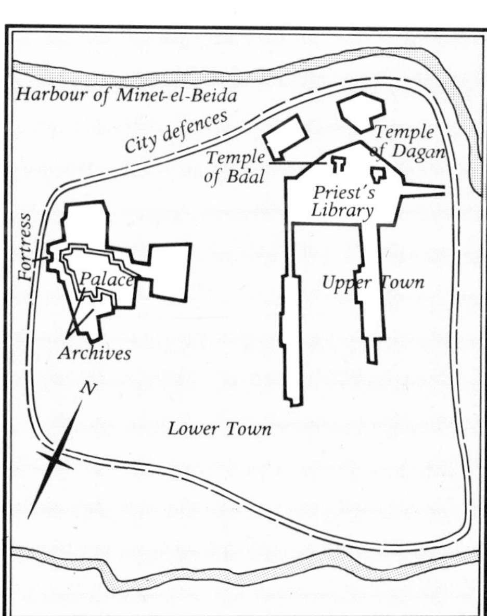

the next phase, Late Ugarit I (about 1600–1450 BC), the pottery includes painted ware similar to the so-called *bichrome ware* which was typical of 16th-century BC Palestine.

For some time it seemed that Ugarit's heyday, in the Late Ugarit II phase of about 1450–1365 BC, coincided with the dominance of 18th-dynasty Egypt. However, the chance discovery in the earlier seasons at Ugarit of tablets, mostly from the Late Ugarit II period, gave an impression of decline in the 13th century BC, ending in the city's fall at the time of the collapse of the Hittite empire. The recovery of archives dating from Late Ugarit III proved this to be a misconception.

This Late Ugarit III period, of about 1365–1170 BC, was a phase of almost 200 years of Hittite suzerainty and followed the imposition of a treaty on Niqmaddu, king of Ugarit, by the Great King of Hatti, Suppiluliumas. To this treaty the city remained loyal throughout Niqmaddu's long reign. Ugarit sent a contingent to fight alongside the Hittite army against the pharaoh Rameses II at the battle of Kadesh in 1300/1286 BC. The city undoubtedly benefited from the long peace which ensued between Egypt and Hatti, sealed by the treaty of the 21st year of Rameses II. Mycenaean trade and cultural connections, already strong in Late Ugarit II, continued. Ugarit was allowed virtual independence within the Hittite sphere.

The end of Ugarit

Some tablets, most of which were never filed in the archives but were found left where they lay, in a tablet oven, give dramatic evidence of the last days of Ugarit. By then only nominally a vassal of the Hittite kings, the city had yet gone to aid Hatti in its moment of mortal danger. This was to prove fatal also to Ugarit itself. Ammurapi, last king of Ugarit, wrote to the king of Alashia (Cyprus):

> 'My father, behold, the enemy's ships came here, my cities were burned and they did evil things in my country. Does not my father know that all my troops and chariots (?) are in the Hittite country and all my ships are in the Lukka land? Thus the country is abandoned to itself. May my father know it: the seven ships of the enemy that came here inflicted much damage upon us . . .'.

This letter from Ammurapi reveals the extent to which Ugarit was involved as an ally of the Hittites, with its fleet deployed on the periphery of the Aegean Sea to try to prevent the Sea Peoples from overrunning the Mediterranean. Unfortunately, these tablets do not give the names of the Sea Peoples in the Ugaritic alphabet. But it seems clear that one group, the Pursata, can be identified with the Peleset of the Egyptian account, and so with the people who gave their name to Palestine, the Philistines. The Medinet Habu temple inscriptions, from Thebes in Egypt, declare that:

> 'The foreign countries made a conspiracy in their lands. Removed and scattered in the fray were the lands at one time. No land could stand before their arms from Hatti, Qadi (Kadesh), Carchemish, Arzawa and Alashia on.'

Carchemish had been the seat of the Hittite viceroy, and looked after the interests of Ugarit in the last decades of the Hittite empire, when the Sun, as the Hittite king styled himself, was busy with enemy infiltrations from the west.

Thus ended Ugarit. Unlike many other cities destroyed by the Sea Peoples, it was never to rise again. The Phoenician cities were to take its place in sea trade with the Mediterranean lands. The role of the great emporium of Ugarit had ceased for ever.

Ugarit Revealed

The palace was both the centre of government in Ugarit and the employer of many craftsmen. Eventually it covered a hectare, and, according to the ruler of Byblos, the palace at Tyre alone equalled it. There were eight entrance staircases, over 90 rooms and nine courtyards, the staircases each having a columned portico. Piped water was laid on to parts of the palace; and there was a large walled garden.

Social stratification in Ugarit is implied by the differing sizes of private houses, those of the highest palace officials and of the royal family standing east and south of the palace, in large blocks. One such had 35 rooms and its own library. Drainage, bathrooms and lavatories were normal features. In the north-east and north-west quarters of the city, however, houses were smaller and crowded together in the manner of older parts of Near Eastern towns today.

Collective burial, one generation of the family following another, was customary. This tradition, widespread in the Mediterranean lands, had its antecedents in the Levant, exemplified at Jericho.

Tablets and seal-impressions

Several archives have been found, among them contracts and diplomatic correspondence. These records, in the form of clay tablets, had first to be baked in an oven in one of the palace courtyards, and were then filed. Akkadian was the language of international relations, even in Egypt, but Ugaritic was the vernacular, into which some of the more important correspondence was translated on receipt. Tablets incorporating pictures and scripts in Akkadian, Ugaritic and occasionally Hurrian assisted the scribal students who were housed and taught in the palace.

Diplomatic contacts were strongest with Egypt in the Late Ugarit II period, and evidence of these is supplied by a fragment of an alabaster vessel depicting, it seems, the marriage of an Egyptian lady to Niqmaddu, ruler of Ugarit. This was found in the stratum associated with the rebuilding of the palace on a larger scale, which followed destruction by fire. The royal seal-impressions of the Hittite overlords are among the finest found in Ugarit. They are of stamp-seals in the Anatolian tradition and in a distinctively Hittite style. These royal seals are bilingual, with the royal monogram in the centre, written in the so-called Hittite hieroglyphs, surrounded by two or even three concentric lines of cuneiform.

Trade and economy

The economy of Ugarit was not by any means based solely on external trade, for grain, oil, wine, wool, flax and timber were produced in the hinterland under its rule. However, textual evidence reveals the existence of at least three ports. The ships of Ugarit plied their trade along the Levant coast to Phoenicia, Palestine and Egypt; and they brought the fashionable Mycenaean pottery from the Aegean. The clearest traces of Mycenaean influence were found in the first season's excavations at the ancient port of Minet-el-Beida, and in the city itself, when masonry tombs were discovered containing numerous familiar Mycenaean vessels. The adoption of this Mycenaean type of underground tomb by the wealthier inhabitants of Ugarit shows the cultural influence of these foreigners. Merchants came to the city from Egypt, Cyprus, Cilicia, Beirut, Ashdod and even Assyria. Some may have established trading centres and settled in their own enclaves in Ugarit. Alashian (Cypriot) traders left Cypro-Mycenaean tablets.

Ugarit was the focus of the metal trade over a wide zone of the Near East, and seems to have enjoyed the advantages of an international centre, where speculation in gold and silver flourished. Copper, bronze, silver and perhaps also tin were imported from Hittite Anatolia, and finished goods in metal exported back again. This trade was naturally conducted by land, using donkey caravans.

While the wealth of Ugarit rested on trade, its government could command considerable forces in time of danger. In the 13th century BC, the army of Ugarit had 1,000 chariots, each drawn by two horses. This was a far greater number than the average of 40 owned by the small city-states of Canaan in the Amarna period of early 14th-century BC Egypt. Its navy, too, was very strong, with perhaps as many as 150 ships. Such a total can be compared with the contingent from Mycenae of 100 ships, the largest mentioned in Homer's *Iliad*.

The craftsmen of Ugarit

Unlike the art of Boğazköy, Nineveh or Persepolis, that of Ugarit was created for the market-place, and was not monumental or public art intended to impress or over-awe. Artisans – goldsmiths, silversmiths and bronze-smiths – producing finished wares for the Ugaritic export trade lived, with seal cutters and sculptors, round a square in the bazaar quarter of the south part of the city. Ivory-workers also produced for export and for the home market alike. Wood-working was a fashionable skill, as panelling of cedar and other woods was used in the palace. In the artisans' quarters, heaps of crushed shells from the *murex* fish are evidence of the dyeing of linen and wool in the famous 'Tyrian purple', which ranged from violet to purple-red. For cheaper textiles a dye was made from the root of the madder plant.

The technical skills and artistic receptiveness to external tastes of the artisans of Ugarit are well demonstrated by the tools, weapons and vessels which the workers in bronze, gold and other metals produced. It is the bronze- and goldsmiths' manufactures which are represented in the excavated material. Already in the Middle Ugarit I period, torques and toggle-pins, largely inspired by those from Byblos and presumably also from centres nearer Ugarit, had been manufactured in some quantities.

A large hoard of bronze tools and weapons is dated to the 14th century BC. Long bronze swords mark an advance in weaponry. One, inscribed with the *cartouche* of Merneptah of Egypt, successor to Rameses II, was not an import but was intended for the Egyptian market. It never reached its destination. Two ornate gold bowls of the Late Ugarit II period illustrate the eclectic character of art in Ugarit. One has an elaborate, overcrowded design resembling certain ivory-work; the other depicts a chase, the hunter riding a light chariot of Egyptian type.

Stonework and building

The technical accomplishments of the people of Ugarit, native and incomer alike, may be seen in their stoneworking, especially in the mason's craft. In the stone-built tombs, the vault varies from tall and steep to low and rounded. It is always a false vault, however, in that it is built by *corbelling*, with each course stepped out from that beneath until they meet at the top. The technique is disguised by carving the ceiling.

The palace, temples and richer houses of Ugarit were constructed of very fine masonry, suggesting that here lies the origin of the Phoenicians' expertise as stonemasons. Wooden or metal dowels give additional bonding for some of the large blocks of the fortifications, which resemble in some degree those of the southern extension of Hattusas, not much later in date.

Among the most important houses excavated in Ugarit is that of the chief priest, in the middle of the temple area. Its library included not only religious and mythological texts, but also school exercise tablets, vocabularies and syllabaries, indicating a priestly school. On either side of this house, on the summit of the mound, stood the massive temple of Dagan and, to the west, that of Ba'al, the youthful storm-god of the Canaanites, whose cult may have been a recent innovation in the 14th century BC. The temples are of simple plan, not unlike those of Hazor, in the extreme north of Israel. The Old Testament supplies considerable, if hardly impartial, evidence for the native religions of the region; and cult equipment, such as that from Hazor, has been unearthed at many sites in the Late Bronze Age Levant.

Mythology and religion

The myths and poetry of the Canaanites as revealed at Ugarit are astonishing for their metaphor and imagery; and later epic poetry is foreshadowed in stylistic conventions. The language of the Old Testament psalms is not wholly dissimilar, just as Hebrew and Ugaritic are very close in their vocabularies.

There is evidence indicating a considerably older origin for the myths, possibly as far back as the early 2nd millennium BC, the period of Middle Ugarit II, and well before they were copied on clay tablets for the city's libraries. Lists of up to 60 deities, in connection with temple rituals, and the use of divine elements in hundreds of personal names suggest discrepancies between the popular religion of Ugarit after about 1400 BC and the world of the myths. Babylonian and Hurrian deities are absent from these, although they were popular in the heyday of Ugarit, where a spirit of tolerance pervaded. Many offering lists show Canaanite, Mesopotamian and Hurrian deities happily together. The very plain dominance of Ba'al, in the pantheon and in state religion alike, was probably achieved only after a successful struggle with the older 'father of the gods', El.

Left: A stone cylinder-seal with gold setting from Ugarit demonstrates how seals were worn around the neck as pendants. This usage was for security as well as ornament, such seals commonly being bequeathed as heirlooms.

Below: On this seal impression, a narrow-waisted male figure stands before a god wearing the horned headdress which is the symbol of divinity.

Above: Gold dish from Ugarit which demonstrates the artistic taste of the city's goldsmiths in the 14th century BC. Its design has a vigour less obvious in some products of the Levant. The light chariot is similar to those of early 18th-dynasty Egypt (c. 1550-1410 BC).

Boğazköy
TURKEY

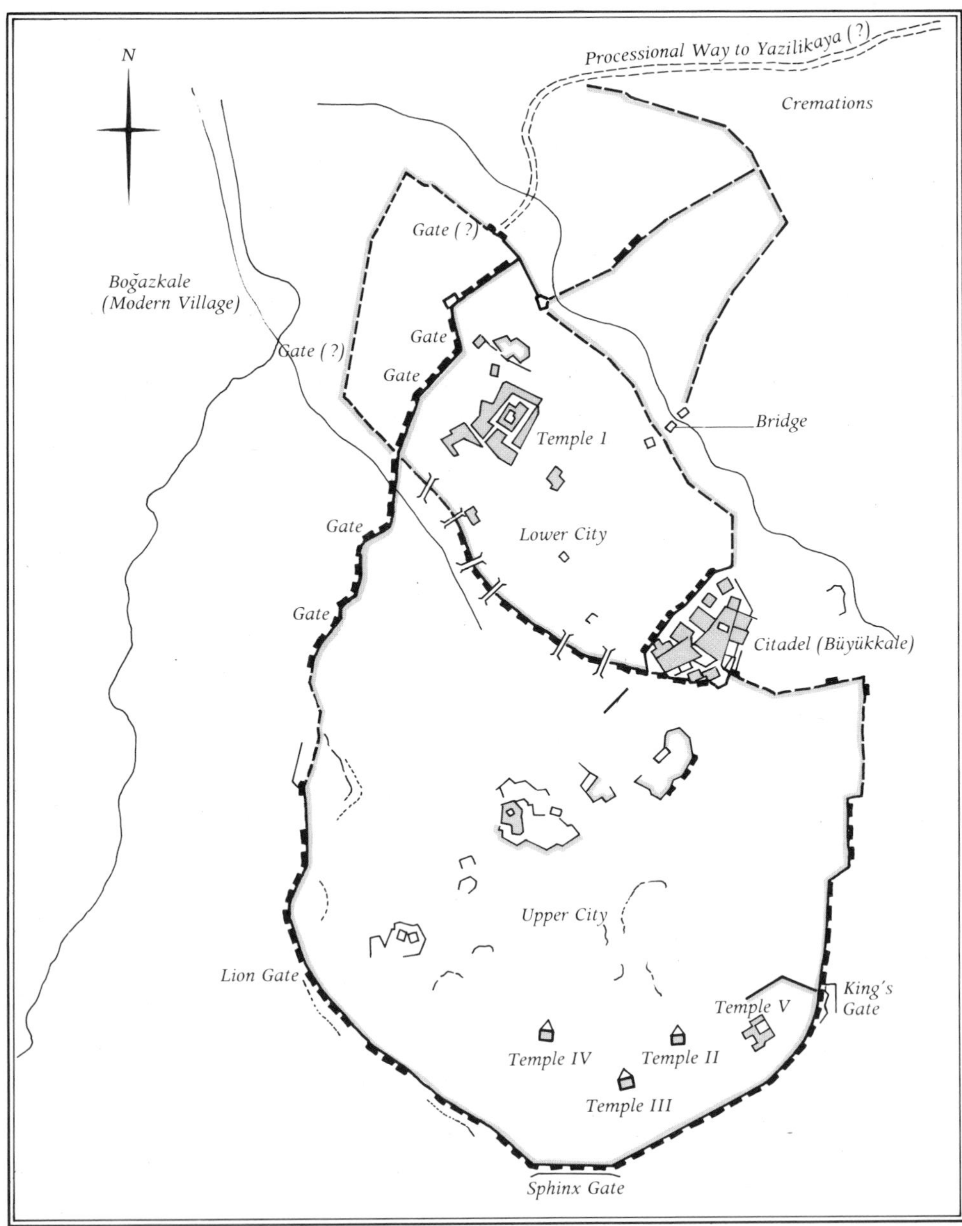

The widely spreading ruins at Boğazköy, site of the ancient Hittite capital of Hattusas, are today one of the most popular tourist sites of Turkey. Situated only some three hours east of Ankara by road, they are easily approached from Sungurlu, a district town on the Ankara-Çorum-Samsun road. The modern village lies immediately at the foot of the main site, with the famous rock shrine of Yazilikaya about 1,200 metres to the north-east. The circuit of this site, which was the principal residence of the Hittite kings of the New Kingdom, or Empire, extends in massive defences over 5 kilometres.

The peoples of Boğazköy

Charles Texier (1802–71), the French traveller and artist, first brought the ruins of Boğazköy to the attention of the Western world in 1834. Fifty years later, the English philologist Archibald Henry Sayce (1845–1933) connected the remains, which were recognized as pre-Classical from the character of the masonry, with the Kheta of the Egyptian records and the Hittim of the Old Testament. Thus began the work of detection which ultimately led to the Hittites being identified as the builders of Boğazköy.

The next stage came in 1894, with the discovery in the ruins of cuneiform tablets. Some were written in a language not then understood; others were recognized as being in the language known as Akkadian, and as contemporary with tablets discovered at Tell el-Amarna, in Upper Egypt, in 1887. For a time Boğazköy was seen as a city of the kingdom of Arzawa, known from the Amarna archive of 14th-century BC Egypt as an Anatolian state, and the unknown language was thought to be Arzawan. The Norwegian scholar J. A. Knudtzon (1854–1917) was the first to recognize the language's affinities to the Indo-European group.

The excavations

The German scholar Hugo Winckler (1863–1913) initiated the systematic investigation of Boğazköy, beginning excavations in 1906 in collaboration with the Turkish archaeologist Theodore Makridi. Results came with sensational speed. On the west slope of the citadel, Büyükkale, some 2,500 tablets were unearthed. Although largely fragmentary, those in Akkadian could swiftly be deciphered, and it was plain that the royal archives had been located.

On 20 August, 1906 Winckler and Makridi found the Akkadian version of a treaty made in the 21st year of the Egyptian ruler Rameses II with the Great King of Hatti, Hattusilis III (reigned about 1275–1250 BC). This treaty was already known from an Egyptian text at Karnak. Now it was obvious that Boğazköy, the site of ancient Hattusas, was the centre of a state based not in Syria but on the Anatolian plateau, and that this state was not Arzawa but Hatti.

Although the technical challenge presented by the Boğazköy excavations was less severe than that involved in the uncovering of a mud-brick site, the German tradition of painstakingly recording architectural evidence, first developed in Mesopotamia, bore fruit in the work at Boğazköy. Several people, including the British archaeologist John Garstang (1876–1956), did much to set Hattusas in its correct historical and geographical settings. This task became gradually more comprehensible after 1915, when Bedrich Hrozny, the decipherer of cuneiform Hittite, published the tablets found by Winckler. The work at Boğazköy has continued for many years, despite interruption by war, and an outstanding contribution to the excavations has been made by the German archaeologist Kurt Bittel.

The history of Hattusas

The long history of Hattusas stretched back for many centuries before the Hittites converted this former Assyrian trading colony into their seat of royal power, around the 16th century BC. During the 19th century BC it had been a trading centre for Assyrian merchants, but some time after 1800 BC it was sacked by Anitta, an early Hittite king, and laid in ruins. The city was refounded and made the Hittite capital by Hattusilis I, who reigned from 1650 BC to about 1620 BC. Following the end of the Assyrian trade, a dark age began in Anatolia, during which the cuneiform script, used for the Old Assyrian tablets of Kanesh and the other merchant colonies, seems to have been abandoned. Only after renewed contacts with Mesopotamia, stimulated by the raid on Babylon in about 1595 BC of Mursili I, grandson of Hattusilis, was cuneiform again brought into use, for the archives of the Hittite state. For about 400 years or so, Hattusas remained the capital, apart from one brief interlude when Muwatallis (1315–1290 BC) moved it south to a site near Karaman, in the eastern Konya plain. References to the history of the city during this period are all too few, although it is known that in the 16th century BC one king, Hantili, fortified Hattusas, which 'was in no way protected by walls before'.

The city was sacked again in about 1400 BC by invaders from the north and east, including the Gasga tribes from the region later to become Pontus. However, in the early 14th century BC, under Suppiluliumas, the Great King of Hatti, Hattusas was rebuilt and enormously enlarged, to an area of 160 hectares. It remained as the imperial capital for 200 more years, before falling in obscure circumstances in the early 12th century BC, as the result of internal pressures and invasions from outside.

A dark age followed, when the whole Anatolian plateau seems to have relapsed for a while into barbarism. In two parts of the site, Büyükkaya and the early citadel rock of Büyükkale ('great castle'), reoccupation has been attributed to the Phrygians, a people who settled in north-west Anatolia late in the 2nd millennium BC and who dominated the area after the Hittite collapse. Some scholars, however, disagree with this attribution. The great southern extension of Hattusas was never resettled. In its last years the town is identifiable as Pteria, which, according to the Greek historian Herodotus, was sacked by Croesus of Lydia in his ill-judged campaign of 547 BC, when he crossed the River Halys into Median territory. Croesus was to pay for this venture with the loss of his kingdom and his life.

Discovering the Hittites

A word of caution is appropriate here on the use of the name 'Hittite' and also 'Phrygian'. These are not to be equated simply with 'Bronze Age' and 'Iron Age' respectively in Anatolia as a whole, but refer to geographically more restricted regions, the centre of Hittite settlement being in central Anatolia, in and near the great bend of the River Halys (Kizil Irmak). The Hittites gave much to Anatolian civilization, most significantly in government, law and literature. However, their material culture was not essentially different from that of the other Anatolian peoples around them, the history of whose settlement long preceded the arrival of the Hittites.

To the wider public the best-known Hittite was Uriah, sent to his death in the forefront of battle by David, king of Israel. Since 1906, however, the excavations of Hattusas by successive German expeditions have brought into the limelight a people previously known only in this biblical context. Scholars at the time of Atatürk (1880–1938), founder of the modern Turkish republic, looked upon this nation as providing evidence for long-lost ancestors of the Turkish people. Such a theory is still acceptable if the Hittites are seen as one of many groups whose descendants have mingled to form the present-day population of Turkey. Another such group comprised the Celtic Galatians, who settled round Ankara, as it is today, in the 3rd century BC.

Statues and shrines

Among the monuments of Boğazköy it is the massive defences of the outer town, with their gates and ditch and postern tunnel, which perhaps most immediately impress the visitor. The muscular figure, in fact a god, carved in very high relief on one side of the so-called King's Gate is an outstanding example of the sculptural style which can legitimately be termed not merely Anatolian but Hittite. His sturdy proportions somehow convey an impression of a hardy highland race, even if he may have been carved by sculptors imported from Babylonia.

The rock-cut shrine of Yazilikaya ('written or carved rock') presents the supreme manifestation of the state cult. Here appear reliefs dedicated by Tudhaliyas IV in the late 13th century BC, and other reliefs dedicated to this ruler after his death. It is generally accepted that these display Hurrian influence, introduced from the eastern Anatolian kingdom of Kizzuwatna (Cilicia) through the king's mother Puduhepa.

The general impression created by the ruins of Boğazköy is of massive construction amid a rather bleak, windswept landscape, where the heat of summer is far briefer than the winter cold. The Hittites, as newcomers at the end of the 3rd millennium BC, were unable to find a better home.

Above: Rock carvings in the open-air sanctuary of Yazilikaya, dedicated to the Hurrian pantheon and possibly to a royal cult. To the left is the 'dagger god'; to the right, the Hittite king embraced by his protector god.

Above: The figure in typically Hittite ultra-high relief represents a muscular warrior-god armed with a battle-axe. It flanks the 'King's Gate' in the southern defensive perimeter of Boğazköy.

The Hittites

The life of the ordinary people of Anatolia in the 2nd millennium BC was principally determined by whether they dwelt in village or town, with villagers forming the vast majority of the population. Within the towns there is some evidence of attempts at overall street planning, even if the houses themselves were individually aligned.

By the 14th century BC the monarchy and administration of the Hittite state was, in its essentials, typical of the Near East. However, before this date, there were features indicating indigenous traditions of government and law. Political power rested in the aristocracy, whose possession of horses and a chariot outwardly denoted their status. At the centre of power was the royal family itself. Of Hittite extraction in the Old Kingdom (around the 16th century BC), it had, by the period of the New Kingdom or Empire (about 1400–about 1200 BC) become Hurrian in descent. The assembly of notables, the 'pankush', probably originated in the meeting of tribal leaders, but by the time of the earliest surviving records its powers had become vestigial. Changes, frequently alluded to in the Hittite laws, tended towards leniency. On the other hand, slavery seems to have become more severe, in that the rights of the slave in the Old Kingdom had largely vanished by the New Kingdom, when the master had power of life and death. Scarcity of reliable native population was a constant weakness of the Hittite state, and was solved by the settlement of deportees, who were retained under royal control even when put beside native communities.

The laws of the Hittite kings are set out in order, 100 laws on each of two tablets found at Hattusas, with other tablets showing variants of this code. It would be fair to say that the spirit pervading the Hittite laws was more humane than that of the Babylonian or Assyrian legal codes, wherein the *lex talionis*, the principle of an eye for an eye, was fundamental.

Building and technology

The royal citadel of Büyükkale reveals a plan cleverly adapted to the steep contours of the rock surface, with the typically Anatolian feature of open-pillared rooms surrounding courtyards. One building comprised a square audience-hall with 25 wooden columns above a basement of narrow store-rooms. Two other buildings on Büyükkale housed archives of clay tablets stored on wooden shelves. One text, of the later 13th century BC, contains instructions for the royal bodyguard, with much detail on the personnel employed in the palace. The indirect evidence of its layout confirms that it was a complex of buildings rather than one great single structure, and fits well with the remains excavated by the German expedition on Büyükkale.

The outstanding evidence of Hittite technology lies in the masonry of their fortifications, temples and relief-carved *orthostats*. Indeed, the use of such slabs as architectural decoration, set on edge as a dado, may well have been initiated by the craftsmen of Hattusas and those of other settlements, such as Alaca Hüyük, 27 kilometres away. The term 'cyclopean' is often used to describe the massive polygonal masonry which comprises the gates and walls of the outer town of Hattusas. This reference to the Cyclops, the legendary one-eyed giants of Greek tradition, is also associated with the masonry's general resemblance to that found at Mycenae and Tiryns by the German archaeologist Heinrich Schliemann (1822–90). Such an association is very misleading, however, if it is taken to imply any link between Mycenaean and Hittite building techniques.

The method employed to span the great gates of Hattusas was technically primitive, although visually impressive. A unique elliptical form was obtained by using single vertical blocks as jambs, while corbelling was employed for crowning the gates and also for the 70-metre-long postern tunnel through the rampart. The wall itself was of stone surmounted by mud brick, with crenellated brick battlements reinforced by wooden beams – as indicated by surviving though fragmented models of fired clay. Such a combination of stone, brick and timber was very much in the Anatolian architectural tradition and not peculiar to the Hittites.

Preliminary shaping of statues and masonry blocks was carried out at the quarry, as at Yesemek, for example. Here, half-way between Carchemish and the Mediterranean, lay hundreds of half-finished statues dating variously from about 1250 to 750 BC, doubtless awaiting transportation. It seems that metal-workers followed a comparable procedure, and traces of metallurgy are found at Boğazköy and also at Tarsus. Textual and material evidence alike indicate the activities of craftsmen ranging from goldsmiths to shoemakers. Pottery became ever more mass-produced and inferior to the comparable Middle Bronze Age vessels with their metal prototypes.

The Hittite vocabulary contains many agricultural terms, including the names of many tools, for the economy of the Hittites was based on agriculture, the main crops being emmer wheat and barley. For example, up to 22,000 hectares of arable land were under cultivation for the annual needs of Hattusas. Honey was also a significant item in the people's diet. Domestic livestock comprised cattle, sheep, goats, pigs and perhaps water-buffalo. Donkeys served as pack animals.

The one detailed narrative of a military engagement comes to us from the enemy side. In 1285 BC the indecisive but famous battle of Kadesh took place. The Hittites were led by their king Muwatallis, and the Egyptians by the 19th-dynasty pharaoh, Rameses II. Neither side deployed its full strength. The Egyptians used light, manoeuvrable chariots; but the heavier Hittite chariots, with solid wooden wheels, served mainly as troop-carriers, bringing the infantry to the front line.

Religion

The religion of the Hittites was an amalgam. It incorporated popular elements indigenous to central Anatolia with external influences, largely of Hurrian origin, appealing particularly to the royal court and most clearly evident in the rock-cut shrine of Yazilikaya. Water was never far from people's thoughts, at least in the heat of summer, and shrines or reliefs near water occur widely in Anatolia. Among the most important of these is the shrine of Plato's Spring (Eflatun Pinar) near Beyşehir, west of Konya. This is of fine masonry with drafted edges, probably surmounted by colossal statues, one of which was found about 50 kilometres away at Fassilar.

Right top: Boğazköy was not a typical Near Eastern settlement mound but a village, later a trading post, under the shadow of a hilltop fortress, which in the early 14th century BC was extended to the south and strongly fortified. Temple I, perhaps dedicated to the cult of Teshub, weather god and head of the Hittite pantheon, was of distinctive plan and surrounded by store-rooms for offerings.

Right centre: The Lion Gate at Boğazköy, perhaps designed under Babylonian influence.

Right: Reconstruction of the impressive defences at the southern, outer area of Boğazköy resulted from the pre-World War I seasons of German excavations. Massive masonry of 'cyclopean' style was a native Anatolian building technique. Elliptical gateways, using lofty vertical monoliths, are unique to this city. The main wall, of casemate construction, stood on top of a high rampart and was reinforced by towers, with smaller ones along the lower outer wall.

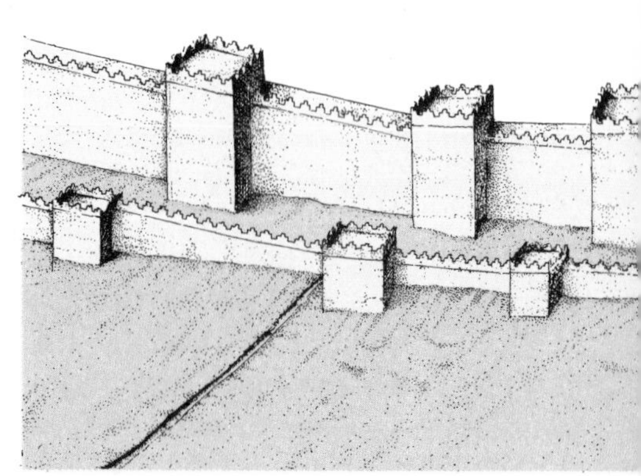

Temple I at Hattusas, very probably dedicated to the weather god Teshub and thus the home of his cult, was approached by a typically Hittite gateway, with a small porter's lodge on either side. Beyond was a paved area surrounding the temple proper. It comprised rooms along three sides of a rectangular central court with a colonnade of square stone piers on the fourth side, through which the visitor had to pass to reach the sanctuary. Within, and shielded from public gaze as was the entire sanctuary, must have stood the cult statue. Only its base remains. Granite was used for this, the most sacred part of Temple I, and limestone for the remainder. Ritual ablutions and liquid offerings, or libations, played an important part in the temple ceremonies of Hattusas as elsewhere in the Hittite dominions. In this context must be seen a square stone basin, within Temple I and on the axis of the gate, to which water was brought from a well by baked clay pipes.

The reliefs of Yazilikaya show gods and goddesses wearing the horned headdress, which was an originally Mesopotamian characteristic emblem of divinity. The most imposing is worn by the weather god Teshub, with goddesses wearing their own distinctive crowns. The tradition of depicting divinities standing on an animal is of Hurrian origin.

An interpretation of Yazilikaya naturally depends on understanding the shrine's purpose. It is therefore hardly remarkable that opinion has changed radically since Charles Texier suggested in 1834 that here was represented a meeting of the Amazons and Paphlagonians (a people from a Roman province on the Black Sea). The prevailing view today is that the reliefs of the first chamber are associated with a great spring festival, most probably the Hittite New Year festival, comparable with the Babylonian 'akitu' ceremonies, and held each year outside the city. The function of the inner chamber seems very different, and is associated with a funerary cult, probably that of Tudhaliyas IV.

Cremation, widespread in central Anatolia from the early 2nd millennium BC, is known from textual sources to have been the funerary custom of the Hittite kings. The ordinary people of Hattusas, however, were either cremated or buried. Funerary offerings were rather meagre, except for traces of animal bones, which may be the remnants of funeral feasts. The remains of horses suggest a possible link with the practices of the *kurgan* people of the steppes of southern Russia. The first Indo-European settlers in Anatolia, to whom the Hittites were related, came from this region, although they are no longer seen as the first Indo-Europeans in the Near East.

Nineveh

IRAQ

The vast ruins of Nineveh stand on the east bank of the River Tigris, opposite Mosul, the second city of Iraq. If the reasonable estimate of the prophet Jonah is to be believed, in the days of its power as the centre of the Assyrian empire, Nineveh boasted a population of 120,000. No city of the ancient Near East strikes a chord so sharply at the mere mention of its name, and nowhere is reaction to it more clearly expressed than in the biblical book of Nahum, from which later generations gained their picture of the fall of the great city,

> 'Woe to the bloody city! It is all full of lies and robbery . . . Thy shepherds slumber, O king of Assyria; thy nobles shall dwell in the dust; thy people is scattered upon the mountains, and no man gathereth them. There is no healing of thy bruise; thy wound is grievous . . .'.

Of the two names most closely associated with the city, the first is that of Sennacherib (d. 681 BC), the king who enlarged it, making it his principal royal residence; the second is Austen Henry Layard (1817–94), the early Victorian traveller, archaeologist and artist.

Layard's excavations

Layard was 28 years of age when on 9 November, 1845, he began excavating Nimrud, 35 kilometres south of Nineveh. In the summer of 1846 he made his first trial excavations on the great mound of Kuyunjik, the citadel of Nineveh, where French excavations had been in progress for some time, following the work of Paul-Emile Botta (1802–70). Having been appointed consul at Mosul, Botta became the first archaeologist to investigate the ruins of Assyria, at Khorsabad, and so began the large-scale excavations of ancient Mesopotamia. Botta's work at Khorsabad (1843–45) was completed before Layard arrived in Mosul to prepare for his own excavations at Kalhu (Nimrud). It is likely that, had Botta been allowed to remain in Mosul, Anglo-French relations in the field would have been much better than they subsequently became. As it was, by the time that Layard turned his attention to Nineveh, he found that the efforts of his French rivals were being largely wasted, because they had not fully appreciated the surface evidence – traces of the platforms of the Assyrian palaces – especially in the south-west corner of Kuyunjik. Layard refused to accept the French consul's claim to the whole mound of Kuyunjik. Nevertheless, since the first results failed to yield treasures comparable to those so quickly unearthed at Nimrud, Layard temporarily lost heart. He did, however, find winged guardians when he opened the Nergal Gate in the north-west sector of the outer rampart, acting on evidence left by Claudius Rich (1786–1821), who had made the first plan of the ruins.

'Palace Without a Rival'

The uncovering of a bas-relief in 1847 revealed the existence of a palace on Kuyunjik, and Layard began intensive work in order to secure his claim to that area of the mound. A customary agreement had evolved that the discoverer of a palace was entitled to continue its excavation, irrespective of any prior right to the site as a whole. Layard returned to London by Christmas of the same year, having been rapturously received en route in Paris. Two years were to elapse before he resumed excavations at Nimrud, which he and Henry Rawlinson (1810–95) erroneously identified with Nineveh, and at Kuyunjik. The publication early in 1849 of *Nineveh and its Remains*, nearly 900 pages long and written in under a year, made Layard a household name, and his fortunes took a turn for the better.

Layard summed up his discoveries in the palace of Sennacherib at Nineveh:

> 'I had opened no less than 71 halls, chambers and passages, whose walls, almost without exception, had been panelled with slabs of sculptured alabaster recording the wars, the triumphs and the great deeds of the Assyrian king. By a rough calculation, about 9,880 feet, or nearly two miles, of bas-reliefs, with 27 portals formed by colossal winged bulls and lion-sphinxes, were uncovered in that part alone of the building explored during my researches'.

Excavations some 80 years later, under R. Campbell-Thompson, were to reveal that Layard had in fact uncovered all the more important areas of Sennacherib's 'Palace Without a Rival'.

Layard was primarily interested in the art of the Assyrian palaces, a bias with which Rawlinson, though admiring his work, could not agree. Rawlinson's appreciation of ancient art stopped short at Greece and Rome, and for him the major significance was in the 'tablets', a term at that time applied to all inscriptions, not merely to those on clay.

Layard the archaeologist

Much stress has been laid on the limitations of Layard's methods, particularly his habit of tunnelling along wall faces to uncover the reliefs. He has also been criticized for not excavating down to floor level, having discovered that beneath the long sequences of the reliefs there was only a plain dado. Yet he was the greatest archaeologist of his pioneering generation, through his writings and above all by the display of his most sensational finds in the British Museum, where they still form the world's finest collection of Assyrian sculpture.

Layard retired from fieldwork at the age of 36. He had never spared himself, although weakened in the end by fever. Among others who have worked in the ruins of the Near East, he frequently found his local workmen more congenial company than his staff, who were not invariably suited to their tasks and the working conditions. 'I frequently feasted the workmen', said Layard, '. . . I endeavoured, as far as it was in my power, to create a good feeling amongst all, and to obtain their willing co-operation in my work'.

Excavations after Layard

It fell to Layard's chief assistant Hormuzd Rassam, a native of Mosul, to carry on the excavations at Nineveh after Layard's departure, beginning in 1852. Rassam had wished to investigate the northern area of Kuyunjik, claimed by the French, and finally resolved on the bizarre tactic of excavating under cover of night. The finding of a well-preserved relief slab led him to inform Victor Place (1819–75), Botta's successor as French consul and excavator of Khorsabad, who hastened to the spot. Place was obliged to

Left: Life-size head, cast in bronze and commonly attributed either to Sargon of Agade or to his grandson Naram-Sin, the most powerful kings of the great Akkadian dynasty. They established their rule through provincial governors, whose unpopularity may be reflected in deliberate mutilation of the eyes. The hairstyle partially resembles that of the helmet of Meskalamshar from Ur.

Right: Relief of a lion hunt, rendered in the traditional 'register', or 'strip' style. Lion hunting was a favourite sport of the Assyrian kings, and was portrayed in agonized detail on the masterpieces achieved by the sculptors of Assurbanipal, who preferred a plain background to heighten the effect. The herding of lions into cages before being released to be slaughtered seems to indicate their being bred specially for the hunt. Elephants and ostriches were among species preserved in Assyrian zoological parks.

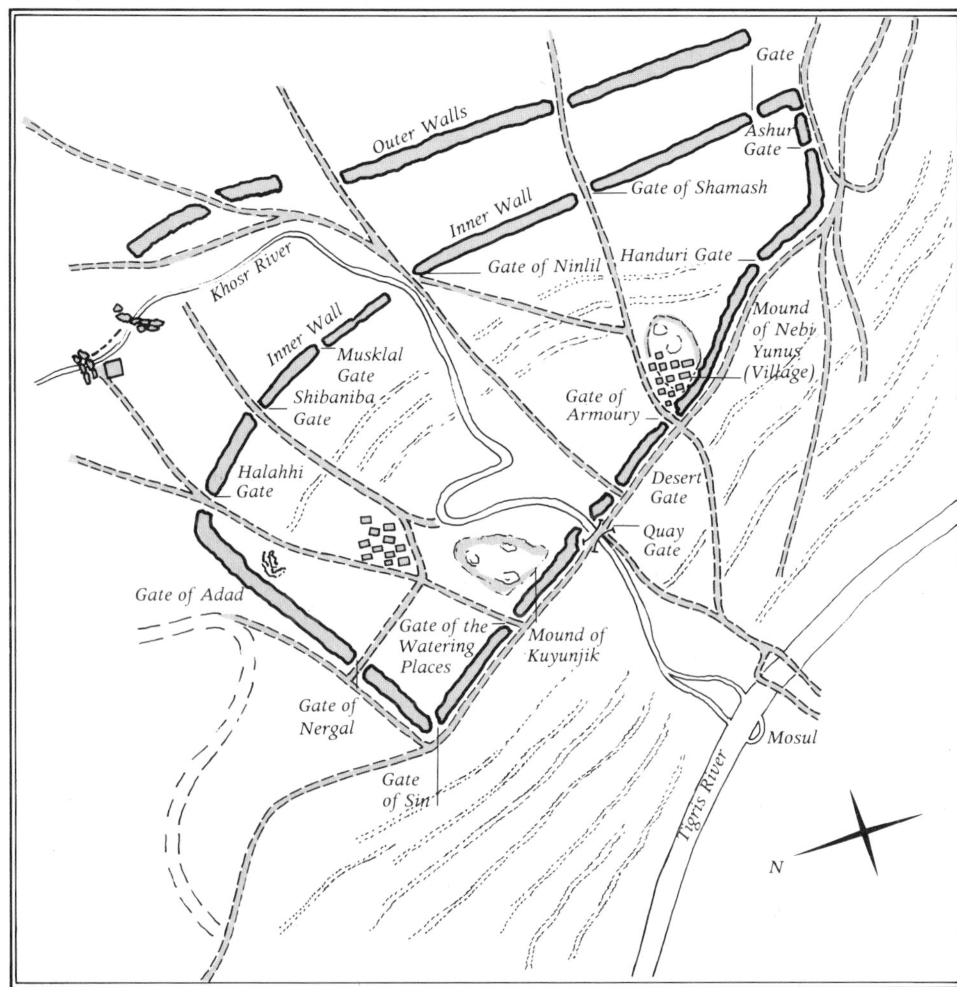

concede the site, which was that of the palace of Assurbanipal (668–627 BC), to Rassam and the British Museum. Thus in due course the library of this king, as well as that of his grandfather found by Layard in the 'Palace Without a Rival', went not to the Louvre but to the British Museum.

The story of Nineveh is almost as much in its rediscovery as in the long centuries of its occupation. Of Assyria's four leading cities, it was almost certainly the oldest by far. The great sounding made by Campbell-Thompson on Kuyunjik went down over 20 metres and revealed occupation dating back into the early 6th millennium BC. Nineveh's importance derived from its situation on a natural east-west trade route, at a crossing over the Tigris. A hint of its wealth in the 3rd millennium BC is provided by a magnificent bronze head, tentatively identified with Sargon of Agade.

Sennacherib's inscriptions

Further large-scale work at Nineveh is inhibited by the sheer scale of the city, which extends for 730 hectares, and the depth of disturbed strata. Yet there is an additional source of information, not normally available for an ancient Near Eastern city, to be found in the building inscriptions of Sennacherib himself. This king spent the first years of his reign (705–703 BC) in restoring and enlarging the city of Nineveh, not least the palace itself. 'Lest in the passing of days its platform should give way before the floods of high water', Sennacherib wrote of the River Tigris.

'I set up great slabs of limestone around its walls, and strengthened its structure; over these I filled in the terrace to a height of 170 courses of brickwork, I added to the site of the former palace . . . Thereon I had them build a palace of ivory, maple, boxwood, mulberry, cedar, cypress, spruce and pistachio, the "Palace Without a Rival" for my royal abode . . .'.

Numerous Sumerian and Akkadian texts from the 2nd and even the 3rd millennium BC were copied in Nineveh. Assyria therefore played a cultural role not unlike that performed later by Byzantium in preserving the literature of Greece and Rome.

As shepherds of their people, the Assyrian kings diligently improved the irrigation and livestock of their homeland; and their religious duties brought them under the influence of the Babylonian south. It was arguably his change to repression and his destruction of Babylon (689 BC) which led to the assassination of Sennacherib (681 BC) in 'the house of Nisroch his god', as the Bible relates. Layard plausibly identified Nisroch with the bird-headed protective genii, holding bucket and fir-cone and sprinkling the king with holy water.

Nineveh's Glory

The economic basis of Assyrian civilization was the land, its agricultural produce and its livestock. Indeed, the king saw and depicted himself as the shepherd of his people. Both archaeological and textual evidence also attest the role of successive kings in the collection and cultivation of plants. Sennacherib, for example, introduced cotton (the 'wool bearing tree'). These rulers also constructed irrigation works for the fertile land in the districts surrounding Nineveh and Nimrud. What Assurnasirpal II had done for Nimrud, Sennacherib was to carry out on a more ambitious scale for the larger city of Nineveh, even drawing water from another river to add to that of the Khosr, which joined the Tigris at Nineveh. Sennacherib's work is described in his own words.

> 'To give these waters a course through the steep mountains, I cut through the difficult places with pickaxes and directed their outflow to the plain of Nineveh . . . I had all of the orchards watered in the hot season . . . Within the orchards, more than in their native habitat, the vine, every fruit-bearing tree and herbs throve luxuriously . . . The mulberry and cypress, the product of the orchards, the reeds of the brakes in the swamps I cut down and used them as desired, in the building of my royal palaces. The wool-bearing trees they sheared and wove the wool into garments . . .'.

Engineering and technology

The aqueduct of stone built at Jerwan by Sennacherib is the most remarkable piece of Assyrian engineering, for there survives one *ogival arch*, proof that the Assyrians had mastered a structural technique widely supposed to have been introduced by the Romans.

The palaces, however, were of simpler construction, roofed by massive cedar beams which dictated the use of relatively narrow rectangular rooms. They were probably constructed by a well-established, conservative building profession, working under royal control. This is suggested both by a recurrent arrangement, now termed the standard reception suite, in which the most important component was the throne room, and by the general adherence to a division between public rooms (*babanu*) and private residential quarters (*bitanu*), although this was not new to the Near East.

The employment of forced labour on public works is nowhere more vividly recorded than in a relief showing gangs of labourers, watched by the royal guards, carrying their baskets of stones and clods of earth for the construction of the platform on which the new palace of Sennacherib was to stand. It was the decay of such foundations which often necessitated the rebuilding of Assyrian palaces.

Iron technology was advanced in the Assyrian empire, and there is even evidence of the production of steel. However, this skill can hardly be used to explain Assyrian military strength, since iron was certainly worked in Urartu also, and had been used earlier by the Philistines and others. The economic implications of one statement by Sennacherib are clear, when he says: 'I built a form of clay and poured bronze into it, as in making half-shekel pieces'. Although Greek tradition credited the Lydians with the invention of coinage, could Sennacherib have a better claim?

The people of Nineveh

Craftsmen were the most numerous class of native Assyrians, their numbers maintained by hereditary succession and a system of apprenticeships. As in all old cities of the Near East today, Nineveh seems to have included quarters occupied by artisans of one trade, and the jealous defence of their status may have been reinforced by the fact that native Assyrians formed a minority of the city population. Goldsmiths, potters, bleachers and gardeners are among those known to have had their own quarters, as was probably the case with weavers, carpenters and workers in non-precious metals. There are references also to guilds and their officers.

The libraries of Sennacherib and Assurbanipal include tablets recording legal decisions and private contracts, such as property transfers, which cast much light on the lives of ordinary people. Census records from Harran in the 7th century BC contribute towards an Assyrian 'Domesday book', registering cultivators and their families, together with the area and type of land farmed. A list from Nimrud connected with military mobilization or levy for public works gives 30 to 50 men for each of a number of villages. Another tablet lists deportees according to profession, age, sex and stature. The royal household made regular demands on the economy, for all its members had to be fed. Grain, wine and other items had to be issued to charioteers, guards, scribes, musicians, diviners, exorcists, leather-workers, seal-cutters, messengers, lieutenants, adjut-

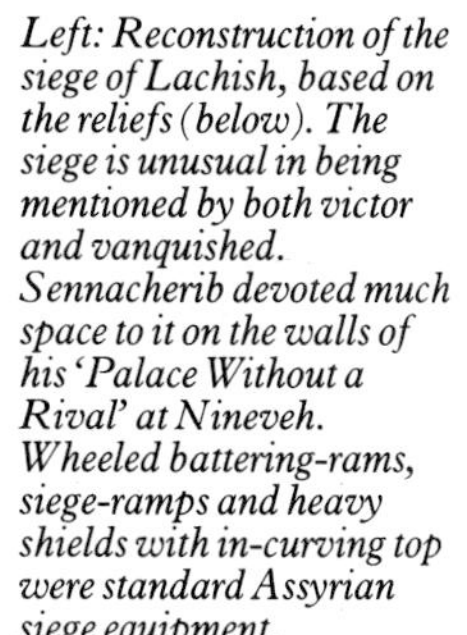

Left: Reconstruction of the siege of Lachish, based on the reliefs (below). The siege is unusual in being mentioned by both victor and vanquished. Sennacherib devoted much space to it on the walls of his 'Palace Without a Rival' at Nineveh. Wheeled battering-rams, siege-ramps and heavy shields with in-curving top were standard Assyrian siege equipment.

Right: Reliefs of Assurbanipal's defeat of the Elamites have crowded scenes clarified by inscriptions.

ants, and, not least, the donkey-driver for a litter.

Defence and warfare

Among the many reliefs at Nineveh is that of the siege of Lachish by Sennacherib (701 BC), in the campaign against Judah of which the Old Testament also gives an account. The clothing, weapons, shields and chariots of the Assyrian army had been the object of detailed attention from the time of the first Assyrian palace reliefs. In the reign of Sennacherib (705–681 BC), the sculptors began to break away from their traditional adherence to registers and to attempt some rendering of the landscape background. Another of Sennacherib's campaigns took him into the marshes at the head of the Gulf, where the Tigris and the Euphrates join. This gave an opportunity to depict the local population, the ancestors of today's marsh Arabs, squatting on their reed platforms in the cover of the marshes. Under Assurbanipal, the melée of a major battle was nowhere better conveyed than in the scenes of his defeat of the Elamites, who were the ancestral enemies of Mesopotamia. Separate short inscriptions were now set beside individual incidents depicted on the reliefs. Some of the reliefs of Assurbanipal record another menace, less serious but demanding different tactics, presented by the camel-riding nomads of the Arabian desert. However, the apex of the Assyrian sculptor's achievement is surely marked by the pathos in the scenes of Assurbanipal's lion-hunts.

On Tell Nebi Yunus, the smaller of the two citadel mounds of Nineveh, remains have been partially uncovered of an army headquarters and arsenal in use through three successive reigns (705–627 BC). The native Assyrian population was too small for security against enemies, and Sennacherib relates how he imported 208,000 settlers to his newly enlarged city. Even if this seems an exaggerated figure, the growing role of Aramaic as a spoken tongue shows the largely non-Assyrian affinities of the population.

Nineveh's defences were the most massive in the ancient Near East, if only in their length and the labour involved in their construction. The inner wall which encircled the whole city was the work of Sennacherib. It was constructed of masonry surmounted by mud brick, with stone stepped parapets and towers. Layard estimated the height of the north gate, including the towers, as 'full 100 feet'. The south sector of Nineveh's east side was further reinforced by two ditches and two walls in alternation. Probably the work of Sinsharishkun (627–612 BC), last king of Assyria, these were never completed.

The techniques of battering rams, siege ramps, dismantling chariots and using inflated goat-skins for river crossings had all been developed by the reign of one of the earlier kings, Assurnasirpal II (883–859 BC), although improvements were introduced from time to time. Chariots became ever more massive, those of Assurbanipal having enormous wheels and sometimes four men in their crew. The armour and helmets of the military units varied both according to their duties and their places of origin.

Religion

The religious centre and royal burial place of the kingdom was at Assur, further down the Tigris, although the temple on Kuyunjik of Nabu, Babylonian god of writing, was restored by Assurbanipal.

The national god Ashur first appears in the guise of a god of vegetation and crops. Only later did he assume the role of war god and patron of the throne, shown on the reliefs and seals as hovering in a winged nimbus above the king. Religious scenes on the palace walls were virtually confined to the theme of protection by *genii*. Human- or bird-headed, these characteristically Assyrian figures hold a bucket, and with a fir cone sprinkle the king with holy water. In some scenes they appear with a tree, and from this, the sacred tree so long an element in Near Eastern iconography, they are drawing magical power. Similar small-scale statuettes buried at the corners of buildings served as watchmen against evil influences. Dreams, divination and soothsaying all had their part in Assyrian life. Oracles were consulted frequently, and were fulsomely reassuring to the king, in marked contrast with prophecy in Israel. For, despite all their physical power, the Assyrian kings were fearful of the forces of demons and magic.

According to a Babylonian tablet, Nineveh fell in 612 BC, following an attack by combined forces of Babylonians, Scythians and Medes. Traces of ash which represent the disaster are to be found in many parts of the site.

Persepolis

IRAN

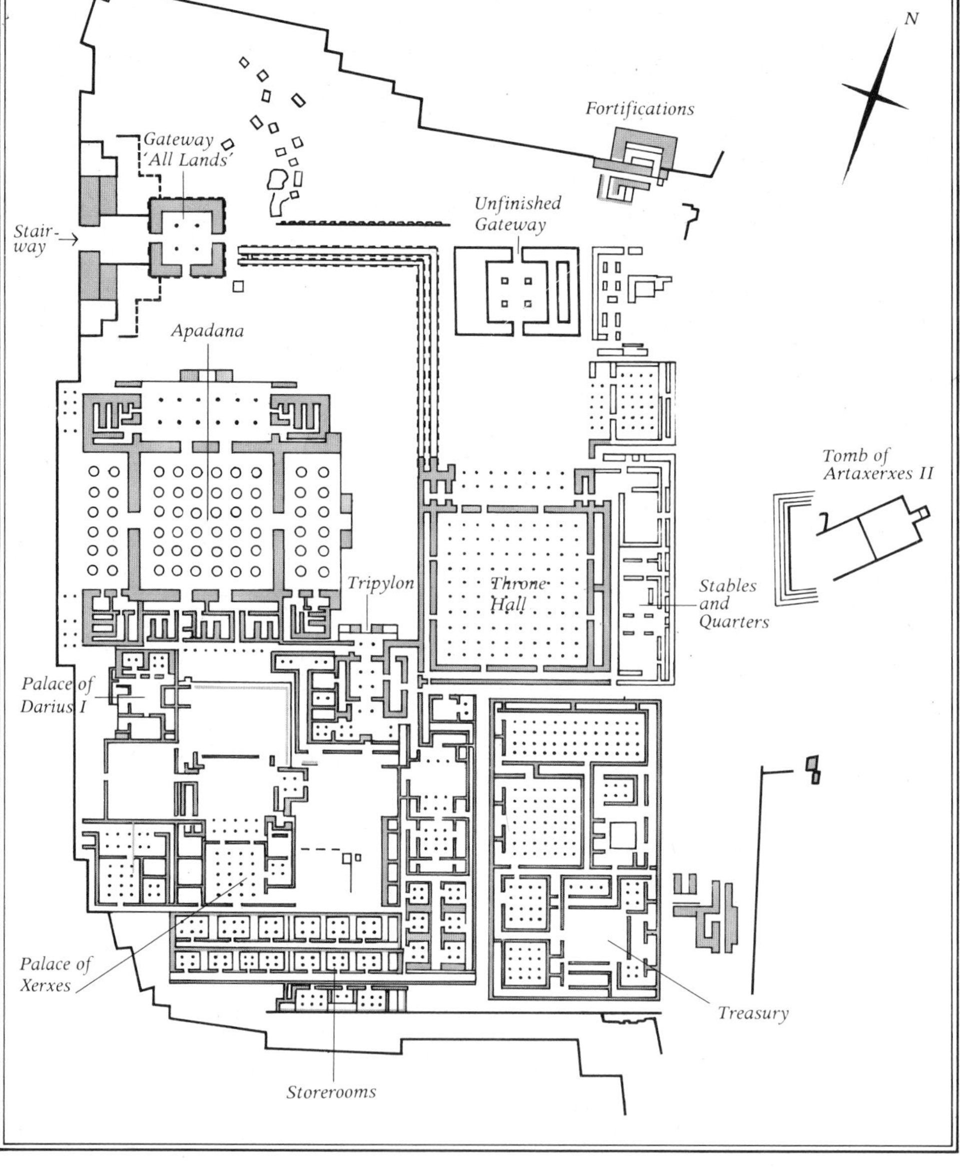

The ruins of the royal monument of the Achaemenid Persian empire are best known by their Greek name – Persepolis. One of the outstanding attractions in the Near East, they are situated in the plain called Marv-i-Dasht, 60 kilometres north-east of the city of Shiraz, where the high altitude, over 2,500 metres, makes for hot dry summers but bitterly cold winter nights. To the Persians themselves the ruins were called Parsa and to their Islamic descendants, Takht-i-Jamshid, 'throne of Jamshid', after a legendary king and mighty hunter of Iranian folklore. Almost personifying the oppressive power of the Persian empire and its threat to the Greek world, Persepolis was the natural target for Alexander the Great's revenge, supposedly for the Persian attack on Greece which led to the battle of Marathon in 490 BC. The fire which consumed its columned halls, however, and which was celebrated so lyrically in Handel's oratorio *Alexander's Feast*, may simply have resulted from a drunken spree by Alexander's troops.

The buildings of Persepolis are constructed on a vast terrace on three different levels. Situated on a spur at the foot of a mountain, they extend over an area of 13 hectares and were built over a period (518–460 BC) which spanned the reigns of Darius I, his son Xerxes and grandson Artaxerxes I. However, the inspiration of the whole is commonly attributed to Darius I. Work started after the suppression of a revolt at the opening of his reign. Following it, Darius reorganized the administration of the provinces, or satrapies, in his vast empire, which stretched from the Danube to the Indus.

Stranger than the fame of the ruined monument through later centuries is the ignorance of it during its days of glory, among the Greeks and others outside the domain of the King of Kings, as the Persian ruler called himself. This may be connected with the mystery of its function, or may merely reflect its remoteness compared with the capital cities of Susa, Babylon and Ecbatana (Hamadan).

Exploring Persepolis

In later years the ruins were mentioned from time to time by various travellers. Geographers of the Islamic period carefully noted the details of the capitals and sculptures, especially those of the king, although these accounts may have been based for the most part on a common source. An Italian traveller of the 15th century remarked on the symbol of Ahuramazda, the leading god of the Persian pantheon, comparing it with God the Father. The modern era of travel in Iran, beginning about AD 1800, opened up the area further to outsiders. Excavations on a large, though scarcely scientific, scale were carried out by Farhad Mirza, governor of Fars province, from about 1878. Mirza employed 600 workmen, but kept no records.

Work began anew at Persepolis in 1924, with an invitation from the Iranian government to Ernst Herzfeld, director of the Oriental Institute of the University of Chicago. He was asked to prepare a report on a long-term plan for excavating the site, as well as for conserving the standing remains. He was also asked to prepare plans of the site and a reconstruction of the monuments, a fact which shows the relative backwardness of archaeology in Iran at that time, compared with other Near Eastern states.

The greatest period of work at Persepolis was that sponsored by the Oriental Institute of the University of Chicago which took place from 1931 to 1939. The Institute was then involved in simultaneous fieldwork in Egypt, Palestine, Syria, Turkey and Iraq as well as Persepolis, first under Herzfeld and later, from 1935, under Erich Schmidt. Schmidt had previously dug Tepe Hissar, in north-east Iran, and had made brilliant use of aerial photography throughout Iran. Work at Persepolis was resumed in the 1940s by the Archaeological Service of Iran, and in recent years restoration work has been led by Giuseppe and Ann Britt Tilia, of the Italian Institute for the Middle and Far East.

Persepolis has presented fewer technical problems than most major Near Eastern sites, for the excavations were mostly a matter of removing accumulated wind-blown dust, ash and building debris. There is no stratigraphy to be unravelled. Interpretation is the challenge.

Gate House stood the Apadana, begun by Darius I, on its own terrace. To the east stood the Throne Hall, or Hall of 100 Columns, of Xerxes. Between these two led the approach south to a fine, relief-decorated staircase of the square plan usual at Persepolis. Through its south door this gave access to the royal apartments, and through its east door to the Harem. West, beyond a ruined building, stood the small palace of Darius I. To the south-east was the palace of Xerxes. Across a court from the Harem was a complex perhaps serving as quarters for the royal guard or else as robing rooms for the Throne Hall. Across a street, and occupying the whole south-east corner of the terrace, stood the royal store-house and arsenal. The excavator named this the Treasury, from the clay tablets found inside.

Above: The ruins of Persepolis seen through the Throne Hall of Xerxes to the Tripylon (rear left), Palace of Darius I (far left) and Audience Hall, or Apadana (rear right).
Right: The Apadana reliefs are in Near East style (lion attacking bull); and tribute-bearers represent the lands then ruled by Darius.

The tombs of Cyrus and Darius

Cyrus the Great, son of Cambyses I of the clan of the Achaemenidae, the chief clan of the Persian tribe of the Pasargadai, was founder of the Persian empire. In 550 BC he reached the climax of his career and united the two Iranian kingdoms of Media and Persia under his leadership. He then sought to centralize at least some of his imperial power, or to symbolize its prestige, in the construction of the city of Pasargadae, which is seen by some as a translation into stone of a nomad encampment. It would be an exaggeration to say that Persepolis represents a different cultural ethos from Pasargadae, although the impression made on the visitor by the two sites is inevitably one of great contrast.

Cyrus saw no need of a grander tomb than he built for himself at Pasargadae, the modest dimensions of which are a far cry from the imposing, inaccessible cliff tombs of Naqsh-i-Rustam, 10 kilometres from Persepolis. Each of these has a façade representing a building, clearly a palace at Persepolis. In Darius I's tomb there is a middle panel above which is a vast throne-stand supported by 30 peoples of the empire arranged in two tiers. This throne is probably as it stood in the Apadana, or audience hall, of Persepolis. All the Naqsh-i-Rustam tombs have rock-cut chambers, and in the tomb of Darius I every finished one has a gabled ceiling. Thus in the contemporary tradition of rock-cut tombs was preserved a feature of the free-standing tombs of Iran.

Layout

Persepolis was sited on a plain where some early Achaemenid buildings already stood. Underground channels add to the evidence that the whole complex was planned to one master design. The public sector was on the north side, reached through the Gate-House called 'All Lands', which was the work of Xerxes (reigned 486–465 BC). Inside the Gate House stood the Apadana, begun by Darius I, on its own terrace.

Architecture

Persian architecture owes much to Assyria and Babylon and to the civilization of Elam (Susiana), yet it remains distinctive. Its outstanding feature is the use of very tall stone columns to support wooden ceilings, the painted decoration of which contrasted with the better preserved reliefs. The slender columns of the Throne Hall, in 10 rows of 10, were almost 12 metres high, compared with the Apadana's rather stouter columns, over 18 metres high. Both were poorly lit. The Throne Hall had seven windows in its front wall, which faced north through the portico. The other three walls incorporated niches rather than windows, but each wall had two doors. On the inside were reliefs showing the king enthroned or fighting monsters.

As long ago as 1789, the German theologian Johann Gottfried von Herder wrote that the processions of gift-bearers on the façades of the Apadana at Persepolis revealed 'a statistical map of the lands of the then Persian empire . . . a living map of its provinces and peoples'.

Among the extravaganzas of Achaemenid Persian architecture were the capitals crowning the columns. Composite in design and top-heavy in appearance, they incorporated palm leaves and papyrus flowers; a long section with pairs of double volutes (spiral scrolls); and the impost block (the horizontal block resting on the uprights) adorned with doubled animal forequarters. The columns of the Apadana had bell-shaped bases with floral designs. Within the halls the wall faces were decorated with a dado, perhaps with coloured designs and probably with rich hangings above. The biblical Book of Esther describes a banquet at Susa, where 'there were hangings of white cloth, of green and of blue, fastened with cords of fine linen and purple'. The same source makes mention of a polychrome marble pavement, but none such occurs in the Apadana at Persepolis.

Royal City

Archaeologists have tended to agree that Persepolis was almost certainly associated with the Persian New Year festival, which today falls at the end of March in the Western calendar. According to this interpretation, the King of Kings spent at least part of every spring at Persepolis, on his annual travels from his summer residence of Hamadan (Ecbatana) to Babylon and Susa in autumn and winter. An alternative theory is that the scenes at Persepolis depict no single event, but rather the presentation of gifts which took place wherever and whenever the Persian king made camp on one of his journeys, with rich and poor alike bringing gifts according to their means and the season.

Whatever the interpretation, the whole complex represented the shrine of the royal clan, the Achaemenids. Darius the Great was an Achaemenid, of the tribe of Pasargadai, of the land of Parsa, of the Aryan people, and the supremacy of the Iranian peoples over other races of the empire is shown by their place in the depiction of rows of gift-bearers, whatever the precise significance of these.

The inscriptions

The official inscriptions of the empire were written in Old Persian, Elamite and Akkadian. The alphabetic character of the Old Persian text helped the English archaeologist Sir Henry Rawlinson when he deciphered the cuneiform script in the late 19th century. Rawlinson had copied the rock inscription of Darius I at Bisutun (Behistun), not far from Kermanshah in the homeland of the Medes. Old Persian was the vernacular of the Achaemenids, but was used only for royal inscriptions. Initial records at court were prepared on papyrus or parchment in Aramaic, the relatively simple alphabetic script of which had made it an increasingly popular language from the last century of the Assyrian empire (600s BC). Later these records were translated into Elamite cuneiform on clay tablets. Aramaic, however, was the language of diplomacy throughout the Persian empire. The Bisutun inscription underlines the Iranian concepts which Darius I set down as governing the conduct of the king. The duty of the ruler was to follow the Truth, eschew the Lie and practise the arts of horsemanship and archery, these knightly accomplishments being set out in the inscriptions on Darius I's tomb at Naqsh-i-Rustam. There justice and the rule of law are stressed.

Administration

The economy of each satrapy, or province, of the Persian empire evolved largely on its own lines, that of Mesopotamia and the west being by and large more sophisticated than that of the less civilized east. Babylonia remained prosperous, although the sack of Babylon itself by Xerxes in 478 BC dealt a blow from which, in spite of better treatment under his son Artaxerxes I (465–425 BC), the city may never have recovered.

The imperial administration was founded on the law of the Medes and Persians, 'which changes not', supported by a system of communications partly inherited from the Assyrians. The famous royal road, running 2,700 kilometres from Sardis to Susa, aided the dispatch of royal messengers. The Medes and Persians were born to the saddle; but for their maritime endeavours they relied on the Phoenicians, the traditional seafarers of the Near East, whom they conscripted for their disastrous invasion of Greece in 480 BC. It is not necessary to take literally Herodotus's estimate of the size of the Persian war machine – six corps of 60,000 men each in six divisions, plus 10,000 Immortals, the élite royal bodyguard – to understand the vast resources in manpower and materials available to the Achaemenid kings.

There is ample evidence for the many groups of foreign workers brought by force or otherwise into the employment of the King of Kings. They included Egyptians; Babylonians; Assyrians; Hattians from north

Above: Ten kilometres from Persepolis lies the cliff of Naqsh-i-Rustam – the place chosen by Darius I, Xerxes, Artaxerxes I and Darius II for their inaccessible tombs, the façades of which imitate a palace surmounted by a throne. In a Sasanian relief (lower right) the Roman emperor Valerian kneels before Shapur I (c. 240-272 AD).

Left: The ruins of the Apadana provide fitting evidence of the power and prestige of the first world empire. Its surviving 18-metre-high stone columns originally supported a brightly painted wooden ceiling.

Right: Although the decoration of Persepolis owed much to Assyrian influence, especially marked in the top-heavy capitals of the Apadana, even these were an Achaemenid form, and the columned halls of Persepolis were a radical architectural innovation. Here the Great King had ample space to receive delegations in audience.

Syria; Carians, Ionians, Sardians and especially Cappadocians from Anatolia; and Skudrians, shown on the reliefs of the Apadana wearing Thracian helmets. Cambyses, the son of Cyrus, is said to have deported to Persia many craftsmen as well as much loot from Egypt after its conquest in 525 BC. Almost certainly some of the foreigners employed at Persepolis were slaves.

The craftsmen

The technical skills evident at Persepolis cannot be understood without first examining Pasargadae, Cyrus's capital. Here clear traces abound of the use of the toothed chisel, which was employed in Greece as early as 570 BC, but it appears to have been used after, not during, the reign of Cyrus in Pasargadae. Close examination of the masonry at Pasargadae, together with textual references, indicates that Greek and Lydian craftsmen worked there, if only for a relatively brief period in the formative stage of Achaemenid art and architecture. The main direction was almost surely Iranian, with foreign advice and craftsmanship, the latter given a freer hand at Pasargadae than Persepolis. The Greek influence seems to have extended beyond the use of the toothed chisel and it is hard to ignore the similarities between the treatment of clothing in Greece and the folding of the Persian robe at Persepolis. Sculptors were paid on the same scale as other craftsmen at Persepolis. They were also paid monthly, not by piece work as in later 5th-century BC Athens. Payment was primarily in silver, supplemented by goods in kind.

The range of skills exploited by the Persian rulers is hinted at by a royal inscription of Darius I concerning a palace he built at Susa. The inscription was on a fired clay tablet from the ruins of the same building. On it specific mention is made of stonemasons from Ionia and Sardis; from the latter also came woodworkers, making wood inlays. More reliable is the evidence of the Persepolis Treasury tablets on sculptors and other workers, supplemented by the Persepolis Fortification tablets and by Greek inscriptions in a quarry. From these is learned the existence of sculptures of wood, utterly perished in the flames which reduced Persepolis after Alexander's feast. Hence too the cedar ash in the 3 metres of debris covering the ruins of the Throne Hall of Xerxes.

Gods and sanctuaries

The religion of Darius I, in its essence, cannot have been far removed from that of Zoroaster, the Iranian prophet. Zoroaster is traditionally believed to have been born '258 years before Alexander', that is, before the burning of Persepolis in 330 BC, and to have lived for 77 years (about 628–551 BC). Whatever his precise date, Zoroaster certainly drew upon older beliefs and practices. At the heart of his ideas lay the moral struggle between the Truth and the Lie. Although Ahuramazda was the great god of the Aryans, by whom Zoroaster claimed to have been chosen, his cult did not survive the end of the Persian empire. Other Aryan divinities, Anahita and Mithra, did survive, the last destined to become popular throughout the Roman world. The symbol of Ahuramazda was not of Aryan derivation, however. The remote god in the sun disc was borrowed from the symbol of Assur, national god of Assyria.

The sanctuaries of the Persians are best exemplified by the well-preserved 'Cube of Zoroaster' at Naqsh-i-Rustam, with an earlier prototype, the Zendan-i-Suleiman, at Pasargadae. Three rows of false windows give the appearance of a storeyed building, in fact solid in its lower part, with 29 steps up to one single high room. The whole structure stands 14.15 metres high and measures 7.25 metres square. Its ground-plan and some details reveal almost undeniable influence from the kingdom of Urartu (Van), the Assyrian name for what was later Armenia.

The tomb of Cyrus the Great at Pasargadae, originally 11 metres high, comprised a gabled tomb chamber only 6.40 by 5.35 metres at its base, on a high plinth of six receding tiers. Any attempt to seek its origin in the west, in Lydia, conquered by Cyrus in 547 BC, can be discounted. There were adequate prototypes in western Iran in the tradition of simple gabled houses, and gable-roofed tombs occur elsewhere in Iran. The simplicity of design accords well with the lost inscription described as having been on or near the tomb. The Classical geographer Strabo (60 BC–AD 21) interpreted the inscription as: 'O man, I am Cyrus, who founded the empire of the Persians and was king of Asia. Grudge me not therefore this monument'.

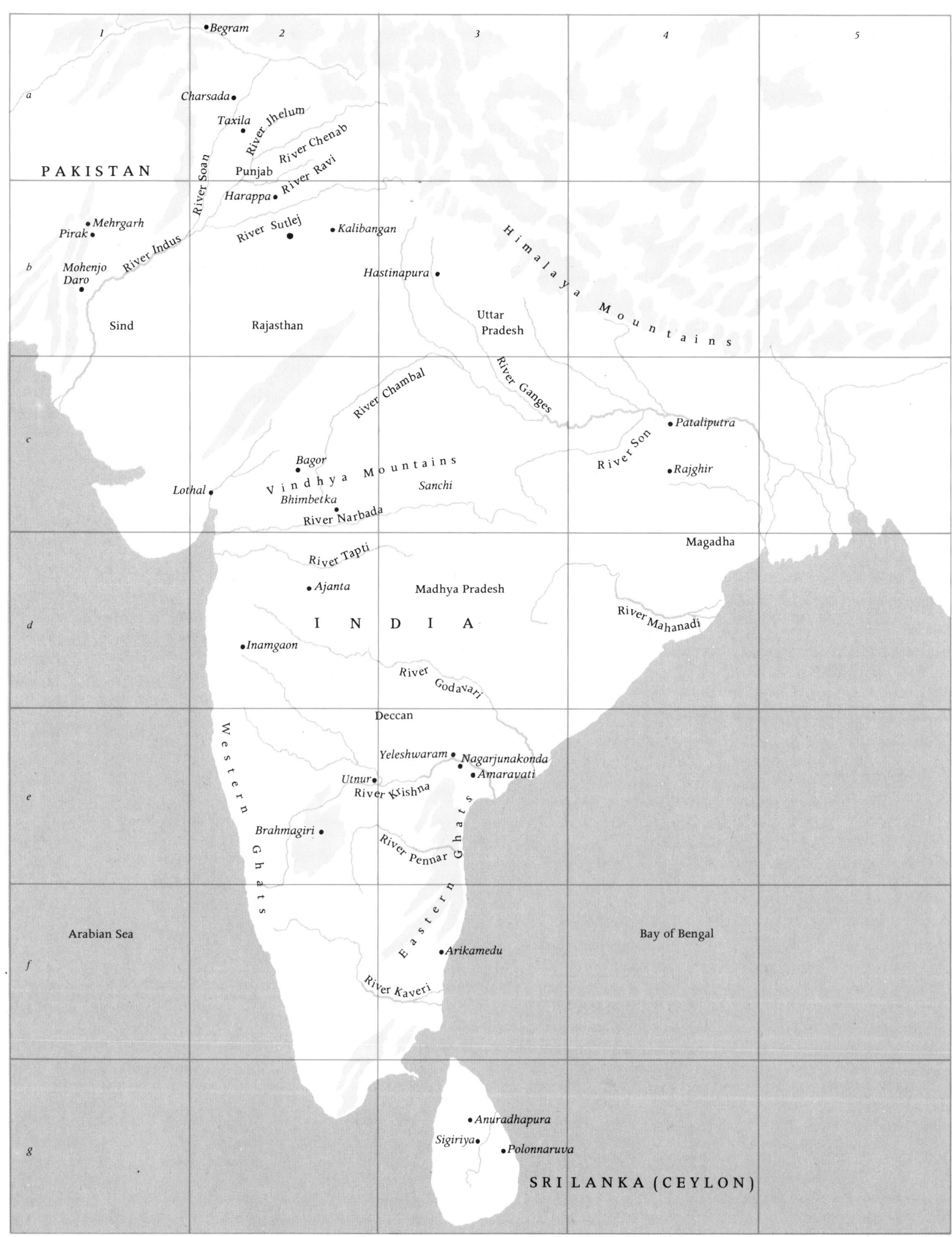

1
2
3
4
5
a
b
c
d
e
f
g
Begram
Charsada
Taxila
River Jhelum
River Chenab
PAKISTAN
River Soan
Punjab
River Ravi
Harappa
Mehrgarh
Pirak
River Sutlej
Kalibangan
River Indus
Mohenjo Daro
Hastinapura
Himalaya Mountains
Sind
Rajasthan
Uttar Pradesh
River Ganges
River Chambal
Pataliputra
River Son
Rajghir
Bagor
Vindhya Mountains
Sanchi
Lothal
Bhimbetka
River Narbada
Magadha
River Tapti
Ajanta
Madhya Pradesh
INDIA
River Mahanadi
Inamgaon
River Godavari
Deccan
Western Ghats
Yeleshwaram
Nagarjunakonda
Amaravati
Utnur
River Krishna
Brahmagiri
River Pennar
Eastern Ghats
Arabian Sea
Bay of Bengal
Arikamedu
River Kaveri
Anuradhapura
Sigiriya
Polonnaruva
SRI LANKA (CEYLON)

The Indian Subcontinent

2500 BC–AD 1150

Remains of early hominids are rare in India, although the Siwalik hills of the north have revealed fossils of *Ramapithecus*, regarded by some as among man's earliest ancestors. Later evidence is mainly from surface finds of stone tools, although a few occupied cave sites are also known. Early Stone Age industries show affinities with those of Europe and East Asia. Flake tools predominated in Middle Stone Age times, while Late Stone Age (Mesolithic) tools were generally microlithic. These stages are also known from Sri Lanka.

People practising farming and animal husbandry spread to India from the Near East by the 6th millennium BC, when occupation began at Mehrgarh. During the 4th and 3rd millennia, prosperous settlements developed in the Indo-Iranian borderlands, and their sophisticated agriculture, monumental architecture and rich material culture foreshadow the civilized culture of the Indus region. To this period also belong the earliest settlements in the Indus valley, where mixed farming provided the staple base. Further south, in the Deccan, villagers relied more heavily on keeping cattle.

By 2300 BC, a civilization had developed in the valley of the Indus and its tributaries, related to the flourishing communities of Baluchistan, but owing its greater prosperity to the enormous agricultural potential of the riverine environment. Two cities, Mohenjo Daro and Harappa, and some smaller towns, such as Kalibangan, provide most of what is known of the Indus civilization, although it seems that the majority of the population lived in villages.

The geography of the Indus civilization indicates a spread eastwards and south in the early centuries of the 2nd millennium BC, and a gradual abandonment of settlement in the original heartland of the civilization. In part, this may be related to environmental deterioration in the Indus valley, resulting from over-exploitation. The cultivation of rice allowed agricultural colonization of the Ganges-Jamuna region and other areas south of the Indus valley.

Little is known of the Ganges-Jamuna region during the 2nd millennium BC, although finds of copper artefacts and pottery indicate quite sophisticated communities. Contemporary groups in the west are better known. Evidence from substantial settlements like Inamgaon indicates a prosperous agricultural society with some social differentiation and well made copper artefacts. Copper tools were much less common in the south. By the end of the 2nd millennium BC, iron working was beginning, but the Deccan culture seems to have declined. Further north, the 2nd millennium BC saw the first incursions of Indo-European speaking Aryans. Literary sources indicating their gradual spread eastwards are supported by 1st millennium archaeological traces in the Ganges-Jamuna area.

The iron-using descendants of the southern Neolithic cultures are known mainly from burials including cists, urns, sarcophagi and pit graves. Such 'Megalithic' graves are also known in Sri Lanka, which also received a mid-1st millennium BC influx of settlers from North India. A series of warring city states had developed in the north at this time, their history preserved in semi-legendary accounts which are given some historical reality by finds from sites like Hastinapura. This period is also known from later Buddhist literature. Constant warfare led to fewer and larger states, culminating in the Mauryan empire, which controlled all India as far south as the Deccan.

The third Mauryan emperor, Ashoka, was a Buddhist convert whose patronage and evangelical missions, including one to Sri Lanka, gave this religion wide support. Buddhism continued to prosper after the collapse of the Mauryan empire. Monasteries, such as Ajanta, became increasingly wealthy, from donations and from developing trade, in which the Romans were active, establishing stations in South India to trade with the growing towns of Tamilnadu (Madras) and Sri Lanka. In the extreme north, the cities of Charsada and Taxila had been involved in east-west trade since at least the mid-1st millennium BC and their art and architecture reflect a blend of native and foreign traditions. This area also bore the brunt of successive invasions by Greeks, Parthians and Central Asian peoples, particularly the Shakas and Kushans. The Gupta empire, which emerged in the 5th century AD, combined many traditions to create the finest flowering of Indian civilization, which laid the foundations of modern Indian life.

Mohenjo Daro

PAKISTAN

Mohenjo Daro was one of the two major cities of the Indus civilization. It lay close to the Indus River in Sind, modern Pakistan, in the southern portion of the area occupied by the Indus culture. Today, the area's great tracts of salt-encrusted desert seem arid and inhospitable. To a considerable extent, however, this harsh environment has resulted from four millennia of human exploitation: through deforestation, overgrazing and the salination that results from prolonged irrigation. During the Indus period these processes were in their infancy, and the environment would therefore have appeared less uninviting. In addition, in Indus times, as today, the main area of occupation lay beside the river and its tributaries – a rich, productive zone. Evidence also suggests that rainfall was somewhat higher in the past, providing an extremely favourable environment for settlement.

Not only has the plant-cover been denuded during the past few millennia, but there has also been a considerable reduction in the local fauna. In Indus times a rich variety of wildlife existed, including tigers and rhinoceros, often depicted on the seals. In localized patches of marsh, there would have been dense gallery forest, while more arid areas had a cover of grass and small shrubs which provided rough grazing.

The history of Mohenjo Daro cannot be completely reconstructed as the local water-table has risen since the city's first occupation, waterlogging its lowest levels and rendering their excavation impossible. The earliest excavated deposits belong to the mature period of the Indus civilization, around 2500 BC. It appears that occupation continued until sometime in the early 2nd millennium, when architectural and cultural deterioration preceded the final abandonment of the city.

In the 50 years since most of the remains were revealed, the site has sadly deteriorated, mainly as a result of salt deposits which have encrusted the bricks and caused them to disintegrate. In 1973, a large-scale conservation programme began, sponsored by Unesco, to save the city.

Excavations

In the later 19th century, General Alexander Cunningham of the Archaeological Survey, and his contemporaries, discovered a few Indus artefacts at Harappa in the Punjab, but

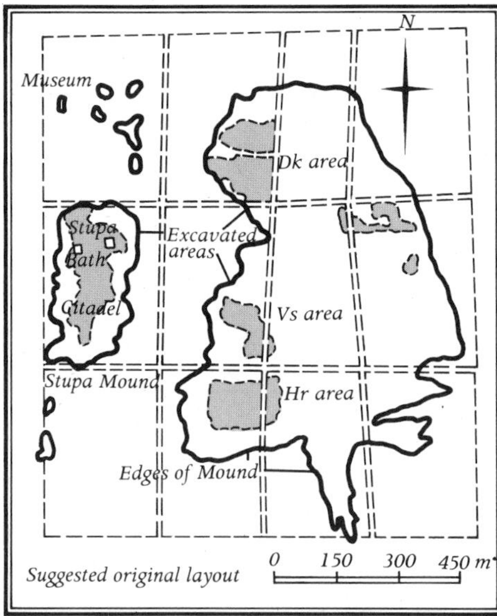

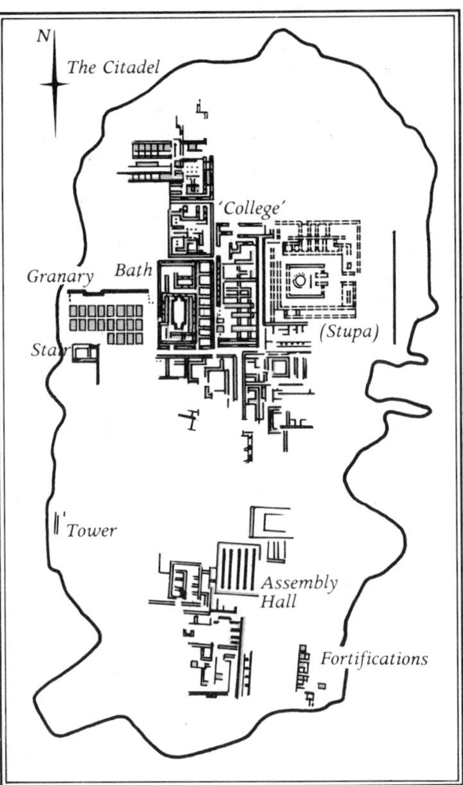

Below: Beads of carnelian, steatite and faience are common at Indus sites. Etched carnelian beads remained a particularly Indian speciality through the ages.

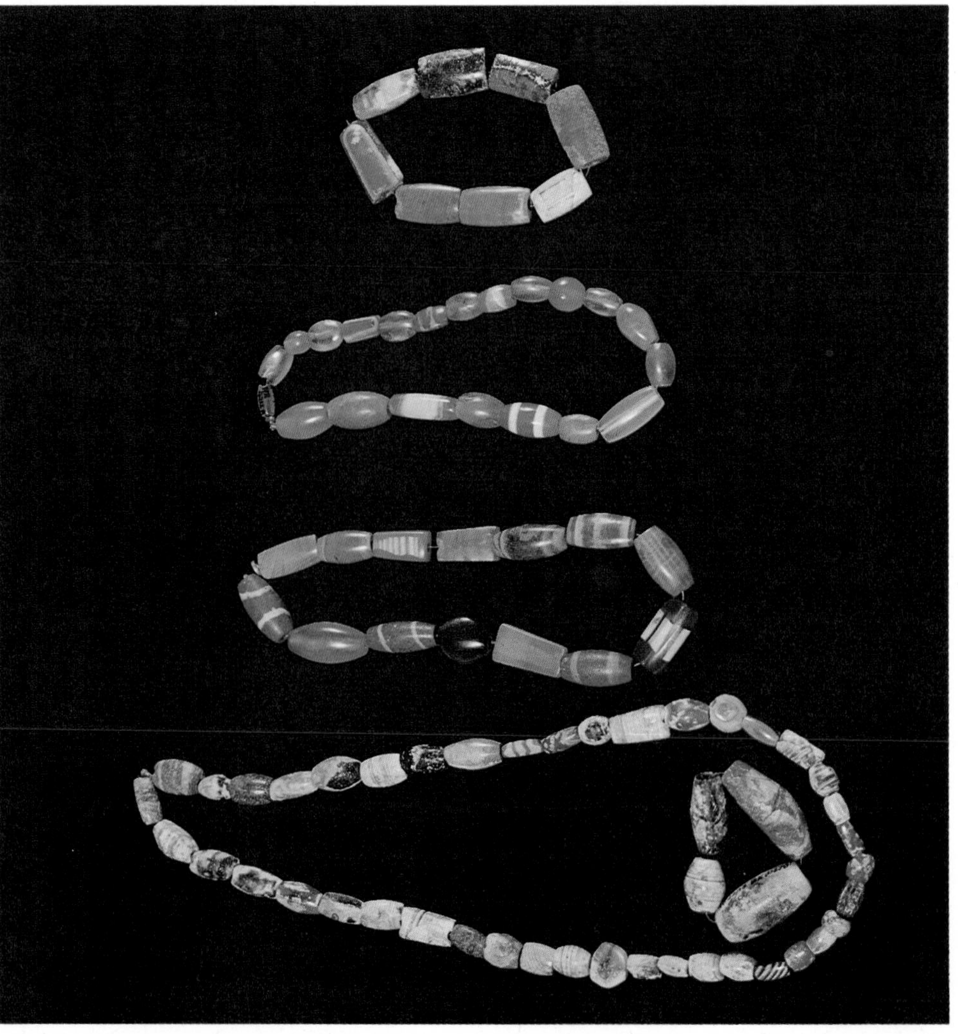

failed to appreciate their age. Even in 1922, when the *Cambridge History of India* was published, it still seemed that India was a cultural backwater until well into the 1st millennium BC. However, excavations which began at Harappa in 1921 revealed monumental Bronze Age remains and the following year, excavations below the Buddhist remains at Mohenjo Daro revealed similar structures and artefacts. Interest was quickly aroused and in the years succeeding, a number of excavators undertook work at Mohenjo Daro, under the general direction of Sir John Marshall until 1927, and then under Mackay. The new discoveries were announced with some excitement by Marshall in the *Illustrated London News* in 1924 and were greeted with great enthusiasm. It was quickly established that the newly-discovered civilization had been in its prime around 2300 BC, the date of the Mesopotamian contexts in which Indus seals had previously been found.

The site of Mohenjo Daro consists of two mounds, the lower and larger of which was the city. The higher mound, which included a number of public buildings, was the so-called citadel. The excavations of Marshall and Mackay uncovered several important structures on the citadel mound. Principal among these was the Great Bath, a well-built brick stepped tank with a fine corbelled vaulted drain. Associated with this were a number of small rooms interpreted by Marshall as the residence of the priestly rulers. Between the Great Bath and the edge of the mound was a structure resembling a Roman *hypocaust*, which Marshall believed had been a steam-bath. In the southern section of the citadel, Marshall uncovered a pillared hall, seemingly a place of assembly, which was surrounded by various structures.

Buildings discovered

In the lower mound, four areas were selected for excavation. These yielded the remains of a remarkable city laid out in a pattern that has remained common in India, with houses presenting a blank frontage to the main thoroughfares of the city, their doors opening off minor lanes. Inside rooms were arranged around a central courtyard which provided lighting for them. The sturdiness of the foundations made it clear that most houses formerly had an upper storey and it is likely that these incorporated projecting balconies. Such features would have relieved the grim appearance presented by the remaining blank façades. In one respect, the city of Mohenjo Daro differed somewhat from its modern counterparts, for there was an almost obsessive concern with cleanliness. Many houses had latrines and every house was equipped with wells and brick-floored bathrooms, with fine brick drainage pipes leading into covered drains along the streets. The houses ranged from small two-roomed structures to huge mansions incorporating three or four courtyard blocks. In the floor of one large building were five pits set with wedge-shaped bricks, probably intended to support jars with pointed bases. This building may have been a restaurant or business premises. In addition to the domestic structures, Marshall uncovered several buildings which he interpreted as temples. One was a high oblong platform which had two staircases leading to it, fronted by a monumental double gateway. Here several stone sculptures were discovered, which possibly represented a deity.

Above the level of the mature Indus city, Marshall and Mackay identified the remains of a 'Squatters'' town. Its buildings were of very poor quality, suggesting both overcrowding and a greatly lowered level of sanitation. Potteries and other industrial premises had been erected amid areas of habitation. A number of skeletons were found thrown into the streets or into the rubble of collapsing buildings, instead of being decently buried. Evidence such as this bears witness to the apparent cultural degeneration of the final occupation.

In 1950, Sir Mortimer Wheeler undertook a small excavation at Mohenjo Daro, one of his main objectives being to uncover remains of the period preceding the mature phase of the city. Remains of this 'pre-Indus' period had already come to light at Harappa, the other main city of the Indus civilization. Unfortunately, although the trench he opened was continuously pumped out, the high water-table caused the trench walls to collapse and so the attempt was abandoned. However, Wheeler was at least able to determine that there had been continuous uninterrupted occupation at the site. He also established that the structure identified by Marshall as a steam-bath was probably a huge granary, the under-floor ducts providing ventilation to prevent the grain from rotting. In the south-eastern corner of the citadel, Wheeler excavated fortification walls with towers. Although he interpreted these as defensive structures, it now seems more probable that they were intended to protect the citadel against flooding.

Similar massive walls were uncovered in the area of the lower city excavated by Dales in 1964. Like those of the citadel, they were of baked brick laced with timbers. Two test bores revealed occupation material to a depth of 12 metres below the present ground level. In all, the lower mound measures 23 metres from top to bottom, equivalent to the height of a seven-storey building.

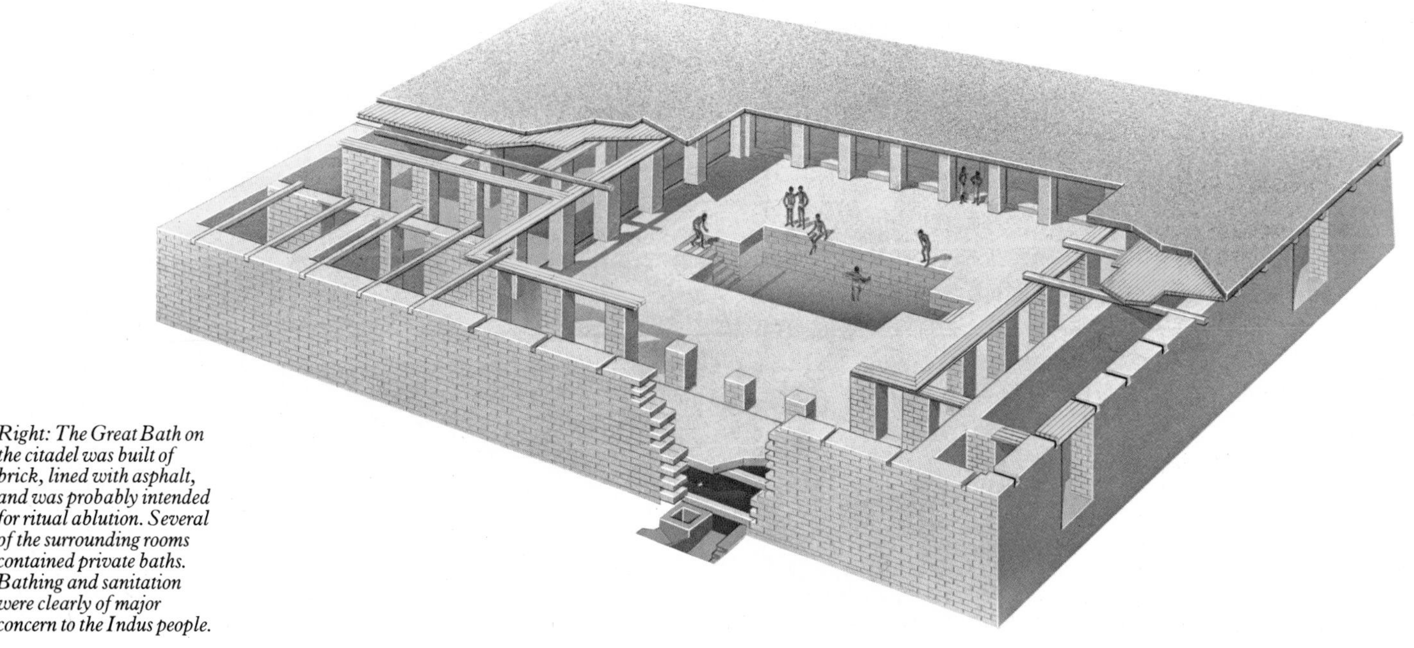

Right: The Great Bath on the citadel was built of brick, lined with asphalt, and was probably intended for ritual ablution. Several of the surrounding rooms contained private baths. Bathing and sanitation were clearly of major concern to the Indus people.

The Indus People

In the late 4th millennium BC the Indus valley probably supported a small population of hunter-gatherers. At the same time there was a dense spread of prosperous farming communities in the uplands of Baluchistan, some of which, such as Mehrgarh, had been established several millennia earlier. During the early 3rd millennium BC, such settlements began to spread over the lower Indus valley, and it is to a settlement of this period that the waterlogged deposits at Mohenjo Daro belong. The abundance of water in the Indus River allowed a much higher population density than could be maintained in Baluchistan, with its problems of fluctuating rainfall. Consequently it was in this region that 'civilization' emerged. Further evidence for this progression has come from the recently excavated town of Kalibangan, which was found to overlie a well-built settlement of mud-brick buildings that belonged to pre-Indus times.

The majority of Indus people must have lived in villages, but there were also a few towns, and these seem to have fulfilled specialized roles as well as mirroring some of the functions of the cities, Mohenjo Daro and Harappa. Mohenjo Daro reflects a high standard of urban organization, for even the lowest levels excavated have been deliberately laid out. Variation in the size of houses seems likely to reflect social divisions. On the outskirts of the city were craftsmen's quarters, incorporating workshops and accommodation. In the centre, houses comprising several courtyards surrounded by rooms must have accommodated large households, perhaps including servants or slaves. The total population of the city probably approached 40,000 people.

Below: The white limestone 'Priest-King' is one of the few surviving pieces of Indus sculpture. He wears a garment decorated with trefoils which were originally filled with red paste: this design also appears on some beads. His hair is held back by a fillet round his head.

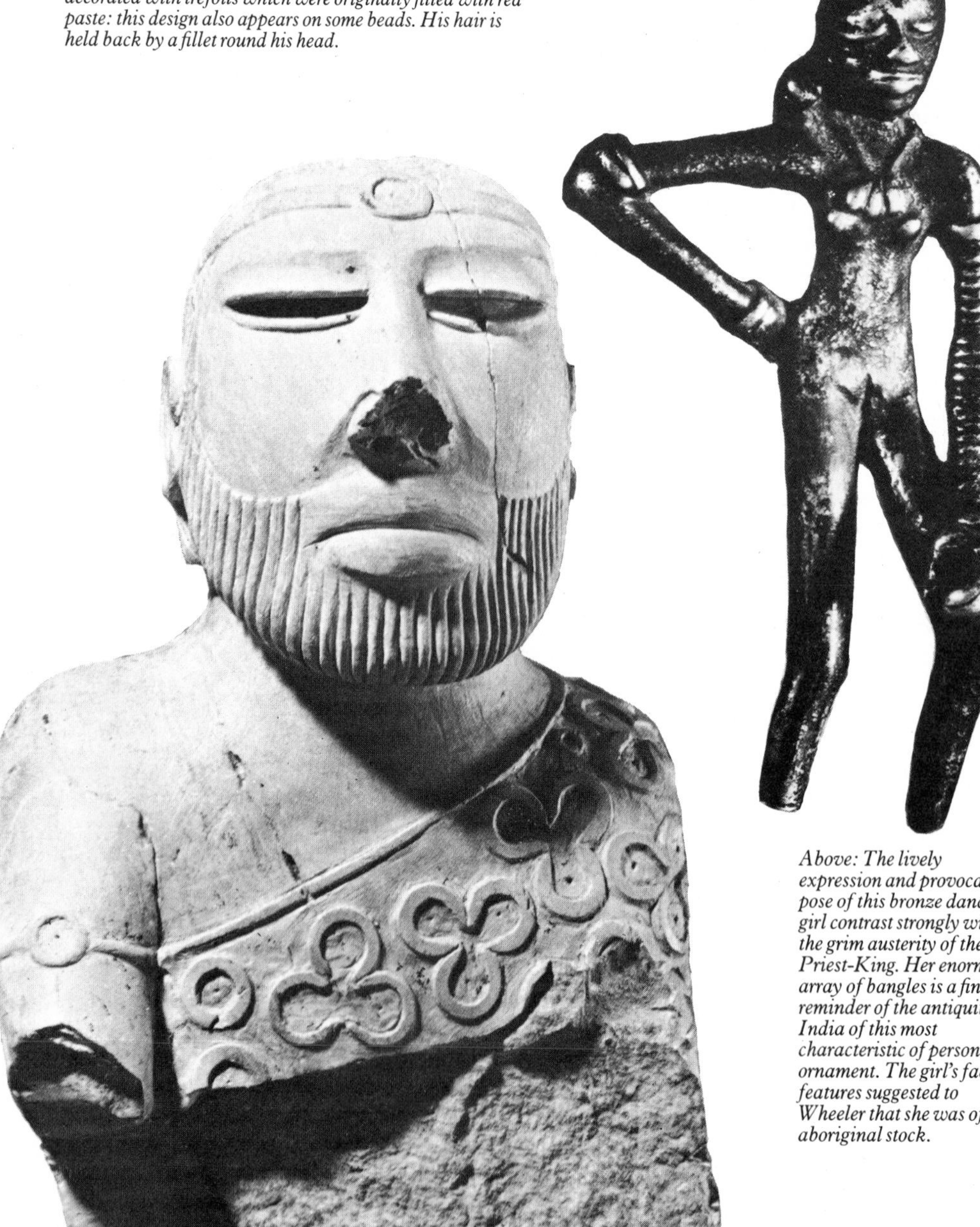

Above: The lively expression and provocative pose of this bronze dancing girl contrast strongly with the grim austerity of the Priest-King. Her enormous array of bangles is a fine reminder of the antiquity in India of this most characteristic of personal ornament. The girl's facial features suggested to Wheeler that she was of aboriginal stock.

Government and society

The nature of the political organization of the Indus civilization is still unclear. However, although the Indus script still remains undeciphered, recent work on it suggests that many seals bear names or titles related to those of later royal dynasties who claimed divine descent. If this is the case, it supports the hypothesis generally in vogue, that the Indus people were ruled by a priestly oligarchy. All the major settlements excavated included a citadel, set apart from the main town, which was probably both the residence of the priesthood and the focus of public life. At Mohenjo Daro, the citadel contained a vast granary (although there is now some doubt about this identification), most probably housing the grain paid as tribute or offered to the gods. Other structures on the citadel seem connected with worship, for instance the pillared hall and the Great Bath.

Trade and economy

Centralized regulation of trade and commerce is well attested by the finding at Mohenjo Daro and other Indus settlements of a large number of standardized weights. Trade links with another great civilization, that of Mesopotamia, are indicated by Indus seals from mid-3rd millennium Sumer, while Sumerian texts mention trade with Meluhha, which may be identified with the Indus civilization. Although there was a probable Indus trading settlement in Sumer near Lagash, it seems that much of the exchange was conducted through middlemen, in particular by traders from Bahrein. Principal among the commodities imported from India by the Sumerians was copper. Other imports included carnelian, ivory, shell, lapis, pearls and spices. Of these, only copper was not available from the Indus area, but could have been obtained from nearby Baluchistan or Rajasthan. What the Indus people received in exchange is uncertain. Sumerian texts mention woollen and linen textiles, leather goods, oil and dried fish as exports; such perishable goods may well have reached India, but would leave no trace. At Mohenjo Daro, part of a house-shaped vessel carved in green stone must be a western import.

The Indus people obtained raw materials from a wide area: copper and lead from Rajas-

Above: The so-called 'unicorn', probably a conventionalized representation of a two-horned cow, is a common subject on Indus seals. It is always shown with a curious design on its fore-quarters, perhaps representing a necklace, and with an altar in front of it. It is thought to have been a sacred animal.

Right: All houses at Mohenjo Daro had fine brick wells and bathrooms; many also had latrines. Water was carried away by well-built drains which ran down the main streets. The remarkable civic organization of the Indus civilization is indicated by the existence of regular inspection covers on the drains.

than, turquoise from north-east Iran and gold from south India. Many of these may have been obtained from the indigenous hunter-gatherer population in exchange for Indus beads, copper tools and pottery, which have been found in their settlements.

The economic basis of the Indus civilization was mixed farming. Animal and plant remains show that wheat and barley were the main cereals cultivated; rice was grown only in a few southern, border settlements. In addition the Indus people ate peas, sesame and mustard, dates and melons; they also grew cotton. Humped and humpless cattle were the main domestic animals, providing not only meat and milk but also dung for fuel and fertilizer and, most important, traction for ploughing and for transport. Buffaloes, sheep, dogs and pigs were kept, and perhaps camels, horses and elephants.

Farmers were probably not included among the inhabitants of Mohenjo Daro. Most of these would have been craftsmen, priests, administrators and other such people, who probably received grain and other essentials in return for their services.

Mohenjo Daro has also yielded a range of tools and weapons of stone and bronze, but almost no metal jewellery or statuary. Personal ornaments were rare apart from numerous beads in a variety of materials, especially steatite. An exceptional find was a superb bronze figurine of a dancing girl, her hand resting on her hip and her head flung back. The stone statues from Mohenjo Daro have none of the liveliness of this figure, but include some fine pieces, for example the 'Priest-King', whose face expresses the calm of meditation. The ability of the Indus artist to give life to his subject-matter is amply shown by a delightful series of terracotta figurines of humans and animals, and by the depiction of plants and animals on the terracotta seals. A few exquisite animal models in faience were also found. Plants, animals and birds figure largely on the black-painted red pottery, most of which was wheel-turned. It is probable that wooden artefacts and textiles, now vanished, were also vehicles for such artistic expression.

Religion

Although the religious beliefs of the inhabitants of Mohenjo Daro can never completely be ascertained, some clues exist. Among the subjects depicted on the seals is a horned figure, surrounded by animals, which seems closely akin to the Hindu god Shiva. The 'lingam' and 'yoni' (which represent the male and female principals respectively) associated with the worship of Shiva are also known from Mohenjo Daro. Other objects possibly related to fertility cults include female figurines which may represent Mother Goddesses, and numerous figurines and seal-representations of bulls, some with an altar before them. The Great Bath and its associated complex on the citadel seem likely to be connected with religious practices. Ritual ablution plays an important part in modern Indian religion, and the Great Bath strongly suggests that this ritual use of water goes back to Indus times.

It is only at Harappa that any cemetery of the mature Indus period has been found: it contained extended burials with a few personal possessions. At Mohenjo Daro it is possible that the cemetery has yet to be located. The only burials found at the site come from the latest phases of occupation, when civic sense was rapidly declining and bodies were flung into old streets or into carelessly-dug pits. The negligent disposal of these bodies suggested to the early excavators that they represented hastily-buried victims of the sack of the city by the invading Aryans. Although it is possible that the Aryans clashed with the Indus people, they cannot have been responsible for more than the final destruction of the already degenerate remnants of the Indus civilization. The squalid dwellings of the late phase at Mohenjo Daro are a vivid indication of this cultural decline, the reason for which is much debated. One possible factor may have been deterioration of the environment as a result of over-exploitation. Other explanations include earth movements causing extensive flooding, changes in the course of the Indus River, or disease. Whatever the reason, it seems that around the 19th century BC the elevated culture of the Indus valley fell into a decline. Beyond the Indus valley itself, related cultures continued to flourish, but the city of Mohenjo Daro was abandoned.

Taxila

PAKISTAN

Above left: Seated Buddha in the attitude of Meditation, with standing Buddhas to the right and left and with two attendant figures behind, one holding a fly whisk and the other a thunderbolt. The figures are of lime plaster on a clay and rubble core. The central Buddha is an impressive example of the conventional images of its period and the finest, in a complete state, at Taxila.

Above: Plaque of gold and coloured glass from Taxila. This finely wrought object comes from the Kushan dynasty period, about the 3rd century AD, and portrays Hariti, protectress of children.

Left: Male head, made of limestone. An example of the Gandharan art style, the sculpture represents work of the 4th to 5th centuries AD.

Taxila lies in the Kabul valley about 35 kilometres north-west of Rawalpindi, in today's Pakistan. The area is extremely rich and fertile, its well-watered soils producing abundant crops, fruits and flowers. The valley in which Taxila lies is formed by two spurs of the Muree hills, while a smaller third spur divides the fertile larger northern part from the southern area. Taxila was sited at a major crossroads from which ran three great highways: to western Asia and Europe, to central and eastern India, and to central Asia and China. It was the development of trade along these routes that gave Taxila the preeminence it enjoyed for nearly 1,000 years.

Taxila's period of greatness began in the 6th century BC, when it became part of the Persian empire. The roads which the Persians built to link the farthest corners of their empire with the administrative centre served also to promote trade. By the time of Alexander the Great (326 BC), Persian rule in north-west India had given way to small independent kingdoms and republics. The king of Taxila allied himself with Alexander but after the latter's death in 323 BC, all the cities of the north-west were conquered by Chandragupta Maurya (about 321–297 BC), who laid the foundations of the first Indian empire. Around 189 BC, the whole Taxila area fell to Greeks who had settled in Bactria, an area in present north-east Afghanistan. Two rival dynasties disputed Taxila during the century of their rule; nevertheless, the city enjoyed a period of considerable prosperity under them. Shaka nomads from central Asia overran much of north-western and western India in the earlier 1st century BC and were themselves overcome by the Parthians around AD 19. Under both invaders, however, Greek administrative organization was continued and Greek culture and Buddhism were encouraged. A second wave of central Asian nomads, the Kushans, swept northern India in the mid-1st century AD. They adopted the flourishing Indo-Greek culture and, under Kanishka (whose reign began in the late 1st or early 2nd century AD) became leading patrons of Buddhism. Although they suffered setbacks, the Kushans continued to rule prosperously at Taxila until its destruction by the White Huns around AD 460.

Excavations

The first excavations at Taxila took place under Sir John Marshall during the 1920s. Further work, to clear up problems left by these excavations, was undertaken by Sir Mortimer Wheeler and A. Ghosh in 1944–45. Most recently, exploration by the Cambridge University Archaeological Mission to Pakistan has disclosed remains of a settlement far earlier than anything hitherto suspected, within the heart of the ancient city.

The sites of Taxila comprise three main cities, successively occupied, together with a number of monasteries and stupas scattered throughout the valley. Local tradition held that the Bhir Mound was the site of the earliest city, and this was confirmed by excavation. Marshall sank one main trench and a number of test pits in the Bhir Mound, which revealed evidence of four phases of occupation, from the 6th to 2nd centuries BC. However, the main excavations were concentrated at Sirkap, which was built by the Indo-Greeks in the 2nd century BC and flourished until around the 2nd century AD. The third city, Sirsukh, was established by

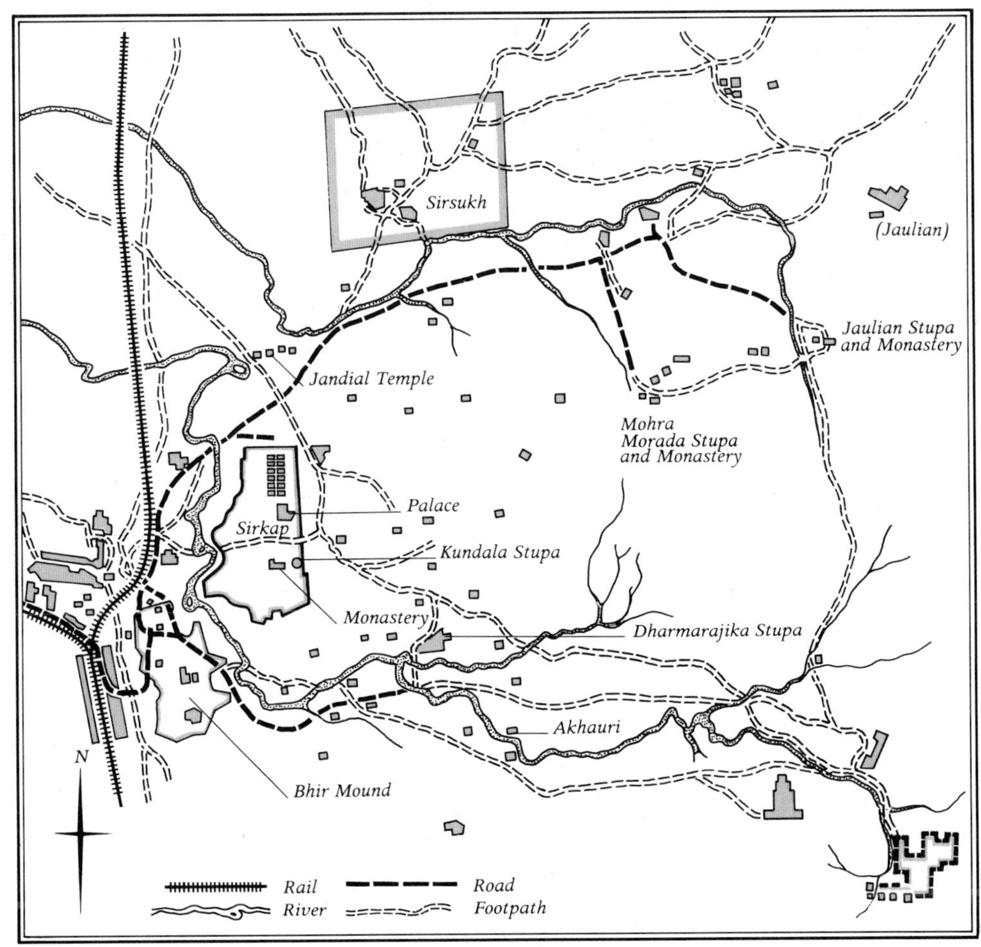

the Kushans. As it lies mainly under several modern villages, Marshall cleared only the city wall and a small interior area. As well as the three cities, Marshall explored and excavated a number of religious establishments in the valley. Notable among these are the Dharmarajika stupa and its associated monasteries, the Jandial temple and the monasteries of Kalawan and Jaulian.

The later excavations at Sirkap showed that the city wall was built in its present alignment at the same time as the earliest Indo-Greek architecture, although the existing wall may be a later replacement. These excavations also revealed that around 50 BC, settlement at Sirkap expanded south to include the Hathial hill.

The Bhir Mound

The earliest city on the Bhir Mound may have been founded by the Persians, while the city which was built subsequently can be identified as that visited by Alexander the Great in 326 BC. However, the majority of buildings excavated at the site belonged to the third period, when the city was under Mauryan rule. Although Marshall made distinctions between these various phases, occupation was continuous, with buildings being constantly replaced. Thus, the layout of the Mauryan town corresponds quite closely to that of the original Persian settlement. Four narrow main streets lined with houses and shops were uncovered, crossed by a network of narrower lanes. In addition to the houses of various sizes, one possibly religious structure was found – a pillared hall surrounded by a number of small rooms. Artefacts from the Bhir Mound reflect changes in its overlords: Persian scaraboid beads from the earliest period, Hellenistic coins and pottery from the time of Alexander, and polished stone vessels from the succeeding era of Mauryan rule.

The uppermost level at the Bhir Mound contained only flimsy structural remains from the earliest years of the Bactrian Greeks. From this period also came a rich hoard of silver coins and exquisite jewellery, as well as two fine Hellenistic pots.

Sirkap

Sirkap was built by the Bactrian Greeks and occupied also by their Shaka and Parthian successors. Although the need to preserve the later buildings prevented Marshall from investigating thoroughly the Indo-Greek remains, he excavated enough to establish that the later occupation closely followed the original Indo-Greek layout of the city. This conformed to the standard Greek 'chessboard' plan, in which the streets were set at right angles dividing the city into rectangular blocks. Also typical of Greek cities was the enclosure of an area of high ground within the city walls to form the acropolis, a place of refuge in times of trouble. Later excavations revealed an inner fortification wall dividing the acropolis from the lower city.

Several monasteries were discovered both within the acropolis and in the main city, as well as numerous temples and stupas. A royal palace with public chambers and private apartments lay in the centre of the city, while a similar palace was found in the acropolis. Discoveries from the upper palace included a hoard of copper vessels, apparently the property of monks fleeing before the Kushan armies. Among other valuables buried when the Kushans threatened the city were an Alexandrian bronze figure of the Egyptian child-god Harpocrates and a silver dish depicting Dionysus. Other finds relate to the everyday life of Taxila's inhabitants —tools, pottery, seals and gaming pieces.

Sirsukh and other sites

The early Kushans settled in Sirkap but soon shifted their main settlement to Sirsukh, in the northern part of the valley. There they built walls on a parallelogram plan typical of their central Asian homeland. Inside the walls, a small excavation revealed part of a large building, although its identity was not established. Finds here were almost confined to coins.

At Jandial, between Sirkap and Sirsukh, Marshall excavated an imposing temple. It faithfully followed the standard Greek temple in plan, except for its inclusion of a large masonry platform, which originally supported a tower about 12 metres high. This was probably a Zoroastrian fire temple, built by the Bactrian Greeks, who may have adopted the religion during the centuries they had lived in Bactria.

Many of the Buddhist monasteries and stupas were built by the Indo-Greeks and their successors in the south of the valley around Sirkap, for instance those around the great Dharmarajika stupa. This shrine was erected by the Mauryan emperor Ashoka and was enlarged and embellished by the Kushans, who also founded or extended most of the stupas and monasteries in the valley. Many of their monasteries, for example Kalawan and Jaulian, occupy secluded spots in the hills around the valley – a fact which reflects the liberal patronage of the Kushans, under whom it became unnecessary for monasteries to be situated near the city in order that the monks could beg their daily bread. These religious foundations contained a wealth of art, mainly depicting Buddhist subjects but also including much of Classical Western origin. The Kushan school of Gandharan art, to which the sculptures and stuccos of Taxila belong, is justly famous as a sublime blend of Eastern and Western traditions.

Life in the Cities

The Mauryan empire was divided into four provinces, ruled by viceroys, one of which had Taxila as its capital. The emperor Ashoka (about 274–about 236 BC) was viceroy there during the reign of his father, and his son Kunala after him. According to legend, it was here that Kunala was blinded, on the orders of his wicked step-mother. To mark the spot where this act allegedly occurred, the Kunala stupa above Sirkap and its associated monastery were built at a later date.

The Mauryans established an efficient administration, based on agriculture. Taxila, situated in the fertile Kabul valley and with a dense population, was the centre of a flourishing farming economy. Heavy taxes supported a huge standing army and the machinery of bureaucracy, as well as irrigation schemes and many other public works. Among these was the great highway linking Taxila with the capital at Patna, which contributed greatly to Taxila's importance since it acted as a major market centre handling trade from central and southern India and from western Asia and Bactria. Mauryan rule was efficient but harsh, and among many revolts recorded, two were at Taxila. After the death of Ashoka, the last strong ruler, many parts of the empire seceded and Taxila enjoyed a brief period of independence.

The early Mauryan emperors were probably Hindus. In the Bhir Mound a pillared hall was excavated in which were found a large number of terracotta reliefs depicting male and female deities. This is probably the earliest known Hindu temple. Across the street was a small structure which seems to have been a shop selling such images to worshippers, a practice that is common beside Hindu temples today. The third emperor, Ashoka, became a convert to Buddhism, which at this time was gaining widespread support, its egalitarian approach allowing more social flexibility than the gradually petrifying caste system associated with Hinduism. From this time, Buddhism developed as the main religion of the wealthy commercial class in Taxila, and as such was adopted by the succession of later rulers.

The Bhir Mound city had a rather haphazard arrangement of streets and lanes. The central main street acted also as the main drain, while smaller covered drains along the minor streets carried off rainwater. Liquid waste was disposed of in soak-wells within the houses, but public bins were provided in the streets for rubbish. The houses followed a common oriental pattern in which small rooms opened from private interior courtyards, while the external walls presented a blank façade with only tiny slit windows. They probably had upper storeys with verandahs, although these have not been preserved. Bathrooms were a common feature, although there were apparently no wells within the city and water had to be brought from the Tamra Nala stream which flowed around the east side of the city.

Many houses had small shops set into their outside walls. One excavated by Marshall was a shell-worker's shop, in which were found pieces of cut shell and mother of pearl. Among the most highly developed crafts of this period was that of making polished stone vessels. The polished black pottery of the period was also of exceptionally high quality. On the other hand, gold and silver jewellery and bronze objects were rare, most domestic metalwork being made of iron. The most elaborate articles of this period were reliquaries. Several examples were discovered reverently enshrined in later stupas, their original stupas probably having been destroyed in the brief period of Brahminical fanaticism that followed the fall of the Mauryans in 185 BC.

Left: Stupas of the Jaulian monastery with decorative motifs and figures, shown under the protective covering of a modern wooden roof.

Below: Ruined dome of the Dharmarajika stupa. The remains, including the ornamental band seen at its centre base, illustrate the evolution of stone masonry from the 1st century BC to the medieval period.

Right: Layout of the ruined city of Sirkap.

The Indo-Greeks and their successors

Under Mauryan rule, Taxila's links were with the Indian world. However, after breaking away from the Mauryan empire, Taxila reverted to its previous position as a melting pot in which Western (and later also central Asian) ideas and ways of life were subtly blended with Indian traditions. Notable among the products of this fusion was the Gandharan art style. The subjects treated are

almost entirely Buddhist, although occasional Classical scenes also appear, but the style shows a marked affinity with the contemporary art of Greece and Rome. Many examples of Gandharan art were found in the stone sculptures adorning the religious buildings around the valley.

Taxila was frequently mentioned in Buddhist literature as having an important university. This may have resembled the Academies of Greece, which had buildings and formal instruction, or may have been an extension of the broad education offered by Buddhist monasteries.

Successive rulers at Taxila adopted the locally predominant Buddhist religion. The wealthy Kushans were particularly liberal patrons who endowed numerous establishments in the valley. Indeed the monks eventually became so affluent that they had to fortify their monasteries against the Sassanians and Huns who threatened the valley in the 3rd to 5th centuries AD. The danger from invaders was vividly illustrated by a discovery in the courtyard of the monastery near the Dharmarajika stupa, where skeletons of five massacre victims were found. Many of the richest finds at Sirkap, the Bhir Mound and in the monasteries were the treasures hidden when the inhabitants were threatened by invaders. Among these were coins, silver vessels, gold and silver jewellery and imported and local luxuries such as an ivory comb from Sirkap and a fine terracotta of a lady holding a lamp.

Foreign invaders were not the only danger to the well-being of Taxila's people. Late in the reign of the Shakas, Sirkap was devastated by an earthquake. The neatly planned Indo-Greek city comprised mainly several-storeyed structures of rubble masonry with shallow foundations. These collapsed. After the earthquake, a new style of architecture was adopted. Deep foundations were dug, and the lower storey of the houses was partially sunk below ground level. The masonry was made more solid, with trimmed blocks set among carefully coursed small flat stones.

Although the arrangement of streets in Sirkap was far more regular than that of the Bhir Mound, the houses were similar in plan. Many incorporated private shrines, but there were also numerous public Buddhist shrines within the city as well as the monastic complexes scattered around the valley. In addition, there were Jain stupas and the Parthian fire temple at Jandial.

According to Christian legend, the Parthian ruler of Taxila, Gondophares, employed St Thomas to build him a palace. The saint squandered all the funds allocated to him on works of charity, informing the enraged Gondophares that he had built him a palace in Heaven. This was confirmed by the king's brother, recently deceased, who was miraculously restored to life to impart this information, whereupon Gondophares and his brother were converted to Christianity. The presence of foreign craftsmen, such as St Thomas, at Taxila was extremely probable. Foreign merchants were certainly a common sight at Taxila: both Sirkap and Sirsukh had a *caravanserai* outside the city walls to accommodate these travellers.

Owing to frequent hostilities between Rome and Parthia, the most direct east-west trade route through Parthia was often closed. As a result, there developed a major route by sea from Alexandria to Barbaricum on the Indus and thence to Taxila. Taxila therefore handled not only much of the trade between India and the West, as in the previous period, but also the lucrative Far Eastern trade, notably in Chinese silks. Under the Kushans, who controlled much of central Asia, this trade was particularly prosperous.

Taxila was overwhelmed around AD 460 by the White Huns. Comparable in their ferocity to the dreaded Huns of Attila, they dealt the city a blow from which it could not recover. It was incorporated in dominions of subsequent rulers of the north-west, but never regained any great importance.

Ajanta
INDIA

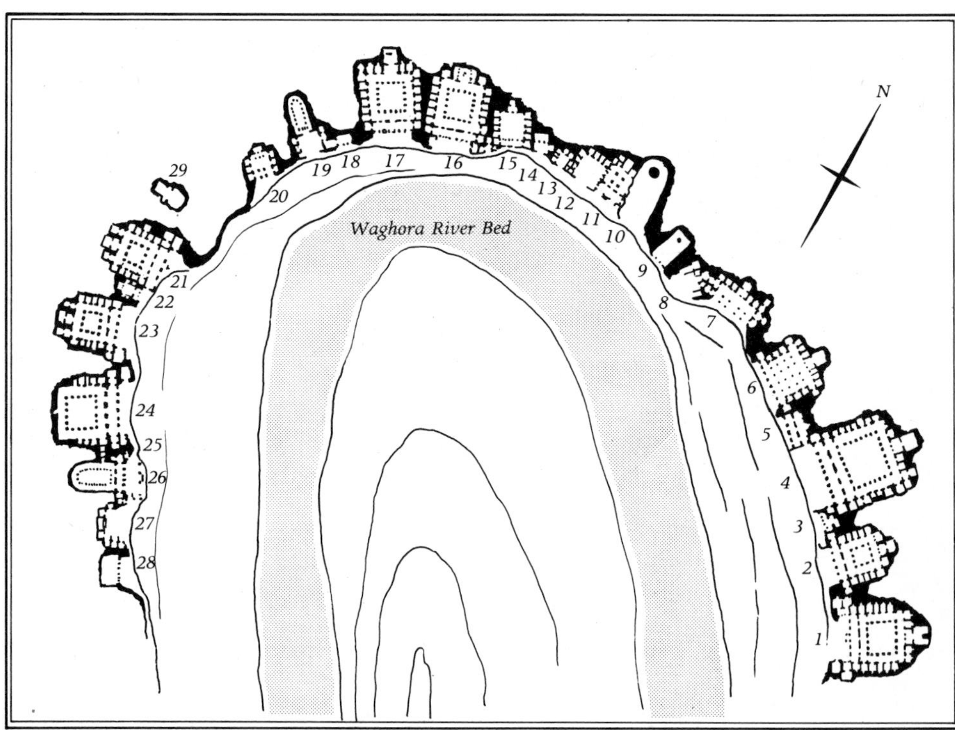

The rock-cut monastic complex at Ajanta in the state of Maharashtra is justly one of India's most famous artistic treasures. A short climb from the modern tourist centre leads the visitor to view a broad, horseshoe shaped valley basking in the tropical sun. The valley floor is clad in lush vegetation, watered by the blue Waghora stream which enters the valley in a series of seven waterfalls. In the natural walls of this setting, about 30 magnificent temples and monasteries have been created from rock-cut caves.

The hewing of Buddhist temples and monasteries from the rock of the Ghats of western India began during the 2nd century BC and continued well into the 1st millennium AD. After the collapse of the great Mauryan empire in 185 BC, the western Deccan came under the rule of the Satavahanas. Although this dynasty suffered a period of defeat at the hands of the Shakas, who were then ruling at Taxila, it regained control of the whole Deccan in the 2nd century AD, and reigned for about a century. It was during the early years of Satavahana rule that the first caves at Ajanta were excavated, creating two temples and four monasteries. These contain the earliest surviving Indian paintings, which are uniquely important not only for their artistic interest, but also for their information on contemporary life.

The Satavahana collapse signalled a long period of political upheaval, during which no new caves were cut. By the early 4th century AD, however, the Vakatakas had established authority in the Deccan, ruling over a large empire. They concluded a matrimonial alliance with the great Gupta dynasty of northern India and continued as subordinate allies of the Guptas until their decline in the later 6th century. The later caves at Ajanta were constructed mainly during this period by the kings and subjects of the southern branch of the Vakatakas, whose territory included Ajanta. This period, when much of India was unified under the direct or indirect authority of the Guptas, is regarded as the Golden Age of the country's history. During this second phase of activity at Ajanta, almost all the caves were painted, and they present fine examples of the artistic renaissance of the Gupta period.

Discovery and preservation

The first Europeans to see the caves at Ajanta were some officers of the Madras army in 1819. Many other visitors followed, and by 1844 it was recorded by Burgess that 'Unfortunately the damp, bats, natives and other ignorant visitors have wrought sad ravages among these pictures.' Sufficient was the concern felt about their deterioration that an artist was employed to record them. He had succeeded in making about 30 copies of portions of the frescoes when his work was abruptly interrupted by the outbreak of the Indian Mutiny in 1857. However, his admirably executed copies were sent to London and exhibited in the Sydenham Crystal Palace, where they were destroyed by fire in 1866. As Burgess writes:

> 'They were, of course, the labour of years, and it was hoped they would perpetuate the most interesting portions of the painting that for a long while past had been decaying. Alas for official wisdom and forethought! no copy, tracing or photograph was taken from them before sending them to be exhibited, and finally burnt'.

Meanwhile the destructive forces were still at work and in 1872 Mr. Griffiths took up the task of making copies, which he completed in 1885. These were sent to the South Kensington Museum where, by some extraordinarily unfortunate coincidence, most were destroyed by fire in the same year. Destruction of the paintings themselves accelerated, unscrupulous individuals actually cutting away portions for sale to tourists. However, in 1903–04, wire screens were fitted, the process of decay and destruction was halted, and that of restoration and conservation begun under the auspices of the Hyderabad Archaeological Department. As a result of this work, many new frescoes have emerged.

Below and right: Most paintings at Ajanta depict scenes from the life of the Buddha or from his former incarnations. Below, prince Mahajanaka sits within a pavilion, while attendants pour lustral waters over him. Another scene (above right) shows Buddha as prince Vishvantara, banished for his excessive generosity. The ceiling above is exuberantly decorated with floral designs. In a delightful domestic scene (below right) princess Irandati swings as she awaits her lover.

The site and its monuments

Buddhist worship is centred on the 'stupa'. In its original form this was an earthen mound covering corporeal remains of the Buddha. The simple mound soon developed into a standardized form: a hemispherical dome containing a reliquary, raised on a circular drum. The stupa, even without relics, came to be regarded as holy in itself. Many stupas

were built in the open air, but wooden temples to house smaller stupas were also erected, and it is their form which is copied in minute detail in the rock-cut temples. These comprised a long apsidal hall with the stupa at the far end. A row of pillars on either side separated the congregational area in the centre from a passage at the side. The main element of the façade was a large, horse-shoe shaped window above the door, which shed an ethereal light inside the temple. In contrast to the plain interior, the façade was usually elaborately decorated.

The two early cave temples at Ajanta, which conform to this plan, are grouped together with four early monasteries in the centre of the valley. The earliest of these, temple 10 and monastery 30, were constructed during the later 2nd century BC. The temple walls were painted soon after its completion and depict two stories of former incarnations of the Buddha. Another painting shows a prince and his entourage worshipping the Bodhi tree under which the Buddha gained enlightenment. This scene gives a vivid picture of contemporary dress: the prince with a high, elaborate hair style, the women loaded with jewels. Temple 10 lacks a façade. In antiquity there would have been a wooden façade, pegged to the front of the temple, which would probably have closely resembled the fine horseshoe-shaped stone façade of the slightly later and considerably smaller temple 9. The paintings here are in the same style: a procession of votaries approaching a stupa and a lively frieze of herdsmen and animals. The four monasteries associated with these temples are simple in form, comprising a central square courtyard hall for congregational purposes, with individual cells opening off it on three sides. The cells contained rock-cut platforms which served as beds for the monks.

After some 400 years, a second phase of cave excavation was initiated at Ajanta, and the 21 monasteries of this period were more complex in form. The central hall became pillared and the simple door of the early type was now preceded by a verandah with a frontal colonnade and porch. Cells surrounded the court as before, but the central cell in the back wall projected further back into the hillside and housed an image of the Buddha. Sometimes this shrine was preceded by a porch or antechamber. Monastery 6 had two storeys, the upper floor being reached by a staircase from the front aisle.

Decoration

Sculptured decoration was extremely rare in the early caves but was lavishly used in the second period. Friezes of delicate tracery adorn the pillars of both halls and temples and the pillars bear richly-carved capitals. Figures of the Buddha cover the walls of temple 26 and the Buddha is carved on the stupas of the two later temples. The façade of the second temple, 19, is exquisitely carved and beautifully proportioned, its pillared portico supporting the delicate, sinuous arch of the window.

Although excavation of some caves was never completed, almost all are painted, including caves of the earlier period, where the original paintings were often obliterated. In addition to scenes of the Buddha and representations of Buddhist devotees on the walls, the ceilings are painted in richly coloured designs depicting flowers, animals, and human and divine individuals. The ceiling artwork is divided into panels by a painted lattice which meticulously reproduces the beams of a wooden ceiling.

The Valley Caves

Buddha and his followers practised a way of life typical of the religious ascetics of their time. They renounced worldly possessions and travelled the land as beggars, preaching their religious message. For three months of the year, however, the rains obliged them to remain in one place. Lay devotees of Buddhism donated to these early monks land on which they could live in simple huts during the rains, and these were the original Buddhist monasteries. Despite the emphasis on absolute poverty, the monasteries attracted generous donations from people in all walks of life – members of the ruling dynasty, local guilds, craftsmen, fishermen and even foreigners – who thus acquired spiritual merit. Donations included both wooden or stone structures to shelter the monks and grants of land revenue to support them. The monasteries rapidly became wealthy, self-supporting establishments, despite opposition from religious purists.

Left: The beautifully decorated façade of cave 9 faithfully reproduces the details of its wooden prototypes. The large, horseshoe-shaped window is the main source of light for the temple's interior. A large figure of the Buddha stands on each side of the window.

Right: The interior of cave 19, one of the two later temples, is divided by two rows of pillars decorated with floral bands. Images of the Buddha adorn their capitals while a large figure of the Buddha signalling universal peace stands at the front of the stupa.

Below: Few sights can rival the natural beauty of the secluded Ajanta valley, the idyllic setting chosen as their home by Buddhist monks 2,000 years ago. Their temples and monasteries are cut into the rock walls high above the valley floor.

Preparing the caves

The use of caves has a long history in India, and their modification for religious purposes predates the time of the Mauryan emperor Ashoka (3rd century BC). Additionally, the clay-like laterite rock of the Ghats, which is soft and easily worked until exposure to the air hardens it, was an ideal medium in which to create temples and monasteries and explains the preference in this area for excavated, rather than free-standing, structures.

Construction of the temples and monasteries was directed by a master craftsman who was either a monk or a lay follower of the monastic community for which the work was being undertaken. This individual organized the layout of the caves, which was always very precisely executed, and directed the work of the craftsmen. Such workmen were organized into guilds, which played an important part in the structure of contemporary society. 'Workers' co-operatives', including all the specialists required for a particular enterprise, would also frequently be employed.

The cave paintings were first sketched in red outline on a clay surface covered with white plaster. Individual colours, made from local minerals, were then applied within the outlines and these were redrawn in black or brown. Finally, the surface was burnished. Most of the paintings at Ajanta depict scenes from the life of Buddha. One shows the reunion of the Buddha with his wife and his son, Rahula, who was born on the day that Buddha renounced the world and set out on his quest for enlightenment. Other paintings tell stories of previous incarnations of the Buddha, such as one in which the future Buddha was an enormous white elephant. Details from the paintings often give an exquisite picture of contemporary life, particularly the portrait of a princess on a swing or palace scenes.

The monastic life

Buddha himself framed a series of rules for monastic life, to which many others were added over the centuries. If free from certain disabilities, an individual, male or female, could be admitted as a novice after the age of 15 and could be ordained on reaching the age of 20. A monk wore simple yellow robes made of pieces of cloth donated by lay devotees. He rose early and spent several hours of the morning and afternoon in meditation. Much of the morning was spent in begging food for the single daily meal at midday. Large portions of the day were also taken up with teaching both disciples and laymen, and in philosophical disputation with fellow monks. Other restrictions in-

cluded chastity, honesty and abstinence from alcohol. A fortnightly assembly was held at which the monks confessed their offences and received absolution for minor misdeeds, although major ones earned an official reprimand. Larger monasteries included bathing places, storerooms, a refectory, wells and a place where the monks could take exercise by walking.

The stupas which were built to house the relics of the Buddha continued an earlier tradition of burial under mounds. Remains of leading Buddhist monks and philosophers were also buried under stupas, within the monastic grounds. Cremation was the usual rite for the dead, as it is largely today, and the monk's cremated remains were buried with the only possessions he was permitted. These were his water pot, food bowl and begging bowl.

Prosperity through trade

The wealth of the Deccan was derived to a considerable extent from trade with the West. Itinerant monks followed the main trade routes in the course of their annual journeys, and it was a matter of convenience that the monasteries should be sited beside these routes. Monasteries also provided accommodation for traders. Merchants gave generous donations to the monasteries and in turn, the wealth accumulated there made the monasteries a chief market for the merchants' goods. This wealth also provided capital which could be lent out to support private or guild enterprises.

Ajanta lay on a main trade route linking the prosperous town of Paithan, 100 kilometres to the south, with ports on the west coast, such as Broach, from which trade with the West was conducted. The Roman empire provided a demanding market for many Indian products and raw materials, including spices, precious stones and the diaphanous cotton cloth worn by the people in the Ajanta paintings. In exchange, wine, silver, young slaves and especially gold were imported.

Trade with the Far East was also important, the imports being destined both for the domestic market and for export to the West. Buddhism became firmly established in the Far East as a result of trade and evangelical missions, for the two functions were often associated. By the later 1st millennium AD, Chinese Buddhists were frequent visitors to India, making pilgrimages to the holy places of Buddha's life and studying texts in the monasteries, which often functioned as universities.

The wealth and luxurious life of later monastic establishments contrasted sharply with the complete asceticism advocated by the Buddha. So great did activity at the monasteries become that many found it necessary to employ hired labourers and slaves. Although no written record survives of life at Ajanta, the 7th-century Chinese pilgrim Hsian-tsang, a learned Buddhist scholar, has left an account of one such monastery, at Nalanda. Here he stayed in a comfortable guest house and was provided with a generous allowance of high quality food for his daily fare. A servant and a Brahmin were allocated to attend his needs. The monastery of Nalanda, which housed 10,000 monks in all, was supported by revenues from more than 100 villages, each of which had 200 families who daily provided for the monastery's needs. Within the monastery, religious disputation, which had been developed to a high art, was the main activity of the monks.

Ajanta is only one of many Buddhist monastic establishments of the 1st millennium AD in India. It is distinguished from the remainder, however, by its paintings, which are among the finest achievements of Indian art.

Nagarjunakonda
INDIA

Nagarjunakonda lies in a secluded valley of Andhra Pradesh, southern India, surrounded on three sides by hills of the Nallamallai ('Black Hill') range. On the fourth side the River Krishna divides it from the valley of Yeleshwaram, with which it was intimately connected throughout prehistory.

Tradition has it that the valley was named after Nagarjuna, a Buddhist philosopher of the 2nd century AD. Nagarjuna is said to have spent his latter days in this area, in a monastery built for him on Sriparvata hill by his royal patron, a member of the Satavahana dynasty. Legend claims that this king impoverished his kingdom by expending his entire wealth on the monastery, which was tunnelled into the hillside. In this crisis Nagarjuna himself came to the rescue, by turning the local rocks into gold.

The valley was occupied sporadically from the earliest times. Crude stone tools of the Lower and Middle Palaeolithic periods and the less crude microlithic tools of the Upper Palaeolithic period have been found on both sides of the river. However, no dwellings have been discovered before those of the Neolithic period, during which a permanent settlement and cemetery were established in the Nagarjunakonda valley. Graves of the subsequent Iron Age occur on both sides of the river, but apparently there was no contemporary settlement.

During the rule of the Satavahanas in the early centuries of the Christian era, a well organized town was established at Yeleshwaram. At the beginning of the 3rd century AD, increasing external pressure from the Shakas led to the collapse of the Satavahana empire and its western portion was seized by the Ikshvakus, probably already viceroys of this region. They established their capital at Nagarjunakonda and it was during their period of power, which lasted about 100 years, that Nagarjunakonda and Yeleshwaram experienced the height of their greatness. Numerous religious buildings, both Hindu and Buddhist, sprang up and the valley became a centre of pilgrimage, as well as a focus for intense artistic activity.

Nagarjunakonda lost its importance after the collapse of the Ikshvakus in the 4th century AD, although Yeleshwaram later became a centre of Hindu pilgrimage.

Longhurst's excavations

In March 1926, A. R. Saraswati came upon a few brick mounds and marble pillars in the Nagarjunakonda valley. An initial investigation seemed so promising that Longhurst, superintendent of the Archaeological Survey, undertook excavations at the site from 1927 until 1931.

At the start, the early promise seemed unlikely to be fulfilled. The monuments had been systematically destroyed by followers of the medieval Hindu philosopher, Sankaracharya, and treasure-hunters had completed the devastation. However, during five seasons' excavations, Longhurst was able to clear a number of impressive structures and to recover a quantity of sculptures.

As it was impossible for wheeled transport to gain access to the valley, Longhurst guessed that the River Krishna served as the main highway linking Nagarjunakonda with the outside world. He was therefore delighted to discover on the banks of the river a stone-built pillared hall beside a huge wharf of stone: this he took to be a goods and customs shed for river traffic.

Most of his work, however, was concentrated in the central area of the valley, where he uncovered a number of Buddhist stupas, temples and monasteries. Principal among these were two large complexes, both comprising a monastery with a central hall, individual cells and small shrines, and a large external stupa (relic mound) for public worship. One complex had been built by a lay worshipper called Bodhisiri, thus indicating the considerable wealth of private individuals in the city. The other was the gift of the princess Chamtisiri, sister of the first king of the hitherto unknown Ikshvaku dynasty. At the latter site the dedicatory inscription proved hard to interpret. It was not clear whether Chamtisiri had built the Great Stupa or had only renovated and added to it. Longhurst began its excavation, hoping to solve this problem, but with little confidence:

> 'When first discovered, the Great Stupa at Nagarjunakonda was a large mound of earth and broken brick overgrown with grass and jungle . . . As the whole of the dome of the stupa had been demolished, the *ayaka* pillars and platforms thrown down and broken by treasure seekers, the chances of finding any relics in the edifice appeared very remote indeed'.

However, by a stroke of good fortune the builders of Nagarjunakonda had deviated from the normal practice of depositing the reliquary in the centre of the stupa. Instead they had placed it under the north side and the treasure hunters, who had searched only at the centre, were foiled. In the Great Stupa, Longhurst found a small, broken pot which enclosed a silver reliquary in the form of a stupa. Inside this was a tiny gold casket that encapsulated a fragment of bone, a Corporeal Relic of the Buddha, rendering the stupa exceptionally holy. Since there was no claim by Chamtisiri to have deposited the relic, this seemed to prove conclusively that the stupa had been built over it at a considerably earlier date, and that by Chamtisiri's time the stupa was already a well-known shrine.

No further remains of the Buddha were recovered but other stupas, to Longhurst's continuing surprise and satisfaction, yielded gold and silver reliquaries accompanied by golden flowers and precious stones. One particularly fine reliquary was found in stupa 8. It contained the bones of some unnamed individual and was composed of a nest of five miniature stupas, of stone, glazed pottery, copper, silver and gold respectively.

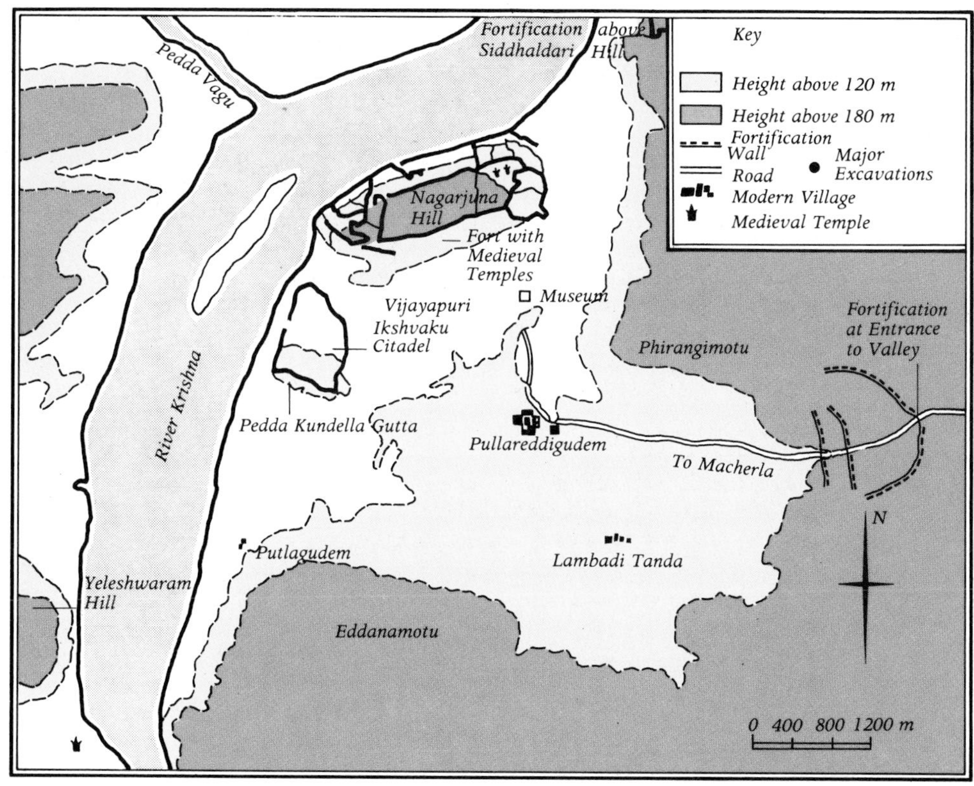

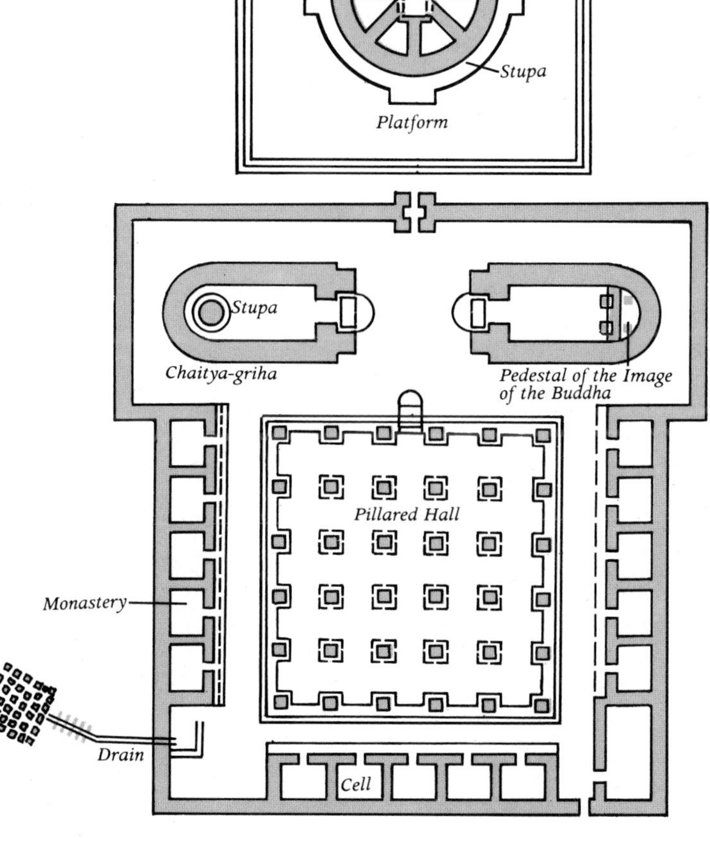

Right: Plan showing the arrangement of a typical monastic complex at Nagarjunakonda. The monks lived in small cells around a central pillared hall. The front courtyard housed two chaityas or shrines, containing stupas or images of the Buddha. Outside the entrance was a platform on which was a large stupa for public worship. The ayaka platforms arranged at the four cardinal points of the stupa had rich carved decoration and were often garlanded with flowers.

Left: The Buddhist monasteries at Nagarjunakonda usually incorporated several chaityas. These were small shrines which housed miniature stupas or images of the Buddha, as in this partially reconstructed example. The shrines were used by monks for their private devotions, public worship being concentrated on the large stupas outside the monasteries. In the background can be seen a few surviving pillars of the central pillared hall in which the monks conducted many of their daily activities, shaded from the sun and cooled by fresh breezes.

Rescuing the remains

No other major work took place until 1954, when it was made known that the huge Krishnasagar Dam was to be built 10 kilometres downstream. This would result in the submerging of the valley, so rich in prehistoric remains and one of the major concentrations of Buddhist art and architecture in India. Under the direction of Dr Subramaniyan, superintendent of the Archaeological Survey, a project was formed with the mammoth intent to recover the archaeological material from the entire valley, including Yeleshwaram. In the six years of intensive exploration and excavation which followed, a phenomenal quantity of material and information was salvaged. In order that the magnificent architecture should not be lost for ever beneath the waters of the reservoir, the Archaeological Survey dismantled nine of the most important structures and rebuilt them on the hilltop which is the only unsubmerged remnant of the valley. These buildings are supplemented by a model of the valley showing 50 excavated sites, and a magnificent museum.

These rescue excavations yielded many interesting results. The large pillared hall thought by Longhurst to have been a customs house was found on closer inspection to be a temple to the Hindu god of war, Karttikeya. A number of shrines to this deity and to other members of the Hindu pantheon were uncovered along the banks of the river. Prior to these discoveries, only the evidence of inscriptions had indicated that the Ikshvaku kings were of the Brahminical faith, although their wives and sisters were generally Buddhists.

The project's excavations also uncovered a considerable number of domestic buildings, allowing a more complete picture of life in the city to be formed. These included a number of stone-faced tanks and bathing places linked by covered drains to soak-pits. Some seem to have been attached to the residence of the Ikshvaku kings within the citadel, although the actual palace was not positively identified.

Evidence for other periods in the valley's history was also revealed in these more recent excavations. Longhurst had discovered and excavated one megalithic grave; now no less than 14 of these Iron Age burials were discovered at Nagarjunakonda, and a large number scattered over four sites at Yeleshwaram. Finds of the preceding Neolithic and earlier Palaeolithic periods were recovered on both sides of the river. Later temples high up in the Nagarjunakonda valley and at Yeleshwaram showed that Hinduism continued to flourish in the valley for many centuries, whereas the Buddhist complexes seem to have lost their importance with the fall of the Ikshvakus.

A Sacred Valley

The earliest settlement at Nagarjunakonda existed during the 3rd and 2nd millennia BC. In this era, the villagers cultivated their land with primitive ploughs and lived by keeping cattle, buffaloes, sheep and goats, as well as hunting and fishing. They lived in huts with walls of mud packed around wooden posts, storing their grain in pits beneath the house floors. Here they also buried their children, in urns, while the adults were interred, with spouted pots and other artefacts, in a separate cemetery.

In the earlier 1st millennium BC, the valley was occupied, probably on a seasonal basis, by iron-using people. They buried their dead in a variety of graves: pits, stone slab cists and urns, often covered by a cairn and surrounded by a stone circle. Little is known about the way of life of these people, but the presence of horse bones in a grave at Yeleshwaram supports the idea that they were nomads. However, the apparent lack of permanent settlements did not prevent them from making a rich variety of artefacts. Among these were fine pottery, iron tools and weapons, and jewellery including a fine gold necklace and spiral gold earrings.

After the collapse of the vast Mauryan empire in 185 BC, the Satavahanas, a local dynasty, seized power in the Deccan, where they ruled for about 300 years. During this time, a town grew up at Yeleshwaram comprising a citadel surrounded by fortified walls pierced by a large north gateway with two guardrooms. When the Satavahana empire fell, the Ikshvakus seized power in the area and selected Nagarjunakonda as the site of their capital, Vijayapuri or 'City of Victory'. The century of their reign marked the heyday of prosperity for Nagarjunakonda and Yeleshwaram.

The Ikshvakus did not reign unopposed. Inscriptions in the temples record their wars and victories, but heaps of elephant bones around the citadel and an inscription of a foreign monarch dated AD 278 attest a brief period of defeat, and they were finally conquered by the Pallavas in the 4th century AD. However, the wealth of the Ikshvaku city indicates a generally peaceful existence.

Commerce

Although the Nagarjunakonda valley contains some fertile arable land, it is mainly arid. The city's evident prosperity indicates that the community depended upon more than the agricultural produce of the valley. In part it drew on the resources of the rest of the kingdom, in the form of taxes; however, much of its wealth stemmed from the monastic communities. Since they received grants and gifts from royal and private donors, these communities accumulated wealth which played a major part in providing capital for merchants and traders and a market for their trade goods. During the early centuries of the Christian era, trade between East and West flourished. Southern India not only exported its own products – spices, fine cloth, ivory and leather goods – but also acted as a commercial centre for trade from the Far East. Roman coins and pottery, and terracotta figurines showing clear Western influences, reveal Nagarjunakonda's participation in this trade. Inland trade was also well developed.

Architecture and technology

The town and monasteries of Nagarjunakonda conform to a high standard of architecture and town-planning. Not least among the achievements of the Satavahanas and Ikshvakus was an elaborate drainage system of numerous fine tanks and paved cisterns linked by underground drains to wells and soak-pits. Public architecture was well developed: the tanks and the steps which led into them and down into the river were stone-faced. At various places in the city, shade and rest were provided by flat-roofed pillared halls open on all sides. Fine stone-faced and elaborately carved stupas for public worship were attached to many of the monastic establishments. From one of these comes a delightful representation of a *mithuna* couple, a common subject developed from the earlier figures of earth spirits. A rectangular amphitheatre, probably used both for dramatic performances and for sporting events, had tiered stone-faced brick

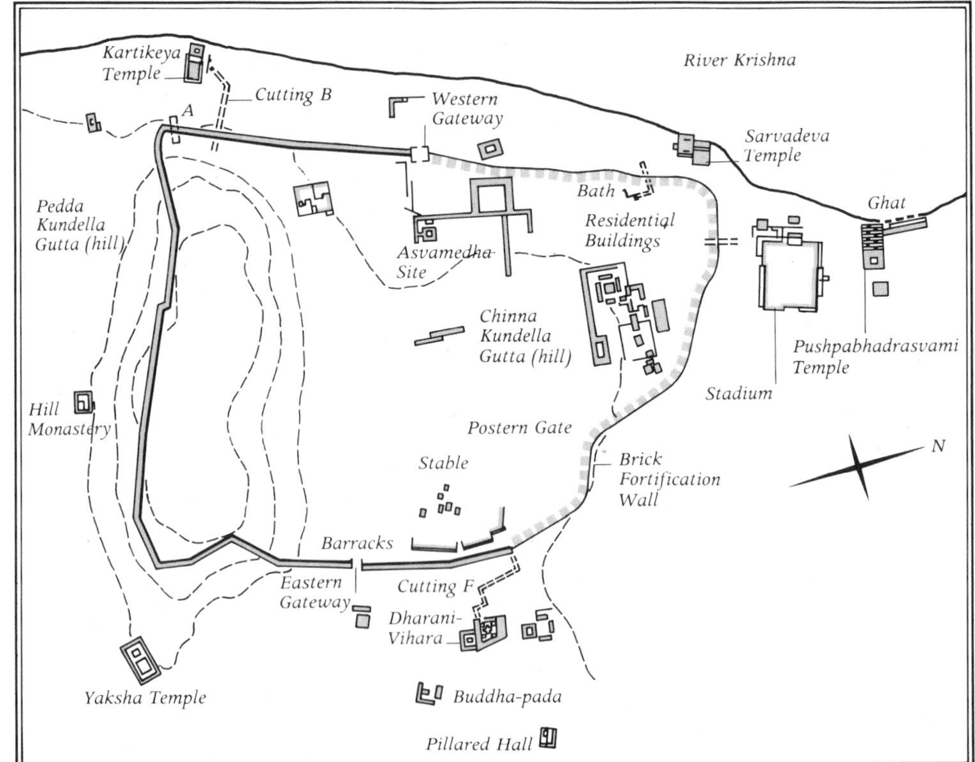

Right: The figure of the Buddha stands in the gateway to the stone railing surrounding a stupa. Behind him rises one of the ayaka platforms with its five pillars. The stupa is richly decorated and hung with garlands. It is surmounted by a series of umbrellas.

Left: The Buddha, standing serenely, converts the aggressive Naga king Apalala, who is in the midst of his harem. On the right, a bashful Mithuna yields to her lover's embrace. Such a mixture of didactic scenes and folk art was common in the decoration of Buddhist stupas.

seats on all four sides, seating about 1,000 spectators. Entertainment was also provided by gaming boards laid out in the stone casing slabs of several public buildings.

Domestic architecture, too, was of a high standard. The citadel contained barracks, stables and residential quarters; it also presumably included the royal palace, although only the bath complex attached to this has been identified. Outside the citadel, the houses of merchants, craftsmen and others were laid out along broad streets cut by lanes. The most common house-type comprised a linear arrangement of rooms with a shared verandah. They were mainly built of rubble and mud although a few were of brick.

The finest jewellery at Nagarjunakonda, a gold necklace and filigree earrings, came from the Ikshvaku period. In the Ikshvaku city, a goldsmith's workshop was found, his stock-in-trade, including moulds and crucibles, still in place. At Yeleshwaram, an iron-smelting factory was discovered: two circular brick ovens, the outer walls of which were pierced with an air-vent. Iron nails were used extensively in building, particularly to join roof-tiles. Fine glazed and often decorated pottery in a multitude of shapes was common. Terracotta figurines representing humans and animals were produced from moulds. Clay moulds were also used to produce the lead and *potin* coins used in everyday exchange.

Religious life

Although Buddhism was becoming well established by Satavahana times, it was as yet an ascetic religion with little popular appeal. Most people still worshipped the Mother Goddess, and many figurines of this deity were found in the excavations. By Ikshvaku times a doctrinal change in Buddhism had broadened its appeal and it attracted many adherents from all walks of life. The large Buddhist monastic community at Nagarjunakonda numbered about 450. They were housed in about 30 monasteries, which generally conformed to the standard plan of a central square or rectangular courtyard, either open or pillared and roofed, off which opened a number of individual cells. A dining room, store rooms and washing facilities were attached at one side and two shrines flanked the entrance, containing respectively a stupa and an image of the Buddha. Outside the entrance stood a large stupa for public worship. At each of the four entrances to the stupa, flower sellers would supply garlands to lay on the four 'ayaka' platforms that projected from the stupa at the cardinal points and which functioned as altars. Each supported five pillars, symbolizing the five great events in the life of the Buddha: Birth, Renunciation, Enlightenment, the First Sermon and Death. The ayaka platforms provided the main focus of decoration, bearing sculptures which represented scenes from the life of the Buddha. For example, the Temptation of Buddha shows Buddha meditating beneath the Bodhi tree. The demon Mara sends his daughters, in the form of irresistible women, to seduce the Buddha in the hope that he will fail to achieve enlightenment and thence the salvation of mankind. However, the Buddha is not moved by their charms, nor is he deterred by the host of demons who raise a tempest round him. Mara retreats, and the Buddha attains enlightenment. Such scenes provided a lively and forceful moral example to worshippers.

The excavations at Nagarjunakonda have laid bare one of India's most important Buddhist centres, a place of great sanctity visited by pilgrims not only from other parts of India and Ceylon, but also from as far away as China. This centre of rich artistic creativity is comparable in quality to the earlier Buddhist artistic masterpieces at Sanchi and Amaravati.

Anuradhapura
SRI LANKA

Anuradhapura, the ancient capital of Ceylon (Sri Lanka), lies in the centre of the island. Today the emphasis of settlement has shifted to the coast, leaving Anuradhapura stranded in a jungle similar to that from which it was won by the first settlers. Although abandoned in the 11th century AD, since the 19th century the site has been a major Buddhist religious centre. In its heyday, however, it was a vast city covering more than 4,000 hectares.

The original inhabitants of Ceylon were the Veddas, and small numbers of these people still dwell in the island. However, during the 1st millennium BC, the island was colonized by Aryans from northern India. They intermarried with the native people and it is their descendants who form the basis of the present Ceylonese population. Legend attributes this colonization to the year of Buddha's death, around 486 BC, and to prince Vijaya, who, together with 700 followers, had recently been expelled from his native land. Under Pandukabhaya, one of his successors, Anuradhapura city was founded. However, it did not become the capital until the reign of Dutthagamini in the 2nd century BC. The entire history of the city see-sawed between prosperity under strong rulers and devastation by South Indians under weaker kings. In 1017, a major invasion by the South Indian Tamil dynasty of Chola made it impossible to continue life at Anuradhapura and the capital was shifted further inland to Polonnaruva.

Many clues to the identity of the buildings at Anuradhapura are provided by several major texts which shed light on much Ceylonese history, in particular the *Mahavamsa*, which covers the period until the 4th century AD.

The excavations

Excavations at Anuradhapura were undertaken from 1890 by Mr. Bell, who traced the outline of the citadel and uncovered the temple in which Buddha's tooth was enshrined. A number of stupas (Buddhist relic shrines) were also cleared of earth and rubble, which often encased them to a height of 3 or 3.5 metres.

In 1913–14, work at Anuradhapura was taken over by Ayrton. He excavated a number of small monastic complexes to the west of the citadel and part of one of the major monasteries, the Abhayagiri vihara. Within the citadel he also revealed foundations of houses from the 16th century AD. No earlier domestic structures have been found: it seems probable that they would have been built mainly of wood and earth and are therefore difficult to detect.

In 1928, Paranavitana resumed excavations in the citadel area. He investigated the Temple of the Tooth, which had been almost completely robbed out for building-stone, the Mahapali (great Alms Hall), and a large area to the north-west of the Mahapali which yielded a pillared hall and a shrine, both probably part of the palace complex.

During 1934–36, the Archaeological Survey of Ceylon carried its investigations to the nearby Mihintale hill, excavating the Kantaka stupa and its associated monastic cells, and the early Ambasthala stupa. A small excavation in 1969 revealed evidence of the early occupation of the citadel area, and although no very accurate chronology was forthcoming, this supports the traditional account of the North Indian colonization of Ceylon in the 5th century BC.

Monuments of Anuradhapura

History at Anuradhapura began when the great Mauryan emperor Ashoka sent his son Mahinda from India to preach Buddhism in Ceylon. Mahinda easily converted king Devanampiya Tissa (247–207 BC) and many of his followers, and in order to set up a monastic establishment for women he sent for his sister, Sanghamitta. With her she brought a cutting from the Bodhi tree under which the Buddha had attained enlightenment. It was planted with great ceremony at Anuradhapura and is still living. Devanampiya Tissa donated his royal pleasure garden to Mahinda and his monks and here the first Buddhist stupa, Thuparama, was built. Enshrined in it were the Buddha's right collarbone and his alms bowl, given by Ashoka. The Thuparama is a bubble-shaped dome surmounted by a conical spire, set on a three-tiered platform. Around it are rows of pillars which originally supported a wooden roof over the stupa.

In order to maintain the Buddhist monks, who were supposed to live by begging, Devanampiya Tissa founded a royal alms hall, the Mahapali. This building was maintained until the city was abandoned in the 11th century. According to the *Mahavamsa*, food was served here in enormous stone troughs: one such trough was found outside the ruins of the building identified as the Mahapali. The wooden superstructure of this building has gone but some stumps of its stone pillars remain, indicating that the lowest floor was in the form of a pillared hall. It was rebuilt at least once in the course of its existence, the uppermost level belonging to the 10th century AD.

Abutting the Mahapali, the excavators discovered a deep well shaft. A passage led from the Mahapali to the top of the well and descended in a flight of steps around three sides of the well to a stone platform by the water's edge. In its present form the well is a 10th-century reconstruction; originally it had been smaller and less elaborate.

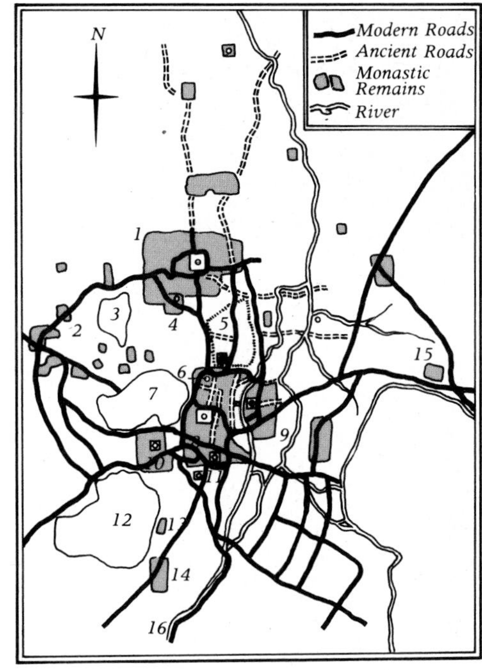

Key

1 Abhayagirivihara
2 Western monasteries
3 Bulankulam
4 Lankarama
5 Citadel
6 Thuparama
7 Basavakkulam
8 Mahavihara
9 Jetavanavihara
10 Mirisavativihara
11 Dakkhinavihara
12 Tisavava
13 Isurumuniya
14 Vessagiriya
15 Paginatissapabbata
16 River Malvatuoya

Mahinda's historic meeting with Devanampiya Tissa took place at Mihintale hill, 13 kilometres outside Anuradhapura. Here he set up his monastic community in 68 rock-cells and when he died, his cremated remains were enshrined beneath the Ambasthala stupa. The somewhat later Kantaka stupa here is one of the finest monuments of the Anuradhapura area. Similar to the Thuparama in form, it has four platforms projecting at the compass points. These were profusely decorated with friezes of plants and animals which make a pleasing contrast to the general austerity of Ceylonese monuments.

Some of the finest sculpture at Anuradhapura was found at Isurumaniya vihara, a rock-cut monastery originally founded by Devanampiya Tissa. Here, beside the pool at the foot of the cliff, are delightful relief carvings of elephants desporting themselves in the water, while on the rock above is a magnificent representation of a man and a horse, perhaps the cloud-god Parjanya and his horse Agni, god of fire.

Left: High on the rock of Isurumaniya vihara is a fine carving of a kingly figure, the cloud-god Parjanya, gazing out over the important Tisaveva irrigation tank. Behind the god is his horse Agni, his head visible and his body vanishing into the rock.

Right: The Kuttampokuna, or Twin Baths, are a pair of beautifully restored pools in the Abhayagiri vihara. Water played an important part in the life of Anuradhapura, in rituals, for irrigation and simply to keep cool.

Below: Around the pool in Isurumaniya vihara are delightful relief carvings of elephants, which appear to be playing in the water. One group comprises two adults and a baby; opposite frolics this lone individual. The carvings date from the 7th century BC.

More religious foundations

Dutthagamini (101–77 BC) was born into the royal family at a time when Ceylon had been conquered by Tamil invaders under Elara. After a long war, Dutthagamini eventually defeated and killed Elara, and unified the island, making Anuradhapura the capital. Dutthagamini was a noted patron of Buddhism and among his many religious foundations was the Lohapasada, a vast nine-storey monastic building. The entire superstructure was of wood, but some of the 16,000 granite pillars of its foundations survive, covering an area 230 metres square. Among Dutthagamini's other foundations was the Ruvanveli dagoba or Great Stupa, in the Mahavihara precinct (the pleasure garden donated to the Buddhists for their monastery by Devanampiya Tissa). This resembles the Kantaka stupa at Mihintale, its platforms richly sculptured at some later date, probably in the 3rd or 4th century AD. The *Mahavamsa* claims that in this stupa a richly jewelled model of the Bodhi tree was enshrined.

Dutthagamini's nephew, Vatthagamini, founded another stupa, the Abhayagiri dagoba, and its associated monastic complex. This was built for the followers of the schismatic Mahayana sect, which was rapidly gaining pre-eminence in contemporary India. Considerable rivalry grew up between the Mahayana monks and the orthodox monks of the original Mahavihara establishment. Later kings sometimes took the side of one of these sects, occasionally persecuting the adherents of the other. Among these was Mahasena, (AD 334–362), who founded the Jetavana monastery and its stupa. Both the Jetavana and Abhayagiri stupas are immense. Jetavana stupa was originally 120 metres high, while the slightly smaller Abhayagiri stupa is said to contain enough bricks to build a wall 3 metres high from London to Edinburgh.

A number of smaller monasteries cluster round the western fringes of the citadel. Most were built during the later Anuradhapura period, after the 5th century AD. However, they seem to conform to an earlier design – a main residential building approached across a bridge from an open pillared hall, with a number of subsidiary structures clustered in the vicinity.

The Island's Capital

Above: Thuparama is the oldest shrine at Anuradhapura, built by Devanampiya Tissa to house the relics of the Buddha brought here by Ashoka's son, Mahinda. It forms part of the Mahavihara, the original monastic complex, which also includes the sacred Bodhi tree planted by Mahinda's sister, the Lohapasada monastery and the Great Stupa.

The population of Ceylon was initially ruled at village level by local chiefs, but by the reign of Dutthagamini, the king at Anuradhapura had come to exercise political control over the entire island. Descendants of the village chiefs now formed a new class, maintaining hereditary overlordship and filling the role of royal officials in the new social order. By the 5th century AD this feudal system had become completely established, with an accompanying rise in the power and wealth of the nobility. Consequently, the period until the fall of Anuradhapura was marked by a succession of dynastic struggles. In these wars the support of South Indian rulers, in particular the employment of South Indian soldiers, led to the involvement of the Tamils on their own behalf. Nevertheless, under the strong rulers of the 9th and 10th centuries, the country enjoyed stability and prosperity. It is to this period that most of the surviving architecture at Anuradhapura can be attributed. Many pre-existing buildings were restored or renovated at this time, and new edifices built.

Engineering and water control

Among the most impressive monuments to the skill of the builders at Anuradhapura are their complex irrigation systems. An engineer called Parker, working for the Irrigation Department of Ceylon in the late 19th century, was full of admiration for the skill of his distant Ceylonese counterparts. Not only had they successfully created large reservoirs by the 4th century BC, but by at least the 3rd century BC, they had developed a highly sophisticated discharge system, the valve-pit. This was a stone-lined sluice in which a gate could be raised or lowered to control the discharge of water from the reservoir. Its stones were extremely finely worked, creating a completely smooth internal face which was probably originally lined with wood to make the sluice completely watertight. Parker marvelled at the highly competent way in which the prehistoric engineers had coped with the problems of gravity and speed of flow.

Three large tanks (lakes) lie to the west of Anuradhapura and a vast reservoir to the south-east. The earliest was built by king Pandukabhaya; the other smaller tanks are the work of his successors and the main reservoir, Nuvaravava, was completed by the early 1st century BC. This main reservoir was supplemented by a further tank 6 kilometres below the Nuvaravava dam.

Such tremendous feats of engineering and water control were essential to the prosperity of northern Ceylon. The south-west of the island receives abundant rainfall but the rest (the 'Dry Zone') lies in the rainshadow of the central mountains and depends largely upon irrigation for the staple rice cultivation. Such has been the case since the earliest days of farming settlement in Ceylon. Early occupation in the island was fairly evenly distributed, but once the irrigation works were well developed, the Dry Zone became the main area of settlement, its high productivity maintaining a large population. The importance of water control is emphasized by details from the texts. These refer to an Inspector of Reservoirs and to a whole body of officials whose task it was to supervise the use and prevent the abuse of water resources, to collect water dues from landowners and to ensure that the peasants' fields were ploughed, ready for the precious water to be released.

Above: An impressive elephant wall, built in the 8th century AD, runs around the platform on which the Ruvanveli dagoba, or Great Stupa, stands.

The monasteries

As we have no knowledge of the domestic structures of the common people, little can be deduced about secular life at Anuradhapura. Nevertheless, the large number of immediate converts to Buddhism which Mahinda made on his arrival, including more than 1,000 women, indicates a large population. Fa Hien, a Chinese Buddhist pilgrim of the 5th century AD, claimed that the city accommodated some 50,000 or 60,000 monks, as well as the secular inhabitants. In describing Pandukabhaya's original foundation of the city the *Mahavamsa* mentions four suburbs, several cemeteries, a place of execution, hospitals and several villages outside the city walls, as well as monastic establishments.

The chronicles, written by Buddhist monks, give a detailed picture of life in the monasteries. The citadel area was surrounded by monastic complexes all of the same general form: a fence or wall bounding a number of buildings which included the stupas, a shrine surrounding a Bodhi tree grown from Sanghamitta's original cutting, and pillared halls for public or monastic worship and discussion. Each monk had a private cell in one of the rectangular residential buildings, with a bedstead, bedding and a seat. His personal possessions were limited to bare essentials, including an alms bowl, clothing and a toothbrush. Other buildings within the monastic complex comprised a hospital, storerooms, kitchens, a refectory, bathrooms and privies. These last are finely and elaborately decorated, since everything connected with the monks, including their excreta, was considered holy.

Other fine sculptures included the entrance stones to buildings. These were in the shape of a half-moon (hence their name, moonstones) and usually depicted the four sacred animals, lion, horse, bull and elephant, representing the four cardinal points, and the goose, representing the zenith. The entrance to most buildings was flanked by a pair of janitor stones, carved with dwarfs or *Nagas*, both supposed to act as guardians.

Of the monastic buildings, undoubtedly the finest was the Lohapasada. Originally this had nine floors, although later reconstructions, following fires, reduced the number of storeys to seven and then to five. The monks were accommodated on different floors on the basis of seniority. Inside, the Lohapasada was richly decorated with gold, silver, precious stones and ivory, while the exterior was said to have been clad in copper plates. A roughly contemporary rock-cut building from Mahabalipuram in southern India gives some idea of the original appearance of the Lohapasada.

Right: Entrances to buildings were usually flanked by pairs of guardstones, which were carved slabs representing benevolent supernatural beings. Sometimes these were dwarfs, but more commonly Nagas were shown, as in this example. A terrified evil spirit, its arm raised begging for mercy, crouches at the Naga's feet.
The scene is symbolic of the Naga's role as guardian against evil. In his hands the Naga carries a vase full of flowers and a flowering branch, symbolic of prosperity.

Trade and overseas links

Overseas trade from Ceylon was well developed by the early centuries of the Christian era. The communication between Ashoka and Devanampiya Tissa is itself evidence that the Aryan colonists of Ceylon had maintained ties with their homeland in northern India. Despite frequent hostilities between Ceylon and the kingdoms of southern India, more friendly relations were also maintained, for a community of Ceylonese Buddhist monks was known at Nagarjunakonda.

Relations were established with Rome when four envoys from Ceylon were received at the court of the Roman emperor Claudius. Their expedition was said to have taken place as a result of curiosity aroused by the arrival in Ceylon of a Roman freedman who had been swept there by the monsoon winds while sailing round Arabia. The king of Ceylon is said to have shown admiration for Roman honesty, because the coins carried by the freedman were all of a standard weight, despite having been minted by different emperors. The development of trade with Rome dates from this time, Ceylon's exports including precious stones.

Trade with the Far East was also important. The Chinese pilgrim Fa Hien relates how he wept with homesickness at seeing a Chinese green jade image in a shrine at Anuradhapura. Among the scanty finds from the citadel excavations was a Chinese porcelain box of the 10th century.

On the whole, however, artefacts from Anuradhapura have been disappointing in their nature and number. Excavation has yielded only a few pots and sherds, numerous beads, a few objects of glass, shell and crystal, a number of coins and a few tools and domestic articles of bronze or iron. Among less mundane items was an interesting seal from the Mahapali, depicting a dancing girl holding a flower. Another attractive piece, from the Temple of the Tooth, was a stone lion in a sitting position.

Anuradhapura was the capital of Ceylon for a period of nearly 1,500 years. The ruins of its royal and monastic structures are all that now remain of its former greatness. Artefacts from these buildings are rare and nothing remains of the houses of the common people in the city. Nevertheless, the grandeur of the buildings and the high quality of the sculptures are sufficient testimony of its former glory.

1
2
3
4
5
a
b
c
d
e
f
Lake Baikal
M o n g o l i a
Inner Mongolia
Turfan
Yungang
Ordos
Sjara Osso Gol
Mancheng
Huang He (Yellow River)
Wuwei
T i b e t
Wei He (Wei River)
Xian
Lantian
Banpocun
Longmen
Yangtze River
C H I N A
Shizhaishan
Mandalay
Pagan
Hmawla
Sriksetra
Hanoi
Dong-son
Hue
Mi-son
Tra-kieu
Dong-duong
Rangoon
Thaton
Nakhon Savan
Phimai
Sukhotai
Lopburi
Ayutthaya
Vat Phu
Banteay Chmar
Angkor
Phra Pathom
Bangkok
Siem Reap
Sambor Prei Kuk
Phnom Penh
Banteay Prei Nokor
Phnom Da
Oc-eo
Chaiya Grahi
Ligor

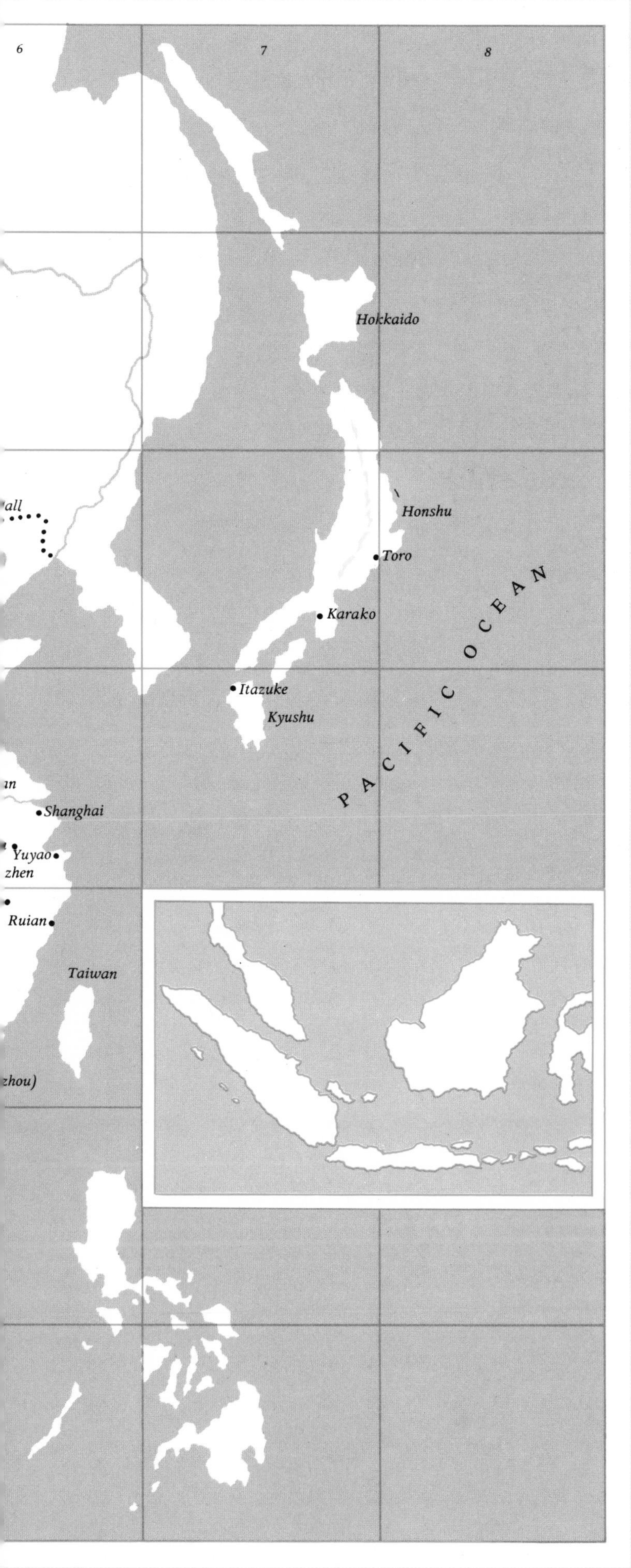

The Far East

c.500,000 BC–AD 1644

The Chinese sites chosen here represent three phases in the history of East Asian civilization. Zhoukoudian confirmed the existence of early man in China; Anyang witnessed the move of a highly advanced bronze-using people to a new capital; the imperial Ming Tombs symbolize the re-establishment of traditional rule after the expulsion of the alien Yuan, Mongol, dynasty. Toro, not unrelated to south Chinese sites, shows specific and essentially Japanese Neolithic traits, while Angkor Thom in Kampuchea exemplifies the use of all the disciplines at the archaeologist's disposal, including art history and documentary studies.

Changing geographical and climatic factors have been significant throughout the history of East Asia. The Huang He (Yellow River) is so called because it carries large quantities of loess, a yellow earth blown from the Gobi Desert, which, enriched with salts and minerals, is redeposited on its banks. The river bed thus forms flood terraces of fertile soil across the great north China plain, supporting agriculture from the Neolithic to the present. Similarly, the Yayoi farmers of Japan depended on water to grow their rice crops, a method derived from the paddy cultures of south China.

Although the Huang He valley was long regarded as an isolated 'cradle of Chinese civilization', the Neolithic communities which sprang up along its eastern end seem to bear a close affinity to proto-Neolithic sites of settled hunter-gatherers along the maritime province of the Soviet Union into north and east China. A coarse, cord-marked pottery, net weights, clubs and shell mounds are typical finds which link them. Similarly, desert locations stretching into north-west China post- and pre-date the Peking Man finds of Zhoukoudian, some 500,000 years old, while the source of the great metal-using civilization of Shang China (about 1850–1027 BC) probably lies in cultures stretching across the Siberian wastes. Such contact and cultural borrowing is even more evident in the historical period. Discoveries of Chinese bronze mirrors of the Han period (206 BC–AD 220) suggest even stronger links between Japan and the Chinese landmass across the bridgehead of Korea. To China's south, interesting connections are being made between the kingdom of Dian, a group culturally different from the contemporary Han people, and the Dong-son culture of South-East Asia and Indonesia.

Zhoukoudian

CHINA

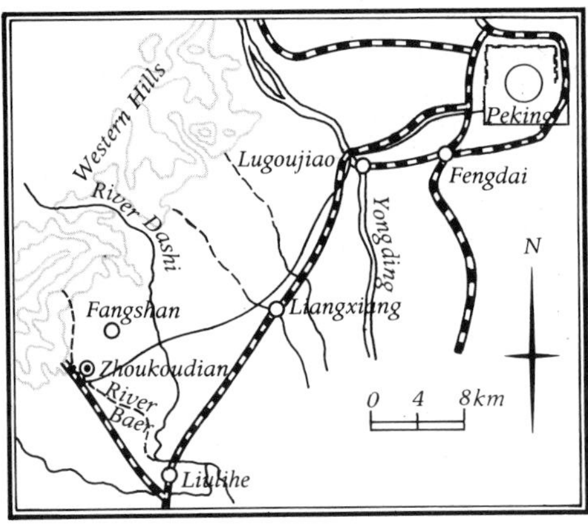

The name of China's capital, Peking, is associated for many with one of the most dramatic of all archaeological discoveries – that of Peking man. The city lies on the northern part of the dry, dusty central plain of northwest China which continues south beyond the great Huang He, or Yellow River, in Hebei province. Approximately 45 kilometres south of Peking a line of mountains, the Western Hills, curves from east to west, and at the point where these slope gently down to meet the Hebei plain is the village of Zhoukoudian. Close by are limestone hills, remnants of massive movements in the Earth's crust some 100,000,000 years ago, which have been a rich source of coal and building materials for many years. As layers of red clay were deposited in the cracks and fissures, they trapped a record of animal and plant life. But it was in the larger caves, high above the ground, that were found the skulls and bones of about 40 individuals – men, women and 15 children – together with the tools and fire they had used.

Of the 15 distinct locations at the site, Locality 13 is the earliest and Locality 15 the latest. All the skeletal remains and most of the tools occurred in Locality 1. When the site was occupied, 450,000–500,000 years ago during the Middle Pleistocene, the level of the plain was some 60–70 metres higher than the modern surface. Thus the caves were more easily accessible to the community of prehistoric people – variously called *Sinanthropus* or *Pithecanthropus pekinensis*, or, more properly, *Homo erectus pekinensis* – than to the excavators, who were compelled to use bamboo scaffolding and ladders during their work in the 1920s.

Clues to the site

The trail that led to the discovery of early man in China was long and slow. It began with the appointment by the Chinese government in 1914 of an eminent Swedish geologist, J. Gunnar Andersson, to investigate coal and ore resources. Palaeontology was a natural extension of Andersson's profession, and increasingly held a fascination for him. The foreign community in Peking had long recognized that the 'dragon bones' found in apothecaries' shops were in fact a source of fossils. The name was given to any ancient relics, including bones and fossils, which occurred naturally in the fields and hills. According to the Chinese pharmacopoeia, the dragon, an auspicious creature important in folklore, periodically shed its scales. Once ground up and used as poultices, these were prescribed for all manner of ailments. The 'dragon bones' played a significant role in the discovery not only of the home of Peking man, but also the Bronze Age capital of the Shang dynasty at Anyang.

In 1918, Andersson visited Jigushan, 'Chicken-bone Hill' at Zhoukoudian, and was shown a pillar of red clay which, owing to local superstition, had been left behind as workmen had quarried the limestone. This characteristic deposit revealed many fossilized bird bones, which were of minor interest only. By the time that Andersson's interest was revived, in 1921, he had persuaded the Geological Surveyor of China to take an interest in the 'dragon bones' source at Zhoukoudian, and had also invited two palaeontologists, a young Austrian called Otto Zdansky, and Dr Walter Granger from the Museum of Natural History, New York, to join him in an excursion to Jigushan. By chance, the local guide led them to a place where they could find 'much better and larger dragon bones'. The vertical side of the abandoned quarry near by presented a horizontal fissure filled with lumps of clay and limestone in which were embedded large bones. That evening, the three palaeontologists drank a toast to their future good fortune in excavating the site.

The finds were mainly of mammalian fossils and, although these were published, Andersson was not satisfied. A return visit in 1923 produced fossils of sabre-tooth tigers, wolves, bears and other, mostly extinct, animals. The rich haul now began to approach original expectations.

It was not until 1926, however, that the most important of these discoveries was recognized. Reporting that year from the laboratory in Uppsala, Sweden, which had been specially established for studying the finds, Zdansky informed Andersson that two of the teeth discovered, a molar and premolar (bicuspid), added a new dimension to their researches. At a reception in Peking for the Crown Prince of Sweden, Andersson made the startling announcement to the assembled dignitaries and scientists that the teeth in question were hominid, or man-like. In the absence of a formal or specific identification, their owner came to be known as 'Peking man'.

Several eminent palaeontologists advocated great caution in drawing conclusions from the evidence, among them the Jesuits Père Pierre Teilhard de Chardin and Père Emile Licent, who were at that time undertaking research in west China. Such advice did not, however, prevent Professor Davidson Black, a neuroanatomist who had helped with the controversial problem of the fake Piltdown man studies in England, from publishing his findings. In the British periodical *Nature* and the American journal *Science*, he agreed with the identification of the teeth as hominid. An extensive scientific operation was now undertaken at Zhoukoudian under Chinese and foreign specialists, backed by the Chinese government with guaranteed funding by the Rockefeller Foundation.

Discovering Peking man

A well-defined programme was continued at Zhoukoudian in the face of skirmishes between powerful rival warlords and the problem of banditry, but it yielded very little. Then, three days before the season was due to close, the effect of removing thousands of cubic metres of soil suddenly proved its worth. A perfectly preserved, unworn hominid lower molar, comparable to that of a modern eight-year-old child, was discovered by the general director of the enterprise, Dr Birgir Bohlin, from Sweden, who had been asked to join the team. With the formal announcement of the find, Dr Davidson Black assigned to the hominid the name *Sinanthropus pekinensis* – 'the Chinese man from Peking' – a completely different and hitherto unknown genus of man.

Any doubts voiced by the cautious as to whether or not Peking man represented a new genus were expelled during the following season when Bohlin returned, accompanied by two Chinese palaeontologists, Pei Wen-chung and C. C. Young. An abundant array of teeth at various stages of development was found. Bohlin observed that the fossil remains of the mandible bones were even more primitive than the teeth they supported. In 1929, the fieldworkers' greatest hopes were realized when Pei Wen-chung discovered an almost complete skull.

Excavations continued for nearly ten years, during which 20,000 cubic metres of the hillside were removed, completely changing its shape, and 6,116 cubic metres were carted away and sifted. Five almost complete crania, 152 teeth and other skeletal remains were collected, representing some 40 men, women and children. *Children of the Yellow*

Left: Close-up view of the eroded limestone hill which overlooks the village of Zhoukoudian, once the home of Peking man. The surrounding plain was then much higher, making access for its inhabitants easier during the period of occupation some 500,000 years ago. The grid of 2-metre squares used by Birgir Bohlin, Pei Wen-chung and the excavation team can be seen marked out on the vertical inner face which was so sheer as to make fieldwork very awkward. Half of the hillside was eventually removed in the 10-year search.

Earth, Andersson's unique saga of the preceding two decades, had to be revised twice before its publication in 1934 to accommodate all the newly-discovered material. The difficult circumstances under which the excavation had been carried out were magnified in 1937, however, when the invasion of north China by the Japanese brought an abrupt halt to the operations. Although excavations continued spasmodically until 1939, it became clear that the fossil treasures should be removed to a place of safety.

Fate of the bones

The history of archaeology is punctuated by mysteries of many kinds, including the loss of unique finds. In the turmoil of the times, the complete set of Peking man fossils disappeared without trace after they had, reportedly, been carefully crated up for shipment to America. Immediately after the invasion, Japanese experts had been assigned to the Cenozoic Research Laboratory in Peking where the fossils were housed and some staff members were closely interrogated concerning the objects' whereabouts. However, to this day, the fossils have never been recovered. It is probable that the crates vanished in the confusion of transportation to America. In China, it is still a sore point that the fossils were removed at all, even though plaster casts of them had been taken to America by Professor Franz Weidenreich, who took on the task of studying the fossils after the death of Davidson Black. When stability returned to China in 1949, excavations were reopened at Zhoukoudian, but only a few fragments of similar age have come to light.

Left: One of the fossilized skull fragments of Peking man is carefully removed. Birgir Bohlin developed methods for extracting fossils from their rocky casings, as well as for bandaging the fragile finds in cotton paper and wheat flour paste for transportation. At his Peking laboratory, Davidson Black evolved a technique to remove encrustations from teeth with a dentist's drill, without damaging the surface.

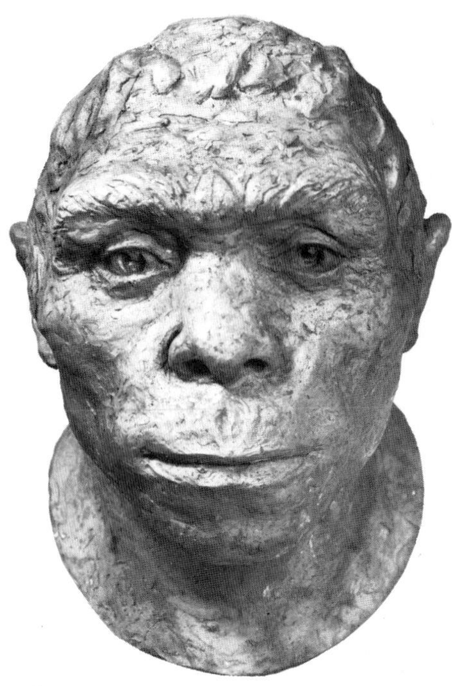

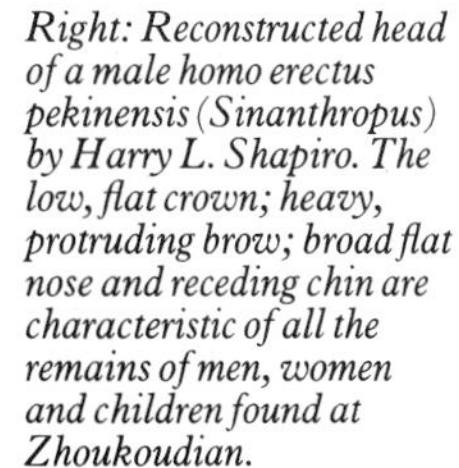

Right: Reconstructed head of a male homo erectus pekinensis (Sinanthropus) by Harry L. Shapiro. The low, flat crown; heavy, protruding brow; broad flat nose and receding chin are characteristic of all the remains of men, women and children found at Zhoukoudian.

Peking Man

Despite the tragic loss of the Peking man remains, sufficient information had been gleaned in scientifically controlled conditions to give the Zhoukoudian site a unique importance in two ways. First, the existence of early man in East Asia had been unquestionably proved. Second, and perhaps of even more value archaeologically, this was the oldest example of man's remains occurring in association with some of the implements he used. Unlike the places where, for example, Neanderthal man and Java man were discovered, Peking man was found at the dwelling site he occupied for hundreds of millennia.

Of all the discoveries, perhaps none was more exciting than evidence of the use of fire. Traces of charcoal, charred bones and ash reflect a new stage in the evolution of man. Pei Wen-chung produced this evidence in 1931 and in the same year his excavations also revealed the first stone tools shaped by Peking man. Lying near human bones, these mostly occurred in Locality 1. Their frequency, shape and material were the only signs that they were not natural products. Apart from smooth 'core-tools', flattish in shape and 15 to 18 centimetres in length, 'flake-tools', which were chips of stone struck from core-tools to form a rough cutting edge, were also found. These were, naturally, much smaller and one bore evidence of further trimming, as well as practical wear and use. At Locality 15 were found tools of a new kind, made of chert. These had been skilfully retouched and were more purposeful in shape. Their technical refinement, and the animal bones found with them, indicate a later date than the others.

Thus, at a time when many field trips were being undertaken throughout the world, the discovery of Peking man had a tremendous impact not only in terms of the sciences which it involved, but also on man's view of himself and his descendants. Although Darwin's theory of evolution had gained currency since the 19th century, with the result that fossils attracted a kind of veneration, Christian religious teaching had not yet managed to accommodate this view of man's development. Père Teilhard de Chardin, for example, had suffered much agony when prevented from taking the Mass, although this brilliant palaeontologist had received acclaim in intellectual circles for his study of evolution and his conclusions and thoughts on man's future direction. Such discoveries as that of Peking man significantly influenced the formation of modern thinking concerning human evolution. With subsequent discoveries of much older fossils – of *Australopithecus* at the Olduvai Gorge in Tanzania, for example – the excitement caused by the Zhoukoudian finds has been much overshadowed. This does not mean that *Homo erectus pekinensis*, 'the man from Peking of upright stance', has been displaced, but that in the context of other major discoveries and with the reciprocation of knowledge gained, he is now better understood.

The hunter-gatherer

As we have seen, the assemblage of fossils at the cave home of Peking man were, not unexpectedly, limited in type. It therefore required all the combined powers of specialists such as anthropologists, botanists, archaeologists and palaeontologists to attempt a reconstruction of Peking man and his mode of existence. Moreover, the period of occupation at Zhoukoudian spanned many millennia. Although a distinction has been made between the 15 localities excavated, there remain more questions than answers.

Climate seems to have been a significant factor in the advent of Peking man and his unexplained disappearance from the caves. The occupation at Zhoukoudian falls neatly between two Ice Age glacials. An analysis of pollen through the sedimentation cycles, that is, the clay infills in the limestone fissures, shows that temperate-loving species of trees such as oak, ash and elm were present during the warmer middle phase. The resulting change in surrounding forest and vegetation, perhaps producing more seeds, berries and fruit, together with a more genial climate, would have provided more favourable conditions for Peking man's existence.

The fossil record presents a large number of animal bones, many belonging to extinct species. These are too numerous to have died from natural causes and, in particular, the concentration of bird bones in one place can only point to Peking man being a hunter who brought the kill back to eat in the caves where his family lived. Sabre-tooth tigers and other felines which inhabited the hills to the north, would, in turn, have preyed on him. Buffalo, deer and sheep grazed the plain that stretched away to the south, while wild pig and rhinoceros would have demanded the thick vegetation allowed only by a north temperate climate. Other species, such as the horse, bear, dingo, hare and wolf, shared the local terrain. While most of these could be trapped, snared or brought down by organized hunting with sticks, birds would have been much less easily caught.

Of all the bones, the highest proportion, approximately 70 per cent, belong to a type of deer with massive spreading antlers. We must assume, therefore, that this deer formed a large part of the hunters' diet and the antlers would have provided useful additional implements. Apart from the flesh, splits made in the bones show that the nutritious marrow found between their walls was also prized. It seems, too, that Peking man was not averse to partaking of the sweet, succulent brain of his contemporaries. It has been noted that the majority of Peking man fossils consist of parts of the skull with very few long bones or vertebrae. Perhaps, as recently observed in some tribal societies, victims were brought back as trophies by headhunters, and the cracks which are visible in the crania of the fossils are the result of heavy blows. Marrow and brain are soft, but the flesh would not have been an easy proposition for the teeth and mandibles discovered. Peking man was the first to possess the controlled use of fire. In the absence of crude cooking utensils, he may have roasted the flesh he ripped from the carcasses, thus tenderizing the meat and enhancing the taste. An analysis of his fossilized faeces has shown that he also garnered and ate seeds, fruits and nuts.

The presence of a hearth situated in a cave dwelling in which bones of hunter and hunted are found side by side suggests a communal life, with individuals sharing the meat. However, a hunter-gatherer existence also raises the question of whether or not it was necessary to lead, if not a completely full, then a partial or periodic, nomadic existence. Until the advent of Neolithic agriculture, seeds were not to be found in the quantity or quality that we now accept as

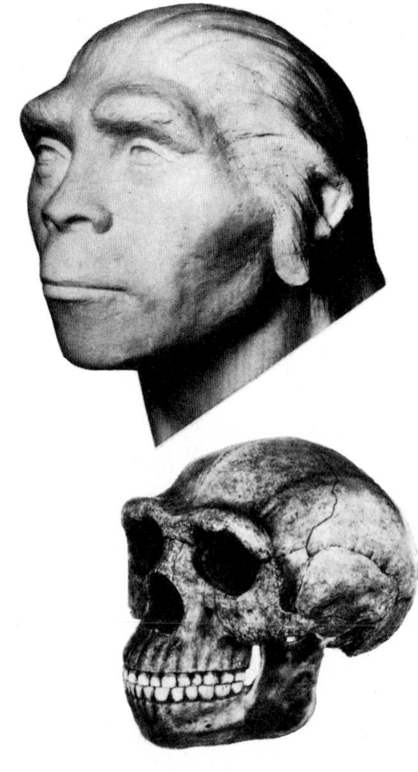

Above: Reconstruction of a female homo erectus pekinensis (Sinanthropus) by Franz Weidenreich, together with the restored skull on which the head was based. The characteristic features of the face and body seem not to have changed during the 500,000 years that Peking man occupied the Zhoukoudian caves.

usual. Seeds, as well as fruits, roots, berries and nuts would only be found in adequate amounts over a relatively large area, and even then would be governed by their season. Peking man probably ate as he gathered. Hunting expeditions would also mean an enforced absence from home, and there may well have been a division of labour in this context, the men hunting while women and children harvested wild plants. All such activity, however, points to a social organization, whether consciously directed or not, and, therefore, to a primitive form of society.

The toolmaker

Although his studies were necessarily limited to teeth, crania and a few other fragments of fossilized bones, Franz Weidenreich was able to tell us something of what Peking man looked like. The average height of the male was 1.56 metres, while the female stood about 1.44 metres. Their posture was erect and although the proportions of the limbs were comparable to those of modern humans, the arms were more obviously developed. A fleeting chin; large, thrusting teeth on great jaws; broad, flat nose; heavily ridged and uneven brow and low forehead curving back flatly to a bulging occiput gave Peking man rather a savage appearance. Although his body was covered with hair, there seems to be little evidence of a thick, fatty subcutaneous layer. Given his knowledge and use of stone tools, and his hunting activities, it does not seem unreasonable to assume the use of animal skins as protection against the typical long, cold winters of even the more temperate period. The brain box was about two thirds the size of that of modern humans, and from the formation of the skull, it is generally agreed that Peking man possessed some form of speech.

It has been estimated that the skeletal remains of the Zhoukoudian site represent some 40 individuals (not all necessarily contemporaneous). This figure is not incompatible with the number needed for a successful community. Unfortunately, not all the skeletons of the site would have been fossilized for posterity. Of those found (15 were children) less than 3 per cent seem to have reached the age of 60, and 40 per cent died before the age of 14.

The assemblage of stone tools used by Peking man represented a tradition independent of any other Palaeolithic stoneworking traditions. The implements might appear crude, but untutored attempts to reproduce them would soon meet with difficulty. Examples of these tools, ranging from the earliest to the latest, would seem to fulfil most of Peking man's needs: for example, the chopping of branches for firewood, while garnering the additional benefit of nuts and fruit; digging or burrowing for roots; killing animals; splitting bones or paring meat and fur. The quartz 'core-tool', flaked on both sides to give a cutting edge, was the one tool most common to all layers of the deposits. Later, quartz and quartzite 'flake-tools' are found in various shapes. In his studies, Père Teilhard de Chardin noticed a rather elongated form with a 'beaked' end that was probably used as a burin or chisel. He also grouped together other distinctly shaped pieces of limestone which were, apparently, hammering stones. Nearby streams may have been the source of the vein quartz and green sandstone used, whereas longer journeys to granite massifs lying north-east and south of the caves would have been undertaken for the quartzite that was also used. Antlers, horn and bone, as well as wood, if worked in a similar way to the stone tools, would have provided additional awls and borers.

As no relics of his art or similar activities have been left, Peking man's life appears to have been rather brutish. It was not until the discovery in 1930 by Pei Wen-chung of an 'upper-cave man', recognized as *homo sapiens*, that evidence of a shift to more 'civilized' activities was found. Living approximately 25,000 years ago, these people not only buried their dead but also performed a funeral rite by sprinkling red haematite dust over the corpse. Such awareness, exclusively human, is also shown in the discovery of painted beads, perforated and polished shell ornaments and tooth pendants.

Above: Communal life at Zhoukoudian. Scattered human fossils suggest a primitive hunter-gatherer society which used stone tools, with evidence of the use of fire.

Anyang

CHINA

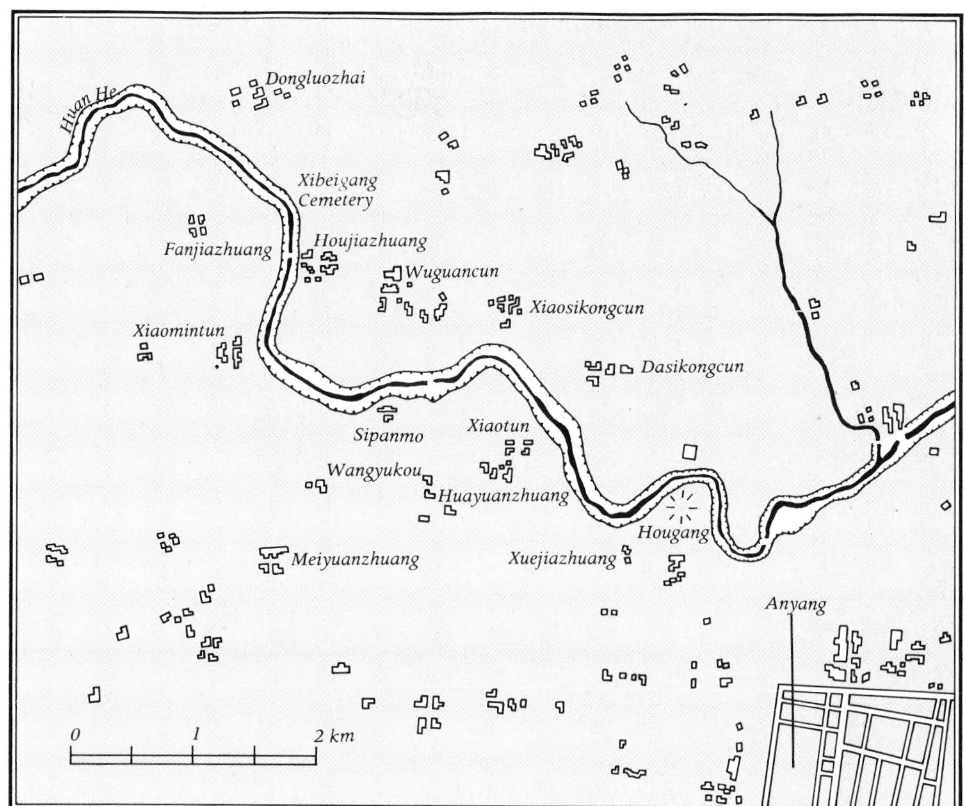

The modern city of Anyang lies in north Henan province on the fertile central plain of north-west China, not far from the Huan He, a tributary of the Huang He (Yellow River). Archaeologists use the name 'Anyang' as a generic term for a group of 17 sites of the Shang civilization (about 1850–1027 BC). The sites take their name from nearby villages, which formed a closely organized unit.

Suspicions that Anyang was the last of the seven capitals of the Shang-dynasty kings were confirmed by two discoveries. One was of large-scale subterranean tombs at Wuguancun; the other of rectangular stamped-earth foundations at Xiaotun, more grand than other dwelling foundations in the area. Both were characterized by many sacrificial burials of humans and animals. Known from ancient historical records as Yin, the walled city was the seat of power for 12 kings who ruled over a large, as yet incompletely delineated, domain for 273 years. Excavations have shown, however, that the site was occupied long before this.

'Dragon bones' and Bamboo Annals

In his 'Records of the Grand Historian', the first of 24 dynastic histories, Sima Qian, archivist at a court of the Han dynasty (206 BC–AD 221) reconstructed Chinese history even to the point of including a genealogy of the Shang kings. The Bamboo Annals, written on slips of bamboo and discovered 600 years after being buried in a prince's tomb in AD 281, gave a revised chronology which is used as a basis for current dating. When antiquarianism became popular from about the 12th century AD onwards, these texts were used to gain information from inscriptions on bronze vessels of the Zhou dynasty (1027–221 BC), but not for those of the Shang. In the heady rush to reform which took place during the early 20th century, Chinese historians cast doubt on information in the dynastic histories and other traditional texts, so that the age of the legendary emperors and the Xia and Shang dynasties were relegated to the realms of myth.

In 1899, however, the attention of several scholars had been drawn to strange markings scratched on the surface of 'dragon' bones, which were being sold as medicine according to prescriptions included in the Chinese pharmacopoeia. Dragons were auspicious creatures, and therefore the scales they had

Left: 'Jia', ritual bronze wine vessel, excavated at Anyang: 14th-11th centuries BC. This was one of the many important ceremonial vessel shapes of the Shang rulers. Bands of disintegrated parts of mythical animals on a 'thunder pattern' ground, forming an integral design, are common to most Shang bronzes. In the lower two bands here, confronting 'kui' dragons form the eyes, snout and horns of the gluttonous 'taotie' monster.

Above: Chariot burial from Wuguancun, Anyang: 11th century BC. The shape of the decayed wooden construction is shown by the excavated recesses originally cut in the pit base to receive the chariot. The charioteer, lying prone, rode in the square box over the axle, at the two ends of which are bronze axle caps. Lines of bronze discs and ornaments indicate the harness.

supposedly shed were thought to be endowed with potent medicinal properties. A search for the source of these bones led to Xiaotun, near Anyang. Here, local farmers, annoyed by the bones constantly clogging their ploughshares, had found that they could be readily sold for cash at apothecaries' shops.

Painstaking research by subsequent scholars, convinced that the scratchmarks were ancient inscriptions, resulted in several thousand modern equivalents for the markings being published in 1917. More significantly, there was also verification of Sima Qian's list of the Shang kings. The scratched fragments proved to be oracle bones on which kings (divination being a royal occupation) questioned various deities on a number of subjects, including hunting, childbirth and the weather. Unfortunately, in the hostile climate of the times, the 80,000 pieces of mostly ox or goat scapulae and femurs, together with tortoise plastrons and carpaces, were disregarded for a decade.

Discovery of a lost capital

Scientific interest in the remains only began with the formation in 1928 of Academia Sinica, China's first institute of scientific research, when Tung Tso-pin was given leave to follow up the clues left by the oracle bones. Even so, he was accused of mere 'grave-grubbing'. But he persevered with his investigations at Anyang. The first excavations proved disappointing, and it was only on discovering a rich source in a village headman's private plot that 300 bones were brought to light. The 'dragon' bones were proving more lucrative than agriculture in the face of failed crops and bandits!

The excavation team returned to Anyang for a fourth time in 1931, following the appointment of Li Ji, field director at Zhoukoudian, the cave-home of Peking man, as head of the newly-formed Department of Archaeology. Prevented from excavating at Anyang because of a dispute with the provincial authorities in 1930, the excavation team had gained immeasurable experience at another, Neolithic, site. On their return to Anyang they began a more systematic and scientific approach to the featureless site at Xiaotun, by dividing it into three sectors, A, B and C. This proved successful in making more sense of the complex foundations at different levels.

The significance of the sites at Anyang cannot be overstated. Most important of all, the excavations proved beyond a shadow of doubt the existence not only of a Shang civilization, but also that the site, called Yin, was the last seat of the Shang kings.

No more effort or money has been expended on excavations at any other site in China, with the exception perhaps of the tomb of the first emperor, than was spent at Anyang between 1928 and 1935. Excavation has continued at the site since 1949, and equally significant is the role it has played in training many of China's first generation of archaeologists.

Since 1953, many sites excavated around the modern city of Zhengzhou, 160 kilometres south of Anyang, have proved to predate the royal occupation at Xiaotun and to have served as the capital until its removal to Anyang in 1300 BC. However, successes achieved in this area owe a debt to knowledge acquired at the Anyang excavations. Comparison of information from the two sites has produced a tentative but useful chronology for five phases of the Shang period, dating back to 1500 BC.

The Metal Workers

The characteristic grey pottery of the Shang dynasty directly overlies pottery of the Neolithic period at many sites in China, including the Anyang group. Although this demonstrates a continuity between the two traditions, they are divided, nonetheless, by a radical change in society and technology which transformed a previously egalitarian society into one which was strictly defined and hierarchical. The cause of this change is unknown.

At the pinnacle of Shang society was the king, who, assuming also a priestly role, asked for guidance on how to rule from various powers, including an ancestral deity and the Sun and Moon. From this situation we can see the emergence of a kind of ancestor worship or veneration, later sanctioned in the 6th century BC by the great philosopher Confucius. There is also the factor of royal power being invested with divine authority – thereby granting a mandate to rule.

Questions which appear on the oracle bones are concerned with all aspects of life: for example, hunting trips; sickness; birth; and travel. Divination was made by applying a hot point to a small, oval-shaped depression drilled into the bone or shell. This produced a long crack with a spur, a mark reproduced by the ancient and modern Chinese characters 'pu', to divine.

The symbols of royal power lay in the magnificent bronze vessels which formed altar sets. Mounted in such places as the area in Sector C at Xiaotun defined as containing ceremonial buildings and altar platforms, they were used by a class of 'priests' authorized to perform the rites and ceremonies. Such was the awesome power of the pantheon of Shang gods, including the monsters and animals which decorate the bronzes, that they demanded human and animal sacrifices. In one tomb alone, 247 of these were found. Such sacrifices were demanded especially during the consecration of buildings and when accompanying a lord into the afterlife. This coercive character of Chinese Bronze-Age society is also apparent in other warlike activities, and reflected in the fact that huge walls were constructed around cities against marauders.

The 'ge' halberd, another mark of Shang civilization, is found at sites all over China, in places not necessarily in the Shang domain. These halberds, together with the construction of chariots, show in their beautiful and intricate decoration a concern with pomp and ceremony, as well as with warfare itself.

The artisans

At the top of Shang society was the 'warrior class', and at the bottom the great mass of people who supported it and provided the vast amount of 'slave' labour needed to build the cities from which power was wielded. Between the two there is evidence of a privileged artisan group. These people seem to have worked, and may have lived, close to the political and ceremonial centres, as bronze foundry floors and other workshops occur in conjunction with royal habitation sites. Later ritual texts mention six clans possessing metalworking monopolies. This suggests the existence of metalwork guilds in which industrial practices were regulated by rules, combined with an efficient division of labour. Similar workshop organization existed for potters and bone and jade workers. From the nature of the oracle bones, it may be deduced that writing was a jealously guarded secret, as in many early civilizations. However, evidence of a clerical group may lie in the different styles of characters (ideographs or pictographs) found on bronze

Above: Artist's impression of a Shang Bronze-Age foundry. Molten metal flowed from a conical clay crucible (centre) in the domed furnace directly into the mould. Ceremonial vessels, in their original bright-bronze state, were further worked after cooling. Shown finished here are (left to right) fang ding, ding, gu and jue vessels.

Right: Fang ding, 14th–11th centuries BC, excavated at Anyang in 1950 and approximately 20 centimetres high. The 'square ding' sacrificial vessel was a variant of the ubiquitous ding tripod vessel produced during the later Shang and early Western Zhou periods. The key fret pattern, long-tailed birds, nipples and flanges are cast in high relief, anticipating the bold plastic designs favoured by the Zhou-dynasty conquerors.

Below: Augural inscription on Shang oracle bone. Questions put to the gods concerning daily life provide the earliest evidence of writing in China. Many of the pictograms, such as that resembling a man at the top of the fourth column, are easy to determine and bear a close affinity with the modern Chinese characters used today.

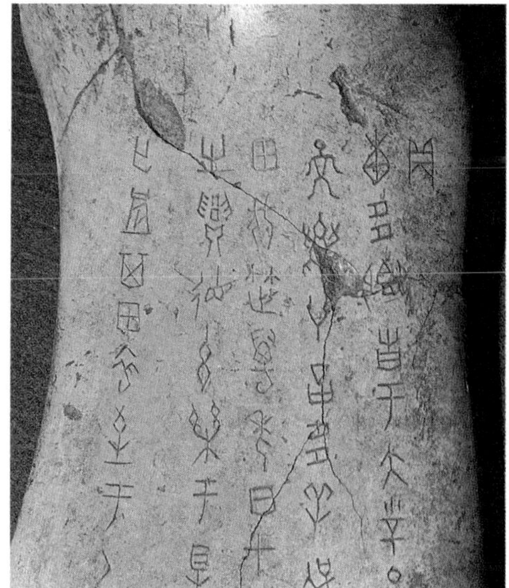

vessels and the more abstract styles of those found on the oracle bones.

Efficient pottery kilns which could produce temperatures up to 1100°C were developed during the Neolithic period. These kilns were responsible for producing the fine white wares, reserved for noble vessels, of the Shang. Together with the early ability to distinguish between the oxidizing and reducing flame, they also directly enabled the production of bronze. Copper is reduced from ore at 1045°C. A foundry floor was investigated at Xiaotun which bore similarities to the dome-shaped pottery kilns of the Neolithic and Shang periods, although its precise nature can only be guessed at. What we do know is that the earliest bronzes discovered so far, at Zhengzhou, were already products of a peak of technical refinement not seen at such early stages in the metal-working development of other cultures. No 'practice' pieces have been discovered. The main development discerned in the later, Anyang, finds lies in the extent and intricacy of ornamentation, including inlays of turquoise, and the variety of prescribed forms.

Casting

Methods of casting bronze during the Shang period are the subject of much debate. The wider variety of forms and detailed decoration of the Anyang vessels and weapons seem to argue for the 'cire perdue', or lost wax, method. In this, soft clay is applied to a wax model. When heated in order to harden the clay, the wax runs out from holes in the mould which is thus left behind. On the other hand, clay fragments of piece-moulds found at Anyang have smooth edges, which easily fitted together. These show that the use of composite clay moulds was one method almost certainly employed. It is an issue that awaits further evidence before being finally resolved.

One fact which points to the importation of more or less refined copper and tin is the absence of slag heaps proportionate to the amount of casting which must have taken place. These materials may have come from west China, for example, the traditional mining area of more recent times. The high proportion of lead discovered in vessels and weapons would both have reduced the melting point and produced sharper casts. If this was accidental, as some argue, the lead being naturally present in the ore, then it was an occurrence more than fortunate as it helped to produce some of the finest bronzes in the world. Although details of the early bronze industry are not fully known, it is clear that it involved a highly organized series of operations covering a wide area.

Economy and contacts

When compared to the abundance of evidence provided in other directions, it is perhaps surprising that archaeology has shed little light on the economy of the Shang state. The oracle sentences casually mention millet and rice, but there is scant proof of the extensive irrigation systems which would have been required for cultivation of the latter.

The flood plain of the Huang He in northern China is known as the 'nuclear area' of Chinese civilization. Here, a highly fertile deposit of loess, 'yellow earth', blown eastwards from the Gobi Desert, gave rise to extensive, settled farming communities in the 6th millennium BC and continued to provide a good growing medium during the Bronze Age, as it does today. In spite of the fact that the Shang élite used bronze implements, these farmers still lived in the Neolithic age, as shown by the evidence of their dwellings and discoveries of stone hoes, digging sticks and stone reaping knives.

Something of royal hunting trips is known from the oracle bones. Hunting provided practice for warfare and, in the process, almost certainly added to the food store. The abundance of sacrificial animals, mainly goat, ox, pig and deer, suggests a surplus of meat and that, possibly, some of these animals were herded for their meat and skins.

Strings of cowrie shells are recorded as gifts, but whether or not these were used as currency cannot finally be proved. Such a donation, however, indicates that wealth among the relatively small aristocratic élite was accrued by means of royal favour and the use of 'slave' labour in the form of *corvée*, extracted by fear. The theory of a slave society as practised by the Romans and Egyptians is not borne out by the evidence.

The search to locate a source for the abrupt introduction of bronze technology in early China has centred attention on contemporary bronze-using cultures to the north and west of the Shang sphere. During this period, the climate over northern China was much warmer than today. It would have allowed, for example, if not migration then at least cultural links in this direction across the Siberian pine forests. More evidence for external links has been found. For example, one tortoiseshell found at Anyang could only have come from the Malay peninsula, perhaps representing some form of tribute.

It appears that although Shang rule was characterized by terror, the economy must have been highly successful. It would never otherwise have been possible to expend so much time and effort in producing so many magnificent artefacts, best exemplified by the bronze ceremonial vessels.

Ming Tombs

CHINA

The tombs of the emperors of the Ming dynasty (1368–1644) of China are situated in a tranquil valley 45 kilometres north-west of Peking. The valley's Chinese name is 'Shisan (thirteen) ling' (mound, or, specifically, imperial tomb). The site was chosen in 1409 by the third Ming emperor, Yong Le, who had removed the capital from Nanking to Peking following his successful challenge to the power of the second emperor, his weak 22-year-old nephew, Jian Wen. Covering an area approximately 5 by 3 kilometres and bounded by mountains to the north, the special characteristic of the site is that it comprises two quite distinct elements. The first is its surface architecture and sculpture which, closely allied to the rebuilding of Peking by Yong Le in the 15th century, has remained more or less intact since the fall of the Ming dynasty. Second, and perhaps more tantalizing, are the subterranean burial chambers of the emperors and their wives. These were so successfully protected by the mounds which characterize the mausolea that no archaeological excavation had been attempted before the founding of modern China in 1949.

It was therefore with a sense of eager anticipation that in 1956, archaeologists began to excavate Ding Ling ('ling' – Tomb; 'ding' – of Security), the mausoleum of the Wan Li emperor who reigned from 1572 to 1620. Ding Ling was the first, and remains the only, tomb to be fully excavated to date.

The way in

Lacking the experience of excavating such an imperial tomb, yet not wishing to despoil the fabric of the burial chamber, the archaeologists were hindered by the problem of locating the entrance, which was covered by earth forming the tumulus. Investigating the fortified wall which surrounded it, they noticed an area where the bricks were weak and falling away. Once these had been carefully removed, an arched entrance was revealed. The theory that this was the first entrance was reinforced when a stele, or engraved stone tablet, was found which recorded the length and direction of the corridor leading into the tumulus. After following brick walls and digging away the soil infill, however, the excavators were disappointed at being brought to an abrupt halt. Disheartened, they came to the conclusion that the true entrance was a good many metres below them. In a moment of great good fortune, another stele was found at the bottom of their trench. This carried the inscription 'the diamond wall' (the outer wall of the burial chamber) 'is 16 zhang away and 3.5 zhang down', a zhang being a Chinese foot. Such clues are an archaeologist's dream.

Cutting away the soil, they did indeed find the 'diamond wall', just as described. At this point, bricks which had been hastily replaced by workmen as the burial party left the tomb were again carefully dismantled to reveal a protective antechamber. It seemed as if the featureless mound and puzzle of the concealed entrances had fulfilled their purpose in foiling any attempt at looting in the past. Inside, double doors of polished marble presented themselves, tightly shut, at the far end of the long chamber. Such doors were known from historical texts, and, armed with this knowledge, the excavators managed to push a rod through the narrow gap between the doors. They levered back the large stone block which acted as a securing crossbar on the inside, falling into place and effectively sealing the doors across the back as they were pulled shut. They were reopened without damage to either doors or crossbar. At the far end of the outer hall, another set of similar doors opened on to a sacrificial chamber 32 metres long and 6 metres wide.

Here were glimpsed for the first time since the sealing of the tomb the three 'precious thrones' of white marble. The central one, decorated with carved interlacing dragons amid clouds, was for the emperor. Those of his two wives, decorated with phoenixes, stood in front and behind. An altar set and a huge blue-and-white porcelain tub full of sesame oil and complete with wick lay before each throne. As the stone blocks were meant to ensure the preservation of the palace, so these 'everlasting lamps' were to light it for eternity. Lack of oxygen, however, had extinguished the flames.

In 1957, another set of marble doors, decorated with nine rows of round bosses and a monster mask in relief, was opened to reveal the grey limestone burial chamber of the Wan Li emperor. Each door, cut from a single slab, weighed between 6 and 7 tonnes. The emperor's coffin was placed between those of his wives who, dying before him, had not been carried to the specially prepared chambers built for them at the end of two corridors lying at right angles to the main north-south axis of the palace. Entrances to the surface of the tumulus, by means of the characteristic doors with self-activating crossbars, had been incorporated into their construction in order to deal with the possibility of their outliving the emperor.

Right: One of four stone guardian warriors of the Spirit Way. All wear the prescribed court uniform of a Ming general. The texture and detail of leather thongs and interlocking armour, as well as the cloth of the robe, show the sculptor's skill at its best.

Above right: Key to Ming Tomb (inset)

1 *Tumulus*
2 *Stele Tower and Pavilion*
3 *Altar*
4 *Protective Screen*
5 *Triple Doorway*
6 *Sacrificial Hall*
7 *Ceramic Ovens*
8 *Gate of Heavenly Favours*
9 *Triple Entrance Gate*
10 *Tortoise Stele*
11 *1st Courtyard*
12 *2nd Courtyard*
13 *3rd Courtyard*

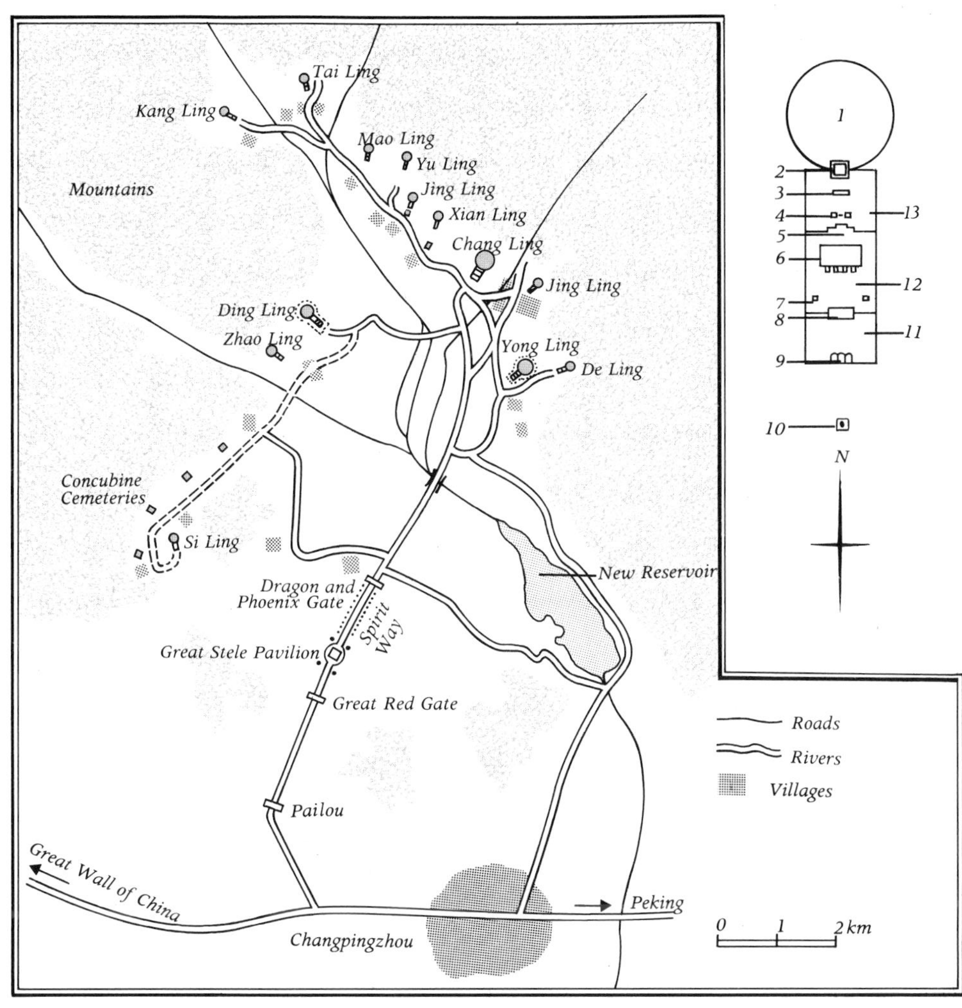

Below: The stone pailou, or triumphal arch, marking the main entrance to the valley of the Ming tombs. The highly decorated pillars still bear the residue of paint, reproducing similar wooden gateways known throughout China.

In the event of that happening, access could be obtained without disturbing the emperor's tomb.

All three corpses lay in a traditional (one inner and one outer) double coffin made of special 'nanmu', a hard, fragrant wood from Sichuan province, painted with red lacquer which was still in pristine condition. The grave goods surrounding the caskets provided a dazzling array of porcelain, jade, gold and silver ceremonial objects. The collapsed coffin of the second empress contained her skeleton, lying on variegated silks, the skull adorned with a gold headdress. The coffin of the emperor's first wife contained silver and gold chopsticks, as well as other equally fine, and sometimes finer, objects. Those goods found in the coffin of the emperor himself were, as would be expected, of a quality and quantity beyond compare.

The group of imperial 'dragon' robes recovered from the burial chamber, together with the rolls of silk bearing the date and place of manufacture, has provided one of the most important collections of Ming dynasty textiles. Examples of the comparatively rare 'sancai', or three-colour, porcelain and of the more well known blue-and-white porcelain contributed to a further understanding of the development of Chinese ceramics. Among the most spectacular finds, however, were the ornate headdresses. One, for use by the emperor when making official journeys, was made of gold thread worked into a mesh forming a bonnet shape, with wing-like projections pointing upward at the back. One of the female headdresses was covered in kingfisher feathers, of a piercing blue, and jewels. It was surmounted by gold dragons and a phoenix, symbols of the emperor and empress respectively, with aerial projections from which hung strings of pearls at the sides.

Approach to the tombs

The gleaming white stone 'pailou' is the first of the monuments on the approach road to the tombs. This is a kind of triumphal arch consisting of six square pillars, 5.5 metres high, supporting horizontal lintels, each surmounted by ornate, palace-style roofs. One kilometre away stands the Great Red Gate, a red-painted building pierced by three arches and roofed with yellow glazed tiles, at the point where the wall surrounding the necropolis joined up with it on two sides. At this main entrance, even the reigning emperor was obliged to dismount and walk. The Great Stele Pavilion houses a single slab stone stele which, at 10 metres high, is the tallest example in China. Inscribed with a dedication to the Ming dynasty, it stands proudly atop a stone tortoise and marks the beginning of the Spirit Way. Here, stone sculptures of guardian animals – mythical and real – civil and military officials and beacons flank the roadway for 1,100 metres, guiding the spirit to its resting place. At this point, the Dragon and Phoenix Gate stands full square across the road, in order to deflect malevolent spirits which can only fly in straight lines. The first tomb is another 4 kilometres away. Many more reception buildings, pavilions and stone columns form part of the complex in the valley of the Ming tombs. At the time when the last Ming emperor was finally laid to rest, the valley was comparable only to the Forbidden City, home of the living emperors, in old Peking.

Imperial China

The burial mounds of the Ming are related to such tombs as that of Qin Shihuangdi, first emperor of China, who reigned from 221 to 210 BC. Excavations of his tomb have revealed a huge lifesize army of terracotta statues, among other spectacular finds. However, elements of imperial burials characteristic of the Ming period are first found during the Han period (206 BC–AD 221) through to the end of the glorious Tang dynasty (AD 618–907), which the Ming administration was attempting to emulate. During the Han period, a square wall (symbol of the Earth) surrounded a circular grave tumulus (symbolical of heaven) with hardly any space between the two. By the Ming period, several main developments had taken place. The square wall to the south of the tumulus was removed to form rectangular courtyards containing ceremonial buildings – a feature probably directly related to the development of the unique Chinese landscape garden. A cluster of tombs was built to form a huge necropolis and the approach area was extended to include gates, triumphal arches and stele pavilions to commemorate the dynasty, and a 'spirit way' flanked by guardian stone figures. This last was also a feature of Han tombs.

Right: Reconstruction of Ding Ling, tomb of the Wan Li emperor (d. 1620) and his two empresses (d. 1611, 1620). The huge outer wall, originally enclosing the whole complex, and the administrative side buildings, are no longer standing. Begun in 1584, it took 600,000 men six years to complete and cost 8,000,000 taels (ounces) of silver. In keeping with the dissipation of his reign, the emperor held a grand banquet within its precincts after it was finished.

Below: Central sacrificial chamber of the underground palace of Ding Ling. The three marble thrones were for the spirits of the emperor and his wives to hold audiences. Wan Li's coffin was behind the portal and the empresses' in vaults to the right and left.

Right: View along the Spirit Way towards the Ming tombs, flanked by alternately sitting and standing stone guardian animals. The 'xie zhai' in the foreground is a mythical animal symbolizing justice, while the camels and elephants were not uncommon in north China during the Ming period as beasts of burden and ceremony respectively. All the sculptures, including the remaining civil and military officials which average 3 metres high, were carved from single stone blocks.

Selecting a site

Widely-held beliefs concerning the nature of the environment and siting of buildings within it were taken from a quasi-science called 'fengshui', meaning 'wind and water', or geomancy. Accompanied by much hocus-pocus, the geomancer made sure that: lying on a north-south axis, the building faced south; there were mountains to the north, containing auspicious dragons to ward off evil influences – usually the north wind; water ran in front of, and not through, the site; there was a pleasant view. The plan of the whole mausoleum reveals that, allowing for the lie of the land, the site chosen in 1409 following several years' investigation accords with these beliefs. Although dismissed as superstition by early European observers, the Canon of Dwellings, handbook of geomancy, contained a core of common sense.

Administration

During the period of relative peace and prosperity under the Ming, China was the largest unified political unit in the world, with a population approaching 200,000,000. Palace politics involving increasingly autocratic emperors and eunuchs hardly touched the peasant, except in the form of harsh taxes. To a certain extent, the administration of the Ming tombs reflected the methods employed in running the empire.

One of the main functions of the tombs was to provide a location for the enactment of the ritual sacrifices and, to that end, an inspectorate was housed to the east of the entrance of each tomb. Here, red tape abounded. Officials carried out duties minutely prescribed by edicts which were issued by the Imperial Ministry of Works and the Board of Rites. The main administrative office for the whole valley stood by the first tomb, Chang Ling.

Although these officials were responsible for carrying out the more minor ceremonies during the year, large imperial delegations journeyed from Peking to observe such important sacrifices as the Day of Frost's Descent, when people throughout the empire burnt paper clothes to ensure their ancestors' warmth during winter. After the long journey from Peking, the purely utilitarian buildings within the tombs' precincts were put to good use. Such events would necessarily place intolerable pressure on the local population.

The practice of forcibly resettling whole families and giving them hereditary guardian status over the tombs, which dated back to the Han period, was employed to provide labour for construction and agriculture. The lives of the people were extremely hard and governed by strict laws. For example, they were forbidden to hunt or gather fuel within the area designated by the lines of concentric coloured posts around the mausoleum. Unable to bury their dead nearby, sons were prevented from carrying out their most important filial duty, an irony that drew no sympathy from the bureaucracy.

The village of Changping, situated southeast of the tombs, was originally the military headquarters of a general who commanded some 7,000 troops. It was specially built to protect the tombs and surrounding imperial lands, as well as the agriculture which sustained the local population, from marauders and bandits. Several villages form part of, and encroach upon, the tombs to this day.

Ancestor worship

By far the most important factor in consideration of the Ming tombs is that of ancestor worship. Although not a religion in the usual sense (Buddhism and Taoism fulfilled this role more satisfactorily), it served to perpetuate the state and family systems and formed the very fabric of Chinese society.

After death, the ancestral spirit assumed a more substantial form than that of its Western counterpart and was capable of exerting evil influences on its descendants. As the head of both his own and a national family, the Yong Le emperor met his moral duty to provide a burial chamber for the corpse, containing items for use after death. For example, the coffins of the two empresses entombed in Ding Ling contained a wash-basin, spouted ewer and gold chopsticks. Outside this sealed residence, the surface site came into its own. Appeasement of the spirit was of paramount importance, and therefore the sacrificial hall was a necessary feature of the complex. Here, rites were performed according to a strictly regulated code which reached back in time far beyond the Zhou dynasty (1027–221 BC). Also prescribed were dishes of specially prepared food, such as soup, rice, saffron, 'dried fish from an island near Dalian (Port Arthur)' and celeriac. These were placed on one table by officials, according to rank, while biscuits and sweets were placed on another. A placard informing the spirit of who was present was burnt in the same way as paper models of everything from gold ingots – in traditional China – to models of automobiles – in modern Hong Kong – have been burnt as offerings.

The inclusion of pottery figurines in burials superseded the human and animal sacrifices of the Shang period (about 1850–1027 BC) and continued for a thousand years. The introduction of burnt-paper offerings made the rituals more accessible to ordinary people. As it was the responsibility of each emperor to provide for himself, it is recorded that tombs tended to reflect the excesses or economies marking particular reigns.

Technology

The technological achievements of the Chinese up to the Ming period included early use of bronze and the invention of high firing kilns, paper and gunpowder, to name only a few. During this 'rebirth' of a purely Chinese culture, the Ming tombs are not remarkable for any major technological innovation. Instead, their construction and contents serve to demonstrate the continuation of traditional Chinese expertise. The most obvious achievements lie in the engineering and construction of the whole necropolis. Stone, timber and soil would need to have been dragged over great distances, while the marble doors and huge steles were carved from single stone blocks. The vaulted burial chamber of Ding Ling, made from tightly-fitting, often mortarless, stone blocks, was still in good condition after 300 years. Precious objects of metal, jade and lacquer attest the continuing traditions of fine craftsmanship over many centuries. Of particular interest were the porcelain finds, as it was during this period that the techniques of porcelain making and the controlled firing of polychrome enamels and glazes were first perfected. China of this period was to have a great impact upon the West.

Toro

JAPAN

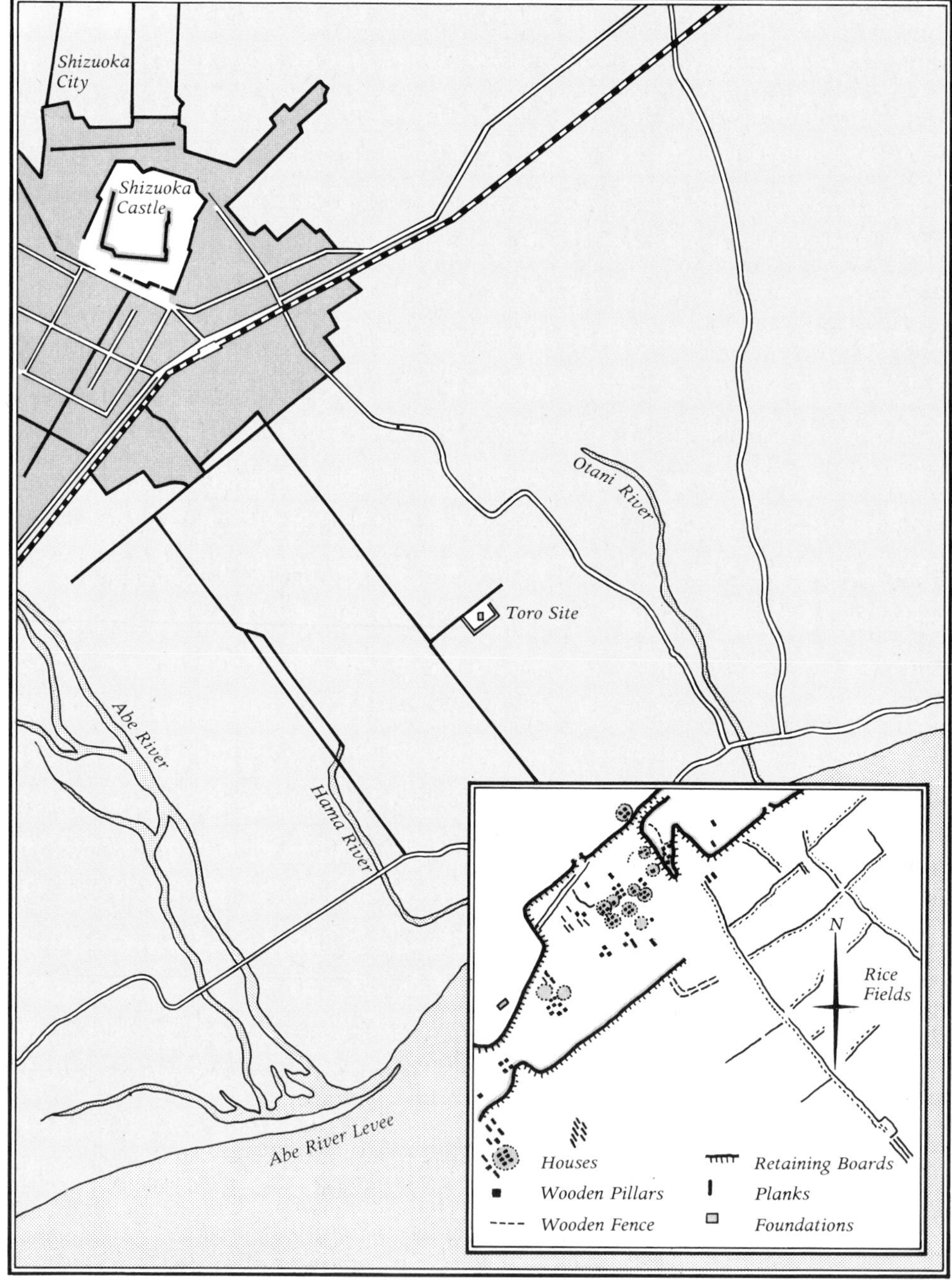

Toro is the site of a prehistoric agricultural village in Japan, occupied by Yayoi rice farmers in the early 1st millennium AD. It lies approximately 2 kilometres inland from the present Pacific seaboard, near the modern city of Shizuoka. The locale has variously been identified as a natural levee of the Abe River, flowing into the Pacific at that point, or a series of low terraces, or a coastal swamp margin. However, it is better understood as an extension of high ground from the hill range curving off to the north-east behind the site. Areas of low ground on both sides of the site are today drained by the small Otani and Hama rivers. An understanding of this topographical setting is crucial to interpreting both the use of land for settlement and cultivation during the site's occupation, and to the site's discovery and investigation.

The site's excavation – from 1947 to 1950 by the Toro Site Investigation Committee, and in 1965 in conjunction with the building of the Tomei expressway – started interdisciplinary archaeological investigation in Japan. It also revolutionized our understanding of early East Asian wet-rice agricultural life, through the recovery of wooden artefacts and the revelation of ancient field systems.

Discovery and importance

In 1943, the piece of ground containing the Toro site was being farmed as rice paddy, along with the rest of the lowland coastal area of Shizuoka City. The land was sought for wartime factory construction, and in order to lay a firm base, paddies close to the shoreline were dredged to a depth of a metre in order to provide earth fill for the foundations. As a result of this work, the underlying remains were revealed. Although a team was immediately formed to investigate the newly-discovered site, its activities were discontinued after the excavation of one dwelling because of the war.

It is interesting to note that the way in which the Toro site was discovered – at the point where earth fill was being obtained rather than at the point of actual construction – is common to many incidents of archaeological recovery in Japan. This is because traditional architectural practices and topography often require the mounding of firm bases for foundations rather than extensive foundation digging. At the Toro site, moreover, it was the heavy gravel overburden originally intended for the factory base that caused the most difficult problems in excavating the area four years later.

A second spate of construction activities during the mid-1960s resulted from Toro's location on the coastal margin, where a super-expressway from Tokyo to Nagoya was planned. By this time, however, a national preservation movement was active in trying to rescue and protect archaeological resources from the government's intense construction and expansion programme. The southern portions of the ancient field system, which were to be crossed by the path of the projected highway, were therefore excavated thoroughly in conjunction with the highway building. The preservation movement also prompted the making of Toro into an historical park, with an on-site museum displaying the farm tools and articles of daily life recovered during excavations. At least two of the thatched dwellings and a raised storehouse have been reconstructed, while the ancient paddy field divisions south-east of the village lie exposed as they were excavated. Toro is one of several historical park and museum complexes built with government encouragement and support throughout the 1970s, each showing a particular temporal and regional aspect of Japan's early history. The significance of Toro is that it supplies the most comprehensive information on Yayoi agricultural life, which formed the basis of traditional rural life in Japan. This way of life lasted through the 19th century and still lingers on to the present day in some aspects of architecture and food preparation.

The excavation

The excavation of Toro was revolutionary in its organization, in the nature of its discoveries, and for our understanding of how a subsistence economy based on wet-rice agriculture was established.

In 1947, knowing the potential of the site from the wartime excavation, archaeologists from several universities in Tokyo joined under the leadership of Imai Toshiki to form the Society for the Investigation of the Toro Sites. This society eventually grew to include ethnologists, sociologists, architectural historians, geographers, botanists, zoologists, agricultural scientists and historians from a variety of eminent institutions in Tokyo. An inter-disciplinary excavation was planned and carried out for 50 days between July and September 1947, resulting in the recovery of unprecedented remains, which were analysed by an unprecedented battery of specialists. In 1948, the Toro Site Investigation Committee was incorporated into the Japan Archaeologists Association (Nihon Kokogaku Kyokai), and a new five-year plan of investigation at Toro under Goto Shuichi was begun.

The remains found

The nature and variety of remains recovered through the Toro excavations were not only outstanding for their time, but are still impressive today. The site's prehistoric paddies were the first to be excavated in Japan, and even now there are few similar examples in the country, let alone in greater East Asia. Again, the fact that the relationship between the field system and contemporary settlement could be revealed is rarely duplicated in archaeological situations. Only the lack of burial remains prevents us from completing a picture of the settlement layout at Toro.

One of the greatest contributions of the Toro excavations was the recovery of quantities of wooden materials and objects. Such artefacts were not entirely unknown, even in the early post-war period, since excavations at the Karako site in western Japan in 1936 provided some wooden objects. But Toro exceeded Karako in the number and variety found. This material added an entirely new dimension to the information on prehistoric society, especially concerning woodworking and lathe technology, and the tools needed for early rice paddy farming, weaving, and architectural construction. Only at lowland waterlogged sites, which Toro became after its abandonment, can such implements be recovered. This fact shows the poverty of evidence relied upon when only stone, or even bone and metal, survive.

The remains at Toro are concentrated in a 10-hectare area. To the north-west lay the dwelling area, where 12 houses, two granaries and several clusters of pillar base-boards (wooden planks set underneath posts to stabilize them) were identified. Interspersed among these were stumps of various trees, including cryptomeria, camphor and evergreen oaks, indicating a warm climate and relatively stable ground. Immediately to the south-east lay over 40 paddy fields, constructed on either side of a central canal which runs north-west to south-east for 400 metres. The paddies were separated by bunds, or embankments, which also served as raised paths, and in some cases by short canals running perpendicular to the central one. The bunds were reinforced by vertical planks, while stakes lined the canals.

Such methods of diking were also seen in the dwellings, where interior floors were surrounded by earthen embankments. These were lined with vertical boards on the interior walls and stakes around the exterior walls. At first glance, the dwellings appear to be pit houses, owing to the illusion of depth created by the embankment walls. In reality, the interior floors and exterior ground surface are on the same level. These Toro houses have served to define one kind of surface house in use as early as the Yayoi period (300 BC–AD 300). In contrast, the structures identified as granaries were raised about 2 metres off the ground on pillars. Rat guards set between the pillar tops and floors served to deter rodents, and the buildings' contents were accessible to humans only by notched-log ladders.

The superstructures of the dwellings and granaries are known both through the recovery of architectural materials – planks, posts and thatching – and through actual illustrations of such buildings on contemporary bronze mirrors, bronze bells and ceramics. The recovery of rat guard and ladder components from the granaries not only enabled the buildings' forms to be reconstructed, but also helped archaeologists to discern their function. The board-wall construction of the raised granaries is a landmark in Japanese architectural development. Together with the planks reinforcing the dwelling embankments and bunds, the granary construction implies skilled use of iron woodworking tools and joinery techniques in what has been called 'the village that iron built'.

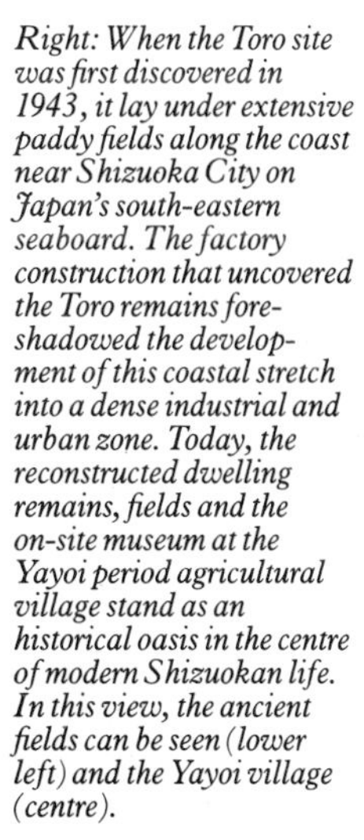

Right: When the Toro site was first discovered in 1943, it lay under extensive paddy fields along the coast near Shizuoka City on Japan's south-eastern seaboard. The factory construction that uncovered the Toro remains foreshadowed the development of this coastal stretch into a dense industrial and urban zone. Today, the reconstructed dwelling remains, fields and the on-site museum at the Yayoi period agricultural village stand as an historical oasis in the centre of modern Shizuokan life. In this view, the ancient fields can be seen (lower left) and the Yayoi village (centre).

Early Rice Farmers

The population of Toro is estimated by the archaeologist Suenaga Masao to have been between 50 and 90 individuals. These figures assume that each oval dwelling, with an average interior floor space of 5 by 7 metres or 28 square metres, housed a family of five, and that only 65 per cent of the dwellings in the village have been archaeologically identified. Each family apparently cooked inside over a central fire pit, using such implements as pedestalled cooking-pots – encrusted with soot – wooden single-lip pouring bowls, ladles, beakers and double-ended grain pounding pestles. Wooden pedestalled bowls are noted in contemporary Chinese dynastic histories as the serving implements of the Yayoi farmers, and those from Toro were made in separate parts – bowl, pedestal and base – showing advanced lathe skills.

Crafts carried on at the site included weaving, woodworking and bead-polishing. Unfortunately, no unfinished wooden artefacts were recovered from Toro as they were from Karako. Only the wooden hafts of axes and adzes remained from woodworking tools, but among the wooden artefacts were weaving implements, including fabric and thread beams, shuttles and reeds from simple *back-strap* looms, and the low stools upon which the weavers sat. Carbonized fragments of woven vegetable fibre, probably hemp, were also preserved in the damp mud of the site. Finally, both sandstone bead-polishing stones and curved beads of serpentine, perforated at one end for suspending on a cord, occurred at Toro, indicating that craft production superseded the utilitarian and that raw materials from outside came into the site through trade.

These and other remains, particularly the Toro ceramics, raise questions concerning self-sufficiency and craft specialization. It has been speculated whether or not the ceramics were wheel-thrown products, which would imply the presence of specialist potters. However, the wheel, or more accurately, a turntable, was used only for finishing the vessel rim and applying the fine corded or combed decoration. The vessels themselves were made by the coil method. Although Toro weaving implements reflect some level of household or village self-sufficiency, the villagers were integrated into a regional social network that involved trade of utilitarian, as well as decorative, goods. Serpentine, as mentioned above, bronze bracelets and finger rings, glass beads and iron were probably imported from western Japan, where they are known to have been available.

Although Toro is most often characterized as an egalitarian village, with even the granaries belonging to the community as a whole, it is possible to imagine an elevated ranking of some families or heads of families. The mere presence of status goods in the form of serpentine curved beads, bronze body ornaments and glass beads does not divulge this kind of information, however. Furthermore, without burial data, no definitive statements can be made.

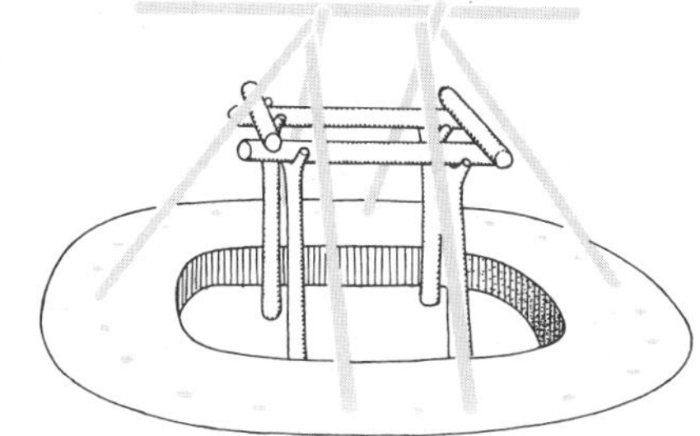

Above: The thatch of a Toro dwelling was supported by a central four-post and beam construction and shaped by diagonally-laid poles.

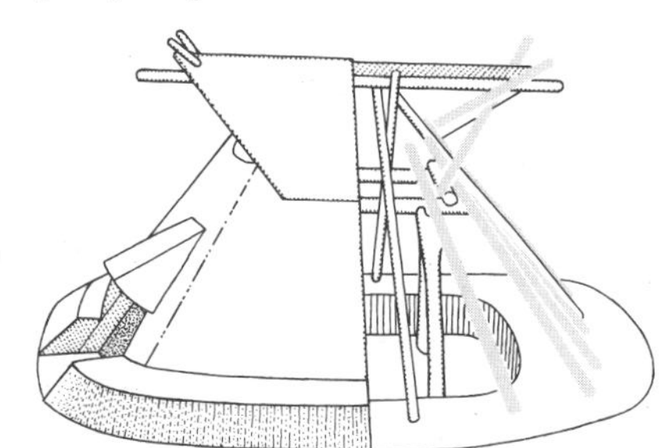

Above: The roof incorporated ventilation holes at the gabled ends, and the thatch extended to the raised embankment outlining the interior floor area.

Above: Stilted buildings at Toro are thought to be granaries for storing rice grown in the nearby paddies. Built off the ground to avoid moisture and rodent pests, they were accessible by notched logs serving as ladders.

Radiocarbon Dates from Toro

HALF-LIFE DATE (Uncorrected C14 date)	CALIBRATED DATE (Corrected C14 date)	MATERIAL	DATE COLLECTED
2100±70	150 BC	Cryptomeria plank	1947
1720±90	AD 440	Wood fragment	1950
1940±120	AD 50	Wood fragment	1945–50
1940±100	AD 50	Wood fragment	1945–50
1950±130	AD 50	Wood bowl	1945–50
1960±80	AD 50	Wood fragment	1950
2010±120	AD (50)	Wood board	1945–50
2060±90	AD (50)	Wood fragment	1950
2240±90	400 BC	Wood fragment	?
2300±120	440 BC	Wood fragment	?
2590±100	800–900 BC	Wood fragment	?

Right: Excavations at Toro have revealed extensive evidence of a Japanese agricultural village of the 3rd century AD. Thatched dwellings and stilted storehouses clustered at the edge of geometrically planned rice fields.

Development of rice farming

The date of the Toro site is important in assessing its relationships to other known settlements and remains. According to the standard Yayoi pottery chronology, the Toro site belongs to the early part of the Late Yayoi period, conventionally dated between AD 100 and 300. This assignment is thought by Japanese archaeologists to be more accurate than radiocarbon dates obtained from the site. These show a wide range, but it will be noted that at least six dates cluster around AD 50, a date which is within the estimate based on ceramic styles. In addition to much earlier dates, four samples have also yielded dates in the 4th and 5th centuries AD, when state organizations were beginning to form in western Japan. There may therefore have been some overlap and mutual influence between eastern seaboard farming communities and western political organizations. Such a relationship is suggested also at Toro by imitation wooden sword blades and scabbards, shields, and polished stone arrowheads of kinds uncovered in western Japanese tombs.

Wet-rice farming communities such as Toro were established on the eastern seaboard of Japan during the first two centuries AD. They represent the final stage of lowland colonization in the first radiation of rice technology from Kyushu, where it was introduced from mainland Asia. Toro lies at the northernmost boundary of this first radiation, a boundary determined both by favourable conditions for growing the available strains of rice, and the willingness of former hunter-gatherer populations to take up farming as their major form of subsistence. Nevertheless, the villagers at Toro did not survive on rice alone; hunting bows, bone fish hooks, grooved stone net weights, as well as a variety of fish, turtle, shellfish, red deer and wild boar remains attest to the exploitation of animals for food. Vegetable foods included red azuki beans, melons, peaches and chestnuts.

It is significant that the rice grown at Toro or other Late Yayoi period sites was not harvested with perforated stone reapers, as it was earlier, but with iron sickle blades. Although few, if any, of the latter have been recovered, no stone reapers are commonly associated with Late Yayoi sites. This change in tool use indicates a shift from harvesting each head of grain as it matured to harvesting an entire field of stalks simultaneously. In turn this suggests a more homogeneous crop, as well as the production of a new source of manufacturing material: rice stalks. Artefacts made of wood and other natural products – including nets, baskets, field clogs and a paddy boat – also give evidence of a fairly advanced and integrated method of wet-rice agriculture. A comparison of some of the field clogs with pre-modern farming equipment in Japan suggests that they were used for trampling green manure into the fields; and the small paddy boat is similar to ones used until recently to drag seedlings or equipment into the paddies. Recovery of bone fragments of the domestic cow at Toro has led Japanese archaeologists to postulate the animal's use in field preparation.

Other advances are more difficult to define, and one aspect of Toro subsistence technology that remains elusive is the paddy canal system. The prehistoric paddies, averaging about 1,500 square metres in size, slope upwards from the central canal which lies in the lowest point of the field divisions. Japanese archaeologists generally agree that at least this central canal (if not others yet undiscovered) was used for draining, rather than for supplying water to the fields. An understanding of this agricultural technology is important in investigating the beginnings of wet-rice agriculture in the lowland and delta areas of South-East and East Asia, particularly in the Yangtze River floodplains whence Japanese rice culture derives. It also contrasts with the subsequent development of community organizations around river drainage systems made for the express use of river-diverted water in irrigation systems. The evidence at Toro indicates that the initial facilities to be developed for wet-rice cultivation were drainage facilities; that the presence of canals cannot be construed as indicating irrigation; and that community organization even in the Late Yayoi period had not yet developed around river drainage systems for irrigation use.

Toro, lying at the intersection of marshy coastal lowlands and higher, drier ground towards the hill ranges, eventually succumbed to the accumulation of shoreline sediment and equalization of land surface heights which resulted in a rise in ground water level. Houses rebuilt three times on successively higher ground, together with the site's burial under a metre of mud and gravel washes, are circumstances which have been cited by Japanese archaeologists as indicating that Toro was abandoned because of flooding. As with so many other Middle and Late Yayoi sites in Japan, water was the source of the inhabitants' way of life as well as its demise; and water is the agent that has nevertheless preserved the remains of that way of life for our inquiry.

Angkor Thom
KAMPUCHEA

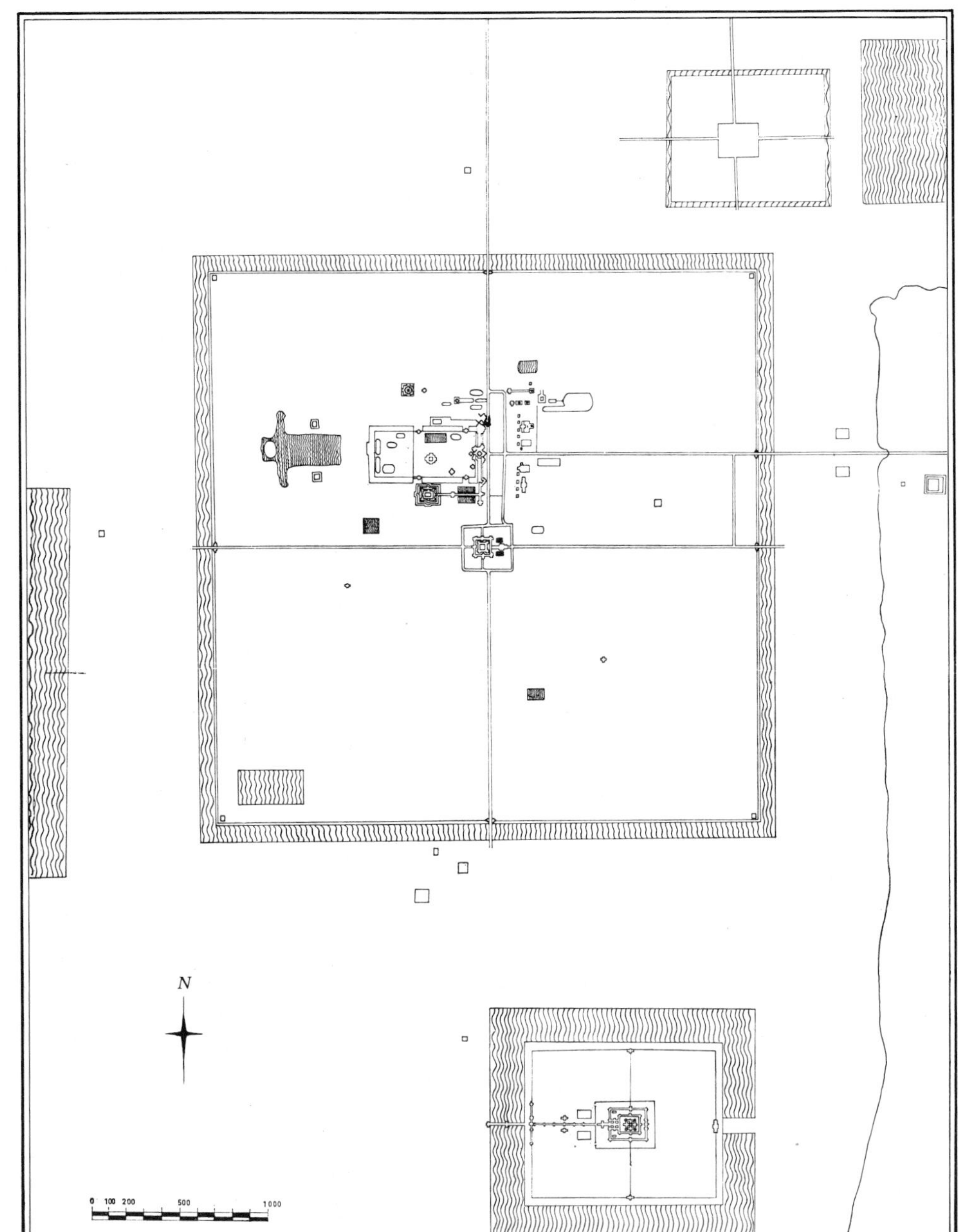

Near the present-day city of Siem Reap in Kampuchea (formerly Cambodia) lie several ruined centres of the ancient Khmer kingdom. Some are grouped in the walled enclosure of Angkor Thom, the enormous capital city built by Jayavarman VII (reigned 1181–about 1218). Near it are other capitals and shrines, including the great temple complex of Angkor Wat. Created by Suryavarman II (reigned 1113– after 1150) as his sepulchre and shrine, Angkor Wat is one of the world's greatest religious buildings.

The Bayon

It was at the exact centre of the square city of Angkor Thom that Jayavarman VII began about AD 1200 to build his greatest temple – the Bayon. The first visitor to leave an account of the Bayon was a Chinese envoy, Chou Ta-kuan, at the end of the 13th century. Chou wrote that at the centre of the Khmer kingdom was a golden tower flanked by more than 20 stone towers and several hundred rooms. On the east side was a golden bridge with a gold lion on either side. Eight gold Buddhas were arranged below the stone rooms. He also recorded the great enclosing wall, 3 kilometres in perimeter, with its moat crossed by five bridges.

Of these bridges, Chou Ta-kuan mentioned 54 spirits like generals in stone, gigantic and terrifying. The stone parapets were carved in the form of serpents, and the spirits held the serpents in their hands, appearing to prevent them from escaping. This last observation is noteworthy. Once study of the monument and its enclosure began, it was soon decided that the giants on either side of the bridges were depicting the well-known Hindu theme of the Churning of the Ocean. Using the world serpent as churn-rope and Mount Mandara as churn-stick, the gods and demons, directed by Vishnu, churned the Ocean of Milk in order to obtain 'amrita', the nectar of immortality.

Such an interpretation was not surprising; the motif is a favourite of Khmer art and is splendidly depicted on the cloister at Angkor Wat. But in this case, all the figures on each side of the five bridges face outwards. Churning, on the other hand, implies a tug-of-war-like confrontation. It has been shown that these bridges are actually rainbows (snakes are rainbows in South-East Asian beliefs) which link Earth and Heaven. This theme is crucial to an understanding of the Bayon,

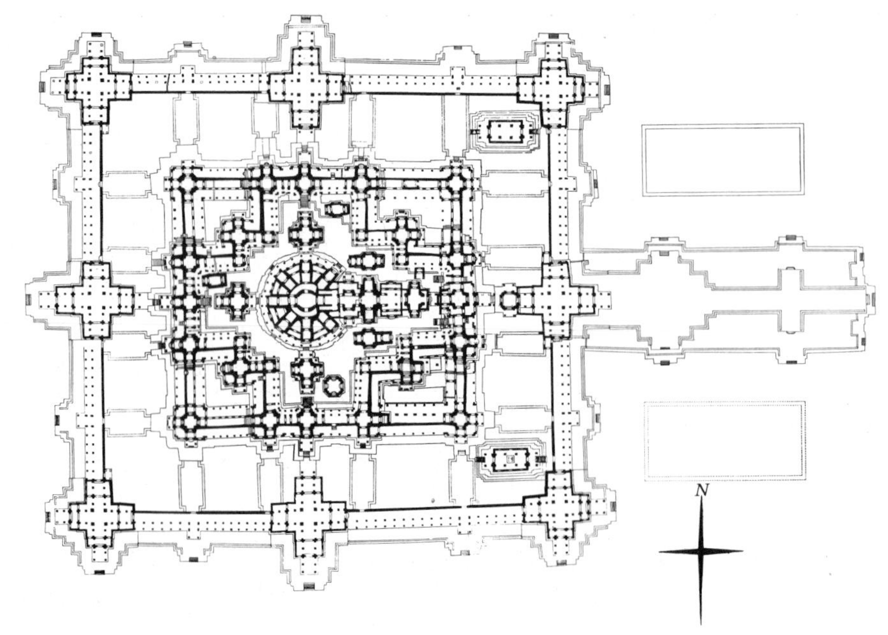

with its walls and moats, as a sacred microcosm at the centre of the 'real' world.

After the time of Chou Ta-kuan, the Khmer kingdom entered a period of decline. Following Angkor's devastation by the Thais in AD 1431, the king and his people fled, leaving the city, palaces and temples to be reclaimed by the jungle. Apart from one brief interlude, the city remained lost until the 19th century, when a French naturalist called Henri Mouhot stumbled upon it during an expedition to the Cambodian interior in 1860. Almost singlehanded, he worked to clear the ruins from the stranglehold of creepers, tendrils and roots. Over the next few decades, archaeologists followed his path. The work of restoring the ruins and learning of their significance was begun.

The religious nature of the Bayon was quickly recognized, although one scholar was convinced that it had been the royal harem. Others suggested that it had been a giant tomb consecrated to Brahma, or that it was connected with Shiva rather than Brahma, being a type of Shiva *linga*.

In the meantime, work had begun on restoration and physical study of the structure. In 1925, a relief over a doorway was recognized as being of Lokeshvara, the great Buddhist *bodhisattva*, whose supreme concern is compassion towards mankind. The Bayon could not be a Hindu linga temple. This was the crucial moment.

It slowly became clear that the building was associated with the Khmer king Jayavarman VII. This great ruler, a devout Buddhist, had restored Khmer fortunes after a series of disastrous foreign attacks and internal conflicts. His naval victory against the Chams is recorded in reliefs on the walls of the Bayon. Not content with restoring his kingdom, Jayavarman extended it as far as Burma in the west, to the South China Sea in the east and to Vientiane in the north. He also claimed that the kings of Vietnam and Java paid him tribute.

Revealing the temple

The work of restoring the monument was not without danger in so hastily constructed a mass of stone. As it proceeded, it became clear that the building had suffered several changes of plan. A simple temple on a Greek-cross plan, perhaps located over an earlier structure which cannot be investigated, was converted into a rectangle by adding extra galleries to fill the corners. Outside this, a further gallery was then constructed and linked to the inner one by passageways. A great platform was built in the middle to support the main shrine. This was circular and had 12 radiating subsidiary chapels, unique in Khmer architecture. A succession of halls linked the centre to the main entrance on the east. The whole building was oriented to the four compass points, and lesser corridors ran to the south, west and north fronts.

The junctions in the galleries and the intersections in the central structure were crowned with towers which have faces on their visible sides, facing the compass points. There were 52 towers in all, that over the centremost shrine being 43 metres high. Under the floor of the central shrine was a deep pit from which was recovered a large seated Buddha image, broken in antiquity. This was the central image of the complex. The absence of images from the site – almost certainly the result of a reaction after the king's death – is a major problem. It means that any attempt to determine the pantheon installed in the Bayon must rely on other evidence. Fortunately, there are a number of inscriptions, mostly short and often badly, sometimes deliberately, eroded. These list, often cryptically, the images in the various shrines.

Left: The moated enclosure of Angkor Thom (top) with the Bayon (shown in detail below) at its centre. To the south-east lies the great temple of Angkor Wat, built by Suryavarman II. Immediately north-east is the Preah Khan, built by Jayavarman VII as a temple in honour of his relatives, with a large reservoir to the east. A much larger reservoir lies to the west of the enclosure and another (not shown) to the east. One duty of the Khmer king was to ensure the water supply. Inside the main enclosure, immediately north-west of the Bayon, is the Baphuon (c. 1050) and to its north the Phimeanakas (c. 1000), two earlier central temples. The royal palace was also in the north-west quadrant. Parade grounds and small ceremonial shrines lay to the east.

Right: One of the five gateways to Angkor Thom, the Great City. The entrance has a typical Khmer corbelled arch (the true arch was unknown), while the tower repeats the face motif of the Bayon. Gods and demons on either side of the approach bridge hold serpents, probably symbolizing the rainbow which links heaven and earth.

The Khmer

Above: Elevation from the north side, showing something of the Bayon's original appearance.

Left: Part of the reliefs carved on the cloisters surrounding the first level of the Bayon. These depict the king's struggle for power, his restoration of the kingdom and his victory over the Chams. This panel shows a naval battle on the Tonle Sap. The reliefs give much information on the Khmer forces, their allies and foes, dress, buildings, flora and fauna, boats, vehicles and other aspects of life.

Right: The faces carved upon the many towers of the Bayon have been an intriguing enigma for years. It now seems reasonably certain that they portray Lokeshvara samantamukha, whose compassionate gaze in all directions offers salvation to all beings. The four faces, directed at the compass points, symbolize universality. It seems likely that the face is that of Jayavarman VII, thereby asserting his claim to universal sovereignty also.

The history of a brahmin family over 250 years from around AD 800 appears on a very long inscription which also tells of the kings whom they served as royal chaplains. 'It recounts how king Jayavarman II came from Java to reign in the city of Indrapura (perhaps modern Banteay Prei Nokor) where he took Shivakaivalya as his priest. After a while, the court moved north of the Tonle Sap, the great lake in central Cambodia. Here, 100 years later, was built the great city of Angkor, the name being a corruption of the Sanskrit word 'nagara', city or capital. The court moved once again, to Hariharalaya, modern Roluos. From here they went to Mahendraparvata (Phnom Kulen), the mountain from which building stone for the countless temples around the Angkor region was brought down the Siem Reap river.

Upon this mountain, certain rituals were carried out by a specialist priest which freed the kingdom of Kambujadesa (Cambodia) from the overlordship of Java. The priest then taught the king a new cult of the 'devaraja' (God-king). Its symbol was the Shiva linga, the sacred phallus embodying the kingship, and of this cult, Shivakaivalya became the first priest.

The linga was set on a mountain, but mountains were not really very suitable as sites for a capital. The court moved back to Hariharalaya, where the idea was adopted of building at the centre of the city an artificial mountain on which the royal linga, the dynastic palladium, could be installed.

The temple-mountains

The king died in 850. In the first example of what was to become normal Khmer practice, he was given a posthumous name identifying him with the god Shiva. It is likely that his image, in the form of the god, was set up in the temple which had once housed his devaraja.

In 889 king Yashovarman came to the throne. Having reigned for a time in Hariharalaya, he then founded the city of Yashodarapura. He established a 'Central Mountain' where the royal priest – a descendant of Shivakaivalya – 'erected the sacred linga in the middle'. For many years it was thought that this recorded the founding of the great enclosure of Angkor Thom with the Bayon at its centre. However, it was demonstrated in 1927 that stylistically this identification was impossible. Instead, it was shown that the new city, probably the first at Angkor, formed a great quadrangle at the centre of which was a hill, Phnom Bakheng, with a pyramid structure on its top. Indeed, it is possible that Jayavarman did spend a brief period there, but this is still to be proved.

Barring a brief interlude (921–40), the capital was to remain at Angkor until the Khmer finally withdrew southwards under pressure from the Thais in 1431. It is interesting that during the interlude there was a return to a natural mountain, Koh Ker, north of Siem Reap. Here the king built an enormous pyramid which, with its linga, reached a height of 35 metres. During the greatest part of this 500-year period each king, unless his reign was too brief, built a central temple and set up his royal linga. The temple would serve as his memorial with his image in the form of the god to whom he had rendered personal devotion.

Khmer kings might worship any of a number of Hindu, or, occasionally, Buddhist deities. But almost always the royal palladium was the Shiva linga. Because of the constant need to initiate work which ended with each builder's death, few of the major Khmer temples were ever finished and many show signs of hasty and unsatisfactory work.

Development of the shrine

At first, the central shrine was a simple pyramid on which a single shrine housed the linga. Subsidiary shrines were added on the top platform to symbolize the five-fold peak of Sumeru, the cosmic axis. Surrounding walls and a moat represented the mountains and ocean which ring the world. Within the enclosure thus formed, other buildings were erected, including libraries for the sacred texts, and sometimes the royal palace. Such a building was of wood, for only the gods were entitled to stone.

Minor shrines were also added to the steps of the pyramid. These were joined by corbelled corridors to form cloisters, which in some cases carried narrative bas-reliefs. Sometimes there were multiple enclosures, creating a long access way to the temple proper. This pattern of building reached its epitome at Angkor Wat, the temple that is a city. This temple, which became a Buddhist shrine after its original dedication to Vishnu, was the one which created so great an impression on the first European visitors to reach the site in the mid-19th century.

Jayavarman VII's temple

The Bayon was the temple that served as Jayavarman VII's Buddhist version of the devaraja shrine (a project that none of his few Buddhist predecessors appears to have conceived) and a magic centre for his kingdom. It was a microcosm that expressed and supported his role as a 'chakravartin', a world ruler. The same claim had been made by the earlier Jayavarman when the linga was initiated on Phnom Kulen at the beginning of the 9th century.

The Bayon pantheon is arranged in three tiers over which are the towers of Lokeshvara samantamukha, Lord of the World, who looks in all directions. Jayavarman identified himself with Lokeshvara. The monument was divided into four quadrants, each subdivided into four. At ground level the 16 subdivisions were represented by rectangular chapels located between the outermost cloister and the inner. There is evidence to show that the deities were drawn from both Buddhism and Hinduism; that the subdivisions respond to a theoretical model of the Khmer kingdom; and that the layout of the images corresponded to the relative positions of the regions they represented when seen from Angkor.

It can also be shown that Hindu deities were thought of as gods of the soil, while those of Buddhist origin represented images set up by the king at various points in his empire. As his inscriptions tell us, this was an activity of which he was very proud.

On the second tier the images, often in groups, represented royal kin – ancestors (real or those claimed to enhance the king's legitimacy) – and royal chaplains with their wives, who were often princesses. The layout was again geographical. Those chosen spanned the whole of Khmer history back to the beginnings of the devaraja cult. At the third level we find esoteric royal Buddhism: the Buddha, seated on the serpent with the king before him. In the major shrines are the great gods of Hinduism. The small chapels around the centres seem to have housed images of the chief queens, and those of the gods, protectors of the concept of kingship. Other deities with such a function were also on this tier. The Sun and Moon, the summer and winter solstices, important in ritual, were also identified.

The great reliefs of the outer cloister, which tell the story of Jayarvarman's rise to power, are also arranged so that the panels face the regions where the events took place.

The first tier, then, is history; the second asserts the royal authority; the third is a unique Buddhist version of the cult of the devaraja.

Not the least of the fascinations of the Bayon are the genre scenes which are to be found among the majestic depictions of the royal reliefs. Among these pictures of everyday life in the Khmer kingdom are tumblers and jugglers, gamblers and cockfights, markets and hunters, animals and birds, including a cassowary. Perhaps it was for that world that Jayavarman, who appears on the reliefs and in four statues as a thickset, heavy-featured man with a chignon, built his many roads with their resthouses, 102 hospitals and countless shrines. For them he also built the mystical powerhouse of the Bayon, to guarantee the prosperity of Kambujadesa.

1
2
3
4
5
a
b
c
d
e
f
g
Rocky Mountains
River Colorado
Mesa Verde
Pueblo Bonito
Rio Grande
Sierra Madre
River Mississippi
River Ohio
Mound City
Newark
Hopewell
Adena
McGraw
Appalachian Mountains
Gulf of Mexico
Tajín
Tula
Teotihuacán
Mayapan
Uxmal
Chichén Itzá
Palenqué
Uaxactún
Tikal
Monte Alban
Piedras Negras
Bonampak
River Pasion
Seibal
Quiriguá
River Motagua
Copán
Caribbean Sea
River Orinoco
Andes Mountains
River Amazon
Chicama Valley
Chan Chan
Huaca del Sol
Casma Valley
Chavín de Huantar
Kotosh
PACIFIC OCEAN
Machu Picchu
Pachacámac
Huari
Cuzco
Paracas
Ayacucho
Nazca Valley
Lake Titicaca
Tiahuanaco

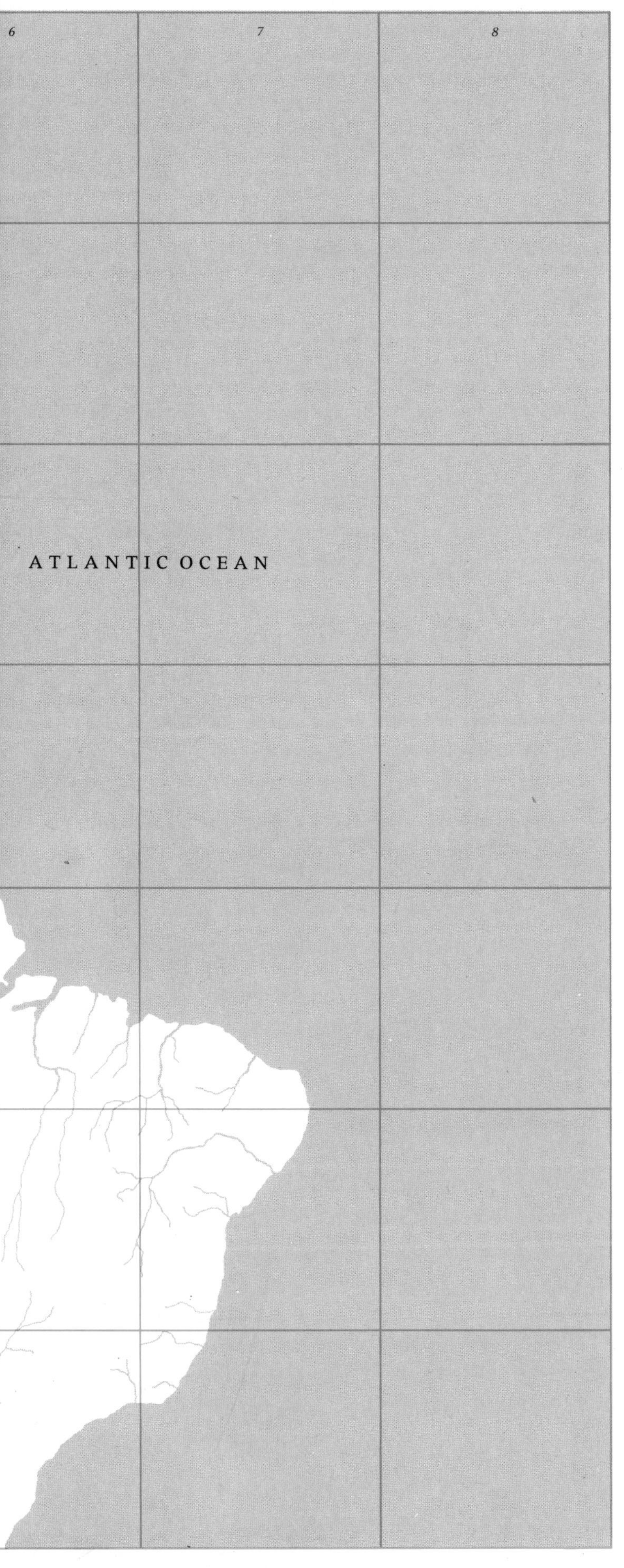

The Americas

AD 400–AD 1500

The first immigrants to the Americas reached Alaska 40,000–25,000 years ago from Siberia via the Bering Straits land bridge. They used crude flake tools to hunt woolly mammoth and giant buffalo, but left few traces. More is known of the specialized 'Big Game Hunters' who, 10,000–8,000 years ago, used spears and bows. By about 10,000 years ago, the entire continent had been populated by hunter-gatherers who faced dwindling food supplies as a result of climatic change. About 5000 BC, communities such as those in the Tehuacán valley of Mexico began to cultivate important New World crops – maize, beans, squash, chili peppers and avocados. With a few domesticated animals, these formed the subsistence economy of village life and, ultimately, the economic base of the great pre-Columbian civilizations.

Clues to early settlement come from accidental finds and from scientific excavations such as those at Fells Cave, Patagonia, and Ayacucho in Peru. Their meagre remains are usually of less interest to the non-specialist than later, better-preserved sites. The selection here aims to show the greater achievements of pre-Columbian peoples.

The high cultures of the Americas were in Central America and the Andes. In Central America the Olmecs were followed by the Maya (AD 300–900) and the empire of the great city of Teotihuacán. Next came the Toltecs, Mixtecs and Aztecs, who were destroyed by Cortés. In the eastern Andes the first great temples were built at Kotosh around 2000 BC, only to be eclipsed by the religious imperium of Chavín de Huantar from about 1000 BC onwards. For a thousand years before the Incas engulfed their territory, the Andes and Pacific coast were under the control of the rulers of Moche, Tiahuanaco, Huari and Chimor. The Inca empire fell in turn to Pizarro in 1532.

In North America the achievements of indigenous cultures were less obvious. Those such as the Hopewell had flowered long before the arrival of Europeans, who were mystified by such monumental earthworks as Adena and Mound City. Prehistoric town sites such as Pueblo Bonito, and the cliff-dwellings of Mesa Verde, remained unremarked until the 19th century, when, once again, the skill and sophistication of the underrated American Indians were revealed.

Copán
HONDURAS

Copán is the most southerly of the major Classic Maya cities of Central America. Although it occupies a fringe position in the Maya zone, it is an outstandingly beautiful and important site. Copán lies in the Motagua valley of northern Honduras, only a few kilometres from the Guatemalan border. The archaeological zone centred on Copán extends over a plain approximately 13 kilometres long and 3.2 kilometres wide, which lies at an altitude of about 600 metres. The encircling steep hills bear the remains of Maya altars and stelae, and the plain itself is covered with low mounds concealing the ruins of houses and burial mounds. The Main Group, or city centre of Copán, lies on the right bank of the Copán River. Much of the eastern part of the Acropolis has been eroded by the river, leaving a cliff-like section, 30 metres high, through the massive platform.

The city consists of four well-proportioned plazas, or courts, surrounded by stone-faced platforms and terraces which support pyramids, temples and subsidiary courts. Copán, which flourished between AD 450 and AD 800, is famous for its two stone stairways carved with long hieroglyphic inscriptions and for its unique style of stone sculpture.

Rediscovery and restoration

In 1835, Colonel Juan Galindo, an officer of the Guatemalan army, published his *Description of the Ruins of Copán*, which contained many drawings of the site and its architecture. During the 1830s he had contributed greatly to the scanty knowledge of ancient Maya sites, and was the first to identify the hieroglyphic writing at Copán and Palenque as a purely Maya achievement. His 1834 excavations at Copán were the first scientific investigations there, and it was his work that inspired John L. Stephens and Frederick Catherwood to explore the forests of the Maya heartland. During their travels in Central America, Stephens and Catherwood spent several weeks at Copán, drawing, excavating and taking notes on the ruins, which, incidentally, they bought for $50. Catherwood's illustrations, made with the help of a *camera lucida*, are exquisitely accurate and still of use to scholars. Stephens did not, however, recognize the true nature of the ruins, thinking that they were collapsed city walls. Their *Incidents of Travel in Central America, Chiapas and Yucatán*, 1839, was a classic book of archaeological discovery.

Just as Stephens and Catherwood were prompted to visit Copán after reading Galindo, so the great English archaeologist, Alfred Percival Maudslay, was led to the site by Stephens' description. Maudslay spent only three days there in 1881, but returned in 1885 with the stated aim:

> 'to gather together and publish such a collection of accurate copies of the monuments and inscriptions as would enable scholars to carry on their work of examination and comparison, and to solve some of the many problems of Maya civilization, whilst comfortably seated in their studies at home'.

Maudslay was not so mindful of his own comfort, however, as he spent a large part of the next seven years at Copán, enduring the tropical climate, insects and fevers, and coping with the technical difficulties of taking moulds and photographs. Under his direction the dense forest was cleared from the entire Main Group ruins and the first accurate map and survey were made. In 1885 he excavated Pyramid 4, a small structure but in a very important position between the Great Plaza and the Middle Court. Finds were few, but the dig produced potsherds, jade beads, sea shells and the red-painted bones of a jaguar. In the same year Maudslay discovered the 30-metre-high Hieroglyphic Stairway, which, hidden beneath a landslip, had not been seen by earlier explorers.

Major investigations were also made in Temple 22, the Temple of Meditation. Sited on the northern terrace of the Eastern Court, this large building, 28 metres long and 12.3 metres wide, was probably the main temple of the city. The tumbled main façade was discovered and proved to have been decorated with sculptures of human figures above the entrance, which itself was carved in the shape of a serpent's large-fanged open mouth. One of the most famous pieces of Maya sculpture came from Temple 22: the statue of the young Maize God.

Maudslay's critical work was superb, but he chose to publish his work at Copán as one of the five volumes in the *Biologia Centrali Americana*, with very little text, in order to allow other students to make unbiased judgements. His photographs, in particular, have proved of immense use; after an earthquake in 1934, reconstruction of Temple 22 was only possible from his illustrations.

For some of his time at Copán, Maudslay worked with a team of archaeologists from the Peabody Museum of Harvard, Massachusetts. In 1891, the museum had acquired custody of the site, with the rights and obligations to explore and restore the ruins on the understanding that one half of the finds was to be removed to the museum's collection in the United States. During the Peabody period, 1891–94, most of the important structures in the Main Group were excavated and restored.

Little work was done at Copán between 1894 and 1935, but two of the seminal works of Maya archaeology, Spinden's *A Study of Maya Art*, and Sylvanus G. Morley's *The Inscriptions at Copán*, were published in 1913 and 1920, based on evidence found at the site. On Morley's recommendation, excavations resumed in 1935 under the supervision of the Carnegie Institution of Washington. Annual expeditions led by Gustav Stromsvik and Alfred V. Kidder worked at Copán between 1935 and 1946, excepting the war years 1943–45.

Work during the first season's programme included repair of stelae damaged by the 1934 earthquake and excavation of many test pits and stratigraphic trenches. In 1936 the major engineering work of diverting the Copán River away from the eastern parts of the Acropolis was begun, and Temple 22 was repaired and restored to its present form to show the sculptured doorways and ceremonial stairways. The Hieroglyphic Stairway was restored during the following year, when a stronger dam was built to control the

Left: The late 8th-century AD *Ball Court, seen from the platform of the Acropolis. Two earlier Ball Courts are concealed beneath it. In the background is the Great Plaza.*

Right: Stela H has stood in the Great Plaza since it was erected in AD *782. It is unique at Copán in portraying a female figure. The high relief sculpture clearly shows the complexity of Maya ceremonial costume: Quetzal feather headdress, jade beads, bracelets, and girdle worn over an ocelot fur tunic decorated with jade, and tasselled sandals.*

Below: Statue of the Young Maize God carved in greenish volcanic stone. This masterpiece of Classic Maya sculpture was discovered by Maudslay in the Temple of Meditation.

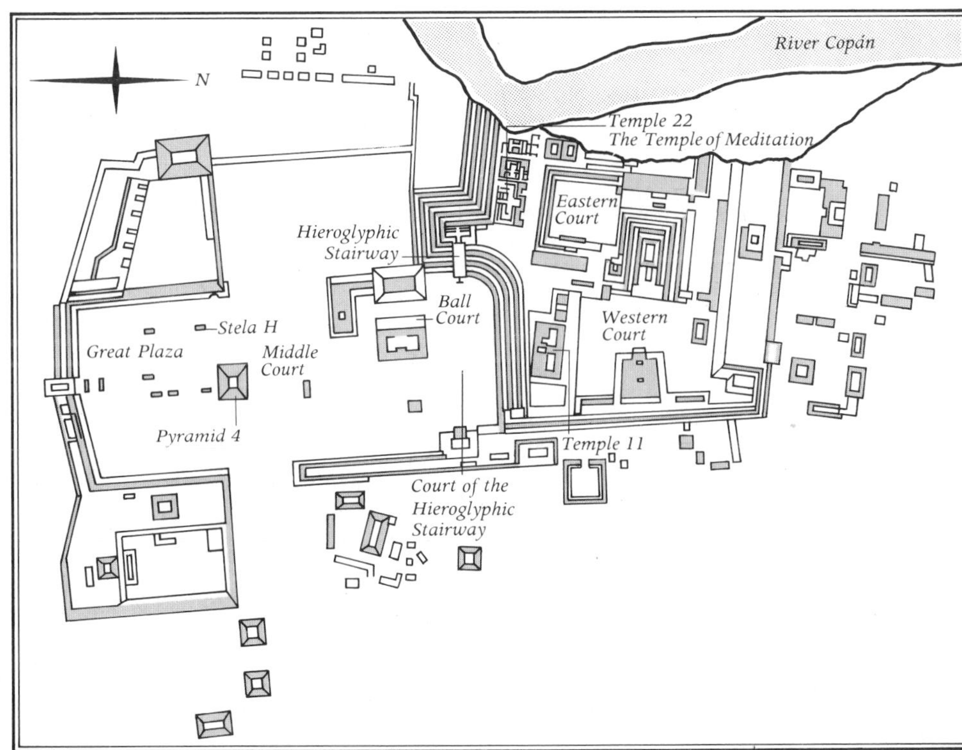

Copán River. Over the next decade the Ball Court and Temple 11 were excavated, and the Eastern and Western Courts were restored to some of their original splendour. A museum was built by the Carnegie Institution. Since 1947, Copán has been maintained by the Honduran government, which has conducted no major excavations.

Development of the city

As at many Maya sites, dated inscriptions on stelae (shaft-like stone monuments set upright in the ground) and altars aid the dating of archaeological remains. It is evident that Copán developed in three main stages, and that its location and character have changed with each phase.

The earliest stelae at Copán are Stelae 20 and 24, dated AD 465 and AD 485. These are not situated in the Main Group, but lie some distance away in the area of the present-day city of Copán. During the following two centuries, monuments were erected only in this area, known as Old Copán, which was the original administrative and religious centre occupied by an élite of warlords, priests and traders. In AD 652, six stelae were erected in different parts of the valley, and a temporary decentralization took place as people moved away from Old Copán and built smaller villages near the river. One of these, about 2.5 kilometres east of the old ceremonial centre, eventually became the Main Group.

The oldest stela in the Central Court, Stela 1, is dated AD 667, and it seems that this was the starting place for the growth of the whole complex. The Acropolis and Main Group grew while Old Copán declined. This middle, active phase ended at the beginning of the 8th century and coincided with the foundation of Quiriguá, another Maya city about 50 kilometres north of Copán. At Quiriguá, the architectural plan and sculptural style indicate very strong Middle Period Copán influence, and it seems that much energy was diverted from Copán to its new colony.

After AD 725, Copán flowered into a brilliant city. The Main Group became a magnificent ceremonial centre, the Ball Court was rebuilt and enlarged, the Hieroglyphic Stairway was constructed and stelae continued to be erected at regular intervals. During its Great Period, Copán was second only to Tikal among Maya cities, and was particularly famous for the accuracy of its astronomical observations.

The last dated inscription at Copán is 26 May AD 800. A few years after this date the city was abandoned. There is no archaeological evidence of any attack or violence, no hasty burials, lost weapons or valuables, no demolished houses or forgotten household goods. The ancient Maya seem simply to have moved away, leaving the city to the ravages of the jungle.

The Maya

The ancient Maya were fascinated by the passage of time. They developed an advanced arithmetical system and made accurate observations of the heavens which allowed them to compute astronomical events. Their science, however, cannot honestly be called astronomy. It was far more like astrology, being based on a firm belief in the cyclical nature of time and its control by supernatural forces which could be influenced by the actions of mankind.

The timing of every ritual and ceremonial act, such as sacrifice, marriage or baptism, was dictated by the Maya calendar, which was one of the most complicated ever devised. The basic unit of time was the day, and in the most commonly-used calendar, the 260-day cycle, a series of 20 day names ran consecutively with a number 1–13 as a prefix. Thus for the same combination of day name and number to occur, 260 days must elapse. The 260-day cycle is not based on any natural phenomenon; it does not tie in with solar or lunar movements and its origin still baffles Maya experts.

A 365-day cycle, similar to our solar year, ran concurrently with the 260-day cycle. The 365-day cycle was divided into 18 months of 20 days, plus five days of bad omen at the end of each year. Months were named and days were numbered 0–19. The two calendars of 260 and 365 days were intermeshed, and 52 years (18,980 days) would have to elapse before a date was repeated in both systems. This 52-year cycle is called the Calendar Round, and was of great significance to the Maya and other Central American peoples. At the end of a Calendar Round, fires were put out, pregnant women were locked up for fear they turn into wild animals, pottery was broken, all in expectation of the end of the world.

The ultimate elaboration of Central American calendrics was the Maya Long Count, which combined the 260- and 365-day cycles of the Calendar Round with calculations of lunar months and observations of the 584-day cycle of the planet Venus, believed to be a sinister influence on human affairs.

The great accuracy of Maya calculations is evident at Copán, where in AD 682, computation of the lunar year and its correlation with the solar year was improved. Astronomers at Copán, famous for its clear night skies which aided observation, calculated that a lunation averaged 29.53020 days (the actual value is 29.53059 days). Copán was probably the most advanced astronomical centre of the Maya world. Altar Q, in the western court of the Acropolis, is dated AD 776 and probably commemorates an astronomical conference held at the city. The figures of 16 important men are carved on the sides of the stone, each sitting on an emblem glyph indicating which city he was from. The delegates are all in serious discussion, probably trying to reconcile the 365-day cycle with the solar year.

Numbers, days, months and other periods of time were each under the patronage of gods, some benevolent, some malevolent, and all with differing strengths, powers and influences. The accuracy and elaboration of the calendar allowed the Maya to be quite certain which were the gods of each day and therefore which should be prayed and sacrificed to. Other gods, such as the Death God; Chac, the Rain God; the Maize God; Ix Chel, the Goddess of Medicine, and Itzamná, the chief of them all, populated the Maya pantheon and demanded worship.

Ceremonies in the temples included prayer, dancing, feasting and the burning of copal incense. Blood sacrifices were made by pulling a string threaded with aloe thorns through the tongue or ears; the blood dropped on to leaves of paper which were then burnt. Human sacrifice was unusual among the Maya; wild turkeys, dogs, quail, squirrels and iguana were more normal offerings.

Sculpture and architecture

One of the most remarkable features of Copán is its richness in superb quality stone sculp-

ture. The abundant carvings are in unusually high relief, deep cut and almost in the round, quite unlike the flat, slab-like stelae at other Maya sites. Most of the sculpture at Copán is found on stelae which, though stylized, are portraits of individuals, probably rulers of the city. The stelae stand on cruciform vaults in open courtyards and usually have an altar in front of them. They were erected at regular intervals, at the end of each Katun (19.71 years) or at each half or quarter Katun.

There are 38 stelae at Copán. All but one show the main personage, much larger than life-size and wearing stiff, dignified dress, in a full frontal view. The rulers wear elaborate headdresses of animal heads topped with sweeping quetzal feathers, ear plugs and pendants, wrist and ankle bands, wide collars and girdles and aprons. Many of the ornaments would have been made of green jade, and the skirts sometimes have spots on them, hinting that they were of jaguar skin. The hands often hold to the breast a 'ceremonial bar', a sort of sceptre with a serpent head on either end. Hieroglyphic inscriptions often cover the sides and sometimes the back of the stelae, giving dates and presumably biographical details about the person commemorated. Work still continues in an attempt to decipher the enigmatic Maya glyphs.

Portrait stelae show us the Maya ideal of beauty. The serene faces peering from a baroque tangle of carved stone have prominent noses, artificially flattened foreheads, squinting almond-shaped eyes and receding chins. The contrast between faces and clothing is echoed by the effect of the richly carved monuments against the simple and graceful architecture of Copán.

Apart from the unique Hieroglyphic Stairway, Copán does not contain the gems of Maya architecture. Tikal and Chichén Itzá are both bigger and more complex; the stucco decoration is better at Palenque. The Maya were, however, splendid architects, and at Copán they had good local stone (andesite) which was easy to work and even textured. After the early phase of the city's development, most buildings were entirely stone constructions; wood was only used for lintels, cross beams and to bind the rubble fill of the huge temple and palace platforms. Walls were decorated with stucco work, and white plaster was used as a final smooth surface on floors. Traces of red paint on walls and red and emerald green paint on stelae show that Copán must have gleamed eye-dazzlingly bright in the tropical sun.

The architects of Copán were primarily concerned with grouping their buildings to form the most magnificent effects. Earlier structures were incorporated into pyramids and platforms to form the base of higher, more impressive buildings. Exteriors of temples were decorated with sculpture: the Temple of Meditation has singing girls, skulls, human figures and serpents; the Temple of the Inscriptions is ornamented with larger than life-size humans and alligators. In contrast, the interiors of buildings were plain and neglected. The use of the corbelled vault (in which two approaching series of stone blocks each have one end deeply embedded in masonry while the other end is free and unsupported, giving the vault a stepped appearance) precluded any rooms being wider than 5 metres. Rooms were therefore dark and narrow, with simple rectangular doorways closed by curtains: the cord holders and tie holes remain carved in the walls of some structures.

Little is known about the everyday life of the inhabitants of Copán. This is mainly because archaeological work has been concentrated on the magnificent buildings of the ceremonial centre and its monuments rather than on the house mounds of more ordinary size. For many years it was thought that cities such as Copán were only visited by large numbers of people on special religious festivals, and that for the rest of the year the temples were looked after by caretaker priests. After investigations at Tikal, however, it is evident that such Maya sites were genuine cities with large, permanent populations. The fault lay with archaeologists who had been looking for concentrated, rather than dispersed, settlements surrounding the ceremonial centres.

Left: A reconstruction of the nucleus of Classic Maya Copán shows the Great Plaza in the left foreground, the Acropolis centre and right.
Below: Grotesque carved stone altars such as this depicting Ah Puch, the god of death, were paired with tall stelae commemorating dead rulers.
Right: Not all the works of art at Copán are convoluted: this jade portrait of a young Maya with an artificially flattened forehead is said to have come from Copán. It weighs nearly 2 kilos and is pierced for suspension so that it can be worn as a breast or waist ornament. The reverse is covered with undeciphered glyphs.

Chichén Itzá

MEXICO

The Maya and Toltec city of Chichén Itzá rises from the flat, dry plain of the Yucatán Peninsula about 120 kilometres south-east of Mérida, capital of the Mexican state of Yucatán. An arid landscape of tangled scrub owes its appearance to the horizontal bed of limestone on which it is based. There is almost no surface water; underground streams and rivers have honeycombed the limestone, and here and there the roofs of caverns have collapsed to reveal deep, vertically-sided holes in the ground with small lakes at the bottom. These 'cenotes' are still the principal source of water supply in the Yucatán, and it is probable that the large cenote now called the Cenote of Sacrifice attracted the Maya and Toltec settlers to the site of Chichén Itzá.

Abundant supplies of local stone were used by the ancient Maya and, to a lesser extent, by the later Toltecs, to erect many exquisite ceremonial centres in the Yucatán during the period AD 800–1180. As at most Central American sites, the spectacular temples and buildings at the centre of the settlement have been excavated and restored, making a major tourist attraction. This work has provided archaeologists with information about the techniques of monumental architecture, styles of religious and ceremonial structures and sculpture, but has left the less glamorous residential area surrounding the ceremonial centre untouched. Thus comparatively little is known about the everyday life of the inhabitants of Chichén Itzá.

The site consists of two cities, distinct in style, builders and time. The Late Classic Maya constructed 'Old Chichén', built in the *Chenes* and *Puuc* styles, where the Caracol observatory, the 'Church', the 'Nunnery', and the House of the Three Lintels still stand. This settlement was abandoned by the Maya in about AD 900. In AD 987 the Toltecs, a warlike Mexican tribe originating from near present-day Mexico City, arrived at Chichén Itzá and began to construct 'New Chichén', 1.5 kilometres north-east of the Maya centre. The Castillo (Temple of Kukulcan – the Feathered Serpent), the Temple of the Warriors, the Great Ball Court and the Temple of the Jaguars all show in their design and decoration the very close links between the Toltecs of Chichén Itzá and their city of origin, Tula. The end of Toltec rule came in AD 1180 when control of the area passed to the city of Mayapán.

Stephens and Catherwood

Unlike many sites in the Americas, Chichén Itzá was never 'lost' after the Spanish conquest. In Mexico, the missionary Bishop Diego de Landa described the ruins in his *Relación de las Cosas de Yucatán,* written in the last half of the 16th century. But it was not until 1843 that publication by John L. Stephens and Frederick Catherwood of *Incidents of Travel in the Yucatán* drew scientific interest to the site. Wrote Stephens:

'In half an hour we were among the ruins of this ancient city, with all the great buildings in full view, casting prodigious shadows over the plain, and presenting a spectacle which, even after all that we had seen, once more excited in us emotions of wonder. . . The buildings were large, and some were in good preservation; in general the façades were not so elaborately ornamented as some we had seen, seemed of an older date, and the sculpture was ruder, but the interior apartments contained decorations and devices that were new to us, and powerfully interesting. All the principal buildings were within a comparatively small compass; in fact, they were in such proximity, and the facilities for moving among them were so great, that by one o'clock we had visited every building, examined every apartment, and arranged the whole plan and order of work'.

Stephens' excellent accounts of the archaeological monuments of Central America, illustrated by Catherwood's accurate engravings, opened up the field of Maya and Mexican archaeology. Their understanding of the sites sometimes seems to have been inspired. At Chichén Itzá they quickly realized that the site was not as ancient as some they had visited, and stated that the place had been built by the ancestors of the present indigenous population – a rare piece of common sense for this period.

Further investigations

Chichén Itzá remained unexcavated until 1875, when Auguste Le Plongeon, digging in the Tomb of Chacmool, discovered a stone statue of a semi-reclining figure, the hands joined on the stomach. Le Plongeon called this type of figure 'Chacmool', although its meaning, 'Red Jaguar', has nothing to do with the subject of the sculpture. Many other Chacmools have been found at Chichén Itzá and Tula; they are one of the most characteristic features of Toltec art. The connection between Tula and Chichén Itzá was first noticed by Désiré Charnay, the earliest photographer of Maya ruins. In 1940, excavations at Tula confirmed his views.

The most exciting early project, amounting to little more than treasure hunting, was the dredging of the Cenote of Sacrifice by E. H. Thompson, American Consul in Yucatán, 1904–07. The cenote measures some 62

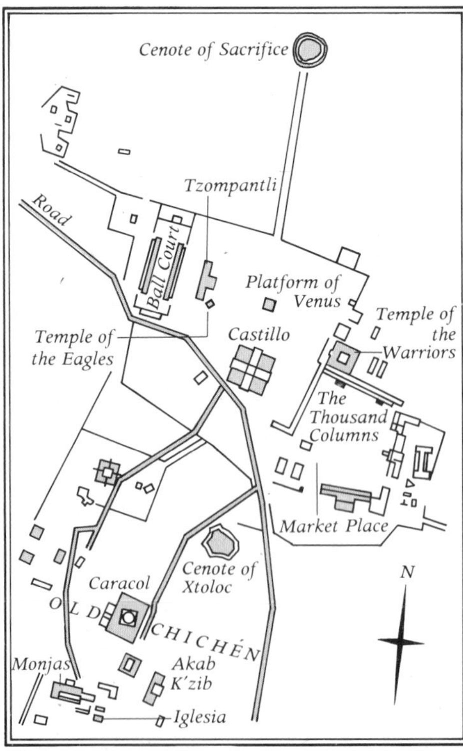

Left: Each face of the square-sectioned stone columns in front of the Temple of the Warriors is carved with reliefs of armed men in typical Toltec style.

Above: The Temple of the Warriors is built on a Toltec-style pyramid, with a steep ceremonial stairway leading from the Plaza to the summit. In front of the temple doorway is a chacmool figure flanked by feathered serpent columns. To the right of the Temple, rows of cylindrical columns border the market place.

Above: Repoussé gold disc dredged from the Cenote of Sacrifice. A Toltec chief is shown conquering his Maya enemies. Many such discs were found.

metres across and is surrounded by near-vertical cliff walls rising 20 metres high. Its waters have received offerings of gold, jade, pottery, copal incense, copper bells, statuettes, animals and human beings. In 1962, under the patronage of the National Geographic Society, a second, scientific, exploration was made. Over 4,000 objects were retrieved, among them many thin gold discs made in Panama and embossed with ritual scenes of both Maya and Toltec figures.

Below: The Cenote of Sacrifice was an important pilgrimage place in pre-Columbian America. The offerings and sacrifices it received were dredged by archaeologists.

Exploration and restoration

The most important phase in the investigation of Chichén Itzá began in 1924 when Sylvanus G. Morley and Alfred V. Kidder, for the Carnegie Institution of Washington, carried out the enormous task of exploring and rebuilding the site. Work continued for 17 years and many of the great figures in Maya archaeology, including J. E. S. Thompson, assisted. The project was significant because it laid the foundations of modern archaeological practice in Mexico. Morley's aims were:

> . . . to conduct the work in a manner calculated to create a feeling of confidence by the Mexican government and people in the good faith of foreign scientific agencies; to handle the site in such a way as to make it a permanent record of the artistic achievement of the Maya; and to develop Chichén Itzá as a focal point for correlated researches'.

Morley's and Kidder's programme at Chichén spans the gap between the older style of archaeology and the wider-ranging 'New' archaeology. It began as part of an epigraphic study of Maya hieroglyphs and developed into a multi-disciplinary research project in which geographical, ecological, racial, medical and linguistic topics were investigated to give an holistic view of the site in its setting.

Arrival of the Toltecs

In the third quarter of the 10th century AD, Topíltzin Quetzalcoatl, founder of the Toltec capital, Tula, and devotee of the Feathered Serpent god, Quetzalcoatl, was expelled from his city by the hostile followers of the god Tezcatlipoca, Smoking Mirror. Topíltzin and his supporters left Hidalgo and sailed away, promising to return one day. It was this legend that was remembered at the court of Montezuma when the Spanish adventurer Hernán Cortés arrived in Mexico more than five centuries later. Maya legends tell of the arrival in Yucatán in AD 987 of a foreign warlord called Kukulcan with a host known as the Itzá, and it is certain that Quetzalcoatl and Kukulcan, whose names both mean 'Feathered Serpent', were one person.

Scenes of the conquest of Chichén Itzá by the Mexican invaders are shown on painted and carved reliefs found during excavations inside the Temple of the Warriors. The Toltecs were famous warriors, organized into two military orders: the Eagles and the Jaguars. Details of their military equipment can be clearly seen on the low-relief carvings which decorate every side of the 60 rectangular columns surrounding the Temple of the Warriors. Ornate, almost uniform parade costumes of ankle-tied sandals, kilts, breastplates, leather belts and shields are completed by nose bars and huge headdresses of turquoise, quetzal feathers and serpents. Each warrior carries a javelin and 'atlatl' (spear thrower) in his right hand. This style of dress, decorated with motifs of butterflies, eagles and jaguars clutching hearts, and monsters symbolizing Quetzalcoatl in his guise of the Morning Star, are all closely paralleled at Tula. Other Toltec elements found at Chichén Itzá include Chacmools, feathered-serpent columns such as those flanking the entrances to the Temple of the Warriors and the Castillo, and long colonnaded courts such as the Thousand Columns, which probably formed part of the marketplace of the city. It is interesting that Maya motifs such as carvings of long-nosed rain gods (Chacs) were adopted by the Toltecs and incorporated into their iconography.

Human sacrifice

A creation myth told the Toltecs that the world had been lit by four previous suns which had been destroyed in turn by jaguars, fire, wind and water. Each time all life on Earth was extinguished. In order to create the present Sun, Quetzalcoatl, the great god, sacrificed himself and gave his heart and blood for the world. He could not ensure that this fifth creation would not also be obliterated, but the catastrophic earthquake signalling its end could be delayed by sacrificing human hearts and blood to the gods. One of the principal features of militaristic Toltec society became large-scale human sacrifice. Although Topíltzin, the founder of Chichén, was ousted from Tula because he objected to the waste of human life in sacrifices, it is clear that human sacrifice was practised at Chichén Itzá. His plan to substitute the sacrifice of butterflies, snakes and jades for that of people was never a success.

Sacrifices to Quetzalcoatl, to Tezcatlipoca, the god of the Night and the North, and Xipe, the Flayed One, were carried out with the maximum pomp and ceremony. Human sacrifice was believed to be to the good and the glory of the people, its victims usually slaves or prisoners taken in battle. At the top of the Temple stairway, four assistants held the arms and legs of the victim as he arched his back over a stone cone. The chest was thus presented to the priest, who cut a long incision beneath the victim's ribs with a flaked flint knife. He then tore out the still-beating heart and offered it to the gods. It is probable that the dished or plate-like areas on the stomachs of Chacmools were made to receive these offerings. The head was then cut from the body and taken to a small platform in the Plaza known as 'Tzompantli' (skull rack). At Chichén the Tzompantli measures 51 metres long and 15 metres wide and is situated near the Castillo. It is covered with a relief of human skulls and once supported a wooden fence on which the heads of sacrificial victims were impaled. The Tzompantli

Left: A relief on the eastern side of the Sacred Ball Court depicts the final stage of a ball game. The victorious captain (standing, left) holds in his hand the head of the rival team's leader. The loser's decapitated body (right) spurts blood in snake-headed gushes from the neck. Between them is the large ball, decorated with a skull, symbol of death.

Left: Chichén Itzá reconstructed, seen from a point near the Cenote of Sacrifice along the Causeway to the Castillo. On the left is the Temple of the Warriors.

Below: Reclining Chacmool figures received the hearts of sacrificial victims in the dish-like hollows of their stomachs.

was all too literally a 'head count' or tally of offerings to the gods. After decapitation, the victim's body was cut into pieces and thrown down the Temple steps to the surrounding crowd. It has been suggested that this continuous need for sacrificial victims was an important cause of the Toltecs' (and later the Aztecs') bellicosity. By the time of Cortés, human flesh may well have formed an important part of the diet of urban Mexicans.

The Ball Game

Most Maya and Toltec cities contain a Ball Court, and that at Chichén Itzá is the largest and most impressive in Central America. Although it would superficially appear to be a type of sporting activity, the Ball Game was in fact a form of religious ceremony.

The game was played by two opposing teams consisting of from one to seven players. It took place between two parallel stone walls, sloping in Maya Ball Courts, vertical in Toltec examples. Although we are not certain of the rules of the game, we do know that a solid rubber ball was passed from player to player, that it must not touch the ground, and that it could be hit only with certain parts of the body: the hips, elbows and thighs. Team members, shown on painted vases, friezes and on Ball Court markers, wore a gauntlet on the right hand, a pad on the right knee and a shoe on the right foot. These seem to have been protective padding to cushion the player against falls on the stone playing surface. The highest score, which instantly won the game, was gained by putting the ball through one of the two vertical stone rings set high in the centre of each playing wall. Whichever team scored this remarkable goal won not only the game but also the clothing and jewellery of all the spectators.

At Chichén Itzá, the I-shaped playing field measures 128 metres long and is bounded by walls 8 metres high and 61 metres apart. Two small temples look down the length of the playing area, one at the northern end, the other at the southern. Above the eastern wall of the Ball Court rises the Temple of the Jaguars. These three temples must have afforded fine grandstand views of the game.

Below each of the vertical playing walls of the Ball Court is a low, inclined wall decorated with low relief carvings. The same scene is repeated three times on each side of the court. Opposing teams of Maya and Toltecs face each other on either side of a large disc decorated with a skull, representing a ball. The leader of the left-hand, Toltec, team holds a sacrificial flint knife in his left hand. In his right hand is the head of the leader of the Maya team. On the right side of the ball is the kneeling, decapitated body, blood gushing from its neck being represented by seven snakes. It is quite possible that the game was played 'for keeps', and that the entire losing team was sacrificed and their heads put on the Tzompantli. On the other hand, less important matches could have been played as a form of divination, or as a re-enactment of a myth, or perhaps as a symbol of the daily passage of the Sun across the sky.

Tiahuanaco
BOLIVIA

Above: Conventionalized human faces carved on stone tenons were inserted in walls to break their monotony.

Left: The restored walls of the sunken inner courtyard of the Kalasasaya are built in typical Tiahuanaco-style long-and-short work. Many of the monumental structures have been resited to give theatrical effects rather than a true picture of the site in antiquity. Here the Bennett monolith (shown opposite) has been dramatically positioned inside a stone gateway at the top of a flight of megalithic steps. Other statues have been erected inside the courtyard.

The ruins of Tiahuanaco are 21 kilometres from the southern end of Lake Titicaca, high in the bleak Bolivian Andes. The standing monuments comprise four main structures: the Kalasasaya compound, the Gateway of the Sun, the Akapana pyramid and the East or Underground Temple. These cover an area measuring about a kilometre by half a kilometre. The site is famous for its monolithic gateways, megalithic steps and large stone sculptures carved in red sandstone and andesite. Tiahuanaco sculpture has a very distinctive, rigid style which was applied to monolithic standing figures, kneeling animal figures, seated figures and tenons ornamented with heads which were inserted into walls.

A wide spread of archaeological debris extends for 2.5–3 square kilometres around the central structures, indicating that Tiahuanaco may have been a populous city as well as an important pilgrimage place. Tiahuanaco was certainly the paramount ceremonial centre in the Andes during the period AD 300–700. It lies at an altitude of 3,660 metres in the cold altiplano between the mountain ranges of the Kisma-Chatta to the south and the Achuta to the north. The location of the city is important, as it controls passage from the lake basin into the altiplano. The city could therefore monitor the transit of goods between different environmental zones. Tiahuanaco's orbit of influence, shown by the widely disseminated Tiahuanacoid iconography and styles of ceramic, metal, stone and textile decoration, spread throughout southern Bolivia, the south coast of Peru, the Atacama area of the southern Andes and even as far as north-west Argentina. It was not an empire of military conquest, as was the later Inca empire, but seems to have been based on trade and religion.

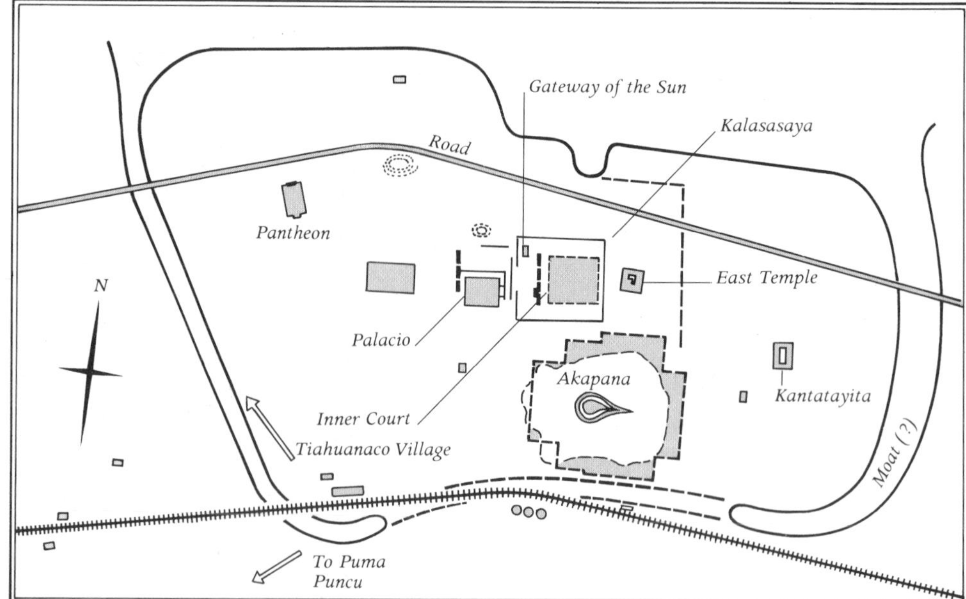

Early work at Tiahuanaco

The exact nature, layout and function of Tiahuanaco are still unknown, although excavations and research by Bolivian archaeologists over the past 20 or so years have clarified the picture and corrected many misconceptions about the site. Unfortunately, the reports are not easily obtainable and Tiahuanaco remains the most enigmatic archaeological site in the Andes.

The earliest reference to Tiahuanaco is found in the works of Cieza de León, a Spanish chronicler who travelled through the former Inca empire shortly after the Conquest. He visited the ruins of Tiahuanaco before 1550, and wrote down the creation myths of the local Aymara Indians. These described how the god Ticci Viracocha, 'Maker of all things created and Prince of all things, Father of the Sun', came to them and had temples built for him. Cieza de León was informed that the great monolithic statues at Tiahuanaco were made during this early period and that the site was already in ruins when the Incas arrived in the 15th century.

It is probable that the central figure on the Gateway of the Sun is Ticci Viracocha, but apart from his name we know nothing about the religious beliefs and practices of his cult.

The site must have been visited many times by local people and treasure hunters before the first professional archaeologists arrived there in 1877. Many shaped stones, including sculptures, had been incorporated into the fabric of the village church, and the summit of the pyramid-like Akapana was transformed into a small lake by the zealous activities of tomb robbers. In the late 19th century, European scholars played a critical role in the development of South American archaeology. Alphons Stübel, who with Wilhelm Reiss, his colleague from Dresden, had excavated the cemetery at Ancón on the Peruvian coast, stayed in Peru to study and photograph the famous ruins at Tiahuanaco in 1877. He returned to Germany where a young philologist, Max Uhle, helped him to organize his research into the first book about the site, *Die Ruinenstaette von Tiahuanaco*, published in 1892.

During the years of preparation, Uhle assimilated a vast amount of knowledge about Inca and Tiahuanaco pottery and art styles. This enabled him to make important judgements about Peruvian chronology, based on ceramic and stratigraphic evidence from his first field work at Pachacámac on the Peruvian coast. Between 1892 and 1912, Uhle devised a four-period chronological scheme for the whole of Peru. His pioneer work, which has only been slightly modified into today's system of 'Horizon Styles', earned him the title of 'Father of Peruvian archaeology'.

Two non-scientific archaeologists excavated at Tiahuanaco in the 1900s. Georges Courty directed a largely destructive three-month-long dig in 1903. He unearthed many previously unseen features, such as the monolithic stairway, the small eastern temple, the 'cloaca maxima' of the Akapana and the Palacio. As Stübel's work had consisted of detailed descriptions, measurements and illustrations of only those structures already visible in 1877, Courty's investigations could have greatly enlarged our knowledge of the site. Unfortunately, he published only a brief summary of his work. Thirty years of research on Tiahuanaco (1900–1930) culminated in the publication of Arthur Posnansky's beautifully-produced but fancifully-written work *Eine Praehistorische Metropole in Sudamerika*. In this he claimed, for example, that Tiahuanaco was immensely ancient and that it was the place of origin of all American and probably all world civilizations.

Until 1932, all factual knowledge about Tiahuanaco was encapsulated in the maps and plans of Stübel, Uhle and Posnansky. The most serious gap in the archaeology of the site was the lack of a pottery sequence from stratigraphic excavations. However, Tiahuanaco pottery could be linked with coastal Peruvian pottery styles which already had an established chronology, and so the site could at last be dated.

Above: Monolithic figure (7.3 metres tall) excavated by Wendell C. Bennett in 1932.

Statues from Pit VII

In June–July 1932, Wendell C. Bennett, a young American student, carried out 10 test excavations at Tiahuanaco. Each trench measured 3 metres by 3.3 metres, and they were situated inside the Kalasasaya, inside the East Temple and Puma Puncu, and in areas outside the ruins. The most spectacular find was made in Pit VII, dug into the East Temple (Underground Temple), which is a 21-metre by 22-metre semi-subterranean structure about 1.8 metres below the base of the monolithic stairway. Only 50 centimetres below the surface of the northern interior of the temple, Bennett uncovered the head of a monolithic figure lying on its back. He extended the trench and revealed a statue, 7.3 metres long, carved from a single block of red sandstone. It was of the finest quality Classic Tiahuanaco workmanship, having features, arms, legs and feet modelled in the round but with no attempt at realism which would destroy the overall columnar effect. Delicate designs were incised on the headband, chest and waist, representing multicoloured patterned textiles. East of the feet of the monolith, and parallel to it, lay a second statue, 2.5 metres long and also of red sandstone. Much cruder in technique, it is of later date than the larger statue. A circular blue stone was found at the feet of the monolith, beneath which was buried a carved stone head and some lapis lazuli beads.

As the two statues from Pit VII are so closely aligned, it is reasonable to assume that they were pushed over or fell simultaneously. From the mixture of Classic and Late styles, it seems probable that the East Temple was built late in the development of Tiahuanaco, and that the statues and stonework were brought from other parts of the ceremonial centre to be erected in the new building. Bennett appreciated that one of the greatest problems in unravelling the archaeology of Tiahuanaco was its long history, during which monuments were dismantled and moved, perhaps several times, or cannibalized and incorporated into new structures.

In the late 1950s, the Bolivian government established the Centro de Investigaciones Arqueológicos en Tiahuanaco (CIAT). During excavations directed by Ponce Sanginés, tens of thousands of cubic metres of soil have been moved. Sanginés and his team, using modern excavation techniques and aided by radiocarbon dating, have revolutionized our understanding of the site. It is on his work that this description of Tiahuanaco is based.

City of Pilgrimage

The earliest radiocarbon date from Tiahuanaco indicates that there was a pre-ceramic occupation of the site about 1500 BC. By 500 BC, the inhabitants of pre-Classic Tiahuanaco used painted pottery and placed silver, gold, and sodalite beads in burials. The first major structure to be built was the Kalasasaya enclosure, erected in the period defined by Ponce Sanginés as Phase III. Tiahuanaco IV is the Classic period, when the city was enhanced and perfected and the arts of statuary and ceramics reached their heights. Radiocarbon dates show that Tiahuanaco IV lasted for approximately 400 years, from AD 300–700. Sanginés suggests that during this phase, Tiahuanaco was a great city covering 420 hectares and with a population of 40,000–100,000. Excavations of outlying, presumably residential, areas have yet to confirm this opinion.

The central zone of the city is organized along east-west and north-south axes, and buildings are arranged with consideration for bilateral symmetry. None of the major buildings correspond to these axes, however, so it seems likely that the avenues were laid out after the major monuments were built, in an attempt to organize the city centre. The Akapana stepped pyramid was in the centre of the city; the Kalasasaya in the north-east; and the Puma Puncu, another great temple, in the south-west. In the southern part of the site were many small pyramids, while palaces lay to the east and west of the Akapana. Cemeteries and the dwellings of ordinary people were located on the city's outskirts.

Construction techniques at Tiahuanaco are the equal of those of the late Chimú and Inca builders in Peru. Red sandstone was the most commonly used building stone, followed by andesite which had to be transported from the shore of Lake Titicaca. The stone was shaped and dressed with great accuracy, and fitted together with notches and joints in a manner reminiscent of wood construction techniques. Copper clamps were used as tie-bolts. One block of red sandstone in the platform of the Puma Puncu weighs 131 tonnes. Ponce Sanginés estimated that 2,620 people would have been needed to move it (20 persons to each tonne) and that they hauled it 10 kilometres over specially laid wet clay, using twined skin or hide ropes. The block is held in place by H-shaped copper clamps weighing a total of 15 kilograms. They were formed by pouring molten copper, which was then allowed to cool, into grooves carved in contiguous blocks. In some buildings, adobe, or sun-dried bricks, were used. Architectural elements were coloured with white, grey, red and green paint. Structures were probably roofed with large, flat slabs of stone supported by square stone columns when rooms were too big to be covered by single slabs. Corbelled vaulting was also probably used.

The monuments

Contrary to earlier opinion, the Akapana is a totally man-made monument, not a modified natural hill. At the base it measures 210 metres square, and rises 15 metres above ground level. The earthen interior was shaped to form a stepped pyramid and faced with fitted stone blocks. A wide stairway led to a great square temple on the summit. During the colonial period, treasure hunters dug a big hole in the top of the Akapana, which filled with water and was believed by earlier investigators of the site to be a reservoir. The excavations of Ponce Sanginés show that the foundations of the temple extend from one side of the 'reservoir' to the other.

The Kalasasaya was originally a large rectangular raised earthen platform, 126.2 metres long and 117.5 metres wide, faced with a dressed stone wall. Over the centuries the earthen core eroded away leaving rows of free standing stones surrounding an empty enclosure. After excavation by the CIAT team, the monument has been restored to its original state and is now about 3 metres high. On the eastern side of the Kalasasaya, near where the Puerta del Sol now stands, is a grand flight of six megalithic steps, leading to a central patio within the platform and occupying about one third of its area. One of the most fascinating discoveries at Tiahuanaco was made in the remains of a palace called the Kantatayita, east of the Akapana. Here a monolithic maquette, or designer's model, of the Kalasasaya was found, comparable with later Inca architects' plans made in stone or clay.

The best known monument at Tiahuanaco is the Gateway of the Sun, which now stands inside the Kalasasaya. Its original position is not known. The monolithic gateway probably formed the entrance to the sanctuary of a temple; the doorway is very small. The upper part of the structure bears a series of distinctive relief carvings, and the central figure above the doorway is an anthropomorphic being, probably a god. It faces forward and has a rectangular head and face with a jaguar mouth and serpent ray headdress. In each hand is a staff or sceptre. The central figure is flanked by four rows of smaller running winged figures holding staves. They wear masks and flowing capes. Traces of red indicate that the stonework was originally painted. Recent research has confirmed the idea first proposed by Posnansky that the figures on the gateway have a calendrical significance. The CIAT team suggests that they represent 12 months, each

Above: Classic Tiahuanaco pottery kero, or beaker, with a modelled jaguar head and painted polychrome motifs. The 'divided eye', half black, half white, of the painted animal is a feature of Tiahuanaco iconography.

with 30 days, divided into 36 weeks of 10 days.

A few metres west of the Kalasasaya lies the Temple of the Sarcophagi, in fact a square palace with many rooms opening from a central patio and entered by a small stairway on the eastern side. Nearby, in a group of four small pyramids, is the Gateway of the Moon, a second monolithic doorway. South-west of the Akapana is the Puma Puncu, a large pyramid about half the height of the Akapana and also damaged by treasure hunters. It was originally surrounded by a dressed stone retaining wall. To the eastern side of the Puma Puncu is a terrace made of the largest worked stones used in pre-Columbian America. They appear to have first formed the main wall of a large temple, and fell in one piece. Beneath these huge stones, Ponce Sanginés discovered the broken remains of three monolithic gateways, similar to the Gateway of the Sun but without decoration.

Economy and society

From environmental evidence it seems that there have been no significant climatic changes in the Tiahuanaco area since its period of greatness. It has always been a cold, bleak, wet area, suitable for the cultivation of oca, quinoa and potatoes, and the herding of llamas and alpacas. The low fertility of the soil was always considered a strong argument against Tiahuanaco ever having been a city rather than a pilgrimage centre; the area simply could not feed a high population. But the discovery of 8,000 hectares of irrigated agricultural plots near the shores of Lake Titi-

Above: The Gateway of the Sun, constructed about AD *600, is the most famous monument at Tiahuanaco. It stands 3 metres high and is decorated with low relief carvings which are dominated by a standing figure holding two staves. This is thought to be Viracocha, the creator god.*

Left: Statues at Tiahuanaco wear intricately detailed patterned costumes. Although no textiles have survived in the Highlands, examples such as this exquisite embroidery from Paracas on the Pacific Coast have been found.

caca, and of a network of raised earth ridges several metres wide and 100 metres or more long prepared for intensive agriculture, tells us that the ancient productivity of the area was far greater than today's.

The competent organization of labour required to build the huge structures at Tiahuanaco indicates that the society was hierarchical, with an élite class to plan the construction of major monuments. The artistic skill displayed by the masons, potters, metal workers and weavers indicates craft specialization. These economic factors, combined with details of the extent of settlement at Tiahuanaco, can only be interpreted as proof that Tiahuanaco was a city with a developed urban society, even though nothing is known about its political, administrative and commercial facets.

The harsh climate has destroyed all traces of organic materials at the site, leaving only pottery, stone and metal artefacts for the archaeologist. The pottery is very attractive: flaring-sided goblets, ring-based libation bowls, modelled puma and llama vessels and open bowls were hand-made without the use of a potter's wheel. They were well fired and highly polished. Many vessels were *red-slipped* and painted with polychrome designs of geometric steps, steps and scrolls, and conventionalized puma, condor and human figures or heads. The designs were usually outlined in black or white paint and filled in with tones of yellow, grey and brown. Some pots bore decoration in eight colours.

No textiles or cloth are preserved in the rainy altiplano, but from indirect evidence it is certain that weaving was a highly developed craft at Tiahuanaco. Brightly coloured figures on the ceramics and anthropomorphic figures on carved stone monoliths and reliefs are shown wearing intricately patterned garments. Indeed, Tiahuanaco must have been a colourful place when the buildings were painted and the populace wore multi-coloured clothing. Many textiles have, however, been preserved in the dry, sandy soil of the desert coast of southern Peru. Although far from Tiahuanaco, some of these show definite inspiration from the Bolivian highland city. Similarly, the pottery shows Tiahuanaco influence, although the designs and forms have been slightly modified. Uhle first noted this long-distance connection, which is identified as Coastal Tiahuanaco. Gold, silver and copper were used by the people of Tiahuanaco to make ornaments and small tools. Axes and disc-shaped pectoral ornaments or mirrors were made of copper. Gold and silver were hammered into sheet, decorated with repoussé and incised designs and made into plaques, cups, masks and cut-out shapes to be sewn on to textiles. Stone bowls, vases, pounders, axes, arrow heads and snuff tablets have been found. Narcotic snuff was sniffed from the tablets through bone tubes, which have been found in large numbers. The use of hallucinogenic snuff as part of religious ritual is well known throughout the Andes.

Tiahuanaco and Huari

The rise of Tiahuanaco and the extent of its influence in South American culture must have been due to a complex pattern of trade, religious conversion and military expansionism. Ponce Sanginés believes that Tiahuanaco was a city state with subject colonies, but others consider its influence to have been more subtle and intrusive, probably based on the propagation of a religious faith. During the 6th century AD, missionaries from Tiahuanaco reached Huari, a town in the south-central highlands of Peru. They introduced new ideas and a new iconography which were quickly accepted and adapted by the people of Huari. They produced a distinctive, derivative art style using themes familiar from Tiahuanaco, such as running winged figures carrying staves. Huari itself rose to control a great empire extending from the Urubamba Basin to the Middle Marañon, and on the coast from Ocoña to Chicama. By about AD 900, the Huari empire was in decline and the capital city abandoned.

Mesa Verde

USA

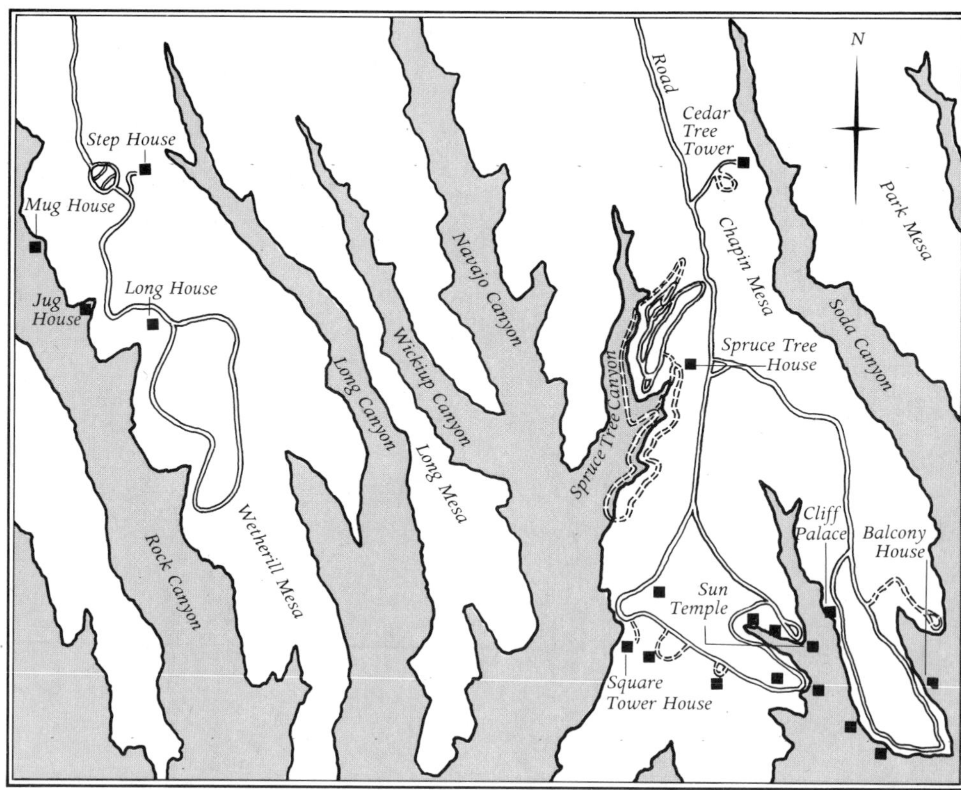

Perhaps the best-known and most intensively researched archaeological area in the United States is a large south-sloping sandstone plateau called Mesa Verde. It lies in the Four Corners area, where the state boundaries of Utah, Colorado, Arizona and New Mexico meet. The Mancos River has cut a 300-metre-deep canyon along the east and south sides of the plateau, which has been further dissected by about 15 steep-sided, almost parallel, canyons. Long finger-like projections of land between the canyons have been named Wetherill Mesa, Long Mesa, Chapin Mesa and Park Mesa, and were settled and cultivated by the Anasazi Indians between AD 350–1300.

The most remarkable features of Mesa Verde are its cliff-dwellings: villages of stone, mud mortar and wood. Some have multi-storeyed buildings and semi-subterranean circular 'kivas', constructed in natural caves or rock shelters in the near vertical sandstone walls of the canyons.

The first surveys

In 1874–75, Mesa Verde was explored and mapped for the United States Geological and Geographical Survey of the newly-settled Territory. It was not until 1888, however, that major ruins were discovered in the area when the Wetherill brothers, who were local cattle ranchers, found the Cliff Palace and Spruce Tree House. The Wetherills explored and excavated the cliff-dwellings, selling their finds to the Historical Society of Colorado. The sites were full of archaeological finds. 'It appeared as though the people had been frightened away with no opportunity to carry anything with them. All seemed to have been left just where it had been used last', said one of the first explorers.

The first scientific study of Mesa Verde was made by Gustav Nordenskiöld, who spent the summer of 1891 excavating and mapping cliff-dwellings and 'mesa'-top sites. This 23-year-old Norwegian, helped by John Wetherill, dug at the Cliff Palace, Long House, Mug House, Step House, Spruce Tree House and Balcony House, and then went on a two-week exploration of the whole of Mesa Verde. He took over 150 photographs which were published alongside detailed maps and plans in 1893, in what was the first scholarly work on the archaeology of the area.

Nordenskiöld's description of the ruins and their contents remains one of the best:

> 'Throughout the entire length of Mancos Cañon and in all its subdivisions, fortress-like buildings have been erected of hewn blocks of sandstone on narrow ledges, often high up the cliffs on inaccessible situations. These structures, in consequence of their position under a sheltering vault of rock, are very well preserved, though they have been abandoned by their inhabitants for several centuries. . . . Among the fine, dry dust or the fallen blocks of sandstone that have filled the rooms, we find still in a wonderful state of preservation the household articles and implements once used by the inhabitants of the cliff-dwellings. Even wooden articles, textile fabrics, bone implements and the like are well preserved although they have probably lain in the earth for more than five centuries'.

Nordenskiöld also observed that the cliff-dwellings were contemporary with the ruins on the mesa-top. In fact the two types of site complement each other and composed an economic unit. The apparent eclipse of a 'higher' culture by a 'lower' one, that is, the disappearance of settled village life to be replaced by a nomadic one, intrigued Nordenskiöld as it ran contrary to the theory of social evolution then current. Evidence from excavations carried out during the past 30 years shows that the cliff-dwellings were abandoned after severe climatic changes which made agriculture impractical.

In 1906, 106 square kilometres of Mesa Verde were declared a National Park in order to protect the ruins and ensure that research was carried out only by properly qualified bodies. The archaeologist appointed to the National Park was J. W. Fewkes, who excavated Spruce Tree House, discovering about 130 rooms and eight kivas; Cliff Palace, containing about 200 rooms and 23 kivas; Balcony House, with about 25 rooms; and the Sun Temple. Fewkes' technique was to clear the ruins of loose stones, dirt and debris, to repair dangerous walls and carry out restoration work as seemed necessary for the preservation of the buildings. Numerous finds made during his operations were sent to the National Museum in Washington. During 1906–16, the sites were protected from, and restored for, tourists.

Recent excavations

Mug House and eight other sites were excavated by Jesse L. Nusbaum in 1928, and tree-ring samples for *dendrochronological dating* were collected in 1932. However, little work was done apart from conservation until 1959, when the National Parks Service and the National Geographic Society began an intensive field study of Wetherill Mesa.

It was decided to develop Wetherill Mesa for more tourists to visit the cliff-dwellings as those of Chapin Mesa, particularly the Cliff Palace, were becoming too crowded and damaged. A major five-year project was initiated with the final aim of excavating, stabilizing and preparing for exhibition three major cliff-dwellings and six or more mesa-top features of various periods. Many experts were involved in the project, under the direction of O. D. Osborn. They included

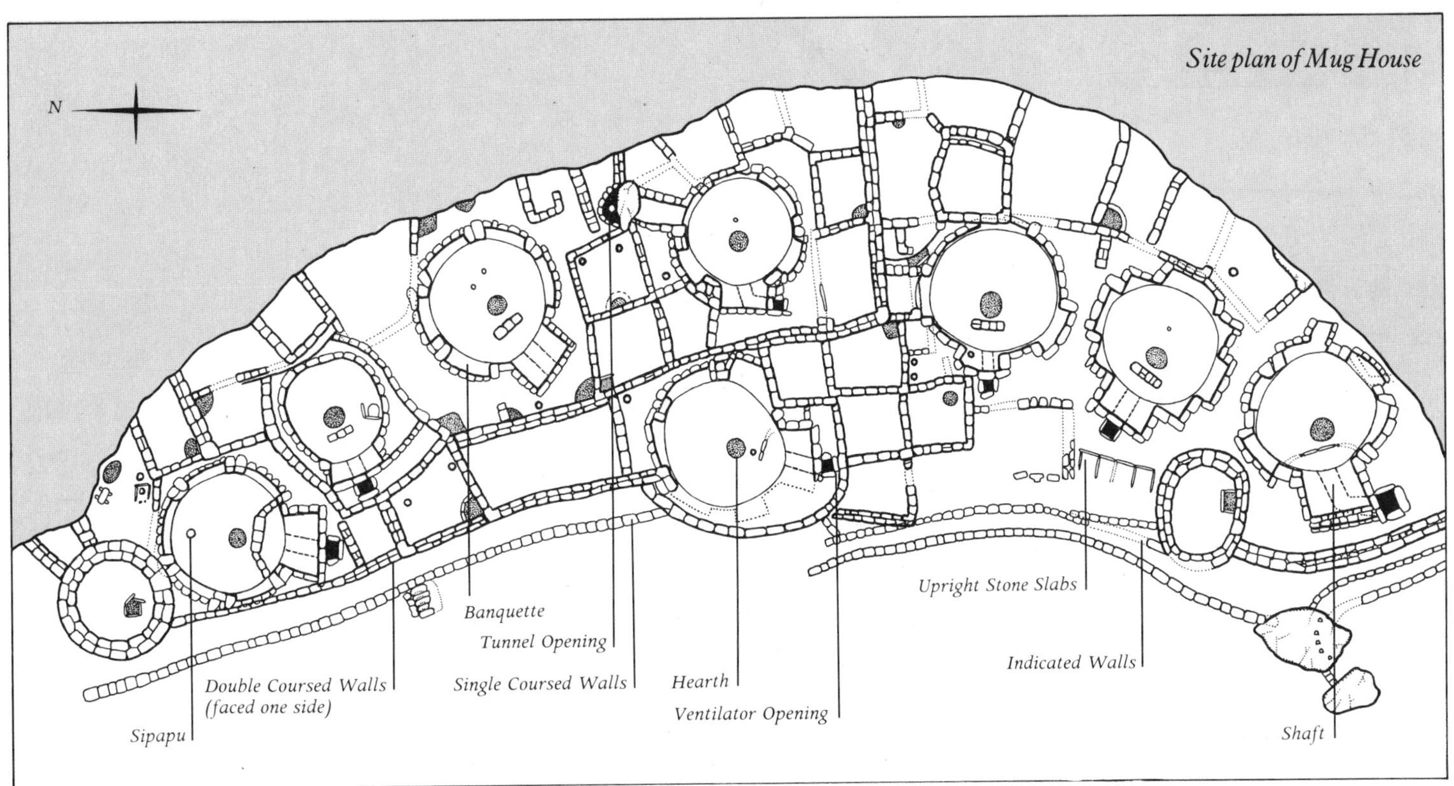

Below: At Mug House, 46 burials were found, most in the midden in front of the cave. Few had grave goods, but these offerings accompanied burial M6. They include typical Mesa Verde black-on-white painted ceramics (a mug and two bowls), and a corrugated jar. The smaller bowl contained 16 stone objects; arrow points, petrified wood, haematite, paintstones, pebbles and a red shale pendant. These may have been part of a medicine man's kit.

specialists in geology, geomorphology, soil science, archaeological excavation techniques, pollen analysis, animal bones, hair and hides, entomology, tree-ring dating and feathers. The results published by this expert team are among the most exhaustive and informative in the literature of south-western archaeology, and allow a near-total reconstruction of life in Anasazi cliff *pueblos*.

Chronology and human settlement

There is some evidence of human occupation at Mesa Verde between 100 BC–AD 400 (Basketmaker II), but population of the area really began at about AD 600 (Basketmaker III) when pit house villages of six to 12 dwellings were built on the tops of mesas. The houses were normally sub-circular, about a metre deep, with four roof supports and internal benches. Gradually, house-building styles changed and by AD 1000, all living accommodation was constructed above ground. At first, 'jacal' (poles lined with reeds and branches coated with mud) was used, then mud mortar with some stone, and finally the typical Mesa Verde style of dressed stone blocks. Only kivas continued to be built in the semi-subterranean tradition. These ceremonial chambers, dug into the ground to represent man's emergence from the underworld to the surface of the Earth, were used by men for purification and initiation rites. By AD 1100, multi-storey blocks of rooms were associated with kivas and hydraulic engineering works such as irrigation ditches, water storage tanks, terraces, field boundaries and check dams were constructed to aid the cultivation of maize, beans and squash.

The large cliff-dwellings and mesa-top villages for which Mesa Verde is best known were built and occupied mainly between AD 1200–1300, when the population of the area was far higher than even today. During the Pueblo III period, hunting and gathering continued to play an important part in the economy of the ancient Anasazi, who relied on seasonal gluts of wild food in the varied ecological zones surrounding them. A decline in food resources resulting from long droughts, increasing aridity and a fall in the water table recorded in the tree rings for AD 1276–99, combined with a rising population, has been suggested as the prime reason for the abandonment of the area in about AD 1300. Other possible causes might have been disease, caused by the insanitary living conditions in the damp, dark cliff-dwellings; inter-puebloan warfare; or attacks by the hunting and gathering Athapascan peoples who eventually replaced them.

The Cliff Dwellers

Mug House, so called because in their 1890 visit the Wetherills found four or five mugs tied together with a string through their handles, is one of the best preserved and excavated of the cliff-dwellings, and an excellent example of the later type of site found all over Mesa Verde. It lies in a large, shallow alcove 62 metres long and up to 12 metres deep, on the eastern side of Wetherill Mesa. The cliff wall rises about 28 metres to the mesa top, and a rocky slope descends 185 metres to the bottom of the canyon. There is no water source within the alcove; a reservoir containing 27,000–32,000 litres of water was built on the mesa-top, 200 metres from the cliff-dwelling. Very little light penetrates to Mug House because of its orientation and the cliff overhang. Consequently it is cool and draughty, especially during the winter.

The dwellings

A total of 94 rooms, two towers and eight kivas were discovered at Mug House. All the walls are of stone masonry with mud mortar, and were plastered where the stonework was not of very high quality. Some of the plaster was painted red or pink, using red loess from the mesa-top for colouring. Living and storage rooms were usually rectangular, averaging about 5 square metres in area, with a ceiling about 1.5–1.8 metres high. About half of the rooms used the low cave roof as a ceiling; others had beams supporting poles covered with shingles and coated with adobe to make flat roofs. Ground floors were of sandstone bedrock, adobe or packed earth; upper storeys had wooden floors. Doorways were rectangular or T-shaped, with raised sills which reduced their height to 0.5–1.2 metres. Sandstone slabs fastened with wooden bars served as doors.

Furniture was sparse. Occasional masonry shelves and niches have been found, and there were also suspension poles, similar to those used by today's Pueblo Indians for attaching looms, cradles and storage racks. Wooden pegs were set in the walls to hang things from, and loops of oak twigs similarly set may have been used for anchoring backstrap looms. Cooking was done on open hearths consisting of pits lined with sandstone slabs, and the cooking pots stood on stone pot supports over the embers. Food and water were stored in large corrugated-ware jars which were buried up to their mouths in the floor and covered with stone lids.

In Pueblo III settlements at Mesa Verde, rooms are arranged around courtyards. In some cases there are sets of courtyards linked with kivas, indicating some kind of supra-household unit of social organization. Results of the excavations at Mug House show this pattern clearly. Household Units, comprising suites of three to nine contiguous rooms with an adjacent open space, were used by a group of related individuals, not necessarily nuclear families, who shared the work of getting and preparing food, using and making household tools, and shared living and sleeping places. Blocks of living rooms (several Household Units) were associated with kivas and rubbish heaps to form Courtyard Units, where the roof of the kiva formed a flat open space around which the rooms clustered. These Courtyard Units probably represent kin groups connected with kiva ownership and use. A further division at Mug House illustrates the duality which forms the basis of much Indian ceremonial life. The site can be divided into north and south zones, with no direct communication between the two apart from the path along the outermost terrace of the cave. This separation probably indicates a division of ceremonial responsibilities between two groups, as among the present-day Hopi.

Kivas

Kivas developed from the ordinary pit houses used in Pueblo I (AD 700–900). These small, circular, semi-subterranean rooms, up to 4 metres in diameter, were all built to a similar pattern. An encircling stone bench or banquette, too high to be a comfortable seat, was probably used as a shelf by the men meeting in the kiva. Pots, axes, scrapers and bone awls have been found on the banquettes, supporting this idea. Each kiva has six masonry columns rising from the banquette to hold up the flat roof, which was high enough to allow plenty of room for a man to stand. A narrow L-shaped ventilator tunnel to the outside allowed fresh air to be drawn inside the kiva, which would quickly become hot and stuffy from the central fire. To prevent a draught blowing on to the fire, small walls or vertical sandstone slabs were positioned to deflect any breeze from the ventilator. Opposite the ventilator, and recessed into the banquette, were niches in which ceremonial objects may have been kept. A small hole up to 15 centimetres in diameter and about 30 centimetres deep was sometimes dug into the floor of the kiva. Called a 'sipapu', it represented the entrance to the spirit world beneath the Earth's surface.

The people of Mesa Verde

Archaeologists have been able to glean much information about the prehistoric occupants of Mesa Verde. Evidence comes from their physical remains in burials and from their well-preserved possessions. The Anasazi had straight black hair, prominent cheek bones, and they flattened the back of the skull, a deformity produced by the use of a cradle board for infants. Adults were 1.5 to 1.75 metres tall, and many ankle bones show facets on the talus indicating that they habitually squatted rather than sat. Many adults suffered from arthritis and from tooth decay caused by grit in the diet which exposed the dentine and pulp cavity and so encouraged abscesses. Most people lost their teeth because of widespread pyorrhoea. Infant mortality was high; 50 per cent of children died in the first four years of life. The dead were buried in refuse heaps, under the floors of abandoned houses, or randomly in the village. The graves were normally unfurnished.

Some articles of clothing have survived six centuries. Sandals of twilled yucca and feathered socks for winter wear have been found, also warm feathered blankets made of brown and white turkey down fixed in a yucca twill. Cotton yarn was woven into cloth on backstrap looms, and animal skins were made into pouches and bags. Very few ornaments have been found in excavations, perhaps indicating that they were highly valued. Beads were made from lengths of tubular bird bone, from snail shells and from stone. Flat stone pendants, circular or rectangular in shape, were worn, and exotic imports, such as a marine shell pendant (*conus* sp.) came from as far away as the Gulf of California. Paint stones indicate that body painting was practised.

A vast variety of cordage and netting was made from yucca and human hair. Coiled baskets made of willow were common containers, as were fibre pot rests, head rings and tumpline head bands. Sleeping mats of willow were sewn with yucca cordage and used with wooden pillows. No metals were known. Stone *manos* and *metates* were used for grinding grain; chopping and pounding tools were made of stone, as were knives and scrapers. Perforating tools such as awls and needles tended to be made of bone.

Perhaps the greatest artistic skill of the Anasazi was shown in their ceramics. At Mesa Verde, white wares were made in large numbers and decorated in black or brownish paint made from mineral and organic substances. Between AD 1050–1150 a typical regional style developed at Mesa Verde; it involved filling rounded spaces with dots and squiggles to produce sophisticated abstract designs.

The economic base

Most of the evidence about the ancient inhabitants' diet comes from the scientific study of dried human faeces, which was found in large quantities in abandoned houses and on ledges at the back of the cave. The coprolites contained remains of cultivated plants, including corn kernels and seeds from squash and beans, as well as gathered pigweed seeds, goosefoot seeds, ground cherry, stink bush, miner's lettuce and prickly pear. Tiny fragments of animal bone, parts of cicadas and white eggshell were also discovered in coprolites. Animal bones were found in the rubbish heaps and show that turkeys, cottontail, rock squirrel, wood rat and deer were eaten. Of these, only the turkey was domesticated and there is no trace of the dog. Stray human bones discovered in rubbish deposits may indicate cannibalism, but microscopic examination has yet to confirm this possibility.

Above: View of the Cliff Palace at Mesa Verde.

Below right: Multi-storeyed buildings of stone, mud mortar and wood are common at Mesa Verde, where maximum use had to be made of the cave space in which the villages were located. Apartment blocks, look-out towers and circular, semi-subterranean kivas, or religious meeting places (below, left), are the most common types of construction. T-shaped doors with raised thresholds are a characteristic architectural feature.

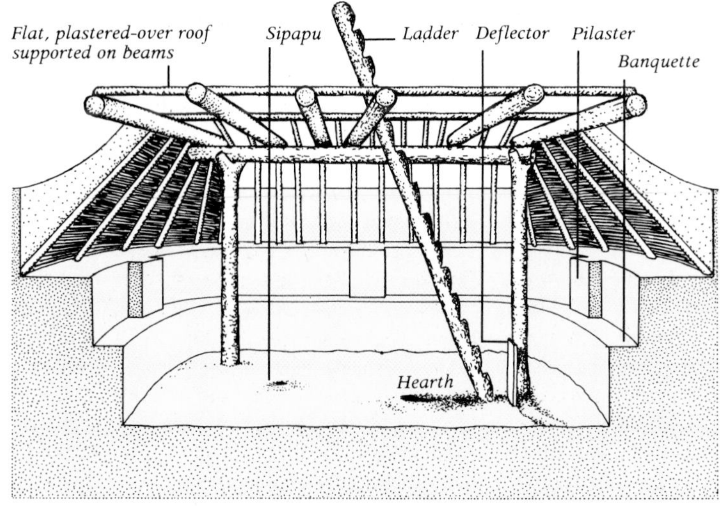

Machu Picchu

PERU

Machu Picchu, the 'Lost City of the Incas', is the most famous archaeological site in Peru. Much of its renown depends upon its romantic and spectacular setting and its near complete state of preservation.

Machu Picchu lies in the south-west Andes, about 100 kilometres north of Cuzco, the ancient capital of the Inca empire. It covers 40 hectares of carefully terraced slopes on a saddle of land between two Andean peaks, Machu Picchu and Huayna Picchu. The city was a fortress and refuge with remarkable natural defences. Sheer cliffs drop 600 metres to the Urubamba River on three sides of the site, while on the fourth a dry moat and two defensive walls run from precipice to precipice. Although the city lies at 2743 metres above sea level, the climate is warm, and sub-tropical food crops can be grown on the tiers of agricultural terraces which surround the site.

Machu Picchu was an Inca citadel built after AD 1438 when Pachacuti Inca, architect of the Inca empire, was crowned. It was occupied until the Spanish Conquistadores subdued the last royal leader of native resistance, Tupac Amaru, in 1572. Inside the fortifications the city appears a labyrinthine tangle of rock-cut and megalithic stairways, water channels, fountains and basins. These interlink the many house groups which cluster round the edges of the city and the central ceremonial areas such as the Great Plaza and the Intihuatana. This is a carved granite boulder, the name of which means 'stone to which the sun is tied'. Machu Picchu contains much distinguished architecture which demonstrates the great engineering and stone-cutting skills possessed by its Inca builders.

Hiram Bingham's expedition

In 1911 Hiram Bingham led a small expedition to Peru from Yale University, with the aim of discovering Vilcabamba, the last stronghold of the Incas. Rumours of large, unexplored ruins in the inaccessible Urubamba valley had been current since 1875, and fortunately for the Yale Peruvian Expedition, a mule trail had been cut through the area shortly before their arrival. Consequently they were the first archaeologists to penetrate the unknown zone. After a journey of five days from Cuzco they made their great discovery. Bingham told the story thus:

> 'Although it was drizzling, the promise of a *sol* (50 cents gold) to be paid to him on our return from the ruins, encouraged Arteaga to guide me up to Machu Picchu . . . we had a fearfully hard climb, a good part of the distance I went on all fours. The path was in many places a primitive stairway or crude step ladder. The heat was excessive, but the view magnificent after we got above the jungle . . . on both sides tremendous precipices fell away to the white rapids of the Urubamba River below. In front was the solitary peak of Huayna Picchu, seemingly inaccessible on all sides. Behind us were rocky heights and impassable cliffs . . . . Around a slight promontory the character of the stone-faced *andenes* (agricultural terraces) began to improve and suddenly we found ourselves in the midst of a jungle-covered maze of small and large walls, the ruins of buildings made of white granite, most carefully cut and fitted together without cement. Surprise followed surprise until there came the realization that we were in the midst of as wonderful ruins as ever found in Peru'.

As workmen cleared away the bushes and trees which choked the plazas and overran the ruined walls, Bingham suspected that the site might have even greater significance than he had initially thought. One structure, known as the Temple of the Three Windows, was particularly striking and unusual. Its very large trapezoidal windows, 1.3 metres high and 1 metre wide, looked out over the mountains and Bingham believed that this was possibly the legendary Tampu Tocco of Inca tradition. The Incas who founded Cuzco claimed to have originated from this place, the name of which means Tavern of Windows. The history of Machu Picchu seemed to have embraced the whole length of Inca history, from the foundation of the state to its final conquest by the Spanish.

Determined to excavate and map the ruins thoroughly, Bingham returned to the United States to raise funds for a second expedition. Outstanding photographs taken by his team illustrated reports in the popular press and ensured that the great discovery caught the public imagination.

The 1912 excavations

Backed by the National Geographic Magazine and Yale University, a larger team of specialists began work again in 1912. The expedition had two aims: to clear the ruins of all vegetation and prepare accurate plans of the site, and to find archaeological evidence which would date the site and prove or disprove Bingham's theories.

Clearing the bush which covered open spaces and filled the insides of buildings

Left: Inca architects and builders had to make the best possible use of the difficult terrain of the Andes. At Machu Picchu much of the town is built on artificial terraces such as these, connected by steep stone stairways, sometimes cut into the living rock. Houses at Machu Picchu were unusually well preserved; the walls and steep gable-ends still stand. Some have been re-thatched with ichu grass to give an impression of what the town looked like 500 years ago.

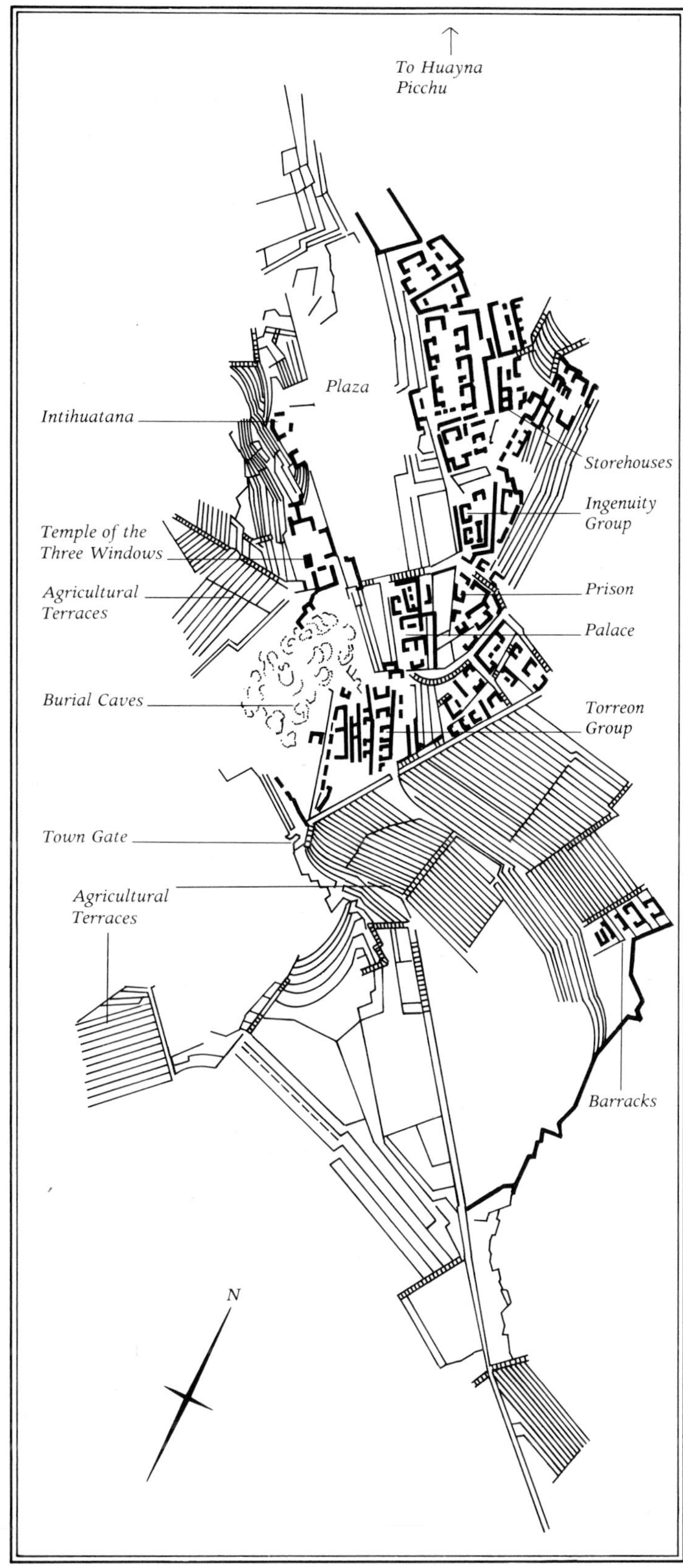

Left: Hiram Bingham was disappointed by the very small number of artistic treasures brought to light by his excavations at Machu Picchu. This cast bronze knife is considered one of his best finds. Not only is it attractive as a caricature of a boy fishing, but also demonstrates the high quality and competence of Inca metalworkers.

proved easy. Problems were encountered where large trees had grown on the walls themselves. Deep root systems penetrated the carefully fitted, mortarless stonework and it was difficult to extract them without destroying the masonry. Bingham decided to begin excavation inside the Principal Temple and the Temple of the Three Windows, but although workers dug to a depth of 3 metres in some places, they found nothing whatsoever. This disappointment led the archaeologists to offer a reward to any workman who could show them a cave or tomb containing a skull *in situ*. Furnished graves would yield the fastest hard evidence about the date of occupation of the city. On the first day of the new reward scheme, eight caves with human remains were reported. A total of 102 burials were found at Machu Picchu, most in the natural caves of the slopes below the city. All burials were meticulously recorded. The cave entrances and interiors were photographed, skeletons and grave goods carefully excavated, catalogued, drawn and photographed. An *osteologist* was on site to determine the sex and age at death of each skeleton.

Evidence of burials

Of the 173 skeletons found, 150 were of females, and all the more richly furnished graves belonged to women. The dead were buried in a sitting position, with knees drawn up to the chest. Grave goods, such as painted polychrome drinking vessels, bronze tweezers and shawl pins with flat, circular heads, were often placed with the body. Some burials were found within the city itself, in artificial caves hollowed out beneath huge granite boulders. These were places of religious importance to the Inca, and Bingham thought that such unusually situated graves were the tombs of the Chosen Women, an Inca religious order dedicated to the worship of the Sun.

The most richly equipped grave was discovered beneath an overhanging rock some 300 metres above the city. There was found the skeleton of a middle-aged woman, who had possibly suffered from syphilis, accompanied by two large bronze shawl pins, bronze tweezers and a bronze knife with an ornamental handle in the form of a flying bird. Nearby, a concave bronze mirror was found, along with two polychrome painted pots decorated with painted and modelled human faces and a cooking pot bearing a modelled snake. Traces of wool and vegetable fibre were noted as the remains of clothing. This assemblage indicates, as does all the other datable material from burials found at Machu Picchu, that the city was only occupied during the later part of the Inca period.

More recent research and excavation has proved that Bingham's assessment of Machu Picchu's importance was wrong. Vilcabamba was found by an American expedition in 1964, and it lies not among the high peaks of the Andes, but in the steamy jungle of the beginnings of Amazonia. In fact, Machu Picchu was a place of little importance, a small town of perhaps 1,000 inhabitants, situated on a minor road within the huge Inca empire. Its significance to us is so great because it was never sacked or occupied by the Conquistadores. It remains unaltered and complete, presenting a full picture of an Inca town of the 15th and 16th centuries AD.

The Incas

The urban planning of Machu Picchu neatly illustrates the hierarchical basis of the Inca social system. The head of state, who had absolute power, was the divine Inca himself. At the bottom of the system was the ordinary household which paid taxes in labour, food and goods to supply the Inca's storehouses. Each intermediate grade in the hierarchy was clearly defined and had strictly observed rights, privileges and duties. Detailed laws imposed uniformity throughout the empire's 3,500-kilometre length. Even styles of dress were restricted and codified. For example, only the nobility and members of the royal family were allowed to wear large disc-shaped ear plugs.

Inca architecture

At Machu Picchu the focus of the town is the Great Plaza, where the Inca's representative would make proclamations and call public meetings. Surrounding the plaza are large, elegant buildings which served as residences and offices for nobles and government officials. Away from the central area are smaller household units which were occupied by artisans and workers. Such social grading was normal in Inca towns, but at Machu Picchu the terrain made it necessary to build on many different vertical levels and this allowed a hierarchical arrangement of buildings from high to low ground, as well as from central areas to the fringes of the town.

Architecture was a highly respected art among the Incas, whose professional architects were drawn from the ranks of the nobility. For large-scale public works, such as the planning of Machu Picchu, clay or stone models were made as blueprints to guide the builders. There was no problem in finding a work-force to carry out such major enterprises; the system of paying tax by labour in the army, mines or on public works ensured a large number of men always available.

Building methods were very simple. Blocks of white granite were carefully cut to shape using stone hammers, and polished using sand and water. The stone blocks were fitted together without mortar, and to position them, rollers, ramps and small bronze crowbars were used. This method of stone fitting allowed the blocks to move during the frequent earth tremors of the Andes, but to settle back into place afterwards. The edges of the granite blocks were bevelled to emphasize the extremely tight-fitting joints between the ashlars, or squared stones, which gives a decorative effect to the massive walls. Two styles of precision-cut stone block walling were used; irregular or polygonal in ordinary buildings, and rectangular in important public structures.

Most buildings had only one storey and at Machu Picchu, where the rainfall is high, the roofs were steeply pitched and made of thick layers of 'ichu' grass tied on to a wooden frame. The whole roof was anchored against high winds by being lashed to stone pegs projecting from the gables.

Trapezoidal niches, windows and doorways are the hallmark of Inca architecture after AD 1470, and they abound at Machu Picchu. Even in the most splendid Inca buildings there is little carving or ornamentation of the stonework. Decorative effect depended more upon the arrangement of niches in inside walls, and, outstandingly at Machu Picchu, the use of trapezoidal windows to frame beathtaking views.

Some two-storey structures were built, in which entry to the upper room was usually made by using a rope ladder or rope, although some houses have stones set in the outer gable wall to serve as a ladder.

Despite the simplicity of their technology, the builders of Machu Picchu took difficult constructional problems in their stride. For example, in the Torreon house group, a semicircular structure needed to be joined to a two-and-a-half storey house. The uniting wall was built of white granite, using matching ashlars which are not exactly rectangular but which key together perfectly at the points of greatest stress. Interlocking hook stones prevent the ashlars from slipping and stop the tall house from leaning away from the curved building. In another part of the town, two large boulders projected through the area that was to be the floor of a house. Instead of changing the plan or cutting the boulders away, the builders carved the outcrops into two mortars in which maize, potatoes and other foods could be mashed. Bingham aptly gave this the name of 'Ingenuity Group'.

Domestic life

The main residential areas of Machu Picchu are built on terraces in the northern and southern sectors of the site, with other house groups lying in the west and south-west. Houses normally consisted of a single rectangular room occupied by one family. Between two and eight houses were grouped around a courtyard to form a compound which was shared by the members of the extended family, who were all members of one 'allyu' or descent group. The house groups were often surrounded by a wall broken by only a single gateway approached through an alley or stairway. Cooking, weaving and other activities took place in the courtyard

Left: Perhaps the most sacred place in Machu Picchu was the Intihuatana, the Sun stone. The Sun was the chief god of the Incas, who believed it to be the dynasty's divine ancestor.

Below: The Temple of the Three Windows looks out over one of the most breathtaking views in the world. The windows themselves are trapezoidal in shape, a characteristic of Inca architecture. White granite was cut to irregular but precisely-shaped blocks, which key together without the use of mortar.

Above: Machu Picchu clings to a saddle of land below the peaks of Huayna Picchu and Machu Picchu. Public buildings are arranged around the only comparatively level open space, an irregular-shaped plaza. Domestic and military buildings are located on surrounding terraces.

rather than inside the poorly-lit houses. The interiors must have been smoky, dark and damp, since only a cloth hung over the doorway to shut out the elements and there were no smoke-holes or chimneys to clear the air when small clay stoves were used during bad weather. These stoves had a stoke-hole at the front and circular holes on the top to steady typically round-based cooking pots. The only other furniture in a normal house would be a stone bench built as part of the wall. There were no chairs or beds; people usually slept in their clothes on reed mats on the floor. Possessions were kept in wall niches and hung on stone pegs projecting from the wall, while food supplies and water were stored in large jars.

In the Andes most clothing was made of alpaca and llama wool spun and woven at home by women. Many clay and stone spindle whorls, shuttles and tools for beating up the weft of cloth on the loom have been found at Machu Picchu. Lengths of untailored cloth were held in place by pins, the most common type of which, called 'topo', is long and disc-headed. Braziers still containing traces of metal and slag show that bronze working was practised at Machu Picchu. The smiths had excellent control of their medium. They used a higher proportion of tin to copper in alloys required for casting, in order to improve ductability, and a lower tin content for beaten-out objects such as tweezers, topos, axes, chisels and 'tumis', or ceremonial knives. Perhaps the most exquisite find from Machu Picchu is a cast bronze tumi. Its handle is in the form of a child playing a large fish on the end of a line, and the crescent-shape blade has been hammered to a sharp edge. Although the Incas had expert knowledge of metallurgy, stone continued to be important as a tool-making material. Diorite hammers, scrapers, knives and polishing stones abound at Machu Picchu, and green schist was carved into decorated stone dishes, beads and pendants.

Inca religion

The Incas were at pains to appease the supernatural forces which they believed ruled their environment. Without the correct ceremonies and sacrifices it was feared that natural disasters such as earthquakes and landslides would be loosed on the world. In particular they were anxious to protect the food supply. The planting and harvesting of oca, quinoa, maize and potatoes were surrounded by ritual actions which ensured the success of the crops. The supreme god, source of all divine power, was Viracocha the Creator God. His main servant was the Sun God, who was popularly worshipped in the mountains where his warmth and light matured and ripened the crops. He was also believed to be the divine ancestor of the Inca royal house. The Sun God was served by the Mamacunas, or Chosen Women, who lived a life of chastity at Sun Temples, weaving intricate textiles for priestly vestments and preparing special 'chicha', maize beer, for festivals. At times of great insecurity, one of the Mamacunas would be sacrificed as well as the usual offerings of llamas, guinea pigs, maize flour and coca leaves.

Other important gods included the Moon, Stars, Thunder, Venus, Mother Earth and the spirits of lakes and water. Many places were revered as having supernatural powers and were called 'huacas'. Huacas could take many forms; mountain peaks, hills, tombs of ancestors, fountains and large stones. At Machu Picchu huge granite boulders were worshipped as huacas, as were natural caves in the cliffs surrounding the town.

Gazetteer

Figures in bold denote sites named on the regional maps. Other grid references serve as a guide to the general location of a site.

Europe Map, 28-29

Aachen, West Germany; Roman spa which became Charlemagne's capital and burial-place, and the coronation place of German kings from 813 to 1531. **4d/e**

Abbeville, France; historic 19th-century excavations by Boucher de Perthes located the rough handaxes of Palaeolithic date now named after this site. **3d**

Altamira, Spain; cave located first in 1868, filled with over 150 painted figures of bison and other mammals in clear, bright colours. **2f**

Ampurias, Spain; Greek colony, later a Roman town; widespread remains of the city and the cemeteries. **3f**

Arene Candide, Italy; cave site with Upper Palaeolithic finds and burials, Mesolithic burials and 3 Neolithic levels with shell-impressed pottery; also Bronze Age, Iron Age and Roman finds. **4f**

Avebury, England; one of the most famous megalithic monuments of Europe comprising a massive bank and ditch, large circle of untrimmed stones with alignments and circles within. **3d**

Bath, England; the major religious site of Roman Britain with a temple to Sulis Minerva; new excavations are in progress. **3d**

Birka, Sweden; earliest trading centre of Sweden, 9th–10th century AD; enclosed settlement site with exterior cemetery of 2,500 graves and traded goods from Russia and the Far East as well as Europe. **5c**

Bologna, Italy; early Iron Age centre with many cemeteries containing thousands of graves; from the 6th century it became the Etruscan Felsina. **4f**

Bylany, Czechoslovakia; large, well-excavated Neolithic settlement site covering 25 hectares which yielded 105 structures of some 14 phases, and two possible ritual areas. **5e**

Carnac, France; area of great density of megalithic monuments comprising graves, standing stones and the famous alignments which may have some astronomical significance. **2e**

Čertomlyk, USSR; Scythian tomb, excavated 1862/3; the main chamber had been robbed, but side chambers contained horse and horsemen burials and silver and gold vessels. **7e**

Châteauneuf-les-Martigues, France; rock shelter with a long sequence of Mesolithic and early Neolithic levels, including some of the earliest impressed wares in the west Mediterranean in the 6th millennium BC. **3f**

Colchester, England; first Roman city in Britain, a Belgic town occupied in AD 43 which eventually became a 'colonia' with houses with piped water. **3d**

Cortaillod, Switzerland; lakeside settlement with well-preserved organic material. Gives its name to the Neolithic culture of Switzerland. **4e**

Cresswell Crags, England; gorge with several cave sites containing Middle and Upper Palaeolithic material. Gives its name to the Cresswellian culture. **3d**

Dimini, Greece; walled town of the Neolithic period with megaron-style houses and painted pottery. **5g**

Dolní Věstonice, Czechoslovakia; Upper Palaeolithic habitation site of mammoth hunters with burials, a rich flint industry, variety of modelled clay figures and pierced shells for ornaments. **4e**

Dublin, Ireland; one of the most important Viking towns with evidence, some recently destroyed, in the form of timber buildings and wharves, of the original layout. **2d**

Egolzwil, Switzerland; Neolithic lakeside settlement of the 3rd millennium BC having evidence for rectangular houses with animal stalls; many wooden tools and equipment were recovered. **4e**

El Argar, Spain; small fortified Early Bronze Age site with rectangular houses and nearly 1,000 burials belonging to 2 main phases. **2g**

Ensérune, France; town occupied over many periods from the Neolithic to the Roman, especially important as a walled town in the Iron Age. **3f**

Entremont, France; Celtic-Ligurian town particularly prominent in the 3rd and 2nd centuries BC; apart from houses there were ritual monuments with human skulls attached. **3f**

Ertebølle, Denmark; site of great mounds or middens of discarded mussel shells, the food debris of a Mesolithic group using pottery in a developed phase. **4c**

Este, Italy; centre of Iron Age settlement datirfg from the 10th century BC onwards, with many cemeteries and a particularly rich metalworking tradition. **4f**

Feddersen Wierde, Germany; farmstead site of the 1st century BC which grew larger until there was a large house with a palisade surrounded by other smaller houses. **4d**

Fère-en-Tardenois, France; eponymous site of the Tardenoisian Mesolithic flint industry which consisted in large part of microliths. **3e**

Fishbourne, England; Roman palace of the 1st century AD, probably that of Cogidubnus, with many fine internal features and evidence for a formal garden. **3d**

Franchthi Cave, Greece; cave site currently under investigation. Contains Upper Palaeolithic, Epipalaeolithic and Neolithic material including imported Melian obsidian. **5g**

Gemeinlebarn, Austria; early Bronze Age flat-grave inhumation cemetery of Unetice type, followed by a cremation cemetery and finally an Iron Age tumulus cemetery. 5e

Gokstad, Sweden; Viking ship burial excavated in the 1880s, possibly that of the 9th-century AD king Olaf. **4c**

Grimes Graves, England; centre of Neolithic flint mining with more than 350 shafts dug; finds include antler picks and lamps. **3d**

Hallstatt, Austria; cemetery of over 2,000 graves, excavated since 1824, associated with extensive salt workings. Site gives its name to the earlier European Iron Age. **4e**

Hamwih, England; forerunner of modern Southampton. One of the major European trading ports in the 7th–10th centuries AD, handling goods from France and the Rhineland. **3d**

Hedeby (Haithabu), Germany; 9th century AD Viking trading centre with major finds of bronze and glass manufacturing as well as timber structures. 4d

Heuneburg, Germany; fortified hilltop princely residence of the Iron Age which has produced many Mediterranean imports as well as evidence for metalworking; one phase of the defences has bastions, and walls of sun-dried brick. **4e**

Karanovo, Bulgaria; massive tell with 12.5 metres of stratigraphy covering the Neolithic, Copper and Bronze Ages; rectangular houses, later sub-divided, and the remains of early gold and copper working. **6f**

Kiev, USSR; Russian town founded in the 9th century AD, possibly by Viking traders, with evidence for goldworking and pottery-making. **6e**

Köln, Germany; centre of the Ubii in the 1st century BC, the town became a Roman 'colonia' with a wall, temples, baths and amphitheatre; later it became a Frankish royal centre. **4d**

Köln-Lindenthal, Germany; large settlement of the Neolithic linear pottery culture with 50 long-houses; the latest of the several phases was the largest and produced some graves. **4e**

Kostienki, USSR; an area of dense Upper Palaeolithic settlement of several phases and on many sites, with some burials, evidence for houses, and finds including carved bone 'Venus' figurines. **7d**

Lagozza, Italy; lakeside settlement site which gave its name to the early Neolithic culture of North Italy. **4f**

La Tène, Switzerland; in Lake Neuchatel was found a great deposit of metalwork including swords and ornaments, and the name of the site was coined for the later Iron Age of Europe. **4e**

Le Moustier, France; type-site for the middle Palaeolithic Mousterian industry, this cave yielded a burial of a young adult with flint implements in 1908. **3e**

Lengyel, Hungary; fortified settlement of the Neolithic period with sunken-floored houses and many artefacts, together with some 90 Copper Age graves of the Lengyel culture. **5e**

Lepenski Vir, Yugoslavia; 7th-millennium BC Mesolithic village of fishing people comprising trapezoidal houses and some burials; there were also many carved stone heads. **5f**

Les Trois Frères, France; cave investigated by Begouen and his three sons (hence the name) in 1914, which contained several hundred engravings including the so-called 'sorcerer'. **3f**

London, England; Roman Londinium had a fort, forum and basilica, and traces of the waterlogged riverside wharves have been found in recent excavations. **3d**

Los Millares, Spain; early Bronze Age settlement site with rectangular houses and a cemetery of over 100 megalithic graves; finds include imports from Egypt. **2g**

Magdalenska Gora, Yugoslavia; large Iron Age cemetery rich in finds, including decorated bronze buckets and arms and armour. **4f**

Maglemose, Denmark; post-glacial Mesolithic settlement site which produced flintwork, bone and antler tools including hooks and harpoons. **4d**

Maiden Castle, England; hillfort of the Iron Age (with earlier Neolithic occupation) with massive ramparts, complex entrances and a final phase war cemetery. **3d**

Manching, Germany; town dating from the 3rd to the 1st centuries BC, a large centre of population as well as a major industrial centre. **4e**

Mas d'Azil, France; cave site which gives its name to the Azilian industry of Mesolithic date. **3f**

Massilia, France; Greek colony founded c. 600 BC (now Marseilles), a key site in the transmission of Mediterranean goods into Iron Age Europe. **3f**

Mezhirich, USSR; Upper Palaeolithic settlement site comprising 2 and probably more huts constructed of mammoth bones, containing hearths, flints, ornaments and figurines. **6e**

Mycenae, Greece; Late Bronze Age city which gave its name to the culture; remains of palaces, houses and graves including the shaft graves excavated by Schliemann. **5g**

Nea Nikomedia, Greece; early Neolithic settlement site, 7th millennium BC, with rectangular buildings, crouched burials, figurines and painted pottery. **5g**

Neanderthal, Germany; eponymous site for Neanderthal man, this cave site, now quarried away, yielded in 1856 part of a skull and some other bones. **4d**

New Grange, Ireland; remarkable megalithic passage grave with decorative carved kerb- and other stones, and a slit allowing the sun to illuminate the chamber on midsummer's day. **2c/d**

Niaux, France; cave painting site with a main chamber decorated with 25 bison, 16 horses and 6 ibex; there is also a fish engraving. **3f**

Nîmes, France; Roman town flourishing in the 2nd century AD, with amphitheatre, temples and aqueduct. **3f**

Novgorod, USSR; possibly a Viking foundation in the 9th or 10th century AD, with many finds of metalwork, bone and leather. **6c**

Nydam, Denmark; clinker-built rowing boat of the 4th to 5th centuries AD was found in a peat bog in the 1860s; over 25 metres long, it had no keel and no mast. 4d

Olbia, USSR; city founded in the 7th century BC by the Greeks and taken over by the Scythians, in the heart of whose area it was; it continued into Roman times. **6e**

Orange, France; Celtic settlement which became Romanized, with famous triumphal arch, theatre and temple. **3f**

St Acheul, France; open-air Palaeolithic site, first excavated 1854, which produced several thousand artefacts of the type now called Acheulian. **3e**

Sarmizegethusa, Romania; powerful citadel comprising houses, workshops and sanctuaries; the site was the centre of the Dacian state. **6f**

Sesklo, Greece; Neolithic tell of several periods, an unwalled town with houses of stone and clay being succeeded by a walled settlement with first megaron-style and later rectangular houses. **5g**

Seven Brothers, USSR; group of 7 Scythian tumuli dating between the 5th and 4th centuries **7e**

BC which contain, apart from the usual magnificent gold and silver objects, a large number of horse burials.

Skara Brae, Scotland; stone-built Neolithic village where the furniture, also built in stone, survives – beds, dressers, cupboards, hearths and seats. **3c**

Star Carr, England; Mesolithic habitation site of c. 8000 BC comprising a brushwood platform with many well-preserved waterlogged items including harpoons, and the remains of a domesticated dog. **3d**

Staré Hradisko, Czechoslovakia; fortified Celtic town with inner and outer areas containing timber buildings, and a manufacturing area for metal-working, enamelling and pottery making. 5e

Steinheim an der Murr, Germany; a skull with Neanderthal features such as a protruding brow ridge was found in gravel digging in 1933. **4e**

Stonehenge, England; multi-phase monument of Neolithic and Bronze Age date, refashioned several times; trilithons of trimmed sarsens, and bluestones imported from Wales. **3d**

Sutton Hoo, England; rich boat burial excavated in 1938/9, probably of Redwald (d. AD 625); in a timber chamber in the clinker-built boat was a remarkable treasure of gold, silver and enamelled objects. **3d**

Swanscombe, England; Palaeolithic open-air site of more than one phase, which yielded fragments of skulls with Neanderthal features. **3d**

Syracuse, Sicily; founded in the 8th century by Corinthian Greeks, the town flourished in the Iron Age and was later Romanized; walls, theatre and temple still stand. **4g**

Terra Amata, France; multi-phase open-air Palaeolithic camp-site on dunes with remains of shelters, hearths, flint-making areas and a footprint in the sand. **3f**

Tollund, Denmark; in a bog in 1950 was found the complete body of an Iron Age man, fully preserved with a hat on his head and a rope around his neck; analysis of his stomach contents showed his last meal to have been a sort of gruel. **4d**

Trelleborg, Denmark; Viking military establishment with a ringwork containing 16 convex-sided longhouses arranged in squares, and 15 more outside the wall in a radial pattern. **4d**

Trier, Germany; the main economic and political centre of north-east Gaul, with evidence for a forum, stone bridge, amphitheatre, public baths and an aqueduct. **3/4e**

Tripolye, USSR; settlement site of the Neolithic and Copper Ages, comprising some 100 longhouses and producing the renowned decorated pottery. **6e**

Ullastret, Spain; fortified hilltop settlement site with a line of towers dating from the 6th century BC enclosing rectangular drystone houses; many Greek imports. **3f**

Unetice, Czechoslovakia; early Bronze Age cemetery of more than 30 graves, richly furnished with daggers, amber beads, pins and armrings, which gave its name to the Central European Bronze Age culture. **4e**

Val Camonica, Italy; area with widespread rock carvings which have been dated to the Neolithic, Bronze Age and Iron Age, showing warriors, vehicles, etc. **4e**

Veii, Italy; Etruscan city dating from the 7th century BC, later fortified with walls and towers; the cemeteries with their hundreds of graves are the focus of current research. **4f**

Vila Nova de São Pedro, Portugal; fortified settlement site of the Neolithic and Copper Age with thick multiple walls encircling the houses. **1f**

Villanova, Italy; cemetery excavated in 1853 of 179 cremation and 14 inhumation graves which gives its name to the culture of these parts in the early Iron Age. **4f**

Vinča, Yugoslavia; Neolithic settlement site on the banks of the Danube which gave its name to the culture, characterized by small rectangular houses and crouched burials, pottery and clay figurines. **5f**

Vix, France; site of a rich 6th-century BC burial containing a 4-wheeled wagon, gold and amber objects and several Greek imports including the famous giant crater. **3e**

York, England; Roman and Saxon town conquered by the Vikings, with recent excavations producing a wealth of new evidence, particularly of organic materials. **3d**

Classical World — Map, 50-51

Akragas, south Sicily; sub-colony of Gela. Important, well-preserved temples; housing. 2e

Aleria (Alalia), Corsica. Short-lived Greek colony, taken over by Etruscans, later 6th century. **1b**

Alexandria, Egypt; great Greek and Roman coastal city founded by Alexander, 332 BC; many remains including theatre, temples, cemetery, sculpture. **7g**

Amphipolis, north Greece; rebellious colony of Athens, 437 BC, strategically located at mouth of Strymon. Piles of wooden bridge are a recent find. 5c

Antakya (Antioch on the Orontes), south Turkey; Greek and Roman city, streets, houses, mosaics. 8e

Apamea, Syria; Greek and Roman town ruins. 8e

Aphrodisias, west Turkey; fine ruins of Roman marble and limestone city, sculptures. 6d

Apollonia, Albania; Corinthian colony of c. 600 BC, by fertile plain. Walls, kilns, tombs, etc. 4c

Argos, Peloponnese; site near sea, controlling fertile plain; habitation of many periods. 4d

Athens, Greece; Bronze Age centre and leading classical city. Acropolis, Agora, cemeteries. **5d**

Baalbek (Heliopolis), Lebanon; Greek and Roman colony; fine Roman temple ruins. 8e

Beirut (Berytus), Lebanon; Augustan Roman colony; colonnade. 8e/f

Benevento, Italy; Roman town with theatre of Hadrian and fine arch of Trajan (AD 114). 2c

Byzantium, later Constantinople; city dominating the Bosphorus; Megarian colony, c. 650 BC. Capital of eastern Roman empire, taken by crusaders in 1204. Walls, churches, cisterns, etc. **6c**

Capua, Italy; city controlling Campanian plain passing from Etruscan to Roman control. 2c

Carthage, Tunisia; great Phoenician, then Roman coastal city; vast area of ruins. **1d**

Cherchell (Iol-Caesarea), Algeria; Punic and Roman town; baths, theatre, statuary, mosaic. (p.92) 2b

Chios, Greece; Aegean island, prosperous in Iron Age; early town at Emborio. Nea Moni monastery with important 11th-century mosaics. **5d**

Coimbra, Portugal; Celtic, then Roman town; later imperial walls and houses with mosaics. (p.28) 1f

Corcyra (Corfu), Greece; island on route to Italy colonised by Corinth c. 700 BC. Important pedimental sculptures of 6th century BC. 4d

Corinth, Peloponnese; strategically located at Isthmus; formidable acropolis. Prosperous city from 8th century BC; later a Roman colony. **4d**

Corunna, Spain; only extant Roman lighthouse. (p.28) 1e

Cumae, Italy; Greek colony of c. 725 BC, controlling coastal Campania; Sibylline oracle. **2c**

Cyrene, east Libya; ruins of city from Archaic Greek (temple of Apollo) to Roman eras. **4f**

Delos, Greece; islet of Cyclades, birthplace of Artemis and Apollo; important trade centre, 200–80 BC. Temples, housing, theatre. **5e**

Demetrias, Greece; main port of Thessaly. Previously named Iolkos (home of Jason) and Pagasae. Extensive fortifications; painted grave stelae. 5d

Didyma, west Turkey; oracular shrine of Apollo, south of Miletus. Massive temple in Ionic order. 6e

Djemila (Cuicul), Algeria; Roman imperial colony, rich remains of limestone buildings. (p.92) 2b

Dodona, north-west Greece; oracular sanctuary of Zeus amid oak groves; religious centre of Epirus. 4d

Dougga (Thugga), Tunisia; Punic, then Roman town; fine stone ruins, forum, temples. (p.92) 3b

El Djem (Thysdrus), Tunisia; Roman town, with huge surviving limestone amphitheatre. (p. 92) 3b

Eleusis, Greece; town and plain west of Athens, important cult centre of Demeter and Persephone with secret rituals for initiates only. 5d

Epidamnos (later Dyrrhachium); Corinthian colony on main route between Greece and Italy. Roman amphitheatre and early wall mosaics. 4c

Epidauros, Peloponnese; city-state on south side of Saronic Gulf, noted for nearby sanctuary of Asclepius; fine theatre, 4th century BC. 5d

Fréjus, south France; Roman colony of Augustus; ruins of walled town, amphitheatre, port. (p.28) 3f

Gela, south Sicily; colony of Rhodes and Crete, 688 BC. Finely preserved 4th-century walls and houses. 2e

Halicarnassus, south-west Turkey; Greek/Canan town, promoted by Mausolus (d. 353 BC); remains of his monumental tomb – the Mausoleum. **6e**

Hatra, Iraq; Roman-period Arab city destroyed AD 241; fine walls, tombs, temple ruins. (p.136) 6c

Herculaneum, Italy; Campanian Roman town buried by eruption of Vesuvius, AD 79; streets, houses with mosaics, sculptures, paintings. 2c

Himera, Sicily; Greek colony on north coast, destroyed, 409 BC. Temples, planned housing. **2d**

Histria, Romania; city on Danube delta founded by Miletus, c. 620 BC. Walls, housing, kilns, etc. 6a

Huelva, Spain; important outlet for Rio Tinto mining area, in contact with Phoenicia, 750 BC. (p.28) 1g

Itálica, Spain; Roman colony, ruins of imperial baths, amphitheatre, houses with mosaics. (p.28) 1g

Ithake (Ithaca), Greece; island south of Corfu, mythical home and assured cult-place of Odysseus. 4d

Jerash (Gerasa), Jordan; Greek, then Roman town; temples, theatres, oval forum, streets. (p.136) 4d

Kition, Cyprus; Bronze Age town and sanctuaries. Phoenician colony, 10th–4th centuries BC. **8e**

Kos, Greece; Aegean island. Roman houses in city (founded 366 BC); important sanctuary of Asclepius set on terraces on hills beyond. **6e**

Lambèse (Lambaesis), Algeria; ruins of Roman legionary camp and nearby town, in limestone. (p.92) 2b

Larisa, Greece; early Greek and Roman relics. 4d

Lyon (Lugdunum), France; Roman colony (Caesar); walls, theatres, amphitheatre, houses. (p.28) 3e

Maktar (Mactaris), Tunisia; Roman town with fine stone ruins, forum, temples, arch, baths. (p.92) 3b

Mallia, Crete, Greece; Minoan palace site on north coast, controlling upland Lasithi plain. **5e**

Marathon, Greece; dependency of Athens with small plain, site of famous battle in 490 BC. 5d

Melos, Greece; Aegean island, major source of obsidian. Phylakopi, Bronze Age centre. **5e**

Mérida, Spain; Roman town, fine remains of bridge, theatre, amphitheatre, house mosaics. (p.28) 1f

Messene, south-west Peloponnese; city founded in 370 BC on being liberated from Sparta. Walls. 4e

Miletus, west Turkey; major Greek city on now-silted Maeander river. Grid-plan, theatre, Agora. **6e**

Motya, west Sicily; Carthaginian post with unusual harbour, sited on island. Destroyed by Syracuse in 398 BC. 1d

Mycenae, Peloponnese; major Bronze Age centre; walls, palace, shaft graves and tholos tombs. 4d

Naxos, Greece; large and fertile island of Cyclades. Marble, emery; early, unfinished sculpture *in situ* in quarries. **5e**

Naxos, east Sicily; earliest Greek colony on Sicily. Walls, kilns. Replaced by Taurominion (Taormina) on hills behind in 4th century BC. 2d

Nicopolis, Greece; city founded by Octavian (Augustus) on northern arm of bay of Actium. 4d

Oenoanda, west Turkey; ruins of Greek and Roman town, home of philosopher Diogenes. 6e

Olbia, USSR; Greek city, founded by Miletus, c. 600 BC, at mouth of Bug/Dnieper estuary. **7a**

Olympia, north-west Peloponnese; major sanctuary of Zeus, site of premier Hellenic games. Stadion, architectural remains, sculpture of Zeus temple. **4e**

Olynthos, north Greece. Grid-plan town destroyed by Philip in 348 BC. 'Typical' Greek housing. 5c

Orange, France; Roman colony founded 36/5 BC; decorated arch of Tiberius (AD 26), theatre. (p.28) 3f

Orchomenos, central Greece; centre of north Boeotia, especially in Bronze Age. Tholos tomb, walls. 5d

Orvieto, Italy; Etruscan city above Tiber valley. Grid-plan cemetery of rock-cut tombs. 2b

Paestum, Italy; Greek colony of c. 600 BC. Three 6–5th century temples; painted tombs. **2c**

Palmyra, Syria; Roman oasis town, later capital of queen Zenobia, destroyed AD 273; ruins of fine limestone temples, tombs, sculptures. (p.136) 4c

Panticapaeum, USSR; Greek city at entrance to sea of Azov. Trading post in touch with local Scythian tribes. Rich 4th-century tomb finds. 8a

Paphos, Cyprus; town with major shrine of Aphrodite (her birthplace); remains of Bronze Age temple. Persian siege-mound, 499 BC. **7e**

Paris, France; small Roman town, with ruins of forum, amphitheatre and fine (Cluny) baths. (p.28) 3e

Paros, Greece; Cycladic island noted for marble. 6th-century BC architecture reused in Venetian walls. Bronze Age centre near Naoussa. 5e

Patras, north-west Peloponnese; city rose to prominence as Roman colony – well sited for trade to Italy. 4d

Pella, north Greece; Alexander's capital, now stranded inland. 4th–3rd century houses and mosaics. **4c**
Pergamon, west Turkey; centre of kingdom 282–133 BC. Rich architecture and sculpture; theatre. **6d**
Perge, south-west Turkey; city in plain of Antalya. Roman baths, theatre, etc; earlier walls. 7e
Petra, south Jordan; Nabataean Arab, then Roman 'rose-red city' ringed by mountains; temples, baths, fine rock-cut tombs, sculptures. 8g
Phaestos, Crete, Greece; Minoan palace site; inland position, dominating Mesara plain. **5f**
Philippi, north Greece; battle site; Roman town ruins, public buildings, houses, latrine. 5c
Populonia, Italy; Etruscan and Roman town on mainland, servicing iron mines of Elba. **1b**
Priene, west Turkey; town once on coast north of Miletus. Grid-plan, housing, market-place etc. 6d
Pylos, south-west Peloponnese; best harbour in area. Bronze Age palace at Ano Englianos inland. 4e
Rhegion, Italy; Greek colony on the straits of Messina, which it was founded to control, c. 710. **2d**
Rhodes, Greece; large strategically important island. Athena sanctuary at Lindos; town at Kamiros; remains of city of Rhodes, founded in 407 BC, extensively quarried by crusaders. **6e**
Sabratha, Libya; Phoenician, then Roman coastal town; fine ruins, theatre, art. **1f**
Sagunto, Spain; Iberian, then Roman coastal town, ruins of amphitheatre and fort. (p.28) 2f
Salamis, Cyprus; Bronze Age city (Enkomi) with important Iron Age successor; 8–7th century tombs. **8e**
Salona, Yugoslavia; Roman town, ruins. 3b
Samos, Greece; Aegean island, powerful in 6th century BC. Temple of Hera, walls, water tunnel. 6d
Sbeïtla (Sufetula), Tunisia; Roman town with fine stone ruins of temples, arch, gate. (p.92) 3b
Segovia, Spain; fine Roman granite aqueduct. (p.28) 2f
Seleucia on the Tigris, south Iraq; Greek, then Parthian city; mud-brick ruins. (p.136) 5c
Selinus, south-west Sicily; Greek colony, 628 BC. Impressive temples and walls. Controlled by Carthage after 409. Illicit excavations rife. **2d**
Side, south Turkey; Greek, then Roman town; ruins of stone buildings, theatre, sculptures. 7e
Smyrna, west Turkey; Greek colony; changed site c. 300 BC. 6th-century temple, Roman market-place. **6d**
Sparta, south Peloponnese. Dominant state in the area in Iron Age, with a highly militarized society. Chronic enemy of Athens in 5th century. **4e**
Spina, Italy; Etruscan 'Venice' on Po delta, find-spot of fine Athenian 5th-century vases. **2a**
Split, Yugoslavia; Greek, then Roman coastal town; palace of emperor Diocletian (AD 295) of which much remains, incorporated in later town. 3b
Sybaris, Italy; Greek colony in Italian instep, destroyed 510 BC, refounded as Thurii, 443. Under deep alluvium, below sea level; part-excavated in recent years using well-point drainage system. **3d**
Taras (Taranto), Italy; fine harbour site on heel of Italy, settled by Spartans. Rich tomb finds. **3c**
Tarquinia, Italy; Etruscan city with many painted tombs; Greek trading post down by sea. **2b**
Tarragona, Spain; Iberian, then Roman coastal town; walls, palace, necropolis and aqueduct. 2f
Tébessa (Theveste), east Algeria; Punic, Roman town; arch, basilica, temple, amphitheatre. (p.92) 2b
Tegea, central Peloponnese; main centre of Arcadia; sanctuary of Athena, 4th-century temple. 4e
Tharros, Sardinia; important Phoenician colony founded to exploit mineral resources of island. 1c
Thasos, Greece; north Aegean island, colonised by Paros, c. 675 BC. Walls, early sculpture. 5c
Thebes, central Greece; agriculturally rich centre of Boeotia in Bronze and Iron Ages. 5d
Thera (Santorini), Greece; Aegean island rent by volcanic explosion, c. 1450 BC, burying a 'Bronze Age Pompeii'. Iron Age town, theatre. **5e**
Thessaloniki, north Greece. City founded c. 300 BC; particularly important in later Roman period. Roman civic centre; early Christian churches. **4c**
Thuburbo Maius, Tunisia; Roman town, ruins. (p.92) 3b
Timgad (Thamugadi), Algeria; founded by Roman emperor Trajan, AD 101; classic town layout, stone ruins, forum, arch, temples, houses. (p.92) 2/3b
Tipasa, Algeria; Punic, then Roman coastal colony; ruins, temple, amphitheatre, houses. (p.92) 2b
Tiryns, near Argos, Peloponnese; important Bronze Age town with imposing fortifications. 4d
Trebenischte, Yugoslavia; tumulus burials, near Lake Ochrid with rich 6th-century Greek imports. 4c
Tripoli(s), Libya; arch of Marcus (c. AD 165). (p.92) 3b
Troy, north-west Turkey; major Bronze Age site, controlling Dardanelles; destroyed (by Mycenaeans?) c. 1200 BC. Greek colony later. **5d**
Verona, north Italy; Etruscan, then Roman town with early imperial theatre and amphitheatre. 2a
Volubilis, Morocco; Roman town, fine ruins. (p.92) 2b
Vulci, Italy; Etruscan city, find-spot of countless Greek vases in its vast cemeteries. **1b**
Xanthos, south-west Turkey; main Lycian centre up Xanthos valley. Sculpted tombs of 6th-5th centuries BC. 6e
Zakro, Crete, Greece; Minoan palace site, set in small bay on route to Egypt and Near East. **5e**

Africa — Map, 92

Aksum, Ethiopia; capital of South Arabian colonists in contact with Mediterranean and Indian Ocean trade, having its own distinctive decorative styles and stelae. From c. AD 100 to 19th century. 5c
Benfica, Angola; so far the most westerly occurrence of southern Early Iron Age pottery overlies Stone Age levels on a coastal shell midden. c. ad 140. 4f
Benin, Nigeria; sites in modern city have yielded medieval bronzes and art. Even more striking are the extensive earthworks from the same period surrounding the city. Late contacts with Portuguese traders are reflected in the art. **2d**
Bigo, Uganda; extensive and massive earthworks (others exist in the area) apparently constructed by pastoralists of the same pottery tradition as found locally today; substantiates oral histories of early kingdoms. c. AD 1290–1575. 4d
Broederstroom, South Africa; large Early Iron Age village with evidence of joint occupation by representatives of two peoples: Khoisan and Negro. c. AD 400. 4f
Cave of Hearths, South Africa; long Early Stone Age to Iron Age tool sequence, with geological indicators of climate changes. **4f**
Daima, Nigeria; long permanent settlement of cattle keepers and fishermen, showing continuity through such technological changes as the coming of iron and agricultural intensity around AD 400, virtually to present. From c. 800 bc. 3c
Dhlo-Dhlo, Zimbabwe; successor to Khami and Great Zimbabwe. From late 17th century. 4f
Die Kelders, South Africa; evidence for Middle Stone Age hunting. More important for first sub-equatorial evidence of domestic sheep around 2,000 BP, along with pottery and, slightly later, domestic cattle. **3g**
Engaruka, Tanzania; extensive stone walling and ditching indicates a powerful Late Iron Age people with a system of intensive agriculture. From c. AD 1500. 4d
Gamble's Cave, Kenya; bone harpoons with early, 'wavy line' pottery, overlaid by more typical pastoralists using bushy terrain. From c. 6000 BC. 4d
Gobedra, Ethiopia; long sequence starting in Middle Stone Age; around 2000–4000 bc pottery appears and seeds of cultivated crops, also camel remains, with domestic cattle later. 4c
Hadar, Ethiopia; open site with upright hominid 'Lucy' and 'First Family', *Australopithecus afarensis* – ancestral to later hominids, but probably more than one species. c. 2,500,000–3,000,000 years BP. **5d**
Howieson's Poort, South Africa; gives its name to ubiquitous later Middle Stone Age tool type. **4g**
Hyrax Hill, Kenya; stone bowls and pottery associated with cattle pastoralists using grassy terrain. Nearby is a 'Sirikwa hole', Iron Age dwellings, often in stone, around sunken stockpen of much later period. c. 3000 bc. 4e
Igbo Ukwu, Nigeria; c. 9th-century AD characteristic bronzes, some clearly cast, and evidence of extensive trade. 2d
Ijebu Ode, Nigeria; trading centre with Europe, c. 15th century AD. **2d**
Ingombe Ilede, Zambia; important trading centre between copper and gold areas and the coast, with a sophisticated metal technology of its own. Woven fabrics found with elaborate burials. Goats more common than cattle. From c. ad 1200. 4f
Isamu Pati, Zambia; a 'mound' site in the Kalomo area, showing how villagers tended to group circular dwellings around a stockpen, use storage pits for crops, engage in long-distance trade, produce lathe-turned ivory and ironwork away from settlement. Clay figurines show humped cattle. c. ad 1000. 3f
Ishango, Zaire; Middle Stone Age sedentary or semi-sedentary community with finely developed artefacts, like harpoons, and possible early counting system. 4d
Isimila, Tanzania; from Early to Middle Stone Age, a long sequence of open-site occupations important for the horizontal variation in the assemblages. **4e**
Kalambo, Zambia; only Early Stone Age open site with well preserved organic remains and good evidence of fire use; also possible windbreak. Shows long sequence of cultural development into Late Iron Age. **4e**
Kanapoi, Kenya; open site with possible *Australopithecus africanus*; no tools. c. 4,000,000 BP. **4d**
Kansyore, Tanzania/Uganda; gives its name to early pottery usually thought to be very Early Iron Age; found on shell middens around Lake Ukerewe/Victoria. 4d
Khami, Zimbabwe; site of stone ruins successive to Great Zimbabwe. Gives its name to a more widespread style of building with similar associations. From c. AD 1500. 4f
Kilwa, Tanzania; Arab/Swahili trading settlement, from around 9th century AD. 5e
Kintampo, Ghana; seasonal hunter-gatherers with pottery, overlain by 'polished stone' eponymous culture with pottery and food-processing equipment (cultivation not sure), as well as small types of bovine and goat, around 1400 bc. 2d
Koobi Fora, Kenya; open site with *Homo erectus* and huge bone and stone collection; indications of food processing. c. 150,000 years BP. **4d**
Kumadzulo, Zambia; Early Iron Age settlement characterized by small implements and some copper; smelting carried out in middle of large, enduring village with 'sub-rectangular' structures. 4f
Kwale, Kenya; gives its name to distinctive 'fluted' pottery found on Early Iron Age sites much further south in eastern Africa. c. ad 200. 5e
Laetoli, Tanzania; open site, footprints and mandibles of upright hominid, relating to Hadar finds. **4e**
Lothagam, Kenya; open site, with possible *Australopithecus africanus*, no tools; also Late Stone Age fishing settlement. c. 5,500,000 years BP. **4d**
Lydenburg, South Africa; series of Early and Late Iron Age sites, including early instance of remarkable modelled clay heads. Later period shows dense settlement with stone walls typical of a large area of South Africa. From c. AD 500. 4f
Machili, Zambia; pottery sequence from various sites associated with iron-working agriculturalists, some seemingly more dependent on cattle than others. 3f
Magosi, Uganda; gives its name to a Late Middle Stone Age tool type widely distributed in East Africa; a long sequence ending with polished stone axes of Late Stone Age. 4d
Makapan Limeworks, South Africa; only South African early hominid site yielding date (palaeomagnetic), and fauna probably older by 2,000,000 years than in the others. Cave site with *Australopithecus africanus*. c. 2,500,000 years BP. **4f**
Manyikeni, Mozambique; outlying establishment of the Shona state, with building styles relating to those of Great Zimbabwe. From c. ad 1200 until 1600. **4f**
Mapungubwe, South Africa. In some ways duplicating the development at Great Zimbabwe, this smaller, more local variant site has been plagued by debate over the racial type (Khoisan or Negro) of its builders and occupants. **4f**
Melkhoutboom, South Africa; here the 'Albany' industry of the Late Stone Age was first identified; rich in plant remains reflecting economy. **4g**
Nachikufu, Zambia; gives its name to a series of ubiquitous microlithic and Late Stone Age assemblages, especially north of the Zambezi. c. 16,000 bc. 4e

Narosura, Kenya; gives its name to a 'pastoral Neolithic' pottery type widespread in East Africa, and dated elsewhere around 1000 bc. 4d
Nderit, Kenya; gives its name to a 'pastoral Neolithic' pottery type elsewhere dated to around 5000 bc; also provides good climatic evidence for earlier periods. 4d
Ngwenya, Swaziland; in a series of caves, Middle Stone Age deposits above which are signs of Late Stone Age mining (around 7000 bc) for haematite, possibly for use as body pigment. Above this, 5th century AD Early Iron Age. 4f
Ntabazingwe, Zimbabwe; type site of 'Leopard's Kopje' tradition of pottery and settlement thought to be ancestral to builders of Great Zimbabwe. From c. AD 900. 4f
Olorgesailie, Kenya; open site with rich collection of artefact types and a few bones. c. 100,000 BP. **4d**
Omo, Ethiopia; c. 2,000,000 years BP, simple stone tools. **4d**
Oyo, Nigeria; successor to Ife, from c. 16th century AD. **2d**
Pomongwe, South Africa; gives its name to inland Late Stone Age finds, contemporary with Albany industry nearer southern coast. 4f
Sanga, Zaire; long Iron Age pottery sequence, starting with the unique and beautiful 'Kisalian' funeral ware, with elaborate burials and sophisticated metal technology. Its people apparently hunted and fished rather than farmed. From c. ad 700. 4e
Sango, Uganda; gives its name to widespread tool type representing transition to Middle Stone Age in Africa. c. 50,000 BP. 4d
Sofala, Mozambique; Arab/Swahili trading port, from c. 10th century AD. 4f
Sterkfontein, South Africa; cave site with australopithecines, but also *Homo habilis*-like skull associated with stone tools around 2,000,000–1,500,000 years BP. Faunal analysis shows climate becoming drier c. 2,000,000 years BP. **4f**
Stillbay, South Africa; gives its name to African Middle Stone Age ubiquitous tool type. **3g**
Swartkrans, South Africa; cave site. Study of bones has shown *Australopithecus africanus* more hunted than hunting. **4f**
Tada, Nigeria; collection of bronzes related to Ife heads, but portraying whole figures, perhaps as late as 16th century AD. A very northerly appearance in the savanna area of a culture otherwise mainly associated with rainforest. **2d**
Taruga, Nigeria; around 300 bc, one of few datable sites in Nok area, where an extraordinary series of modelled clay heads has been found associated with ironworking and agriculture, although there is evidence of stone axes being used well into the Iron Age. 2d
Tichitt-walata, Mauretania; dense distribution of stone-built villages, active in fishing and grain-processing. By c. 1000 bc, evidence of more reliable domestic grains and small domestic cattle and goats. Important responses to climate change reflected. 1c
Timbuktu, Mali; ancient and modern trading settlement and site of medieval Islamic university. **2c**
Urewe, Uganda; gives its name to 'dimple-based' pottery, dated elsewhere c. AD 200–300 and associated with Early Iron Age, mainly to west. 4d
Uvinza, Tanzania; salt-processing centre. From c. ad 420–1740. 4e
Wilton, South Africa; gives its name to ubiquitous Late Stone Age assemblage type. **4g**
Ziwa, Zimbabwe; gives its name to more widespread Early Iron Age pottery c. AD 300, here associated with some stone building but succeeded c. AD 1000 by elaborate stone building and terracing distinct from the Great Zimbabwe tradition and concentrated in this mountainous area, called 'Inyanga'. 4f

Nile Valley — Map, 114

Abu Gurab; site of the Sun-Temples of the kings of the 5th dynasty (2494–2345 BC). The central feature of these structures comprised a podium surmounted by a truncated obelisk. **2b**
Abu Rawash; desert location of the 4th-dynasty pyramid of king Djedefre (c. 2500 BC), who for unknown reasons preferred this site for his tomb to the necropolis at Giza. **2b**
Abusir, site south of Abu Gurab at which several 5th-dynasty kings constructed their pyramids. These tombs are inferior in size and accuracy to the earlier pyramids at Giza. **2b**
Akhmim; important city in Upper Egypt; the cemeteries have yielded numerous antiquities of the Graeco-Roman Period (after 332 BC), particularly funerary stelae and textiles. **2e**
El-Amarna; site of the city named Akhetaten, founded by king Akhenaten when he moved here from the older capital at Thebes. Occupied for only a short time, between c. 1375 and 1362 BC, and deserted under Tutankhamun. **2d**
El-Amra; name given to the southern extension of the Abydos necropolis, in which graves of the Predynastic Period (before 3100 BC) have been excavated. **3e**
Armant; cult-centre of the warrior-god Monthu, principal deity of the Theban area during the 11th dynasty (2133–1991 BC). Burial-place of the sacred Buchis bulls. **3f**
Ashmunein; important town in Middle Egypt, occupied from early times and completely re-developed in the Roman Period (after 30 BC). Chief centre of the cult of Thoth, god of writing and wisdom. **2d**
Aswan; modern town around the site of the ancient Elephantine, often regarded as the southern limit of Egypt proper. Its quarries provided the black and red granite used in monumental buildings. **3g**
Asyut; the ancient city is covered by its modern counterpart, but in the nearby cemeteries are the important tombs of the local princes of Asyut during the First Intermediate Period (2181–2040 BC). **3e**
El-Badari; cemetery site at which the first evidence for the existence of the earliest Predynastic culture was discovered by Guy Brunton. The culture is named 'Badarian' after the site. **3e**
El-Bahnasa; site of the Graeco-Roman city of Oxyrhynchus, famous for the discovery of Greek and Latin papyri. The thousands of documents found by the Graeco-Roman Branch of the Egypt Exploration Society at the beginning of this century are steadily being published. **2c**
Ballas; extensive early cemetery site of the Predynastic and Early Dynastic Periods (from before 3100 to 2700 BC). **3f**
Beni Hasan; middle-Egyptian necropolis of the local governors during the 12th dynasty (1991–1786 BC). The decorated tomb-chapels are cut into the cliffs on the east bank of the Nile. **2d**
El-Bersha; similar site to Beni Hasan, containing more rock-cut tombs of local administrators from the Middle Kingdom. **2d**
Bet Khallaf; desert cemetery a short distance north of Abydos, chiefly noted for several massive mud-brick mastaba-tombs of the 3rd dynasty (2686–2613 BC). **2/3e**
Bubastis; delta city and chief centre of the goddess Bastet, with remains of temples from the Old Kingdom onwards. Major rebuilding took place under king Osorkon II (c. 860 BC). **3b**
Busiris; original centre of Osiris-worship in the Delta. Very few remains of the site can be seen at the present day. **2a**
Buto; city in the Nile Delta, one of the traditional early centres of the Predynastic Period, and site of the twin towns of Pe and Dep. The town-mound remains largely unexcavated. **2a**
Cairo; capital of modern Egypt, founded by the Arabs on the site of the ancient fortress of Babylon. The situation of Cairo at the junction of Upper and Lower Egypt is well-suited for an administrative centre. **2b**
Daphnae; site of a fortified camp built by Psamtik I (664–610 BC) for his Greek mercenaries. Mentioned in biblical texts under the name Tahpanhes. **3b**
Dashur; part of the Memphite necropolis to the south of Saqqara, marked by the two pyramids of king Sneferu (c. 2600 BC) and certain brick-built pyramids of the 12th dynasty. **2b**
Deir El-Bahari; site of the mortuary temple of queen Hatshepsut (1503–1482 BC) on the west bank of the Nile at Thebes. The temple was built in a series of terraces, modelled on the adjacent temple of king Mentuhotpe II of the 11th dynasty (c. 2025 BC). **3f**
Deir el-Gebrawi; provincial cemetery in Middle Egypt, containing rock-tombs of the late Old Kingdom (c. 2200 BC). **2d**
Denderah; important town from early times, but now chiefly known for its Ptolemaic temple of the goddess Hathor. Cemeteries of earlier date lie in the desert behind the temple. **3f**
Edfu; the well-preserved temple of Horus at the site dates from the Ptolemaic Period (305–30 BC) but the town was occupied much earlier. Much of the early town is beneath the modern village, but the Graeco-Roman town-site is visible to the west of the temple. **3g**
Ehnasiya; important city during the First Intermediate Period (2181–2040 BC) when its rulers were in conflict with the Thebans for control of Egypt. Developed in the Roman Period as the city of Heracleopolis. **2c**
Esna; town on the west bank of the Nile in Upper Egypt and site of a temple of the Graeco-Roman Period, dedicated to the god Khnum. In the desert west of the town are cemeteries of earlier date. **3f**
Gebelein; site to the south of Thebes, at which are the remains of brick constructions dating from the time of the High-Priest of Amun, Menkheperre (c. 970 BC). **3f**
Gebel es-Silsila; quarry region in Upper Egypt from which the Egyptians obtained sandstone for building projects. The area contains numerous chapels, shrines and inscriptions. **3g**
Hawara; site of the pyramid of king Amenemhat III (c. 1800 BC), whose vast mortuary temple greatly impressed the Greek historian Herodotus. Extensive Roman cemetery from which many of the so-called 'mummy-portraits' are derived. **2c**
Heliopolis; cult-centre of the Sun-god, Re. Heliopolis was of particular importance in the 5th dynasty, when the solar cult gained influence. Now a suburb of modern Cairo. **2b**
Hierakonpolis; city of very early foundation in Upper Egypt, opposite El-Kab. The temple remains contain building phases of the Early Dynastic Period and Old Kingdom beneath later reconstructions of the New Kingdom. Important Predynastic tombs have been found near the town. **3f**
Hu; the Roman Diospolis Parva, excavated by Flinders Petrie in 1898. His most important results concerned the Predynastic cemeteries, used as the basis for the sequential dating of the Predynastic cultures. **3f**
Illahun; site of the brick-built pyramid of king Sesostris II (1897–1878 BC), the first of the pyramids to have its entrance on other than the north side. **2c**
El-Kab; town on the east of the Nile, opposite Hierakonpolis. Occupation dates from very early times to the latest, and the most striking feature is the great mud-brick enclosure-wall of the 30th dynasty (c. 350 BC) around the temple-area. Important rock-tombs of the New Kingdom lie in the nearby cliffs. **3f**
Kom Abu Billo; site of the ancient Terenuthis, the cemeteries of which have produced very many tomb-stelae of the 3rd and 4th centuries AD, showing clear intermixing of Greek and Egyptian motifs. **2b**
Kom Ombo; site of a town and temple in Upper Egypt. Only the Graeco-Roman temple, dedicated to Sobek and Horus, is clearly visible today. **3g**
El-Lisht; administrative capital of Egypt during the 12th dynasty (1991–1786 BC). Site of the pyramids of kings Amenemhat I and Sesostris I. **2c**
Luxor; name of the modern town on the site of ancient Thebes, around the ruins of the temple of Luxor, initiated by Amenophis III (c. 1390 BC) and enlarged by Rameses II (c. 1250 BC). **3f**
Maidum; chief monument of the site is the pyramid of uncertain ownership, considered in ancient times to belong to Sneferu, but now sometimes ascribed to Huni, last king of the 3rd dynasty (c. 1613 BC). **2c**
Medinet el-Faiyum; modern town on the site of the ancient Crocodilopolis, main cult-centre of the crocodile-god Sobek. The area was important in the Middle Kingdom, when land-reclamation works were carried out in the district. **2c**
Medinet Habu; name given to the area around the mortuary temple of Rameses III at Thebes (1198– **3f**

1166 BC). In the Third Intermediate Period, the temple became the centre for the administration of the Theban necropolis.

Meir; local necropolis of rock-cut tombs, chiefly of the late Old Kingdom and the First Intermediate Period (c. 2200–2040 BC). Such regional cemeteries became established as central power declined in the 6th dynasty. **2d**

Memphis; traditionally founded by Menes c. 3000 BC as the capital of Egypt, it continued to be an important centre throughout later periods. The city's principal god was Ptah, to whom large temples were dedicated. **2b**

Mendes; town in the central Delta, with remains from the Predynastic (before 3100 BC) to the late Roman Period (5th century AD). The Roman and Pharaonic towns are marked by the adjacent mounds of Thmuis and Tell er-Ruba respectively. **3a**

Minya; modern town which serves as the administrative centre of Middle Egypt, having taken over this role from the ancient Ashmunein a little to the south. **2d**

Naqada; a short distance to the south of Ballas, and site of an important Predynastic cemetery and town, at which the distinctive products of the Predynastic cultures were first encountered. **3f**

Naq ed-Deir; extensive cemeteries of the ancient city of Thinis, covering the whole range of Egyptian history. **3e**

Naucratis; town established in the 26th dynasty (664–525 BC) as the sole Greek trading centre in Egypt. Many objects of purely Greek manufacture have been recovered from the site. **2a**

Nebesha; the ancient town of Imet and cult-centre of the goddess Wadjit in the eastern Delta. Excavated by the Egypt Exploration Fund in 1886. **3b**

Pelusium; town in the marshy district on the northern coast of Sinai, near which the Persians defeated the Egyptians in 525 BC and gained control of Egypt. **4a**

Philae; island site south of Aswan, occupied by an ancient town and several temples, chief among which is the temple of Isis. The temples have recently been transferred to a new island site to save them from the waters of Lake Nasser. **3g**

Qantir; new royal residence established in the 19th dynasty (c. 1300 BC) in the eastern Delta. Mentioned in the Bible under its Egyptian name of Pi-Ramesse. **3b**

Qaw el-Kebir; site noted for cemeteries of all periods, containing mostly small graves, but during the First Intermediate Period (2181–2040 BC) some very large and monumental tombs were constructed for the nobility of the district. **2e**

Qena; modern town situated at the end of the Wadi Hammamat, a route into the eastern desert used by ancient mining expeditions. **3e**

Qift; the ancient town of Coptos, cult-centre of the fertility-god Min. Remains of the temple in the city showed evidence of repeated phases of rebuilding down to the Roman Period. **3f**

Rosetta; town at the mouth of the western branch of the Nile, where the bilingual decree, now known as the Rosetta Stone, was discovered in 1799. **2a**

Sebennytus; ancient town in the Delta, now marked by the modern Sammanud. Home-town of the kings of the 30th dynasty (380–343 BC). **3a**

Sedment; cemetery of the ancient city of Heracleopolis with tombs from all periods. **2c**

Sheikh Ibada; Roman town on the east bank of the Nile, opposite Ashmunein. From the cemeteries of the town a number of important late Roman and early Christian antiquities have been recovered. In Roman times the town was called Antinoopolis. **2d**

Tanis; large city in the eastern Delta, identified with the biblical Zoan. Chiefly developed from the 22nd dynasty (c. 850 BC) and embellished with monuments removed from the New Kingdom site at Qantir. **3a**

Tarkhan; desert cemetery excavated by Flinders Petrie in 1911–13, containing important tombs of the 1st dynasty (3100–2890 BC) and other graves of later date. **2c**

Tell el-Rataba; site on the eastern side of the Nile Delta, marked by a fortified enclosure and traces of a New Kingdom temple. **3b**

Tell el-Yahudiya; town site, chiefly known for the remains of a palace of Rameses III (c. 1198–1166 BC), now destroyed. Coloured tile inlays from the palace are scattered through the museums of the world. **3b**

Tuna el-Gebel; the cemetery of Ashmunein, noted for tombs of the Late Period and the Graeco-Roman age (from 380 BC). Subterranean galleries contain the burials of the sacred ibises and baboons of Thoth. **2d**

Xois; town in the Delta from which the kings of the 14th dynasty (c. 1786–1603 BC) ruled a part of Egypt during the Second Intermediate Period. **2a**

Near East

Map, 136-137

Alaca Hüyük, Turkey; rich burials show mingling of Anatolian craftsmanship in gold, silver and bronze with burial customs from the northern steppes; monumental gateway with guardian sphinxes is comparable with Boğazköy. **4a**

Arin-Berd; major Urartian citadel founded by king Argishti I (early 8th century BC), and designed to control Yerevan plain; excavated by K. Oganesyan (Yerevan); palace with murals. 6a

Ashdod (Tell Mor); one of the five main cities of the Philistines, with earlier Canaanite cults and a burnt layer marking Israelite destruction. **3d**

Arslantepe (Malatya); shrine with Late Uruk (Mesopotamian) links, with later levels of the Early Trans-Caucasian culture centred in highlands to the east. 4b

Assur; ancient religious centre of Assyria, founded mid-3rd millennium BC on west bank of Tigris; excavated from 1903 by German team under Andrae and recently by Iraqi State Organization. **3c**

Babylon; excavation under Robert Koldewey (1898–1917) set example for treatment of Near Eastern stratified sites with architectural remains and revealed Neo-Babylonian town, Ishtar Gate, etc. Current Iraqi work of excavation and restoration. **3d**

Bahrein (Dilmun); major trading centre of the Gulf region from c. 2500 BC; evidence of sea trade with Indus valley cities; vast cemeteries of tumuli suggest burial of many from Mesopotamia in Dilmun, sacred to the Sumerians; Danish excavations for many seasons (Bibby and others). **7f**

Bastam, north-west Iran; Urartian fortress dug by W. Kleiss (1969–), mainly 7th-century BC. 6b

Brak, Tell; huge city-mound on upper Khabur River excavated by Mallowan and currently by Oates; prehistoric temples with eye-idols; arsenal built by Akkadian kings (24th–23rd centuries BC). 5b

Byblos; port for cedar trade from Lebanon to Egypt, prosperous trading city from 4th millennium BC; Canaanite temples; rich metalwork; almost unbroken settlement through prehistoric periods and beyond; French excavations (Dunand). **4c**

Carchemish; excavated by Woolley and T. E. Lawrence, but work could not be completed; Bronze Age city; became viceregal centre of Hittite rule in north Syria; then (c. 900 BC) again extended; richest Syro-Hittite city under strong Hittite cultural legacy; sculptured slabs in various styles. **4b**

Ebla (Tell Mardikh); excavated since 1964 by Italian expedition under Paolo Matthiae. In 1974 a burnt level was found to comprise a palace with a remarkable cuneiform archive, helping to set Syria in a cultural context comparable with the Sumerian homeland; palace destroyed by Sargon of Agade or by his grandson Naram-Sin. **4c**

Eridu; by Sumerian tradition the oldest city of southern Mesopotamia, excavations confirmed its early origins (6th millennium BC), with a unique sequence of shrines demonstrating development to the characteristic Sumerian design. **6d**

Godin Tepe, central western Iran; excavated by Royal Ontario Museum (T. C. Young, 1967–73), this mound revealed occupation from prehistoric settlement of merchants from Susa to a Median chieftain's residence and fort. 6c

Gordion; capital of Phrygian kingdom, at its height in 8th century BC; excavated by American team under R. S. Young; massive gateway; rich tumulus burials with much woodwork. 3a

Hacilar; prehistoric village near Lake Burdur; excavated by James Mellaart (1957–60); fine painted pottery and female statuettes. **2b**

Hama; excavated in 1930s by Danish expedition; long sequence from Neolithic to Iron Age, with main period c. 900–720 BC, having large palace and gateways of typical Syro-Hittite design, under Aramaean rather than Hittite influence. 4c

Hasanlu; excavated (1956–) by American expedition under R. H. Dyson; 5 public buildings in major burnt level (IV), c. 1100–800 BC; strangely decorated gold bowl betrays Hurrian traditions; training ground of many North American excavators. 6b

Hazor; excavated by Yigael Yadin; major Canaanite city (citadel and lower city), with much less extensive settlement after Israelite conquest, even under Solomon and Ahab; sequence of Canaanite temples (compare Temple of Jerusalem). **3c**

Jericho; earlier excavations followed by those under Kathleen Kenyon (1952–58) marked new approach to stratigraphic problems of a major Near Eastern mound; 9 millennia of occupation; Neolithic plastered skulls. **3d**

Jerusalem; Middle Bronze Age (Jebusite) defences remodelled by Hezekiah under threat of Assyrian attack; city captured by David and made capital of united kingdom. **3d**

Kadesh (Tell Nebi Mend); major city on Orontes, scene of drawn battle between Hittites and Rameses II. **4c**

Karmir-Blur; Urartian stronghold replacing Arin-Berd; sacked by Scyths; massive storerooms; many bronzes; excavated by B. B. Piotrovskii. 6a

Khorsabad; unfinished residence of Sargon II of Assyria (722–705 BC); French and American excavations. **5b**

Kültepe (Kanesh); most famous for the period of the Assyrian merchant colony, centre of Anatolian trade network (c. 2100–1750 BC); tablets recording trade. 4b

Lachish (Tell ed-Duweir); siege by Sennacherib, king of Assyria (700 BC), recorded in relief and text on walls of his palace at Nineveh and in Old Testament. **3d**

Lagash; important Sumerian trading city of later 3rd millennium BC; its governor Gudea left basalt statues, now in the Louvre, Paris; deadly rival of neighbouring city Umma; Stele of Vultures records military action. **6d**

Mari; famous for palace of last king, Zimri-Lim, with administrative, residential, educational, religious and economic functions; large archive, published by French expedition started (1933) by André Parrot; murals; city sacked by Hammurabi of Babylon (c. 1757 BC). **5c**

Mersin; excavated by John Garstang before and after World War II; Neolithic to Bronze Age sequence of occupation. **3b**

Nimrud (Calah); one of the major Assyrian cities, excavated by Layard and (1949–63) by Mallowan and Oates; north-west Palace and Fort Shalmaneser yielded reliefs and ivories respectively. **5c**

Nippur; religious centre of Sumerian homeland, seat of god Enlil; long history of American excavations, currently under McGuire Gibson. 6d

Nush-i Jan, Tepe, central western Iran; Median site excavated by David Stronach; comprises fortress, columned hall and fire temple (7th century BC). 6c

Pasargadae; capital of Cyrus the Great, who employed Greek and Lydian masons for his new residence. 7d

Samaria; Israelite city founded by Omri (c. 880 BC) as new capital for kingdom of Israel; archaeological sequence relates well to historical events. 3d

Sardis; American excavations have revealed remains of Lydian and Byzantine occupation; gold-working nearby; royal tombs; capital of rich king Croesus of Lydia and his predecessors. **2b**

Sidon; **Tyre**; major Phoenician cities historically attested. **3c**

Sippar; second city of kingdom of Babylon; major archives. **5d**

Susa; French excavations since later 19th century; major prehistoric centre, with evidence of early urbanization and interconnections (from early 4th millennium BC) between highland Elam (southern Iran) and Mesopotamia. **6d**

Tarsus; American excavations (Goldman) revealed sequence supplementing neighbouring Mersin with special importance for Early and Middle Bronze Age (c. 3500–1600 BC) cultural links. **3b**

Tyre, see Sidon.
Van (Tushpa); capital of kingdom of Urartu, c. 850–600 BC. Rock fortress; rock-cut tombs and open-air shrine. 5b
Warka (Uruk/Erech); largest Sumerian city, excavated for many seasons by German expedition; earliest evidence of cylinder-seals and writing; temple-governmental complex of 4th millennium BC; Uruk pottery (bevelled-rim bowls etc.). 6d

Indian Subcontinent — Map, 162

Amaravati, Andhra Pradesh; site includes exquisite sculptured decoration representing the later great flowering of Indian Buddhist art. **3e**
Arikamedu, near Pondicherry, on Tamilnadu coast; acted as port for export of Indian material to the West; throws light on Roman trading activities in Southern India. **3f**
Bagor, south-east Rajasthan; shows development of local Mesolithic people contemporary with Indus civilization; provides evidence of trade between the two cultures. **2c**
Begram, Kabul valley; location at foot of Hindu Kush on branch trade route from Bactria to India gave it an important position in international trade; evidence from later 1st- to 3rd-century finds in 'palace', which seems to have been a customs depot. **2a**
Bhimbetkar, near Bhopal, Central India; focus of artistic activity from Upper Palaeolithic until recent times, especially during the Mesolithic; 480 rock-shelters spread over 7 localities. **2c**
Brahmagiri, near Siddapur, Karnataka; first scientific excavation, in 1947, of graves of Megalithic culture; one of the few sites at which a contemporary settlement was excavated. **2e**
Charsada, near Peshawar; ancient Pushkalavati, capital of Gandhara, traditionally founded at same time as Taxila and enjoying similar importance politically and as a trading centre. **2a**
Harappa, Punjab, Pakistan; twin capital of Indus civilization and first site at which remains of the civilization were recognized. Citadel mound and lower town of mature Indus civilization comparable in importance to Mohenjo Daro, but less well preserved. Occupation before and after mature Indus civilization provides fuller picture of cultural sequence than available from Mohenjo Daro. Evidence of Indus funerary rites found here were absent at Mohenjo Daro. **2b**
Hastinapura, Uttar Pradesh; four main periods of occupation, of which the 2nd is Painted Grey Ware, or PGW. The PGW village can be identified as the capital of the Kurus and Pandavas whose legendary feud is described in the *Mahabharata* epic, which mentions Hastinapura's destruction by a flood. Deserted c. 3rd century AD. **3b**
Inamgaon, Poona district; scientifically conducted horizontal excavation of large Chalcolithic settlement with evidence of social stratification and religious practices. Settlement occupied after 1000 BC, when most Deccan Chalcolithic sites were abandoned. **2d**
Kalibangan, Rajasthan; ploughed field of pre-Indus culture shows antiquity of modern farming practices in this area. Similarities to Harappa and Mohenjo Daro except in scale; picture of settlement hierarchy. Important sequence from pre-Indus period; 'fire altars' throw new light on religion; cemetery gives fuller picture of funerary rites than at Harappa. **2b**
Lothal, Gujurat; originally on coast. Southernmost outpost of Indus civilization; 'dock' and coastal location suggest importance in international trade. 'Gateway' trading settlement exchanging manufactured jewellery and copper tools with local Mesolithic people for raw materials. **2c**
Mehrgarh, plateau at foot of Bolan pass, Kachi district, Baluchistan; seven periods of occupation, beginning with ceramic Neolithic of 5th and possibly late 6th millennium BC. Long unbroken cultural sequence shows importance of hitherto little known Kachi plain. Extends known prehistoric occupation of Baluchistan back several thousand years. **1b**
Pataliputra, modern city of Patna; capital city of Mauryan and Gupta empires; seat of power of Shungas and Kushans. Small village at time of Buddha which grew to be Mauryan capital in 3rd century BC. **4c**
Pirak, North Kachi plain, Baluchistan; 12 metres of deposit demonstrate the existence of prosperous post-Indus civilization culture in area previously considered to have been largely uninhabited at this time. **1b**
Polonnaruva, north Central Province, Sri Lanka; succeeded Anuradhapura as capital in 8th century AD and flourished until abandonment in 13th century. As at Anuradhapura, main surviving monuments are religious, mainly Buddhist but also Hindu structures built by Tamil invaders. Shows later stage of Classical Ceylonese art and architecture begun at Anuradhapura. **3g**
Rajghir, south-east of Patna; major metropolis during later 1st millennium BC, when seat of government shifted to Pataliputra. Features prominently in the life of Buddha; many locations associated with him were identified in the excavations. **4c**
Sanchi, near Bhopal, Central India; superlative carvings on gateways are one of the highest achievements of Indian art. Buddhist monastic site, principal monument being the Great Stupa built by Ashoka and enlarged by the Satavahanas in 2nd to 1st centuries BC. **3c**
Sigiriya, near Kandy, central province, Sri Lanka; rock pinnacle about 350 metres high; temporary capital of parricide king Kasyapa in 5th century AD. Frescoes are earliest surviving examples of Ceylonese painting, comparable in artistic merit to the frescoes of Ajanta. **3g**
Utnur, Andhra; one of a group of 'ash-mounds' in this region. Before excavation, 'ash-mounds' were a source of controversy. Now shown to be mounds of cattle dung periodically fired, accumulated in the course of seasonal occupation during Lower and part of Upper Neolithic periods. The burning of dung, now a valuable fuel, indicates more heavy afforestation in the 3rd millennium BC. **2e**

Far East — Map, 184-185

Banpocun, Shaanxi province; type-site of the Yangshao Neolithic culture of west China. Evidence of millet; domestication of sheep and dog. Slash-and-burn agriculture and use of polished stone axes. c. 5000 BC. **5d**
Borobadur, western central Asia, Buddhist monument, c. AD 800. The structure consists of 6 superimposed, square terraces, cardinally orientated, with double projections on each side, supporting 3 circular platforms and a central terminal stupa. In all, the monument housed a total of 505 images of the Buddha. Immediately east of Borobadur are Candi Pawon, now empty, and Candi Mendut, which houses a colossal seated Buddha flanked by two equally large Boddhisattvas. Borobadur and the complex are unique in the Buddhist world and the particular form of Buddhism which they represent is still a matter of controversy after 150 years. **8f**
Dunhuang, Gansu province; 486 cave temples cut into limestone cliffs, richly decorated with sculptures and murals of Buddha's and everyday life by monks at the oasis town. c. 4th–14th centuries AD. 4c
Huixian, Henan province; several sites exist around Huixian, eg. Liulige, the earliest dating from the Middle Shang Bronze Age. More significant are those of the Warring States (475–221 BC) period. Near Guweicun, 27 intact 200-metre-long tombs with lacquered coffins were found. Reconstruction of decayed chariots revealed the use of dish-shaped spoked wheels, predating similar European solutions to stress problems by about 2,000 years. The earliest Chinese iron ploughshare was found here. **5d**
Lantian, Shaanxi province; Palaeolithic site where skull and jawbone of Lantian man were found – the oldest human type in China before Peking man and comparable to *Australopithecus* of East Africa and Java. c. 700,000 years ago. **5d**
Liyu, Shaanxi province. Decoration of *ding* bronze vessels found here is important in the development of the so-called 'Huai style' seen at Shouxian. 7th–6th centuries BC. 5c
Longmen, near Luoyang, Henan province; Wei dynasty capital moved to Luoyang in 494 AD and the emperor built cave temples along the lines of the Yungang caves. Site is important for emergence and transmission of Indian and central Asian art influences and birth of purely Chinese forms. The caves were revitalized at the end of the 7th century when Buddhism reached its final apogee. After AD 494; also end 7th century. **5d**
Longshan, Shandong province; type-site of Longshan Neolithic culture, characterized by thin-wall, wheel-turned pottery burnished black. c. 2,500 BC. **6d**
Luoyang, Henan province; second capital of the Zhou dynasty (1027–221 BC), called Eastern Zhou. First capital at Xian was destroyed by invaders in 771 BC and feudal lords then eroded Zhou power in the Warring States period (402–221 BC). Zhou chariot burials were found there. It was subsequently capital of several dynasties to the 10th century AD. 5d
Mancheng, Hebei province. Hills near the town contained tombs of prince Liu Sheng (d. 113 BC) and his cousin consort Dou Wan. Hewn from solid rock, these were lined with timbers and tiles and sealed off by brick walls. Numerous gold, silver, bronze, lacquer and clay items were found. Most celebrated were 2 jade burial suits, hitherto only known from writings. c. 100 BC. **5c**
Mawangdui, Hunan province; one of the 'fire-pit' graves (from the area's flammable marsh gas) revealed the coffins of the marquess of Dai, lined with charcoal and clay. Her body's excellent state of preservation was due to the nature of the soil. According to X-rays she died, aged 50, from 'biliary colic' – 138 melon pips were found in her stomach. 2nd century BC. **5e**
Ordos, Mongolian name for grasslands in the northward loop of the Huang He, covered by fertile loess deposit. This, with post-glacial warmer temperatures, provided optimum conditions for man and vegetation. Several sites give evidence for 'Ordos man'. **5c**
Shouxian, Anhui province; tomb of marquess of Cai is best known for its magnificent bronze vessels, which best exemplify the 'Huai style'. Distinctive style comprises interlace, studding, dots, wing and feather motifs, etc. Early 5th century BC. **6d**
Shizhaishan, Yunnan province; necropolis of Dian kingdom, a client people of Chinese culture who submitted to Han dynasty supremacy in 109 BC. 2nd–1st century BC. **4e**
Sjara Osso Gol, Ordos region; Palaeolithic site, one of several of Neanderthaloid 'Ordos man'. Notable for microliths bearing evidence of secondary working and an advance on stone tool-making of Peking man. c. 600,000 years ago. **5c**
Tangshan, Hebei province; best known for bronze vessels discovered there – 'hunting *hu*'. c. 500 BC. 6c
Turfan, Xinjiang province; graves excavated here demonstrate the inroads made by Chinese culture along the northern desert route into Central Asia. 3rd–8th centuries AD. **3c**
Wuwei, Gansu province; brick-built tomb of general Zhang Yechang. Finds include a procession of 39 horses, 14 carts and 28 human bronze statuettes, as well as the first discovery of Han-dynasty silks. Most celebrated find was the 'flying horse of Gansu'. 2nd century AD. **4d**
Xian, Shaanxi province; site of first Zhou dynasty (Western Zhou; 1027–221 BC) which overthrew the Shang and set up China's first feudal government. Laid out in chessboard pattern, 12 enormous roads running east–west crossed 9 north–south ways at right angles; the central one was 165 metres wide. Subsequently, as Xianyang, capital of first emperor of China, from 221 BC. Thousands of life-size clay soldiers and horses unearthed from rectangular pit near large unexcavated burial mound of emperor. Also capital of several later dynasties, called Chang'an. **5d**
Xinzheng, Henan province; bronzes found mark the deliberate adoption of a style including spirals, rope patterns, interlace and other characteristics of the later nomad art of the ancient steppes around the Ordos. Xinzheng bronzes are a stage in the development of the 'Huai style'. 8th–7th centuries BC. 5d
Yungang, Shaanxi province; cave temples begun in the 460s but abandoned when the capital moved **5c**

to Luoyang in AD 494. Mainly decorated with Buddhist carvings and massive sculptures – up to 25 metres high – standing in temples cut in cliffs. AD 460s–490s.

Zhengzhou, Henan province; probably Shang dynasty capital Ao or Xiao before the capital was moved to Anyang, 1300 BC. China's oldest excavated city, it covered 3.2 square kilometres, surrounded by a high wall of typically Shang rammed earth. Shang Bronze Age – 1300 BC. **5d**

Americas — Map, 206-207

Adena, USA; type-site of a funerary mound-building culture in the Ohio valley. Exotic grave goods show wide trade contacts and early use of hammered copper tools. c. 500 BC. **4b**

Ayacucho, Peru; caves containing stone tools made by early hunters, associated with bones of extinct animals, eg., elephant, giant sloth. From 14,000 BC. **4f**

Chanchan, Peru; capital city of the Chimú empire, conquered by the Incas. Famed for metalwork, fine textiles and mass-produced pottery. AD 1000–1400. **4f**

Chavín de Huantar, Peru; early religious centre of great influence. The stone temple complex has stylized carvings of jaguars, snakes and birds which were copied throughout Peru. 900–200 BC. **4f**

Clovis, USA; type-site for the first fluted stone lanceolate projectile points in the Americas, made by Palaeo-Indians hunting mammoth. c. 10,000 BC. 3b

Cuzco, Peru; political and religious centre of the Inca empire. c. AD 1200–1532. **4f**

El Inga, Ecuador; obsidian tool workshop site producing Clovis- and Folsom-type points, as well as fishtail points similar to Fell's Cave. 10,000–5000 BC. 4e

Folsom, USA; giant buffalo kill site in New Mexico, type-site for Folsom point, later than Clovis point and with retouched edges. c. 8500 BC. 3b

Huaca del Sol, Peru; huge adobe block pyramid constructed by the Moche of northern coastal Peru. AD 200–700. **4f**

Huaca Prieta, Peru; pre-ceramic village site. Deep middens contain evidence of a fishing economy and early cultivation of cotton, gourds, peppers, beans. Also earliest Peruvian textiles. 2500–1800 BC. 4f

Huari, Peru; capital city of a great empire contemporary with, and influenced by, Tiahuanaco. AD 600–800. **4f**

Kotosh, Peru; multi-phased ceremonial centre beginning in pre-ceramic times and ancestral to Chavín de Huantar. c. 2000–500 BC. **4f**

La Venta, Mexico; important Olmec site with 33.5-metre-high earthern pyramid, jade sculptures and colossal stone heads and altars. 1000–600 BC. 3c

Marajó, Brazil; site on this island at the mouth of the Amazon shows long history of human settlement, with production of fine incised ceramics. 1000 BC–AD 1500. 6e

Mayapan, Mexico; fortified Maya town founded by the Itzá tribe, where Maya and Toltec traditions survived longer than elsewhere in Yucatan. AD 1262–1441. **3c**

Mound City, USA; complex of geometric-shaped earthworks, mounds and enclosures built by the Hopewell people in Ohio. 300 BC–AD 200. **4b**

Nazca, Peru; culture of the south coast of Peru, famed for polychrome painted pottery and the large-scale 'Nazca lines' in the desert, some abstract subjects, others monkeys, spiders, birds. 200 BC–AD 600. **4f**

Pachacamac, Peru; ceremonial centre on central coast of Peru, later an important Inca oracle. AD 0–1534. **4f**

Paracas, Peru; ceramics from the early phases of the site show strong Chavín influence. Later burials of bodies wearing colourful textiles were preserved by the dry desert conditions. 1000–100 BC. **4f**

Poverty Point, USA; complex of massive earthen monuments in lower Mississippi valley, possibly a planned town of the Woodlands culture. 1200–100 BC. 3b

Pueblo Bonito, USA; D-shaped village of multi-storeyed buildings with kivas, built by Pueblo Indians. AD 919–1067. **2b**

Puerto Hormiga, Colombia; site on Caribbean coast which produced the earliest pottery in the Americas. c. 3100 BC. 4d

San Lorenzo Tenochtitlán, Mexico; important Olmec site with huge earthen mounds, ceremonial buildings and stone carvings. 1500–700 BC. 3c

Santa Isabel Itzapán, Mexico; mammoth kill site on shores of old Lake Texcoco. c. 8000 BC. 3c

Snaketown, USA; Hohokam town of wattle and daub houses with associated irrigation schemes. 100 BC–AD 1100. 2b

Tehuacán Valley, Mexico; dry highland valley which produced evidence of early domestication of maize, gourd, avocado and chili peppers. 10,000 BC onwards. 2c

Teotihuacan, Mexico; great city planned around the temples of the Sun and Moon. Religious, industrial, diplomatic and trading centre contemporary with the Maya. 200 BC–AD 700. **2c**

Tikal, Guatemala; one of the largest and best-known Maya cities, covering 123 sq km, famous for its stone stelae and 160-metre-tall pyramids. AD 200–900. **3c**

Tula, Mexico; capital city of the Toltecs, centre of the cult of Quetzalcoatl. AD 900–1156. 2c

Uxmal, Mexico; spaciously planned Maya ceremonial centre built in Puuc architectural style. AD 600–900. **3c**

Valdivia, Ecuador; stratified site on south coast which produced accomplished pottery dated almost as early as Puerto Hormiga. Suggestions of trans-Pacific Japanese contacts have been made. 2700 BC–1500 BC. 4e

Glossary

Absolute chronology, dates given in terms of the calendar, that is, in years before present (or BP).

Acheulean, early Palaeolithic culture identified by two main types of stone hand-axes, pointed and almond-shaped. The name is taken from St Acheul in France.

Acroteria, pedestals of ornaments set at the top or side angle of a pediment.

Amarna period, phase in the late 18th dynasty, comprising the reigns of Akhenaten, Smenkhkare, Tutankhamun and Ay (1379–1352 BC), when notable religious and artistic changes were made. The name is derived from the site of Akhenaten's capital at El-Amarna.

Amino-acid dating, technique used for absolute dating. Living organisms contain amino acids which change their nature over a known time, thus enabling substances to be dated. Temperature alterations affect the process of change, but the technique has been used for dating fossil bones and deep-sea sediments.

Archaeomagnetism, technique used for absolute dating. It depends on knowing that the Earth's magnetic field has been subject to changes in direction and intensity over time, and makes use of the magnetism in archaeological material. Clay and rocks contain magnetic minerals, and when heated above a certain temperature the magnetism is destroyed. On cooling, the magnetism returns, taking on the direction and strength of the magnetic field in which the object is lying. Therefore when clay or rocks are heated, as in the firing of pottery, they 'fossilize' the Earth's magnetic field as it was at the moment of their cooling. In areas where the variations of the Earth's magnetic field are known, it is possible to date a pottery sample, for example, by fitting it to the known curve.

Assemblages, groups of objects of different types found in close association with each other. If the assemblage is found frequently repeated and covers a range of human activity, it is called a culture. Where it is repeated, but is limited in scope, for example to flint tools only, it is called an industry.

Ayaka, group of 5 pillars, carved with representations of Buddhist symbols.

Backstrap, loom most commonly used in the Americas. A continuous warp thread passes between two horizontal poles, one attached to a support and the other to a seated weaver, who adjusts the tension by moving forwards or backwards.

Basilica, large oblong hall with double colonnades and usually a semi-circular apse, used for judicial and commercial purposes.

Battle-Axe culture, stone battle-axes were common throughout Europe in the late Neolithic and Copper Age, associated with corded ware and beakers.

Beaker Folk, named after the characteristic bell-shaped beakers found buried with the dead of a people who spread the knowledge of metal-working in Europe, about 2500 – 2000 BC.

Bedding trenches, those dug into the ground to receive the foundations of walls.

Bichrome ware, material decorated in two colours.

Bodhisattva, in Buddhism, one who postpones entrance into Nirvana in order to help others, a future Buddha.

Burin, pointed tool made of chipped flint or stone and found in Upper Palaeolithic industries.

Camera lucida, system of prisms or mirrors used as an aid in sketching images seen in an optical instrument, such as a microscope.

Caravanserai, a kind of unfurnished inn or large enclosed court where caravans were put up.

Cardinal points, the four chief points of the compass, North, South, East and West.

Carolingian art, style which flourished at the time of the Frankish emperor Charlemagne (died 814), when there was a revival of scholarship and the arts.

Cartouche, in ancient Egypt, an oval figure enclosing the hieroglyphs of a royal or divine name.

Celadon ware, Chinese pottery of pale green glaze.

Chasing, engraving on the outside of raised metalwork.

Chenes, Maya architectural style restricted to the Yucatan peninsula, AD 600-900. Chenes is a flamboyant style of building; façades are elaborately decorated in deep relief and doorways carved into the form of the mouth of a monster.

Cicatrization, process of healing over a wound which results in scars being left on the skin.

Cloisonné, decorative enamelling in which different colours of the pattern are separated by thin strips of metal.

Colossi, gigantic statues, far larger than life size.

Composite, blend of Ionic and Corinthian styles of architecture.

Corbelled, corbelling, technique for roofing stone chambers. Near the top of the wall, each course of stone partly overlaps the one below it, until the stones meet or leave only a small gap to span. The method can also be used for a 'false' corbelled arch or vault.

Corinthian, ornate style of Greek architecture, with acanthus leaves on the capital.

Corvée, obligation to perform labour for a king or overlord.

Cuneiform, from 'cuneus', wedge. A pictographic script, the oldest known in the world, in which characters were formed from strokes like wedges impressed in wet clay with a split reed. The scripts were employed in Mesopotamia and neighbouring areas from the 3rd to the 1st millennium BC.

Cybernetics, comparative study of automatic communication and control in body functions and in mechanical and electrical systems such as computers, thermostats, etc.

Deinotherium, elephant-like animal with down-turned tusks on its lower jaws. It became extinct at the end of the Pleistocene.

Dendrochronological dating, technique based on the fact that trees add a growth ring for every year of their lives. The method is of great use in refining radiocarbon dates (see pages 16-17). By comparing a complete series of rings from a tree of known date (one recently alive) with a series from an earlier, dead tree which overlaps in age, ring patterns from the centre layers of the recent tree and the outer ones of the old tree may show a correlation which makes it possible to date the older tree in calendar years. The central rings of this tree can then be compared with the outer rings of an even older tree, and so on backwards into prehistory.

Diatoms, microscopic, unicellular algae. Different species are associated with different habitats and so examples found in archaeological deposits can give information on changes in environment, especially at coastal sites.

Diffusionism, diffusionists, the spread of a cultural trait from its point of origin, by means of war, trade or imitation. Such movement has played an important part in human history. Indeed, the diffusionist theory was once used to explain the beginning of most new ideas, although the multiple origin of

such significant advances as metal-working, for example, is now accepted.
Doric, Greek order of architecture distinguished by its simplicity and massive strength.
Ethnography, the scientific description of the races of the Earth.
Ethnology, the study of the varieties of the human race; cultural anthropology.
Faience, a glazed paste, made mostly of quartz sand and used for beads and figurines.
False colour infra-red photography, technique used in aerial photography. Infra-red film reacts to the varying degrees of water absorption in different features, so that changes in vegetation, the existence of buried features filled with disturbed soil, the presence of roadways, etc., can be detected. 'False colour' refers to the accentuation of specific features in red, pink, blue, yellow, etc. These do not reflect natural colour but emphasize the contrasts between features.
Fibulae, brooches of safety-pin form, often used for fastening a draped garment such as a toga or cloak.
Filigree, ornamental metal lacework of gold or silver, twisted and united by soldering.
Granulation, method of pouring hot metal through a sieve into water in order to form grains.
Gypsum, a soft mineral which in its finely grained state is known as alabaster. It is also the source of plaster of Paris and other plasters.
Header and stretcher, in building, header is a brick or stone laid in a wall with its end towards the wall-face; stretcher is a brick or stone laid with its length parallel to the wall-face.
Heavy mineral analysis, method used to examine pottery to find the geological source of the sands in its clay. The crushed pot material is floated on a heavy liquid such as bromoform, whereupon the heavy minerals sink and the quartz sand and clay float. The heavy minerals can then be identified and this also often indicates the source of manufacture.
Fission track dating, technique used for absolute dating, applied particularly to volcanic substances such as obsidian, glass and the minerals in pottery. It is based on an isotope of uranium, U238, as it undergoes spontaneous fission and proves a useful method for checking potassium-argon dating.
Hyperboreans, legendary people supposed to live in sunshine beyond the north wind; belonging to the extreme north.
Hypocaust, system of underfloor heating by the circulation of hot air, used in Roman villas.
Impluvia, impluvium, in Roman houses, cistern or tanks for collecting rainwater, situated in the atrium under an opening in the roof.
Ionic, Greek style of architecture characterized by the spiral scrolls of its capitals.
Kurgan, Russian word for a mound or barrow covering a burial in a pit grave, mortuary house or catacomb grave. The earliest kurgans appeared during the 3rd millennium BC among peoples of the Caucasus and soon after 2500 the kurgan cultures affected most of east, central and northern Europe. The tradition persisted in Russia and, in an altered form, was still practised by the Scythians.
Lake villages, dwellings, prehistoric people often built dwellings on marshy ground by lake sides and such villages have been found in Switzerland and Germany, dating from Neolithic times. A remarkable lakeside dwelling was found at Star Carr in Yorkshire, England.
Levallois, technique of flint flaking in which the face of the core is trimmed to shape in order to control the form and size of the intended flake.
Linear A, Linear B, scripts used by the Minoans and Mycenaeans in Crete and Greece during the Bronze Age. Linear A remains undeciphered; Linear B was deciphered in 1952 by Michael Ventris and was found to be an early form of Greek. Linear A has pictograms reduced to formal outline patterns and was replaced about the 14th century BC by Linear B.
Linga, the Hindu phallus, a symbol of Shiva.
Lost wax process, or cire perdue, technique of casting objects in metal. A model of the figure to be cast is made in wax, often on a clay core. This is coated with clay and baked. The wax runs out through vents left in the clay for the purpose, and molten metal is then poured through the same vents into the mould. When the metal is cool, the clay is broken off to reveal the metal casting.
Magdalenian, final Palaeolithic culture of much of western Europe. The culture is famous for its cave art, as at Altamira in Spain, and for decorative work in bone and ivory. It spanned about 15,000 to 10,000 BC.
Magnetometers, instruments for measuring the intensity of the Earth's magnetic field at any point.
Manos, in American archaeology, the upper stone used when grinding maize on a metate, or stone slab.
Metates, in American archaeology, the stone slabs used for grinding maize.
Mimbres, name of an archaeological culture, dated AD 1000–1200, found in the south-western USA, particularly New Mexico. The Mimbres people are particularly renowned for the black-on-white painted pottery bowls which they made especially to be put in burials. These are decorated with abstract designs and with pictures of people, bears, rabbits and other animals.
Mithuna, auspicious pair, male and female, emblematic of fruitful union.
Nagas, in Hindu and Buddhist belief, semi-divine beings, half-human and half-serpent. In Buddhism they are often represented as door guardians.
Nazca lines, in Peruvian desert, geometric and geomorphic patterns created by the removal of surface stones to reveal the pale earth beneath.
Neutron activation analysis, method used to determine the chemical composition of various substances, such as flint, obsidian, pottery, coins, etc. The specimen is bombarded with neutrons to activate the nuclei of its elements in order to form radioactive isotopes. These decay, emitting gamma rays which can be measured to find the constituent elements.
Nome, administrative unit or province of ancient Egypt. Each nome consisted of a town or group of villages with its own guardian deity and symbol or standard.
Oblique photographs, in aerial photography, taken from an angle so as to reveal elevation and contours.
Ogival arch, a pointed arch.
Orthostats, large stone slabs, set vertically. These often formed part of the walls of megalithic chamber tombs.
Osteologist, a person who studies bones.
Overburden, soil overlying a bed of clay or other base to be dug, mined or quarried.
Oxygen isotope examination, analysis, technique based on the fact that the ratio of two of the stable isotopes of oxygen varies according to the material in which it is found. The method can be used to classify glass types and to analyse mollusc shells in order to try and reconstruct their original environment and thus the source of the shell.
Palaeomagnetism, see Archaeomagnetism.
Papyri, manuscripts written on papyrus, a tall plant of the sedge family, the pith of which was cut into strips and pressed together to make writing material by the ancient Egyptians.
Particle accelerator, used mainly in nuclear physics, to increase the velocities of atomic fragments such as electrons, protons and ions.
Pathology, the study of diseases on abnormalities.
Pharaonic period, the entire history of Egypt from the establishment of the monarchy in 3100 BC down to the invasion of Alexander in 332 BC.
Pilasters, square columns which partly project from, and are partly built into, a wall.
Pleistocene, geological period beginning about 1,600,000 years ago and ending about 8000 BC.
Potassium-argon dating, technique for absolute dating which is based on the decay of a radioactive material into a non-radioactive material at a known rate. Potassium is present in most rocks and minerals and has a single radioactive isotope, ^{40}K, which decays into Calcium 40 and Argon 40. The 11 per cent that decays into the gas argon can be measured, together with the potassium left in the sample, to give a date.
Potin, bronze alloy with a high tin content. The term is usually used for a type of coinage current in western Europe in the first centuries BC and AD.
Proton magnetometer, instrument used in magnetic surveying to detect changes in intensity of the Earth's magnetic field. It makes possible the plotting of changes in magnetic field strength often caused by buried iron, kilns, hearths, pits or ditches (topsoil is more magnetic than subsoil). Excavation can then be directed to the most promising areas.
Pueblos, Spanish word for town or village. Also used in American archaeology to describe the prehistoric inhabitants of the south-west.
Puuc, Maya architectural style restricted to the Yucatan, AD 600-900. Its main characteristic is the use of veneer masonry to cover rubble and concrete walls, and the prefabrication of sculpted elements which were assembled to form patterns and masks.
Pylon, monumental gateway to Egyptian temples or palaces, built in stone and often decorated with relief figures and hieroglyphs.
Radiocarbon dating, determination, method for absolute dating which can be used for most organic material up to 70,000 years old (see pages 16-17). Dates given in radiocarbon years are written bc or bp (before present) before they are calibrated. Calibrated dates are written BC or BP.
Red-slipped, slip is a thin layer of fine clay applied to pottery before firing by dipping the pot into a thick liquid mixture of clay and water. Slip decorates the fabric, often chosen to bake to a good colour such as red, yellow or black, and makes the pot more watertight by clogging the pores of the earthenware.
Relieving compartment, usually a rough construction placed in a wall above an arch or opening to relieve it of much of the weight.
Repoussé, in metalwork, a relief or pattern raised by being hammered from the back.
Resistivity meters, techniques, method used for investigating underlying deposits before, or instead of, digging. It is based on the principle that different deposits offer differing resistance to the passage of an electric current, depending largely on the amount of water present. A damp pit gives less resistance, and foundations of a dry stone wall more resistance, than surrounding soil.
Shaft tomb, tomb in which the burials are made at the bottom of a deep, narrow pit. They occur in various parts of the world and at different periods. The most famous are those at Mycenae.
Shell middens, a midden is a refuse heap, normally found on an ancient settlement site.
Spondylus, Mediterranean sea shell from which bangles were made. The material was traded into central Europe during the early Neolithic.
Stele, upright stone slab, tablet or column, often decorated with carvings and inscriptions.
Stereoscope, instrument by which images of two pictures differing slightly in point of view are seen one by each eye, thereby giving a 'solid' effect.
Stratified; stratification, in archaeology, study of the various layers, or strata, of habitation at a site.
Sumach, sumac, tree or shrub of the genus Rhus, the leaves and shoots of which are used for a dye.
Taxonomy, the science of biological classification (into genus, species, etc.) and, by extension, other sorts of classification.
Thermoluminescence, thermoluminescent dates, technique for absolute dating used on pottery and other fired clay artefacts. It is based on the principle that ceramics contain small amounts of radioactive material, absorbed since the pottery was fired, which on heating is released in the form of light. By measuring the amount of light it is possible to find the length of time since the mineral crystals of the pottery were lasted heated, and thus the date it was made.
Thin sectioning, the removal of a thin slice of material from an artefact, usually pottery or stone, for examination under a petrological microscope. It is then possible to identify the source of the raw materials from which the object was made.
Transhumant, transhumance, the transference of cattle from summer to winter pasture and from winter pasture to summer.
Tufa, talc, a porous rock.
Tuscan, Doric style modified by the Romans, with unfluted columns and without triglyphs.
Typological method, typology, technique for classifying objects based on their form and decoration, such as a group of pottery items. It is useful as an aid to relative dating.
Vertical photographs, in aerial photography, taken from directly overhead to reveal plan of site or object.
Way station, small chapel on an avenue in a temple-complex, where the shrine of the god might be placed temporarily during processions.

Index

Figures in bold denote illustrations

Credits

Photographs

Adespoton 96T; 97; courtesy American Museum of Natural History 187T (courtesy of the Geological Survey of China/Dr. Franz Weidereich); 187L; 187R; 188; American School of Classical Studies at Athens (Agora Excavation) 61; Professor Andronikos/Kalliora Iliadis 68; 69; 71; Ardea 18; BBC Hulton Picture Library 25; British Museum 13T; 73; British School of Archaeology in Jerusalem 20; Cambridge University Press 96C; Cambridge University Museum of Archaeology and Anthropology 20L; 220T; Peter Cheze-Brown 107; 108; Peter Clayton 53BR; 122B (Cairo Museum); Cam Culbert 172C; Douglas Dickens F.R.P.S. 159C; 168TR; 172; 176; 178; 179; 181TR; 182B; 204; 205; C.M. Dixon 55BL; 72; 181TL,B; 182T; 183; Edimedia 154; Egypt Exploration Society 133R; Ekdotike Athenon 56; Mary Evans Picture Library 13B; Werner Foreman Archive 43; 44; 45; 87C; 111; 113R; 143BR; 157; French Government Tourist Office 30B; 31; 33; Sonia Halliday Photographs 55BR; 58; 73C; 74; Robert Harding Associates 119; 160; 166R; 170T; 189; 194; 195; 208T; Robert Harding Associates (Rainbird Archive) 12; 19; 119; 134B; 190; 191; 193T; J.D. Hawkins 153T; Michael Holford 143; 147; 213; Michael Holford/Gerry Clyde 173T; 174; R. Inskeep 99R; International Society for Educational Information 199; 200; Alan Johnston 64; 65; 66T; Document Henri Lhote's Expedition 102; 104; 105; Professor Luning/Universitat zum Koln/Institut fur Ur und Fruhgeschichte 35; 36/7; William MacQuitty Collection 130; 193B; Mansell Collection 15; Arlette Mellaart 138B; 138/9; 139B; Metropolitan Museum of Art, New York/Nina Gareth Davies 126; 127; Marion and Tony Morrison 9B (photo Servicio Aerofotografico Nacional, Peru); 216; 217; 219B; 222; 223; Musees Nationaux, France/Louvre 149T; Museum of Mankind/Maudslay Collection (British Museum) 209; 211R; Chris Niedenthal 40T; 41; Oxford Archaeological Unit 8; 27; Peabody Museum Harvard 210; 213B; 214; Peabody Museum of Natural History, Yale University 220R; Pitt Rivers Museum, Oxford 99L; 101; Popperfoto 32T; 155; 170B; 171; 213TR; Josephine Powell, Rome 83B; 151R; 159T; 164; 166L; 167; Royal Commission on Historic Monuments (Crown Copyright) 27(a); Scala 66B (Castello Sforzesco, Milan); 67; 78/9; 79; 146; Ronald Sheridan/Ancient Art and Architecture Collection 53BL; 77B; 85B; 143BL; 149BL & BR; 157B; John Topham Picture Library 30C (Fotogram); 82B (Picturepoint); University Museum of National Antiquities, Oslo 47; 48; 49; U.S. Department of the Interior, National Parks Service 225 (Fred Ming); 227B (Paul Goeldner); Vautier-Decool 9T (Musee de la Universitee de San Marcos); 203; 213T; 215B; 219T; Victoria and Albert Museum (Crown Copyright) 168TL; 168B; Vision International 196 (Paolo Koch); Roger Wood 53TL & TR; 89; 90; 91T; 116; 117T; 121T; 122T; 133L; Wieslaw Zajaczkowski 38C; 39; ZEFA 63T (Goebel); 85T (Schorken); 151L; 153C; 211L (Karl Kummels); 227T (Sunak)

Artists

Marian Appleton 201; Ray Burrows 18; 21; 34; 42; 70; 79; 86; 200; 221; 223; Kai Choi 118; 130, 131; 134; 140, 141; 152, 153; Simon Dalby 81; David Etchell and John Ridyard 55; 58, 59; 62, 63; 74, 75; 196; Will Giles 96; Groom and Pickerill 192; Richard Prideaux 161; Ed Stuart 90, 91; 122, 123; Shirley Willis 77; 112; 129; 144; 156, 157